Computer Accounting

with

QuickBooks® 2021

Twentieth Edition

Donna Kay, MBA, PhD, CPA, CITP

QuickBooks Pro 2021

QuickBooks Premier 2021

QuickBooks Accountant 2021

McGraw Hill

COMPUTER ACCOUNTING WITH QUICKBOOKS® 2021, TWENTIETH EDITION

Published by McGraw Hill LLC, 1325 Avenue of the Americas, New York, NY 10019. Copyright ©2022 by McGraw Hill LLC. All rights reserved. Printed in the United States of America. Previous editions ©2020, 2019, and 2015. No part of this publication may be reproduced or distributed in any form or by any means, or stored in a database or retrieval system, without the prior written consent of McGraw Hill LLC, including, but not limited to, in any network or other electronic storage or transmission, or broadcast for distance learning.

Some ancillaries, including electronic and print components, may not be available to customers outside the United States.

This book is printed on acid-free paper.

1 2 3 4 5 6 7 8 9 LMN 26 25 24 23 22 21

ISBN 978-1-259-91700-4 (bound edition)
MHID 1-259-91700-2 (bound edition)
ISBN 978-1-264-06919-4 (loose-leaf edition)
MHID 1-264-06919-7 (loose-leaf edition)

Executive Portfolio Manager: *Steve Schuetz*
Product Developer: *Sarah Sacco*
Marketing Manager: *Claire McLemore*
Senior Assessment Content Project Manager: *Angela Norris*
Lead Core Content Project Manager: *Susan Trentacosti*
Buyer: *Susan K. Culbertson*
Designer: *Beth Blech*
Lead Content Licensing Specialist: *Melissa Homer*
Cover Image: *©Songquan Deng/Shutterstock*
Compositor: *SPi Global*

All credits appearing on page or at the end of the book are considered to be an extension of the copyright page.

The Internet addresses listed in the text were accurate at the time of publication. The inclusion of a website does not indicate an endorsement by the authors or McGraw Hill LLC, and McGraw Hill LLC does not guarantee the accuracy of the information presented at these sites.

mheducation.com/highered

Computer Accounting with QuickBooks

20th Edition by Donna Kay

Dear QuickBooks Student

Welcome to Learning QuickBooks!

Give yourself a competitive advantage – learn the leading financial software for entrepreneurs using *Computer Accounting with QuickBooks*. Designed using the most effective way to learn QuickBooks, this text streamlines learning QuickBooks because it focuses on you—the learner.

Proven instructional techniques are incorporated throughout the text to make your mastery of QuickBooks as effortless as possible. Using a hands-on approach, this text integrates understanding accounting with mastery of QuickBooks. Designed for maximum flexibility to meet your needs, *Computer Accounting with QuickBooks* can be used either in a QuickBooks course or independently at your own pace.

A Quick Review Guide in Chapter 17 provides a handy resource to seek out additional information as needed. In addition, Chapter 17 streamlines review for the QuickBooks User Certification Exam.

Good luck with QuickBooks and best wishes for your continued success,

Donna Kay

Meet the Author

Donna Kay is a former professor of Accounting and Accounting Systems and Forensics, teaching both undergraduate and graduate accounting. Dr. Kay earned B.S. and MBA degrees from Southern Illinois University at Edwardsville before receiving a Ph.D. from Saint Louis University, where she conducted action research on the perceived effectiveness of instructional techniques for learning technology. Dr. Kay designs her textbooks to incorporate the most effective instructional techniques based on research findings, making your learning journey as productive as possible. Named to Who's Who Among American Women, Dr. Kay holds certifications as both a Certified Public Accountant (CPA) and Certified Informational Technology Professional (CITP) and is an active member of the American Institute of Certified Public Accountants (AICPA).

Donna Kay is also the author of *Computer Accounting with QuickBooks Online*. Visit Dr. Kay's websites www.my-quickbooks.com and www.my-quickbooksonline.com to learn more about her books and available resources.

XPM Mapping

What is the most effective way to learn QuickBooks?

Use a highly effective three-step approach to streamline learning: **eXplore, Practice, Master (XPM)**.

1. eXplore. Providing numerous screen shots and detailed instructions, chapters in *Computer Accounting with QuickBooks* are designed as tutorials for you to explore and learn QuickBooks features.

2. Practice. Designed with fewer instructions, the end-of-chapter exercises provide opportunities for you to practice and test your understanding.

3. Master. Virtual company projects and case studies provide mastery opportunities for you to apply and integrate your QuickBooks skills.

1. e**X**plore	>	2. **P**ractice	>	3. **M**aster
Chapter 1		Exercises 1		Project 1.1
Chapter 2		Exercises 2		Project 2.1
Chapter 3		Exercises 3		Project 3.1
Chapter 4		Exercises 4		Project 4.1
Chapter 5		Exercises 5		Project 5.1
Chapter 6		Exercises 6		Project 6.1
Chapter 7		Exercises 7		Project 7.1
Chapter 8		Exercises 8		Project 8.1
Chapter 9		Exercises 9		Project 9.1
Chapter 10		Exercises 10		Project 10.1
Chapter 11		Exercises 11		Project 11.1 Project 11.2 Chapter 12
Chapter 13		Exercises 13		Project 13.1 Project 13.2 Chapter 14
Chapter 15		Exercises 15		Project 15.1 Project 15.2
Chapter 16		Exercises 16		Chapter 17 Chapter 18

QuickBooks SatNav

QuickBooks SatNav is a feature in the text which functions like a satellite navigation for QuickBooks. It Is intended to provide an easy way to learn the software by helping you zoom out to see the big picture of the entire financial system and zoom in to view the details. If at any time you are feeling lost while using QuickBooks, go to QuickBooks SatNav to help guide you.

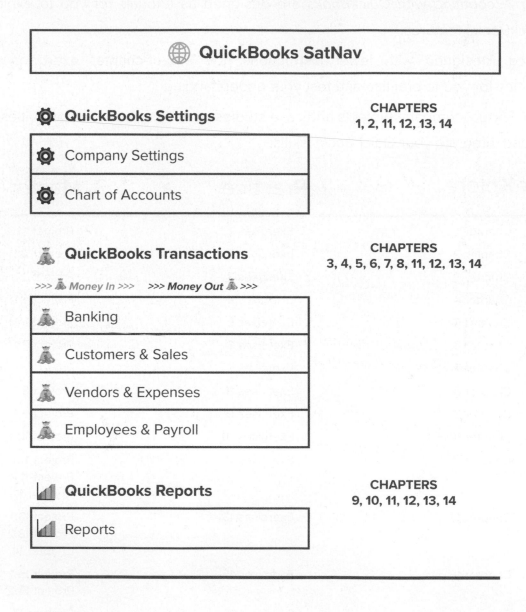

QuickBooks SatNav

QuickBooks Settings

CHAPTERS
1, 2, 11, 12, 13, 14

| Company Settings |
| Chart of Accounts |

QuickBooks Transactions

CHAPTERS
3, 4, 5, 6, 7, 8, 11, 12, 13, 14

>>> Money In >>>   >>> Money Out >>>

| Banking |
| Customers & Sales |
| Vendors & Expenses |
| Employees & Payroll |

QuickBooks Reports

CHAPTERS
9, 10, 11, 12, 13, 14

| Reports |

Hot Dots

Intuitive callouts with matching step-by-step instructions, Hot Dots on screen captures make learning QuickBooks even faster and easier.

Becoming a QuickBooks Certified User

QuickBooks User Certification is certification that is obtained by passing the QuickBooks User Certification Examination. See **Chapter 17** for more detailed information about developing your action plan to review for QuickBooks User Certification.

What is the QuickBooks User Certification examination?

The QuickBooks User Certification examination is an online exam that is proctored at authorized testing centers. The QuickBooks User Certification is a certification focused on QuickBooks users. The QuickBooks ProAdvisor certification is a different certification that is focused more on accountants who provide advisory services to QuickBooks clients.

Why consider the QuickBooks User Certification?

Passing the QuickBooks User Certification examination adds another credential to your resume. Employers often value credentials that indicate skill and a knowledge level as a baseline for employment.

How do I obtain more information about the QuickBooks User Certification exam?

For more information about the QuickBooks User Certification examination, see:

- www.certiport.com
- www.My-QuickBooks.com, QB Certified User
- *Computer Accounting with QuickBooks* Chapter 17

Virtual Activity Mapping

What is the most effective way to learn QuickBooks?

Virtual company cases provide you with a realistic context and business environment to enhance your understanding of QuickBooks. Related learning activities mapping follows.

Company	Chapter	Exercises	Project	Type of Company
Rock Castle Construction	1*, 2*, 3*, 4*, 5*, 6*, 7*, 8*, 9*, 10*	1, 2, 3, 4, 5, 6, 7, 8, 9, 10	--	Service
Larry's Landscaping	--	--	1.1*, 2.1, 3.1, 4.1, 5.1, 6.1, 7.1, 8.1, 9.1, 10.1	Service
Paint Palette	11, 15*	11, 15	--	Service
Paint Palette Store	13	13	--	Merchandising
Mookie The Beagle™ Spa	12	--	--	Service
Mookie The Beagle™ Spa Supplies	14	--	--	Merchandising
Martin Consulting	--	--	11.1, 15.1	Service
Herman LLC	--	--	11.2	Service
Ella's Knittery	--	--	13.1	Merchandising
Johann Enterprises	--	--	13.2	Merchandising
Your Name Botanicals	--	--	15.2	Merchandising

*QuickBooks Starter files are provided for these learning activities.

🛠 ROCK CASTLE CONSTRUCTION

Rock Castle Construction is a business that provides construction services and products to customers. For Rock Castle Construction learning activities, you will restore a Starter file at the beginning of each chapter that will be used to complete the chapter and exercises. Each chapter and corresponding exercises focus on exploration and practice in becoming proficient in a specific area of QuickBooks, such as Banking, Customers and Sales, Vendors and Expenses.

- **Chapter 1* and Exercises 1**
- **Chapter 2* and Exercises 2**
- **Chapter 3* and Exercises 3**
- **Chapter 4* and Exercises 4**
- **Chapter 5* and Exercises 5**
- **Chapter 6* and Exercises 6**
- **Chapter 7* and Exercises 7**
- **Chapter 8* and Exercises 8**
- **Chapter 9* and Exercises 9**
- **Chapter 10* and Exercises 10**

🌴 LARRY'S LANDSCAPING

Larry's Landscaping is a merchandising, service company providing both landscaping services and landscaping products. For Larry's Landscaping projects, you will restore a Project 1.1 Starter file and then use your own QuickBooks files after that to complete the remaining projects. Since you will be using your own file, you will want to check and cross check your work to eliminate errors. If you find you have an issue with your QuickBooks file that you are unable to resolve, contact your instructor.

- Project 1.1*
- Project 2.1
- Project 3.1
- Project 4.1
- Project 5.1
- Project 6.1
- Project 7.1
- Project 8.1
- Project 9.1
- Project 10.1

*QuickBooks Starter files are provided for these learning activities.

🎨 Paint Palette

Paint Palette is a painting service business. With no starter file required, Chapter 11 covers new company setup for a sole-proprietor service business, customer and vendor transactions, adjustments, and reports. Chapter 15, a continuation of Chapter 11, has a Starter file and covers advanced QuickBooks features including estimates, budgeting, progress billing, uncollectible accounts, and the audit trail.

- **Chapter 11 and Exercises 11**
- **Chapter 15* and Exercises 15**

🎨 Paint Palette Store

Paint Palette Store is a paint boutique specializing in custom tint paints. This chapter, requiring no starter file, covers new company setup for a S Corporation merchandising business with beginning balances, opening adjustments, customer, vendor, and inventory transactions,adjustments, and reports.

- **Chapter 13 and Exercises 13**

🐶 Mookie The Beagle™ Spa

Mookie The Beagle™ Spa, a service company, is a mobile pet spa business. A starter file is not required. This comprehensive QuickBooks case covers setting up a new sole proprietor service company, customer and vendor transactions, adjustments, and reports.

- **Chapter 12**

🐶 Mookie The Beagle™ Spa Supplies

Mookie The Beaglc™ Spa Supplies, a merchandising company, sells branded pet spa products. With no starter file required, this comprehensive merchandising case covers new company setup for an S Corporation with beginning balances, opening adjustments, customer, vendor, and inventory transactions, adjustments, and reports.

- **Chapter 14**

MARTIN CONSULTING

Martin Consulting delivers social media marketing services. A comprehensive project that requires no starter file, Project 11.1 covers new service company setup for a sole proprietorship, customer and vendor transactions, adjustments, and reports. Project 15.1 is a continuation of Project 11.1 and uses QuickBooks budget features for Martin Consulting.

- Project 11.1
- Project 15.1

✳ HERMANN LLC

Hermann LLC is a cleaning and sanitizing service. With no starter file required, this project covers new company setup for a sole proprietor service- based business, customer and vendor transactions, adjustments, and reports.

- Project 11.2

ELLA'S KNITTERY

Ella's Knittery is an online and yarn boutique. A comprehensive project that requires no starter file, Project 13.1 covers new company setup for a S Corporation merchandising business with beginning balances, opening adjustments, customer, vendor and inventory transactions, adjustments, and reports.

- Project 13.1

📱 JOHANN ENTERPRISES

Johann Enterprises sells smartphone accessories, including smartphone cases and bluetooth earbuds. Requiring no starter file, Project 13.2 covers new company setup for a merchandising S corporation with beginning balances, opening adjustments, customer, vendor, and inventory transactions, adjustments, and reports.

- Project 13.2

❦ YOUR NAME BOTANICALS

Botanicals is a merchandising and service company specializing in unique orchid arrangements. With no starter file required, this new comprehensive QuickBooks project covers new company setup for a merchandising and service S Corporation, customer, vendor, and inventory transactions, adjustments, reports, budgets, estimates, and progress billing.

• **Project 15.2**

What's New in QuickBooks 2021

Computer Accounting with QuickBooks 2021 continues to offer the features that have made the text a best seller. In addition, this edition also offers:

New! Expanded QuickBooks Troubleshooting (QT) Assistance. Chapter 1 covers new QuickBooks Tool Hub, a feature that offers a launchpad of troubleshooting tools. In addition, new Appendix D: QuickBooks Troubleshooting covers instructions for accessing QuickBooks Help, QuickBooks Tool Hub, and QuickBooks Troubleshooting (QT) Best Practices.

Expanded QuickBooks Troubleshooting (QT) Activities. Chapter 5 offers a new QuickBooks troubleshooting activity to track down an incorrect sales price in QuickBooks and correct it. Chapter 9 Accounting Essentials covers how to make correcting entries for an error in QuickBooks. Exercise activities in Chapter 9 provide an opportunity to practice troubleshooting skills in accounting for one of Rock Castle's oversights. Chapter 15 covers how to use the QuickBooks Audit Log to search for discrepancies and review changed transactions.

New! Expanded Coverage of Aligning the Chart of Accounts with a Tax Return. For most businesses, one of the primary objectives of using QuickBooks is in order to streamline tax preparation. Additional chapter coverage, exercises, and project activities are offered in the new 20th edition focused on aligning the Chart of Accounts with the company's tax return.

New! Expanded Coverage of Bank Feeds. QuickBooks 2021 offers an improved Bank Feeds feature and an advanced Bank Feeds mode. Chapter 4 covers the new improved Bank Feed and how to use both the Advanced Bank Feeds mode and how to create Bank rules for bank feeds. New exercises on Bank Feeds provide an opportunity for students to practice using this increasingly important feature for QuickBooks users.

Expanded Receive Payments Coverage. Chapter 5 offers more extensive coverage of QuickBooks Receive Payments feature and accompany journal entries.

New! QuickBooks Receipt Management Feature. QuickBooks Desktop 2021 rolls out a new Receipt Management feature for capturing and organizing receipt data. Chapter 6 previews this new feature.

QuickBooks Inventory Center Feature Coverage. Chapter 5 introduces the QuickBooks Inventory Center and demonstrates how it can be used for error detection. Chapter 7 revisits and discusses it further. The Inventory Center summarizes inventory item information in one convenient location.

QuickBooks Data Analytics and Graphing. In the new 20th edition, Chapter 10 now includes activities and exercises on data analysis and graphing.

Updated and New Projects. Throughout the text there are updated and new projects, including new comprehensive Project 15.2 featuring QuickBooks estimates, progress invoicing, inventory, and budgets.

Online Learning Resources

Computer Accounting with QuickBooks 2021 is accompanied by both the Additional Student Resources and Instructor Resources that make online learning and teaching QuickBooks easier. They include student starter files, templates, updates, help and support links, video links, assistance with QuickBooks troubleshooting, Instructor supplements and more. **Both the Additional Student Resources and the Instructor Resources are available through Connect.** Below you will find directions for locating these materials within Connect for your uses.

Additional Student Resources (ASR):

Access ASR through the eBook. On the Connect course homepage, select the eBook option from the two eBooks shown. Open the Table of Contents by selecting the three-lined button inthe upper left-hand corner of the screen. Navigate to the bottom of the Table of Contents andselect "Additional Student Resources".

  Access ASR through the SmartBook. On the Connect course homepage, select the SmartBook option from the two eBooks shown. Once the Table of Contents has loaded, navigate down to the "Read only Content" section and select "Additional Student Resources". Additional Student Resources consist of...

- **Student Starter Files:** Use the QuickBooks Starter files (.QBB files) to start QuickBooks assignments. *Note: There are no Starter QBB Files for Chapters 11, 12,13, 14, and 16*

- **Excel Report Templates:** Download the Excel Report Templates to easily export your QuickBooks Reports to Excel for your QuickBooks assignments

- **QuickBooks 2021 Software License Instructions:** Details for requesting, downloading, installing, and registering the QuickBooks 2021 Software/License

- **PowerPoint Presentation Slides:** Chapter presentations

- **Computer Accounting with QuickBooks Updates:** Any updates that may be required when there are software update that affects the text

- **QuickBooks Issue Resolution:** A guided approach to troubleshooting QuickBooks

Instructor Resources:

Instructor Resources and Supplements: The instructor resources are found within Connect by selecting the library tab at the top of your course home page and then choosing "Instructor Resources" from the Menu. The instructor resources consist of...

- **Instructor Resources Guide**
- **PowerPoint Presentation**
- **Excel Solutions**
- **QBB Solution Files**

- **QB Educator Access Codes**
- **Connect Pre-Built Course Key**
- **Test Bank**
- **Updates and more**

Instructors not using Connect in the courses: *Please contact your McGraw-Hill rep for instructor access to Connect for the supplements. You may also provide the ASR file to your students directly.* The ASR Word document, with links to all student resources, can be downloaded on the Instructor Resource page in Connect. The document can then be provided to your students directly or linked in your course's LMS.

Connect

What Kind of student study tools does Connect offer?

SmartBook 2.0. A personalized and adaptive learning tool used to maximize the learning experience by helping students study more efficiently and effectively. SmartBook 2.0 highlights where in the chapter to focus, asks review questions on the materials covered and tracks the most challenging content for later review or recharge. SmartBook 2.0 is available both online and offline.

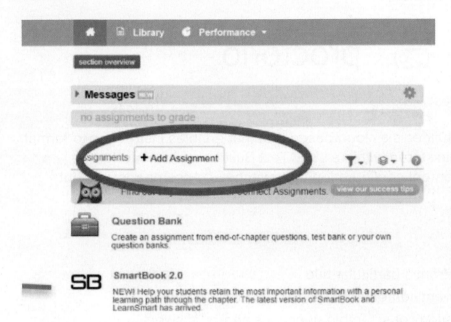

Assignment Materials. After completing assignments, students can enter key elements of their solution into Connect for grading. Based on instructor settings, they can receive instant feedback either while working on the assignment or after the assignment is submitted for grade. Assignable materials include: in chapter activities, exercises, projects, practice quizzes, and test bank materials.

Read Anywhere App. Using McGraw Hill's ReadAnywhere app, you can access the Computer Accounting with QuickBooks 2021 eBook anywhere, both online and offline, data free, by signing in with your Connect credentials. Simply download the entire textbook or only the chapters you need. The app also provides the same tools available on the laptop version of the eBook and any notes or highlights made to the text will sync across platforms so they're available on the app and in Connect.

Connect

What Kind of instructor tools does Connect offer?

Proctorio.
New remote proctoring and browser-locking capabilities, hosted by Proctorio within Connect, provide control of the assessment environment by enabling security options and verifying the identity of the students. These service provide instant and detailed reporting to instructors in an at-a-glance view of potential academic integrity concerns, thereby avoiding personal bias and supporting evidence-based claims.

Test Builder.
Available within Connect, Test Builder is a cloud-based tool that enables instructors to format tests that can be printed or administered within a LMS. Test Builder offers a modern, streamlined interface for easy content configuration that matches course needs, without requiring a download.

Test Builder allows you to:

- Access all test bank content from a particular title.
- Easily pinpoint the most relevant content through robust filtering options.
- Manipulate the order of questions or scramble questions and/or answers.
- Pin questions to a specific location within a test.
- Determine your preferred treatment of algorithmic questions.
- Choose the layout and spacing.
- Add instructions and configure default settings.

Test Builder provides a secure interface for better protection of content and allows for just-in-time updates to flow directly into assessments.

Reporting and Insights.
At-a-glance performance dashboards that use robust visual data displays that are each framed by intuitive question, to provide actionable recommendations and guide students towards behaviors that could increase class performance and enables instructors to give targeted tuition precisely when and where it is needed.

Instructors: Student Success Starts with You

Tools to enhance your unique voice

Want to build your own course? No problem. Prefer to use our turnkey, prebuilt course? Easy. Want to make changes throughout the semester? Sure. And you'll save time with Connect's auto-grading too.

65%
Less Time Grading

Laptop: McGraw Hill; Woman/dog: George Doyle/Getty Images

Study made personal

Incorporate adaptive study resources like SmartBook® 2.0 into your course and help your students be better prepared in less time. Learn more about the powerful personalized learning experience available in SmartBook 2.0 at **www.mheducation.com/highered/connect/smartbook**

Affordable solutions, added value

Make technology work for you with LMS integration for single sign-on access, mobile access to the digital textbook, and reports to quickly show you how each of your students is doing. And with our Inclusive Access program you can provide all these tools at a discount to your students. Ask your McGraw Hill representative for more information.

Padlock: Jobalou/Getty Images

Solutions for your challenges

A product isn't a solution. Real solutions are affordable, reliable, and come with training and ongoing support when you need it and how you want it. Visit **www.supportateverystep.com** for videos and resources both you and your students can use throughout the semester.

Checkmark: Jobalou/Getty Images

Students: Get Learning that Fits You

Effective tools for efficient studying

Connect is designed to make you more productive with simple, flexible, intuitive tools that maximize your study time and meet your individual learning needs. Get learning that works for you with Connect.

Study anytime, anywhere

Download the free ReadAnywhere app and access your online eBook or SmartBook 2.0 assignments when it's convenient, even if you're offline. And since the app automatically syncs with your eBook and SmartBook 2.0 assignments in Connect, all of your work is available every time you open it. Find out more at **www.mheducation.com/readanywhere**

> *"I really liked this app—it made it easy to study when you don't have your textbook in front of you."*
>
> - Jordan Cunningham,
>   Eastern Washington University

Calendar: owattaphotos/Getty Images

Everything you need in one place

Your Connect course has everything you need—whether reading on your digital eBook or completing assignments for class, Connect makes it easy to get your work done.

Learning for everyone

McGraw Hill works directly with Accessibility Services Departments and faculty to meet the learning needs of all students. Please contact your Accessibility Services Office and ask them to email accessibility@mheducation.com, or visit **www.mheducation.com/about/accessibility** for more information.

Acknowledgments

Thank you to all who have helped in advancing this text through 20 editions, especially feedback from students and instructors. Special thanks to:

- The McGraw Hill QuickBooks team Steve, Kevin, Sarah, Angela, and Susan
- Sandy Roman for her cheerful, careful accuracy checking and editing
- Erin Dischler for her attention to detail in accruacy checking the Test Bank and PowerPoints
- Brian Behrens for always being in my corner with greatly appreciated support
- Matt, Michael, Evan, Steve, and Sherri
- Faust and Silvia
- All the QuickBooks educators who share ideas, comments, suggestions, and encouragement. Special recognition to:
  - Aaron Butler, Warner Pacific University
  - Adria Vasquez, Del Mar College
  - Angela Payne, Collin College
  - Cammy Wayne, Harper College
  - Cecile M. Roberti, Community College of Rhode Island
  - Demelece Stewart, Ivy Tech Community College
  - Erin Dischler, Milwaukee Area Technical College
  - Erskine Hawkins, Atlanta Technical College
  - Felicia Baldwin, Richard J. Daley College
  - Heather Lynch, Northeast Iowa Community College
  - James Stanton, LDS Business College
  - Jane Margulies, The Team Group, LLC
  - Jennifer Blalock, Carteret Community College
  - Jennifer L. Sanders, El Centro College
  - Lori Hatchell, Aims Community College
  - NaTunya Johnson, Holmes Community College
  - Phyllis Gilbert, Louisiana Community & Technical College System
  - Scott Birk, Portland Community College
  - Scott Wallace, Blue Mountain Community College
  - Theresa Grover, Northeast Wisconsin Technical College - Green Bay
  - Zach Houk, Des Moines Area Community College - Ankeny

Table of Contents

Computer Accounting with QuickBooks

20th Edition by Donna Kay

Expanded Table of Contents

Designed as hands-on tutorials for learning QuickBooks, *Computer Accounting with QuickBooks* chapters provide screen captures with step-by-step, detailed instructions. To improve long-term retention of your QuickBooks skills, end-of-chapter learning activities are designed with fewer instructions to test your understanding and, when needed, to develop your skills to quickly seek out additional information to complete the task. The ability to find information as needed is an increasingly important skill in a rapidly changing business environment. The design of *Computer Accounting with QuickBooks* seamlessly facilitates your development of this crucial skill.

Chapters 1 through 10 focus on learning the basics of entering transactions and generating reports using the sample company, Rock Castle Construction.

Chapters 11 through 15 build upon the first ten chapters, covering the entire accounting cycle, including new company setup as well as QuickBooks advanced features for accountants. Chapter 11 and 12 cover sole proprietor service businesses, and Chapter 13, 14, and 15 cover a merchandise corporation. Using a progressive approach, the text gradually introduces advanced features while maintaining continuity and interest.

Chapters 16 provides insights into the differences between QuickBooks Desktop covered in this text and QuickBooks Online, including user and accountant versions of each.

Chapter 17 provides assistance in reviewing for the QuickBooks User Certification. In addition, Chapter 17 serves as a Quick Review Guide, providing step-by-step instructions for frequently used customer, vendor, and employee tasks in a convenient, user-friendly resource.

Chapter 18 offers a framework of seven milestones for conducting a QuickBooks Desktop consulting project.

Chapter 1 QuickBooks Quick Tour: Navigation and Settings

Chapter 1 provides a guided tour of QuickBooks Desktop software using QuickBooks Navigation tools, introducing the QuickBooks sample company, Rock Castle Construction. Other topics include how to restore QuickBooks starter files and back up files. A key new topic in this chapter is QuickBooks Troubleshooting, including coverage of QuickBooks Tool Hub, a new QuickBooks 2021 feature that offers a launchpad of troubleshooting tools.

Chapter 2 QuickBooks Chart of Accounts

This chapter introduces how to customize QuickBooks Chart of Accounts to meet specific business needs. For most businesses, one of the primary objectives of using QuickBooks is to streamline tax preparation. Accordingly, additional Chapter 2 coverage, exercises, and project activities are offered in the new 20th edition focused on aligning the Chart of Accounts with the company's tax return.

Chapter 3 QuickBooks Transactions

Chapter 3 provides an introduction to the various types of transactions entered in QuickBooks, including banking, customer, vendor, and employee transactions. A key topic in this chapter is coverage of two ways to enter information into QuickBooks: the onscreen journal and onscreen forms.

Chapter 4 Banking

Focusing on the Checking account and check register for a small business, Chapter 4 topics include making deposits, writing checks, matching bank transactions, and reconciling bank statements. Chapter 4 adds coverage of the new improved QuickBooks 2021 Bank Feed, including using the Advanced Bank Feeds mode and creating Bank rules for bank feeds. New exercises provide an opportunity for additional student practice the new banking features.

Chapter 5 Customers and Sales

Chapter 5 demonstrates how to record customer transactions. Topics include how to create a customer list, create invoices, record customer payments, and make deposits. Customer reports, including the aging of accounts receivable, are covered. Chapter 5 offers a new QuickBooks troubleshooting activity on how to discover an incorrect sales price and correct it.

Chapter 6 Vendors and Expenses

Chapter 6 focuses on recording vendor transactions, such as recording expenses for services received from vendors. Topics include writing checks, entering bills, and paying bills. Vendor reports, including the aging of accounts payable, are covered. QuickBooks 2021 new Receipt Management feature is previewed in Chapter 6.

Chapter 7 Inventory

Chapter 7 focuses on recording transactions related to inventory, including creating purchase orders, receiving inventory items, entering bills for inventory and paying bills. The QuickBooks Inventory Center and inventory reports are also covered in this chapter.

Chapter 8 Employees and Payroll

Chapter 8 covers tracking time using weekly timesheets and processing payroll using QuickBooks payroll service for withholdings. Also covered in this chapter is how to use tracked time to record billable time on customer invoices.

Chapter 9 QuickBooks Adjustments

Chapter 9 covers how to create a trial balance and enter adjusting entries to bring accounts up to date at the end of an accounting period. Four types of adjusting entries covered in the chapter are: prepaid items, unearned items, accrued expenses, and accrued revenues.

Chapter 10 QuickBooks Reports

Chapter 10 completes the accounting cycle, covering the adjusted trial balance and a variety of QuickBooks reports, including memorized reports. The main types of reports covered include financial statements, management reports, and tax reports. In addition, Chapter 10 contains new data analytics and graphing exercises.

Chapter 11 QuickBooks Service Company

Chapter 11 covers how to set up a new company in QuickBooks, create customers, vendors, and items lists, and enter transactions for a service company. The focus of Chapter 11 is on sole proprietorships.

Chapter 12 QuickBooks Service Company Case

Chapter 12 is a QuickBooks company case study that provides an opportunity to integrate QuickBooks skills and knowledge covered thus far in a comprehensive fashion for a sole proprietor service company.

Chapter 13 QuickBooks Merchandise Company

Chapter 13 covers how to set up a new merchandise corporation with inventory in QuickBooks, create customers, vendors, and items lists, and enter transactions for a merchandise company. A key topic covered in this chapter is how to set up a new QuickBooks company for businesses that have opening balances. Topics include how to make opening adjusting entries to properly account for the opening balances. End of period adjusting entries and financial reports are also included.

Chapter 14 QuickBooks Merchandise Company Case

Chapter 14 is a QuickBooks company case study that provides an opportunity to integrate QuickBooks skills and knowledge in a comprehensive fashion for a S Corporation that sells products. Opening balances and opening adjusting entries are included in addition to end of period adjusting entries and reports.

Chapter 15 Advanced QuickBooks Features forAccountants

This chapter covers advanced features of QuickBooks software including budgets, estimates, progress billing, credit card sales, accounting for uncollectible debts, the audit trail, accountant's copy, and the Ask My Accountant account.

Chapter 16 QuickBooks Desktop Versus QuickBooksOnline

Chapter 16 compares and contrasts the QuickBooks Desktop application and QuickBooks Online (QBO). QuickBooks user options and QuickBooks accountant options for QuickBooks Desktop and QBO are presented. Videos to accompany the chapter with discussion questions can be found at www.my-quickbooks.com, QB2021 Videos link.

Chapter 17 Quick Review Guide

Chapter 17 provides step-by-step instructions for frequently used customer, vendor, and employee tasks in a convenient, user-friendly resource that can also be used in preparing for QuickBooks Certification. Twenty-five multiple choice questions accompany the chapter that can be assigned to test understanding. In addition, working through Chapter 17 with the accompanying Starter File provides a simulation experience for better preparation.

Chapter 18 QuickBooks Consulting Project

This chapter outlines the project management milestones for development of a QuickBooks accounting system. Providing you with an opportunity to apply QuickBooks software to a live consulting project gives you hands-on professional experience for your resume.

Appendix A Install and Activate QuickBooks Software

Intuit provides QuickBooks Desktop 2021 software free to qualifying students. Appendix A contains step-by-step instructions for obtaining, installing, and activating QuickBooks Desktop 2021 software to accompany your text.

Appendix B Backup and Restore QuickBooks Files

Appendix B provides step-by-step instructions on how to restore the QuickBooks Starter files to accompany Chapters 1 through 10 of the text. In addition, Appendix B covers the steps to make backup copies of your QuickBooks files.

Appendix C www.My-QuickBooks.com

Appendix C summarizes features to accompany your text that you will find at www.My-QuickBooks.com, including QuickBooks videos, Excel Report templates, and Updates to your text and QuickBooks.

Appendix D QuickBooks Troubleshooting

Appendix D summarizes QuickBooks Troubleshooting resources, including QuickBooks Help, the new QuickBooks Tool Hub, and QuickBooks Troubleshooting (QT) Best Practices. Located as the last appendix in your text, it's convenient when you need assistance with QuickBooks troubleshooting.

Chapter 1

QuickBooks Quick Tour: Navigation and Settings

🔨 Rock Castle Construction

BACKSTORY

Rock Castle, owner of Rock Castle Construction, called to hire you as his accountant. His former accountant unexpectedly accepted a job offer in Hawaii, and Rock Castle Construction needs a replacement immediately. Mr. Castle indicates they use QuickBooks to maintain the company's accounting records. When you tell him that you're not familiar with QuickBooks, Mr. Castle reassures you, *"No problem! QuickBooks is easy to learn. Stop by my office this afternoon."*

When you arrive at Rock Castle Construction, Mr. Castle leads you to a desk as he rapidly explains Rock Castle's accounting.

"Rock Castle needs to keep records of transactions with customers, vendors, and employees. We must keep a record of our customers and the sales and services we provide to those customers. Also, it's crucial for the company to be able to bill customers promptly and keep a record of cash collected from them. If we don't know who owes Rock Castle money, we can't collect it.

"Rock Castle also needs to keep track of the supplies, materials, and inventory we purchase from vendors. We need to track all purchase orders, the items received, the bills received from vendors, and the payments made to vendors. If we don't track bills, we can't pay our vendors on time. And if Rock Castle doesn't pay its bills on time, the vendors don't like to sell to us.

"Also, we like to keep our employees happy. One way to do that is to pay them the right amount at the right time. So Rock Castle must keep track of the time worked by its employees, the amounts owed to the employees, and the wages and salaries paid to them.

"QuickBooks permits Rock Castle Construction to keep a record of all of these transactions. Also, we need records so we can prepare tax returns, financial reports for bank loans, and reports to evaluate the company's performance and make business decisions.

"Your first assignment is to learn more about QuickBooks." Mr. Castle tosses you a QuickBooks training manual as he rushes off to answer a phone call.

Slightly overwhelmed by Mr. Castle's rapid-fire delivery, you sink into a chair. As you look around your cubicle, you notice for the first time the leaning tower of papers stacked beside the computer, waiting to be processed. No wonder Mr. Castle wanted you to start right way.

Mr. Castle bursts back into your cubicle quickly tossing something onto your cluttered desk. *"And here's your new company smartphone—that way I can reach you anytime I need you!"*

Noticing your startled expression, Mr. Castle pauses and then reassuringly says, *"Don't worry—IT has already set up security for your new phone so that all financial communications will be secure."*

Opening the QuickBooks learning guide, you see the following.

Chapter 1

Learning Objectives

Chapter 1 introduces QuickBooks Desktop. In this chapter, you will learn about the following topics:

- What is an Easy Way to Learn QuickBooks?
- Install QuickBooks
- Start QuickBooks
- Restore a QuickBooks File
  - Restore Starter Files
  - Change Company Name
- QuickBooks SatNav
  - QuickBooks Settings
  - QuickBooks Transactions
  - QuickBooks Reports
- QuickBooks Navigation
- QuickBooks Home Page
  - Customers
  - Vendors
  - Employees
  - Banking
  - Company
- QuickBooks Navigation Bar
- QuickBooks Menus
- QuickBooks Reports
  - Create Reports
  - Export Reports to Excel
- QuickBooks Help and Troubleshooting
- Back Up QuickBooks Files
- Restore QuickBooks File Options
  - QBW Workflow
  - QBB Restore
- Close and Exit QuickBooks
- Accounting Essentials: Accounting Systems

WHAT IS AN EASY WAY TO LEARN QUICKBOOKS?

Learning QuickBooks requires integrating knowledge of accounting, financial systems, and financial technology. Don't become discouraged if you find that you need to go over the same material more than once. That is normal. Learning how accounting and financial technology is interrelated often requires repetition.

To make learning QuickBooks easier, we will use an effective three-step XPM approach to streamline learning QuickBooks:

eXplore → Practice → Master

1. **eXplore** QuickBooks Desktop using the chapter with step-by-step walk through screen captures. Don't worry about making mistakes or "breaking" Quickbooks. Instead, focus on learning how to navigate and use QuickBooks.
2. **Practice** entering information and transactions into QuickBooks end-of-chapter exercises.
3. **Master** QuickBooks with virtual company projects. The projects cover QuickBooks tasks from setting up a new QuickBooks company and entering transactions to generating QuickBooks reports.

First, we will eXplore using the Chapter illustrations, then we will Practice using Exercises at the end of the chapter, and finally we will Master QuickBooks by completing Projects. The eXplore Chapter activities use a Starter file. So you do not have to be stressed about errors that might carry forward to subsequent Chapters. The Projects, however, provide an opportunity for you to demonstrate mastery of QuickBooks and your QuickBooks data does carry forward to subsequent Projects.

XPM mapping for this chapter, listing eXplore activities with corresponding Practice and Master activities, follows.

1. eXplore	→	2. Practice	→	3. Master
Chapter 1		Exercises 1.1, 1.2		Project 1.1

💡 **Accounting Essentials appear at the end of the chapter. Tip: Preview Accounting Essentials <u>before</u> starting the chapter and then review Accounting Essentials <u>after</u> completing the chapter.**

Section 1.1

Install QuickBooks

QuickBooks® Desktop (QBDT) is a software-based financial system for entrepreneurs. QuickBooks Desktop Accountant software accompanies your *Computer Accounting with Quickbooks 2021* text.

REQUEST QUICKBOOKS SOFTWARE

To obtain QuickBooks Desktop 2021 software to accompany this text:

1   Go to **https://intuit.me/mh-desktop**. Note: if you have any issue with this url, go to www.mhhe.com/kay2021 for additional information and updates.

2   Follow the onscreen instructions to complete the Intuit request form for your QuickBooks Desktop 2021 student software. Be sure to select the version for this text: **QuickBooks Desktop 2021**.

3   After you receive email confirmation from Intuit Verification, follow the instructions provided to download your free QuickBooks Desktop Accountant 2021. Make a note of your License and Product numbers included in the email. If you don't receive the confirmation email, check your Spam folder.

⚠ **Note: If the new QuickBooks Desktop Manager appears as an option to download your QuickBooks software, do not use it. It is not designed for use with the Intuit QuickBooks Educational version. Use the QuickBooks standard installation instead.**

⚠ **Before installing QuickBooks Desktop software verify that your Windows operating system is compatible with the QuickBooks Desktop software. Note that QuickBooks Desktop 2021 is not compatible with Windows 7 or earlier.**

DOWNLOAD AND INSTALL QUICKBOOKS SOFTWARE

After downloading your QuickBooks Desktop 2021 software installer and verifying that your Windows operating system is compatible, install the QBDT 2021 software as follows:

1 If the installer does not open automatically, double-click on the QuickBooks Desktop 2021 installer to start installation. Follow the onscreen instructions. After the installer is loaded, to accept the license agreement and proceed with installation, select **Accept & Continue**.

2 When prompted to enter your License Number and Product Number, **copy and paste the License number and Product Number** from the Intuit email. Then select **Next**.

3 When the Choose your installation type window appears, select **Express > Next**.

4 Follow the onscreen instructions and select **Install** to install the QuickBooks software.

5 Various screens will appear while the QuickBooks software is installing. When the Installation Complete window appears, select **Open QuickBooks**.

6 After QuickBooks starts, if the Activate Quickbooks Desktop Now window appears, select **Begin Activation**. Follow the onscreen instructions to activate QuickBooks.

Intuit QuickBooks Desktop Installer

intuit quickbooks.

Welcome to QuickBooks

Complete your QuickBooks installation with just a few steps. For smooth installation, it is a good idea to close any open programs, especially virus protection programs.

Once the installer is loaded, accept the license agreement to continue.
View License Agreement

1

| Accept & Continue | Cancel |

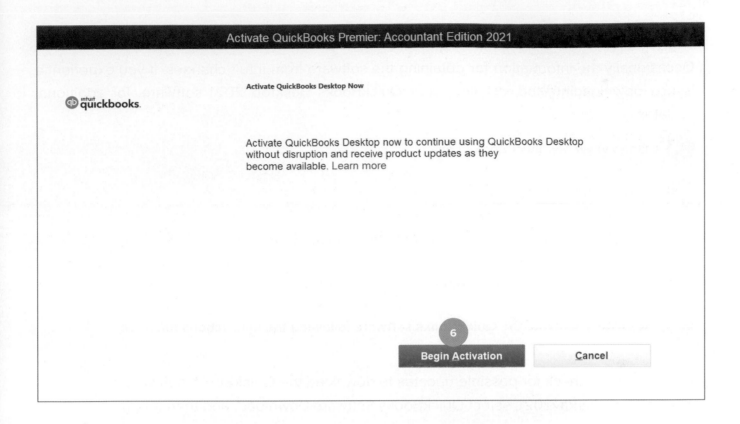

ACTIVATE QUICKBOOKS SOFTWARE

Three ways to activate/register your QuickBooks software are:

1. Activate the software when you install it as shown in the previous section
2. Select **Help menu > Activate QuickBooks Desktop**
3. Activate your QuickBooks software by phone at 800-316-1068 and select the appropriate menu option

> ⚠ **Activate your QuickBooks software! Failure to activate your QuickBooks trial version software may result in the software no longer functioning.**

> ⚠ **If you are locked out from using your QuickBooks software, select Help menu > Activate QuickBooks Desktop. If that is unsuccessful, try uninstalling and reinstalling the QuickBooks software.**

QUICKBOOKS SOFTWARE INSTALL UPDATES

Occasionally the information for obtaining the software from Intuit changes. If you experience issues downloading and installing your QuickBooks Desktop 2021 software, for additional updates:

1. Go to **www.My-QuickBooks.com**

2. Select **QB2021** link

3. Scroll down to **Download and Install QuickBooks Software**

4. Follow the instructions to download and install the QuickBooks software

5. **Register / Activate the QuickBooks software following the instructions provided**

Another site to check for possible updates to download the QuickBooks software is www.mhhe.com/kay2021, select QuickBooks Software Download, and then follow instructions provided.

> **QuickBooks Support. QuickBooks Desktop Installation Support: 888-222-7276. QuickBooks Desktop Registration Support 800-316-1068.**

> ⚠ **Activate QuickBooks software with Intuit after installing or you will be locked out of the software. If registered, you will be able to use the QuickBooks software for up to 1 year. If you fail to register the software, you will be locked out of the software and unable to use it.**

> **QuickBooks Accountant software that comes with your text is Windows-based software. If you have a Mac, see your instructor. Also, go to www.My-QuickBooks.com. Select QB & My Mac for options to consider.**

Section 1.2

Start QuickBooks

To start QuickBooks software, click the **QuickBooks** icon on your desktop. If a QuickBooks icon does not appear on your desktop, from Microsoft® Windows® click **Start** button > **QuickBooks** > **QuickBooks Premier Accountant Edition**.

QuickBooks Accountant includes all the features of QuickBooks Pro plus features for client services. If you use QuickBooks Pro, your screens may appear slightly different than those appearing in this text.

Section 1.3
Restore a QuickBooks File

QuickBooks uses several different types of files. Two types of QuickBooks files that you will be using throughout this text are:

1. **QBW file.** The QuickBooks working file in which you can enter accounting data and transactions.

2. **QBB file.** The QuickBooks backup file used to move a QuickBooks file to another computer or if the working file (QBW) fails. The starter files provided for you with this text are QBB files. Because QBB files are compressed, the QBB file must be restored (unzipped) using QuickBooks software. Unlike Excel files, for example, QBB files cannot be opened by clicking on the file.

The QBW file is the only QuickBooks file in which you can enter data and transactions. When you enter transactions into a QBW file, the information is automatically saved. The typical workflow for a business is to use the QBW file to record transactions and periodically back up to a QBB (backup) file.

RESTORE STARTER FILE

For purposes of this text, we will use QuickBooks Starter files that are QBB files containing the company data needed to complete the assignments in this text. The QBB Starter files are compressed files that must be unzipped, or restored, into QBW files before the files can be used.

For your convenience, **QuickBooks (QBB) Starter files accompany** *Computer Accounting with QuickBooks 2021*.

Go to www.mhhe.com/kay2021 to download the Starter files from the Online Learning Center.

To stay organized, consider adding a folder to your Desktop: QBB STARTER FILES. Then copy the QBB STARTER files to that folder.

For Connect users, the Starter Files are accessible through your Connect Chapter Assignments.

⚠ **Desktop (QBDT) QBB Files** are compressed backup files that can be restored and used. To use QBB Starter files, the compressed file must be restored following the instructions here. Since it is a compressed file, you cannot open and use the QuickBooks Starter files by simply clicking on the file. Instead you must follow the instructions here to unzip and restore the data file before using it.

To restore the Starter File for Chapter 1 from a QBB file to a QBW file:

1 From the No Company Open window, select **Open or restore an existing company**. (If the Let's get your business set up quickly! window appears first, select **Other Options > Open Existing File**.)

2 Select **Restore a backup copy**

3 Click **Next**

4 When the Open or Restore Company window appears, select **Local backup**

5 Click **Next**

6 Identify the location of the **CHAPTER 1 STARTER.QBB** file. If you copied the CHAPTER 1 STARTER file to your desktop, select the **Look in** field to find the location of the .QBB file on your desktop.

7 Select the file: **CHAPTER 1 STARTER.QBB**

8 The Files of type field should automatically display: **QBW Backup (*.QBB)**

9 Click **Open**

10 When the Open or Restore window appears, click **Next**

11 Identify the file name and location of the QBW company file. To save the QBW (working file) on your desktop, select the location to save in: **Desktop**. (Another option is to save your QBW files to Users > Public > Public Documents > Intuit > QuickBooks > Company Files. Be sure you have permissions to save to a folder.)

12 Enter QBW File name: **YourName Chapter 1**. (Insert your name in the QBW file name so you can identify your files.)

13 The Save as type field should automatically appear as **QuickBooks Files (*.QBW)**

14 Click **Save**

15 Click **OK** when the QuickBooks Desktop Information window appears notifying you that **You're opening a QuickBooks sample file**. (If a message appears indicating your file needs to be updated, select Yes. Then follow the onscreen instructions.)

Now that we have restored the QBB file (CHAPTER 1 STARTER.QBB) to a QBW file (Chapter 1.QBW), we can use the QBW file to update settings, enter transactions, and create reports.

CHANGE COMPANY NAME

So that your name automatically appears on reports and checks, update the Company Name setting to add your name to the company name.

To change a company name in QuickBooks, complete the following:

1 From My Shortcuts on the Navigation Bar, select **My Company**

2 When the My Company window appears, select **Edit**

3 When the Company Information window appears, update the Company Name field to: **YourName Chapter 1 Rock Castle Construction**

4 Select **OK** to close the Company Information window

5 **Close** the My Company window

Section 1.4

 ## QuickBooks SatNav

QuickBooks SatNav is your satellite navigation for QuickBooks, assisting you in navigating QuickBooks

Learning QuickBooks will be easier if you have an overview of the entire QuickBooks system. Just like you use your smartphone with satellite mapping to zoom in for detail and zoom out for the big picture, when learning Quickbooks, you may need to adjust your thinking to zoom out to see the big picture of the entire financial system or at other times zoom in to view details.

QuickBooks SatNav is designed to assist you in zooming out and zooming in to successfully navigate QuickBooks. QuickBooks SatNav divides QuickBooks into three main processes:

1. **QuickBooks Settings** include Company Settings and the Chart of Accounts.

   Company Settings involve setting up a new company and selecting company preferences, such as displaying account numbers. QuickBooks uses an EasyStep Interview that asks us questions about our business. QuickBooks then automatically creates a company file for our business. In Chapters 1 through 10 of this text, we will use Rock Castle Construction, a sample company data file, that has already been created for us. In Chapters 11, 12, 13 and 14, we will set up a new QuickBooks company. To learn how to set up a company file, see Chapter 11.

   The Chart of Accounts, a list of all the accounts for a company, is another aspect of QuickBooks Settings. Accounts are used to sort and track accounting information. For example, a business needs one account for cash, another account to track amounts customers owe (Accounts Receivable), and yet another account to track inventory. QuickBooks automatically creates a Chart of Accounts in the EasyStep Interview when setting up a new company. QuickBooks then permits us to modify the Chart of Accounts to customize it for specific company needs.

   QuickBooks Settings are covered in Chapters 1, 2, 11, 12, 13, and 14.

2. **QuickBooks Transactions** involve recording transactions as **input** into the financial system. Transaction types can be categorized as Banking, Customers and Sales,

Vendors and Expenses, and Employees and Payroll. In basic terms, recording transactions involves recording money in and money out of the company.

Transactions are exchanges between the QuickBooks company and other parties, such as customers, vendors, and employees. QuickBooks Home Page is an overview of the most frequently used transactions in a flowchart form.

Typically in a transaction, the company gives something and receives something in exchange. QuickBooks is used to keep a record of what is given and what is received in a transaction. We can enter transaction information into QuickBooks using the onscreen Journal or onscreen forms, such as onscreen invoices and onscreen checks.

QuickBooks Transactions are covered in Chapters 3 through 8, 11, 12, 13, 14, and 15.

3. **QuickBooks Reports** are the **output** of the system. Reports typically provide information to decision makers. For example, accounting information is used to prepare:

- **Financial statements** for external users, such as creditors and investors. Internal users, such as managers, also may use financial statements. Financial statements are standardized financial reports that summarize information about past transactions. The primary financial statements for a business are:
  - **Balance Sheet**: summarizes what a company owns and owes on a particular date.
  - **Profit & Loss Statement** (or **Income Statement**): summarizes what a company has earned and the expenses incurred to earn the income.
  - **Statement of Cash Flows**: summarizes cash inflows and cash outflows for operating, investing, and financing activities of a business.
- **Tax returns** for federal and state tax agencies.
- **Management reports** for company managers and owners to use when making business decisions. Such decisions include: Will we have enough cash to pay our bills on time? Are we collecting customer payments when due? An example of a management report is a cash budget that projects amounts of cash that will be collected and spent in the future.

Quickbooks Reports are covered in several chapters with a focus on reports in Chapters 9, 10, 11, 12, 13, 14, and 15.

This QuickBooks SatNav will be used in the first 15 chapters to illustrate which aspects of QuickBooks the chapter will focus on. If you start to feel lost in QuickBooks, return to the QuickBooks SatNav to assist you in navigating QuickBooks.

In later QuickBooks SatNavs, the portion of the QuickBooks SatNav that is the focus of the chapter will be highlighted on the QuickBooks SatNav.

Learning QuickBooks requires integrating knowledge of accounting, financial systems, and financial technology. Don't become discouraged if you find that you need to go over the same material more than once. That is normal. Learning how accounting and financial tech is interrelated takes repetition.

🌐 QuickBooks SatNav

⚙️ QuickBooks Settings

CHAPTERS
1, 2, 11, 12, 13, 14

⚙️ Company Settings
⚙️ Chart of Accounts

💰 QuickBooks Transactions

CHAPTERS
3, 4, 5, 6, 7, 8, 11, 12, 13, 14, 15

>>> 💰 *Money In* >>>   >>> *Money Out* 💰 >>>

💰 Banking
💰 Customers & Sales
💰 Vendors & Expenses
💰 Employees & Payroll

📊 QuickBooks Reports

CHAPTERS
9, 10, 11, 12, 13, 14, 15

📊 Reports

Section 1.5

QuickBooks Navigation

Taking a few minutes to explore QuickBooks navigation will make learning QuickBooks easier. QuickBooks offers three different ways to navigate QuickBooks software:

1 **Home Page.** Click the Home icon on the Navigation Bar (Icon Bar) to reveal flowcharts of frequently used tasks.

2 **Navigation Bar.** Click on the Navigation Bar (Icon Bar) to display customer, vendor, and employee centers and frequently used windows, such as customer invoices.

3 **Menu Bar.** Click on the Menu Bar to reveal a drop-down menu for each area.

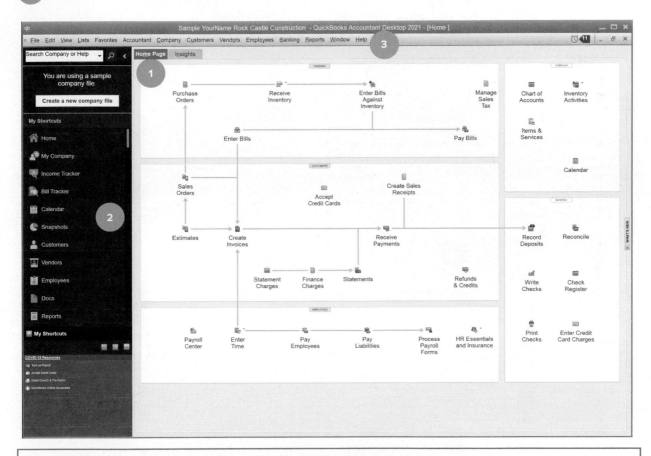

> **What's New may appear on the right side of your Home Page. Open What's New to view the new features in the 2021 version of QuickBooks Desktop. Click the X beside What's New if you wish to remove it from your Home Page.**

Next, we explore navigation in greater detail.

Section 1.6

QuickBooks Home Page

To view the QuickBooks Home Page, click the **Home** icon in the Navigation Bar. The Home Page contains the following main categories of transactions and tasks:

1. Customers and sales transactions

2. Vendors and expenses transactions

3. Employees and payroll transactions

4. Banking and credit card transactions

5. Company tasks

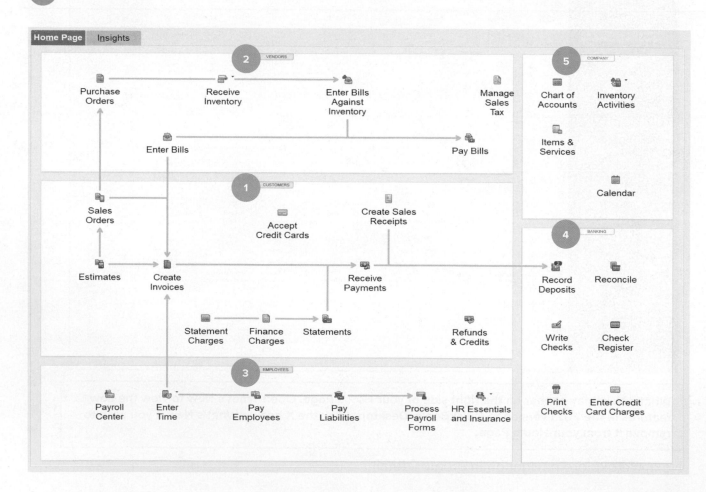

CUSTOMERS

The Customers section is a flowchart of the main activities associated with sales and customers. For example, we can:

1 Create estimates

2 Create invoices to bill customers

3 Record payments received from customers (cash, check, and credit card payments)

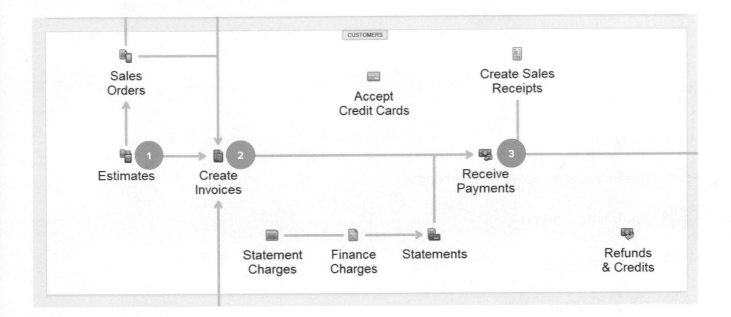

VENDORS

From the Vendors flowchart, we can record:

1 Purchase orders (orders placed to purchase items)

2 Inventory received

3 Bills received for inventory

4 Bills received for services

5 Bills paid

6 Sales tax paid

EMPLOYEES

From the Employees flowchart, we can:

1 Enter time worked

2 Pay employees

3 Pay payroll tax liabilities

4 Process payroll forms

BANKING

From the Banking section, we can:

1. Record deposits

2. Write checks

3. Print checks

4. Reconcile a bank statement

5. View the check register

6. Enter credit card charges

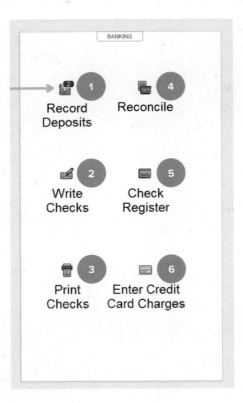

COMPANY

From the Company section, we can access:

1 Chart of Accounts. A list of accounts a company uses to track accounting information.

2 Items & Services. A list of items and services that a company buys and/or sells.

3 Inventory Activities. Perform inventory activities including accessing the Inventory Center or adjusting the quantity of inventory on hand.

4 Calendar. View your to do list and reminders in a calendar form.

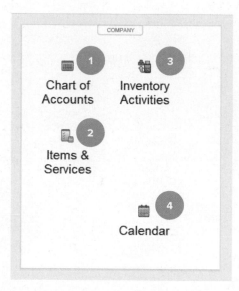

Section 1.7

QuickBooks Navigation Bar

QuickBooks Navigation Bar (or Icon Bar) is located on the left side of your screen. The Navigation Bar permits you to quickly access various QuickBooks screens. The Navigation Bar can be displayed either at the top beneath the Menu Bar or on the left side of the QuickBooks window.

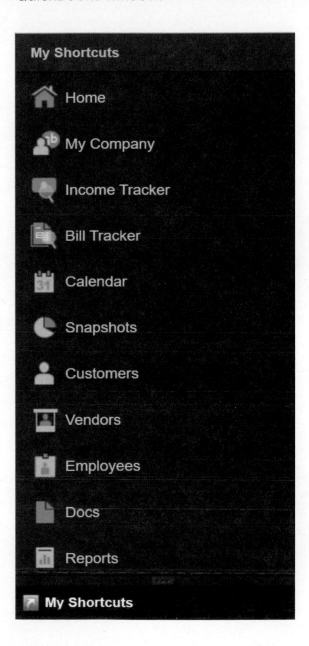

To display the Navigation Bar if it does not appear on your screen:

1   Select **View** on the Menu Bar

2   Select **Left Icon Bar**

The Navigation Bar, or Icon Bar, can be customized to display the tasks that are used most frequently. To customize the Navigation Bar:

1   Select **View** on the Menu Bar

2   Select **Customize Icon Bar**

3   **Drag and drop** to reorder the tasks in the following order:
- Home
- Customers
- Vendors
- Employees
- Reports
- My Company
- Calendar
- Snapshots
- Income Tracker
- Bill Tracker
- Docs

4   Select the **OK** button to close

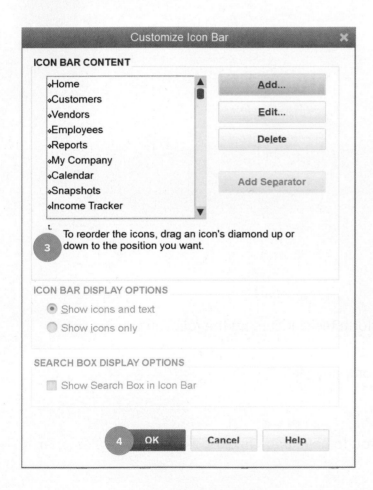

Section 1.8

QuickBooks Menus

We can also access tasks using the Menu Bar across the top of the QuickBooks window.

 Select **File** on the Menu Bar to display the drop-down File Menu

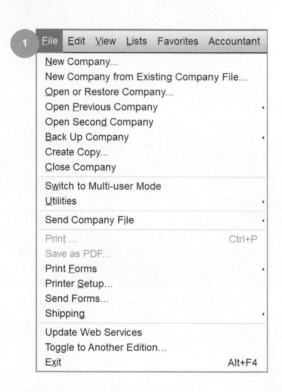

From the drop-down File Menu, you can perform tasks including the following:

- Create a new company file
- Create a new company from an existing company file
- Open or restore an existing company file
- Open a previous company file
- Open a second company file, permitting you to have two QuickBooks company files open at the same time
- Back up your company file
- Create a copy of your company file
- Close a company file

- Switch to multi-user mode when QuickBooks is used on a network
- Use utilities such as importing and exporting files
- Send a copy of your QuickBooks company file to your accountant

QuickBooks output tasks include:

- Print or save as a Portable Document Format (PDF) file
- Print Forms for printing forms, such as invoices, sales receipts, and tax forms
- Printer Setup to select a printer as well as fonts and margins
- Send Forms to email various QuickBooks forms, such as sending invoices to customers
- Ship using FedEx, UPS, and USPS

In QuickBooks Accountant Edition, the File Menu displays Toggle to Another Edition. This command allows you to switch to another QuickBooks edition, such as QuickBooks Pro.

To remove the drop-down File Menu from the screen, click anywhere outside the drop-down menu or press the **Esc** (Escape) key.

2 Select **Edit** on the Menu Bar to display the drop-down Edit Menu

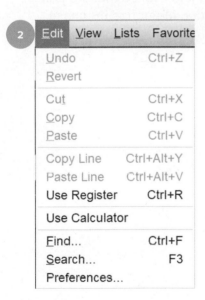

From the drop-down Edit Menu, you can undo, cut, copy, paste, and edit information entered in QuickBooks.

The Edit Menu changes based upon which windows are open. For example:

3 Click the **Home** icon in the Navigation Bar to display the Home Page

4 Click the **Purchase Orders** icon in the Vendors section of the Home Page to display the purchase order form

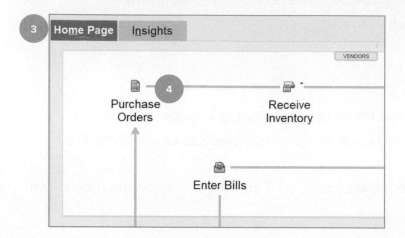

5 Select **Edit** on the Menu Bar to display the drop-down Edit Menu again. Notice that the Edit Menu now contains: New Purchase Order, Duplicate Purchase Order, Memorize Purchase Order, and Change Account Color.

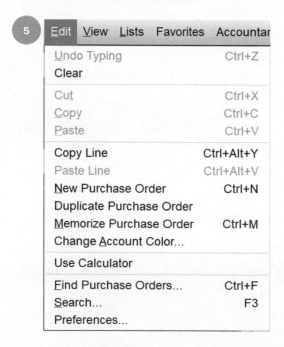

6 Click **Lists** on the Menu Bar to display the drop-down Lists Menu

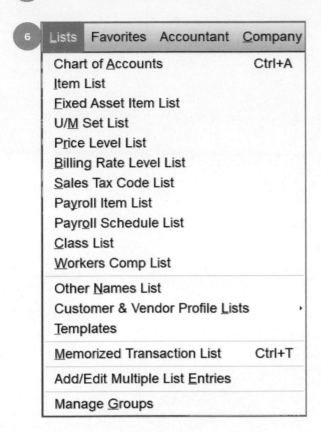

From the drop-down Lists Menu, you can access various lists of information.

- **Chart of Accounts.** A list of accounts used to record transactions.
- **Item List.** A list of inventory items that you buy and sell or a list of services provided to customers.
- **Payroll Item List.** A list of items related to payroll checks and company payroll expense such as salary, hourly wages, federal and state withholding, unemployment taxes, Medicare, and Social Security.
- **Templates.** A list of templates for business forms, such as invoices and purchase orders.
- **Memorized Transaction List.** A list of recurring transactions that are memorized or saved. For example, if your company pays $900 in rent each month, then the rent payment transaction can be memorized to eliminate the need to reenter it each month.

7   Click **Accountant** on the Menu Bar to display the drop-down Accountant Menu

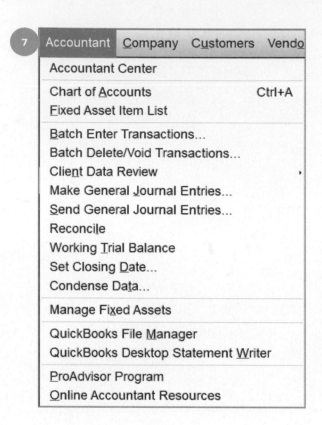

From the drop-down Accountant Menu, you can access features accountants use for client services.

- **Accountant Center.** A central location to organize accountant tools in QuickBooks.
- **Chart of Accounts.** A list of accounts used to record transactions.
- **Client Data Review.** This tool streamlines client file cleanup tasks.
- **Make General Journal Entries.** An onscreen journal for the accountant to make correcting and adjusting entries.
- **Reconcile.** The accountant can reconcile client bank statements.
- **Working Trial Balance.** The accountant can use this to review beginning balances, adjustments, and ending balances.
- **Set Closing Date.** The accountant can set the closing date for the accounting period.
- **Condense Data.** This feature permits the accountant to create a period copy of a client's QuickBooks files. For example, an accountant might create a period copy of a client's 2021 accounting year to provide to the IRS.

- **Online Accountant Resources.** QuickBooks offers desktop and online accounting solutions. See Chapter 16 of this text for more information about QuickBooks Online Accountant.

8   Click **Company** on the Menu Bar to display the drop-down Company Menu

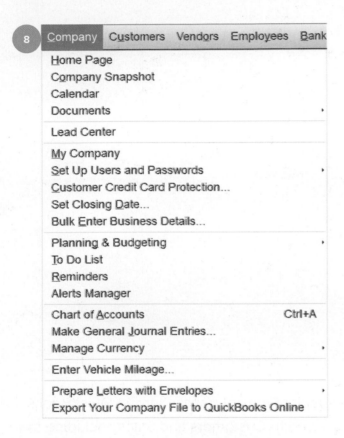

From the Company Menu, you can:
- Access company information and, for example, change the company name
- Set up users and restrict access to certain parts of QuickBooks
- Change your password
- Set up budgets and use planning decision tools
- Create a To Do List and Reminders
- Access the Chart of Accounts and onscreen Journal
- Enter vehicle mileage
- Export Company File to QuickBooks Online

9   Click **Customers** on the Menu Bar to display the drop-down Customers Menu

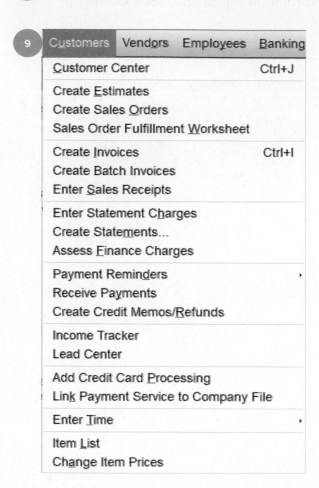

Customers and sales transactions are one of four major types of transactions in QuickBooks. The Customers Menu lists the various activities related to Customers and Sales, including the following. Notice that some of the customer activities on the drop-down Customers Menu can also be accessed from the Home Page.

- Access the Customer Center
- Create estimates
- Create invoices
- Create batch invoices
- Receive payments from customers
- Enter credit memos or refunds
- Access the Item List
- Change item prices

10   Click **Vendors** on the Menu Bar to display the drop-down Vendors Menu

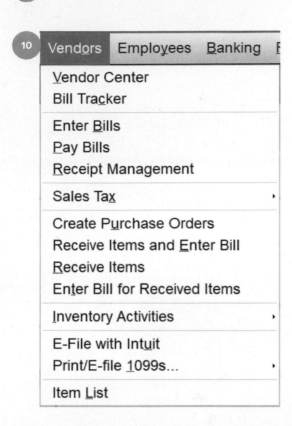

Vendors and expenses transactions are one of four major types of transactions in QuickBooks. The Vendors Menu lists the various activities related to Vendors and Expenses, including the following. Notice that some of the vendor activities on the drop-down Vendors Menu can also be accessed from the Home Page.

- Access the Vendor Center
- Enter Bills
- Pay Bills
- Create Purchase Orders
- Receive Items and Enter Bill
- Receive Items
- Enter Bill for Received Items
- Perform inventory activities, such as entering new items, adjusting quantity or value on hand, and creating a physical inventory worksheet
- Print/E-file 1099s
- Access the Item List

11   Click **Employees** on the Menu Bar to display the drop-down Employee Menu

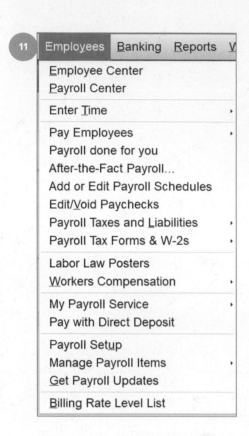

Employees or payroll transactions are one of four major types of transactions in QuickBooks. The Employees Menu lists the various activities related to employees and payroll, including the following. Notice that some of the employee activities on the drop-down Employees Menu can also be accessed from the Home Page.

- Access the Employee Center
- Access the Payroll Center
- Enter time
- Pay employees
- Add or edit payroll schedules
- Edit or void paychecks
- Pay payroll taxes and liabilities
- Prepare payroll tax forms and W-2s
- Pay with direct deposit

Click **Banking** on the Menu Bar to display the drop-down Banking Menu

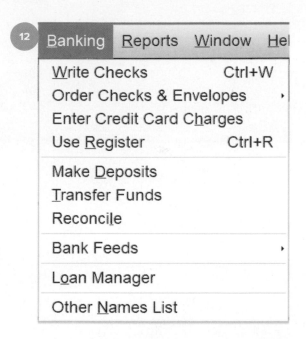

Banking transactions are one of four major types of transactions in QuickBooks. The Banking Menu lists the various activities related to banking, including the following. Notice that some of the banking activities on the drop-down Banking Menu can also be accessed from the Home Page.

- Write checks
- Enter credit card charges
- Use Check Register
- Make deposits
- Transfer funds
- Reconcile bank statements

Click **Reports** on the Menu Bar to display the list of reports that QuickBooks can create for your company

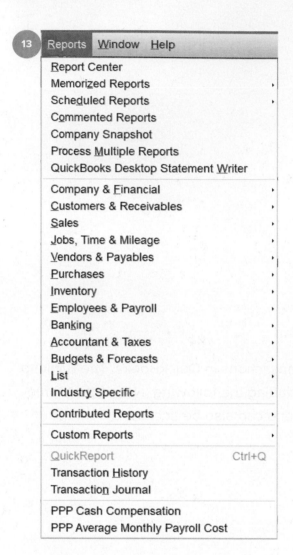

The Reports Menu lists the various activities related to preparing reports, including the following.

- Access the Report Center
- Access memorized reports that have been saved to reuse
- Access scheduled reports that are to be run at specific times
- Access different types of reports, such as company reports, customer reports, sales reports, vendor reports, and employee and payroll reports
- Access the transaction journal

Notice that reports can also be accessed from the Report Center by selecting Reports on the Navigation Bar.

14 Click **Window** on the Menu Bar to display the drop-down Window Menu. From this menu we can switch between windows to display onscreen.

15 If not already selected, select **Create Purchase Orders** window from the drop-down menu. Then **close** the Create Purchase Orders window by clicking the **X** in the upper right corner of the Create Purchase Orders window.

14

Window   Help
Arrange Icons
Close All
Tile Vertically
Tile Horizontally
Cascade
✓ 1 Home
2 Create Purchase Orders

15

Section 1.9

QuickBooks Reports

Preparing reports is an important aspect of an accountant's role. QuickBooks offers many different types of reports that can be customized to meet business needs.

CREATE REPORTS

To prepare a QuickBooks report, such as a Trial Balance, for Rock Castle Construction:

1   To view the Report Center, select **Reports** in the My Shortcuts section of the Navigation Bar

2   Select **Accountant & Taxes** from the report categories on the left of the window

3   Select **Carousel View**

4   Select **Trial Balance** report

5   Select the date range: **11/01/2024 To 11/30/2024**

6   Select **Run** icon to display the Trial Balance report. (Optional) If you would like to print the Trial Balance report, with the Trial Balance displayed on your QuickBooks screen, select Print to print the report. Leave the report displayed on your screen.

EXPORT REPORTS TO EXCEL

QuickBooks offers the option of exporting reports to Microsoft Excel® or PDF format.

To organize your text assignments, first we will download Excel Report Templates so all of your chapter assignments can be exported into one Excel file instead of separate Excel files.

To download Excel Report Templates for QuickBooks assignments:

1 If you are using Connect, download the Excel Report Templates from Connect. If not using connect, go to **www.My-QuickBooks.com**, select **QB2021** link, scroll down to **Excel Reports Templates**. Or go to the Online Learning Center at **www.mhhe.com/kay2021**.

2 Download the **Excel Report Template** for **Chapter 1** to your Desktop

3 **Open** the Excel workbook. (If you receive a Protected Mode message, click Enable Editing.)

4   Select **File > Save As**

5   Enter file name: **YourLastName FirstName CH1 REPORTS**

6   The filename extension should be: **.xls or .xlsx**

7   **Close** the Excel workbook

C1.9.1 Trial Balance. To export the Trial Balance QuickBooks report to the Excel Report Template:

1   To export the Trial Balance from the QuickBooks software, with the Trial Balance report displayed on your screen, select **Excel**

2   Select **Create New Worksheet**

3   When the Send Report to Excel window appears, select **Replace an existing worksheet**

4   Click the **Browse** button and select your **CH1 REPORTS Excel file**. Select **Open.**

5   From the drop-down list, select the sheet: **C1.9.1 TB**

6   Click the **Advanced** button

7   Uncheck **Space between columns**

8   Uncheck **Include QuickBooks Export Guide worksheet with helpful advice**

9   Select **On printed report and screen**

10   Click **OK**

11   Click **Export**

12   When the Export Report Alert window appears, select **Do not display this message in the future**

13   Select **Yes**

14 Click the **X** in the upper right corner of the Trial Balance window to close this report. If asked if you would like to memorize the report, select **No**.

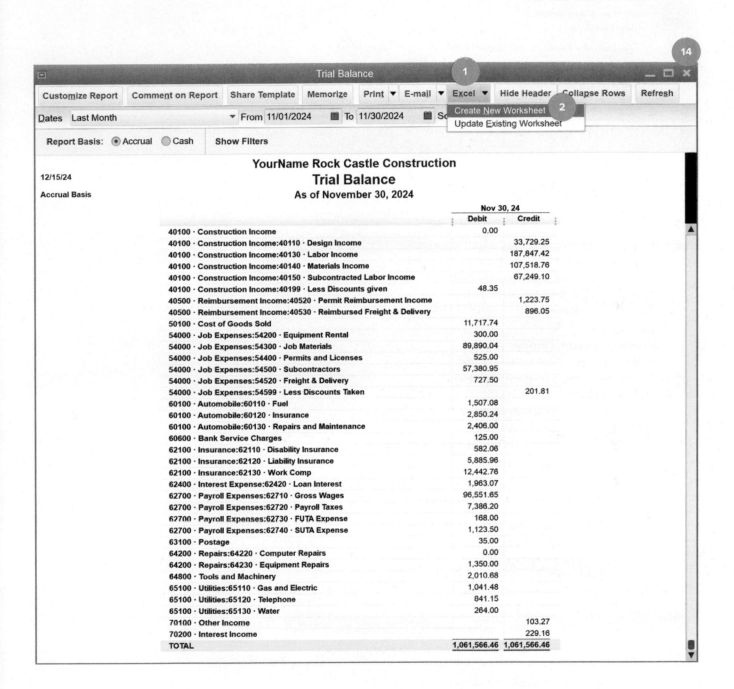

Trial Balance

| Customize Report | Comment on Report | Share Template | Memorize | Print ▼ | E-mail ▼ | Excel ▼ | Hide Header | Collapse Rows | Refresh |

Dates Last Month ▼   From 11/01/2024   To 11/30/2024

Create New Worksheet
Update Existing Worksheet

Report Basis: ● Accrual ○ Cash   Show Filters

YourName Rock Castle Construction
Trial Balance
As of November 30, 2024

12/15/24
Accrual Basis

	Nov 30, 24	
	Debit	Credit
40100 · Construction Income	0.00	
40100 · Construction Income:40110 · Design Income		33,729.25
40100 · Construction Income:40130 · Labor Income		187,847.42
40100 · Construction Income:40140 · Materials Income		107,518.76
40100 · Construction Income:40150 · Subcontracted Labor Income		67,249.10
40100 · Construction Income:40199 · Less Discounts given	48.35	
40500 · Reimbursement Income:40520 · Permit Reimbursement Income		1,223.75
40500 · Reimbursement Income:40530 · Reimbursed Freight & Delivery		896.05
50100 · Cost of Goods Sold	11,717.74	
54000 · Job Expenses:54200 · Equipment Rental	300.00	
54000 · Job Expenses:54300 · Job Materials	89,890.04	
54000 · Job Expenses:54400 · Permits and Licenses	525.00	
54000 · Job Expenses:54500 · Subcontractors	57,380.95	
54000 · Job Expenses:54520 · Freight & Delivery	727.50	
54000 · Job Expenses:54599 · Less Discounts Taken		201.81
60100 · Automobile:60110 · Fuel	1,507.08	
60100 · Automobile:60120 · Insurance	2,850.24	
60100 · Automobile:60130 · Repairs and Maintenance	2,406.00	
60600 · Bank Service Charges	125.00	
62100 · Insurance:62110 · Disability Insurance	582.06	
62100 · Insurance:62120 · Liability Insurance	5,885.96	
62100 · Insurance:62130 · Work Comp	12,442.76	
62400 · Interest Expense:62420 · Loan Interest	1,963.07	
62700 · Payroll Expenses:62710 · Gross Wages	96,551.65	
62700 · Payroll Expenses:62720 · Payroll Taxes	7,386.20	
62700 · Payroll Expenses:62730 · FUTA Expense	168.00	
62700 · Payroll Expenses:62740 · SUTA Expense	1,123.50	
63100 · Postage	35.00	
64200 · Repairs:64220 · Computer Repairs	0.00	
64200 · Repairs:64230 · Equipment Repairs	1,350.00	
64800 · Tools and Machinery	2,010.68	
65100 · Utilities:65110 · Gas and Electric	1,041.48	
65100 · Utilities:65120 · Telephone	841.15	
65100 · Utilities:65130 · Water	264.00	
70100 · Other Income		103.27
70200 · Interest Income		229.16
TOTAL	**1,061,566.46**	**1,061,566.46**

Excel should open on your screen with your QuickBooks Trial Balance inserted. (If you receive an error message when you attempt to export an Excel report, save your Excel report workbook, then close the workbook and Excel software. Then export the report as instructed, saving and closing Excel after each report export. Basically, in some versions of Excel, you must save and close the workbook after each report export, before exporting the next report.)

1 Select the **1 REPORTS** sheet tab

2 Mark the report sheet you completed by inserting an "**X**"

3 Save your **CH1 REPORTS** Excel workbook using the filename: **YourLastName FirstName CH1 REPORTS**

4 (Optional) If you would like to print the Trial Balance report, with the Trial Balance displayed on your QuickBooks screen, select **Print** to print the report

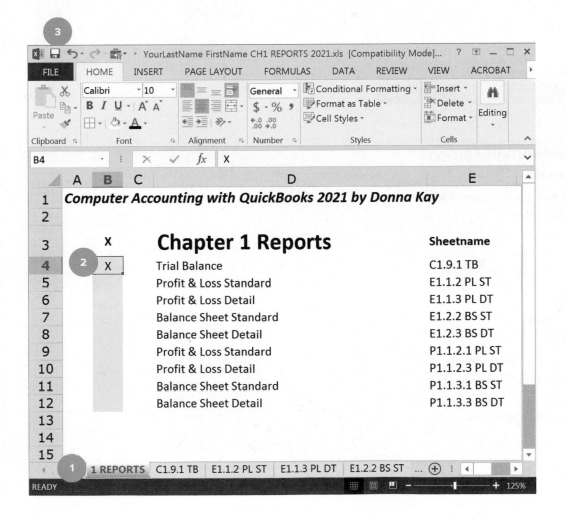

Section 1.10
QuickBooks Help and Troubleshooting

QUICKBOOKS HELP

To use the Quickbooks Help Menu:

1. Select **Help** on the Menu Bar to display the drop-down menu of Help features

2. Select **QuickBooks Desktop Help** from the Help Menu, and the Have a Question? window will appear

3. At the top of the Have a Question? window, you can type in your question and then view the results

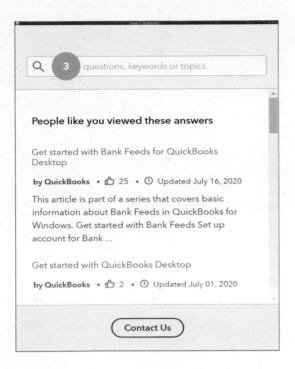

QUICKBOOKS TOOL HUB

QuickBooks Tool Hub is a new feature that is a launchpad for QuickBooks Desktop troubleshooting tools. The QuickBooks Tool Hub is where you can find tools for fixing QuickBooks Desktop issues.

To download and install the QuickBooks Tool Hub:

1. Select **Help** on the Menu Bar to display the drop-down Help menu

2. From the Help menu select **QuickBooks Tool Hub: Fix Setup and File Issues**. If you receive an error message, select **Retry**.

3. Follow the onscreen instructions to **download** the QuickBooks Tool Hub, saving it to your Downloads folder or to your Desktop where you can find it easily

4. **Open** the downloaded file named **QuickBooksToolHub.exe**

5. Follow the instructions on your screen to **install** the QuickBooks Tool Hub

6. After installed, to open the QuickBooks Tool Hub, **double-click on the QuickBooks Tool Hub icon** that appears on your desktop. If the icon does not automatically appear on your desktop, use your Windows search feature to search for the QuickBooks Tool Hub app.

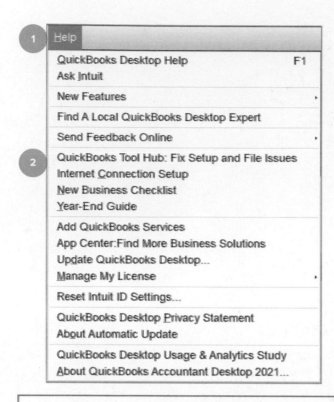

Note: Intuit recommends using QuickBooks Tool Hub on Windows 10, 64-bit for the best experience.

The QuickBooks Tool Hub organizes the tools into categories for different types of problems. To view tools for the various categories, select the tabs on the left side of the Tool Hub.

To use the QuickBooks Tool Hub:

1. Select **Home** tab to view a summary of the tool categories

2. Select the **Company Files Issues** tab. These tools include the QuickBooks File Doctor to repair common company data file issues.

3. Select the **Network Issues** tab. These tools address issues with your network or computers on your network.

4. Select the **Program Problems** tab. These tools resolve performance issues, such as the program crashing, or printing and PDF issues.

5. Select the **Installation Issues** tab. Click this tab to resolve issues with installing and uninstalling QuickBooks Desktop software.

6. Select the **Password Reset** tab. Use this tab if you need to use the password reset tool to reset your QuickBooks Desktop password.

7 Select the **Help & Support** tab. Click this tab to contact QuickBooks support if you have not resolved your issue with the Tool Hub. Also, manage your Intuit QuickBooks account.

8 Select the **Advanced Tools** tab. This tab contains Windows shortcuts for common tasks in troubleshooting QuickBooks errors.

9 Select **Installed Version - Check for Updates** to find the latest updates to the QuickBooks Tool Hub

10 **Close** the QuickBooks Tool Hub by selecting the **X** in the upper right corner of the Tool Hub

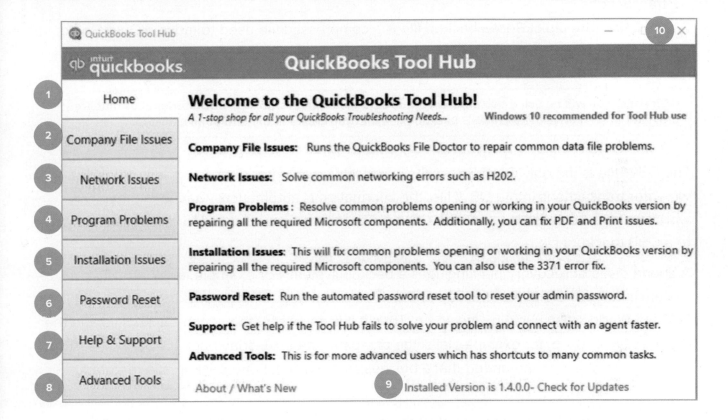

QUICKBOOKS TROUBLESHOOTING (QT) BEST PRACTICES

QuickBooks Troubleshooting (QT) Best Practices can increase your chances of success at troubleshooting QuickBooks. One QT Best Practice is to use a structured, process approach to QuickBooks Troubleshooting to streamline the troubleshooting process and increase effectiveness in resolving issues. For more information about QT Best Practices, see Appendix D: QuickBooks Troubleshooting (QT).

Section 1.11

Back Up QuickBooks Files

As mentioned previously, there are two types of QuickBooks files that we will be using in this text.

1. **QBW file.** The QuickBooks working file in which you can enter accounting data and transactions.
2. **QBB file.** The QuickBooks backup file is a compressed file used to move a QuickBooks file to another computer or if the working file (QBW) fails.

QBB Files. You will be using two different types QBB files with this text: (1) QBB Starter Files that are provided to start an activity (2) QBB Backup Files that you create at the end of an activity.

The QBW file is the only QuickBooks file in which we can enter data and transactions. When we enter transactions into a QBW file, the information is automatically saved. The typical workflow for a business is to use the QBW file to record transactions and periodically back up to a QBB (backup) file.

A sound disaster recovery plan includes a backup system. For example, a good backup system is to have a different backup for each business day: Monday backup, Tuesday backup, Wednesday backup, and so on. Then if it is necessary to use the backup file and the Wednesday backup, for example, fails, the company has a Tuesday backup to use. Furthermore, it is recommended that a business store at least one backup at a remote location.

Typically, the backup file is used only if the company's working file (QBW) fails. Then the backup file (QBB) can be restored and used. So it is important that the backup copy is as up to date as possible in case it must be used to replace lost company data. The backup file (QBB) is compressed and must be restored to a working file (QBW) before you can use it to enter data or transactions.

The backup schedule used with this text is to create a backup QBB file at the end of each chapter, exercise or project.

To save a backup (QBB) file:

1 With your QuickBooks file (*.QBW) open, click **File**

2 Select **Back Up Company**

3 Select **Create Local Backup**

4 When the Create Backup window appears, select **Local backup**

5 Select **Options** to specify your backup settings

6 If asked where to save your files, to make it easier to find your backup files, click the **Browse** button

7 Select **Desktop**. Click **OK** to close the Browse for Folder window.

8 Select **Add the date and time of the backup to the file name (recommended)**

9 Select **Complete verification (recommended)**

10 Click **OK** again to close the Backup Options window. Select **Use this Location** if a QuickBooks warning window appears.

11 Select **Next**

12 Select **Save it now**

13 Select **Next**

14 When the Save Backup Copy window appears, the Save in field should automatically show: **Desktop**

15 Update the File name field as shown to: **YourName Chapter 1 (Backup)**. Depending on your operating system settings, the file extension .QBB may appear automatically. If the .QBB extension does not appear, *do not type it*.

16 The Save as type field should automatically appear as **QBW Backup (*.QBB)**

17 Select **Save**

18 If a QuickBooks Desktop Information message appears, click **OK**

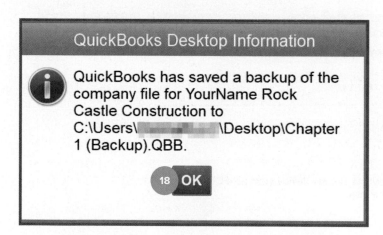

Section 1.12

Restore QuickBooks File Options

The typical workflow for a business is to use the QBW file to record transactions and periodically back up to a QBB (backup) file. The QBB (backup) file is only restored if there is an issue with the QBW file.

For our QuickBooks assignments of *Computer Accounting with QuickBooks*, there are two options for our restore schedule.

1. **Chapters and Exercises.** Chapters and exercises provide opportunities to *explore* and *practice*. If an error results while we are exploring or practicing, it will not affect the next chapter because a new QBB Starter File is provided for each chapter when needed. There is a QBB Starter File for Chapters 1 through 10, 15 and 17. We will restore the QBB Starter File to create a QBW file. Then we will complete the activities in the chapter and exercises. After we complete the activities, we will create a QBB Backup File.

2. **Projects.** Projects provide *mastery* opportunities. We are provided a QBB Starter File for Project 1. After that we will continue to use our own files to complete subsequent Projects 2 through 10. Just as in a business workflow, since we are using the same computer, we can continue to use the same QBW file. We will make backups at the end of each project. However, we will only use our QBB Backup File if our QBW file fails or we need to switch to a different computer. When completing the projects, errors will carry forward, so it is important to check and cross check work as well as track down and resolve errors.

> **If your QuickBooks Project file has an issue that you are unable to fix, contact your instructor for assistance.**

QUICKBOOKS CHAPTERS & EXERCISES		
QBW	**QBB STARTER FILES**	**QBB BACKUP FILES**
Start		
↓		
Restore QBB STARTER FILE	←— **CHAPTER 1 QBB STARTER FILE**	
↓		
Complete Chapter 1		
↓		
Back Up		—→ **QBB BACKUP FILE**
↓		
Complete Exercise 1.1		
↓		
Back Up		—→ **QBB BACKUP FILE**
↓		
Repeat		
↓		
Restore QBB STARTER FILE	←— **CHAPTER 2 QBB STARTER FILE**	
↓		
Complete Chapter 2		
↓		
Back Up		—→ **QBB BACKUP FILE**
↓		
Repeat		
↓		
End		

QUICKBOOKS PROJECTS		
QBW	**QBB STARTER FILES**	**QBB BACKUP FILES**
Start		
↓		
Restore PROJECT 1.1 QBB STARTER FILE	← PROJECT 1.1 QBB STARTER FILE	
↓		
Open QBW File		
↓		
Complete Project 1.1		
↓		
Back Up		⟶ QBB BACKUP FILE
↓		
Complete Project 2.1 Using Same QBW File		
↓		
Back Up		⟶ QBB BACKUP FILE
↓		
Repeat		
↓		
End		

QBW WORKFLOW

If you will be using the same computer to complete Chapter 1 QuickBooks exercises, just as in a business workflow, you can continue to use the same QBW file. You will make backups at the end of each chapter, exercise, or project. However, you will only use the backup if your QBW file fails.

If you are using the QBW approach, **leave your QBW file open and proceed directly to Exercise 1.1.**

QBB RESTORE

If you will be switching computers, after you finish your QuickBooks work session, you will back up to a QBB file in order to move your QuickBooks file to another computer. When you restart your work session on another computer, you will restore the backup (QBB) file.

If you are using the QBB approach and are ending your computer session now, use the following directions to **close** the company file and **exit** QuickBooks. When you restart, you will **restore your backup file** to complete Exercise 1.1.

Section 1.13

Close and Exit QuickBooks

After you have backed up your QuickBooks file, you can close the QuickBooks QBW file and exit QuickBooks software.

CLOSE QUICKBOOKS QBW COMPANY FILE

To close a QuickBooks company file:

1 From the Menu Bar, select **File**

2 Click **Close Company**

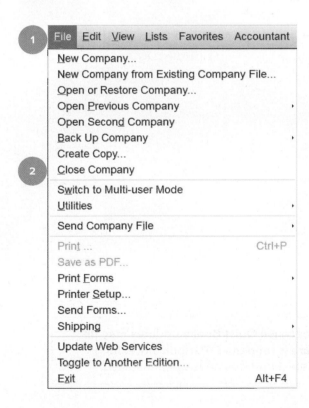

If the company QBW file is left open when you exit QuickBooks, the next time anyone uses the QuickBooks software, the company file might still be open, permitting access to your company accounting records.

EXIT QUICKBOOKS SOFTWARE

To exit QuickBooks software:

1 From the Menu Bar, select **File**

2 Select **Exit**

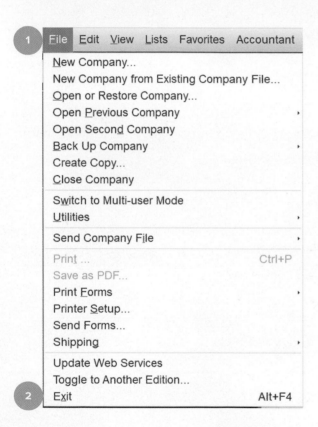

> ⚠ **It is important to periodically exit QuickBooks software because QuickBooks updates may be downloaded but are only installed when QuickBooks software is reopened. Periodically exiting QuickBooks software and reopening it will ensure that the latest updates have been installed.**

Section 1.14

Accounting Essentials: Accounting Systems

Accounting Essentials summarize important foundational accounting knowledge that may be useful when using QuickBooks

What's the language of business?

Accounting is the language of business. Learning accounting is similar to learning a new language, such as Spanish or French. As you use this text, you will learn terms and definitions that are unique to accounting.

What's the objective of an accounting system?

The objective of an accounting system is to collect, summarize, and communicate information to decision makers. Accounting information is used to:

- Prepare tax returns for federal and state tax agencies.
- Prepare financial statements for banks and investors.
- Prepare reports for managers and owners to use when making decisions. Such decisions include: Are our customers paying their bills on time? Which of our products are the most profitable? Will we have enough cash to pay our bills next month?

What are the main components to an accounting system?

Most accounting systems consist of three components:

- Input, such as entering transactions
- Processing, such as the processing that QuickBooks does for you automatically, sorting and posting appropriate accounts when you enter transactions
- Output, such as the QuickBooks report you generate

What are the main advantages of a computerized accounting system?

Before computerized accounting systems, the process component had to be performed manually consuming numerous hours of work to sort, post, calculate balances, and so on. With a computerized accounting system, most of the processing is done automatically saving hours of manual work.

www.My-QuickBooks.com

Go to **www.My-QuickBooks.com** to view additional QuickBooks resources including:

- **Excel Report Templates** to organize QuickBooks reports exported to Excel
- *Computer Accounting with QuickBooks* **updates**, sometimes required when there is a software update that affects the text
- **QuickBooks Video links**
- **QuickBooks Help and Support links**
- **Other QuickBooks Resources** to make learning QuickBooks easier and more effective
- **QuickBooks Troubleshooting (QT) Tips** offering a structured approach to troubleshooting QuickBooks

---

💡 **Troubleshooting QuickBooks and Correcting Errors are crucial QuickBooks skill to acquire. Troubleshooting resources include:**
- **www.My-QuickBooks.com > QuickBooks Troubleshooting (QT) Tips**
- **Chapter 17, Quick Review Guide, contains tips on Correcting Errors**
- **Appendix D, QuickBooks Troubleshooting (QT), provides you with an effective troubleshooting process**

💡 **Bookmark www.My-QuickBooks.com for future use.**

Note that the exercises contain instructions but fewer screen captures than the chapter. Screen captures are included in the chapter for exploring QuickBooks. In the exercises, the focus is on practicing, so instructions are included but fewer screen captures. This learning approach increases retention of material and results in deeper learning.

Exercise 1.1 Profit and Loss Statement

 Rock Castle Construction

BACKSTORY

While working at your computer, you notice Mr. Castle heading toward you. Adding another stack of papers to your overflowing inbox, he says, "*I need a profit & loss statement and a balance sheet for November as soon as possible. I haven't seen any financial statements since our former accountant left.*"

As he walks away, Mr. Castle calls over his shoulder, *"From now on I'd like a P&L and balance sheet by the first of each month."*

E1.1.1 QuickBooks File

If you will be using the same computer and the same Chapter 1.QBW file:

1. If your Chapter 1.QBW file is not already open, open it by selecting **File > Open Previous Company**. Select your **Chapter 1.QBW file**. If a QuickBooks Information window appears with a message about the sample company file, click **OK**.

2. Update the company name to **YourName Exercise 1.1 Rock Castle Construction** by selecting **Company Menu > My Company**.

> Note that the company name appears on reports and can differ from the file name. See Chapter 1 for additional instructions for changing the company name.

> If you are not using the same computer that you used for Chapter 1, you will need to restore your Chapter 1 Backup.QBB file using the instructions in Appendix B: Back Up and Restore QuickBooks. After restoring, update the company name to YourName Exercise 1.1 Rock Castle Construction.

E1.1.2 Profit and Loss, Standard

The Profit & Loss Statement (also called the Income Statement) lists income earned and expenses incurred to generate income. Summarizing the amount of profit or loss a company has earned, the Profit & Loss Statement is one of the primary financial statements given to bankers and investors.

Prepare the QuickBooks Profit & Loss Standard for Rock Castle Construction by completing the following steps:

1. Click **Reports** in the Navigation Bar

2. Select type of report: **Company & Financial**

3. Select report: **Profit & Loss Standard**

4. Select the date range: **Last Month**. The Dates field will now be: **11/01/2024 To 11/30/2024**. Select the **Run** icon.

5. Export the report to **Excel** or **print** the Profit and Loss Standard. (If your Chapter 1 Excel Report workbook is already open, you may receive an error message. Close the Chapter 1 Excel Report worksheet. Then export the report again. If you continue to receive an error message, then close the Excel software, and export the report again.)

6. **Close** the Profit & Loss Standard window

7. **Highlight** the amount of the single largest income item appearing on the Profit & Loss Statement for the month of November

8. **Highlight** the amount of the single largest expense item appearing on the Profit & Loss Statement for the month of November

E1.1.3 Profit and Loss, Detail

Prepare the QuickBooks Profit & Loss Detail for Rock Castle Construction by completing the following steps:

1. Click **Reports** in the Navigation Bar

2. Select type of report: **Company & Financial**

3. Select report: **Profit & Loss Detail**

4. Select the date range: **Last Month**. The Dates field will now be: **11/01/2024 To 11/30/2024**. Select the **Run** icon.

5. Export the report to **Excel** or **print** the Profit and Loss Detail

6. **Close** the Profit & Loss Detail window

7. **Highlight** the amount of the single largest Subcontracted Labor Income item appearing on the Profit & Loss Detail for the month of November

8. **Highlight** the amount of the single largest Utilities Expense item appearing on the Profit & Loss Detail for the month of November

E1.1.4 Back Up Exercise 1.1

Save a backup of your Exercise file using the file name: **YourName Exercise 1.1 Backup.QBB**. See Appendix B: Back Up and Restore QuickBooks Files for instructions.

Exercise 1.2 Balance Sheet

 Rock Castle Construction

E1.2.1 QuickBooks File

If you will be using the same computer and the same QBW file:

1. Select your **QBW file**.

2. Update the company name to **YourName Exercise 1.2 Rock Castle Construction** by selecting **Company Menu > My Company**.

If you are not using the same computer that you used for Chapter 1 and Exercise 1.1, you will need to restore your latest prior Backup.QBB file using the instructions in Appendix B: Back Up and Restore QuickBooks. After restoring, update the company name to YourName Exercise 1.2 Rock Castle Construction.

E1.2.2 Balance Sheet, Standard

The Balance Sheet is the financial statement that summarizes the financial position of a business. Listing assets, liabilities, and equity, the Balance Sheet reveals what a company owns and what it owes.

To prepare the Balance Sheet Standard for Rock Castle Construction at November 30, 2024, complete the following steps:

1. From the Report Center window, select type of report: **Company & Financial**

2. Select report: **Balance Sheet Standard**

3. Select date range: **Last Month** with Dates field **From 11/01/2024 To 11/30/2024**. Select the **Run** icon.

4. Export the report to **Excel** or **print** the Balance Sheet Standard

5. **Highlight** the amount of the single largest asset listed on Rock Castle Construction's November 30, 2024 Balance Sheet

6. **Highlight** the amount of Total Checking/Savings listed on Rock Castle Construction's November 30, 2024 Balance Sheet

E1.2.3 Balance Sheet, Detail

To prepare the Balance Sheet Detail for Rock Castle Construction at November 30, 2024, complete the following steps:

1. From the Report Center window, select type of report: **Company & Financial**

2. Select report: **Balance Sheet Detail**

3. Select date range: **Last Month** with Dates field **From 11/01/2024 To 11/30/2024**. Select the **Run** icon.

4. Export the report to **Excel** or **print** the Balance Sheet Detail

5.   **Highlight** the ending balance for Undeposited Funds listed on Rock Castle Construction's November 30, 2024 Balance Sheet Detail. Undeposited Funds are the amount that the company has accepted, such as from customers, but has not yet recorded as a deposit in a bank account.

E1.2.4 Back Up Exercise 1.2

Save a backup of your Exercise file using the file name: **YourName Exercise 1.2 Backup.QBB**. See Appendix B: Back Up and Restore QuickBooks Files for instructions.

PROJECT 1.1

Larry's Landscaping

BACKSTORY

Larry's Landscaping just hired you as an accounting consultant to maintain its accounting records using QuickBooks financial software. The QuickBooks company file for Larry's Landscaping has already been created and transactions have been entered. Your assignment is to complete the following steps to export reports to Excel and then email them to the finance director at Larry's.

> 💡 **Troubleshooting QuickBooks and Correcting Errors are crucial QuickBooks skill to acquire. Troubleshooting resources include:**
> - **www.My-QuickBooks.com > QuickBooks Troubleshooting (QT) Tips**
> - **Chapter 17, Quick Review Guide, contains tips on Correcting Errors**
> - **Appendix D, QuickBooks Troubleshooting (QT), provides you with an effective troubleshooting process**

🌐 QuickBooks SatNav

The objective of Project 1.1 is to facilitate your mastery of QuickBooks Desktop. As shown in the following QuickBooks SatNav, Project 1.1 focuses on QuickBooks Reports.

QuickBooks SatNav

⚙ **QuickBooks Settings**

⚙ Company Settings
⚙ Chart of Accounts

💰 **QuickBooks Transactions**

💰 Banking
💰 Customers & Sales
💰 Vendors & Expenses
💰 Employees & Payroll

📊 **QuickBooks Reports**

📊 Reports

P1.1.1 Restore Starter File

Restore the Project 1 Starter file. (.QBB file) for Larry's Landscaping. See Appendix B: Back Up and Restore QuickBooks Files for instructions.

1. Restore the **PROJECT 1.1 STARTER.QBB** for Larry's Landscaping

2. Update the Company Name to: **YourName Project 1.1 Larry's Landscaping**

P1.1.2 Profit and Loss

1. Using the Chapter 1 Excel Report Template, export to **Excel** the Profit & Loss Standard for Larry's Landscaping for the Last Fiscal Year, October 1, 2023 through September 30, 2024.

   ⚠️ When exporting to Excel, remember to select Advanced Excel Options:
   - **Uncheck Space between columns**
   - **Uncheck Include QuickBooks Export Guide worksheet with helpful advice**
   - **Select On printed report and screen**

2. **Highlight** the single largest expense item

3. Export to **Excel** the Profit & Loss Detail for Larry's Landscaping for the Last Fiscal Year, October 1, 2023 through September 30, 2024

4. Which type of income from Job Materials is the greatest? Decks & Patios, Fountains & Garden Lighting, Plants and Sod, or Sprinklers & Drip Systems? **Highlight** your answer.

5. Which type of landscaping service produces more revenue for Larry's: Installation or Maintenance & Repairs? **Highlight** your answer.

6. Which type of utilities expense is the greatest? Gas and Electric, Telephone, or Water? **Highlight** your answer.

P1.1.3 Balance Sheet

1. Export to **Excel** the Balance Sheet Standard for Larry's Landscaping for the Last Fiscal Year ending September 2024

2. **Highlight** the single largest asset on the balance sheet

3. Export to **Excel** the Balance Sheet Detail for Larry's Landscaping for the Last Fiscal Year, ending September 2024

4. **Highlight** the largest single liability on the balance sheet

P1.1.4 Back Up Project 1.1

Save a backup of your Project file using the file name: **YourName Project 1.1 Backup.QBB**. See Appendix B: Back Up and Restore QuickBooks Files for instructions.

Chapter 2

QuickBooks Chart of Accounts

🔨 Rock Castle Construction

BACKSTORY

The next morning when you arrive at work, Mr. Castle is waiting for you, pacing in the aisle outside your cubicle.

He looks at you over the top of his glasses, his voice tense when he asks, *"Do you have the P&L and balance sheet ready?"*

"Yes sir!" you reply, handing him the financial statements.

You hit the Send button on your smartphone. *"And I'm sending you a link so you can also view the financials in a spreadsheet."*

The creases in Mr. Castle's brow disappear as his eyes run down the statements, murmuring to himself as he walks away, *"The creditor waiting in my office should like this...."*

As he rounds the corner, he calls back to you, *"See your inbox for account changes we need to make. And we haven't gotten around to password protecting our QuickBooks file yet. But I'm confident you'll be able to figure that out."*

Opening the QuickBooks training manual, you dive into learning how to update the Chart of Accounts and password protect QuickBooks files.

Chapter 2

Learning Objectives

Chapter 2 covers the QuickBooks Chart of Accounts, the list of the accounts used in a company's accounting system. In this chapter, you will learn about the following topics:

- Start QuickBooks and Open QuickBooks Company
- Customize Chart of Accounts (COA)
- Display Chart of Accounts (COA)
- Align QB Chart of Accounts with Income Tax Return
- Add New Accounts
- Edit Accounts
- Delete Accounts
- Create Chart of Accounts Report
- QuickBooks Password Protection
- Back Up QuickBooks Files
- Accounting Essentials: Chart of Accounts

Section 2.1

 QuickBooks SatNav

QuickBooks SatNav is your satellite navigation for QuickBooks, assisting you in navigating QuickBooks

In Chapter 2, we will see how to customize a company's Chart of Accounts, a list of all the accounts used by a company to collect accounting information. In addition, we will learn how to restrict access to our QuickBooks accounting records using passwords to improve security and controls.

QuickBooks SatNav is designed to assist in seeing how all the QuickBooks pieces we learn fit together. As mentioned in Chapter 1, QuickBooks SatNav divides QuickBooks into three processes:

1. **QuickBooks Settings.** This includes Company Settings when setting up a new QuickBooks company and the Company Chart of Accounts.

2. **QuickBooks Transactions.** This includes recording transactions in QuickBooks. Transaction types can be categorized as Banking, Customers and Sales, Vendors and Expenses, and Employees and Payroll. In basic terms, recording transactions involves recording money in and money out.

3. **QuickBooks Reports.** QuickBooks reports are the output of the system, such as commonly used financial statements of Balance Sheet, Income Statement, and Statement of Cash Flows.

In this chapter we focus on customizing:
- QuickBooks Company settings, such as passwords for security, and
- Company Chart of Accounts

QuickBooks SatNav

 QuickBooks Settings

Company Settings
Chart of Accounts

 QuickBooks Transactions

Banking
Customers & Sales
Vendors & Expenses
Employees & Payroll

QuickBooks Reports

Reports

💡 **Accounting Essentials appear at the end of the chapter. Tip: Preview Accounting Essentials before completing the chapter and then review Accounting Essentials after completing the chapter.**

Section 2.2

Start QuickBooks and Open QuickBooks Company

START QUICKBOOKS

To start QuickBooks software, click the **QuickBooks** icon on your desktop. If a QuickBooks icon does not appear on your desktop, from Microsoft® Windows® click **Start** button > **QuickBooks** > **QuickBooks Premier Accountant Edition**.

> **QuickBooks Accountant includes all the features of QuickBooks Pro plus features for client services. If you use QuickBooks Pro, your screens may appear slightly different than those appearing in this text.**

QBB STARTER FILE

The typical workflow for a business is to use the QBW file to record transactions and periodically back up to a QBB (backup) file. The QBB (backup) file is only restored if there is an issue with the QBW file.

To complete the *Computer Accounting with QuickBooks* assignments for chapters and exercises, we will restore the QBB Starter File for the chapter. There is a QBB Starter File for Chapters 1 through 10, 15 and 17. Then we will complete the chapter and exercise assignments, making backups at the end of the chapter or exercise. However, we will only use our QBB Backup File if our QBW file fails or we need to change to a different computer.

QUICKBOOKS CHAPTER 2 & EXERCISES 2		
QBW	**QBB STARTER FILES**	**QBB BACKUP FILES**
Start		
↓		
Restore **QBB STARTER FILE**	← **CHAPTER 2 QBB STARTER FILE**	
↓		
Complete Chapter 2		
↓		
Back Up		→ **QBB BACKUP FILE**
↓		
Complete Exercise 2.1		
↓		
Back Up		→ **QBB BACKUP FILE**
↓		
Complete Exercise 2.2		
↓		
Back Up		→ **QBB BACKUP FILE**
↓		
Repeat		
↓		
End		

RESTORE QBB STARTER FILE

For purposes of this text, we will use QuickBooks Starter files that are QBB files containing the company data needed to complete the assignments in this text. The QBB Starter files are compressed files that must be unzipped, or restored, into QBW files before the files can be used.

For your convenience, QuickBooks (.QBB) Starter files accompany *Computer Accounting with QuickBooks 2021.*

Go to www.mhhe.com/kay2021 to download the Starter files from the Online Learning Center.

To stay organized, consider adding a folder to your Desktop: QBB STARTER FILES. Then copy the QBB STARTER files to that folder.

For Connect users, the Starter Files are accessible through your Connect Chapter Assignments.

⚠ **Desktop (QBDT) Data Files are compressed backup files that can be restored and used. To use Starter Files, the compressed file must be restored following the instructions here. Since it is a compressed file, you cannot open and use the QuickBooks data files by simply clicking on the file. Instead you must follow the instructions here to unzip and restore the data file before using it.**

To restore the Chapter 2 QBB Starter file from a QBB file to a QBW file:

1 From the No Company Open window, select **Open or restore an existing company**

2 Select **Restore a backup copy**

3 Click **Next**

4 When the Open or Restore Company window appears, select **Local backup**

5 Click **Next**

6 Identify the location of the **CHAPTER 2 STARTER.QBB** file. If you copied the CHAPTER 2 STARTER.QBB file to your desktop, select the **Look in** field to find the location of the .QBB file on your desktop.

7 Select the file: **CHAPTER 2 STARTER.QBB**

8 The Files of type field should automatically display: **QBW Backup (*.QBB)**

9 Click **Open**

10 When the Open or Restore window appears, click **Next**

11 Identify the file name and location of the QBW company file. To save the QBW (working file) on your desktop, select the location to save in: **Desktop**. (Another option is to save your QBW files to Users > Public > Public Documents > Intuit > QuickBooks > Company Files. Be sure you have permissions to save to a folder.)

12 Enter QBW File name: **YourName Chapter 2.** (Insert your name in the QBW file name so you can identify your files.)

13 The Save as type field should automatically appear as **QuickBooks Files (*.QBW)**

14 Click **Save**

15 Click **OK** when the QuickBooks Desktop Information window appears notifying you that **You're opening a QuickBooks sample file**. (If a message appears indicating your file needs to be updated, select Yes. Then follow the onscreen instructions.)

CHANGE COMPANY NAME

So that your name automatically appears on reports and checks, update the Company Name setting to add your name to the company name.

To change a company name in QuickBooks, complete the following:

1 From My Shortcuts on the Navigation Bar, select **My Company**

2 When the My Company window appears, select **Edit**

3 When the Company Information window, update Company Name field to: **YourName Chapter 2 Rock Castle Construction**. Select **OK** to close the Company Information window.

4 Select **OK** to close the Company Information window

5 **Close** the My Company window

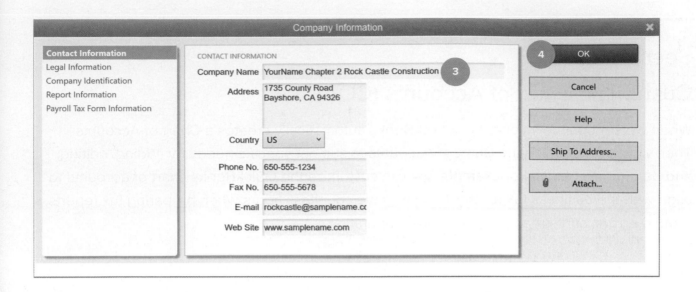

Section 2.3

Customize Chart of Accounts (COA)

When we set up a new company, QuickBooks automatically creates a Chart of Accounts. Then we can customize the Chart of Accounts to suit our specific needs by adding, editing, and deleting accounts. For example, we can customize the QuickBooks chart of accounts to align with the business tax return. This can save countless hours when preparing tax reports, reduce errors, and streamline tax return preparation.

ALIGN QB CHART OF ACCOUNTS WITH INCOME TAX RETURN

In many cases, we are using QuickBooks to track information for tax return preparation. So to streamline the process, it only makes sense to align the QB Chart of Accounts with our company's tax return.

When setting up a Chart of Accounts for a business, it is often helpful to review the tax form that the business will use. Then a company's Chart of Accounts can be customized to track information needed for the tax form.

Our goal is to see that the QB Chart of Accounts feeds into the tax return lines. So first, we need to know which business tax return the company files. The tax form used by type of organization is as follows. For example, if the business is an S corporation, then for federal income taxes the business files Form 1120S. If the business is a sole proprietorship, then Schedule C is attached to the sole proprietor's IRS Form 1040.

Form of Organization	Tax Form
Sole Proprietorship	Form 1040 Schedule C
Partnership	Form 1065
C Corporation	Form 1120
S Corporation	Form 1120S

To view various tax return forms for businesses with the tax lines on each form, go to the Internal Revenue Service (IRS) website: www.irs.gov.

Section 2.4

Display Chart of Accounts (COA)

We can display the Chart of Accounts in different ways:

1. From the Company Menu
2. From the Navigation Bar
3. From the Company section of the Home Page

To view the Chart of Accounts for Rock Castle Construction from the Home Page, complete the following steps:

1 Click the **Chart of Accounts** icon in the Company section of the Home Page

2 In the Chart of Accounts window, for each account, the account name, type of account, and the balance of the account are listed. The **Account** button at the bottom of the window displays a drop-down menu for adding, editing, and deleting accounts.

3 Another option is to right-click in the Chart of Accounts window to display a pop-up menu to add and edit accounts.

The Chart of Account displays account titles. In addition, sometimes companies prefer to also display account numbers for accounts listed in the Chart of Accounts.

DISPLAY ACCOUNT NUMBERS

Account numbers are used to uniquely identify accounts. Usually account numbers are used as a coding system to also identify the account type. For example, a typical account numbering system for a merchandising company that sells products might be as follows.

Account Type	Account No.
Asset accounts	10000 - 19999
Liability accounts	20000 - 29999
Equity accounts	30000 - 39999
Revenue (income) accounts	40000 - 49999
Cost of Goods Sold (Expense) accounts	50000 - 59999
Expense accounts	60000 - 69999

> **Account type determines whether the account appears on the Balance Sheet or Income Statement.**

QuickBooks preferences will determine whether the account number is displayed in the Chart of Accounts. If account numbers are not displayed in Rock Castle Construction's Chart of Accounts, select the QuickBooks preference to view account numbers as follows.

1 Select **Edit Menu**

2 Select **Preferences**

3 When the Preferences window appears, click the **Accounting** icon in the left scrollbar

4 Then select the **Company Preferences** tab

5 Select **Use account numbers** to display the account numbers in the Chart of Accounts

6 Then click **OK**. (If the Chart of Accounts does not appear on your screen, click **Window Menu > Chart of Accounts**.)

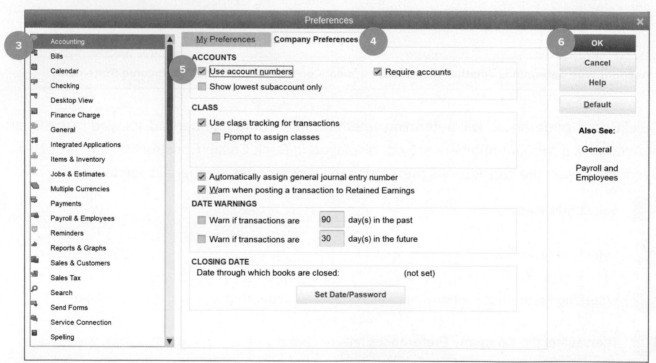

The Chart of Accounts should now list account numbers preceding the account name.

Section 2.5

Add New Accounts

We can customize the Chart of Accounts by adding, editing, and deleting accounts as needed to meet our company's specific and changing needs.

Rock Castle Construction has decided to begin advertising and would like to add an Advertising Expense account to the Chart of Accounts.

To add a new account to the Chart of Accounts:

1. Click the **Account** button at the bottom of the Chart of Accounts window to display a drop-down menu

2. Select **New**

3. Select Account Type: **Expense**

4. Click **Continue**

5. In the Add New Account window, verify the Account Type: **Expense**

6. Enter the new Account Number: **60400**

7. Enter the Account Name: **Advertising Expense**

8. Leave **Subaccount unchecked**. Subaccounts are subcategories of an account.

9. Select Tax-Line Mapping: **Deductions: Advertising**. This indicates the Advertising Expense account balance will appear as a deduction on Rock Castle Construction's tax return. Selecting the appropriate Tax Line ensures that QuickBooks provides the information needed to complete your tax return. Note that Tax Line Mapping options can vary from one QuickBooks company to another depending upon the tax return selected during the new company QuickBooks setup.

10. Click **Save & Close** to save the changes and close the Add New Account window

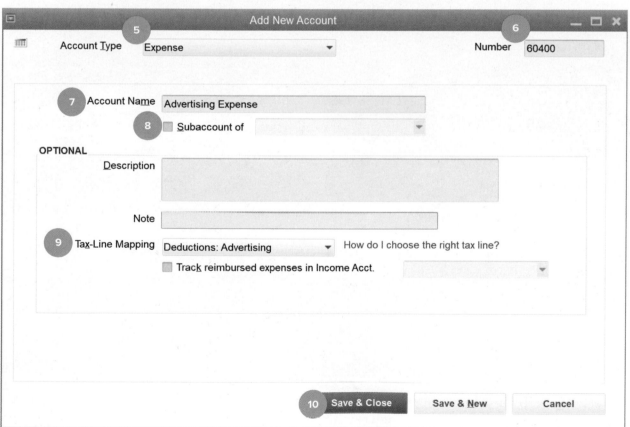

Notice that Account 60400 Advertising Expense now appears on the Chart of Accounts.

If the new account had been a Balance Sheet account (an asset, liability, or equity account), QuickBooks would ask you for the opening account balance as of your QuickBooks start date. Since Advertising Expense is an Expense account that appears on the Income Statement and not the Balance Sheet, QuickBooks did not ask for the opening balance.

Section 2.6

Edit Accounts

Next, we will edit an account. Rock Castle Construction would like to change the name of the Advertising Expense account to Advertising & Promotion.

To change the name of the Advertising Expense account to Advertising & Promotion:

1 Select **View Menu > Open Window List** to display all open windows on the left of the screen. From the Open Window List, select the **Chart of Accounts** window. From the Chart of Accounts window, select the account to edit: **60400 Advertising Expense**.

2 Click the **Account** button in the lower left corner of the Chart of Accounts window or **right-click** the mouse to display the pop-up menu

3 From the pop-up menu, select **Edit Account** to open the Edit Account window

4 Make changes to the account information. In this case, change Account Name to: **Advertising & Promotion**.

5 Click **Save & Close** to save the changes. Advertising Expense should now appear as Advertising & Promotion in the Chart of Accounts window.

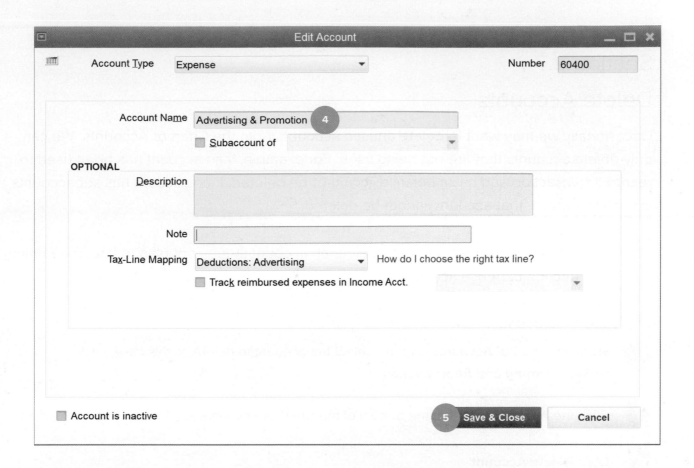

Section 2.7

Delete Accounts

Occasionally we may want to delete unused accounts from the Chart of Accounts. We can only delete accounts that are not being used. For example, if an account has been used to record a transaction and has a balance, it cannot be deleted. If an account has subaccounts associated with it, that account cannot be deleted.

Rock Castle Construction would like to delete an account it does not plan to use, the Printing and Reproduction Expense account.

To delete an account:

1. From the Chart of Accounts window, select the account to delete. In this case, click **63300: Printing and Reproduction**.

2. Click the **Account** button at the bottom of the Chart of Accounts window

3. Click **Delete Account**

4. Click **OK** to confirm that you want to delete the account

Section 2.8
Create Chart of Accounts Report

QuickBooks provides an Account Listing report that lists the Chart of Accounts plus the account balances.

First, re-sort the Chart of Accounts list as follows:

1 From the Chart of Accounts window, select the **Account** button

2 Select **Re-sort List**

3 When the Re-sort List? Window appears, select **OK**

4 **Close** the Chart of Accounts window

C2.8.1 Chart of Accounts. To create the Chart of Accounts (Account Listing) report:

1　Select **Reports** in the My Shortcuts section of the Navigation Bar

2　Select **Accountants & Taxes**

3　Select **Account Listing**

4　Select Date: **12/15/2024**

5　Select **Run**

6　To export the Account Listing report to Excel, at the top of the Account Listing window select **Excel**

7　Select **Create New Worksheet**

8　When the Send Report to Excel window appears, select **Replace an existing worksheet**

9　Browse for **YourLastName FirstName CH2 REPORTS** Excel file

10　From the drop-down list, select the sheet: **C2.8.1 COA**

11　Select the **Advanced** button

12　**Uncheck Space between columns**

13　**Uncheck Include QuickBooks Export Guide worksheet with helpful advice**

14　Select Show report header: **On printed report and screen**

15　Click **OK**

16　Click **Export**

Excel software should open on your screen with your QuickBooks report.

1 Select the **2 REPORTS** sheet tab

2 Mark the report you have completed by inserting an "**X**"

3 Save your **CH2 REPORTS** Excel workbook using the filename: **YourLastName FirstName CH2 REPORTS**. **Close** the QuickBooks Account Listing window.

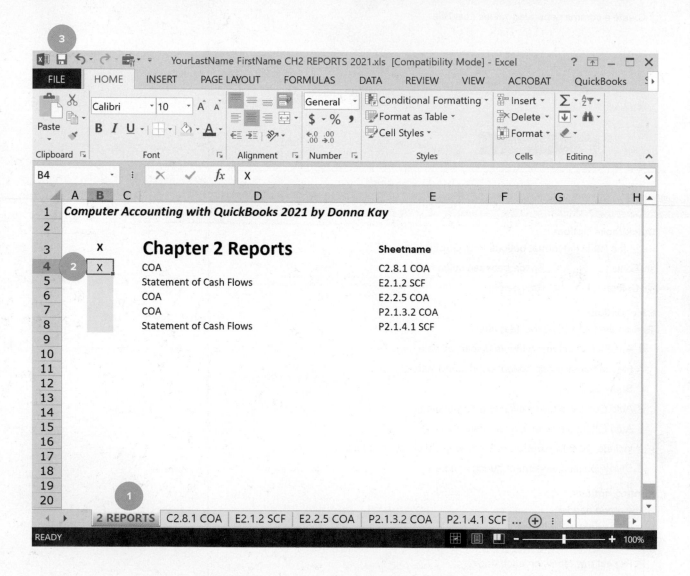

Section 2.9

QuickBooks Password Protection

QuickBooks permits a company to conveniently collect accounting information and store it in a single file. Much of the accounting information stored in QuickBooks is confidential, however, and a company often wants to limit employee access.

Password protection can be used to customize and limit access to company data and improve security and control.

Two ways to restrict access to accounting information stored in a QuickBooks company data file are:

1. Password protect the company file so individuals must enter a user ID and password to open the company file.
2. Limit access to selected areas of the company's accounting data. For example, a user may access accounts receivable to view customer balances but not be able to access payroll or check writing.

Only the QuickBooks Administrator can add users with passwords and grant user access to selected areas of QuickBooks. The QuickBooks Administrator is an individual who has access to all areas of QuickBooks.

To add a new user and password protection to your company file:

1 Select **Company Menu**

2 Select **Set Up Users and Passwords**

3 Select **Set Up Users**

4 First, set up a QuickBooks Administrator who has access to all areas of QuickBooks. The Administrator can then add new users. To add the Administrator password, from the User List window, select **Admin**.

5 Select **Edit User**

6   On the Change user password and access window, enter and confirm a **Password** of your choice. ***Write the password on the inside cover of your text.***

7   Select **Next**

8   Select **Finish**

9   Only the QuickBooks Administrator can add new users. To add another user, click **Add User**.

10   In the following Set up user password and access window, enter **YourName** in the User Name field

11   At this point, if you were adding another employee as a user, you would ask the employee to enter and confirm his or her password. In this instance, enter and confirm a **password** of your choice. ***Write the password on the inside cover of your book.***

12   Click **Next**

13   In the following window, you can restrict user access to selected areas of QuickBooks or give the user access to all areas of QuickBooks. Select: **All areas of QuickBooks**.

14   Click **Next**

15   Select **Yes** to confirm that you want to give access to all areas of QuickBooks

16   The next window summarizes the user's access for each QuickBooks area, indicating access to create documents, print, and view reports. Click **Finish**.

17   Two names (Admin and YourName) should appear on the User List

18   Click **Close** to close the User List window

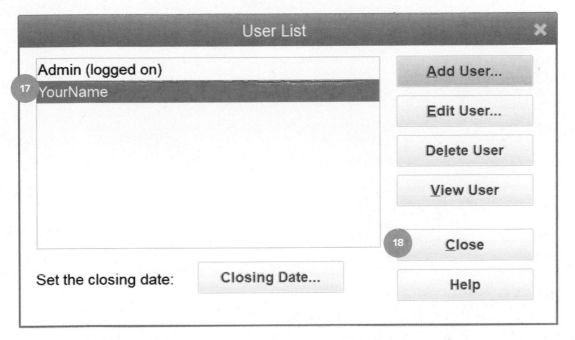

Now whenever you open the company file for Rock Castle Construction, you will be asked to enter your user name and password.

Notice User Access Rights are set by Areas: Create, Print, Reports.

⚠ Write your password on the inside of your book cover. You will not be able to access your company file without your password.

- When restoring a **QBB STARTER FILE**, if QuickBooks requires you to create a password in order to continue, create your own password and record the password in a secure location, such as the inside cover of your textbook.
- If a password is requested when restoring a QuickBooks **QBB STARTER FILE**, try using User ID: Admin and leave the Password field <u>blank</u>
- If you are using the **QBB STARTER FILE** and QuickBooks requires a password and QuickBooks will not accept the password field blank, try User ID: Admin and Password: KayQB2021
- If none of the above approaches permit you to restore the **QBB** file, see your instructor

Section 2.10

Back Up QuickBooks Files

BACK UP QBB

Save a backup of your Chapter 2 file using the file name: **YourName Chapter 2 Backup.QBB**. For further instructions on how to back up your file, see Appendix B: Back Up and Restore QuickBooks Files.

QBW WORKFLOW

If you will be using the same computer to complete Chapter 2 QuickBooks exercises, just as in a business workflow, you can continue to use the same QBW file. You will make backups at the end of each exercise. However, you will only use the backup if your QBW file fails.

If you are using the QBW approach, leave your QBW file open and proceed directly to Exercise 2.1.

QBB RESTORE

If you are using the QBB approach and will be switching computers, after you finish your QuickBooks work session, you will back up to a QBB file in order to move your QuickBooks file to another computer. When you restart your work session on another computer, you will restore the backup (QBB) file.

If you are using the QBB approach, and are ending your computer session now, close your QBW file and exit QuickBooks. When you restart, you will restore your backup file to complete Exercise 2.1.

Section 2.11

Accounting Essentials: Chart of Accounts

Accounting Essentials summarize important foundational accounting knowledge that may be useful when using QuickBooks

What is the primary objective of accounting?

- The primary objective of accounting is to provide information for decision making. Businesses use a financial system, such as QuickBooks Online, to capture, track, sort, summarize, and communicate financial information.

How is financial information for decision making provided?

- Financial reports summarize and communicate information about a company's financial position and business operations.

What is the difference between financial reports and financial statements?

- Financial statements are standardized financial reports that summarize information about past transactions. Financial statements are provided to external users and internal users for decision making. External users include bankers, creditors, and investors.
- Internal users include managers and employees of the business.

What are the main financial statements for a business?

- The primary financial statements for a business are:
  - **Balance Sheet** summarizes what a company *owns* and *owes* on a particular date.
  - **Profit & Loss Statement** (also referred to as P & L or Income Statement) summarizes the income a company has earned and the expenses incurred to earn the income.
  - **Statement of Cash Flows** summarizes cash inflows and cash outflows for operating, investing, and financing activities of a business.

What is a Chart of Accounts?

- **Chart of Accounts (COA)** is a list of all the accounts and account numbers for a business. Accounts are used to sort and track accounting information. For example, a business needs one account for cash, another account to track amounts customers owe (Accounts Receivable), and yet another account to track inventory.

Why use accounts?

- We use **accounts** to record transactions in our accounting system. Accounts (such as the Checking account or Insurance Expense account) permit us to sort, organize, summarize, and track information.
- We can add **subaccounts** for even better tracking. Example: We could add subaccounts Rental Insurance Expense and Liability Insurance Expense as subaccounts to our Insurance Expense account. (It's the best of both worlds. We have additional detail of subaccounts Rental Insurance and Liability Insurance Expense and the subaccounts roll up into the total for the parent account, Insurance Expense.)

What Are the Different Types of Accounts?

- We can group accounts into the following different account types:

Balance Sheet accounts			Profit and Loss accounts	
Assets	**Liability**	**Equity**	**Income**	**Expense**
Bank account	Accounts Payable	Capital Investment	Sales	Supplies Expense
Accounts Receivable	Credit Cards Payable	Retained Earnings	Consulting Fees	Rent Expense
Equipment	Loans Payable		Interest Income	Utilities Expense

What are balance sheet accounts?

- The Balance Sheet is a financial statement that summarizes what a company owns and what it owes.
- Balance Sheet accounts are accounts that appear on the company's Balance Sheet.
- Three types of accounts appear on the Balance Sheet:
    1. Assets
    2. Liabilities
    3. Owners' (or Stockholders') Equity

1. Assets are resources that a company owns. These resources are expected to have future benefit.

Asset accounts include:

- Cash.
- Accounts receivable (amounts to be *received* from customers in the future).
- Inventory.
- Other current assets (assets likely to be converted to cash or consumed within one year).
- Fixed assets (property used in the operations of the business, such as equipment, buildings, and land).
- Intangible assets (such as copyrights, patents, trademarks, and franchises).

How Do We Know if an Account is an Asset?

Ask:
Will our enterprise receive a *future benefit* from the item? (For example, prepaid insurance has future benefit.)

Answer:
If we will receive *future benefit*, the account is probably an *asset*.

---

2. Liabilities are amounts a company owes to others. Liabilities are obligations. For example, if a company borrows $10,000 from the bank, the company has an obligation to repay the $10,000 to the bank. Thus, the $10,000 obligation is shown as a liability on the company's Balance Sheet.

Liability accounts include:
- Accounts payable (amounts that are owed and will be paid to suppliers in the future).
- Sales taxes payable (sales tax owed and to be paid in the future).
- Interest payable (interest owed and to be paid in the future).
- Other current liabilities (liabilities due within one year).
- Loan payable (also called notes payable).
- Mortgage payable. (The difference between a note payable and a mortgage payable is that a mortgage payable has real estate as collateral.)
- Other long-term liabilities (liabilities due after one year).

How Do We Know if an Account is a Liability?

Ask:
Is our enterprise *obligated* to do something, such as pay a bill or provide a service?

Answer:
If we have an *obligation*, the account is probably a *liability*.

---

3. **Equity accounts** (or stockholders' equity for a corporation) represent the net worth of a business. Equity is calculated as assets (resources owned) minus liabilities (amounts owed).

Different types of business ownership include:
- Sole proprietorship (an unincorporated business with one owner).
- Partnership (an unincorporated business with more than one owner).
- Corporation (an incorporated business with one or more owners).

Owners' equity is increased by:
- Investments by owners. For a corporation, owners invest by buying stock.
- Net profits retained in the business rather than distributed to owners.

Owners' equity is decreased by:

- Amounts paid to owners as a return for their investment. For a sole proprietorship or partnership, these are called withdrawals or distributions. For a corporation, they are called dividends.
- Losses incurred by the business.

How Do We Calculate Equity?

Equity = Assets - Liabilities

  Assets
- Liabilities
= Equity

What we *own* minus what we *owe* leaves equity.

What are profit and loss accounts?

- The Profit and Loss Statement (also called the Income Statement or P&L Statement) reports the results of a company's operations, listing income and expenses for a period of time.
- Profit and Loss accounts are accounts that appear on a company's Profit and Loss Statement.
- QuickBooks uses two different types of Profit and Loss accounts:
  1. Income accounts
  2. Expense accounts

1. Income accounts record sales to customers and other revenues earned by the company. Revenues are the prices charged customers for products and services provided.

Examples of Income accounts include:
- Sales or revenues.
- Fees earned.
- Interest income.
- Rental income.
- Gains on sale of assets.

2. Expense accounts record costs that have expired or been consumed in the process of generating income. Expenses are the costs of providing products and services to customers.

Examples of Expense accounts include:
- Cost of goods sold expense.
- Salaries expense.
- Insurance expense.
- Rent expense.
- Interest expense.

How Do We Calculate Net Income?

Net Income = Income (Revenue) - Expenses (including CGS)

   Income (Revenue)
- *Expenses (including CGS)*
= *Net Income (Net Profit or Net Earnings)*

Net income is calculated as income (or revenue) less cost of goods sold and other expenses. Net income is an attempt to match or measure efforts (expenses) against accomplishments (revenues).

Three Names for the Same Thing: Net Income is also referred to as Net Profit or Net Earnings.

What are permanent accounts?

- In general, Balance Sheet accounts are considered **permanent accounts** (with the exception of the Withdrawals or Distributions account which is closed out each year).
- Balances in permanent accounts are carried forward from year to year. Thus, for a Balance Sheet account, such as Checking, the balance at December 31 is carried forward and becomes the opening balance on January 1 of the next year.

What are temporary accounts?

- Profit and Loss accounts are called **temporary accounts** because they are used to track account data for a temporary period of time, usually one year.

- At the end of each year, temporary accounts are closed (the balance reduced to zero). For example, if a Profit and Loss account, such as Advertising Expense, had a $13,000 balance at December 31, the $13,000 balance would be closed or transferred to owners' equity at year-end. The opening balance on January 1 for the Advertising Expense account would be $0.00.

What are non-posting accounts?

- Non-posting accounts are accounts that do not appear on the Balance Sheet or Income Statement. However, these accounts are needed to track information necessary for the accounting system.
- Examples of non-posting accounts include:
  - Purchase orders: documents that track items that have been ordered from suppliers.
  - Estimates: bids or proposals submitted to customers.

💡 **Troubleshooting QuickBooks and Correcting Errors are crucial QuickBooks skill to acquire. Troubleshooting resources include:**
- **www.My-QuickBooks.com > QuickBooks Troubleshooting (QT) Tips**
- **Chapter 17, Quick Review Guide, contains tips on Correcting Errors**
- **Appendix D, QuickBooks Troubleshooting (QT), provides you with an effective troubleshooting process**

Note that the exercises contain instructions but fewer screen captures than the chapter. Screen captures are included in the chapter for exploring QuickBooks. In the exercises, the focus is on practicing, so instructions are included but fewer screen captures. This learning approach increases retention of material and results in deeper learning.

Exercise 2.1 Statement of Cash Flows

 Rock Castle Construction

BACKSTORY

When you return to your cubicle after lunch, you find the following note stuck to your computer screen.

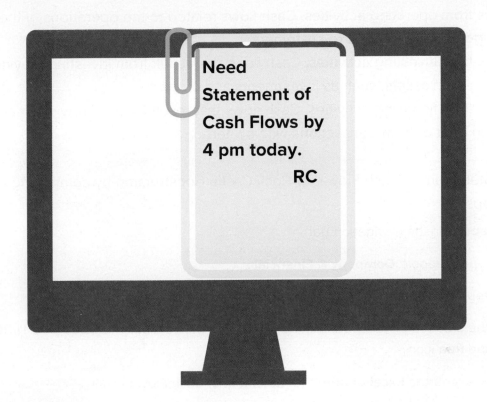

Need Statement of Cash Flows by 4 pm today.
RC

E2.1.1 QuickBooks File

If you will be using the same computer and the same Chapter 2.QBW file:

1. If your Chapter 2.QBW file is not already open, open it by selecting **File > Open Previous Company**. Select your **Chapter 2.QBW file**. If a QuickBooks Information window appears with a message about the sample company file, click **OK**.

2. Update the company name to **YourName Exercise 2.1 Rock Castle Construction** by selecting **Company Menu > My Company**.

> **If you are not using the same computer that you used for Chapter 2, you will need to restore your Chapter 2 Backup.QBB file using the instructions in Appendix B: Back Up and Restore QuickBooks Files. After restoring, update the company name to YourName Exercise 2.1 Rock Castle Construction.**

E2.1.2 Print Statement of Cash Flows

The Statement of Cash Flows summarizes a company's cash inflows and cash outflows. The cash flows are grouped by activity:

- Cash flows from operating activities. Cash flows related to the operations of the business—providing goods and services to customers.
- Cash flows from investing activities. Cash flows that result from investing (buying and selling) long-term assets, such as investments and property.
- Cash flows from financing activities. Cash flows that result from borrowing or repaying principal on debt or from transactions with owners.

Create the Statement of Cash Flows for Rock Castle Construction by completing the following steps:

1. Click **Reports** in the Navigation Bar

2. Select type of report: **Company & Financial**

3. Select report: **Statement of Cash Flows**

4. Select the date range: **Last Month**. The Dates field will now be: **11/01/2024 To 11/30/2024**. Select the **Run** icon.

5. Export the report to **Excel** or **print** the Statement of Cash Flows

6. **Close** the Statement of Cash Flows window

7. **Close** the Report Center window

8. **Highlight** the Net cash provided by Operating Activities for the Statement of Cash Flows

9. **Highlight** the Net cash provided by Financing Activities for the Statement of Cash Flows

10. **Highlight** the net change in cash for the period on the Statement of Cash Flows

E2.1.3 Back Up Exercise 2.1

Save a backup of your Exercise file using the file name: **YourName Exercise 2.1 Backup.QBB**. See Appendix B: Back Up and Restore QuickBooks Files for instructions.

Exercise 2.2 Chart of Accounts

 Rock Castle Construction

BACKSTORY

When you return to your cubicle after your afternoon break, another note is stuck to your computer screen.

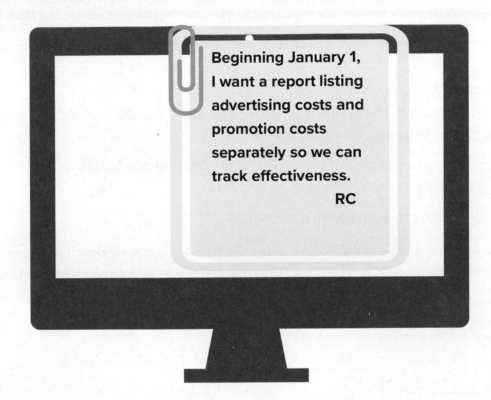

In order to track advertising costs separately from promotion costs, you decide to use subaccounts for better tracking. So you plan the following changes to customize the Chart of Accounts.

- Rename Account 60400 Advertising & Promotion account to: Selling Expense
- Add two subaccounts: 60410 Advertising Expense and 60420 Promotion Expense

After these changes, the Chart of Accounts should list the following accounts:

- Account 60400: Selling Expense
- Subaccount 60410: Advertising Expense
- Subaccount 60420: Promotion Expense

E2.2.1 QuickBooks File

If you will be using the same computer and the same QBW file:

1. Select your **QBW file**.

2. Update the company name to **YourName Exercise 2.2 Rock Castle Construction** by selecting **Company Menu > My Company**.

> If you are not using the same computer that you used for Chapter 2 and Exercise 2.1, you will need to restore your latest prior Backup.QBB file using the instructions in Appendix B: Back Up and Restore QuickBooks files. After restoring, update the company name to YourName Exercise 2.2 Rock Castle Construction.

E2.2.2 Edit Account

Edit the Chart of Accounts to change the name of Account 60400 from Advertising & Promotion to Selling Expense.

1. Open the Chart of Accounts window by clicking the **Chart of Accounts** icon in the Company section of the Home Page

2. Select account: **60400 Advertising & Promotion**

3. Click the **Account** button at the bottom of the Chart of Accounts window, then select **Edit Account** from the drop-down menu (or right-click and select Edit Account from the menu)

4. Change the account name from Advertising & Promotion to: **Selling Expense**

5. Click **Save & Close** to save the changes

E2.2.3 Add Subaccount

Add the Advertising subaccount to the Selling Expense account.

1. Click the **Account** button at the bottom of the Chart of Accounts window, then select **New** to open the Add New Account window

2. Select Account Type: **Expense**. Click **Continue**.

3. Enter Account Number: **60410**

4. Enter Account Name: **Advertising Expense**

5. **Check** the box in front of the Subaccount of field

6. From the drop-down list, select subaccount of: **60400 Selling Expense**

7. From the drop-down list for Tax-Line Mapping, select Deductions: **Advertising**

8. Click **Save & New**

E2.2.4 Add Subaccount

Add the Promotion Expense subaccount to the Selling Expense account.

1. Add the sub account: **60420 Promotion Expense**

2. Click **Save & Close**

E2.2.5 Create the Chart of Accounts (Account Listing) Report

Create the Chart of Accounts (Account Listing).

1. Using the Reports center, export to **Excel** or **print** the revised Chart of Accounts

2. **Highlight** the accounts that you changed or added in this exercise

E2.2.6 Back Up Exercise 2.2

Save a backup of your Exercise file using the file name: **YourName Exercise 2.2 Backup.QBB**. See Appendix B: Back Up and Restore QuickBooks Files for instructions.

Exercise 2.3 Align QB Chart of Accounts with Tax Return

 Rock Castle Construction

BACKSTORY

When customizing the Chart of Accounts for Rock Castle Construction, you decide to explore whether the accounts on the company's Chart of Accounts correspond to expenses shown on the tax return the business files.

First, you need to determine which business tax return Rock Castle Construction files. Then you plan to see how Rock Castle Construction's COA matches to expense lines on the tax form.

E2.3.1 QuickBooks File

If you will be using the same computer and the same QBW file:

1. Select your **QBW file**.

2. Update the company name to **YourName Exercise 2.3 Rock Castle Construction** by selecting **Company Menu > My Company**.

> If you are not using the same computer that you used for Chapter 2, Exercise 2.1, and Exercise 2.2, you will need to restore your latest prior Backup.QBB file using the instructions in Appendix B: Back Up and Restore QuickBooks files. After restoring, update the company name to YourName Exercise 2.3 Rock Castle Construction.

E2.3.2 Identify Tax Return

Identify the income tax form that Rock Castle Construction files with the Internal Revenue Service (IRS).

1. Open the My Company window by selecting **My Company** in the Navigation Bar

2. On the My Company window, find the **Income Tax Form** field

3. The Income Tax Form field should display: **Form 1120S (S Corporation)**. This tells you that for income tax purposes, Rock Castle Construction is a S Corporation and files IRS Form 1120S.

4. **Close** the My Company window

E2.3.3 Compare QB COA with Tax Lines on Tax Return

Display Rock Castle Construction's Chart of Accounts and compare it to IRS Form 1120S.

1. To display the Chart of Accounts, select the **Chart of Accounts** icon in the Company section of the Home Page

2. Form 1120S can be obtained from irs.gov. Using the following sample partial Form 1120S, for the accounts listed, identify:
   - The type of account as Asset, Liability, Equity, Income or Expense
   - The corresponding Line number on the IRS Form 1120S

Form **1120-S**

Department of the Treasury
Internal Revenue Service

U.S. Income Tax Return for an S Corporation

▶ Do not file this form unless the corporation has filed or
is attaching Form 2553 to elect to be an S corporation.
▶ Go to *www.irs.gov/Form1120S* for instructions and the latest information.

OMB No. 1545-0123

A S election effective date	TYPE OR PRINT	Name	D Employer identification number
B Business activity code number (see instructions)		Number, street, and room or suite no. If a P.O. box, see instructions.	E Date incorporated
C Check if Sch. M-3 attached ☐		City or town, state or province, country, and ZIP or foreign postal code	F Total assets (see instructions) $

G Is the corporation electing to be an S corporation beginning with this tax year? ☐ Yes ☐ No If "Yes," attach Form 2553 if not already filed
H Check if: **(1)** ☐ Final return **(2)** ☐ Name change **(3)** ☐ Address change **(4)** ☐ Amended return **(5)** ☐ S election termination or revocation
I Enter the number of shareholders who were shareholders during any part of the tax year . . . . ▶ _____
J Check if corporation: **(1)** ☐ Aggregated activities for section 465 at-risk purposes **(2)** ☐ Grouped activities for section 469 passive activity purposes

Caution: Include **only** trade or business income and expenses on lines 1a through 21. See the instructions for more information.

Income

1a Gross receipts or sales	1a	
b Returns and allowances	1b	
c Balance. Subtract line 1b from line 1a	1c	
2 Cost of goods sold (attach Form 1125-A)	2	
3 Gross profit. Subtract line 2 from line 1c	3	
4 Net gain (loss) from Form 4797, line 17 (attach Form 4797)	4	
5 Other income (loss) (see instructions—attach statement)	5	
6 **Total income (loss).** Add lines 3 through 5 . . . . ▶	6	

Deductions (see instructions for limitations)

7 Compensation of officers (see instructions—attach Form 1125-E)	7	
8 Salaries and wages (less employment credits)	8	
9 Repairs and maintenance	9	
10 Bad debts	10	
11 Rents	11	
12 Taxes and licenses	12	
13 Interest (see instructions)	13	
14 Depreciation not claimed on Form 1125-A or elsewhere on return (attach Form 4562)	14	
15 Depletion **(Do not deduct oil and gas depletion.)**	15	
16 Advertising	16	
17 Pension, profit-sharing, etc., plans	17	
18 Employee benefit programs	18	
19 Other deductions (attach statement)	19	
20 **Total deductions.** Add lines 7 through 19 . . . . ▶	20	
21 **Ordinary business income (loss).** Subtract line 20 from line 6	21	

Source: Department of the Treasury Internal Revenue Service

Rock Castle Construction COA	Account Type	IRS Form 1120S
1. 50100 Cost of Goods Sold	_____	Form 1120S Line ____
2. 60410 Advertising Expense	_____	Form 1120S Line ____
3. 64220 Computer Repairs	_____	Form 1120S Line ____
4. 64230 Equipment Repairs	_____	Form 1120S Line ____
5. 62400 Interest Expense	_____	Form 1120S Line ____

E2.3.4 Select QuickBooks Tax Line for COA

To simplify tax preparation, QuickBooks permits you to select Tax Line Mapping for QuickBooks accounts. The Tax Line Mapping options that QuickBooks offers depends upon which tax return was selected during the new company setup. For example, Rock Castle Construction uses Form 1120S so the Tax Line Mapping options are for Form 1120S.

Next, select the Tax Line Mapping for the following accounts in Rock Castle Construction's Chart of Accounts.

1. From the Chart of Accounts window, select account: **64220 Computer Repairs > right-click** to display the pop-up menu > select **Edit Account** > Tax-Line Mapping: **Deductions: Repairs and maintenance > Save & Close**

2. From the Chart of Accounts window, select account: **64230 Equipment Repairs > right-click** to display the pop-up menu > select **Edit Account** > Tax-Line Mapping: **Deductions: Repairs and maintenance > Save & Close**

3. From the Chart of Accounts window, select account: **62400 Interest Expense > right-click** to display the pop-up menu > select **Edit Account** > Tax-Line Mapping: **Deductions: Interest expense > Save & Close**

E2.3.5 Back Up Exercise 2.3

Save a backup of your Exercise file using the file name: **YourName Exercise 2.3 Backup.QBB**. See Appendix B: Back Up and Restore QuickBooks Files for instructions.

Project 2.1

Larry's Landscaping 🌴

As an accounting consultant for Larry's Landscaping complete the following to customize QuickBooks for the company and create reports.

> 💡 **Troubleshooting QuickBooks and Correcting Errors are crucial QuickBooks skill to acquire. Troubleshooting resources include:**
> - **www.My-QuickBooks.com > QuickBooks Troubleshooting (QT) Tips**
> - **Chapter 17, Quick Review Guide, contains tips on Correcting Errors**
> - **Appendix D, QuickBooks Troubleshooting (QT), provides you with an effective troubleshooting process**

🌐 QuickBooks SatNav

The objective of Project 2.1 is to facilitate your mastery of QuickBooks Desktop. As shown in the following QuickBooks SatNav, Project 2.1 focuses on the first and last of the three processes: QuickBooks Settings and QuickBooks Reports.

QuickBooks SatNav

 QuickBooks Settings

Company Settings
Chart of Accounts

QuickBooks Transactions

Banking
Customers & Sales
Vendors & Expenses
Employees & Payroll

QuickBooks Reports

Reports

P2.1.1 QuickBooks File

1. Use either your QuickBooks Company file (QBW) or restore the backup file (QBB) that you completed for Project 1.1. (If you have issues with your QuickBooks file, contact your instructor.)

2. Update the Company Name to: **YourName Project 2.1 Larry's Landscaping**

P2.1.2 QuickBooks Preferences

1. Using QuickBooks General preferences, select **Use the last entered date as default**

2. Using QuickBooks Accounting preferences, select **Use account numbers** to display account numbers in the Chart of Accounts

P2.1.3 Chart of Accounts

Customize Larry's Chart of Accounts as follows.

1. Enter the following accounts and **re-sort** the Chart of Accounts

Account	**Supplies**
Account No.	**7310**
Account Type	**Expense**
Account Description	**Cleaning Supplies**
Tax Line	**Schedule C: Supplies (not from COGS)**

Account	**Computer Supplies**
Account No.	**7320**
Account Type	**Expense**
Account Description	**Computer Supplies**
Tax Line	**Schedule C: Supplies (not from COGS)**

Account	**Professional Design Fees**
Account No.	**7430**
Account Type	**Expense**
Account Description	**Professional Design Fees**
Subaccount of	**7400 Professional Fees**
Tax Line	**Schedule C: Legal and professional fees**

Account	**Section 179**
Account No.	**6710**
Account Type	**Expense**
Account Description	**Section 179**
Subaccount of	**6700 Depreciation**
Tax Line	**Schedule C: Other business expenses**

Account	**Internet Provider**
Account No.	**7754**
Account Type	**Expense**
Account Description	**Internet Provider**
Subaccount of	**7750 Utilities**
Tax Line	**Schedule C: Office expenses**

2. Export to **Excel** the Chart of Accounts for Larry's Landscaping using the Account Listing report at December 15, 2024

3. **Highlight** the accounts that you added

P2.1.4 Financial Reports

1. Export to **Excel** the Statement of Cash Flows for Larry's Landscaping for the Last Fiscal Year, October 1, 2023 to September 30, 2024

2. **Highlight** the Net cash provided by Operating Activities for the Statement of Cash Flows

3. **Highlight** the Net cash provided by Financing Activities for the Statement of Cash Flows

4. **Highlight** the net change in cash for the period on the Statement of Cash Flows

P2.1.5 Align QB Chart of Accounts with Tax Return

First, determine which business tax return Larry's Landscaping files. Then evaluate how the Chart of Accounts for Larry's Landscaping aligns to expense lines on the tax form.

1. Identify the income tax form that Larry's Landscaping files with the Internal Revenue Service (IRS). Select **My Company** in the Navigation Bar. On the My Company window, find the **Income Tax Form** field. The Income Tax Form field should display: **Form 1040 (Sole Proprietorship)** This tells you that for income tax purposes, Larry's Landscaping is a sole proprietorship and files Form 1040 Schedule C.

2. To display the Chart of Accounts, select the **Chart of Accounts** icon in the Company section of the Home Page.

3. Using the following sample partial Form 1040 Schedule C, for the accounts listed, identify:
   * The type of account as Asset, Liability, Equity, Income or Expense
   * The corresponding Line number on the IRS Form 1040 Schedule C

Larry's Landscaping COA	Account Type	IRS Form 1040 Schedule C
1. 6000 Advertising Expense	_____	Schedule C Line _____
2. 6900 Insurance Expense	_____	Schedule C Line _____
3. 7400 Professional Fees	_____	Schedule C Line _____
4. 7500 Rent	_____	Schedule C Line _____
5. 7550 Repairs	_____	Schedule C Line _____
6. 7551 Gas and Electric	_____	Schedule C Line _____
7. 7552 Water	_____	Schedule C Line _____
8. 7553 Telephone	_____	Schedule C Line _____
9. 7554 Internet Provider	_____	Schedule C Line _____

SCHEDULE C (Form 1040)

Department of the Treasury
Internal Revenue Service (99)

Profit or Loss From Business
(Sole Proprietorship)

▶ Information about Schedule C and its separate instructions is at *www.irs.gov/schedulec*.
▶ Attach to Form 1040, 1040NR, or 1041; partnerships generally must file Form 1065.

Name of proprietor

Social security number (SSN)

A	Principal business or profession, including product or service (see instructions)	B Enter code from instructions ▶
C	Business name. If no separate business name, leave blank.	D Employer ID number (EIN), (see instr.)

E   Business address (including suite or room no.) ▶
    City, town or post office, state, and ZIP code

F   Accounting method: (1) ☐ Cash   (2) ☐ Accrual   (3) ☐ Other (specify) ▶

G   Did you "materially participate" in the operation of this business during 2016? If "No," see instructions for limit on losses   ☐ Yes ☐ No
H   If you started or acquired this business during 2016, check here   ▶ ☐
I   Did you make any payments in 2016 that would require you to file Form(s) 1099? (see instructions)   ☐ Yes ☐ No
J   If "Yes," did you or will you file required Forms 1099?   ☐ Yes ☐ No

Part I   Income

1	Gross receipts or sales. See instructions for line 1 and check the box if this income was reported to you on Form W-2 and the "Statutory employee" box on that form was checked ▶ ☐	1
2	Returns and allowances	2
3	Subtract line 2 from line 1	3
4	Cost of goods sold (from line 42)	4
5	**Gross profit.** Subtract line 4 from line 3	5
6	Other income, including federal and state gasoline or fuel tax credit or refund (see instructions)	6
7	**Gross income.** Add lines 5 and 6 ▶	7

Part II   Expenses. Enter expenses for business use of your home **only** on line 30.

8	Advertising	8	18	Office expense (see instructions)	18
9	Car and truck expenses (see instructions)	9	19	Pension and profit-sharing plans	19
10	Commissions and fees	10	20	Rent or lease (see instructions):	
11	Contract labor (see instructions)	11	a	Vehicles, machinery, and equipment	20a
12	Depletion	12	b	Other business property	20b
13	Depreciation and section 179 expense deduction (not included in Part III) (see instructions)	13	21	Repairs and maintenance	21
			22	Supplies (not included in Part III)	22
			23	Taxes and licenses	23
			24	Travel, meals, and entertainment:	
14	Employee benefit programs (other than on line 19)	14	a	Travel	24a
15	Insurance (other than health)	15	b	Deductible meals and entertainment (see instructions)	24b
16	Interest:		25	Utilities	25
a	Mortgage (paid to banks, etc.)	16a	26	Wages (less employment credits)	26
b	Other	16b	27a	Other expenses (from line 48)	27a
17	Legal and professional services	17	b	Reserved for future use	27b

Source: Department of the Treasury Internal Revenue Service

4. To simplify tax preparation, QuickBooks permits you to select a tax line for QuickBooks accounts. Verify the Tax Line for the following account in the COA of Larry's Landscaping.
    • From the Chart of Accounts window, select account: **7553 Telephone** > **right-click** to display the pop-up menu > select **Edit Account** > Verify Tax-Line Mapping: **Schedule C: Office expenses** > **Save & Close**.

P2.1.6 Back Up Project 2.1

Save a backup of your Project file using the file name: **YourName Project 2.1 Backup.QBB**.

See Appendix B: Back Up and Restore QuickBooks Files for instructions.

Design elements: Dog icon: ©josep perianes jorba/Shutterstock; paint roller icon: ©Netti Buletti/Shutterstock; other icons/symbols: ©Carboxylase/Shutterstock

Chapter 3

QuickBooks Transactions

 Rock Castle Construction

BACKSTORY

As you start sorting through the random stacks of paper on your desk, you hear Mr. Castle's booming voice and rapid pace coming in your direction. You look up just in time to see Mr. Castle plant a huge stack of papers on your desk.

Smiling he says, *"Since you are getting organized I thought you'd want these papers too. And when you are finished there are more in my office. We got a little bit behind."*

Seeing the stricken look on your face, Mr. Castle pauses, putting his hands on his hips. *"Here's the way I look at it, we have all this info we have to get into QuickBooks. But it's basically about entering four, and only four, different types of transactions.*

1. *Banking and credit card transactions*
2. *Customers and sales transactions*
3. *Vendors and expenses transaction*
4. *Employees and payroll transactions*

"And we don't need to worry about payroll for a while yet. So you can focus on three different types of transactions.

"So dive in!" Mr. Castle points at the paperwork smiling.

Chapter 3

Learning Objectives

Chapter 3 introduces QuickBooks Transactions, such as Banking, Customer, Vendor, and Employee transactions. In this chapter, you will learn about the following topics:

- QuickBooks Lists
- Enter QuickBooks Transactions
- Different Types of Transactions
- Banking and Credit Card Transactions
  - Record Deposit
  - Write Check
- Customers and Sales Transactions
  - Create Sales Receipt
  - Create Bank Deposit for Undeposited Funds from Sales Receipt
- Vendors and Expenses Transactions
  - Enter Bill
  - Pay Bills
- Employees and Payroll Transactions
- Other Transactions
- Memorized Transactions
- Accounting Essentials: Double-Entry Accounting

Section 3.1
 QuickBooks SatNav

QuickBooks SatNav is your satellite navigation for QuickBooks, assisting you in navigating QuickBooks

QuickBooks SatNav divides QuickBooks into three processes:

1. **QuickBooks Settings.** This includes Company Settings when setting up a new QuickBooks company and the Company Chart of Accounts.

2. **QuickBooks Transactions.** This includes recording transactions in QuickBooks. Transaction types can be categorized as Banking, Customers and Sales, Vendors and Expenses, and Employees and Payroll. In basic terms, recording transactions involves recording money in and money out.

3. **QuickBooks Reports.** QuickBooks reports are the output of the system, such as commonly used financial statements of Balance Sheet, Income Statement, and Statement of Cash Flows.

Chapter 3 provides an overview of QuickBooks transactions, shown in the following QuickBooks SatNav.

🌐 QuickBooks SatNav

⚙ QuickBooks Settings

⚙ Company Settings

⚙ Chart of Accounts

QuickBooks Transactions

Banking

Customers & Sales

Vendors & Expenses

Employees & Payroll

📊 QuickBooks Reports

📊 Reports

💡 **Accounting Essentials** appear at the end of the chapter. Tip: Preview Accounting Essentials <u>before</u> completing the chapter and then review Accounting Essentials <u>after</u> completing the chapter.

Section 3.2

Start QuickBooks and Open QuickBooks Company

START QUICKBOOKS.

To start QuickBooks software, click the **QuickBooks** icon on your desktop. If a QuickBooks icon does not appear on your desktop, from Microsoft® Windows® click **Start** button > **QuickBooks** > **QuickBooks Premier Accountant Edition**.

> **QuickBooks Accountant** includes all the features of QuickBooks Pro plus features for client services. If you use QuickBooks Pro, your screens may appear slightly different than those appearing in this text.

RESTORE QBB STARTER FILE

Restore the QBB Starter file for this chapter as follows.

1. Select **File** > **Restore**

2. Using the directions in Appendix B: Back Up and Restore QuickBooks Files, restore **CHAPTER 3 STARTER.QBB**

3. After restoring, update the company name to **YourName Chapter 3 Rock Castle Construction** by selecting **Company Menu** > **My Company**

> ⚠ **QuickBooks Desktop (QBDT)** Data Files are compressed backup files that can be restored and used. To use Starter Files, the compressed file must be restored following the instructions here. Since it is a compressed file, you cannot open and use the QuickBooks data files by simply clicking on the file. Instead you must follow the instructions here to unzip and restore the data file before using it.

> - When restoring a **QBB STARTER FILE**, if QuickBooks requires you to create a password in order to continue, create your own password and record the password in a secure location, such as the inside cover of your textbook.
> - If a password is requested when restoring a QuickBooks QBB STARTER FILE, try using User ID: Admin and leave the Password field <u>blank</u>
> - If you are using the QBB STARTER FILE and QuickBooks requires a password and QuickBooks will not accept the password field blank, try User ID: Admin and Password: KayQB2021
> - If none of the above approaches permit you to restore the QBB file, see your instructor

Section 3.3
QuickBooks Lists

As a company conducts business operations, the company enters into transactions with customers, vendors, and employees. Before entering these transactions in QuickBooks, we typically want to make sure our QuickBooks Lists are up to date.

WHAT ARE QUICKBOOKS LISTS?

QuickBooks lists are a time saving feature so that we don't have to continually re-enter the same information for accounts, customers, vendors, and so on, each time we enter a new transaction. Lists permit us to collect information that we will reuse so we don't have to re-enter it.

QuickBooks lists include:

- **Customers List.** Provides information about customers.
- **Vendors List.** Provides information about vendors.
- **Employees List.** Provides information about employees for payroll purposes.
- **Items List.** Provides information about the items or services sold to customers or purchased from vendors.
- **Payroll Items List.** Tracks detailed information about payroll, such as payroll taxes and payroll deductions. The Payroll Item List permits the use of a single or limited number of payroll accounts while more detailed information is tracked using the Item List for payroll.
- **Class List.** Permits income to be tracked according to the specific source (class) of income. An example of a class might be a department, store location, business segment, or product line.

Lists are used so that information can be entered once in a list and then reused as needed. For example, information about a customer, such as address, can be entered in the Customers List. This customer information then automatically appears on the customer invoice.

To view QuickBooks lists, select the lists as follows.

1   Select **Customers** on the Navigation Bar to view the Customers List

2   Select **Vendors** on the Navigation Bar to view the Vendors List

3   Select **Employees** on the Navigation Bar to view the Employees List

4   Select the **Items & Services** icon in the Company section of the Home Page to view the Items & Services List

5   Select the **Chart of Accounts** icon in the Company section of the Home Page to view the Chart of Accounts, a list of accounts

6   Select the **Lists Menu** to view other QuickBooks Lists, such as the Payroll Items List or the Class List

Customers List collects information about customers, such as customer name, customer number, address, and contact information.

Vendors List collects information about vendors, such as vendor name, vendor number, and contact information.

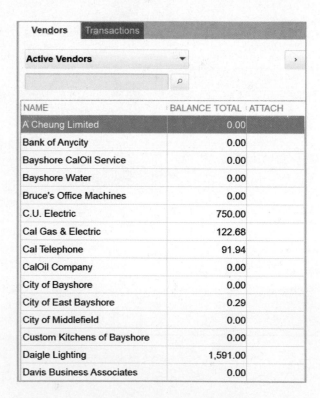

Employees List collects information about employees for payroll purposes including name, Social Security number, and address.

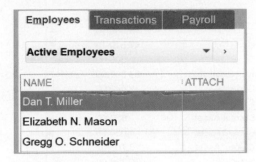

Items and Services List collects information about the products and services sold to customers, such as hours worked and types of products or services.

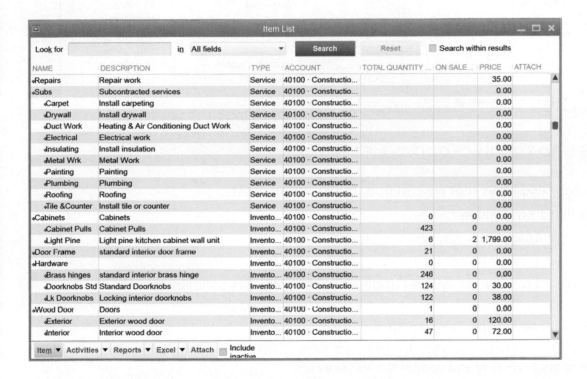

Chart of Accounts is a list of all the accounts a company uses when recording transactions. Accounts (such as the Checking account or Inventory account) permit us to sort and track accounting information.

```
┌─────────────────────────────────────────────────────────────────────────────────────┐
│ ▫                          Chart of Accounts                              _ □ x       │
├─────────────────────────────────────────────────────────────────────────────────────┤
│  Look for account name or number                                                      │
│  ┌──────────────────────┐   ┌──────────────┐   ┌──────────────┐                       │
│  │                      │   │    Search    │   │    Reset     │                       │
│  └──────────────────────┘   └──────────────┘   └──────────────┘                       │
└─────────────────────────────────────────────────────────────────────────────────────┘
```

✖	NAME	⚡	TYPE	BALANCE TOTAL	ATTA...
	10100 · Checking		Bank	46,969.10	
	10300 · Savings		Bank	17,910.19	
	10400 · Petty Cash		Bank	500.00	
	11000 · Accounts Receivable		Accounts Receivable	93,007.93	
	12000 · Undeposited Funds		Other Current Asset	2,440.00	
	12100 · Inventory Asset		Other Current Asset	30,683.38	
	12800 · Employee Advances		Other Current Asset	832.00	
	13100 · Pre-paid Insurance		Other Current Asset	4,050.00	
	13400 · Retainage Receivable		Other Current Asset	3,703.02	
	15000 · Furniture and Equipment		Fixed Asset	34,326.00	
	15100 · Vehicles		Fixed Asset	78,936.91	
✖	1510 · Original Cost		Fixed Asset	0.00	
✖	1520 · Depreciation		Fixed Asset	0.00	
	15200 · Buildings and Improvements		Fixed Asset	325,000.00	
	15300 · Construction Equipment		Fixed Asset	15,300.00	
	16900 · Land		Fixed Asset	90,000.00	
	17000 · Accumulated Depreciation		Fixed Asset	-110,344.60	
	18700 · Security Deposits		Other Asset	1,720.00	
	20000 · Accounts Payable		Accounts Payable	26,636.92	
	20500 · QuickBooks Credit Card		Credit Card	94.20	

Account ▾ Activities ▾ Reports ▾ Attach ☑ Include inactive

HOW DO WE UPDATE QUICKBOOKS LISTS?

There are basically two ways that we can update QuickBooks lists.
1. *Before* entering transactions
2. *While* entering transactions

1. *Before* entering transactions, we can update QuickBooks lists as follows.

1 Select **Customers** to display and update the Customers List

2 Select **Vendors** to display and update the Vendors List

3 Select **Employees** to display and update the Employees List

4 Select the **Items & Services** icon to display and update the Items & Services List

2. *While* entering transactions, we can update lists on the fly from the screen where we enter the transaction. If a customer, for example, has not been entered in the Customer List and is needed for a sales transaction, we can add the customer as follows from an onscreen Invoice form.

1   For example, to view an onscreen form such as an Invoice, select the **Create Invoices** icon to display an onscreen invoice

2   Then select **Customer:Job drop-down arrow > + Add New**

3   Next we would enter **new customer information**

4   Normally, we would select **OK** to save the new customer information. Then we would complete and save the Invoice. In this case, select **Cancel** to leave the New Customer window.

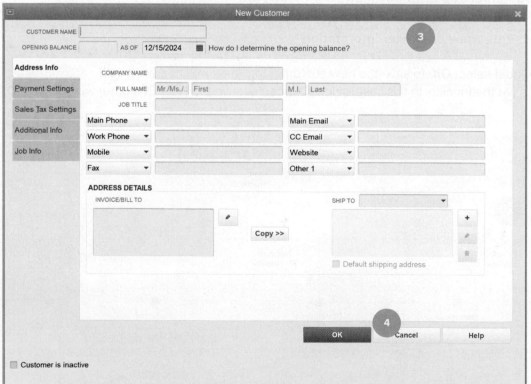

Section 3.4

How Do We Enter Transactions in QuickBooks?

WHAT ARE TRANSACTIONS?

Our QuickBooks financial system needs to collect information about transactions.

Transactions are exchanges. A business enters into transactions or exchanges between the business and other parties, such as customers, vendors, and employers. The business gives and receives something in an exchange.

A business can exchange services, products, cash, or a promise to pay later (Accounts Payable). A transaction must have two parts to the exchange: something must be given and something must be received.
For example, when a business sells 1 hour of consulting services to a customer, the two parts to the transaction are:

1. The business gives the customer 1 hour of consulting services.
2. In exchange, the business receives cash (or a promise to pay later) from the customer.

When we record transactions in QuickBooks we need to record what is exchanged, what is given and what is received.

ONSCREEN FORM OR ONSCREEN JOURNAL

QuickBooks offers us two different ways to enter transaction information:
1. Onscreen Journal
2. Onscreen forms

Onscreen Journal. We can make debit and credit entries in an onscreen Journal as follows.

> The onscreen Journal using debits and credits to enter transactions is accessed from the Accountant Menu > **Make General Journal Entries**.

An onscreen Journal is often used to make adjusting entries at year end to bring accounts up to date before preparing financial statements.

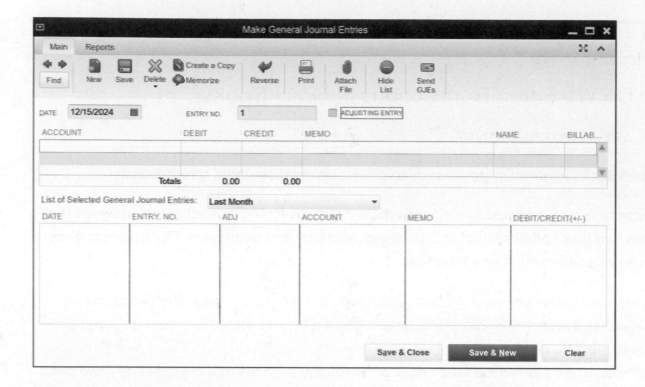

Instead of using the onscreen Journal, we can use onscreen forms to enter transaction information in QuickBooks.

Onscreen forms. We can enter information about transactions using onscreen forms such as the following onscreen form. When we enter information into an onscreen form, behind the screen QuickBooks automatically converts that information into a journal entry with debits and credits. QuickBooks maintains a list of journal entries for all the transactions entered—whether entered using the onscreen Journal or onscreen forms.

1. To view an onscreen form such as an Expense, select the **Enter Bills** icon in the Vendors section of the Home Page

2. From the Enter Bills onscreen form window, select the **Main** tab at the top of the window

3. Click the back **Find** arrow until the bill for Thomas Kitchen & Bath for 12/15/2024 in the amount of $585.00 appears

4. Next select the **Reports** tab at the top of the Enter Bills window

5. Select **Transaction Journal**

6 Behind the screen, QuickBooks automatically converted the information in the Enter Bills onscreen form into a following journal entry with debits and credits. Notice that the journal entry displays a Debit to Job Materials and a Credit to Accounts Payable for $585.00.

7 **Close** the Transaction Journal window and the Enter Bills window

For example, to view the journal entry that QuickBooks created behind the screen for a transaction entered and saved using an onscreen form, complete the following steps.

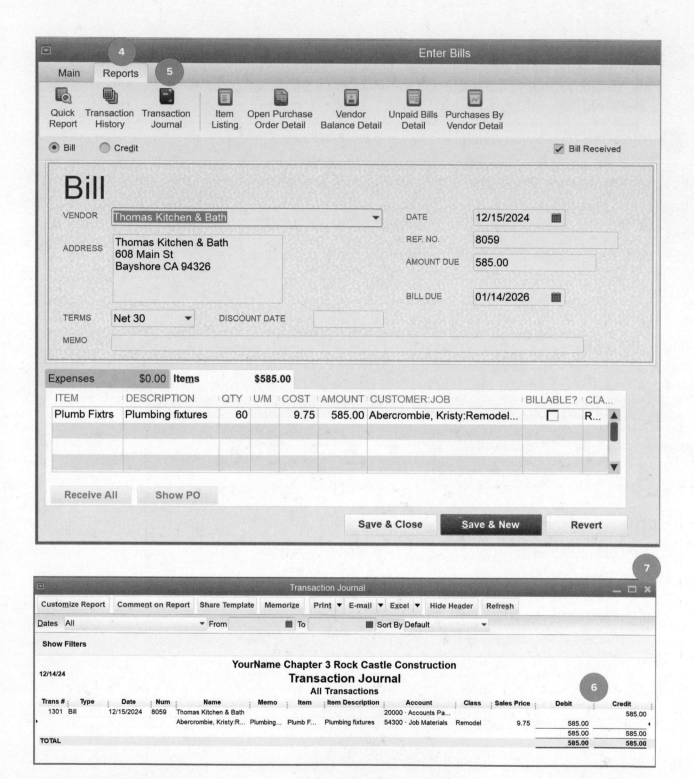

Notice that the Transaction Journal report displays a subtotal and total for the debit and credit columns in order to cross check that debits and credits are equal.

Section 3.5

What Are The Different Types of Transactions?

A transaction is simply an exchange between our QuickBooks business and another party, such as a customer, vendor, or employee. Although there are many different types of transactions, generally we can group transactions into the following different types based upon the other party to the transaction:

1. Banking and Credit Card
2. Customers and Sales
3. Vendors and Expenses
4. Employees and Payroll
5. Other

QuickBooks organizes how we access entering transactions according to the type of transaction and which onscreen form we need to use to enter the transaction.

Section 3.6

Banking and Credit Card Transactions

 QuickBooks SatNav

 QuickBooks Transactions

Banking	*Record Deposits	Write Checks*
Customers & Sales	
Vendors & Expenses	
Employees & Payroll	

Transactions that involve depositing funds or writing checks can be entered using icons in the Banking section of the Home Page.

Banking transactions include:

1. Record Deposits

2. Write Checks

RECORD DEPOSIT

To make a deposit:

1 Select **Record Deposit** icon in the Banking section of the Home Page

2 If a Payments to Deposit window appears, confirm that none of the payments have been selected for deposit, then click **OK**

3 When the Make Deposits window appears, select Deposit To: **10100 Checking**

4 Select Date: **12/15/2024**

5 In the Received From column, enter: **YourName**. Press **Tab** key.

6 Select **Quick Add** to add YourName to the Name List

7 Select Name Type: **Other**

8 Click **OK**

9 Click in the From Account column. From the drop-down list of accounts, select **30100 Capital Stock**. Press **Tab**.

10 Enter Check No.: **999**

11 From the Payment Method drop-down list, select **Check**

12 Enter Amount: **1000**. (QuickBooks will automatically enter the comma in the amount.)

13 Select the **Save** icon to save the deposit. (To print a summary of the deposit just recorded, we would select the Print arrow at the top of the Make Deposits window. In this case, we will not print the Deposit Summary.) Leave the Make Deposits window open on your screen

C3.6.1 Deposit Journal Entry. To view the journal entry that QuickBooks created behind the screen for the deposit entered and saved using the Make Deposits onscreen form above, complete the following steps.

1 From the Make Deposits onscreen form, select the **Journal** icon at the top of the form

2 Behind the screen, QuickBooks automatically converted the information in the Record Deposit onscreen form into a journal entry with debits and credits. Notice that the journal entry displays a Debit to 10100 Checking and a Credit to 30100 Capital Stock for $1,000.00.

3 Export the Transaction Journal report to **Excel** or **print** the report

4 **Close** the Transaction Journal window

5 Normally, we would select Save & Close to save the deposit but in this case close the Make Deposits window without saving. We will enter deposits in the exercises at the end of the chapter.

WRITE CHECK

To write a check:

1   From the Banking section of the Home Page, click the **Write Checks** icon

2   To enter the check information, select Bank Account: **10100 Checking**

3   Select Date: **12/15/2024**

4   For the Pay to the Order of field, select: **Kershaw Computer Services**. (Select Kershaw from the drop-down list or type the first few letters of the name.)

5   Enter the check amount: **500**. Press **Tab**.

6   Click the checkbox preceding **Print Later** so that a check mark appears. The Check No. field will now display: To Print. Notice there is also an option to Pay Online.

7   Next, to record the payment in the correct account using the lower portion of the Write Checks window, select the **Expenses** tab

8   If not already selected, select Account: **64220 Computer Repairs**. Account 64200 Repairs: 64220 Computer Repairs should appear in the Account column and $500 should automatically appear in the expense Amount column.

9   If we wanted to print the check, we would select the Print button located at the top of the Write Checks window. In this case, we will not be printing the check.

10   Select **Save**. Leave the Write Checks window open on your screen.

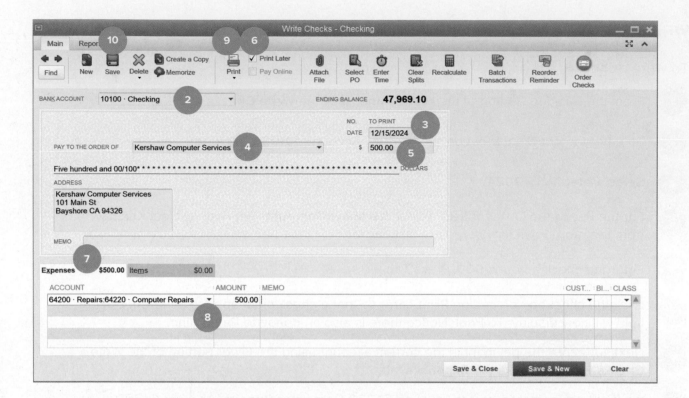

C3.6.2 Check Journal Entry. To view the journal entry that QuickBooks created behind the screen for the check entered and saved using the Write Checks onscreen form above, complete the following steps.

1. From the Write Checks onscreen form, select the **Reports** tab

2. Select the **Transaction Journal** icon

3. Behind the screen, QuickBooks automatically converted the information in the Write Checks onscreen form into a journal entry with debits and credits. Notice that the journal entry displays a Credit to 10100 Checking and a Debit to 64220 Computer Repairs for $500.00. (Notice that the QuickBooks Journal does not always display Debits before Credits in the Journal.)

4. Export the Transaction Journal report to **Excel** or **print** the report

5. **Close** the Transaction Journal window. **Close** the Write Checks window.

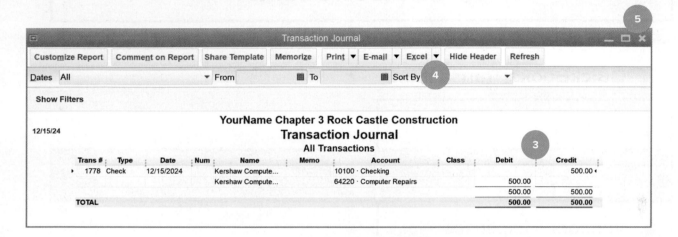

Additional banking activities are covered in the next chapter.

Section 3.7

Customers and Sales Transactions

🐸 **QuickBooks Transactions**	
🐸 Banking	
🐸 Customers & Sales	*Create Sales Receipts > Record Deposits*
🐸 Vendors & Expenses	
🐸 Employees & Payroll	

Customers transactions are exchanges between our company and customers of our company. Typically, these exchanges focus on sales transactions. Customers include parties to whom we sell products or services.

We can enter customers and sales transactions using the Customers section of the Home Page.

Customer transactions include:

1   Enter sales receipts when the customer pays at the same time a sale occurs

2   Record deposit to deposit the funds in the Checking account

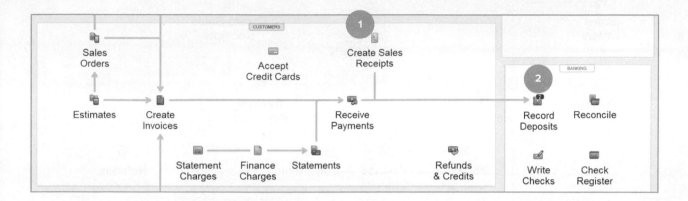

CREATE SALES RECEIPT

One of Rock Castle Construction's customers, Noelani Luke, wants to purchase an extra set of cabinet pulls that match the cabinets that Rock Castle Construction installed. Noelani pays $20 in cash for the extra cabinet pulls.

To create a sales receipt for a customer sale when payment is received at the time of the sale:

1   From the Customers section of the Home Page, click **Create Sales Receipts**

2   In the Enter Sales Receipts window, select Customer & Job: **Luke, Noelani: Kitchen**

3   Select Date: **12/15/2024**

4   Select Payment Method: **Cash**

5   Select item from the Item drop-down menu or Add New Item. In this case, select **Cabinet Pulls**.

6   Select Quantity: **1**

7   Enter Rate: **20.00**

8 Select **Print Later** checkbox

9 Select **Save**. Leave the Enter Sales Receipts window open on your screen.

C3.7.1 Sales Receipt Journal Entry. To view the journal entry that QuickBooks created behind the screen for the sales receipt entered and saved using the Enter Sales Receipts onscreen form above, complete the following steps.

1   From the Enter Sales Receipts onscreen form, select the **Reports** tab

2   Select the **Transaction Journal** icon

3   Export the Transaction Journal report to **Excel** or **print** the report

4   **Close** the Transaction Journal window. **Close** the Enter Sales Receipts window

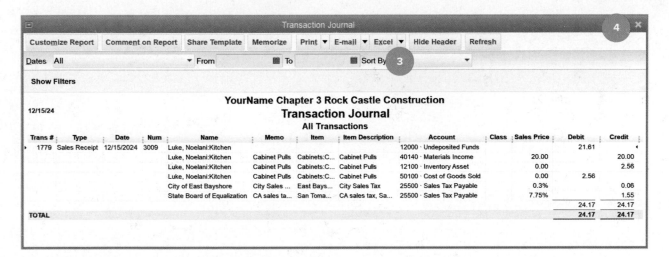

CREATE BANK DEPOSIT FOR UNDEPOSITED FUNDS FROM SALES RECEIPT

When we recorded the sales receipt, QuickBooks recorded a Debit of $21.61 in the Undeposited Funds account. Next, we must record a bank deposit to move the funds from the Undeposited Funds account to the Checking account. The process of using the

Undeposited Funds account for customer payments permits a business to bundle multiple customer payments together into one bank deposit.

To record a bank deposit to transfer a customer payment from Undeposited Funds to the Checking account:

1 Click the **Record Deposits** icon in the Banking section of the Home Page to display the Payments to Deposit window. The Payments to Deposit window lists undeposited funds that have been received but not yet deposited in the bank.

2 Select the payments to transfer from the Undeposited Funds account to the Checking account. In this case select **Luke, Noelani: Kitchen** for the amount of **$21.61**.

3 Click **OK** to display the following Make Deposits window

4 Select Deposit To: **10100 Checking**

5 Select Date: **12/15/2024**

6 Verify the Amount field displays **$21.61**

7 Select **Save**

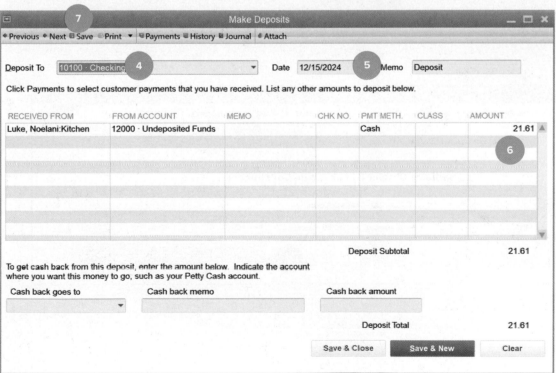

C3.7.2 Deposit Journal Entry. To view the journal entry that QuickBooks created behind the screen for the deposit entered and saved using the Record Deposit onscreen form above, complete the following steps.

1 From the Record Deposit onscreen form, select the **Journal** icon at the top of the form

2 Behind the screen, QuickBooks automatically converted the information in the Record Deposit onscreen form into a journal entry with debits and credits. Notice that the journal entry displays a Debit (increase) to the Checking account and a Credit (decrease) to Undeposited Funds to move the funds from the Undeposited Funds account to the Checking account.

3 Export the Transaction Journal report to **Excel** or **print** the report

4 **Close** the Transaction Journal window

5 On the Make Deposits window, select **Save & Close** to save the deposit

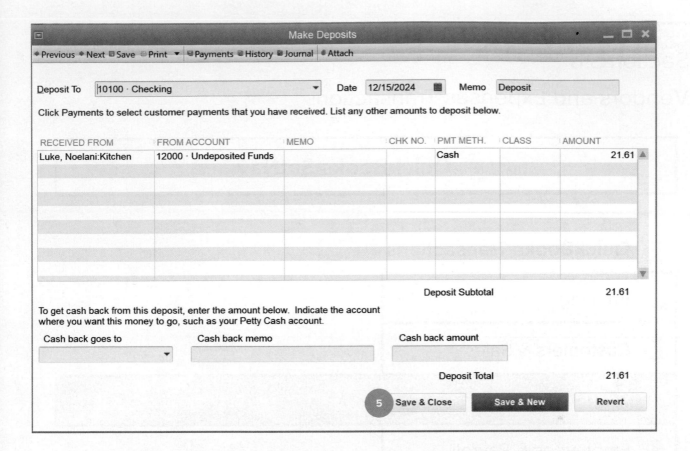

Section 3.8

Vendors and Expenses Transactions

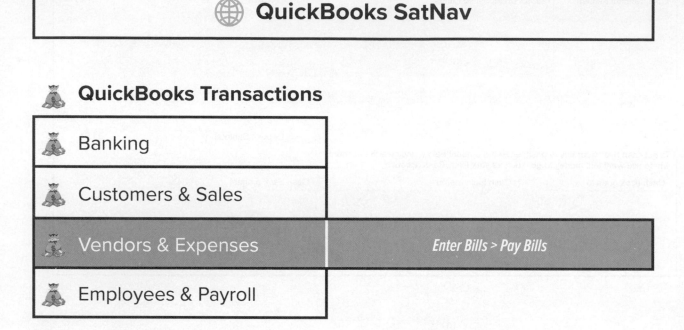

Vendors transactions are exchanges between our company and vendors of our company. Typically, these exchanges focus on expense transactions. Vendors include suppliers who sell products and professionals who provide services to our company.

We can enter vendors and expenses transactions using the Vendors section of the Home Page.

Vendors transactions can include:

1   Enter bills for services received

2   Pay bills

ENTER BILL

To enter bills for expenses:

1   Click the **Enter Bills** icon in the Vendors section of the Home Page

2   When the Enter Bills window appears, click the **Expenses** tab

3   Enter the following information for Rock Castle's water bill in the Enter Bills window.

Vendor	**Bayshore Water**
Date	**12/15/2024**
Amount Due	**$42**
Terms	**Net 30**
Account	**65130: Water**

4   Select **Save**

C3.8.1 Bill Journal Entry. To view the journal entry that QuickBooks created behind the screen for the bill entered and saved using the Enter Bills onscreen form above, complete the following steps.

1. From the Enter Bills onscreen form, select the **Reports** tab

2. Select the **Transaction Journal** icon

3. Export the Transaction Journal report to **Excel** or **print** the report

4. **Close** the Transaction Journal window

5. **Close** the Enter Bills window

PAY BILLS

To select bill to pay:

1 Click the **Pay Bills** icon in the Vendors section of the Home Page

2 Select Show bills: **Show all bills**

3 Typically, you would select the bills that are due first. In this case, however, select the **$42.00 Bayshore Water** bill due on **01/14/2025**.

4 In the Payment section, select Date: **12/15/2024**

5 Select Method: **Check**

6 Select: **To be printed**

7 Select Account: **Checking**

8 Select **Pay Selected Bills**

9 Select **Done**

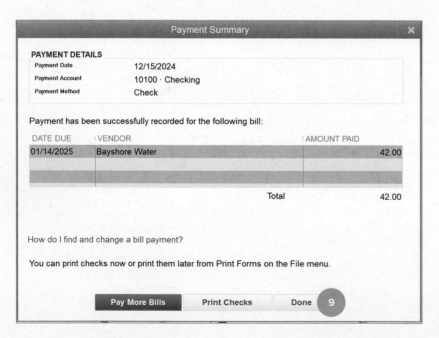

C3.8.2 Pay Bills Journal Entries. Another way to view the behind the screen journal entry is to use the Report Center. To view the journal entries that QuickBooks created behind the screen when bills were entered and selected for payment, complete the following steps.

1. From the Navigation Bar, select **Reports**

2. Select **Accountant & Taxes**

3. Select **Journal**

4. Select **Run**

5. Select Dates From **12/15/2024** To **12/15/2024**

6. Select **Refresh**

7. To add a filter, select **Customize Report**

8. Select **Filters** tab

9. Select Filter: **Amount**

10. Select =

11. Enter **42.00**

12. Select **OK**

13. Export the Journal report to **Excel** or **print** the report

14. Notice that the first journal entry records the expense with a debit and records an account payable of $42.00 with a credit. The second journal entry records paying the bill with a debit (decreases) Accounts Payable and a credit (decreases) the Checking account for $42.00.

15. **Close** the Journal window

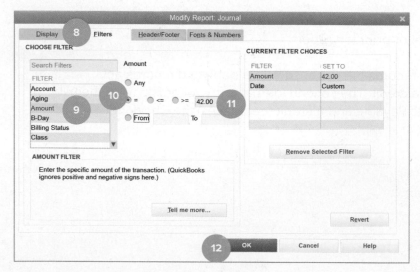

Section 3.9

Employees and Payroll Transactions

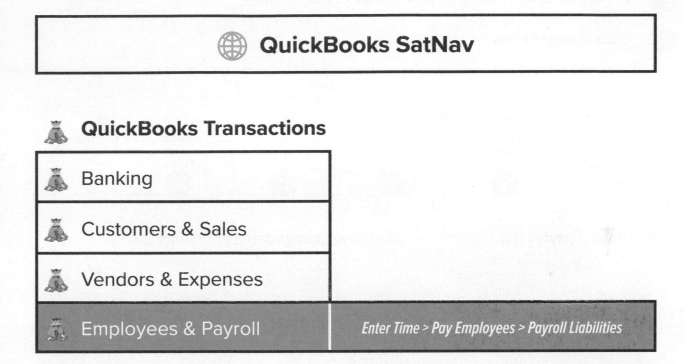

Employee transactions are exchanges between our company and the employees of our company. Typically, these exchanges focus on payroll transactions, including tracking employee time and paying employees for their services to the company.

We can enter employees and payroll transactions using either the Employees section of the Home Page or the Employees Menu.

Employee and payroll activities can include:

1   Enter time that employees have worked

2   Pay employees wages and salaries

3   Pay payroll liabilities owed for withholdings and payroll taxes

4   Process payroll forms

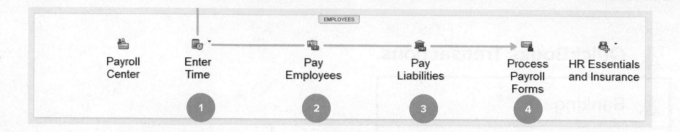

Employee and payroll transactions are covered in greater depth in Chapter 8.

Section 3.10

Other Transactions

If a transaction does not fall into one of the above categories, then it can be classified as other. Other transactions might include adjusting entries that are required to bring our accounts up to date at year end before preparing financial reports. We make adjusting entries using the onscreen Journal accessed as follows.

To access the Journal:

1 Select **Accountant Menu**

2 Select **Make General Journal Entries**

3 Select **Adjusting Entry** to identify the journal entry as an adjustment to accounts. If the journal entry was not an adjusting entry, then you would use the same screen except uncheck Adjusting Entry.

4 Enter the accounts and amounts for the debits and credits in the adjusting entry

5 **Close** the Make General Journal Entries window without saving

Section 3.11

Memorized Transactions

To save time entering transactions, QuickBooks offers a feature that permits us to save a transaction that will be recurring. One way we reduce errors and save time when entering transactions is to save frequently used transactions as memorized transactions.

To access the Memorized Transactions list, complete the following steps.

1   Select **Lists Menu**

2   Select **Memorized Transaction List**

3   To enter a new memorized transaction, select **Enter Transaction**

4   To use a memorized transaction to enter a new transaction, select a memorized transaction in the Memorized Transaction List. For example, to enter the monthly Sergeant Insurance bill, you would select Sergeant Insurance from the Memorized Transaction List. This saves time because you do not have to reenter the entire transaction each month.

5   **Close** the Memorized Transaction List window

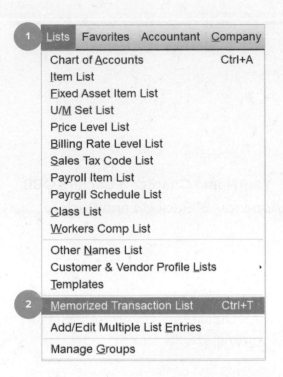

Section 3.12

Back Up QuickBooks Files

BACK UP QBB

Save a backup of your Chapter 3 file using the file name: **YourName Chapter 3 Backup.QBB**. For further instructions on how to back up your file, *see* Appendix B: Back Up and Restore QuickBooks Files.

QBW WORKFLOW

If you will be using the same computer to complete Chapter 3 QuickBooks exercises, just as in a business workflow, you can continue to use the same QBW file.

If you are using the QBW approach, leave your QBW file open and proceed directly to Exercise 3.1.

QBB RESTORE

If you will be switching computers before completing the exercises, after you finish your QuickBooks work session, you will back up to a QBB file in order to move your QuickBooks file to another computer. When you restart your work session on another computer, you will restore the backup (QBB) file.

If you are using the QBB approach and are ending your computer session now, close your QBW file and exit QuickBooks. When you restart, you will restore your backup file to complete Exercise 3.1.

Section 3.13

Accounting Essentials: Double-Entry Accounting

Accounting Essentials summarize important foundational accounting knowledge that may be useful when using QuickBooks

What is double-entry accounting?

- Double-entry accounting is used with a journal to record what is exchanged in a transaction:

  1. The amount received, such as equipment purchased, is recorded with a debit.
  2. The amount given, such as cash or a promise to pay later, is recorded with a credit.

- Each journal entry must balance; debits must equal credits. This is true whether it is a manual accounting system or a computerized accounting system, such as QuickBooks.

In double-entry accounting, how do we know if a debit is an increase or a decrease to an account? How do we know if a credit is an increase or a decrease to an account?

- Whether a debit or credit increases or decreases an account depends upon the type of account.

Account Type	Debit	Credit
Assets	Increase	Decrease
Liabilities	Decrease	Increase
Equity	Decrease	Increase
Revenues (Income)	Decrease	Increase
Expenses	Increase	Decrease

What are the different types of accounts and the effect of debits and credits on the accounts?

- Five different types of accounts are listed below along with the normal balance of the account and whether debit or credit increases the account balance.

Account Type	Debit/Credit	Effect on Balance
Assets	Debit	Increase
Liabilities	Credit	Increase
Equity	Credit	Increase
Revenues (Income)	Credit	Increase
Expenses	Debit	Increase

- For example, if an owner invests $100,000 in a business that is a corporation, the journal entry with debits and credits would be as follows.

Account	Account Type	Debit/Credit	Effect on Balance	Amount
Checking	Asset	Debit	Increase	$100,000
Capital Stock	Equity	Credit	Increase	$100,000

> 💡 **Troubleshooting QuickBooks and Correcting Errors are crucial QuickBooks skill to acquire. Troubleshooting resources include:**
> - **www.My-QuickBooks.com > QuickBooks Troubleshooting (QT) Tips**
> - **Chapter 17, Quick Review Guide, contains tips on Correcting Errors**
> - **Appendix D, QuickBooks Troubleshooting (QT), provides you with an effective troubleshooting process**

Exercise 3.1 Banking Transactions

 Rock Castle Construction

BACKSTORY

As you glance up from your work, you notice Mr. Castle tossing papers into your inbox as he charges past your cubicle. *"Here is another deposit to record."*

E3.1.1 QuickBooks File

If you will be using the same computer and the same Chapter 3.QBW file:

1. If your Chapter 3.QBW file is not already open, open it by selecting **File** > **Open Previous Company**. Select your **Chapter 3.QBW file**. If a QuickBooks Information window appears with a message about the sample company file, click **OK**.

2. Update the company name to **YourName Exercise 3.1 Rock Castle Construction** by selecting **Company Menu** > **My Company**.

> If you are not using the same computer that you used for Chapter 3, you will need to restore your Chapter 3 Backup.QBB file using the instructions in Appendix B: Back Up and Restore QuickBooks Files. After restoring, update the company name to YourName Exercise 3.1 Rock Castle Construction.

E3.1.2 Make Deposits

Rock Castle invests $3,000 in Rock Castle Construction.

1. Record the deposit for Mr. Castle's $3,000 check (No. 556).
   - Use a deposit date of **12/16/2024**
   - In Received From field, select **<Add New>** to add Rock Castle. Select Name Type: **Other**.
   - Record the deposit using From Account: **30100 Capital Stock**
   - Use Memo: **Investment**

2. Select the **Save** icon at the top of the Make Deposit window

3. Select the **Journal** icon to display the journal entry to QuickBooks created behind the screen for the deposit

4. Export to **Excel** or **print** the Transaction Journal

5. **Close** the Transaction Journal and the Make Deposits windows

E3.1.3 Write Checks

Write a check to pay the following bill.

1.   Use the Write Checks window to record the following check.

Date	**12/16/2024**
Vendor	**Express Delivery Service**
Expense Account	**54520 Freight & Delivery**
Amount	**$58.00**
Check No.	**Select: Print Later**

2.   Select the **Save** icon

3.   Select the **Reports** tab

4.   Select the **Transaction Journal** icon

5.   Export the Transaction Journal report to **Excel** or **print** the report

6.   **Close** the Transaction Journal and the Write Checks windows

E3.1.4 Back Up Exercise 3.1

Save a backup of your Exercise file using the file name: **YourName Exercise 3.1 Backup.QBB**.
See Appendix B: Back Up and Restore QuickBooks Files for instructions.

Exercise 3.2 Customers and Sales Transactions

 Rock Castle Construction

E3.2.1 QuickBooks File

If you will be using the same computer and the same QBW file:

1.   Select your **QBW file**.

2.   Update the company name to **YourName Exercise 3.2 Rock Castle Construction** by selecting **Company Menu > My Company**.

> **If you are not using the same computer that you used for Chapter 3 and Exercise 3.1, you will need to restore your latest prior Backup.QBB file using the instructions in Appendix B: Back Up and Restore QuickBooks files. After restoring, update the company name to YourName Exercise 3.2 Rock Castle Construction.**

E3.2.2 Sales Receipts

1. Enter the following sales receipts for Rock Castle Construction.

Date	**12/16/2024**
Customer	**Baker, Chris: Garage Repair**
Item	**Lumber: Trim**
Quantity	**5**
Rate	**$20.00 each**
Payment	**Cash**
Tax	**Taxable Sales**

2. Select the **Save** icon
3. Select the **Reports** tab
4. Select the **Transaction Journal** icon
5. Export the Transaction Journal report to **Excel** or **print** the report
6. **Close** the Transaction Journal and the Enter Sales Receipts windows

E3.2.3 Make Deposit

1. Record the deposit to transfer funds from the Undeposited Funds account to the Checking account for the following sales receipt.

Date	**12/16/2024**
Customer	**Baker, Chris: Garage Repair**
Amount	**$107.75**

2. Select the **Save** icon at the top of the Make Deposits window
3. Select the **Journal** icon to display the journal entry to QuickBooks created behind the screen for the deposit
4. Export to **Excel** or **print** the Transaction Journal
5. **Close** the Transaction Journal and the Make Deposits windows

E3.2.4 Back Up Exercise 3.2

Save a backup of your Exercise file using the file name: **YourName Exercise 3.2 Backup.QBB**. See Appendix B: Back Up and Restore QuickBooks Files for instructions.

Exercise 3.3 Vendors and Expenses Transactions

 Rock Castle Construction

BACKSTORY

When you arrive at work, you decide to sort through the papers stacked in the corner of your cubicle. You discover an unpaid utility bill amid the clutter.

E3.3.1 QuickBooks File

If you will be using the same computer and the same QBW file:

1. Select your **QBW file**.

2. Update the company name to **YourName Exercise 3.3 Rock Castle Construction** by selecting **Company Menu > My Company**.

> If you are not using the same computer that you used for Chapter 3, Exercise 3.1 and Exercise 3.2, you will need to restore your latest prior Backup.QBB file using the instructions in Appendix B: Back Up and Restore QuickBooks files. After restoring, update the company name to YourName Exercise 3.3 Rock Castle Construction.

E3.3.2 Enter Bills

Use the Enter Bills icon in the Vendors section of the Home Page to enter the following bills.

1. Enter the following utility bill for Rock Castle Construction.

Vendor	**Cal Gas & Electric**
Date	**12/16/2024**
Amount Due	**$91.00**
Account	**65110: Gas and Electric**

2. Select the **Save** icon at the top of the Enter Bills window

3. Select the **Reports** tab

4.   Select the **Transaction Journal** icon

5.   Export the Transaction Journal report to **Excel** or **print** the report

6.   **Close** the Transaction Journal and the Enter Bills windows

E3.3.3 Pay Bills

1.   On **12/17/2024**, pay by check the Cal Gas & Electric utility bill that you entered. (Hint: select Show all bills.)

2.   From the Navigation Bar, select **Reports** > **Accountant & Taxes** > **Journal**

3.   Select Dates: **12/16/2024 To 12/17/2024**

4.   Customize the report to add a filter for amount equal to **$91.00**

5.   Export the Journal report to **Excel** or **print** the report

6.   **Close** the Journal window

E3.3.4 Back Up Exercise 3.3

Save a backup of your Exercise file using the file name: **YourName Exercise 3.3 Backup.QBB**. See Appendix B: Back Up and Restore QuickBooks Files for instructions.

Project 3.1

Larry's Landscaping 🌴

As an accounting consultant for Larry's Landscaping, complete the following to enter transactions for the company.

💡 **Troubleshooting QuickBooks and Correcting Errors are crucial QuickBooks skill to acquire. Troubleshooting resources include:**
- **www.My-QuickBooks.com > QuickBooks Troubleshooting (QT) Tips**
- **Chapter 17, Quick Review Guide, contains tips on Correcting Errors**
- **Appendix D, QuickBooks Troubleshooting (QT), provides you with an effective troubleshooting process**

🌐 QuickBooks SatNav

The objective of Project 3.1 is to facilitate your mastery of QuickBooks Desktop. As shown in the following QuickBooks SatNav, Project 3.1 focuses on QuickBooks Transactions.

🌐 QuickBooks SatNav

⚙️ QuickBooks Settings

⚙️ Company Settings

⚙️ Chart of Accounts

💰 QuickBooks Transactions

💰 Banking	*Record Deposits	Write Checks*
💰 Customers & Sales	*Create Sales Receipts > Record Deposits*
💰 Vendors & Expenses	*Enter Bills > Pay Bills*
💰 Employees & Payroll	

📊 QuickBooks Reports

📊 Reports

P3.1.1 QuickBooks File

1. Use either your QuickBooks Company file (QBW) or restore the backup file (QBB) that you completed for Project 2.1. (If you have issues with your QuickBooks file, contact your instructor.)

2. Update the Company Name to: **YourName Project 3.1 Larry's Landscaping**

P3.1.2 Banking Transaction: Make Deposits

Enter the following banking transaction for Larry's Landscaping.

1. Record the following deposit.

Date	**12/16/2024**
Received From	**Larry Wadford**
Account	**3020 Owner's Contributions**
Memo	**Owner Investment**
Amount	**$3,600**
Cash/ Check No.	**Check No. 1558**

2. Select the **Save** icon at the top of the Make Deposit window

3. Select the **Journal** icon to display the journal entry to QuickBooks created behind the screen for the deposit

4. Export to **Excel** or **print** the Transaction Journal

5. **Close** the Transaction Journal and the Make Deposits windows

P3.1.3 Banking Transaction: Write Checks

Enter the following banking transaction for Larry's Landscaping.

1. Use the Write Checks window to record the following check.

Date	**12/16/2024**
Vendor	**Computer Services by DJ**
Account	**7552 Computer Repairs**
Memo	**Computer Repair**
Amount	**$720.00**
Check No.	**1464**

2. Select the **Save** icon

3. Select the **Reports** tab

4. Select the **Transaction Journal** icon

5. Export the Transaction Journal report to **Excel** or **print** the report

6. **Close** the Transaction Journal and the Write Checks windows

P3.1.4 Customers and Sales Transaction: Sales Receipts

Enter the following customers and sales transaction for Larry's Landscaping.

1. Enter the following sales receipts for Larry's Landscaping.

Template	**Sales Receipt - Retail**
Date	**12/19/2024**
Customer <Add New>	**Jean Paulny**
Item	**Pump (Fountain Pump)**
Quantity	**6**
Payment	**Cash**

2. Select the **Save** icon

3. Select the **Reports** tab

4. Select the **Transaction Journal** icon

5. Export the Transaction Journal report to **Excel** or **print** the report

6. **Close** the Transaction Journal and the Enter Sales Receipts windows

P3.1.5 Customers and Sales Transaction: Make Deposit

Enter the following customers and sales transaction for Larry's Landscaping.

1. Record the following deposits transferring funds from Undeposited Funds to the Checking account

Date	**12/21/2024**
Customer	**Jean Paulny**
Amount	**$479.25**

2. Select the **Save** icon at the top of the Make Deposit window

3. Select the **Journal** icon to display the journal entry to QuickBooks created behind the screen for the deposit

4. Export to **Excel** or **print** the Transaction Journal

5. **Close** the Transaction Journal and the Make Deposits windows

P3.1.6 Vendors and Expenses Transaction: Enter Bill

Enter the following vendors and expense transaction for Larry's Landscaping.

1. Use the Enter Bills icon to enter the following bill received by Larry's.

Date	**12/23/2024**
Vendor <Add New>	**Carole Design Media**
Account	**6000 Advertising Expense**
Terms	**Net 30**
Amount Due	**$648.00**

2. Select the **Save** icon at the top of the Enter Bills window

3. Select the **Reports** tab

4. Select the **Transaction Journal** icon

5. Export the Transaction Journal report to **Excel** or **print** the report

6. **Close** the Transaction Journal and the Enter Bills windows

P3.1.7 Vendors and Expenses Transaction: Pay Bill

Enter the following vendors and expense transactions for Larry's Landscaping.

1. Pay the following bills for Larry's on 12/23/2024.

Date	**12/23/2024**
Vendor	**Carole Design Media**
Account	**$648**

2. From the Navigation Bar, select **Reports > Accountant & Taxes > Journal**

3. Select Dates: **12/23/2024 To 12/23/2024**

4. Customize the report to add a filter for amount equal to **$648.00**

5. Export the Journal report to **Excel** or **print** the report

6. **Close** the Journal window

P3.1.8 Back Up Project 3.1

Save a backup of your Project file using the file name: **YourName Project 3.1 Backup.QBB**. See Appendix B: Back Up and Restore QuickBooks Files for instructions.

Design elements: Dog icon: ©josep perianes jorba/Shutterstock; paint roller icon: ©Netti Buletti/Shutterstock; other icons/symbols: ©Carboxylase/Shutterstock

Chapter 4

Banking

 Rock Castle Construction

BACKSTORY

The next morning as you pass the open door of Mr. Castle's office, you notice he's looking at the financial statements you prepared. You try to slip past his door unnoticed, but you take only a few steps when you hear him curtly call your name.

You turn to see Mr. Castle charging toward you with documents in hand.

"I need you to keep an eye on the bank accounts. Cash is the lifeblood of a business. A business can't survive if it doesn't have enough cash flowing through its veins to pay its bills. So it's very important that someone keep an eye on the cash in our bank accounts—the cash inflows into the accounts and the cash outflows from the accounts. That is your job now."

Handing you more documents, Mr. Castle continues, *"We fell behind on our bank reconciliations. Here is last month's bank statement that needs to be reconciled by the end of the workday."*

After you master QuickBooks bank reconciliations, you send Mr. Castle the following quick text.

Today, 12:57 PM

> Bank reconciliation up to date by EOD

Delivered

Chapter 4

Learning Objectives

Chapter 4 covers QuickBooks Banking. In this chapter, you will learn about the following banking topics:

- Banking Navigation
- Check Register
- Make Deposits
- One-Step and Two-Step Approach to Bill Paying
- Write Checks
- Create Journal Report
- Reconcile Bank Statement
- Online Banking and Bank Feeds
- Enter Credit Card Charges
- Accounting Essentials: Debits and Credits

Section 4.1

 ## QuickBooks SatNav

QuickBooks SatNav is your satellite navigation for QuickBooks, assisting you in navigating QuickBooks

QuickBooks SatNav divides QuickBooks into three processes:

1. **QuickBooks Settings.** This includes Company Settings when setting up a new QuickBooks company and the Company Chart of Accounts.

2. **QuickBooks Transactions.** This includes recording transactions in QuickBooks. Transaction types can be categorized as Banking, Customers and Sales, Vendors and Expenses, and Employees and Payroll. In basic terms, recording transactions involves recording money in and money out.

3. **QuickBooks Reports.** QuickBooks reports are the output of the system, such as commonly used financial statements of Balance Sheet, Income Statement, and Statement of Cash Flows.

Chapter 4 focuses on banking transactions as shown in the following QuickBooks SatNav.

QuickBooks SatNav

⚙ QuickBooks Settings

⚙ Company Settings
⚙ Chart of Accounts

💰 QuickBooks Transactions

💰 Banking	*Record Deposits | Write Checks*
💰 Customers & Sales	
💰 Vendors & Expenses	
💰 Employees & Payroll	

📊 QuickBooks Reports

📊 Reports

💡 **Accounting Essentials appear at the end of the chapter. Tip: Preview Accounting Essentials <u>before</u>** completing the chapter and then review Accounting Essentials <u>after</u> completing the chapter.

Section 4.2

Start QuickBooks and Open QuickBooks Company

START QUICKBOOKS

To start QuickBooks software, click the **QuickBooks** icon on your desktop. If a QuickBooks icon does not appear on your desktop, from Microsoft® Windows® click **Start** button > **QuickBooks** > **QuickBooks Premier Accountant Edition**.

> **QuickBooks Accountant** includes all the features of QuickBooks Pro plus features for client services. If you use QuickBooks Pro, your screens may appear slightly different than those appearing in this text.

RESTORE QBB STARTER FILE

Restore the QBB Starter file for this chapter as follows.

1. Select **File** > **Restore**

2. Using the directions in Appendix B: Back Up and Restore QuickBooks Files, restore **CHAPTER 4 STARTER.QBB**

3. After restoring, update the company name to **YourName Chapter 4 Rock Castle Construction** by selecting **Company Menu** > **My Company**

> ⚠ **Desktop (QBDT)** Data Files are compressed backup files that can be restored and used. To use Starter Files, the compressed file must be restored following the instructions here. Since it is a compressed file, you cannot open and use the QuickBooks data files by simply clicking on the file. Instead you must follow the instructions here to unzip and restore the data file before using it.

Section 4.3

Banking Navigation

The QuickBooks Home Page contains a Banking section that displays icons used for Banking functions. If necessary click the **Home** icon in the Navigation Bar to display the Home Page.

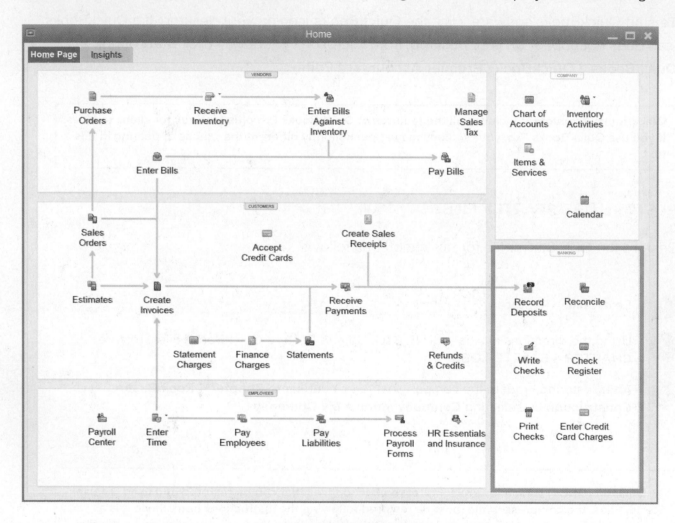

From the Banking section of the Home Page, we can:

- Record deposits (cash flowing into the Checking account)
- Write checks (cash going out of the Checking account)
- Print checks

- Reconcile bank statements
- View Check Register
- Enter credit card charges

A business should establish a *business checking account* completely separate from the owner's *personal checking account.* The company's business checking account should be used only for business transactions, such as business insurance and mortgage payments for the company's office building. An owner should maintain a completely separate checking account for personal transactions, such as mortgage payments for the owner's home.

Section 4.4

Check Register

The Check Register is a record of all transactions affecting the Checking account. The QuickBooks onscreen Check Register looks similar to a checkbook register used to manually record deposits and checks.

VIEW CHECK REGISTER

To view the QuickBooks Check Register:

1 Click the **Check Register** icon in the Banking section of the Home Page

2 When the Use Register window appears asking us to specify a bank account, select **10100 Checking**

3 Click **OK**

4 When the Check Register window appears on the screen, notice that there is a separate column for **Payments (checks)**

5 Notice the column for **Deposits**

6 Notice the **Balance** column that automatically updates to show the Check Register balance

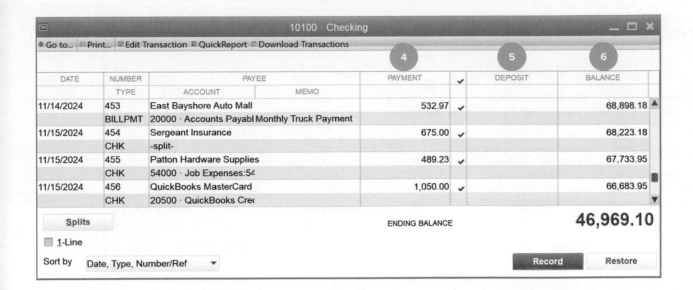

Small enterprises that have strictly cash-based operations sometimes simply use the Check Register to record all transactions. Such enterprises record payments and deposits directly into the Check Register using the Record button. However, most business enterprises require the more advanced features of the QuickBooks accounting software that are covered in the following chapters.

CHECK REGISTER DRILL DOWN

QuickBooks offers a drill-down feature from its registers. QuickBooks drill-down feature permits us to double-click and view the supporting documents. For example, from the Check Register, we can double-click on a transaction to drill down to the source document for that transaction.

To drill down and view the check for the Sergeant Insurance transaction:

1 Double-click the **Sergeant Insurance** entry on **11/15/2024** in the Check Register

2 Notice that the check is stamped **Cleared**, indicating it has already cleared the bank with funds paid to Sergeant Insurance

3 **Close** the Write Checks window by clicking on the **X** in the upper right corner of the window

ADD NEW TRANSACTIONS TO THE CHECK REGISTER

We can record deposits and checks directly in the Check Register. Simply scroll down to the first blank line and enter the transaction information. If the new transaction is a deposit, then we enter the amount in the Deposit column. If the new transaction is a Check, then we enter the amount in the Payment column. The Balance will update automatically.

Another way to enter transactions that will appear in the Check Register is to use the Make Deposits window and the Write Checks window.

Section 4.5

Make Deposits

Deposits are additions to the Checking account. Any cash coming into a business should be recorded as a deposit to one of the company's accounts.

QuickBooks classifies deposits into two types:

1. Payments from customers
2. Nonsales receipts (deposits other than customer payments) such as:
   - Cash received from loans
   - Investments from owners
   - Interest earned
   - Other income, such as rental income

Payments from customers are entered using the Customers section of the Home Page. For more information about recording payments from customers, see Chapter 5: Customers and Sales. Deposits other than customer payments are recorded using the Banking section of the Home Page.

QuickBooks uses a one-step or two-step process to record payments received. One-step process records the deposit directly in the Checking account. When we use the two-step process to record payments received:

1. Record the payment received but not yet deposited in an Undeposited Funds account
2. Record the deposit in the Checking account

The reason QuickBooks uses this two-step process is when our business has multiple deposits on the same day. We can record the payments received in the Undeposited Funds account when we receive the payments. Then when we make the bank deposit consisting of multiple payments, we record the transfer of the total deposit from the Undeposited Funds account to the Checking account.

Mr. Castle wants to invest an additional $72,000 in the business by depositing his $72,000 check in Rock Castle Construction's Checking account.

C4.5.1 Deposit Journal Entry. To record nonsales receipts (a deposit other than a customer payment):

1. From the Banking section of the Home Page, click the **Record Deposits** icon

2. When the Payments to Deposit window appears, notice the payments listed. These are undeposited funds that have been recorded as received but not yet deposited in the bank. Since these amounts will be deposited at a later time, confirm that none of the payments have been selected for deposit, then click **OK**.

3. When the Make Deposits window appears, record Mr. Castle's $72,000 deposit. Select Deposit To: **10100 Checking**.

4. Select Date: **12/15/2024**

5. Click in the Received From column and type: **Rock Castle**. Press the **Tab** key.

6. When prompted, select **Quick Add** to add the name to the Name List

7. Select Name Type: **Other**

8. Click **OK**

9. Click in the From Account column. From the drop-down list of accounts, select **30100 Capital Stock**. Press **Tab**.

10. Enter Memo: **Investment**

11. Enter Check No.: **555** (the number of Mr. Castle's check)

12. From the Payment Method drop-down list, select **Check**

13. Enter Amount: **72000**. (QuickBooks will automatically enter the comma in the amount.)

14. Select the **Save** icon to save the deposit. (To print a summary of the deposit just recorded, we would select the Print arrow at the top of the Make Deposits window. In this case, we will not print the Deposit Summary.)

15. Select the **Journal** icon to display the journal entry that QuickBooks created for the deposit. Notice that the journal entry to record the deposit of Mr. Castle's $72,000 check includes a debit (increase) to the Checking account and a credit (increase) to Account 30100 Capital Stock.

16 Export the Transaction Journal report to **Excel** or **print** the report

17 **Close** the Transaction Journal window and the Make Deposit window

Mr. Castle's $72,000 investment in the company has now been recorded as a deposit in Rock Castle Construction's Checking account.

Section 4.6

One-Step and Two-Step Approaches to Bill Paying

A business needs to track all cash paid out of the company's checking account. Examples of payments include purchases of inventory, office supplies, employee salaries, rent payments, and insurance payments.

Supporting documents (source documents) for payments include canceled checks, receipts, and paid invoices. These source documents provide proof that the transaction occurred; therefore, source documents should be kept on file for tax purposes.

QuickBooks provides two ways to pay bills.

1. One-step approach to bill paying:

1   Record and pay the bill at the same time. When using this approach, the bill is paid when it is received.

2. Two-step approach to bill paying:

1   Record the bill when it is received

2   Pay the bill later when it is due

ONE-STEP APPROACH TO BILL PAYING

1   **Pay Bills When Received:** Record bill and print check to pay bill.

Use the Write Checks window for the one-step approach to bill paying. QuickBooks:

- Records an expense (debit)
- Reduces the Checking account (credit)

The one-step approach to bill paying is covered in this chapter.

TWO-STEP APPROACH TO BILL PAYING

1 **Enter Bills:** Record bills for services, such as utilities

2 **Pay Bills:** Select bills to pay, then print checks

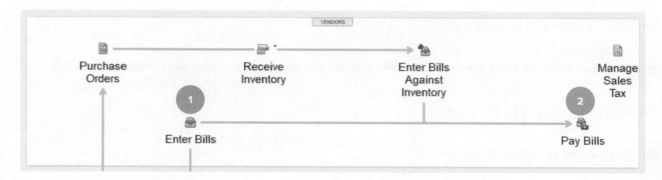

With the two-step approach to bill paying, when bills are entered QuickBooks:

- Records an expense (debit)
- Records an obligation (liability) to pay later (credit)

When the bill is paid and the obligation fulfilled, QuickBooks:

- Reduces the liability (debit)
- Reduces the Checking account (credit)

The two-step approach to bill paying is covered in Chapter 6, Vendors and Expenses.

QuickBooks Desktop has a Check for Bills feature. The purpose of this relatively new feature is to assist us in consistent use of the Write Check (1-step) approach versus the Enter Bills > Pay Bills (2-step) approach.

If we enter a vendor name in the Pay to the Order of field on the Write Check window for a vendor that has an unpaid vendor bill already entered using the Enter Bills window, then the following Check for Bills window will display, listing any unpaid bills already entered for the vendor. If we wish to pay the unpaid bill already entered, then we would select Go to Pay Bills to complete the vendor bill payment instead of using the Write Checks window.

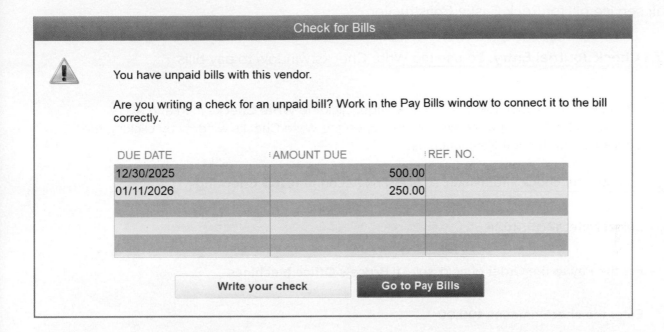

WHEN TO USE THE ONE-STEP APPROACH

The Write Checks window (One-Step Approach) should not be used to pay:

1. Bills already entered in the Enter Bills window. From the Vendors section, use the Pay Bills window
2. Paychecks to employees for wages and salaries. From the Employees section of the Home Page, use the Pay Employees window
3. Payroll taxes and liabilities. From the Employees section, use the Pay Liabilities window
4. Sales taxes. From the Vendors section, use the Manage Sales Tax icon and the Pay Sales Tax window

The Write Checks window (One-Step Approach) can be used to pay:

1. Expenses, such as rent, utilities, and insurance
2. Non-inventory items, such as office supplies
3. Services, such as accounting or legal services

Section 4.7
Write Checks

In this chapter, you will use the Write Checks window (One-Step Approach) to pay a computer repair service bill for Rock Castle Construction.

C4.7.1 Check Journal Entry. To use the Write Checks window to pay bills:

1 From the Banking section of the Home Page, click the **Write Checks** icon and an onscreen check will appear. We can also open the Write Checks window by clicking the Check icon on the left Navigation Bar.

2 To enter the check information, select Bank Account: **10100 Checking**

3 Select Date: **12/15/2024**

4 For the Pay to the Order of field, select: **Bruce's Office Machines**

5 Enter the check amount: **100.00**

6 Click the checkbox preceding **Print Later** so that a check mark appears. This tells QuickBooks to record and print the check later. The Check No. field will now display: To Print. Notice there is also an option to Pay Online.

7 Next, to record the payment in the correct account using the lower portion of the Write Checks window, select the **Expenses** tab

8 If not already selected, select Account: **64230 Equipment Repairs**. Account 64200 Repairs: 64230 Equipment Repairs should appear in the Account column and $100 should automatically appear in the expense Amount column.

FYI: If the payment was related to a specific customer or job, you could enter that information in the Customer: Job column and select Billable.

9 If we wanted to print the check, we would select the Print button located at the top of the Write Checks window. In this case, we will not be printing the check.

10 Select **Save**. QuickBooks automatically records the check in the Check Register. Leave the Write Checks window open on your screen.

11 From the Write Checks onscreen form, select the **Reports** tab

12 Select the **Transaction Journal** icon. The journal entry is displayed to record the check written to Bruce's Office Machines for equipment repair services. This entry debits (increases) the balance of the expense account, Equipment Repairs, and credits (decreases) the Checking account balance. If we double-click on the journal entry, we can drill down to the related source document. **Double-click** on the journal entry for the equipment repair. The Write Checks window should appear, displaying the onscreen check that we just prepared. **Close** the Write Checks window.

13 Export the Transaction Journal report to **Excel** or **print** the report

14 **Close** the Transaction Journal window and the Write Checks window

Section 4.8

Create Journal Report

As we have seen, when we enter information into an onscreen form, QuickBooks automatically converts that information into a journal entry with debits and credits. If we wanted to view all journal entries for specific dates or date ranges, we could create a journal report from the Report Center.

C4.8.1 Journal Report. To view and print the journal entries for specific dates:

1. Click **Reports** in the Navigation bar to open the Report Center

2. Select **Accountant & Taxes**

3. Select **Journal**

4. Select Dates: From **12/15/2024** To **12/15/2024**

5. Select **Run**

6. When the Journal window appears, scroll down to find the journal entry to record the $72,000 deposit. Notice that the journal entry to record the deposit of Mr. Castle's $72,000 check includes a debit to the Checking account and a credit to Account 30100 Capital Stock.

7. **Double-click** on the journal entry for the $72,000 deposit to drill down to the related source document, the Make Deposits onscreen form

8. **Close** the Make Deposits form

9. Export to **Excel** or **print** the Journal report

10. **Close** the Journal window

⑦

Make Deposits

◆ Previous ◆ Next 🗒 Save 🖶 Print ▼ 🗐 Payments 🗐 History 🗐 Journal 🖇 Attach

⑧ ✕

Deposit To | 10100 · Checking ▼ | Date 12/15/2024 📅 Memo | Deposit

Click Payments to select customer payments that you have received. List any other amounts to deposit below.

RECEIVED FROM	FROM ACCOUNT	MEMO	CHK NO.	PMT METH.	CLASS	AMOUNT
Rock Castle ▼	30100 · Capital Stock ▼	Investment	555	Check ▼	▼	72,000.00 ▲
						▼

Deposit Subtotal 72,000.00

To get cash back from this deposit, enter the amount below. Indicate the account where you want this money to go, such as your Petty Cash account.

Cash back goes to | Cash back memo | Cash back amount

▼

Deposit Total 72,000.00

| Save & Close | | Save & New | | Revert |

Section 4.9

Reconcile Bank Statements

Typically once a month, the bank sends a Checking account bank statement to you. The bank statement lists each deposit, check, and withdrawal from the account during the month.

A bank reconciliation is the process of comparing, or reconciling, the bank statement with your accounting records for the Checking account. The bank reconciliation has two objectives: (1) to detect errors and (2) to update your accounting records for unrecorded items listed on the bank statement (such as service charges).

Differences between the balance the bank reports on the bank statement and the balance the company shows in its accounting records usually arise for two reasons:

1. **Errors** (either the bank's errors or the company's errors).
2. **Timing differences.** This occurs when the company records an amount before the bank does or the bank records an amount before the company does. For example, the company may record a deposit in its accounting records, but the bank does not record the deposit before the company's bank statement is prepared and mailed.

Timing differences include:

Items the bank has not recorded yet, such as:

- **Deposits in transit:** deposits the company has recorded but the bank has not.
- **Outstanding checks:** checks the company has written and recorded but the bank has not recorded yet.

Items the company has not recorded yet, such as:

- **Unrecorded charges:** charges that the bank has recorded on the bank statement but the company has not recorded in its accounting records yet. Unrecorded charges include service charges, loan payments, automatic withdrawals, and ATM withdrawals.
- **Interest earned on the account:** interest the bank has recorded as earned but the company has not recorded yet.

The following bank statement lists the deposits and checks for Rock Castle Construction according to the bank's records as of November 20, 2024.

Bank Statement		
Rock Castle Construction 1735 County Road Bayshore, CA 94326		11-20-2024 Checking
Previous Balance	10-20-2024	$71,452.58
+ Deposits	0	0.00
- Checks	4	4,161.56
- Service Charge		10.00
+ Interest Paid		0.00
Ending Balance	11-20-2024	$67,281.02

DEPOSITS		
Date		**Amount**
		0.00

CHECKS PAID		
Date	**No.**	**Amount**
10-31-2024	**433**	**712.56**
10-31-2024	**436**	**24.00**
11-14-2024	**451**	**3,200.00**
11-19-2024	**460**	**225.00**

Thank you for banking with us!

C4.9.1 Bank Reconciliation. To reconcile this bank statement with Rock Castle's QuickBooks records, complete the following steps.

1. From the Banking section of the Home Page, click the **Reconcile** icon to display the following Begin Reconciliation window

2. Select Account to Reconcile: **Checking**

3. Enter date shown on the bank statement: **11/20/2024**

4. Compare the amount shown in the Beginning Balance field with the beginning (previous) balance of **$71,452.58** on the bank statement

5. In the Ending Balance field, enter the ending balance shown on the bank statement: **$67,281.02**

6. In the Service Charge field, enter the bank's service charge: **$10.00**

7. Change the date to **11/20/2024**

8. Select the Account: **Bank Service Charges**

9. Click **Continue**

10. To mark deposits that have been recorded by the bank as shown on the bank statement, simply **click** on the deposit in the Deposits and Other Credits section of the Reconcile window

11. To mark checks and payments that have cleared the bank as shown on the bank statement, simply **click** on the check in the Checks and Payments section of the Reconcile window. (If we use Online Banking, we would click the Matched button to reconcile online transactions and mark online transactions as cleared.)

12. After marking all deposits and checks that appear on the bank statement, **compare** the Ending Balance and the Cleared Balance at the bottom of the Reconcile window

13. If the Difference amount in the lower right corner of the Reconcile window equals **$0.00**, click **Reconcile Now**. If there is a difference between the Ending Balance and the Cleared Balance, then try to locate the error or use QuickBooks Locate Discrepancies feature from the Begin Reconciliation window. (If you are not finished and plan to return to this bank reconciliation later, click Leave.)

14. When the Select Reconciliation Report window appears, select type of Reconciliation Report: **Detail**

15 Click **Display**. If a Reconciliation Report windows appears stating that the report displays current data, select OK.

16 Export to **Excel or print** the Reconciliation Detail report

17 **Highlight** the items on the bank reconciliation report that are marked as cleared for the November bank reconciliation

18 **Close** the Reconciliation Detail report window

You have now completed the November bank reconciliation for Rock Castle Construction.

> **After you click Reconcile Now, you can view the Bank Reconciliation by selecting Reports Menu > Banking > Previous Reconciliation.**
>
> **If you need to make changes to the bank reconciliation:**
>
> 1. **To return to the reconciliation screen to make changes, from the Begin Reconciliation window, click Locate Discrepancies.**
>
> 2. **Another way to change the status of a cleared item: Display the Check Register, then click the Cleared Status column until the appropriate status (cleared or uncleared) appears.**

Section 4.10
Online Banking and Bank Feeds

QuickBooks offers an online banking feature so that you can conduct banking transactions online using the Internet. View online banking features through the Banking Menu.

QuickBooks Desktop permits you to connect to Bank and Credit Card accounts and then automatically download transactions from those connected accounts into QuickBooks. When the transactions are downloaded, we can review the accounts to:

- **Match** the downloaded bank transactions to transactions we have already entered in QuickBooks. For example, if we have already recorded a deposit and it is downloaded into QuickBooks from the bank account, then we Match the downloaded deposit to the transaction we already entered.
- **Add** the downloaded bank transactions. If we have not already entered the transaction into QuickBooks, we can add the downloaded transaction and it will be recorded in our QuickBooks accounts.

The steps for using online banking and bank feeds with QuickBooks are:

1. Set up account for a participating financial institution
2. Enter transactions in QuickBooks and flag online payments
3. Download transactions into the QuickBooks bank feeds center
4. Match or add downloaded transactions into QuickBooks

You can access QuickBooks online banking features from the Banking Menu as follows.

1 Select **Banking** from the Menu Bar

2 Select **Bank Feeds**

3 Select **Bank Feeds Center**

4 If a Bank feeds window appears with a message about Advanced Bank Feeds, select **Skip**

5   Verify that the Bank and Credit card field displays ANYTIME Financial. In the Bank Feeds window, select the **Checking Account ending in ***1235**. Notice that there are 7 transactions pending for review.

6   Select the **Unrecognized** tab to display downloaded transactions that QuickBooks does not automatically recognize as matches to transactions already entered in QuickBooks.
   - **Recognized transactions** are transactions that QuickBooks recognizes and suggests matches to transactions already entered
   - **Partially-recognized transactions** are those that QuickBooks may not find complete matches for but may recognize some of the transaction and make suggestions for you
   - **Unrecognized transactions** are transactions that we need to review because QuickBooks is not finding complete or partial matching transactions.
   - **Added to register transactions** are downloaded transactions that you have added or matched.

7   Downloaded transactions must have accounts assigned to the transaction in order to be entered in to your QuickBooks company records. To assign an account to the deposit of $5,000, select the **Account down-arrow**.

8   Select the account: **11000 Accounts Receivable**

9   In the Payee column, select the **Payee down arrow** for the $5,000 deposit.

10   Select Payee: **Anton Teschner: Sun Room**

11   To add the downloaded transaction to your QuickBooks company, in the Action column, select **Add**. This will add the transaction to your QuickBooks accounts.

12   The number of Unrecognized transactions decreases to **6**

13   Select the **Added to register** tab. Now there is **1** transaction added to the register, the Anton Teschner $5,000 deposit that you just added. Leave the Bank Feeds window open.

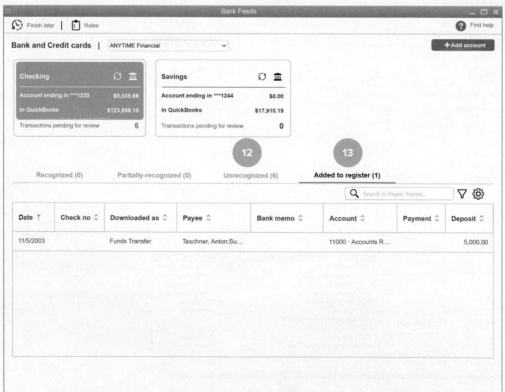

New in QuickBooks Desktop 2021 is an improved bank feeds feature with advanced mode. Advanced mode for bank feeds provides the opportunity for enhanced rules to automatically categorize bank transactions. If your business processes only a few bank transactions a month, manual matching may not be time consuming. However, if your business has a high volume of transactions per month, setting up the advanced mode for automatically categorizing bank feed transactions can save time.

To set the preference for the bank feeds advanced mode:

1 Select **Edit** from the Menu Bar

2 Select **Preferences**

3 Select **Checking**

4 Select **Company Preferences**

5 Select: **Select Advanced Mode**

6 Select **OK** to close the Preferences window

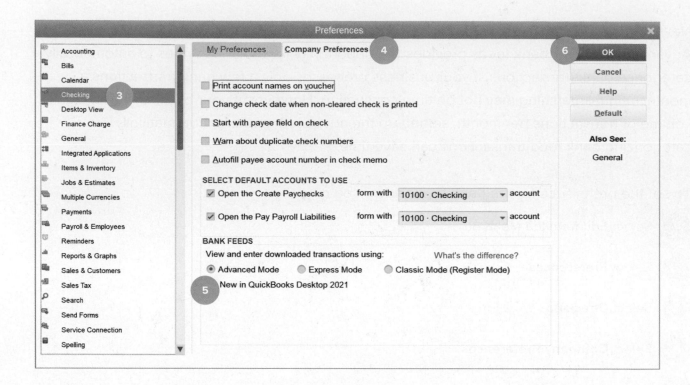

Next, we will create a bank service charges rule that will permit QuickBooks to automatically recognize downloaded bank service charge transactions and identify the correct account to record the transactions in QuickBooks.

To create a bank feed rule:

1. From the Bank Feeds window, select **Rules**

2. From the Rules List window, select **Add rule**

3. Enter Rule name: **Bank Service Charges**

4. Select For: **Money out**

5. Select: When a transaction meets **Any** of these conditions

6. Select **Memo**

7. Select **Begins with**

8. Enter: **Bank Se**

9. Select Categorize in account: **60600 Bank Service Charges**

10 Select **Save**

11 **Close** the Rules List window

12 From the Bank Feeds window, select the **Recognized** tab.

13 Since we created a bank service charges rule, QuickBooks automatically applies the rule and recognizes the downloaded bank service charges. (Notice that the unrecognized transactions tab decreased from 6 to 5.)

14 Note that even though the transaction downloaded with a typo in the bank memo field (Bank Severvice Charge instead of Bank Service Charge), because our rule designated a memo that starts with" Bank Se", the rule was applied.)

15 When applying the created rule, QuickBooks automatically classifies the downloaded transaction in account **60600**.

16 Select **Add** to add the transaction to your QuickBooks accounts

17 Notice the Added to register tab increased to reflect that **2** transactions have been added

18 **Close** the Bank Feeds window

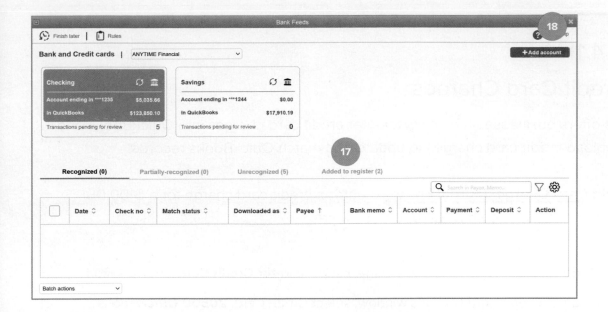

Section 4.11

Enter Credit Card Charges

QuickBooks offers businesses the ability to enter credit card charges into QuickBooks and then to download credit card charges to update and match QuickBooks records.

C4.11.1 Credit Card Charge Journal Entry. To enter a credit card charge for a $100.00 trackpad purchased from Kershaw Computer Services:

1. From the Banking section of the Home Page, click the **Enter Credit Card Charges** icon

2. From the Enter Credit Card Charges window, select Credit Card: **20500 QuickBooks Credit Card**

3. Select **Purchase/Charge**

4. Select Purchased From: **Kershaw Computer Services**

5. Enter Date: **12/15/2024**

6. Enter Amount: **100.00**

7. Enter Memo: **Trackpad**

8. Select the **Expenses** tab

9. In the Account field, enter account number: **63000 - Office Supplies**

10. The Amount field should automatically display the amount of 100.00 dollars

11. Click the **Save** icon

12. Select the **Reports** tab

13. Select the **Transaction Journal** icon. Notice that this entry debits (increases) the balance of the expense account, Office Supplies, and credits (increases) the liability account, QuickBooks Credit Card account.

14. Export the Transaction Journal report to **Excel** or **print** the report

15. **Close** the Transaction Journal window and the Enter Credit Card Charges window

Section 4.12

Back up QuickBooks Files

BACK UP QBB

Save a backup of your Chapter 4 file using the file name: **YourName Chapter 4 Backup.QBB**. For further instructions on how to back up your file, *see* Appendix B: Back Up and Restore QuickBooks Files.

QBW WORKFLOW

If you will be using the same computer to complete Chapter 4 QuickBooks exercises, just as in a business workflow, you can continue to use the same QBW file.

If you are using the QBW approach, leave your QBW file open and proceed directly to Exercise 4.1.

QBB RESTORE

If you are using the QBB approach and will be switching computers and ending your computer session now, close your QBW file and exit QuickBooks. If you are using the QBB approach, when you restart, you will restore your backup file to complete Exercise 4.1.

Section 4.13

Accounting Essentials: Debits and Credits

Accounting Essentials summarize important foundational accounting knowledge that may be useful when using QuickBooks

Why are debits and credits important to understanding QuickBooks?

- For every transaction entered in QuickBooks, there is a corresponding entry using debits and credits. Even if we use QuickBooks online forms, such as invoices and bills, debit and credit entries are the core of the accounting system. Behind the scenes, the information we enter in online forms is converted to debit and credit entries. Understanding these debit and credit entries becomes crucial to understanding the accounting system, tracking errors, and making corrections.

Why can debits and credits be so confusing?

- Sometimes when working with debits and credits, it may seem confusing because sometimes a debit is an increase to an account and sometimes a debit is a decrease. Sometimes a credit is an increase to an account and sometimes a credit is a decrease. So we cannot assume a debit is always an increase, for example.

How do we know whether a debit or credit is an increase or decrease to an account?

- Whether a debit or credit increases or decreases an account depends upon the type of account. So we must know the account type before we know if the debit or credit is an increase or a decrease.

- Five different types of accounts are listed below along with the normal balance of the account and whether debit or credit increases the account balance.

Account Type	Debit/Credit	Effect on Balance
Assets	Debit	Increase
Liabilities	Credit	Increase
Equity	Credit	Increase
Revenues (Income)	Credit	Increase
Expenses	Debit	Increase

- For example, the deposit we recorded in this chapter using the QuickBooks deposit form resulted in a journal entry with debits and credits that we could view in the Journal. Notice that in that entry, the debit to Rock Castle Construction Checking account increased the balance. The credit to the Capital Stock account for $72,000 increased the Capital Stock account balance.

Account	Account Type	Debit/Credit	Effect on Balance	Amount
Checking	Asset	Debit	Increase	$72,000
Capital Stock	Equity	Credit	Increase	$72,000

Rock Castle Construction

BACKSTORY

As you glance up from your work, you notice Mr. Castle charging past your cubicle with more documents in hand. He tosses a hefty stack of papers into your creaking inbox. *"Here is another deposit to record. Also, Washuta called to say they did not receive the check we sent them. You will need to void that check—I believe it was check no. 470. I have already called the bank and stopped payment. Also, here are more bills to pay."*

Exercise 4.1 Make Deposits

E4.1.1 QuickBooks File

If you will be using the same computer and the same Chapter 4.QBW file:

1. If your Chapter 4.QBW file is not already open, open it by selecting **File** > **Open Previous Company**. Select your **Chapter 4.QBW file**. If a QuickBooks Information window appears with a message about the sample company file, click **OK**.

2. Update the company name to **YourName Exercise 4.1 Rock Castle Construction** by selecting **Company Menu** > **My Company**.

> If you are not using the same computer that you used for Chapter 4, you will need to restore your Chapter 4 Backup.QBB file using the instructions in Appendix B: Back Up and Restore QuickBooks Files. After restoring, update the company name to YourName Exercise 4.1 Rock Castle Construction.

E4.1.2 Make Deposits

Rock Castle invests another $5,000 in Rock Castle Construction.

1. Record the deposit for Mr. Castle's $5,000 check (No. 557). Record the deposit in Account 30100 Capital Stock with a deposit date of 12/18/2024. Use Memo: Investment.

2. Select the **Save** icon at the top of the Make Deposit window

3. Select the **Journal** icon to display the journal entry to QuickBooks created behind the screen for the deposit

4. Export to **Excel** or **print** the Transaction Journal

5. **Close** the Transaction Journal and the Make Deposits windows

E4.1.3 Deposit Detail Report

The Deposit Detail report lists all deposited and undeposited funds, including the amount of each payment included in the deposit and the customer who made the payment. The Deposit Detail report can prove useful when tracking customer payments that have been bundled into a single bank deposit.

1. From the Navigation Bar select **Reports > Banking > Deposit Detail**

2. Select Dates: **12/15/2024** To **12/18/2024**

3. Select **Run**

4. Export to **Excel** or **print** the Deposit Detail report

5. **Highlight** in the Deposit Detail report the deposit just recorded

E4.1.4 Back Up Exercise 4.1

Save a backup of your Exercise file using the file name: **YourName Exercise 4.1 Backup.QBB**. See Appendix B: Back Up and Restore QuickBooks Files for instructions.

Exercise 4.2 Write Checks

 Rock Castle Construction

E4.2.1 QuickBooks File

If you will be using the same computer and the same QBW file:

1. Select your **QBW file**.

2. Update the company name to **YourName Exercise 4.2 Rock Castle Construction** by selecting **Company Menu > My Company**.

> **If you are not using the same computer that you used for Chapter 4 and Exercise 4.1, you will need to restore your latest prior Backup.QBB file using the instructions in Appendix B: Back Up and Restore QuickBooks files. After restoring, update the company name to YourName Exercise 4.2 Rock Castle Construction.**

E4.2.2 Write Checks

1. Use the Write Checks window to record the following check.

Date	**12/18/2024**
Vendor	**Davis Business Associates**
Expense Account	**64230 Equipment Repairs**
Amount	**$330.00**
Check No.	**Select: Print Later**

2. Select the **Save** icon

3. Select the **Reports** tab

4. Select the **Transaction Journal** icon

5. Export the Transaction Journal report to **Excel** or **print** the report

6. **Close** the Transaction Journal and the Write Checks windows

E4.2.3 Check Detail Report

1. From the Report Center, select **Banking > Check Detail**
2. Select Dates From: **12/15/2024** To: **12/18/2024**
3. Export to **Excel** or **print** the Check Detail report
4. **Highlight** the transaction you entered in this exercise

E4.2.4 Back Up Exercise 4.2

Save a backup of your Exercise file using the file name: **YourName Exercise 4.2 Backup.QBB**. See Appendix B: Back Up and Restore QuickBooks Files for instructions.

Exercise 4.3 Void Checks

 Rock Castle Construction

Since Washuta did not receive Check No. 470 and Mr. Castle stopped payment on the check, you need to void Check No. 470.

E4.3.1 QuickBooks File

If you will be using the same computer and the same QBW file:

1. Select your **QBW file**.
2. Update the company name to **YourName Exercise 4.3 Rock Castle Construction** by selecting **Company Menu > My Company**.

> If you are not using the same computer that you used for Chapter 4, Exercise 4.1 and Exercise 4.2, you will need to restore your latest prior Backup.QBB file using the instructions in Appendix B: Back Up and Restore QuickBooks files. After restoring, update the company name to YourName Exercise 4.3 Rock Castle Construction.

E4.3.2 Find Check

Find Check No. 470 made out to Washuta & Son Painting in the QuickBooks Check Register by completing the following steps.

1. View the **Check Register**. (Click Check Register icon in the Banking section of the Home Page.)

2. Next, search the Check Register for Check No. 470 using the Go To feature. Click the **Go to** button in the upper left corner of the Check Register window.

3. In the Go To window:
   - Select Which Field: **Number/Ref**
   - Enter Search For: **470**

4. Click the **Next** button. If asked if you want to search from the beginning, click **Yes**.

5. Check No. 470 on 11/28/2024 to Washuta & Son Painting should appear in the Check Register window

6. **Close** the Go To window

7. To view Check No. 470, double-click on the Check Register entry for Washuta & Son Painting to drill down to the check. Leave Check No. 470 open on your screen.

E4.3.3 Void Check

The next task is to void Check No. 470. There are two ways to remove a check amount from the Check Register:

- Delete the check: This removes all record of the transaction.
- Void the check: QuickBooks changes the amount deducted in the Check Register to zero but the voided check still appears in the Check Register, thus leaving a record of the transaction. Should questions about the transaction arise later, a voided check provides a better record than a deleted check.

For Check No. 470 you want to maintain a record of the transaction, so you want to void the check rather than delete it.

Void Check No. 470 by completing the following steps:

1. With Check No. 470 displayed, select the **down arrow** under the Delete icon and select **Void**. The Payment amount should now be $0.00. (Another way to void the check is from the Check Register as follows. With your cursor over Check No 470, **right-click** and from the pop-up menu select **Void Bill Pmt - Check**. VOID should now appear next to Check No. 470 in the Check Register.)

2. Select **Save & Close**

3. When asked if you are sure you want to record the voided check, click **Yes**

E4.3.4 Check Register Report

Next, prepare the Check Register QuickReport to verify the voided check.

1. With your cursor on the voided check No 470, **right-click** and from the pop-up menu, select **QuickReport**

2. Export to **Excel** or **print** the Register QuickReport

3. **Highlight** Check No. 470 on the Check Register report and verify that Check No. 470 is void, showing a check amount of $0.00

4. **Close** the Check Register window

E4.3.5 Back Up Exercise 4.3

Save a backup of your Exercise file using the file name: **YourName Exercise 4.3 Backup.QBB**. See Appendix B: Back Up and Restore QuickBooks Files for instructions.

Exercise 4.4 Bank Reconciliation

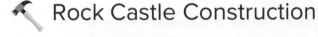 Rock Castle Construction

BACKSTORY

When you arrive at work the next morning, Rock Castle Construction's December bank statement is on your desk with the following note from Mr. Castle attached.

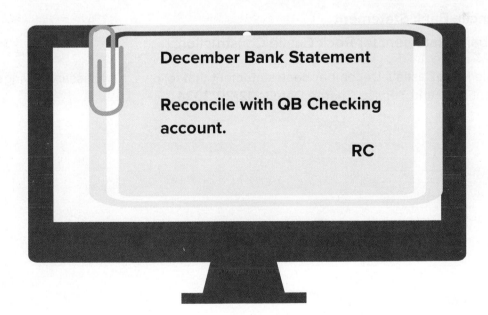

December Bank Statement

Reconcile with QB Checking account.

RC

E4.4.1 QuickBooks File

If you will be using the same computer and the same QBW file:

1. Select your **QBW file**.

2. Update the company name to **YourName Exercise 4.4 Rock Castle Construction** by selecting **Company Menu > My Company**.

If you are not using the same computer that you used for Chapter 4, Exercise 4.1, Exercise 4.2 and Exercise 4.3, you will need to restore your latest prior Backup.QBB file using the instructions in Appendix B: Back Up and Restore QuickBooks files. After restoring, update the company name to **YourName Exercise 4.4 Rock Castle Construction.**

E4.4.2 Export Previous Bank Reconciliation

Export the previous bank reconciliation as follows:

1. Click **Reports > Banking > Previous Reconciliation**. If necessary, select **Run**.

2. Select Type of Report: **Summary**

3. Select: **Transactions cleared plus any changes made to those transactions since the reconciliation**

4. Click **Display**. (If a Reconciliation Report window appears, click **OK**.)

5. Export to **Excel** or **print** the Reconciliation Summary report

E4.4.3 Reconcile Bank Statement

Reconcile a bank statement for Rock Castle Construction.

1. Reconcile Rock Castle's December bank statement that follows. If necessary, change the Statement Date and Service Charge Date to **12/20/2024**.

Bank Statement

Rock Castle Construction 1045 Main Street Bayshore, CA 94326		12-20-2024 Checking

Previous Balance		11-20-2024	$67,281.02
+ Deposits	10		58,413.56
- Checks	12		15,996.28
- Service Charge			10.00
+ Interest Paid			0.00
Ending Balance		12-20-2024	$109,688.30

DEPOSITS

Date	Amount
11-30-2024	4,135.50
12-02-2024	4,706.01
12-03-2024	1,200.00
12-05-2024	5,000.00
12-05-2024	25,000.00
12-10-2024	102.65
12-10-2024	1,000.00
12-12-2024	4,936.12
12-14-2024	4,700.00
12-15-2024	7,633.28

CHECKS PAID		
Date	No.	Amount
11-28-2024	464	300.00
11-28-2024	465	500.00
11-28-2024	466	600.00
11-28-2024	467	800.00
11-28-2024	468	6,790.00
11-28-2024	469	2,000.00
11-30-2024	471	24.00
11-30-2024	472	656.23
11-30-2024	473	686.00
11-30-2024	474	218.00
11-30-2024	475	2,710.90
12-01-2024	476	711.15

Thank you for banking with us!

2. In the Reconcile window (lower left corner) "Items you have marked cleared" should agree with the December bank statement:

- Deposits and Other Credits $58,413.56
- Checks and Payments $15,996.28
- Ending Balance $109,688.30
- Cleared Balance $109,688.30
- Difference $ 0.00

3. If the difference between the Ending Balance and the Cleared Balance is zero, select **Reconcile Now**. (If the difference between the Ending Balance and the Cleared Balance is not zero, and you want to return to the bank reconciliation later, do NOT click Reconcile Now. Instead, click Leave.)

Another way to change the status of a cleared item:
1. Display the Check Register.
2. Click the Cleared Status column until the appropriate status (cleared or uncleared) appears.

After you click Reconcile Now, you can return to this Bank Reconciliation by selecting **Reports Menu > Banking > Previous Reconciliation.**

E4.4.4 Print Bank Reconciliation Report

1. Export to **Excel** the bank reconciliation summary report

2. Export to **Excel** the bank reconciliation detail report

3. In the bank reconciliation detail report, **highlight** the checks and deposits cleared for the December bank statement

E4.4.5 Back Up Exercise 4.4

Save a backup of your Exercise file using the file name: **YourName Exercise 4.4 Backup.QBB**. See Appendix B: Back Up and Restore QuickBooks Files for instructions.

Exercise 4.5 Bank Feeds

 Rock Castle Construction

BACKSTORY

Every month, Rock Castle Construction pays $850 for a lease payment for storage facilities. Since it will be the same amount per month, you see an opportunity to use a bank rule to save time.

First, you will create a bank rule to assign account number 63900 Rent to the downloaded $850 transaction. Then you will review the transaction before adding it to your QuickBooks accounts. If there are any other $850 transactions that are not for storage facilities leasing, then you can reclassify those transactions before adding them to QuickBooks.

E4.5.1 QuickBooks File

If you will be using the same computer and the same QBW file:

1. Select your **QBW file**.

2. Update the company name to **YourName Exercise 4.5 Rock Castle Construction** by selecting **Company Menu > My Company**.

If you are not using the same computer that you used for Chapter 4, Exercise 4.1, 4.2, 4.3, and 4.4, you will need to restore your latest prior Backup.QBB file using the instructions in Appendix B: Back Up and Restore QuickBooks files. After restoring, update the company name to YourName Exercise 4.5 Rock Castle Construction.

E4.5.2 Before Creating Bank Rule

Before creating the new bank rule, open the Bank Feeds window. (Select **Banking** menu > **Bank Feeds** > **Bank Feeds Center**.) Then answer the following questions for the Rock Castle Construction's ANYTIME Financial Checking account.

1. How many **Recognized** transactions are indicated in the Bank Feed window?

2. How many **Unrecognized** transactions are indicated in the Bank Feed window?

E4.5.3 Create New Bank Rule

Complete the following steps to create a new bank rule for Rock Castle Construction.

1. Select the **Rules** icon > **Add rule**

2. Enter Rule name: **Storage Lease**

3. Select For: **Money out**

4. Select: When a transaction meets **Any** of these conditions

5. Select: **Amount Equals to 850.00**

6. Do this and Categorize in account: **63900 Rent**

7. Select **Save** > **Close** the Rules list window

E4.5.4 After Applying Bank Rule

After creating the new bank rule, answer the following questions for the Rock Castle Construction's ANYTIME Financial Checking account.

1. How many **Recognized** transactions are indicated in the Bank Feed window?

2. How many **Unrecognized** transactions are indicated in the Bank Feed window?

3   How many **Added to Register** transactions are indicated in the Bank Feed window?

E4.5.5 Add Recognized Transaction with New Bank Rule

After creating the new bank rule, the next step is to review transactions that QuickBooks has recognized as a result of the new bank rule. Complete the following steps to review and add recognized transactions.

1. From the Bank Feeds window, select the **Recognized** tab

2. Verify that the Match status displays: **Rule Applied Storage Lease**

3. Verify Account displays: **63900 Rent**

4. After verifying the transaction, to add the transaction to your QuickBooks accounts. select **Add**. (Or select transaction > Batch actions > Add / Confirm.)

E4.5.6 After Adding Recognized Transaction with New Bank Rule

After adding to your QuickBooks accounts the storage lease transaction recognized by the new bank rule, answer the following questions for the Rock Castle Construction's ANYTIME Financial Checking account.

1. How many **Recognized** transactions are indicated in the Bank Feed window?

2. How many **Unrecognized** transactions are indicated in the Bank Feed window?

3. How many **Added to Register** transactions are indicated in the Bank Feed window?

E4.5.7 Back Up Exercise 4.5

Save a backup of your Exercise file using the file name: **YourName Exercise 4.5 Backup.QBB**. See Appendix B: Back Up and Restore QuickBooks Files for instructions.

PROJECT 4.1

Larry's Landscaping 🌴

As an accounting consultant for Larry's Landscaping complete the following to enter transactions for the company.

> 💡 **Troubleshooting QuickBooks and Correcting Errors are crucial QuickBooks skill to acquire. Troubleshooting resources include:**
> - **www.My-QuickBooks.com > QuickBooks Troubleshooting (QT) Tips**
> - **Chapter 17, Quick Review Guide, contains tips on Correcting Errors**
> - **Appendix D, QuickBooks Troubleshooting (QT), provides you with an effective troubleshooting process**

🌐 QuickBooks SatNav

The objective of Project 4.1 is to facilitate your mastery of QuickBooks Desktop. As shown in the following QuickBooks SatNav, Project 4.1 focuses on QuickBooks Banking Transactions.

QuickBooks SatNav

QuickBooks Settings

Company Settings
Chart of Accounts

QuickBooks Transactions

Banking	*Record Deposits	Write Checks*
Customers & Sales	
Vendors & Expenses	
Employees & Payroll	

QuickBooks Reports

Reports

P4.1.1 QuickBooks File

1. Use either your QuickBooks Company file (QBW) or restore the backup file (QBB) that you completed for Project 3.1. (If you have issues with your QuickBooks file, contact your instructor.)

2. Update the Company Name to: **YourName Project 4.1 Larry's Landscaping**

P4.1.2 Deposits

Enter the following deposits for Larry's Landscaping.

1. Record the following deposits on the same deposit form.

Date	**12/17/2024**
Received From	**Gussman's Nursery**
Account	**4300 Other Income**
Memo	**Storage Rental Revenue**
Amount	**$500.00**
Cash/ Check No.	**Cash**

Date	**12/17/2024**
Received From <Add New, Other>	**Lynne's Space**
Account	**4300 Other Income**
Memo	**Storage Rental Revenue**
Amount	**$1300.00**
Cash/ Check No.	**Check No. 2200**

2. Select the **Save** icon at the top of the Make Deposit window

3. Select the **Journal** icon to display the journal entry to QuickBooks created behind the screen for the deposit

4. Export to **Excel** or **print** the Transaction Journal. Select **Save & New** on the Make Deposit form.

5. Record the following two deposits on a new deposit form.

Date	**12/18/2024**
Received From	**Conner Garden Supply**
Account	**4300 Other Income**
Memo	**Storage Rental Revenue**
Amount	**$900.00**
Cash/ Check No.	**Cash**

Date	**12/18/2024**
Received From	**Bank of Anycity**
Account	**8000 Interest Income**
Memo	**Interest Revenue**
Amount	**$432.00**
Cash/ Check No.	**Check No. 11818**

6. Select the **Save** icon at the top of the Make Deposit window

7. Select the **Journal** icon to display the journal entry to QuickBooks created behind the screen for the deposit

8. Export to **Excel** or **print** the Transaction Journal

9. Export to **Excel** the Deposit Detail report for December 17 through 18, 2024. (Hint: Report Center > Banking.)

P4.1.3 Write Checks

Enter the banking transactions for Larry's Landscaping using the Write Checks window.

1. Write the following check for Larry's Landscaping.

Date	**12/17/2024**
To	**Computer Services by DJ**
Account	**7320 Computer Supplies**
Memo	**External Hard Drive**
Amount	**$306.00**
Check No.	**1465**

2.   Select the **Save** icon

3.   Select the **Reports** tab > **Transaction Journal** icon

4.   Export the Transaction Journal report to **Excel** or **print** the report

5.   Write the following check for Larry's Landscaping.

Date	**12/17/2024**
To	**Mike Scopellite**
Account	**7430 Professional Design Fees**
Memo	**Professional Design Consulting**
Amount	**$420.00**
Check No.	**1466**

6.   Select the **Save** icon

7.   Select the **Reports** tab > **Transaction Journal** icon

8.   Export the Transaction Journal report to **Excel** or **print** the report

9.   Write the following check for Larry's Landscaping.

Date	**12/18/2024**
To	**Sowers Office Equipment**
Account	**7300 Office Supplies**
Memo	**Special Order**
Amount	**$330.00**
Check No.	**1467**

10.   Select the **Save** icon

11.   Select the **Reports** tab > **Transaction Journal** icon

12.   Export the Transaction Journal report to **Excel** or **print** the report

13.   Write the following check for Larry's Landscaping.

Date	**12/18/2024**
To	**Nye Properties**
Account	**7500 Rent (Expense)**
Memo	**Rent**
Amount	**$900.00**
Check No.	**1468**

14. Select the **Save** icon

15. Select the **Reports** tab > **Transaction Journal** icon

16. Export the Transaction Journal report to **Excel** or **print** the report

17. Export to **Excel** the Check Detail report for December 17 through 18, 2024. (Hint: Report Center > Banking.)

P4.1.4 Bank Reconciliation

Reconcile a bank statement for Larry's Landscaping.

1. Reconcile the following bank statement. Select account to reconcile: **Checking**.

2. Export to **Excel** the bank reconciliation summary report

3. Export to **Excel** the bank reconciliation detail report

4. In the bank reconciliation detail report, **highlight** the checks, deposits, and items cleared for the November bank statement

---

Bank Statement

Larry's Landscaping		11-30-2024
1045 Main Street		Checking
Bayshore, CA 94326		

Previous Balance	10-30-2024	$238,625.29
+ Deposits	2	5,775.80
- Checks	8	2,865.51
- Service Charge		40.00
+ Interest Paid		0.00
Ending Balance	11-30-2024	$241,495.58

DEPOSITS	
Date	**Amount**
11-25-2024	5,000.00
11-30-2024	775.80

CHECKS PAID		
Date	**No.**	**Amount**
10-22-2024	1459	244.13
10-28-2024	1461	550.00
11-22-2024	1460	244.13
11-28-2024	1462	550.00
11-29-2024	1112	177.25
11-30-2024	1113	125.00
11-30-2024	1114	375.00
11-30-2024	1115	600.00

Thank you for banking with us!

P4.1.5 Reports

1. Export to **Excel** the Journal report for December 17 through 18, 2024

P4.1.6 Back Up Project 4.1

Save a backup of your Project file using the file name: **YourName Project 4.1 Backup.QBB**.
See Appendix B: Back Up and Restore QuickBooks Files for instructions.

Design elements: Dog icon: ©josep perianes jorba/Shutterstock; paint roller icon: ©Netti Buletti/Shutterstock; other icons/symbols: ©Carboxylase/Shutterstock

Chapter 5

Customers and Sales

 Rock Castle Construction

BACKSTORY

Just as you are finishing the last bank reconciliation and checking bank reconciliations off your smartphone reminders, Mr. Castle reappears. He always seems to know just when you are about to finish a task.

"While cash flow is crucial to our survival," he says, *"we also need to keep an eye on profits. We are in the business of selling products and services to our customers. We have to be certain that we charge customers enough to cover our costs and make a profit."*

Mr. Castle pulls out a pen and begins scribbling on a sheet of paper on your desk:

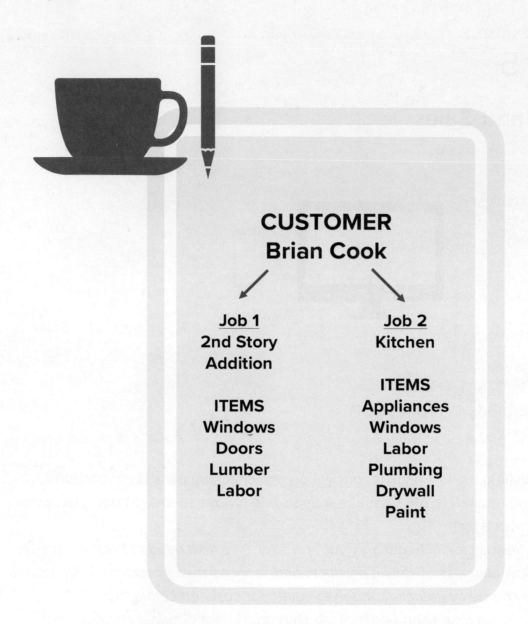

CUSTOMER
Brian Cook

Job 1	Job 2
2nd Story Addition	**Kitchen**
	ITEMS
ITEMS	Appliances
Windows	Windows
Doors	Labor
Lumber	Plumbing
Labor	Drywall
	Paint

"We track the costs of each job we work on. A job is a project for a specific customer. For example, we are working on two jobs for Brian Cook: Job 1 is a second story addition and Job 2 is a kitchen remodeling job.

"In QuickBooks we use items to track the products and services we use on each project. On the 2nd story addition job we used four different items."

Pushing a stack of papers toward you, Mr. Castle says, "Here are some customer transactions that need to be recorded in QuickBooks."

Chapter 5

Learning Objectives

Chapter 5 explores QuickBooks customers and sales transactions, such as creating sales receipts and invoices. In this chapter, you will learn about the following topics:

- Customer Navigation
- Customer List
  - View Customer List
  - Add New Customer
  - Edit Customer Information
  - Add a Job
  - Export Customer List
- Recording Sales Transactions
- Customer Sales Receipts
  - Create Sales Receipt
  - Create Bank Deposit for Undeposited Funds from Sales Receipt
- Customer Invoices
  - Create Invoice
  - Create Receive Payment
  - Create Bank Deposit for Undeposited Funds from Receive Payment
  - Customer Invoice History Tracker
- Customer Reports
  - Accounts Receivable Reports: Which Customers Owe Us Money?
    - Accounts Receivable Aging Summary Report
    - Customers with Open Invoices Report
    - Collections Report: Customers with Overdue Balances
  - Profit and Loss Reports: Which Customers and Jobs are Profitable?
    - Income by Customer Summary Report
- Accounting Essentials: Customer Sales and Accounts Receivable

Section 5.1

 ## QuickBooks SatNav

QuickBooks SatNav is your satellite navigation for QuickBooks, assisting you in navigating QuickBooks

QuickBooks SatNav divides QuickBooks into three processes:

1. **QuickBooks Settings.** This includes Company Settings when setting up a new QuickBooks company and the Company Chart of Accounts.

2. **QuickBooks Transactions.** This includes recording transactions in QuickBooks. Transaction types can be categorized as Banking, Customers and Sales, Vendors and Expenses, and Employees and Payroll. In basic terms, recording transactions involves recording money in and money out.

3. **QuickBooks Reports.** QuickBooks reports are the output of the system, such as commonly used financial statements of Balance Sheet, Income Statement, and Statement of Cash Flows.

Chapter 5 focuses on customers and sales transactions as shown in the following QuickBooks SatNav.

 QuickBooks SatNav

 QuickBooks Settings

Company Settings
Chart of Accounts

QuickBooks Transactions

Banking
Customers & Sales
Vendors & Expenses
Employees & Payroll

QuickBooks Reports

Reports

Accounting Essentials appear at the end of the chapter. Tip: Preview Accounting Essentials <u>before</u> completing the chapter and then review Accounting Essentials <u>after</u> completing the chapter.

Section 5.2

Start QuickBooks and Open QuickBooks Company

START QUICKBOOKS

To start QuickBooks software, click the **QuickBooks** icon on your desktop. If a QuickBooks icon does not appear on your desktop, from Microsoft® Windows® click **Start** button > **QuickBooks** > **QuickBooks Premier Accountant Edition**.

RESTORE QBB STARTER FILE

Restore the QBB Starter file for this chapter as follows.

1. Select **File** > **Restore**

2. Using the directions in Appendix B: Back Up and Restore QuickBooks Files, restore **CHAPTER 5 STARTER.QBB**

3. After restoring, update the company name to **YourName Chapter 5 Rock Castle Construction** by selecting **Company Menu** > **My Company**

Section 5.3
Customer Navigation

The QuickBooks Home Page contains a Customers section that displays icons used for Customers functions. If necessary click the **Home** icon in the Navigation Bar to display the Home Page.

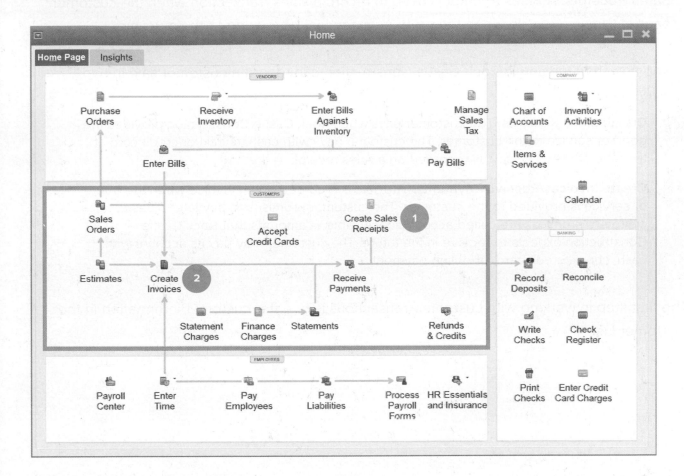

The Customers section of the Home Page is a flowchart of customer transactions.

Types of sales transactions that we can enter using QuickBooks include:

• **Invoices.** A sales transaction is recorded on an invoice when the product or service is provided to the customer, and the customer promises to pay later. These customer promises are called accounts receivable — amounts that we expect to receive in the future.

- **Receive Payments.** The Receive Payment onscreen form is used to record the transaction when the customer pays its account with cash, check, credit card, or online payment.
- **Estimates.** The Estimate onscreen form is used to record estimated costs of products and services to be provided to a customer in the future.
- **Refunds & Credits.** A Credit Memo onscreen form is used when we need to record a credit, or reduction, in the amount the customer is charged, such as when we issue a customer a refund.
- **Sales Receipts.** A Sales Receipt is used to record a sales transaction when the customer pays at the time of sale when the product or service is provided to the customer.

As the flowchart indicates, Rock Castle Construction can record a customer sale in two different ways:

1. **Create Sales Receipts.** The customer pays when Rock Castle Construction provides the good or service to the customer. The customer pays with cash, check, or credit card at the time of sale. The sale is recorded on a sales receipt.

2. **Create Invoices/Receive Payments.** The sale is recorded on an invoice when the good or service is provided to the customer. The customer promises to pay later. These customer promises are called accounts receivable — amounts that Rock Castle Construction expects to receive in the future. The customer may pay its account with cash, check, credit card, or online payment.

The first step in working with customer transactions is to enter customer information in the Customer List.

Section 5.4

Customer List

The Customer List contains customer information such as address, telephone number, and credit terms. Once customer information is entered in the Customer List, QuickBooks automatically transfers the customer information to the appropriate forms, such as sales invoices and sales returns. This feature enables you to enter customer information only once instead of entering the customer information each time a form is prepared.

The Customer List in QuickBooks also tracks projects (jobs) for each customer. For example, Rock Castle Construction is working on two projects for Brian Cook:

- Job 1: 2nd Story Addition
- Job 2: Kitchen

VIEW CUSTOMER LIST

To view the Customer List for Rock Castle Construction:

1 Click **Customers** in the Navigation Bar

2 The following Customer Center window appears, listing customers and jobs. Notice the two jobs listed for Brian Cook:
- 2nd story addition
- Kitchen

3 The Customers & Jobs List displays:
- Customer name
- Job name
- Balance for each job

4 To view additional information about a customer, click the customer or job name. The Customer/Job Information window displays:
- Customer address and contact information
- Transaction information for the customer
- Estimate information (if an estimate for the job was prepared)
- Notes about the job

ADD NEW CUSTOMER

Rock Castle Construction needs to add a new customer, Tracey Kari, to the Customer List.

To add a new customer to the Customer List:

1. Click the **New Customer & Job** button at the top of the Customer Center

2. Click **New Customer** on the drop-down menu

3. When a blank New Customer window appears, select the **Address Info** tab. Enter the following information in the New Customer | Address Info window.

Customer Name	**Kari, Tracey**
First Name	**Tracey**
Last Name	**Kari**
Main Phone	**415-555-1234**
Mobile	**415-555-9999**
Address Details Bill To / Ship To	**99 Reyka Drive Bayshore, CA 94326**

4 To enter payment information for the customer, click the **Payment Settings** tab. Enter the following information in the Payment Settings fields:

Account No.   **7890**

Credit Limit   **50,000**

Payment Terms   **Net 30**

Preferred Delivery Method   **E-mail**

Preferred Payment Method   **Check**

5 To enter sales tax information for the customer, click the **Sales Tax Settings** tab. Enter the following information in the Sales Tax Settings fields:

Tax Code   **Tax**

Tax Item   **San Tomas**

6 Click the **Additional Info** tab to display another customer information window. Enter the following information in the Additional Info field.

Customer Type   **Residential**

7 Click **OK** to add the new customer to Rock Castle Construction's Customer List

8 To sort the Customer List, with your cursor over the Customer List, **right-click** to display the pop-up menu > select: **Re-sort List**. If asked if you want to return this list to its original order, select **OK**.

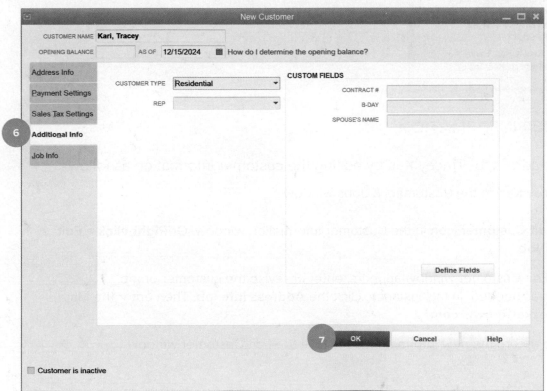

NAME	BALANCE TOTAL	ATTACH

Customers & Jobs | Transactions

Active Customers ▾ | ›

Kari, Tracey

- Find...
- Use   Ctrl+U
- Refresh
- Edit Customer:Job
- New Customer
- Delete Customer:Job
- Add/Edit Multiple Customer:Jobs
- Add Job
- Make Customer:Job Inactive
- Re-sort List   **8**
- ✓ Hierarchical View
- Flat View
- Customize Columns...
- Show Full Customer List Only
- Create Invoices
- Create Estimates
- Show Estimates
- Create Sales Orders
- Receive Payments
- Make Deposits
- Enter Sales Receipts
- Enter Statement Charges
- Create Credit Memos/Refunds
- Create Statements
- Assess Finance Charges
- Use Register
- QuickReport: Kari, Tracey
- Open Balance: Kari, Tracey
- Attach

Customer list names (partially hidden by menu):
- ◆Abercrombie, Kris
  - ◆Family Room
  - ◆Kitchen
  - ◆Remodel Bath
- ◆Allard, Robert
  - ◆Remodel
- ◆Babcock's Music
  - ◆Remodel
- ◆Baker, Chris
  - ◆Family Room
  - ◆Garage Repai
- ◆Balak, Mike
  - ◆Utility Shed
- ◆Barley, Renee
  - ◆Repairs
- ◆Bauman, Mark
  - ◆Home Remod
- ◆Bolinski, Rafal
  - ◆2nd story addi
- ◆Bristol, Sonya
  - ◆Repairs
  - ◆Utility Shed

EDIT CUSTOMER INFORMATION

Enter the email address for Tracey Kari by editing the customer information as follows:

1 Select **Tracey Kari** in the Customers & Jobs window

2 Click the **Edit Customer** icon in the Customer Information window. Or **Right-click > Edit Customer: Job**.

3 When the Edit Customer window appears, enter or revise the customer or job information as needed. In this instance, click the **Address Info** tab. Then enter the Main Email: **traceykari@www.com**.

4 Click **OK** to record the new information and close the Edit Customer window

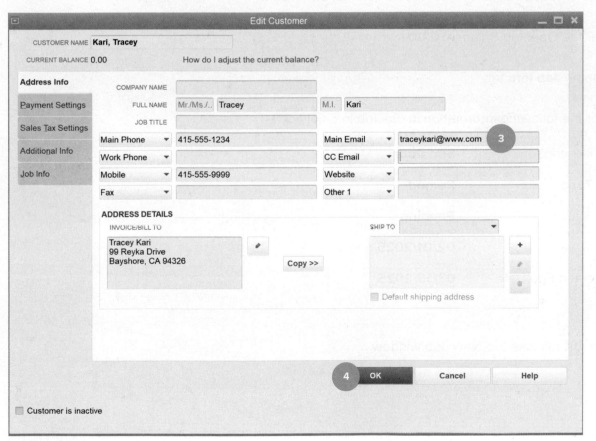

ADD A JOB

Tracey Kari is considering having Rock Castle Construction add a sun room to his home. Tracey is looking to find a way to blend his fondness for the outdoors with working in office space, so he would like to be able to use the sun room for his home office workspace with expansive views of the outdoors.

To add a Sun Room job for Tracey Kari, complete the following steps:

1. Click on the customer, **Tracey Kari**, in the Customers & Jobs window

2. Click the **New Customer & Job** button at the top of the Customer Center window

3. Select **Add Job** from the drop-down menu. (Or right-click > Add Job.)

4. In the New Job window, enter the Job Name: **Sun Room**

5. Enter the Opening Balance: **0.00**

6. Click the **Job Info** tab

7. Enter the following information in the Job Info fields:

Job Description	**Sun Room**
Job Type	**Remodel**
Job Status	**Pending**
Start Date	**02/01/2025**
Projected End Date	**03/15/2025**

8. Click **OK** to close the New Job window

Tracey Kari tells Rock Castle Construction that he will hire them to do the Sun Room job on one condition—he needs Rock Castle Construction as soon as possible to replace a damaged exterior door that will not close. Rock Castle sends a workman out to begin work on replacing the door right away.

To add the Exterior Door job:

1 Click on the customer, **Tracey Kari**, in the Customers & Jobs window

2 **Right-click > Add Job**

3 In the Job Name field at the top of the New Job window, enter: **Exterior Door**

4 Enter Opening Balance: **0.00**

5 Click the **Job Info** tab, then enter the following information

Job Description	**Replace Exterior Door**
Job Type	**Repairs**
Job Status	**Awarded**
Start Date	**12/15/2024**
Projected End Date	**12/18/2024**

6 Click **OK** to record the new job and close the New Job window

7 Rock Castle Construction's Customer List should now list two jobs for **Tracey Kari: Exterior Door** and **Sun Room**. **Close** the Customer Center window.

EXPORT CUSTOMER LIST

C5.4.1 Customer List. To export the Customer List:

1 From Customer Center, select **Excel** > **Export Customer List**

2 Select **Replace an existing worksheet**

3 Export the Customer List to **Excel**

Section 5.5

Recording Sales Transactions

Two main ways to record customers and sales transactions using QuickBooks are:

- Customer Sales using Sales Receipts
- Customer Sales using Invoices

If the customer pays on the spot when purchasing a product or service, then the Sales Receipt can be used to record the sale. If the customer pays later after receiving products or services, then an Invoice is used.

When using QuickBooks, customer sales must be recorded using Sales Receipts or Invoices. The diagrams on the following pages summarize how to record sales transactions in QuickBooks.

> **Bank deposits other than customer sales** are recorded using the **Bank Deposit** onscreen form. **Bank deposits not related to customer sales was covered in the previous chapter.**

Section 5.6

Customer Sales Receipts

 QuickBooks SatNav

 QuickBooks Transactions

Banking	
Customers & Sales	*Create Sales Receipts > Record Deposits*
Vendors & Expenses	
Employees & Payroll	

If the customer payment is *received at the same time* the product or service is provided, we record the customer sale using the Sales Receipt form.

The customer payment may consist of cash, check, or credit card.

When using Sales Receipts to record customer sales:

1 **Create Sales Receipts.** Create a sales receipt record the customer sale for product given and customer payment received in form of cash, check or credit card.

2 **Make Deposit.** Create a Bank Deposit to move customer payment from Undeposited Funds account to the Checking account.

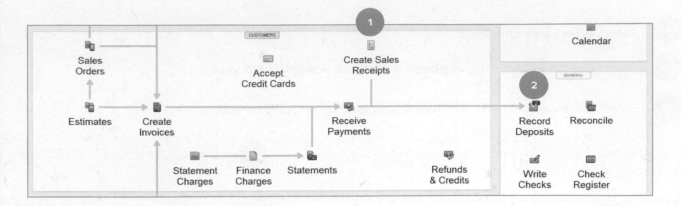

CREATE SALES RECEIPT

One of Rock Castle Construction's customers, Samuels Art Supplies, needs to purchase a replacement brass hinge. Adam Samuels from Samuels Art Supplies picks up the hinge and pays $30 in cash for the hinge.

To create a Sales Receipt for the customer sale:

1. From the Customers section of the Home Page, click **Create Sales Receipts** to display the Enter Sales Receipts window. (If asked if you would like to complete the Payment Interview, select No.)

2. In the Enter Sales Receipts window, select Customer: **Samuels Art Supplies**

3. Select Date: **12/15/2024**

4. Select Payment Method: **Cash**. Other types of payment include Check, Credit Card, Debit Card, or Check. If Payment Method is Check, enter the customer check no. in the **Check No.** field.

5. Select item from the Item drop-down menu or Add New Item. In this case, select **Brass hinges**.

6. Select Quantity: **1**

7. Enter Rate: **30.00**

8. Select Tax: **Tax**

9. Select Tax: **San Tomas**

10 Select **Print Later** checkbox

11 Select Customer Message: **It's been a pleasure working with you!**

12 Select **Save**. Leave the Enter Sales Receipts window open on your screen.

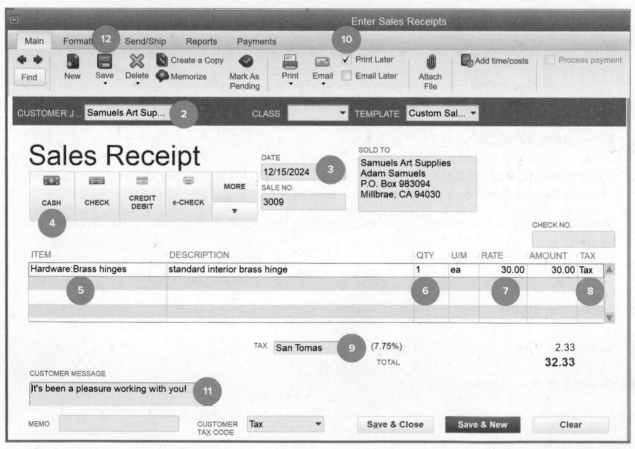

C5.6.1 Sales Receipt Journal Entry. To view the journal entry that QuickBooks created behind the screen for the sales receipt entered and saved using the previous Enter Sales Receipt onscreen form, complete the following steps.

1 From the Enter Sales Receipts onscreen form, select the **Reports** tab

2 Select the **Transaction Journal** icon

3 Export the Transaction Journal report to **Excel** or **print** the report

4 **Close** the Transaction Journal window

5 **Close** the Enter Sales Receipts window

QuickBooks records the $32.33 as undeposited funds. Next, we will record the $32.33 as a bank deposit to Rock Castle's Checking account.

CREATE BANK DEPOSIT FOR UNDEPOSITED FUNDS FROM SALES RECEIPT

When we recorded the Sales Receipt, QuickBooks recorded Undeposited Funds. So we must create a Bank Deposit to transfer the funds from the Undeposited Funds account to the appropriate Checking account. Undeposited Funds is used on the Sales Receipt so that the customer payment will be bundled with other customer payments when deposited. Then our totals will correspond to the bank deposit total shown by the bank.

> When we create a Sales Receipt we *must* create a bank deposit to transfer the funds from the Undeposited Funds account to the appropriate bank account. Otherwise, the funds will remain in the Undeposited Funds account instead of appearing in our Checking account.

To record a bank deposit related to a customer sale when the Sales Receipt onscreen form was used:

1 Click the **Record Deposits** icon in the Banking section of the Home Page to display the Payments to Deposit window. The Payments to Deposit window lists undeposited funds that have been received but not yet deposited in the bank.

2 Select the payments to transfer from the undeposited funds account to the Checking account. In this case select **Samuels Art Supplies** for the amount of **$32.33**.

3 Click **OK** to display the following Make Deposits window

4 Select Deposit To: **10100 Checking**

5 Select Date: **12/15/2024**

6 Verify the Amount field displays **$32.33**

7 Select **Save**

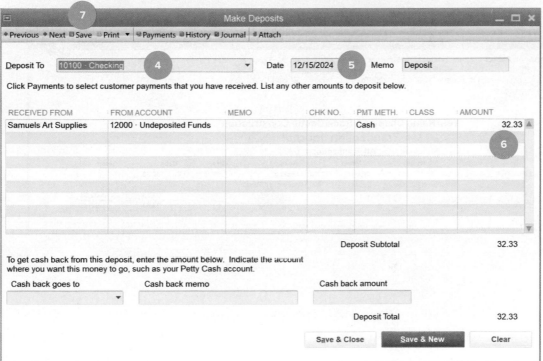

C5.6.2 Deposit Journal Entry. To view the journal entry that QuickBooks created behind the screen for the deposit entered and saved using the Record Deposit onscreen form above, complete the following steps.

1 From the Make Deposits onscreen form, select the **Journal** icon at the top of the form

2 Behind the screen, QuickBooks automatically converted the information in the Make Deposits onscreen form into a journal entry with debits and credits. Notice that the journal entry displays a Debit (increase) to the Checking account and a Credit (decrease) to Undeposited Funds to move the funds from the Undeposited Funds account to the Checking account.

3 Export the Transaction Journal report to **Excel** or **print** the report

4 **Close** the Transaction Journal window

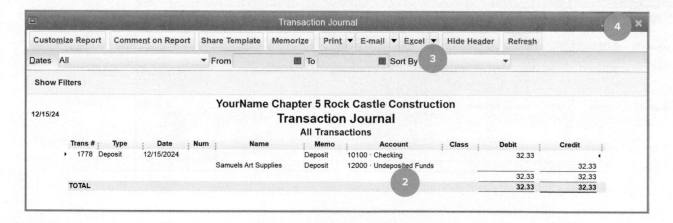

Section 5.7
Customer Invoices

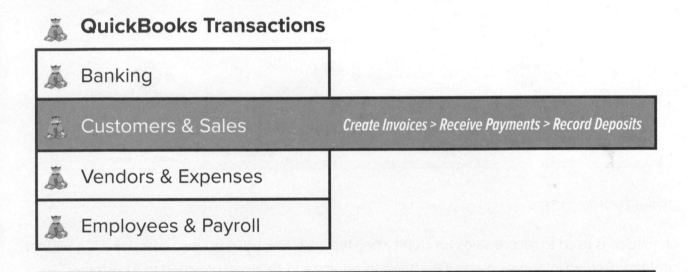

If products or services are given to the customer and the customer will pay later, then we use an Invoice instead of a Sales Receipt to record the sales transaction.

When a customer will pay later after receiving the product or service, theses are often called credit sales. Credit sales occur when Rock Castle Construction provides goods and services to customers and in exchange receives a promise that the customers will pay later. This promise to pay is called an *account receivable* because Rock Castle expects to *receive* the account balance in the future.

Recording a credit sale in QuickBooks requires three steps:

1 **Create Invoices.** Create an invoice to bill the customer for the product or service provided. QuickBooks records accounts receivable and the sales amount.

2 **Receive Payments.** Receive payment from the customer. QuickBooks reduces accounts receivable and increases undeposited funds.

3 **Record Deposits.** Deposit the customer's payment in the bank.

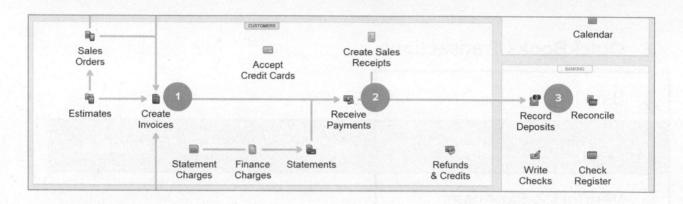

CREATE INVOICE

An invoice is used to record sales on credit when the customer will pay later. An invoice is a bill that contains detailed information about the items (products and services) provided to a customer.

If QuickBooks' time-tracking feature (tracking time worked on each job) is not used, then time worked on a job is entered directly on the invoice. In this chapter, assume that time tracking is not used and that time worked on a job is entered on the invoice form. For more information about time tracking, see Chapter 8.

Next, you will create an invoice for Rock Castle Construction. Rock Castle sent a workman to the Kari residence immediately after receiving the phone call from Tracey Kari requesting an exterior door replacement as soon as possible. The workman spent one hour at the site the first day.

In this instance, Rock Castle Construction was not asked to provide an estimate before starting the work. Charges for products and labor used on the Kari door replacement job will be recorded on an invoice.

When using an Invoice to record customer sales:

1 In the Customers section of the Home Page, click the **Create Invoices** icon to display the Create Invoices window

2 From the Create Invoices window, select the Template: **Rock Castle Invoice**

3 Enter the Customer:Job by selecting **Kari, Tracey: Exterior Door** from the drop-down Customer: Job List. (Make certain to select the customer name and the correct job: Exterior Door. To add new customers from the Create Invoices window: Select <Add New> from the Customer drop-down list.)

4 Select Date: **12/15/2024**

5 Enter charges for the service provided the customer. Enter Item: **Repairs**. Press **Tab**. Description should automatically display: Repair work.

6 Enter Quantity: **1** (hour)

7 The Rate should automatically display **$35.00**. The Amount should automatically display **$35.00**.

8 From the drop-down list, select Tax: **Non-Taxable Sales**

9 Select Customer Message: **It's been a pleasure working with you!**

10 Select **Save** and leave the Create Invoices window open

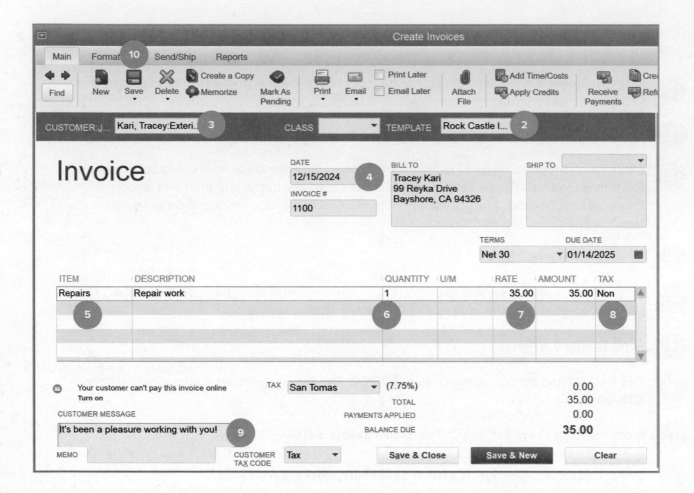

A Pending Invoice can used if the invoice is left open and additional charges will be added later. To mark an invoice as pending, right-click on the invoice and select Mark as Pending from the pop-up menu.

A Progress Invoice is used if the customer is billed as the work progresses rather than when the work is fully completed.

To print envelopes for invoices and shipping labels, click the down arrow by the Print icon on the Invoice.

C5.7.1 Invoice Journal Entry. To view the journal entry that QuickBooks created behind the screen for the invoice entered and saved using the Create Invoices onscreen form, complete the following steps.

1 From the Create Invoices onscreen form, select the **Reports** tab

2 Select the **Transaction Journal** icon

3 Export the Transaction Journal report to **Excel** or **print** the report

4 Notice that the journal entry records an increase (debit) to Accounts Receivable for $35.00, the net amount of the invoice

5 **Close** the Transaction Journal window

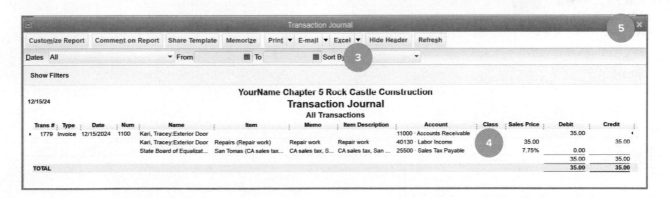

Later in the day on December 15, 2024, one of the Rock Castle Construction crews located an exterior door and finished installing the new door at the Kari residence.

When you learn what the crew is working on you begin to explore how to use QuickBooks to record the new sales transaction on an invoice. First, you decide to check the QuickBooks inventory information related to the exterior door. You notice an apparent discrepancy that requires further investigation.

To view the QuickBooks Inventory record related to the exterior door:

1 From the Company section of the Home Page, select the **Inventory Activities** icon

2 From the pop-up menu, select **Inventory Center**

3 From the Items List on the left of the Inventory Center window, select **Wood Door: Exterior**

4 Notice the cost recorded for the Exterior Wood Door: **$590.39**

5 Notice the sales price charged customers for the Exterior Wood Door: **$120.00**

Inventory Center **2**
Build Assemblies...
Adjust Quantity/Value On Hand...
Learn about serial #/lots and more

The cost of the exterior door is $590.39. The sales price is listed in QuickBooks as $120.00, and the sales price will automatically fill the sales price field for the exterior door on the invoice. You are concerned that if the cost is $590.39 and Rock Castle is only charging the customer $120.00, then Rock Castle Construction will be *losing* around $470 every time it sells and installs an exterior door.

After bringing the exterior door issue to Mr. Castle's attention, he quickly directs you to update the sales price for the exterior wood door to $900.00. To update the sales price for the exterior door:

1. From the Inventory Center window with the Exterior Wood Door selected, click the **Edit** icon

2. From the Edit Item window for the Exterior Wood Door, update the sales price from 120.00 to: **900.00**

3. Select **OK** to close the Edit Item window

4. Notice that the sales price for the Exterior Wood Door now displays as **$900.00**

5. **Close** the Inventory Center window

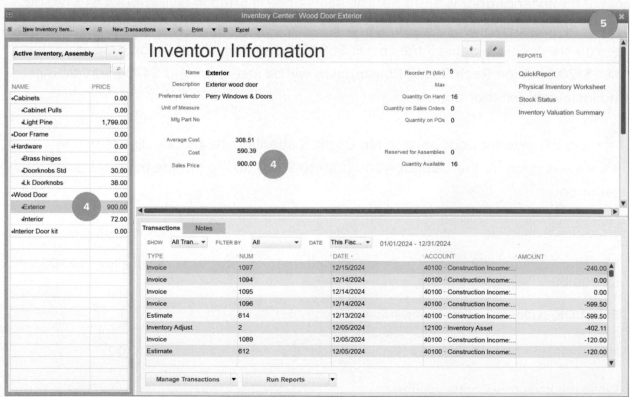

To record on the Kari Exterior Door invoice the additional products and services used:

1. Display **Invoice No. 1100.** If it is not already displayed on your screen, display the invoice for the Exterior Door job again:
- Click the **Create Invoices** icon
- When the Create Invoices window appears, click **Find**
- Enter Invoice No.: **1100**
- Click **Find**

2. Enter the following items as new line items on Invoice No. 1100 for the Kari Exterior Door job:

Exterior wood door	1 @ $900	Taxable Sales
Repair work	4 hours	Non-Taxable Sales

3. If we wanted to email the invoice to the customer, we would select the Email icon

4. If we wanted to turn on options for our customers to pay us online, we would select the Turn on link. This feature would permit us to email invoices to customers and then the customers could pay the invoice online using a bank transfer or credit card payment.

5. Select **Save** and leave the Invoice displayed. If you receive a message stating you have changed the transaction and asking if you want to record your changes, select **Yes**.

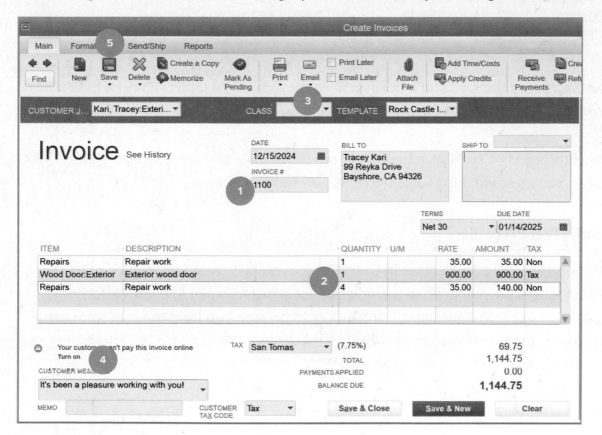

C5.7.2 Invoice Journal Entry. To view the journal entry that QuickBooks created behind the screen for the updated invoice, complete the following steps.

1. From the Create Invoices onscreen form, select the **Reports** tab

2. Select the **Transaction Journal** icon

3. Export the Transaction Journal report to **Excel** or **print** the report

4. Notice that the journal entry records an increase (debit) to Accounts Receivable for $1,144.75, the net amount of the invoice

5. **Close** the Transaction Journal window

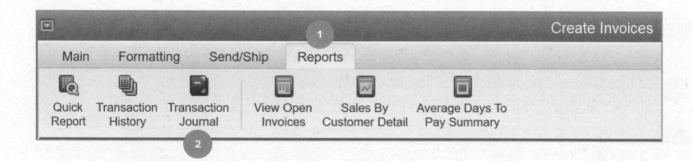

QuickBooks will record the sale and record an account receivable for the amount to be received from the customer in the future.

The Invoice Total is $1,144.75. Notice that the Exterior Door is a taxable item and QuickBooks automatically calculates and adds sales tax of $69.75 for the door.

CREATE RECEIVE PAYMENT

Recall that when recording credit sales in QuickBooks, you first create an invoice and then record the customer's payment. When a credit sale is recorded on an invoice, QuickBooks records (debits) an Account Receivable—an amount to be received from the customer in the future. When the customer's payment is received, the Account Receivable account is reduced (credited).

Customers may pay in the following ways:

1. **Credit card**, such as Visa, MasterCard, American Express, or Diners Club over the phone, in person, or by mail.
2. **Online** by credit card or bank account transfer. Using QuickBooks' Payments service, you can obtain accept credit cards and bank transfers online and then download payments directly into QuickBooks.
3. **Customer check** delivered either in person or by mail.

To record a customer's payment received to pay an outstanding invoice, such as payment by check for the Exterior Door job:

1 Click the **Receive Payments** icon in the Customers section of the Home Page to display the Receive Payments window

2 Select Received From: **Kari, Tracey: Exterior Door**. Invoice No. 1100 for $1,144.75 should appear as an outstanding invoice.

3 Select Date: **12/17/2024**

4 Select Invoice Number **1100** when it appears. QuickBooks will automatically enter the selected invoice amount of $1,144.75 into the Amount field.

5 Select: Pmt. Method: **Check**

6 Enter Check No. **1005**

7 Notice that there is no Save icon on the Receive Payments window. Select **Save & New**.

8 Select the **Find** back arrow to display the customer payment just recorded

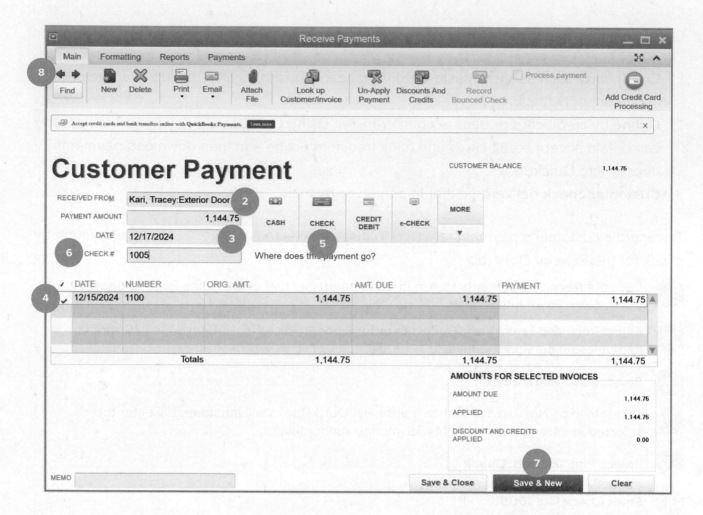

C5.7.3 Receive Payment Journal Entry.
To view the journal entry that QuickBooks created behind the screen for the customer payment received, complete the following steps.

1. From the Receive Payments onscreen form, select the **Reports** tab

2. Select the **Transaction Journal** icon

3. Export the Transaction Journal report to **Excel** or **print** the report

4. Notice that when a customer's payment is recorded as received, QuickBooks increases (debits) the Undeposited Funds account and decreases (credits) the customer's account receivable.

5. **Close** the Transaction Journal and the Receive Payments windows

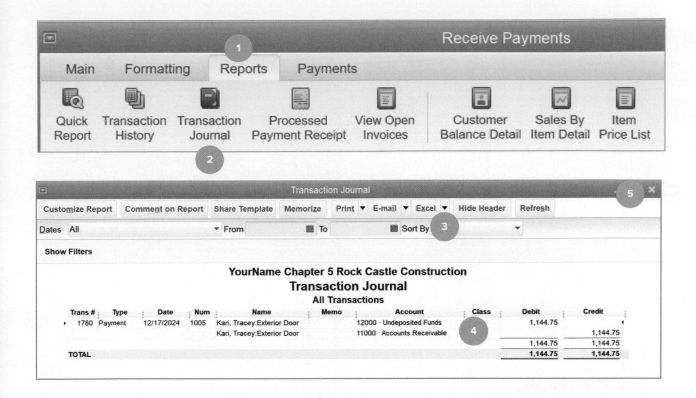

CREATE BANK DEPOSIT FOR UNDEPOSITED FUNDS FROM RECEIVE PAYMENT

By default, customer payments received are recorded in the Undeposited Funds account, so we must create a bank deposit to transfer the funds from the Undeposited Funds account to the appropriate bank account. Otherwise, the funds will remain in the Undeposited Funds account, and we will not be able to use the funds to pay bills, for example.

To record a bank deposit related to a customer payment recorded using the Receive Payment onscreen form:

1. Click the **Record Deposits** icon in the Banking section of the Home Page to display the Payments to Deposit window

2. The Payments to Deposit window lists undeposited funds that have been received but not yet deposited in the bank. From the Select Existing Payments section, select the the **Tracey Kari** payment of **$1,144.75** that was added to undeposited funds when we recorded the customer payment on **12/17/2024**.

3. Click **OK** to display the following Make Deposits window

4. Select Deposit To: **10100 Checking**

5 Select Date: **12/17/2024**

6 Verify the Amount is **$1,144.75**

7 Select **Save** and leave the Make Deposits window displayed

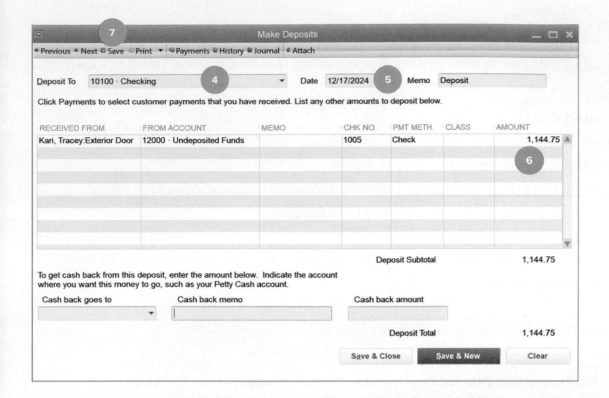

C5.7.4 Deposit Journal Entry. To view the journal entry that QuickBooks created behind the screen for the deposit entered and saved using the Record Deposit onscreen form, complete the following steps.

1. From the Make Deposits onscreen form, select the **Journal** icon at the top of the form

2. Export the Transaction Journal report to **Excel** or **print** the report

3. Notice that the journal entry displays a Debit (increase) to the Checking account and a Credit (decrease) to Undeposited Funds to move the funds from the Undeposited Funds account to the Checking account

4. **Close** the Transaction Journal window

5. On the Make Deposits window, select **Save & Close** to save the deposit

CUSTOMER INVOICE HISTORY TRACKER

The QuickBooks Customer Invoice History Tracker offers real-time invoice status tracking including:

- Invoice created date
- Invoice email date
- Invoice viewed by customer date
- Amount and date of customer Receive Payment recorded in Quickbooks
- Amount and date of Make Deposit recorded in QuickBooks

The real-time customer invoice history tracking information is useful for improving collection of open accounts receivable.

To view the Customer Invoice History Tracker:

1   Display the **Tracey Kari Exterior Door Invoice**, then select **See History**. The Invoice History Tracker summarizes information for tracking the invoice including the following.

2   Invoice created date

3   Invoice sent date (for invoices emailed to customers)

4   Invoice viewed by customer date (for invoices emailed to customers)

5   Amount and date of customer Receive Payment recorded in QuickBooks

6   Amount and date of Make Deposit recorded in QuickBooks

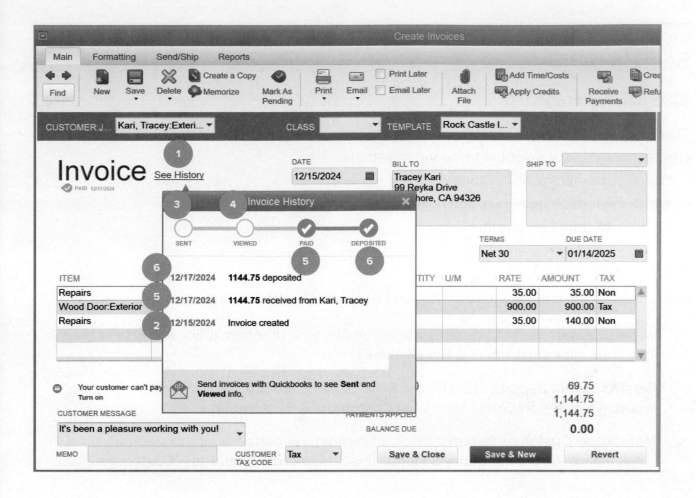

Section 5.8

Customer Reports

There are many different customer reports that a business may find useful. QuickBooks creates reports to answer the following questions:

- Which customers owe us money?
- Which customers have overdue balances?
- Which customers are profitable?
- Which jobs are profitable?

Customer reports can be accessed in QuickBooks in several different ways:

1. **Report Center.** Permits you to locate reports by type of report. (Click **Reports** icon, then click **Customers & Receivables**.)

2. **Reports Menu.** Reports listed on the Reports Menu are grouped by type of report. (From the **Reports** Menu, click **Customers & Receivables**.)

3. **Memorized Customer Reports.** Selected customer reports are memorized for convenience. (From the **Reports Menu**, select **Memorized Reports > Customers**.)

In this chapter, you will use the Report Center to access customer reports.

1 To display the Report Center, click **Reports** on the Navigation Bar

2 Select the **List View** icon

3 Select: **Customers & Receivables** to display customer reports that can be accessed in QuickBooks

4 Scroll down to view the three categories of Customers & Receivables reports:
- Accounts Receivable Aging reports
- Customer Balance reports
- Lists reports

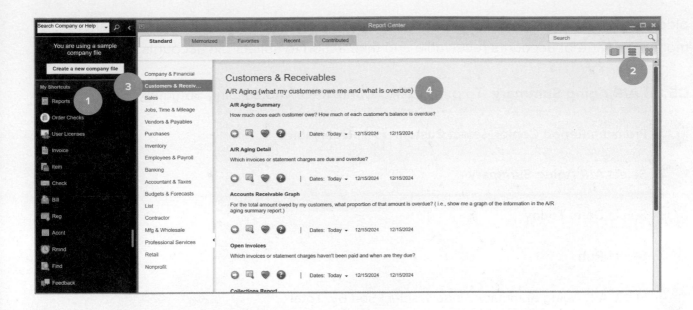

ACCOUNTS RECEIVABLE REPORTS: WHICH CUSTOMERS OWE US MONEY?

Accounts Receivable reports provide information about which customers owe your business money. When Rock Castle Construction makes a credit sale, the company provides goods and services to a customer in exchange for a promise that the customer will pay later. Sometimes the customer breaks the promise and does not pay. Therefore, a business should have a credit policy to ensure that credit is extended only to customers who are likely to keep their promise and pay their bills.

After credit has been extended, a business needs to track accounts receivable to determine if accounts are being collected in a timely manner. The following reports provide information useful in tracking accounts receivable.

1. Accounts Receivable Aging Summary (age of amounts due you by customers)
2. Accounts Receivable Aging Detail
3. Customers with Open Invoices (invoices not yet paid)
4. Collections Report (overdue customer accounts with contact information)

Accounts Receivable Aging Summary Report

The Accounts Receivable Aging Summary report provides information about the age of customer accounts. This report lists the age of accounts receivable balances. In general, the older an account, the less likely the customer will pay the bill. Therefore, it is important to monitor the age of accounts receivable and take action to collect old accounts.

C5.8.1 A/R Aging Summary. To print the Accounts Receivable Aging Summary:

1 From the Report Center, select **Customers & Receivables**

2 Select **A/R Aging Summary**

3 Select Date: **Today**

4 Select **Run**

5 In the A/R Aging Summary window, select Sort By: **Total**

6 Sort in **Descending** order, listing the customers with the largest accounts receivable balances first. If necessary, click and drag to adjust the column widths

7 Export the report to **Excel** or **print**

8 **Close** the A/R Aging Summary window

Customers with Open Invoices Report

Customers with open invoices are those who have an unbilled or unpaid balance. It is important to track the status of open accounts to determine:

- Are these amounts unbilled? The sooner the balances are billed, the sooner your company receives cash to pay your bills.
- Are these amounts billed but not yet due?
- Are these amounts billed and overdue? These accounts should be monitored closely with an action plan for collecting the accounts.

C5.8.2 Open Invoice Report. The Open Invoices report lists all customers with open balances and can be printed as follows:

1. From the Customers & Receivables section of the Report Center, click **Open Invoices**

2. Select Date: **Today**

3. Select **Run**

4. Export to **Excel** or **print** the Open Invoices report

5. Notice the Aging column in the report. This column indicates the age of overdue accounts.

6. **Close** the Open Invoices window

Collections Report: Customers with Overdue Balances

When reviewing the age of accounts receivable, a business should monitor overdue accounts closely and maintain ongoing collection efforts to collect its overdue accounts. The Collections Report lists customers with overdue account balances. In addition, the Collections Report includes a contact phone number for convenience in contacting the customer.

C5.8.3 Collections Report. To print the Collections Report summarizing information for all customers with overdue balances:

1. From the Customers & Receivables section of the Report Center, select: **Collections Report**

2. Select Date: **Today**

3. Select **Run**. No customers have overdue balances so it appears that you are doing a good job collecting customer payments on accounts.

4. Export to **Excel** or **print** the Collections report

5. **Close** the Collections Report window

The Collections Report provides the information necessary to monitor and contact overdue accounts and should be prepared and reviewed on a regular basis.

PROFIT AND LOSS REPORTS: WHICH CUSTOMERS AND JOBS ARE PROFITABLE?

To improve profitability in the future, a business should evaluate which customers and jobs have been profitable in the past. This information permits a business to improve profitability by:

- Increasing business in profitable areas
- Improving performance in unprofitable areas
- Discontinuing unprofitable areas

The following QuickBooks reports provide information about customer and job profitability:

1. Income by Customer Summary
2. Income by Customer Detail
3. Job Profitability Summary
4. Job Profitability Detail

Income by Customer Summary Report

To determine which customers are generating the most profit for your business, it is necessary to look at both the sales for the customer and associated costs.

C5.8.4 Income by Customer Summary Report. To print the Income by Customer Summary Report:

1. From the Report Center, select **Company & Financial > Income by Customer Summary**

2. Select: **This Fiscal Year-to-date**

3. Select **Run**

4. In the Income by Customer Summary window, select Sort By: **Total**

5. Sort in **Descending** order with the customer with the greatest income listed first. If necessary, click and drag to adjust the column widths.

6. Export to **Excel** or **print** the report

7. **Highlight** Rock Castle Construction's customer generating the most income

8. **Close** the Income by Customer Summary window

QuickBooks offers other additional reports about customers that provide information useful to a business. These reports can be accessed from the Report Center.

Section 5.9

Back up QuickBooks Files

BACK UP QBB

Save a backup of your Chapter 5 file using the file name: **YourName Chapter 5 Backup.QBB**. For further instructions on how to back up your file, *see* Appendix B: Back Up and Restore QuickBooks Files.

QBW WORKFLOW

If you are using the QBW approach, leave your QBW file open and proceed directly to Exercise 5.1.

QBB RESTORE

If you are using the QBB approach and ending your computer session now, close your QBW file and exit QuickBooks. When you restart, you will restore your backup file to complete Exercise 5.1.

Section 5.10

Accounting Essentials: Customer Sales and Accounts Receivable

Accounting Essentials summarize important foundational accounting knowledge that may be useful when using QuickBooks

What are accounts receivable?

- Accounts Receivable are amounts that a customer owes our business. When our business makes a credit sale, our business provides goods and services to a customer in exchange for the customer's promise to pay later.
- When a credit sale is recorded on an invoice, QuickBooks records (debits) an Account Receivable—an amount to be received from the customer in the future. When the customer's payment is received, the Account Receivable account is reduced (credited).
- Sometimes the customer breaks the promise and does not pay. So a business should have a credit policy to ensure that credit is extended only to customers who are likely to keep their promise and pay their bills.
- After credit has been extended, a business needs to track accounts receivable to determine if accounts are being collected in a timely manner.

How can a business track accounts receivable to make certain customers are paying on time?

- Accounts Receivable Aging reports provide information about which customers owe our business money, how much the customer owes, and the age of the customer accounts receivable balances.
- In general, the older an account, the less likely the customer will pay the bill. So it is important to monitor the age of accounts receivable and take action to collect old accounts.

What happens if a customer does not pay the accounts receivable balance?

- When a customer does not pay the accounts receivable balance, then it is called a bad debt or uncollectible account.
- At the time a credit sale occurs, it is recorded as an increase to sales and an increase to accounts receivable.
- Occasionally a company is unable to collect a customer payment and must write off the customer's account as a bad debt or uncollectible account. When an account is uncollectible, the account receivable is written off or removed from the accounting records.
- There are two different methods that can be used to account for bad debts:
  1. **Direct write-off method.** This method records bad debt expense when it becomes apparent that the customer is not going to pay the amount due. If the direct write-off method is used, the customer's uncollectible account receivable is removed and bad debt expense is recorded at the time a specific customer's account becomes uncollectible. The direct write-off method is used for tax purposes.
  2. **Allowance method.** The allowance method estimates bad debt expense and establishes an allowance or reserve for uncollectible accounts. When using the allowance method, uncollectible accounts expense is estimated in advance of the write-off. The estimate can be calculated as a percentage of sales or as a percentage of accounts receivable. (For example, 2% of credit sales might be estimated to be uncollectible.) This method should be used if uncollectible accounts have a material effect on the company's financial statements used by investors and creditors.
- To record a bad debt, make a journal entry to remove the customer's account receivable (credit Accounts Receivable) and debit either Bad Debt Expense (direct write-off method) or the Allowance for Uncollectible Accounts (allowance method).

Rock Castle Construction

BACKSTORY

"I just finished the Merriman job, Mr. Castle." A workman tosses a job ticket over your cubicle wall into your inbox as he walks past. *"Ms. Merriman's black and tan German Shepherd, Kuno, really did a number on that door. No wonder she wanted it replaced before her party tonight. Looks better than ever now!"*

You hear Mr. Castle reply, *"We want to keep Ms. Merriman happy. She will be a good customer."*

Exercise 5.1 Customer and Job List

First, you will need to add Ms. Merriman as a new customer and then add a new job.

E5.1.1 QuickBooks File

If you will be using the same computer and the same Chapter 5.QBW file:

1. If your Chapter 5.QBW file is not already open, open it by selecting **File > Open Previous Company**. Select your **Chapter 5.QBW file**. If a QuickBooks Information window appears with a message about the sample company file, click **OK**.

2. Update the company name to **YourName Exercise 5.1 Rock Castle Construction** by selecting **Company Menu > My Company**.

> If you are not using the same computer that you used for Chapter 5, you will need to restore your Chapter 5 Backup.QBB file using the instructions in Appendix B: Back Up and Restore QuickBooks Files. After restoring, update the company name to YourName Exercise 5.1 Rock Castle Construction.

E5.1.2 Add New Customer

1. Add the following customer to the Customer List.

Customer	**Merriman, Angel**
Address Info:	
First Name	**Angel**
Last Name	**Merriman**
Main Phone	**415-555-7579**
Address	**623 Thorsmork Road** **Bayshore, CA 94326**
Payment Settings:	
Account No.	**12736**
Payment Terms	**Net 30**
Preferred Delivery	**E-mail**
Preferred Payment Method	**VISA**
Credit LImit	**20,000**
Sales Tax Settings:	
Tax Code	**Tax**
Tax Item	**San Tomas**
Additional Info:	
Customer Type	**Residential**

2. **Close** the New Customer window

E5.1.3 Add New Job

Add a new job for Angel Merriman.

1. Add the new Angel Merriman job using the following information.

Job Name	**Door Replacement**
Job Description	**Interior Door Replacement**
Job Type	**Repairs**
Job Status	**Closed**
Start Date	**12/17/2024**
Projected End	**12/17/2024**
End Date	**12/17/2024**

E5.1.4 Customer List

1. **Sort** the Customer List. (Hint: Right-click > Re-sort List.)

2. Export to **Excel** or **print** the Customer List

E5.1.5 Back Up Exercise 5.1

Save a backup of your Exercise file using the file name: **YourName Exercise 5.1 Backup.QBB**.
See Appendix B: Back Up and Restore QuickBooks Files for instructions.

Exercise 5.2 Invoice

 Rock Castle Construction

E5.2.1 QuickBooks File

If you will be using the same computer and the same QBW file:

1. Select your **QBW file**.

2. Update the company name to **YourName Exercise 5.2 Rock Castle Construction** by selecting **Company Menu > My Company**.

> If you are not using the same computer that you used for Chapter 5 and Exercise 5.1, you will need to restore your prior Backup.QBB file using the instructions in Appendix B: Back Up and Restore QuickBooks Files. After restoring, update the company name to YourName Exercise 5.2 Rock Castle Construction.

E5.2.2 Create Invoice

Create an invoice for Angel Merriman for the interior door replacement.

1. Create an invoice for an interior door replacement using the following information:

Customer: Job	**Merriman, Angel: Door Replacement**
Customer Template	**Rock Castle Invoice**
Date	**12/17/2024**
Invoice No.	**1101**

Items
- **1 Wood Door: Interior @ $72.00**
- **1 Hardware: Standard Doorknob @ 30.00**
- **Installation Labor: 3 hours @ $35.00**

2. Select the **Save** icon

3. Select the **Reports** tab

4. Select the **Transaction Journal** icon

5. Export the Transaction Journal report to **Excel** or **print** the report

6. **Close** the Transaction Journal and the Invoice windows

E5.2.3 Back Up Exercise 5.2

Save a backup of your Exercise file using the file name: **YourName Exercise 5.2 Backup.QBB**. See Appendix B: Back Up and Restore QuickBooks Files for instructions.

Exercise 5.3 Customer Credit

 Rock Castle Construction

BACKSTORY

"It's time you learned how to record a credit to a customer's account." Mr. Castle groans, then rubbing his temples, he continues, *"Ms. Merriman called earlier today to tell us she was very pleased with her new bathroom door. However, she ordered locking hardware for the door, and standard hardware with no lock was installed instead. Although she appreciates our prompt service, she would like a lock on her bathroom door. We sent a workman over to her house, and when the hardware was replaced, she paid the bill.*

"We need to record a credit to her account for the standard hardware and then record a charge for the locking hardware set. And we won't charge her for the labor to change the hardware."

E5.3.1 QuickBooks File

If you will be using the same computer and the same QBW file:

1. Select your **QBW file**.

2. Update the company name to **YourName Exercise 5.3 Rock Castle Construction** by selecting **Company Menu > My Company**.

> If you are not using the same computer that you used for Chapter 5, Exercise 5.1 and Exercise 5.2, you will need to restore your latest prior Backup.QBB file using the instructions in Appendix B: Back Up and Restore QuickBooks files. After restoring, update the company name to YourName Exercise 5.3 Rock Castle Construction.

E5.3.2 Record Customer Credit

Record a credit to Ms. Merriman's account for the $30.00 she was previously charged for standard door hardware by completing the following steps:

1.   Click the **Refunds and Credits** icon in the Customers section of the Home Page

2.   Select Customer and Job: **Merriman, Angel: Door Replacement**

3.   Select Template: **Custom Credit Memo**. Credit No. 1102 should automatically appear.

4.   Select Date: **12/20/2024**

5.   Select Item: **Hardware Standard Doorknobs**

6.   Enter Quantity: **1**

7.   Select the **Save** icon

8.   When the Available Credit window appears, select **Apply to an invoice**. If an Apply Credit to Invoices window appears, select the credit of $32.33 for Invoice 1101, then select Done.

9.   Select **Reports** tab > **Transaction Journal**

10.   Export the Transaction Journal report to **Excel** or **print** the report

11.   **Close** the Transaction Journal and the Create Credit Memos/Refunds windows

E5.3.3 Create Invoice

1.   Create a new invoice (Invoice No. 1103) for Angel Merriman: Door Replacement on 12/20/2024 to record the charges for the interior door locking hardware

2.   Select the **Save** icon

3.   Select the **Reports** tab > **Transaction Journal**

4.   Export the Transaction Journal report to **Excel** or **print** the report

5.   **Close** the Transaction Journal and the Invoice windows

E5.3.4 Back Up Exercise 5.3

Save a backup of your Exercise file using the file name: **YourName Exercise 5.3 Backup.QBB**. See Appendix B: Back Up and Restore QuickBooks Files for instructions.

Exercise 5.4 Receive Customer Payments

 Rock Castle Construction

BACKSTORY

"Oops! Almost forgot to give you this," Rock Castle says as he drops a scrap of paper into your inbox. In Mr. Castle's handwriting, the paper contains the following: *On 12/20/2024 Angel Merriman prepaid $223.53 for door replacement using her VISA credit card.*

E5.4.1 QuickBooks File

If you will be using the same computer and the same QBW file:

1. Select your **QBW file**.

2. Update the company name to **YourName Exercise 5.4 Rock Castle Construction** by selecting **Company Menu > My Company**.

> If you are not using the same computer that you used for Chapter 5, Exercise 5.1, Exercise 5.2 and Exercise 5.3, you will need to restore your latest prior Backup.QBB file using the instructions in Appendix B: Back Up and Restore QuickBooks files. After restoring, update the company name to YourName Exercise 5.4 Rock Castle Construction.

E5.4.2 Receive Payment

Record the payment received from Angel Merriman for the net amount due for the door replacement.

1. Record Ms. Merriman's payment for the door replacement by VISA credit card for $223.53 on 12/20/2024.

   Card No.   **4444-5555-6666-7777**

   Exp. Date   **07/2025**

2. Select **Save & New**

3. Select the **Find** back arrow to display the customer payment just recorded

4. From the Receive Payments onscreen form, select the **Reports** tab > **Transaction Journal**

5. Export the Transaction Journal report to **Excel** or **print** the report

6. **Close** the Transaction Journal and the Receive Payments windows

E5.4.3 Back Up Exercise 5.4

Save a backup of your Exercise file using the file name: **YourName Exercise 5.4 Backup.QBB**. See Appendix B: Back Up and Restore QuickBooks Files for instructions.

Exercise 5.5 Make Deposits

 Rock Castle Construction

E5.5.1 QuickBooks File

If you will be using the same computer and the same QBW file:

1. Select your **QBW file**.

2. Update the company name to **YourName Exercise 5.5 Rock Castle Construction** by selecting **Company Menu > My Company**.

> If you are not using the same computer that you used for prior Chapter 5 and Exercises, you will need to restore your latest prior Backup.QBB file using the instructions in Appendix B: Back Up and Restore QuickBooks files. After restoring, update the company name to YourName Exercise 5.5 Rock Castle Construction.

E5.5.2 Make Deposit

1. On 12/20/2024, record the deposit from Angel Merriman's payment for $223.53

2. Select the **Save** icon at the top of the Make Deposits window

3. Select the **Journal** icon to display the journal entry to QuickBooks created behind the screen for the deposit

4. Export to **Excel** or **print** the Transaction Journal

5. **Close** the Transaction Journal and the Make Deposits windows

E5.5.3 Deposit Detail Report

1. Export to **Excel** or **print** the Deposit Detail report for 12/20/2024

E5.5.4 Back Up Exercise 5.5

Save a backup of your Exercise file using the file name: **YourName Exercise 5.5 Backup.QBB**. See Appendix B: Back Up and Restore QuickBooks Files for instructions.

Exercise 5.6 Customer Reports

 Rock Castle Construction

In this exercise, we create additional customer reports that a business might find useful.

E5.6.1 QuickBooks File

If you will be using the same computer and the same QBW file:

1. Select your **QBW file**.

2. Update the company name to **YourName Exercise 5.6 Rock Castle Construction** by selecting **Company Menu > My Company**.

> If you are not using the same computer that you used for prior Chapter 5 and Exercises, you will need to restore your latest prior Backup.QBB file using the instructions in Appendix B: Back Up and Restore QuickBooks files. After restoring, update the company name to YourName Exercise 5.6 Rock Castle Construction.

E5.6.2 Average Days to Pay Summary

Prepare the Average Days to Pay Summary report for Rock Castle Construction as follows.

1. From the Report Center, select **Customers & Receivables**

2. Select **Average Days to Pay Summary** report

3. Select Dates: **All**

4. Export to **Excel** or **print** the Average Days to Pay Summary report

5. **Highlight** how many days on average it takes for a customer to pay Rock Castle Construction

E5.6.3 Transaction List by Customer

Prepare a Transaction List by Customer report as follows.

1. From the Report Center, select **Customers & Receivables**

2. Select **Transaction List by Customer** report

3. Select Dates **From: 12/15/2024 To: 12/20/2024**

4. Export to **Excel** or **print** the report

E5.6.4 Journal

Prepare the Journal as follows.

1. From the Report Center, select **Accountant and Taxes > Journal**

2. Select Dates **From: 12/17/2024 To: 12/20/2024**

3. Export to **Excel** or **print** the Journal

E5.6.5 Back Up Exercise 5.6

Save a backup of your Exercise file using the file name: **YourName Exercise 5.6 Backup.QBB**. See Appendix B: Back Up and Restore QuickBooks Files for instructions.

Project 5.1

Larry's Landscaping 🌴

As an accounting consultant for Larry's Landscaping complete the following to enter customers and sales transactions for the company.

💡 **Troubleshooting QuickBooks and Correcting Errors are crucial QuickBooks skill to acquire. Troubleshooting resources include:**
- **www.My-QuickBooks.com > QuickBooks Troubleshooting (QT) Tips**
- **Chapter 17, Quick Review Guide, contains tips on Correcting Errors**
- **Appendix D, QuickBooks Troubleshooting (QT), provides you with an effective troubleshooting process**

🌐 QuickBooks SatNav

The objective of Project 5.1 is to facilitate your mastery of QuickBooks Desktop. As shown in the following QuickBooks SatNav, Project 5.1 focuses on QuickBooks Customers and Sales Transactions.

🌐 QuickBooks SatNav

⚙️ QuickBooks Settings

⚙️ Company Settings
⚙️ Chart of Accounts

💰 QuickBooks Transactions

💰 Banking
💰 Customers & Sales
💰 Vendors & Expenses
💰 Employees & Payroll

📊 QuickBooks Reports

📊 Reports

P5.1.1 QuickBooks File

1. Use either your QuickBooks Company file (QBW) or restore the backup file (QBB) that you completed for Project 4.1. (If you have issues with your QuickBooks file, contact your instructor.)

2. Update the Company Name to: **YourName Project 5.1 Larry's Landscaping**

P5.1.2 Sales Receipts

1. Enter the following sales receipt for Larry's Landscaping.

Template	**Sales Receipt - Retail**
Date	**12/20/2024**
Customer	**Dave Perry**
Item	**Fertilizer (Lawn & Garden)**
Quantity	**45**
Payment	**Check (No. 622)**

2. Select the **Save** icon

3. Select the **Reports** tab > **Transaction Journal**

4. Export the Transaction Journal report to **Excel** or **print** the report

5. Enter the following sales receipt for Larry's Landscaping.

Template	**Sales Receipt - Retail**
Date	**12/22/2024**
Customer	**Jean Paulney**
Item	**Rocks (Garden Rocks)**
Quantity	**22**
Payment	**Cash**

6. Select the **Save** icon

7. Select the **Reports** tab > **Transaction Journal**

8. Export the Transaction Journal report to **Excel** or **print** the report

P5.1.3 Invoices

1. Enter the following invoice for Larry's Landscaping.

Date	**12/22/2024**
Customer	**Anne Loomis**
Item	**Pest Control Service**
Quantity	**5**
Price Each	**$60.00**
Tax	**Non**

2. Select the **Save** icon

3. Select the **Reports** tab > **Transaction Journal**

4. Export the Transaction Journal report to **Excel** or **print** the report

5. Enter the following invoice for Larry's Landscaping.

Date	**12/22/2024**
Customer	**Russell Chiropractic**
Item	**Weekly Gardening Services**
Quantity	**3**
Price Each	**$75.00**
Tax	**Non**

6. Select the **Save** icon

7. Select the **Reports** tab > **Transaction Journal**

8. Export the Transaction Journal report to **Excel** or **print** the report

9. Enter the following invoice for Larry's Landscaping.

Date	**12/22/2024**
Customer	**Gwen Price**
Item	**Tree Removal**
Quantity	**8**
Price Each	**$90.00**
Tax	**Non**

10. Select the **Save** icon

11. Select the **Reports** tab > **Transaction Journal**

12. Export the Transaction Journal report to **Excel** or **print** the report

13. **Close** the Transaction Journal and the Invoice windows

P5.1.4 Receive Payments

1. Record the following customer payment received by Larry's Landscaping.

Date	**12/19/2024**
Customer	**Susie Rummens**
Invoice No.	**No. 128**
Amount	**$1438.56**
Payment Method	**Check (No. 321)**

2. Select **Save & New**. Use the **Find** arrow to display the payment just recorded.

3. Select the **Reports** tab > **Transaction Journal**

4. Export the Transaction Journal report to **Excel** or **print** the report

5. Record the following customer payment received by Larry's Landscaping.

Date	**12/20/2024**
Customer	**Bob Heldt**
Invoice No.	**No. 137**
Amount	**$101.82**
Payment Method	**Check (No. 823)**

6. Select **Save & New**. Use the **Find** arrow to display the payment just recorded.

7.   Select the **Reports** tab > **Transaction Journal**

8.   Export the Transaction Journal report to **Excel** or **print** the report

9.   Record the following customer payment received by Larry's Landscaping.

Date	**12/22/2024**
Customer	**Mike Balak**
Invoice No.	**No. 116**
Amount	**$180**
Payment Method	**Check (No. 1281)**

10.   Select **Save & New**. Use the **Find** arrow to display the payment just recorded.

11.   Select the **Reports** tab > **Transaction Journal**

12.   Export the Transaction Journal report to **Excel** or **print** the report

13.   **Close** the Transaction Journal and the Receive Payments windows

P5.1.5 Make Deposits

1.   Record the following deposits transferring funds from Undeposited Funds to the Checking account.

Deposit Date	**12/22/2024**
Customer	**Jean Paulney**
Amount	**$228.44**

Deposit Date	**12/22/2024**
Customer	**Susie Rummens**
Amount	**$1,438.56**

Deposit Date	**12/22/2024**
Customer	**Bob Heldt**
Amount	**$101.82**

Deposit Date	**12/22/2024**
Customer	**Dave Perry**
Amount	**$90.58**

Deposit Date	**12/22/2024**
Customer	**Mike Balak**
Amount	**$180.00**

2. Select the **Save** icon at the top of the Make Deposits window

3. Select the **Journal** icon to display the Transaction Journal

4. Export to **Excel** or **print** the Transaction Journal

5. **Close** the Transaction Journal and the Make Deposits windows

P5.1.6 Reports

1. Export to **Excel** the Journal report for December 19 through 22, 2024

2. Export to **Excel** the Open Invoices report for Larry's Landscaping for December 22, 2024

3. Export to **Excel** the Deposit Detail report for December 19 through 22, 2024

P5.1.7 Back Up Project 5.1

Save a backup of your Project file using the file name: **YourName Project 5.1 Backup.QBB**. See Appendix B: Back Up and Restore QuickBooks Files for instructions.

Design elements: Dog icon: ©josep perianes jorba/Shutterstock; paint roller icon: ©Netti Buletti/Shutterstock; other icons/symbols: ©Carboxylase/Shutterstock

Chapter 6

Vendors and Expenses

 Rock Castle Construction

BACKSTORY

Mr. Castle walks up to your desk with another stack of paperwork. At this point, you are wondering if he has file cabinets full of never-ending paper just waiting to bring it to you one stack at a time.

Setting the stack onto your desk, Mr. Castle jovially says, *"Now that you are almost caught up with customers and sales transactions, here are some vendor transactions for you. To make it a bit easier on you, I've been thinking we can work on inventory later. Let's just focus on getting caught up on vendors and expense transactions and save inventory transactions until later.*

"How does that sound to you? We don't want to overwhelm you... not just yet anyway," he laughs.

"Absolutely Mr Castle." You nod in agreement.

Chapter 6

Learning Objectives

Chapter 6 explores QuickBooks vendors and expenses transactions, such as entering bills and paying bills. In this chapter, you will learn about the following topics:

- Vendor Navigation
- Vendor List
  - View Vendor List
  - Add New Vendor
  - Export Vendor List
- Vendor Transactions
- Enter Bills
- Pay Bills
- Vendor Reports
  - Accounts Payable Reports: How Much Do We Owe?
- Accounting Essentials: Vendor Transactions, Accounts Payable, and 1099s

Section 6.1

 QuickBooks SatNav

QuickBooks SatNav is your satellite navigation for QuickBooks, assisting you in navigating QuickBooks

QuickBooks SatNav divides QuickBooks into three processes:

1. **QuickBooks Settings.** This includes Company Settings when setting up a new QuickBooks company and the Company Chart of Accounts.

2. **QuickBooks Transactions.** This includes recording transactions in QuickBooks. Transaction types can be categorized as Banking, Customers and Sales, Vendors and Expenses, and Employees and Payroll. In basic terms, recording transactions involves recording money in and money out.

3. **QuickBooks Reports.** QuickBooks reports are the output of the system, such as commonly used financial statements of Balance Sheet, Income Statement, and Statement of Cash Flows.

Chapter 6 focuses on vendors and expenses transactions as shown in the following QuickBooks SatNav.

QuickBooks SatNav

⚙ QuickBooks Settings

⚙ Company Settings
⚙ Chart of Accounts

💰 QuickBooks Transactions

💰 Banking
💰 Customers & Sales
💰 Vendors & Expenses	*Enter Bills > Pay Bills*
💰 Employees & Payroll

📊 QuickBooks Reports

📊 Reports

💡 **Accounting Essentials appear at the end of the chapter. Tip: Preview Accounting Essentials** <u>before</u> **completing the chapter and then review Accounting Essentials** <u>after</u> **completing the chapter.**

Section 6.2

Start QuickBooks and Open QuickBooks Company

START QUICKBOOKS

To start QuickBooks software, click the **QuickBooks** icon on your desktop. If a QuickBooks icon does not appear on your desktop, from Microsoft® Windows® click **Start** button > **QuickBooks** > **QuickBooks Premier Accountant Edition**.

> **QuickBooks Accountant** includes all the features of QuickBooks Pro plus features for client services. If you use QuickBooks Pro, your screens may appear slightly different than those appearing in this text.

RESTORE QBB STARTER FILE

Restore the QBB Starter file for this chapter as follows.

1   Select **File** > **Restore**

2   Using the directions in Appendix B: Back Up and Restore QuickBooks Files, restore **CHAPTER 6 STARTER.QBB**

3   After restoring, update the company name to **YourName Chapter 6 Rock Castle Construction** by selecting **Company Menu** > **My Company**

Section 6.3

Vendor Navigation

The QuickBooks Home Page contains a Vendors section that displays icons used for vendor functions. If necessary click the **Home** icon in the Navigation Bar to display the Home Page.

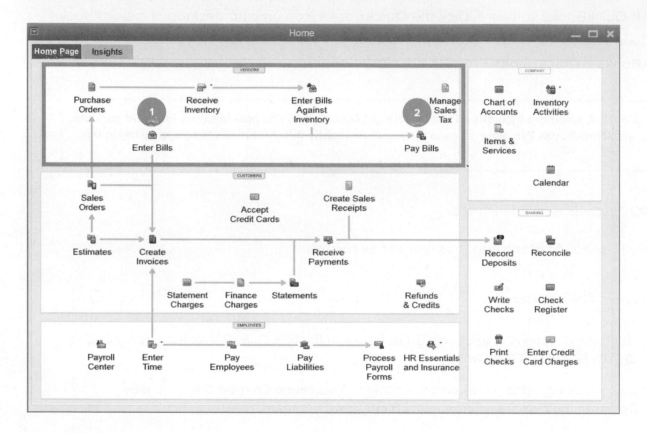

The Vendors section of the Home Page is a flowchart of vendor transactions. In this chapter we are going to focus on the following vendor transactions:

1. **Enter Bills.** Use the Enter Bills window to record bills for services received. Examples include rent, utilities expense, insurance expense, and accounting and professional services. QuickBooks will record an obligation (accounts payable liability) to pay the bill later.

2. **Pay Bills.** Use the Pay Bills window to select the bills that are due and you are ready to pay.

Section 6.4

Vendor List

The first step in working with vendor transactions is to enter vendor information in the Vendor List.

The Vendor List contains information for each vendor, such as address, telephone number, and credit terms. Vendor information is entered in the Vendor List and then QuickBooks automatically transfers the vendor information to the appropriate forms, such as purchase orders and checks. This feature enables you to enter vendor information only once in QuickBooks instead of entering the vendor information each time a form is prepared.

QuickBooks considers a vendor to be any individual or organization that provides products or services to your company. QuickBooks considers all of the following to be vendors:

- Suppliers from whom you buy inventory or supplies
- Service companies that provide services to your company, such as cleaning services or landscaping services
- Financial institutions, such as banks, that provide financial services including checking accounts and loans
- Tax agencies such as the IRS. The IRS is considered a vendor because you pay taxes to the IRS
- Utility and telephone companies

VIEW VENDOR LIST

To view the Vendor List for Rock Castle Construction:

1 Click **Vendors** in the Navigation Bar

2 Click the **Vendors** tab. The following Vendor List appears listing vendors with whom Rock Castle Construction does business. The Vendor List also displays the balance currently owed each vendor.

3 To view additional information about a vendor, click the vendor's name, and Vendor Information will appear on the right side of the Vendor Center.

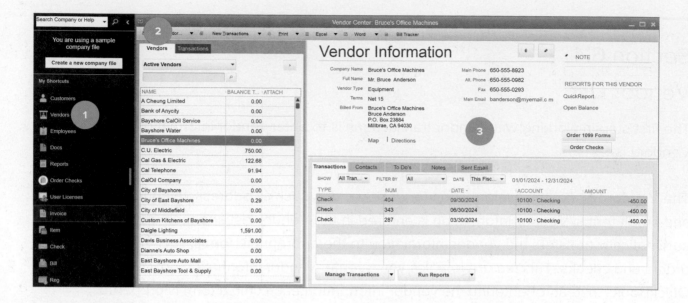

ADD NEW VENDOR

Rock Castle Construction needs to add a new vendor, Andre Window & Door, to the Vendor List.

To add a new vendor to the Vendor List:

1 Click the **New Vendor** button at the top of the Vendor Center

2 Click **New Vendor** on the drop-down menu

3 Select the **Address Info** tab in the New Vendor window. Enter the following information.

Vendor Name	**Andre Window & Door**
Company Name	**Andre Window & Door**
Full Name	**Andre LaFortune**
Main Phone	**415-555-1955**
Mobile	**415-555-1988**
Main Email	**andre@windowdoor.com**
Address	**27 Beach Street** **Bayshore, CA 94326**

4   Select the **Payment Settings** tab and enter the following information

Account No.	**58101**
Payment Terms	**Net 15**
Print on Check as	**Andre Window & Door**

5   Select the **Tax Settings** tab and enter the following information

Vendor Tax ID	**37-1958101**
Vendor Eligible for 1099	**Yes**

6   Select the **Additional Info** tab and enter the following information

Vendor Type	**Materials**

7   Click **OK** to add the new vendor to Rock Castle Construction's Vendor List and close the New Vendor window

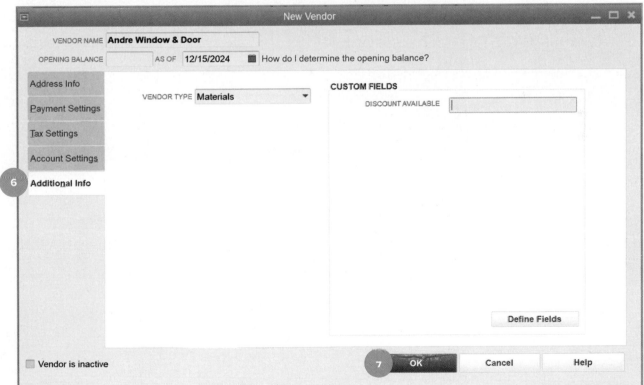

> To edit vendor information later, simply click the vendor's name in the Vendor List window. The vendor information will appear on the right side of the Vendor Center. Click the Edit Vendor button, make the necessary changes in the Edit Vendor window that appears, and then click OK to close the Edit Vendor window.

> The Vendor List can also be imported from Excel into QuickBooks.

EXPORT VENDOR LIST

C6.4.1 Vendor List. Export the Vendor List as follows:

1 From Vendor Center, select **Excel > Export Vendor List**

2 Select **Replace an existing worksheet**

3 Export the Vendor List to **Excel**

Section 6.5

Vendor Transactions

After creating a Vendor List, you are ready to enter vendor transactions. There are two basic ways to enter vendor transactions using QuickBooks.

1. **Enter Bills > Pay Bills.** This is used to record services, such as utilities or accounting services. After the bill is entered, it is paid when it is due.

2. **Enter Purchase Orders > Receive Inventory > Enter Bills Against Inventory > Pay Bills.** This approach is used to record the purchase of inventory items. The purchase order provides a record of the items ordered.

This chapter focuses on entering vendor transactions for services using the Enter Bills and Pay Bills onscreen forms. The next chapter covers how to record the purchase of inventory items using Purchase Orders.

Recording bills for services, such as utilities, in QuickBooks requires two steps:

1 **Enter Bills.** Record bills received for services.

2 **Pay Bills.** Select bills to pay.

Section 6.6

Enter Bills

To record bills related to services instead of inventory, use the Enter Bills icon. Expenses that can be recorded using the Enter Bills window include utilities, insurance, and rent.

ENTER BILLS FOR SERVICES

To enter bills for expenses related to services received:

1. Click the **Enter Bills** icon in the Vendors section of the Home Page

2. When the Enter Bills window appears, click the **Expenses** tab

3. Enter the following information for Rock Castle's water bill in the Enter Bills window

Vendor	**Bayshore Water**
Date	**12/24/2024**
Amount Due	**$86.00**
Terms	**Net 30**
Account	**65130: Water**

4. Select **Save** and leave the Enter Bills window open

C6.6.1 Bill Journal Entry. To view the journal entry that QuickBooks created behind the screen for the bill entered and saved using the Enter Bills onscreen form, complete the following steps.

1. From the Enter Bills onscreen form, select the **Reports** tab

2. Select the **Transaction Journal** icon

3. Export the Transaction Journal report to **Excel** or **print** the report. Notice that the entry shows a debit (increase) to Water Expense and a credit (increase) to Accounts Payable for the amount of the entered bill.

4. **Close** the Transaction Journal window

5. **Close** the Enter Bills window

The next time you pay bills in QuickBooks, the water bill will appear on the list of bills to pay.

RECEIPT MANAGEMENT

QuickBooks Desktop 2021 rolled out a new receipt management feature. Receipts are important source documents for some purchases from vendors. For example, if you are at the local office supply store to pick up items for your business, the receipt for the purchase is easily lost or misplaced before you can return to your office to enter the transaction in QuickBooks Desktop.

The QuickBooks Desktop mobile app permits you to take a photo of the receipt with your phone or mobile device to capture the receipt data. The QuickBooks Desktop app then syncs with your QuickBooks Desktop. When you return to QuickBooks Desktop on your computer, you can review and attach the digital receipt to your expense (bill) transactions in QuickBooks Desktop.

To use the new QuickBooks Receipt Management feature requires the use of the QuickBooks Mobile app and a QuickBooks account.

To access the Receipt Management feature from QuickBooks:

1 Select **Vendors** from the Menu Bar

2 Select **Receipt Management**. Close the Receipt Management window. Refer to QuickBooks Help for more information about the new Receipt Management feature.

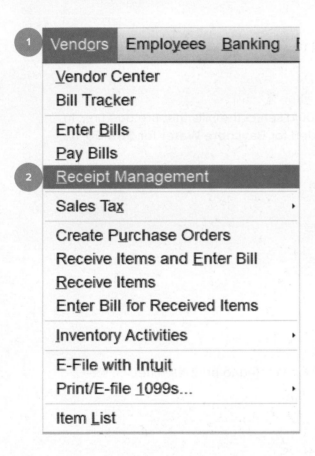

Section 6.7

Pay Bills

After entering a bill into QuickBooks, the next step is to pay the bill.

SELECT BILLS TO PAY

To select the bills to pay:

1 Click the **Pay Bills** icon in the Vendors section of the Home Page

2 Select Show bills: **Show all bills**

3 Select the bills you want to pay. Typically, you would select the bills that are due first. In this case, however, select bill that you just recorded for **Bayshore Water** for **$86.00**. If necessary, scroll down to view this bill.

4 In the Payment section, select: Date: **12/24/2024**

5 Select Method: **Check**

6 Select: **To be printed**

7 Select Account: **Checking**

8 Click **Pay Selected Bills**

9 When the Payment Summary window displays, if we wanted to print the checks, we would select Print Checks. In this case, select **Done**.

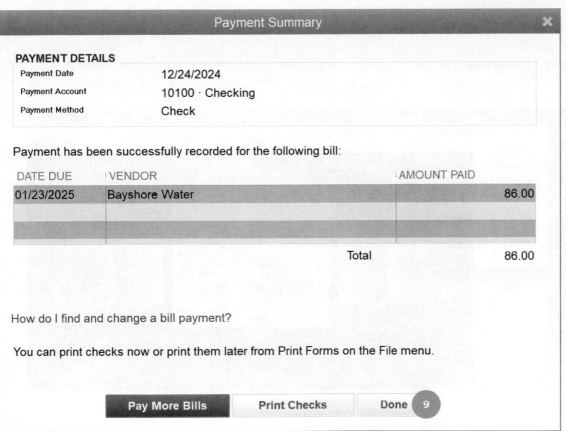

To pay by debit card, **select Method: Check > Assign check number. Then use DC (for debit card) as the check number.**

C6.7.1 Pay Bills Journal Entries. Another way to view the behind the screen journal entry is to use the Report Center. To view the journal entries that QuickBooks created behind the screen when bills were entered and selected for payment, complete the following steps.

1   From the Navigation Bar, select **Reports**

2   Select **Accountant & Taxes**

3   Select **Journal**

4   Select Date: **12/24/2024**

5   Export the Journal report to **Excel** or **print** the report

6   Notice that the first journal entry records the expense with a debit and records an account payable of $86.00 with a credit. The second journal entry records paying the bill with a debit (decreases) Accounts Payable and a credit (decreases) the Checking account for $86.00.

7   **Close** the Journal window

Section 6.8

Vendor Reports

QuickBooks provides vendor reports to answer the following questions:

- How much do we owe? (Accounts Payable reports)
- How much have we purchased? (Purchase reports)
- How much inventory do we have? (Inventory reports)

QuickBooks offers several different ways to access vendor reports:

1. **Vendor Center.** Summarizes vendor information in one location (Access the Vendor Center by clicking the Vendors icon on the Navigation Bar.)

2. **Report Center.** Permits you to locate reports by type of report (Click the Reports icon on the Navigation Bar, then see Vendors & Payables, Purchases, and Inventory reports).

3. **Reports Menu.** Reports are grouped by type of report (See Vendors & Payables, Purchases, and Inventory reports).

ACCOUNTS PAYABLE REPORTS: HOW MUCH DO WE OWE?

Accounts payable consists of amounts that your company is obligated to pay in the future. Accounts Payable reports tell you how much you owe vendors and when amounts are due.

The following Accounts Payable reports provide information useful when tracking amounts owed vendors:

1. Accounts Payable Aging Summary
2. Accounts Payable Aging Detail
3. Unpaid Bills Detail

The Accounts Payable Aging Summary summarizes accounts payable balances by the age of the account. This report helps to track any past due bills as well as provides information about bills that will be due shortly.

Although you can access the vendor reports in several different ways, we will access this report from the Report Center.

C6.8.1 A/P Aging Summary. To prepare the A/P Aging Summary report:

1 Select **Reports** in the Navigation Bar

2 Select: **Vendors & Payables**

3 Select: **A/P Aging Summary**

4 Select Date: **12/24/2024**

5 Select **Run**

6 Export to **Excel** or **print** the report. **Highlight** the vendors and amounts of any past due accounts payable

7 **Close** the A/P Aging Summary window

Section 6.9

Back Up QuickBooks Files

BACK UP QBB

Save a backup of your Chapter 6 file using the file name: **YourName Chapter 6 Backup.QBB**. For further instructions on how to back up your file, *see* Appendix B: Back Up and Restore QuickBooks Files.

QBW WORKFLOW

If you are using the QBW approach, leave your QBW file open and proceed directly to Exercise 6.1.

QBB RESTORE

If you are using the QBB approach and ending your computer session now, close your QBW file and exit QuickBooks. When you restart, you will restore your backup file to complete Exercise 6.1.

Section 6.10

Accounting Essentials: Vendors Transactions, Accounts Payable, and 1099s

Accounting Essentials summarize important foundational accounting knowledge that may be useful when using QuickBooks

What are accounts payable?

- Accounts payable consists of amounts that our business is obligated to pay in the future. When our business makes purchases on credit, our business is promising to pay that amount in the future.
- When a purchase is made and recorded as a bill, accounts payable is increased by a credit. When the bill is paid, the accounts payable is decreased by a debit.

How can a business track accounts payables to make certain it is paying on time?

- Accounts Payable reports provide information to track amounts we owe vendors. An Accounts Payable Aging report summarizes accounts payable balances by the age of the account. This report helps us to track how much we owe vendors and when amounts are due, including the age of past due bills.

What is a 1099 and when does my company need to prepare 1099s?

- IRS Form 1099 must be completed for sole proprietorships and partnerships to which we paid $600 or more for services in a year. The vendor's Tax ID No. is required to complete the 1099. QuickBooks can assist in tracking amounts and preparing 1099s for appropriate vendors. To learn more about preparing 1099s, see www.irs.gov.

Exercise 6.1 Enter Bills

 Rock Castle Construction

BACKSTORY

When you arrive at work, you decide to sort through the papers stacked in the corner of your cubicle. You discover another unpaid utility bill amid the clutter.

E6.1.1 QuickBooks File

If you will be using the same computer and the same Chapter 6.QBW file:

1. If your Chapter 6.QBW file is not already open, open it by selecting **File > Open Previous Company**. Select your **Chapter 6.QBW file**. If a QuickBooks Information window appears with a message about the sample company file, click **OK**.

2. Update the company name to **YourName Exercise 6.1 Rock Castle Construction** by selecting **Company Menu > My Company**.

> **If you are not using the same computer that you used for Chapter 6, you will need to restore your Chapter 6 Backup.QBB file using the instructions in Appendix B: Back Up and Restore QuickBooks Files. After restoring, update the company name to YourName Exercise 6.1 Rock Castle Construction.**

E6.1.2 Enter Bills

Use the Enter Bills icon in the Vendors section of the Home Page to enter the following bill.

1. Enter the following utility bill for Rock Castle Construction.

Vendor	**Cal Telephone**
Date	**12/26/2024**
Amount Due	**$77.00**
Account	**65120: Telephone**

2. Select the **Save** icon at the top of the Enter Bills window

3. Select the **Reports** tab

4. Select the **Transaction Journal** icon

5. Export the Transaction Journal report to **Excel** or **print** the report

6. **Close** the Transaction Journal and the Enter Bills windows

E6.1.3 Back Up Exercise 6.1

Save a backup of your Exercise file using the file name: **YourName Exercise 6.1 Backup.QBB**. See Appendix B: Back Up and Restore QuickBooks Files for instructions.

Exercise 6.2 Pay Bills

 Rock Castle Construction

E6.2.1 QuickBooks File

If you will be using the same computer and the same QBW file:

1. Select your **QBW file**.

2. Update the company name to **YourName Exercise 6.2 Rock Castle Construction** by selecting **Company Menu > My Company**.

> If you are not using the same computer that you used for Chapter 6 and Exercise 6.1, you will need to restore your latest prior Backup.QBB file using the instructions in Appendix B: Back Up and Restore QuickBooks files. After restoring, update the company name to YourName Exercise 6.2 Rock Castle Construction.

E6.2.2 Pay Bills

1. On **12/26/2024**, pay by check the Cal Telephone bill that you entered. (Hint: Select Show all bills.)

2. From the Navigation Bar, select **Reports > Accountant & Taxes > Journal**

3. Select Date: **12/26/2024**

4. Export the Journal report to **Excel** or **print** the report

5. **Close** the Journal window

E6.2.3 Back Up Exercise 6.2

Save a backup of your Exercise file using the file name: **YourName Exercise 6.2 Backup.QBB**. See Appendix B: Back Up and Restore QuickBooks Files for instructions.

Exercise 6.3 Vendor Reports

 Rock Castle Construction

E6.3.1 QuickBooks File

If you will be using the same computer and the same QBW file:

1. Select your **QBW file**.

2. Update the company name to **YourName Exercise 6.3 Rock Castle Construction** by selecting **Company Menu > My Company**.

> If you are not using the same computer that you used for Chapter 6, Exercise 6.1 and Exercise 6.2, you will need to restore your latest prior Backup.QBB file using the instructions in Appendix B: Back Up and Restore QuickBooks files. After restoring, update the company name to YourName Exercise 6.3 to Rock Castle Construction.

E6.3.2 Check Detail Report

To review the transactions you entered, print a Check Detail report as follows.

1. From the Report Center, select **Banking > Check Detail**

2. Select Date **From: 12/24/2024 To: 12/26/2024**

3. Export to **Excel** or **print** the report

4. **Close** the Check Detail window

E6.3.3 Accounts Payable Aging Detail Report

The Accounts Payable Aging report summarizes accounts payable balances by the age of the account.

1. From the Report Center, select **Vendors & Payables > A/P Aging Detail**

2. Select Date **12/26/2024**

3. Select **Run**

4. Export to **Excel** or **print** the report

5. **Highlight** the vendors and amounts of any past due accounts payable

6. **Close** the A/P Aging Detail window

E6.3.4 Back Up Exercise 6.3

Save a backup of your Exercise file using the file name: **YourName Exercise 6.3 Backup.QBB**. See Appendix B: Back Up and Restore QuickBooks Files for instructions.

PROJECT 6.1

Larry's Landscaping

As an accounting consultant for Larry's Landscaping complete the following to enter vendors and expenses transactions for the company.

> 💡 **Troubleshooting QuickBooks and Correcting Errors are crucial QuickBooks skill to acquire. Troubleshooting resources include:**
> - **www.My-QuickBooks.com > QuickBooks Troubleshooting (QT) Tips**
> - **Chapter 17, Quick Review Guide, contains tips on Correcting Errors**
> - **Appendix D, QuickBooks Troubleshooting (QT), provides you with an effective troubleshooting process**

🌐 QuickBooks SatNav

The objective of Project 6.1 is to facilitate your mastery of QuickBooks Desktop. As shown in the following QuickBooks SatNav, Project 6.1 focuses on QuickBooks Vendors and Expenses Transactions.

🌐 **QuickBooks SatNav**

⚙️ **QuickBooks Settings**

⚙️ Company Settings
⚙️ Chart of Accounts

💰 **QuickBooks Transactions**

💰 Banking	
💰 Customers & Sales	
💰 Vendors & Expenses	*Enter Bills > Pay Bills*
💰 Employees & Payroll	

📊 **QuickBooks Reports**

📊 Reports

P6.1.1 QuickBooks File

1. Use either your QuickBooks Company file (QBW) or restore the backup file (QBB) that you completed for Project 5.1. (If you have issues with your QuickBooks file, contact your instructor.)

2. Update the Company Name to: **YourName Project 6.1 Larry's Landscaping**

P6.1.2 Enter Bills

1. Use the Enter Bills icon to enter the following bill received by Larry's Landscaping.

Date	**12/23/2024**
Vendor	**Carole Design Media**
Account	**6000 Advertising Expense**
Terms	**Net 30**
Amount Due	**$450.00**

2. Select the **Save** icon

3. Select the **Reports** tab > **Transaction Journal**

4. Export the Transaction Journal report to **Excel** or **print** the report

5. Enter the following bill for Larry's Landscaping.

Date	**12/23/2024**
Vendor	**Brown Equipment Rental**
Account	**7120 Equipment Rental**
Terms	**Net 15**
Amount Due	**$960.00**

6. Select the **Save** icon

7. Select the **Reports** tab > **Transaction Journal**

8. Export the Transaction Journal report to **Excel** or **print** the report

9. Enter the following bill for Larry's Landscaping.

Date	**12/23/2024**
Vendor	**Campion Patrick, CPA**
Account	**7410 Accounting Expense**
Terms	**Net 30**
Amount Due	**$224**

10. Select the **Save** icon

11. Select the **Reports** tab > **Transaction Journal**

12. Export the Transaction Journal report to **Excel** or **print** the report

P6.1.3 Pay Bills

1. Pay the following bills for Larry's on 12/23/2024.

Vendor	Brown Equipment Rental
Amount Due	**$960.00**

Vendor	Carole Design Media
Amount Due	**$450.00**

Vendor	Campion, Patrick CPA
Amount Due	**$224.00**

Vendor	Townley Insurance Agency
Amount Due	**$427.62**

Vendor	Great Statewide Bank
Amount Due	**$699.12**

2. From the Navigation Bar, select **Reports > Accountant & Taxes > Journal**
3. Select Date: **12/23/2024**
4. Export the Journal report to **Excel** or **print** the report
5. **Close** the Journal window

P6.1.4 Reports

1. Export to **Excel** the Unpaid Bills Detail report for December 23, 2024
2. Export to **Excel** the Check Detail report for Larry's Landscaping for December 23, 2024
3. Export to **Excel** the Accounts Payable Aging Detail report as of December 23, 2024

P6.1.5 Back Up Project 6.1

Save a backup of your Project file using the file name: **YourName Project 6.1 Backup.QBB**.
See Appendix B: Back Up and Restore QuickBooks Files for instructions.

Design elements: Dog icon: ©josep perianes jorba/Shutterstock; paint roller icon: ©Netti Buletti/Shutterstock; other icons/symbols: ©Carboxylase/Shutterstock

Chapter 7

Inventory

Rock Castle Construction

BACKSTORY

As you work your way through stacks of paper in your desk's inbox, you hear Mr. Castle's rapid footsteps coming in your direction. He whips around the corner of your cubicle with another stack of papers in hand.

In his usual rapid-fire delivery, Mr. Castle begins, *"This is the way we do business."* He quickly sketches the following:

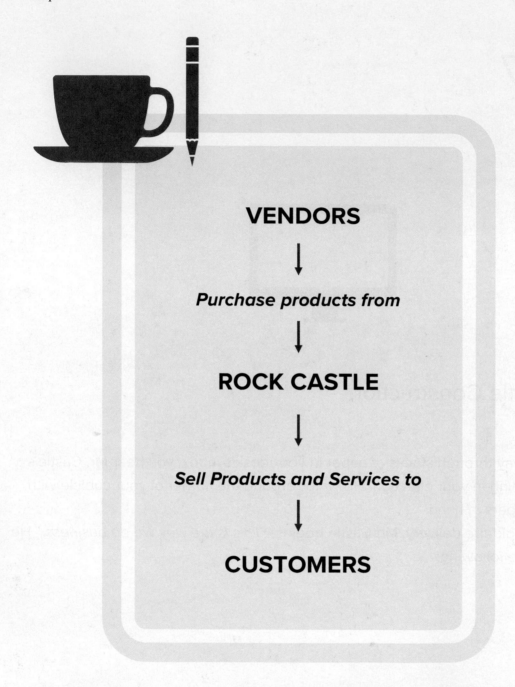

VENDORS

↓

Purchase products from

↓

ROCK CASTLE

↓

Sell Products and Services to

↓

CUSTOMERS

"We purchase products from our vendors and suppliers, and then we sell those products and provide services to our customers. We use QuickBooks to track the quantity and cost of items we purchase and sell."

Mr. Castle tosses the papers into your brand new inbox on your desk. *"Here are vendor and purchase transactions that need to be recorded."*

Mr. Castle races past, engaged in an intense conversation on his mobile phone.

Chapter 7
Learning Objectives

Chapter 7 explores using QuickBooks for inventory. In this chapter, you will learn about the following topics:

- Vendor and Customer Transactions
- Vendor Navigation
- Items & Services List
  - View Item List
  - Add New Item
  - Generate Item List
  - View Inventory Center
- Vendor Transactions
- Create Purchase Orders
- Receive Inventory
- Enter Bills Against Inventory
- Pay Bills
- Pay Sales Tax
- Vendor Reports
  - Purchase Reports: How Much Have We Purchased?
  - Inventory Reports: How Much Inventory Do We Have?
- Accounting Essentials: Inventory and Internal Control

Section 7.1

 ## QuickBooks SatNav

QuickBooks SatNav is your satellite navigation for QuickBooks, assisting you in navigating QuickBooks

QuickBooks SatNav divides QuickBooks into three processes:

1. **QuickBooks Settings.** This includes Company Settings when setting up a new QuickBooks company and the Company Chart of Accounts.

2. **QuickBooks Transactions.** This includes recording transactions in QuickBooks. Transaction types can be categorized as Banking, Customers and Sales, Vendors and Expenses, and Employees and Payroll. In basic terms, recording transactions involves recording money in and money out.

3. **QuickBooks Reports.** QuickBooks reports are the output of the system, such as commonly used financial statements of Balance Sheet, Income Statement, and Statement of Cash Flows.

Chapter 7 focuses on inventory which is a type of vendor and expense transaction as shown in the following QuickBooks SatNav.

 QuickBooks SatNav

⚙️ **QuickBooks Settings**

⚙️ Company Settings
⚙️ Chart of Accounts

💰 **QuickBooks Transactions**

💰 Banking	
💰 Customers & Sales	*Create Invoices > Receive Payments > Record Deposits*
💰 Vendors & Expenses	*PO > Receive Inventory > Enter Bills Inventory > Pay Bills*
💰 Employees & Payroll	

📊 **QuickBooks Reports**

📊 Reports

💡 **Accounting Essentials** appear at the end of the chapter. **Tip: Preview Accounting Essentials <u>before</u>** completing the chapter and then review Accounting Essentials <u>after</u> completing the chapter.

Section 7.2

Start QuickBooks and Open QuickBooks Company

START QUICKBOOKS

To start QuickBooks software, click the **QuickBooks** icon on your desktop. If a QuickBooks icon does not appear on your desktop, from Microsoft® Windows® click **Start** button > **QuickBooks** > **QuickBooks Premier Accountant Edition**.

> **QuickBooks Accountant** includes all the features of QuickBooks Pro plus features for client services. If you use QuickBooks Pro, your screens may appear slightly different than those appearing in this text.

RESTORE QBB STARTER FILE

Restore the QBB Starter file for this chapter as follows.

1 Select **File** > **Restore**

2 Using the directions in Appendix B: Back Up and Restore QuickBooks Files, restore **CHAPTER 7 STARTER.QBB**

3 After restoring, update the company name to **YourName Chapter 7 Rock Castle Construction** by selecting **Company Menu** > **My Company**

Section 7.3

Vendor and Customer Transactions

If our company is a merchandising business that buys and resells goods, then we must maintain inventory records to account for the items we purchase from vendors and resell to customers.

The following diagram summarizes vendor and customer transactions.

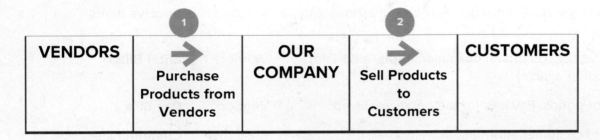

We can use QuickBooks for inventory to record:

1   **Vendor transactions**, including placing product orders, receiving products, and paying bills

2   **Customer transactions**, including recording sale of product on invoices and receiving customer payments

The following table summarizes how to record Rock Castle Construction's business operations using QuickBooks.

	Activity	Type	Record Using...
1	Record vendor information	Vendor	**Vendor List**
2	Record inventory information: Set up inventory records to track the quantity and cost of items purchased	Vendor	**Item List**
3	Order goods: Use purchase orders (POs) to order goods from vendors	Vendor	**Purchase Orders**
4	Receive goods: Record goods received as inventory	Vendor	**Receive Items**
5	Receive bill: Record an obligation to pay a bill later (Account Payable)	Vendor	**Enter Bills**
6	Pay for goods: Pay bills for the goods received	Vendor	**Pay Bills**
7	Record customer information	Customer	**Customer List**
8	Sell goods and bill customers: Record customer's promise to pay later (Account Receivable)	Customer	**Invoice**
9	Receive customer payment: Record cash collected and reduce customer's Account Receivable	Customer	**Receive Payments**
10	Deposit customers' payments in bank account	Customer	**Deposit**

Section 7.4

Vendor Navigation

After opening the company file for Rock Castle Construction, click **Home** in the Navigation Bar.

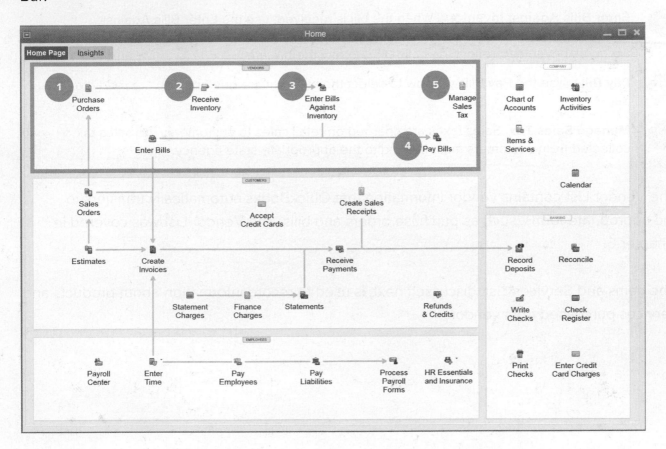

The Vendors section of the Home Page is a flowchart of vendor transactions. Chapter 6 covered how to enter bills for services, such as utilities or professional services. Chapter 7 covers how to use QuickBooks to record the purchase of products, instead of services.

As the flowchart indicates, vendor transactions for purchasing products can be recorded using QuickBooks as follows.

1. **Purchase Orders.** Use the Purchase Orders window to record an order to purchase goods.

2. **Receive Inventory.** Use the Receive Items window to record goods received.

3. **Enter Bills Against Inventory.** When the bill is received, use the Enter Bills Against Inventory window to record the bill. When the bill is entered, QuickBooks records accounts payable to reflect the obligation to pay the bill later.

4. **Pay Bills.** Use the Pay Bills window to select the bills that are due and you are ready to pay.

5. **Manage Sales Tax.** Sales taxes are charged on retail sales to customers. The sales tax collected from customers must be paid to the appropriate state agency.

The Vendor List contains vendor information that QuickBooks automatically transfers to the appropriate forms, such as purchase orders and bills. The Vendor List was covered in Chapter 6.

The Items and Services List, discussed next, is used to record information about products and services purchased from vendors.

Section 7.5
Items & Services List

QuickBooks defines an item as anything that your company buys, sells, or resells including services, products, shipping charges, and sales taxes. Items provide supporting detail for accounts.

QuickBooks classifies products and services purchased and sold into three different categories of items:

1. **Service Items.** Service items can be services that are purchased *or* sold. For example, service items include:

   - Services you buy from vendors, such as cleaning services

   - Services you sell to customers, such as installation labor

2. **Inventory Items.** Inventory items are products that a business purchases, holds as inventory, and then resells to customers. QuickBooks traces the quantity and cost of inventory items in stock.

   For consistency, the same inventory item is used when recording sales and purchases. QuickBooks has the capability to track both the cost and the sales price for inventory items. For example, in Chapter 5, we recorded the sale of an inventory item, an interior door. When the interior door was recorded on a sales invoice, QuickBooks automatically updated our inventory records by reducing the quantity of doors on hand. If we purchased an interior door, then we would record the door on the purchase order using the same inventory item number that we used on the invoice, except the purchase order uses the door cost while the invoice uses the door selling price.

3. **Non-inventory Items.** Non-inventory items are products that a business purchases, but QuickBooks does not track the quantity on hand for non-inventory items. Non-inventory items include:

   - Items purchased for a specific customer job, such as a custom countertop

- Items purchased and used by your company instead of resold to customers, such as office supplies or carpentry tools

- Items purchased and resold (if the quantity on hand does not need to be tracked)

The Items and Services List (Item List) summarizes information about items (inventory items, non-inventory items, and service items) that a company purchases or sells.

> **QuickBooks tracks inventory costs using the weighted-average method. QuickBooks does not use FIFO (First-in, First-out) or LIFO (Last-in, First- out) inventory costing. The average cost of an inventory item is displayed in the Edit Item window.**

> **QuickBooks does not track the quantity of non-inventory items. If it is important for your business to know the quantity of an item on hand, record the item as an inventory item.**

VIEW ITEM LIST

To view the Item List in QuickBooks:

1 Click the **Items & Services** icon in the Company section of the Home Page

2 The Item List window will appear

3 Notice the **Type** column in the Item List, displaying Service, Inventory and Non-inventory items

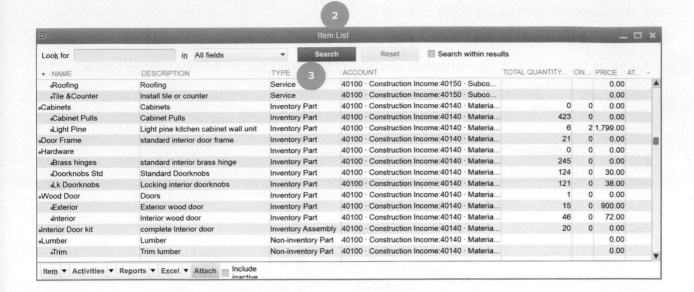

The Item List contains the following information:

- Item name
- Item description
- Item type (service, inventory, non-inventory, other charge, discount, sales tax item)
- Account used
- Quantity on hand
- Price of the item

ADD NEW ITEM

Rock Castle Construction needs to add two new items to the Item List: bifold doors and bifold door hardware. Because Rock Castle Construction wants to track the quantity of each item, both will be inventory items.

To add an inventory item to the Item List:

1 From the Item List window, **right-click** to display the following pop-up menu. Select **New**.

2 In the New Item window that appears, enter information about the bifold door inventory item. From the Type drop- down list, select **Inventory Part**. Then enter the following information in the New Item window.

Item Name/Number	**Bifold Doors**
Subitem of	**Wood Door**
Manufacturer's Part Number	**BD42**
Description on Purchase Transactions	**Bifold interior door**
Description on Sales Transactions	**Bifold interior door**
Cost	**45.00**
COGS Account	**50100 – Cost of Goods Sold**
Preferred Vendor	**Andre Window & Door**
Sales Price	**72.00**
Tax Code	**Tax**
Income Account	**40140 Materials Income**
Asset Account	**12100 – Inventory Asset**
Reorder Point (Min)	**2**
On Hand	**0**
Total Value	**0.00**
As of	**12/15/2024**

3 Click **Next** to record this inventory item and clear the fields to record another inventory item

4 Enter bifold door knobs as an **Inventory part** in the Item List using the following information:

Item Name/Number	**Bifold Knobs**
Subitem of	**Hardware**
Manufacturer's Part Number	**BK36**
Description on Purchase Transactions	**Bifold door hardware**
Description on Sales Transactions	**Bifold door hardware**

Cost	**6.00**
COGS Account	**50100 – Cost of Goods Sold**
Preferred Vendor	**Patton Hardware Supplies**
Sales Price	**13.00**
Tax Code	**Tax**
Income Account	**40140 Materials Income**
Asset Account	**12100 – Inventory Asset**
Reorder Point (Min)	**2**
On Hand	**0**
Total Value	**0.00**
As of	**12/15/2024**

5 Click **OK** to record the item and close the New Item window

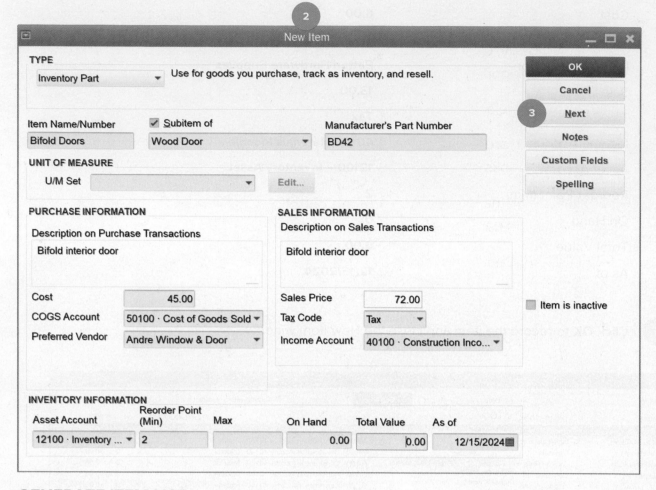

GENERATE ITEM LIST

C7.5.1 Item List. Prepare the Item List as follows:

1 Sort the Item List by selecting **Item** button > **Re-sort List**

2 Click the **Reports** button at the bottom of the Item List window. Select **Item Listing**.

3 Export to **Excel** or **print** the Item List

4 **Close** the Item List window

VIEW INVENTORY CENTER

As mentioned previously, QuickBooks classifies products and services purchased and sold into three different categories of items:

1. Service Items that are services purchased or sold

2. Inventory Items that are products that a business buys from vendors and then resells to customers. QuickBooks traces the quantity and cost of inventory items in stock

3. Non-inventory items that are products a business purchases, but QuickBooks does not track the quantity on hand for non-inventory items

QuickBooks Inventory Center lists only items that are classified as Inventory Items. To view the Inventory Center:

1 From the Company section of the Home Page, select **Inventory Activities**

2 From the pop-up menu, select **Inventory Center**

3 Select **All Inventory** to view items from the Items List that are classified as Inventory Items

4 Select **Exterior Wood Door** item

5 The **Inventory Information** screen displays item information such as Preferred Vendor, Average Cost, Cost, Sales Price, and Quantity on Hand. Notice the sales price of the Exterior Wood Door is $900, which you updated in Chapter 5.

6 Notice that because the **Bifold Doors** item you added in this chapter is an inventory item, it appears in the Inventory Center

7 Notice the **Bifold Knobs** inventory item you added in this chapter also appears in the Inventory Center

8 Note the section of the Inventory Center labeled **Reports**. In addition to accessing inventory reports from the Report Center, you can also create selected inventory reports from the Inventory Center.

9 **Close** the Inventory Center window

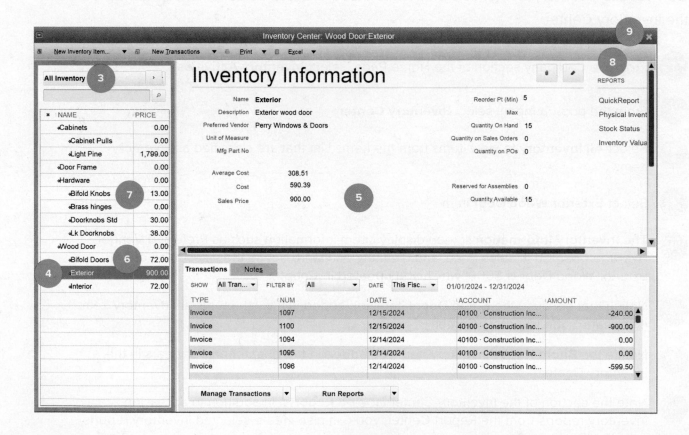

Section 7.6

Vendor Transactions

After creating a Vendor List and Item List, we are ready to enter vendor transactions. There are two basic ways to enter vendor transactions using QuickBooks.

1. **Enter Bills > Pay Bills.** This is used to record services, such as utilities or accounting services. After the bill is entered, it is paid when it is due.

2. **Enter Purchase Orders > Receive Inventory > Enter Bills Against Inventory > Pay Bills.** This approach is used to record the purchase of inventory items. The purchase order provides a record of the items ordered.

Chapter 6 focused on entering vendor transactions for services using the Enter Bills and Pay Bills onscreen forms. This chapter covers how to record the purchase of inventory items using Purchase Orders.

Display the Home Page to view the flowchart of vendor transactions. Recording the purchase of inventory using QuickBooks involves the following steps:

① **Purchase Orders.** Create a purchase order to order items from vendors.

② **Receive Inventory.** Record inventory items received.

③ **Enter Bills Against Inventory.** Record bill received and the obligation to pay the vendor later (accounts payable).

④ **Pay Bills.** Select bills to pay. Since the obligation is fulfilled, accounts payable is reduced.

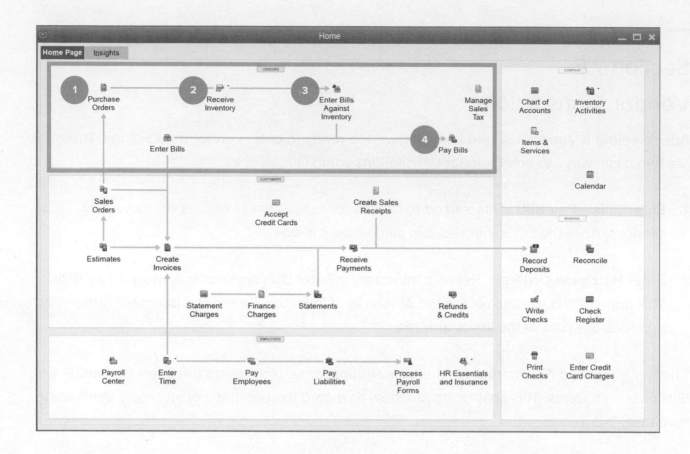

Section 7.7

Create Purchase Orders

A purchase order is a record of an order to purchase inventory from a vendor.

Rock Castle Construction wants to order 8 bifold interior doors and 8 sets of bifold door hardware to stock in inventory.

To create a purchase order:

1. Click the **Purchase Orders** icon in the Vendors section of the Home Page

2. From the drop-down Vendor List, select the vendor name: **Andre Window & Door**

3. Select Template: **Custom Purchase Order**

4. Enter the Purchase Order Date: **12/20/2024**

5. Select item ordered: **Wood Door: Bifold Doors**. ($45.00 now appears in the Rate column.)

6. Enter Quantity: **8**. ($360.00 should now appear in the Amount column.)

7. Select the **Save** icon. Leave the Create Purchase Orders window open on your screen.

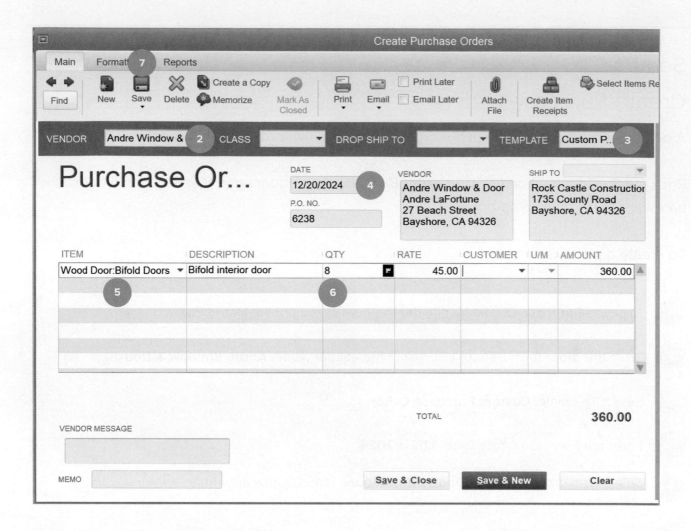

C7.7.1 Purchase Order Journal Entry. To display the journal entry that QuickBooks created behind the screen for this purchase order, complete the following steps.

1. From the Create Purchase Orders form, select the **Reports** tab

2. Select the **Transaction Journal** icon

3. Export the Transaction Journal report to **Excel** or **print** the report

4. **Close** the Transaction Journal window

To create a purchase order for bifold door hardware:

1. Click **Save & New** on the open Create Purchase Orders window

2. From the drop-down Vendor List, select the vendor name: **Patton Hardware Supplies**

3. Select Template: **Custom Purchase Order**

4. Enter the Purchase Order Date: **12/20/2024**

5. Select item ordered: **Hardware: Bifold Knobs**

6. Enter Quantity: **8**

7. Select the **Save** icon. Leave the Create Purchase Orders window open on your screen.

C7.7.2 Purchase Order Journal Entry. To display the journal entry that QuickBooks created behind the screen for this purchase order, complete the following steps.

1. From the Create Purchase Orders form, select the **Reports** tab

2. Select the **Transaction Journal** icon

3. Export the Transaction Journal report to **Excel** or **print** the report

4. **Close** the Transaction Journal window

5. Select **Save & Close** to close the Create Purchase Orders window

Section 7.8

Receive Inventory

To record inventory items received on 12/22/2024 ordered from the vendor, Andre Window & Door, complete the following steps:

1 Click the **Receive Inventory** icon in the Vendors section of the Home Page

2 Select: **Receive Inventory without Bill**

3 In the Create Item Receipts window, select vendor: **Andre Window & Door**

4 If a purchase order for the item exists, QuickBooks will display the following Open POs Exist window. Click **Yes**.

5 When the following Open Purchase Orders window appears, select the purchase order for the items received

6 Click **OK**

7 The Create Item Receipts window will appear with a total of $360. If necessary, change the Date to: **12/22/2024**.

8 Although Rock Castle Construction ordered 8 bifold doors, only 6 were received. Change the quantity from 8 to **6**.

9 The Total in the Create Item Receipts window is now **$270.00**.

10 Click the **Save** icon and leave the Create Item Receipts window open

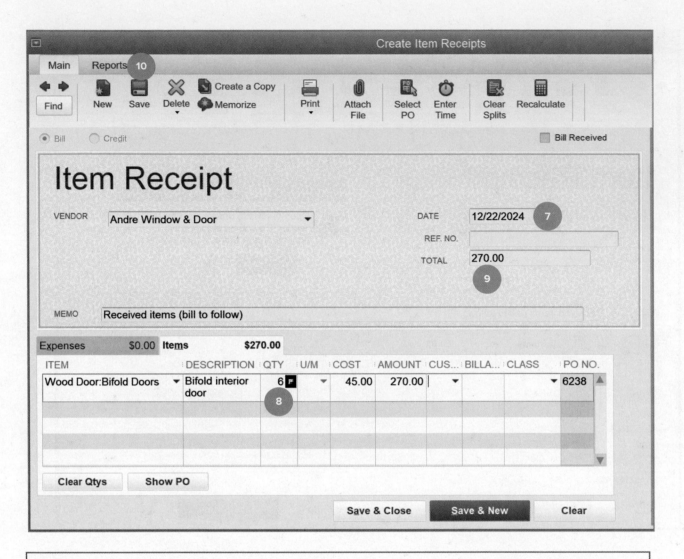

If we receive inventory and the bill at the same time, then we would select Receive Inventory > Receive Inventory with Bill (instead of Receive Inventory without Bill). Basically we are combining the two steps of Receiving Inventory and Entering Bills. When inventory and the bill are received at the same time, **Bill Received** is checked on the Item Receipt window.

C7.8.1 Receive Inventory Journal Entry. To display the journal entry that QuickBooks created behind the screen when recording receipt of inventory, complete the following steps.

1. From the Create Item Receipts form, select the **Reports** tab

2. Select the **Transaction Journal** icon

3. Export the Transaction Journal report to **Excel** or **print** the report. Notice that the journal entry debits (increases) Inventory Asset for $270.00, and credit (increases) Accounts Payable by $270.00.

4. **Close** the Transaction Journal window

To record receipt of the bifold door hardware:

1. Click **Save & New** on the open Create Item Receipts window

2. From the drop-down Vendor List, select the vendor name: **Patton Hardware Supplies**

3. Select PO No.: **6239**

4. Enter Date: **12/22/2024**

5. Item ordered should appear in the Create Item Receipts window: **Hardware: Bifold Knobs**

6. Enter Quantity: **8**

7. Select the **Save** icon. Leave the Create Item Receipts window open on your screen.

C7.8.2 Receive Inventory Journal Entry. To display the journal entry that QuickBooks created behind the screen for receiving this inventory, complete the following steps.

1. From the Create Item Receipts form, select the **Reports** tab

2. Select the **Transaction Journal** icon

3. Export the Transaction Journal report to **Excel** or **print** the report

4. **Close** the Transaction Journal window

5. **Close** the Create Items Receipt window

Section 7.9

Enter Bills Against Inventory

We may receive bills at three different times:

Receive Bill...	Record Using...
1 We receive a bill for services and no inventory items will be received, as for example, if the bill is for security services.	**Enter Bills**
2 We receive a bill at the same time we receive inventory items.	**Receive Inventory with Bill**
3 We receive inventory without a bill, and we receive the bill later.	**a. Receive Inventory without Bill** **b. Enter Bills Against Inventory**

In Chapter 6, we learned how to record bills for services (situation 1 above).

If we receive inventory and the bill at the same time (situation 2 above), then we would select Receive Inventory > Receive Inventory with Bill (instead of Receive Inventory without Bill). Basically we are combining the two steps of Receiving Inventory and Entering Bills.

In many cases, inventory is shipped to one location (for example, the Shipping and Receiving Department) and the bill sent to another location (the Accounting Department). So typically the situation where inventory and the bill are not received at the same time (situation 3 above) is a common occurrence.

Next, we will record the bill received for the bifold doors ordered and received from Andre Window & Door (situation 3 above).

To enter a bill received after inventory items are received:

1 Click the **Enter Bills Against Inventory** icon on the Vendors section of the Home Page

2 When the Select Item Receipt window appears, select Vendor: **Andre Window & Door**. If necessary, press **Tab**.

3 Select the **Item Receipt** that corresponds to the bill

4 Click **OK**

5 The Enter Bills window will appear. Notice that the Enter Bills window is the same as the Create Item Receipts window except:
- Bill Received in the upper right corner is checked
- The title of the form changes from Item Receipt to Bill
- The window name changes from Create Item Receipts to Enter Bills

6 At this point, you can make any changes necessary, such as:
- Change the date if the bill is received on a date different from the date the item was received. In this instance, the item and bill are both received on **12/22/2024**.
- Terms should be **Net 15**
- Ref. No.
- Memo

7 The Amount Due of **$270.00** should agree with the amount shown on the vendor's bill

8 The Item displayed should be **Wood Door: Bifold Doors** with a quantity of **6**, the number received. A 3-way match typically occurs at this point before the bill is approved for payment by comparing the:
1. Purchase Order (PO)
2. Item Receipt
3. Bill

In this case:
1. The PO displays a quantity of 8 bifold door.
2. The Item Receipt shows that we only received 6 bifold doors.
3. Since we only want to pay for what we have received, the bill should be 6, not 8, bifold doors.

9 Click the **Save** icon. If asked if you want to record your changes, select **Yes**. Leave the Enter Bills window open.

C7.9.1 Enter Bill Journal Entry. To display the journal entry that QuickBooks created behind the screen when recording the bill, complete the following steps.

1   From the Enter Bills form, select the **Reports** tab > **Transaction Journal**

2   Export the Transaction Journal report to **Excel** or **print** the report

3   **Close** the Transaction Journal window

To record receipt of the bifold door hardware:

1 Click **Main** tab > **Find arrows** in the upper left of the Enter Bills window to advance to the Item Receipt for the bifold door hardware purchased from Patton Hardware Supplies for $48.00

2 With the Create Item Receipts window displaying Patton Hardware Supplies for $48.00, to record the bill received for the bifold door hardware, check **Bill Received** in the upper right corner of the window. (Notice that the Item Receipt form title changes to Bill and the window name changed from Create Item Receipts to Enter Bills.)

3 Verify PO No.: **6239**

4 Verify Date: **12/22/2024**

5 Verify Item: **Hardware: Bifold Knobs**

6 Verify Quantity: **8**

7 Verify Terms: **Net 30**

8 Select the **Save** icon. Leave the Enter Bills window open on your screen.

C7.9.2 Enter Bill Journal Entry. To display the journal entry that QuickBooks created behind the screen when recording the bill, complete the following steps.

1 From the Enter Bills form, select the **Reports** tab > **Transaction Journal**

2 Export the Transaction Journal report to **Excel** or **print** the report

3 **Close** the Transaction Journal window and the Enter Bills window

Notice that the journal entries for Item Receipts and Enter Bills are the same, except the Type column in the Journal changes from Item Receipt to Bill.

Section 7.10

Pay Bills

After receiving the items and entering the bill, the next step is to pay the bill.

To select the bills to pay:

1 Click the **Pay Bills** icon in the Vendors section of the Home Page

2 Select Show bills: **Show all bills**

3 Select the bills you want to pay. Typically, you would select the bills that are due first. In this case, however, select the bill that you just recorded for:
  - **Andre Window and Door** for **$270.00**
  - **Patton Hardware Supplies** for **$48.00**

  If necessary, scroll down to view these two bills.

4 In the Payment section, select: Date: **12/23/2024**

5 Select Method: **Check**

6 Select: **To be printed**

7 Select Account: **Checking**

8 Select **Pay Selected Bills**

9 When the Payment Summary window displays, if we wanted to print the checks, we would select Print Checks. In this case, select **Done**.

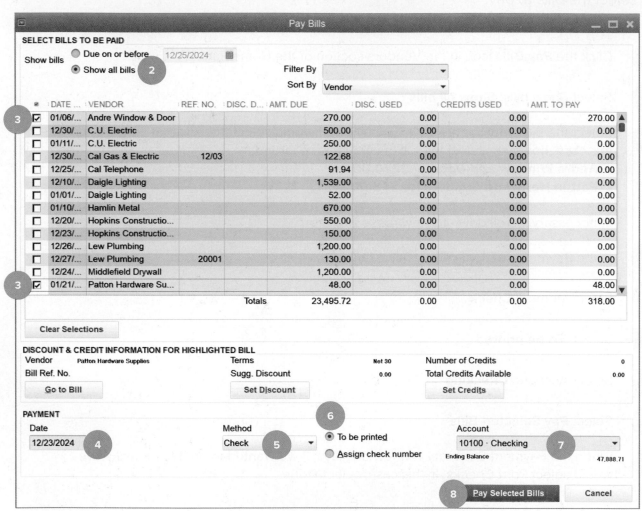

To pay by debit card, select Method: Check > Assign check number. Then use DC (for debit card) as the check number.

C7.10.1 Pay Bills Journal Entries. Another way to view the behind the screen journal entry is to use the Report Center. To view the journal entries that QuickBooks created behind the screen when bills were entered and selected for payment, complete the following steps.

1. From the Navigation Bar, select **Reports**

2. Select **Accountant & Taxes**

3. Select **Journal**

4. Select Date: **12/22/2024 To 12/23/2024**

5. Export the Journal report to **Excel** or **print** the report

6. **Close** the Journal window

Section 7.11
Pay Sales Tax

QuickBooks tracks the sales tax that you collect from customers and must remit to governmental agencies. When you set up a new company in QuickBooks, you identify which items and customers are subject to sales tax. In addition, you must specify the appropriate sales tax rate. Then whenever you prepare sales invoices, QuickBooks automatically calculates and adds sales tax to the invoices.

Rock Castle Construction is required to collect sales tax from customers on certain items sold. Rock Castle then must pay the sales tax collected to the appropriate governmental tax agency.

QuickBooks uses a two-step process to remit sales tax:

1. **Pay Sales Tax.** The Manage Sales Tax window lists the sales taxes owed and allows you to select the individual sales tax items you want to pay.
2. **Print Checks or E-Pay.** Print the check to pay the sales tax or if you are using a QuickBooks Payroll Service, your company may be able to e-pay the sales tax liability electronically.

To select the sales tax to pay:

1. Click the **Manage Sales Tax** icon in the Vendors section of the Home Page

2. When the Manage Sales Tax window appears, in the Pay Sales Tax section of the window, click the **Pay Sales Tax** button

3. When the following Pay Sales Tax window appears, select Pay From Account: **10100 Checking**

4. Select Check Date: **12/31/2024**

5. Show sales tax due through: **12/31/2024**

6. Check **To be printed**

7 Select: **Pay All Tax**

8 Click **OK**

9 Click **Close** to close the Manage Sales Tax window

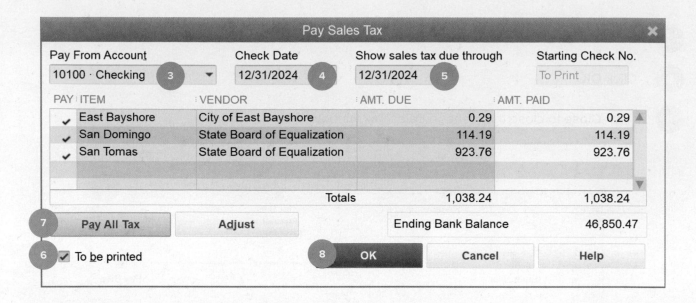

Section 7.12

Vendor Reports

QuickBooks provides vendor reports to answer the following questions:
- How much do we owe? (Accounts Payable reports)
- How much have we purchased? (Purchase reports)
- How much inventory do we have? (Inventory reports)

QuickBooks offers several different ways to access vendor reports:

1. **Vendor Center.** Summarizes vendor information in one location (Access the Vendor Center by clicking the Vendors icon on the Navigation Bar.)

2. **Report Center.** Permits you to locate reports by type of report (Click the Reports icon on the Navigation Bar, then see Vendors & Payables, Purchases, and Inventory reports).

3. **Reports Menu.** Reports are grouped by type of report (See Vendors & Payables, Purchases, and Inventory reports).

VENDOR CENTER

The Vendor Center summarizes vendor information in one convenient location. For convenience, some vendor reports can be created directly from the Vendor Center.

C7.12.1 Vendor Transaction Report. Display the Vendor Center as follows:

1. From the Navigation Bar, select **Vendors**

2. Select Vendor: **Andre Window & Door**

3. The Vendor Information section summarizes information about the vendor selected, including a list of the transactions for the specific vendor. In this case, you recorded three transactions for Andre Window & Door:
   - Purchase order on 12/20/2024
   - Bill received on 12/22/2024
   - Bill paid on 12/23/2024

4. Select **Bill Pymt – Check** on **12/23/2024** for **Andre Window & Door**. (Double-click on the Bill Pymt - Check to drill-down and view the check form to pay Andre Window & Door.)

5. With the cursor over the Vendor Transactions section of the window, **right-click** to display the pop-up menu. Select **View as a Report**.

6. Export to **Excel** or **print** the report of all transactions for Andre Window & Door for this fiscal year

7. **Close** the report window

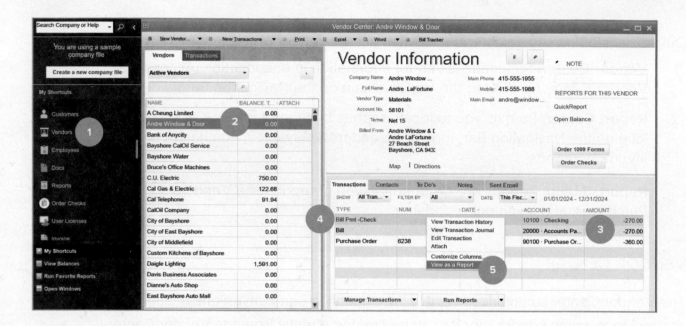

PURCHASE REPORTS: HOW MUCH HAVE WE PURCHASED?

Purchase reports provide information about purchases by item, by vendor, or by open purchase orders. Purchase reports include:

1. Open Purchase Orders (Outstanding Purchase Orders)
2. Purchases by Vendor Summary
3. Purchases by Item Summary

Open Purchase Orders Report

Open purchase orders are purchase orders for items ordered but not yet received. QuickBooks permits you to view all open purchase orders or just those for a specific vendor.

C7.12.2 Open Purchase Orders Report. To prepare the Open Purchase Orders report that lists all open purchase orders:

① From the Report Center, select: **Purchases**

② Select: **Open Purchase Orders**

③ Select Dates: **All**. Click **Run**.

④ Export to **Excel** or **print** the report

⑤ **Close** the Open Purchase Orders window

INVENTORY REPORTS: HOW MUCH INVENTORY DO WE HAVE?

Inventory reports list the amount and status of inventory. Inventory reports include:

1. Inventory Stock Status by Item
2. Physical Inventory Worksheet

Inventory Stock Status By Item

This report lists the quantity of inventory items on hand and on order. This information is useful for planning when and how many units to order.

C7.12.3 Inventory Stock Status Report. To print the Inventory Stock Status by Item report:

① From the Report Center, select: **Inventory**

② Select: **Inventory Stock Status by Item**

③ Enter Date: From: **12/22/2024** To: **12/22/2024**. Click **Run**.

④ Export to **Excel** or **print** the report

⑤ **Close** the Inventory Stock Status by Item window

Physical Inventory Worksheet

The Physical Inventory Worksheet is used when taking a physical count of inventory on hand. The worksheet lists the quantity of inventory items on hand and provides a blank column in which to enter the quantity counted during a physical inventory count. This worksheet permits you to compare your physical inventory count with your QuickBooks records.

C7.12.4 Physical Inventory Worksheet. To prepare the Physical Inventory Worksheet:

1. From the Report Center, select: **Inventory**

2. Select: **Physical Inventory Worksheet**

3. Enter Date: **12/31/2024**. Click **Run**.

4. Export to **Excel** or **print** the report

5. **Close** the Physical Inventory Worksheet window

QuickBooks offers other additional vendor reports that provide useful information to a business. These reports can also be accessed from the Reports Menu or from the Report Center.

Section 7.13

Back up QuickBooks Files

BACK UP QBB

Save a backup of your Chapter 7 file using the file name: **YourName Chapter 7 Backup.QBB**. For further instructions on how to back up your file, *see* Appendix B: Back Up and Restore QuickBooks Files.

QBW WORKFLOW

If you are using the QBW approach, leave your QBW file open and proceed directly to Exercise 7.1.

QBB RESTORE

If you are using the QBB approach and ending your computer session now, close your QBW file and exit QuickBooks. When you restart, you will restore your backup file to complete Exercise 7.1.

Section 7.14

Accounting Essentials: Inventory and Internal Control

Accounting Essentials summarize important foundational accounting knowledge that may be useful when using QuickBooks

How do we improve internal control over inventory?

- Internal control is a set of processes and procedures to safeguard assets and detect errors. Since inventory is one of the main targets of fraud and theft, we want to have a good system of internal control to safeguard inventory.
- One principle of internal control is periodically to compare and reconcile the actual asset with the accounting records to identify and track any discrepancies. So at least once a year, businesses typically reconcile:
    1. inventory on hand confirmed by a physical count of the asset on hand with
    2. inventory recorded in the accounting records

What is a 3-way match?

- Another principle of internal control is to use a 3-way match when ordering, receiving, and paying for inventory.
- Three-way match improves internal control by cross checking amounts across three different documents.
- Three-way match compares:
    1. What was *ordered*?
    2. What was *received*?
    3. What was *billed*?

- Basically, we want to compare what we *ordered* with what we *received*, and what we were *billed*. These three amounts should agree so that we are not paying for more than what we ordered or received.

Exercise 7.1 Vendor and Items Lists

 Rock Castle Construction

BACKSTORY

Mr. Castle tosses you a document as he charges past your cubicle, shouting over his shoulder, *"That's info about our new supplier. From now on, Rock Castle will install closet shelving instead of waiting on unreliable subcontractors. We do a better job and we get it done on time!"*

E7.1.1 QuickBooks File

If you will be using the same computer and the same Chapter 7.QBW file:

1. If your Chapter 7.QBW file is not already open, open it by selecting **File > Open Previous Company**. Select your **Chapter 7.QBW file**. If a QuickBooks Information window appears with a message about the sample company file, click **OK**.

2. Update the company name to **YourName Exercise 7.1 Rock Castle Construction** by selecting **Company Menu > My Company**.

> If you are not using the same computer that you used for Chapter 7, you will need to restore your Chapter 7 Backup.QBB file using the instructions in Appendix B: Back Up and Restore QuickBooks Files. After restoring, update the company name to YourName Exercise 7.1 Rock Castle Construction.

E7.1.2 Add New Vendor

Add a new vendor to Rock Castle Construction's Vendor List.

1. Add the following vendor to the Vendor List.

Vendor	**Ayanna's Closets**
Address Info:	
Company Name	**Ayanna's Closets**
Address	**13 Rheims Road** **Bayshore, CA 94326**
Main Phone	**415-555-5813**

Payment Settings:

Account No.	**58127**
Payment Terms	**Net 30**

Tax Settings:

Vendor 1099	**No**

Additional Info:

Vendor Type	**Materials**

2. From the Vendor Center, export to **Excel** the Vendor List

E7.1.3 Add New Inventory Items

Add the following inventory items to Rock Castle Construction's Items List.

1. Add the following items to the Items List.

Item Type	**Inventory Part**
Item Name	**Closet Materials**
Item Description	**Closet Materials**
COGS Account	**50100 – Cost of Goods Sold**
Income Account	**40140 – Materials Income**
Asset Account	**12100 – Inventory Asset**
Tax Code	**Tax**

2. Add the following three new inventory parts as **subitems** to Closet Materials. Use **Ayanna's Closets** as the preferred vendor and the same accounts for Cost of Goods Sold, Materials Income and Inventory Asset.

Item Type	**Inventory Part**
Item Name	**6' Closet Shelving**
Item Description	**6' Closet Shelving**
Cost	**$33**
Sales Price	**$60**

Item Type	**Inventory Part**
Item Name	**12' Closet Shelving**
Item Description	**12' Closet Shelving**
Cost	**$55.00**
Sales Price	**$100.00**

Item Type	**Inventory Part**
Item Name	**Closet Install Kit**
Item Description	**Closet Installation Kit**
Cost	**$22.00**
Sales Price	**$50.00**

3.   **Sort** the Items List by selecting **Item button > Re-sort List**

4.   Export to **Excel** or **print** the Items List by selecting the **Reports button > Item Listing**

E7.1.4 Back Up Exercise 7.1

Save a backup of your Exercise file using the file name: **YourName Exercise 7.1 Backup.QBB**. See Appendix B: Back Up and Restore QuickBooks Files for instructions.

Exercise 7.2 Purchase Orders

 Rock Castle Construction

E7.2.1 QuickBooks File

If you will be using the same computer and the same QBW file:

1.   Select your **QBW file**.

2.   Update the company name to **YourName Exercise 7.2 Rock Castle Construction** by selecting **Company Menu > My Company**.

> If you are not using the same computer that you used for Chapter 7 and Exercise 7.1, you will need to restore your latest prior Backup.QBB file using the instructions in Appendix B: Back Up and Restore QuickBooks files. After restoring, update the company name to YourName Exercise 7.2 Rock Castle Construction.

E7.2.2 Create Purchase Order

Using the Purchase Orders icon in the Vendors section of the Home Page, record the following.

1. Create a purchase order to order **10** each of the new inventory items for **Ayanna's Closets** from the prior exercise on **12/23/2024**.

12' Closet Shelving	**10**
6' Closet Shelving	**10**
Closet Install Kit	**10**

2. Select the **Save** icon at the top of the Create Purchase Orders window
3. Select the **Reports** tab
4. Select the **Transaction Journal** icon
5. Export the Transaction Journal report to **Excel** or **print** the report
6. **Close** the Transaction Journal and the Create Purchase Orders windows

E7.2.3 Back Up Exercise 7.2

Save a backup of your Exercise file using the file name: **YourName Exercise 7.2 Backup.QBB**. See Appendix B: Back Up and Restore QuickBooks Files for instructions.

Exercise 7.3 Receive Items

 Rock Castle Construction

E7.3.1 QuickBooks File

If you will be using the same computer and the same QBW file:

1. Select your **QBW file**.

2. Update the company name to **YourName Exercise 7.3 Rock Castle Construction** by selecting **Company Menu > My Company**.

If you are not using the same computer that you used for Chapter 7, Exercise 7.1 and Exercise 7.2, you will need to restore your latest prior Backup.QBB file using the instructions in Appendix B: Back Up and Restore QuickBooks files. After restoring, update the company name to YourName Exercise 7.3 Rock Castle Construction.

E7.3.2 Receive Inventory

Using the Receive Inventory icon in the Vendors section of the Home Page, record inventory received.

1. On **12/24/2024**, record the receipt of the closet inventory items ordered on **12/23/2024**. There are no freight charges.

2. Select the **Save** icon at the top of the Create Item Receipts window

3. Select the **Reports** tab

4. Select the **Transaction Journal** icon

5. Export the Transaction Journal report to **Excel** or **print** the report

6. **Close** the Transaction Journal and the Create Item Receipts windows

E7.3.3 Back Up Exercise 7.3

Save a backup of your Exercise file using the file name: **YourName Exercise 7.3 Backup.QBB**. See Appendix B: Back Up and Restore QuickBooks Files for instructions.

Exercise 7.4 Enter Bills Against Inventory

 Rock Castle Construction

E7.4.1 QuickBooks File

If you will be using the same computer and the same QBW file:

1. Select your **QBW file**.

2. Update the company name to **YourName Exercise 7.4 Rock Castle Construction** by selecting **Company Menu > My Company**.

> If you are not using the same computer that you used for Chapter 7 and Exercises 7.1 - 7.3, you will need to restore your latest prior Backup.QBB file using the instructions in Appendix B: Back Up and Restore QuickBooks files. After restoring, update the company name to YourName Exercise 7.4 Rock Castle Construction.

E7.4.2 Enter Bills Against Inventory

Using the Enter Bills Against Inventory icon in the Vendors section of the Home Page to record the following.

1. Record the receipt of the bill for the closet items on **12/27/2024**

2. Select the **Save** icon at the top of the Enter Bills window

3. Select the **Reports** tab

4. Select the **Transaction Journal** icon

5. Export the Transaction Journal report to **Excel** or **print** the report

6. **Close** the Transaction Journal and the Enter Bills windows

E7.4.3 Back Up Exercise 7.4

Save a backup of your Exercise file using the file name: **YourName Exercise 7.4 Backup.QBB**. See Appendix B: Back Up and Restore QuickBooks Files for instructions.

Exercise 7.5 Pay Bills

 Rock Castle Construction

E7.5.1 QuickBooks File

If you will be using the same computer and the same QBW file:

1. Select your **QBW file**.

2. Update the company name to **YourName Exercise 7.5 Rock Castle Construction** by selecting **Company Menu > My Company**.

> If you are not using the same computer that you used for Chapter 7 and Exercises 7.1 - 7.4, you will need to restore your latest prior Backup.QBB file using the instructions in Appendix B: Back Up and Restore QuickBooks files. After restoring, update the company name to YourName Exercise 7.5 Rock Castle Construction.

E7.5.2 Pay Bills

Pay the following bills.

1.   Pay the bill for the closet materials ordered from Ayanna's Closets on **12/29/2024**

2.   From the Navigation Bar, select **Reports** > **Accountant & Taxes** > **Journal**

3.   Select Date: **12/29/2024**

4.   Export the Journal report to **Excel** or **print** the report

5.   **Close** the Journal window

E7.5.3 Back Up Exercise 7.5

Save a backup of your Exercise file using the file name: **YourName Exercise 7.5 Backup.QBB**. See Appendix B: Back Up and Restore QuickBooks Files for instructions.

Exercise 7.6 Reports

 Rock Castle Construction

E7.6.1 QuickBooks File

If you will be using the same computer and the same QBW file:

1.   Select your **QBW file**.

2.   Update the company name to **YourName Exercise 7.6 Rock Castle Construction** by selecting **Company Menu** > **My Company**.

> If you are not using the same computer that you used for Chapter 7 and Exercises 7.1 - 7.5, you will need to restore your latest prior Backup.QBB file using the instructions in Appendix B: Back Up and Restore QuickBooks files. After restoring, update the company name to YourName Exercise 7.6 Rock Castle Construction.

E7.6.2 Open PO Report

1.   Export to **Excel** or **print** the Open Purchase Orders report for Rock Castle Construction for **This Month: 12/01/2024 To 12/31/2024**

E7.6.3 Stock Status Report

Prepare the stock status report for Rock Castle Construction at December 31, 2024.

1. Export to **Excel** or **print** an Inventory Stock Status by Item report to check the status of the closet inventory items as of **12/31/2024**

2. **Highlight** the closet inventory items on the Inventory Stock Status printout

3. **Close** the report window

E7.6.4 Back Up Exercise 7.6

Save a backup of your Exercise file using the file name: **YourName Exercise 7.6 Backup.QBB**. See Appendix B: Back Up and Restore QuickBooks Files for instructions.

Exercise 7.7 Sales of Inventory

 Rock Castle Construction

BACKSTORY

"I told you replacing Ms. Merriman's door hardware would pay off. She is going to become one of our best customers. Just wait and see." Mr. Castle appears to be in a much better mood today. *"Angel Merriman just had us install new closet shelving in her huge walk-in closet. She said she wanted us to do it because we stand by our work."*

E7.7.1 QuickBooks File

If you will be using the same computer and the same QBW file:

1. Select your **QBW file**.

2. Update the company name to **YourName Exercise 7.7 Rock Castle Construction** by selecting **Company Menu > My Company**.

If you are not using the same computer that you used for Chapter 7 and Exercises 7.1 - 7.6, you will need to restore your latest prior Backup.QBB file using the instructions in Appendix B: Back Up and Restore QuickBooks files. After restoring, update the company name to YourName Exercise 7.7 Rock Castle Construction.

E7.7.2 Add Customer Job

Add the Closet Shelving job for Angel Merriman to the Customer & Job List.

1. From the Customer Center, select **Merriman, Angel** then **right-click** to display menu, and select **Add Job**.

Job Name	**Closet Shelving**
Job Description	**Replace Closet Shelving**
Job Type	**Repairs**
Job Status	**Closed**
Start Date	**12/27/2024**
Projected End Date	**12/27/2024**
End Date	**12/27/2024**

E7.7.3 Create Invoice

1. Create an invoice for the Merriman closet shelving job using the following information.

Customer: Job	**Merriman, Angel: Closet Shelving**
Custom Template	**Rock Castle Invoice**
Date	**12/27/2024**
Invoice No.	**1104**
Items and Quantities	• **(3) 12' Closet Shelving** • **(3) 6' Closet Shelving** • **(3) Closet Installation Kit** • **(3 hours) Installation Labor**

2. Select the **Save** icon

3. Select the **Reports** tab > **Transaction Journal**

4. Export the Transaction Journal report to **Excel** or **print** the report

5. **Close** the Transaction Journal and the Invoice windows

E7.7.4 Receive Customer Payment

1. Record Angel Merriman payment for the Closet Shelving job (e-Check No. 625) for the full amount on **12/29/2024**

2. Select **Save & New**

3. Select the **Find** back arrow to display the customer payment just recorded

4. From the Receive Payments onscreen form, select the **Reports** tab > **Transaction Journal**

5. Export the Transaction Journal report to **Excel** or **print** the report

6. **Close** the Transaction Journal and the Receive Payments windows

E7.7.5 Make Deposit

1. Record the bank deposit for Angel Merriman's payment on **12/29/2024**

2. Select the **Save** icon at the top of the Make Deposits window

3. Select the **Journal** icon to display the journal entry to QuickBooks created behind the screen for the deposit

4. Export to **Excel** or **print** the Transaction Journal

5. **Close** the Transaction Journal and the Make Deposits windows

E7.7.6 Back Up Exercise 7.7

Save a backup of your Exercise file using the file name: **YourName Exercise 7.7 Backup.QBB**. See Appendix B: Back Up and Restore QuickBooks Files for instructions.

PROJECT 7.1

Larry's Landscaping 🌴

As an accounting consultant for Larry's Landscaping complete the following to enter inventory transactions for the company.

> 💡 **Troubleshooting QuickBooks and Correcting Errors are crucial QuickBooks skill to acquire. Troubleshooting resources include:**
> - **www.My-QuickBooks.com > QuickBooks Troubleshooting (QT) Tips**
> - **Chapter 17, Quick Review Guide, contains tips on Correcting Errors**
> - **Appendix D, QuickBooks Troubleshooting (QT), provides you with an effective troubleshooting process**

🌐 QuickBooks SatNav

The objective of Project 7.1 is to facilitate your mastery of QuickBooks Desktop. As shown in the following QuickBooks SatNav, Project 7.1 focuses on QuickBooks transactions related to the purchase of inventory.

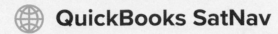

QuickBooks SatNav

⚙ QuickBooks Settings

⚙ Company Settings

⚙ Chart of Accounts

QuickBooks Transactions

Banking

Customers & Sales

Vendors & Expenses | *PO > Receive Inventory > Enter Bills Inventory > Pay Bills*

Employees & Payroll

📊 QuickBooks Reports

📊 Reports

P7.1.1 QuickBooks File

1.   Use either your QuickBooks Company file (QBW) or restore the backup file (QBB) that you completed for Project 6.1. (If you have issues with your QuickBooks file, contact your instructor.)

2.   Update the Company Name to: **YourName Project 7.1 Larry's Landscaping**

P7.1.2 Enter Purchase Orders

1.   Enter the the following purchase order using the Purchase Orders icon.

Date	**12/23/2024**
Vendor	**Conner Garden Supplies**
Item	**1/2" Vinyl Irrigation Line**
Quantity	**600**

2.   Select the **Save** icon

3.   Select the **Reports** tab > **Transaction Journal**

4.   Export the Transaction Journal report to **Excel** or **print** the report

5.   Enter the following purchase order for Larry's Landscaping.

Date	**12/23/2024**
Vendor	**Nolan Hardware and Supplies**
Item	**Plastic Sprinkler Piping**
Quantity	**700**

6.   Select the **Save** icon

7.   Select the **Reports** tab > **Transaction Journal**

8.   Export the Transaction Journal report to **Excel** or **print** the report

9. Enter the following purchase order for Larry's Landscaping.

    Date   **12/23/2024**

    Vendor   **Willis Orchards**

    Item   **Soil (2 cubic foot bag)**

    Quantity   **90**

10. Select the **Save** icon

11. Select the **Reports** tab > **Transaction Journal**

12. Export the Transaction Journal report to **Excel** or **print** the report

P7.1.3 Enter Items Received

1. Record the following items received by Larry's Landscaping.

    Date   **12/23/2024**

    Vendor   **Nolan Hardware and Supplies**

    PO No.   **7**

    Item   **Garden Walkway Lights**

    Quantity   **28**

    Item   **Sprinkler Head**

    Quantity   **36**

    Item   **Plastic Sprinkler Piping**

    Quantity   **115**

2. Select the **Save** icon

3. Select the **Reports** tab > **Transaction Journal**

4. Export the Transaction Journal report to **Excel** or **print** the report

5. Enter the following item received for Larry's Landscaping.

Date	**12/23/2024**
Vendor	**Conner Garden Supplies**
PO No.	**12**
Item	**½" Vinyl Irrigation Line**
Quantity	**600**

6. Select the **Save** icon

7. Select the **Reports** tab > **Transaction Journal**

8. Export the Transaction Journal report to **Excel** or **print** the report

9. Enter the following item received for Larry's Landscaping.

Date	**12/23/2024**
Vendor	**Gussman's Nursery**
PO No.	**11**
Item	**Lemon Tree, Citrus**
Quantity	**1**
Item	**Citrus Tree – Arizona Sweet**
Quantity	**1**
Item	**Fruit Tree – Plum**
Quantity	**1**

10. Select the **Save** icon

11. Select the **Reports** tab > **Transaction Journal**

12. Export the Transaction Journal report to **Excel** or **print** the report

13. Enter the following item received for Larry's Landscaping.

Date	**12/23/2024**
Vendor	**Nolan Hardware and Supplies**

PO No.	**13**
Item	**Plastic Sprinkler Piping**
Quantity	**700**

14. Select the **Save** icon

15. Select the **Reports** tab > **Transaction Journal**

16. Export the Transaction Journal report to **Excel** or **print** the report

P7.1.4 Enter Bills Against Inventory

1. Use the Enter Bills Against Inventory icon to enter the following bills received by Larry's Landscaping.

Date	**12/23/2024**
Vendor	**Gussman's Nursery**
PO No.	**11**
Terms	**Net 15**
Amount Due	**$147.00**

2. Select the **Save** icon

3. Select the **Reports** tab > **Transaction Journal**

4. Export the Transaction Journal report to **Excel** or **print** the report

5. Enter the following bill for Larry's Landscaping.

Date	**12/23/2024**
Vendor	**Conner Garden Supplies**
PO No.	**12**
Amount Due	**$72.00**

6. Select the **Save** icon

7. Select the **Reports** tab > **Transaction Journal**

8. Export the Transaction Journal report to **Excel** or **print** the report

P7.1.5 Pay Bills

1. Pay the following bills for Larry's on 12/23/2024.

| Vendor | **Gussman's Nursery** |
| Amount Due | **$147.00** |

| Vendor | **Conner Garden Supplies** |
| Amount Due | **$72.00** |

| Vendor | **Conner Garden Supplies** |
| Amount Due | **$127.20** |

| Vendor | **Nolan Hardware and Supplies** |
| Amount Due | **$610.00** |

2. From the Navigation Bar, select **Reports > Accountant & Taxes > Journal**

3. Select Date: **12/23/2024**

4. Export the Journal report to **Excel** or **print** the report

5. **Close** the Journal window

P7.1.6 Reports

Prepare the following reports for Larry's Landscaping.

1. Export to **Excel** the Open Purchase Orders report for Larry's Landscaping for This Fiscal Quarter, October 1 - December 31, 2024

2. Export to **Excel** the Check Detail report for Larry's Landscaping for December 23, 2024

3. Export to **Excel** the Accounts Payable Aging Detail report as of December 23, 2024

P7.1.7 Back Up Project 7.1

Save a backup of your Project file using the file name: **YourName Project 7.1 Backup.QBB**.

See Appendix B: Back Up and Restore QuickBooks Files for instructions.

Design elements: Dog icon: ©josep perianes jorba/Shutterstock; paint roller icon: ©Netti Buletti/Shutterstock; other icons/symbols: ©Carboxylase/Shutterstock

Chapter 8

Employees and Payroll

 Rock Castle Construction

BACKSTORY

The next morning on your way to your cubicle, two employees ask you if their paychecks are ready yet. Apparently, Rock Castle employees expect their paychecks today?! Then your smartphone chimes repeatedly with incoming texts from the construction crews asking about their paychecks.

> **We need our paychecks 2day. We have bills 2 pay!**

> Understood.

Deciding that you do not want all the employees upset with you if paychecks are not ready on time, you take the initiative and ask Mr. Castle about the paychecks.

His reply: *"Oops! I was so busy I almost forgot about paychecks."* He hands you another stack of documents. *"Here—you will need these. I'm sure you won't have any trouble using QuickBooks to print the paychecks. And don't forget to pay yourself!"* he adds with a chuckle as he rushes out the door.

Chapter 8

Learning Objectives

Chapter 8 explores QuickBooks employees and payroll transactions, such as creating paychecks and paying payroll taxes. In this chapter, you will learn about the following topics:

- Employee Transactions
- Payroll Setup
  - Turn on QuickBooks Payroll
  - Payroll and Time Tracking Preferences
- Employee List
  - View Employee List
  - Add New Employee
  - Export Employee List
- Employee Navigation and Payroll Processing
- Enter Time
  - Time Single Activity
  - Timesheet
- Pay Employees
  - QuickBooks Payroll Services
  - Create Paychecks
- Pay Payroll Liabilities
- File Payroll Tax Forms
- Transfer Time to Sales Invoices
- Payroll Reports
  - Payroll Reports: How Much Did We Pay for Payroll?
  - Project Reports: How Much Time Did We Use?
- Accounting Essentials: Payroll Liabilities and Payroll Taxes

Section 8.1

QuickBooks SatNav

QuickBooks SatNav is your satellite navigation for QuickBooks, assisting you in navigating QuickBooks

QuickBooks SatNav divides QuickBooks into three processes:

1. **QuickBooks Settings.** This includes Company Settings when setting up a new QuickBooks company and the Company Chart of Accounts.

2. **QuickBooks Transactions.** This includes recording transactions in QuickBooks. Transaction types can be categorized as Banking, Customers and Sales, Vendors and Expenses, and Employees and Payroll. In basic terms, recording transactions involves recording money in and money out.

3. **QuickBooks Reports.** QuickBooks reports are the output of the system, such as commonly used financial statements of Balance Sheet, Income Statement, and Statement of Cash Flows.

Chapter 8 focuses on employee and payroll transactions as shown in the following QuickBooks SatNav.

QuickBooks SatNav

⚙ QuickBooks Settings

⚙ Company Settings
⚙ Chart of Accounts

QuickBooks Transactions

Banking
Customers & Sales
Vendors & Expenses
Employees & Payroll   *Enter Time > Pay Employees > Payroll Liabilities*

📊 QuickBooks Reports

📊 Reports

💡 **Accounting Essentials appear at the end of the chapter. Tip: Preview Accounting Essentials <u>before</u> completing the chapter and then review Accounting Essentials <u>after</u> completing the chapter.**

Section 8.2

Start QuickBooks and Open QuickBooks Company

START QUICKBOOKS

To start QuickBooks software, click the **QuickBooks** icon on your desktop. If a QuickBooks icon does not appear on your desktop, from Microsoft® Windows® click **Start** button > **QuickBooks** > **QuickBooks Premier Accountant Edition**.

> **QuickBooks Accountant includes all the features of QuickBooks Pro plus features for client services. If you use QuickBooks Pro, your screens may appear slightly different than those appearing in this text.**

RESTORE QBB STARTER FILE

Restore the QBB Starter file for this chapter as follows.

1 Select **File > Restore**

2 Using the directions in Appendix B: Back Up and Restore QuickBooks Files, restore **CHAPTER 8 STARTER.QBB**

3 After restoring, update the company name to **YourName Chapter 8 Rock Castle Construction** by selecting **Company Menu > My Company**

Section 8.3

Employee Transactions

In Chapter 8 we will focus on recording employee and payroll transactions. Payroll involves preparing employee paychecks, withholding the appropriate amount in taxes, and paying the company's share of payroll taxes.

To assist in processing payroll, QuickBooks offers a time-tracking feature that permits us to track the amount of time worked. QuickBooks uses time tracked to:

1. Calculate employee paychecks
2. Transfer time to sales invoices to bill customers for work performed

Basically, there are two main aspects to using QuickBooks for Employee and Payroll purposes:

- Setting up payroll
- Processing payroll

PAYROLL SETUP

Payroll setup requires:

1. **Turn on QuickBooks Payroll** (Employees Menu, Payroll Setup)
2. **Turn on Time Tracking preference** (Edit Menu, Preferences, Time & Expenses)
3. **Set up Employees List** (Employees Menu, Employee List)

PAYROLL PROCESSING

Payroll processing consists of the following four main types of tasks:

1. **Enter Time.** QuickBooks permits us to track employee time worked to use in processing payroll and billing customers.
2. **Pay Employees.** Select employees to pay and create their paychecks.
3. **Pay Payroll Liabilities.** Pay payroll tax liabilities due governmental agencies such as the IRS. Payroll tax liabilities include federal income taxes withheld, state income taxes withheld, FICA (Social Security and Medicare), and unemployment taxes.
4. **Process Payroll Forms.** Process payroll forms including Forms 940, 941, W-2, and W-3 that must be submitted to governmental agencies.

Section 8.4

Payroll Setup

Payroll setup in QuickBooks requires the following:

1. Turn on QuickBooks Payroll (Employees Menu, Payroll Setup)
2. Turn on Time Tracking preference (Edit Menu, Preferences, Time & Expenses)
3. Set up Employees List (Employees Menu, Employee List)

TURN ON QUICKBOOKS PAYROLL

Payroll setup in QuickBooks is accessed from the Employees Menu.

1 Select **Employees**

2 Select **Payroll Setup**

3 The QuickBooks Payroll Setup window summarizes the steps to set up QuickBooks payroll and time tracking

4 Select the **payroll setup checklist** link to view a list of information needed to set up payroll into 4 categories: Company information, Employee information, Tax information, and Payroll History information.

5 Click **Finish Later**

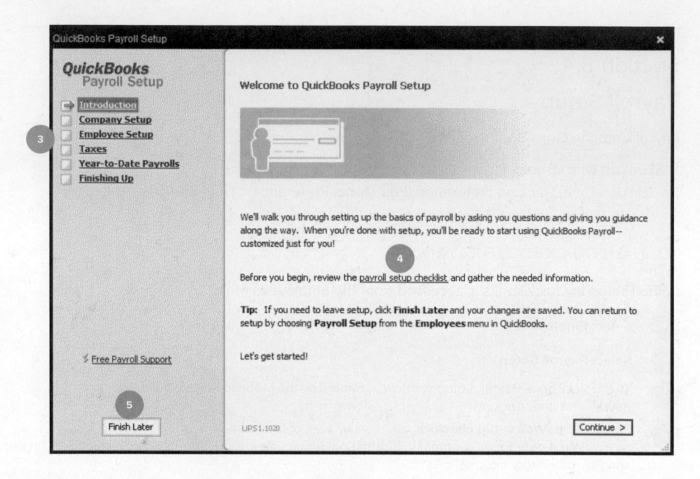

Payroll accounts for Rock Castle Construction have already been established. QuickBooks automatically creates a Chart of Accounts with payroll liability and payroll expense accounts. Payroll Items track supporting detail for the payroll accounts.

In this chapter, we will focus on customizing payroll using preferences and recording employee and payroll transactions.

PAYROLL AND TIME TRACKING PREFERENCES

Use QuickBooks Preferences to customize time tracking and payroll to suit your company's specific needs. There are two types of preferences that affect payroll:

1. Time-tracking preferences
2. Payroll and employees preferences

Time Tracking Preferences

Time tracking is used to keep a record of time that employees and contractors in order to calculate payroll and to bill customers for hours worked on specific jobs. QuickBooks offer time tracking features with different preferences.

To turn on the QuickBooks time-tracking feature, complete the following steps:

1 Select **Edit Menu**

2 Select **Preferences**

3 When the Preferences window appears, select **Time & Expenses** from the left scrollbar

4 Then select the **Company Preferences** tab

5 Select Do you track time? **Yes**

6 Select First Day of Work Week: **Monday**

7 Leave the Preferences window open

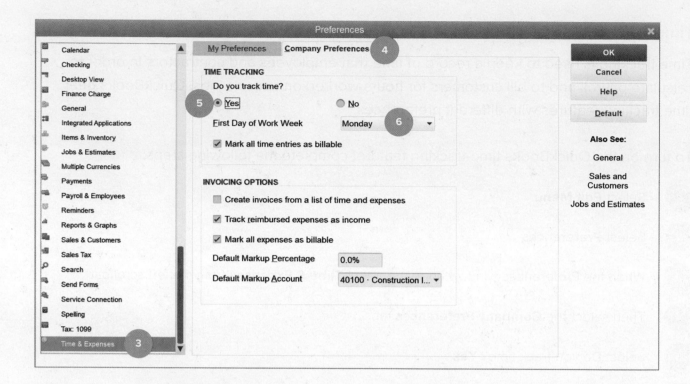

Payroll and Employee Preferences

We can also select preferences for payroll and employees that further customize QuickBooks payroll to better fit specific business needs.

To select QuickBooks payroll and employees preferences for your company:

1 From the left scrollbar of the Preferences window, click on the **Payroll & Employees** icon

2 Select the **Company Preferences** tab

3 Select QuickBooks Payroll Features: **Full payroll**
- Full payroll is selected if you use QuickBooks Desktop Payroll services. Rock Castle Construction uses a QuickBooks Desktop Payroll service where the service calculates withholding and other payroll amounts for you automatically.
- Manual payroll option is when you use QuickBooks Desktop for payroll but you manually calculate the withholding amounts meeting IRS and state requirements.
- No payroll is selected if you do not use a QuickBooks Payroll service, such as outsourcing payroll or your company has no employees.
- Online payroll is selected if you use an Intuit Online Payroll service.

4 Select Display Employee List by: **Last Name**

5 Click the **Employee Defaults** button to select payroll defaults

6 Select the checkbox: **Use time data to create paychecks**. Now QuickBooks will automatically use tracked time to calculate payroll.

7 Click **OK** to close the Employee Defaults window

8 Click **OK** again to close the Preferences window

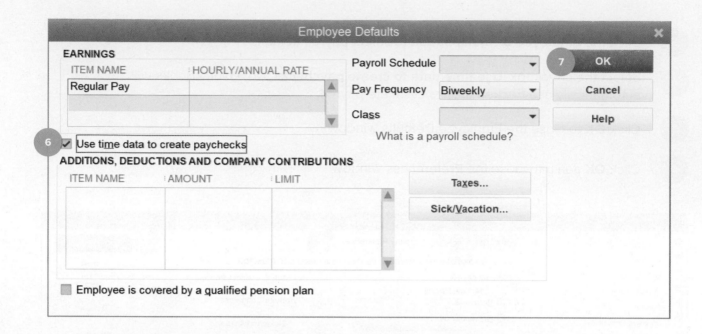

To save time, enter information common to most employees (such as a deduction for health insurance) as an employee default. QuickBooks then records the information for all employees. Later, you can customize the information as needed for a specific employee.

Now that the time-tracking and payroll preferences are set, we will edit and print the Employee List.

Section 8.5

Employees List

The Employees List contains employee information such as address, telephone, salary or wage rate, and Social Security number.

VIEW EMPLOYEES LIST

To view the Employees List for Rock Castle Construction:

1 Click Employees on the Navigation Bar or click the **Employees** button on the Home Page to display the Employee Center

2 From the Employee Center, select the **Employees** tab to display a list of employees

3 To view or edit employee information, **double-click the employee's name**

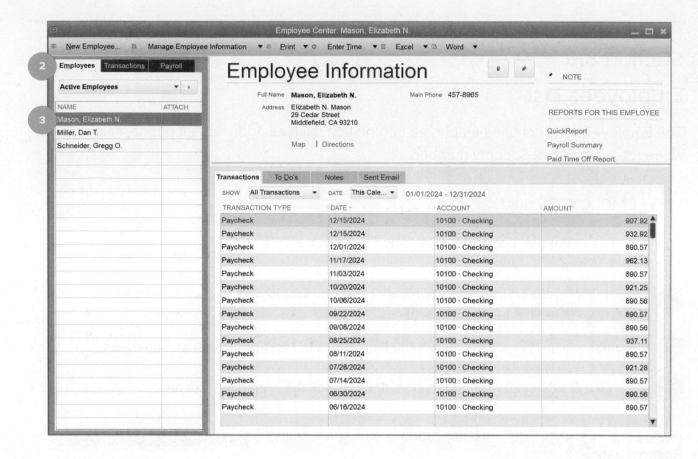

ADD NEW EMPLOYEE

To enter your name as a new employee in the Employee List:

1 Click the **New Employee** button in the Employee Center

2 When the blank New Employee window appears, select **Personal** tab. Enter the following information.

First Name	**[Enter your first name]**
Last Name	**[Enter your last name]**
Social Security No.	**333-22-4444**
Gender	**[Enter gender]**
Date of Birth	**[Enter a fictitious date of birth]**
Marital Status	**Single**
U.S. Citizen	**Yes**

3   Select the **Address & Contact** tab, then enter the following information.

Address	**555 Lakeview Lane** **Bayshore, CA 94326**
Main Email	**[Enter your email address]**

4   Select the **Additional Info** tab, then enter the following information.

Employee ID	**333-22-4444**
B-Day	**[Enter a fictitious birth date]**

5   Select the **Payroll Info** tab, then enter the following payroll information. (Note: if the Payroll Schedule field is not blank, delete the contents of the Payroll Schedule field and enter the following information.)

Earnings Name	**Regular Pay**
Hourly/Annual Rate	**15.00**
Use time data to create paychecks	**Yes**
Pay Frequency	**Biweekly**
Deductions	**Health Insurance**
Amount	**-25.00**
Limit	**-1200.00**

6   Select the **Taxes** button to view federal, state, and other tax information related to your employment, such as filing status and allowances.

7   Select the **Federal** tab and enter the following:
- Form W 4: **2020 and Later**. (If a message about Federal W-4 2020 Form appears, select OK.)
- Filing Status: **Single or Married filing separately**
- Select Subject to:
  - **Medicare**
  - **Social Security**
  - **Federal Unemployment Tax (Company Paid)**

8 Select **State** tab and enter the following:
- State: **CA**
- SUI: **Yes**
- SDI: **Yes**
- Filing Status: **Single**
- Allowances for State: **1**
- Extra Witholding: **0.00**

9 Click **OK** to close the Taxes window

10 Click **OK** again to close the New Employee window and add your name to Rock Castle Construction's Employee List

11 When asked if you want to set up payroll information for sick leave and vacation, click **Leave As Is** to use the employee default information for these items

12 Leave the Employee Center window

New Employee: Payroll Info (other)

Do you wish to set up payroll information for:

* Other or local taxes...
* Sick/vacation...

The payroll information for the item(s) listed above currently matches the employee defaults.

Set Up Now   **Leave As Is**

If you receive a message that you must update QuickBooks before you can use payroll, update QuickBooks, then proceed.

New employees complete Form W-4 to indicate filing status and allowances. To access hiring forms, such as Form W-4, from with QuickBooks, select Payroll Center from the Employee section of the Home Page > Hiring Forms.

EXPORT EMPLOYEES LIST

C8.5.1 Employees List. Export the Employees List as follows:

1 Click the **Name** bar to sort employee names in alphabetical order

2 At the top of the Employee Center, select **Excel**

3 Select **Export Employee List**

4 When the Export window appears, select **Replace an existing worksheet**. Browse and select your **CH8 REPORTS** Excel template. Select the appropriate worksheet.

5 Click **Export**

6 **Highlight** your name and information on the Employees List

7 **Close** the Employee Center window

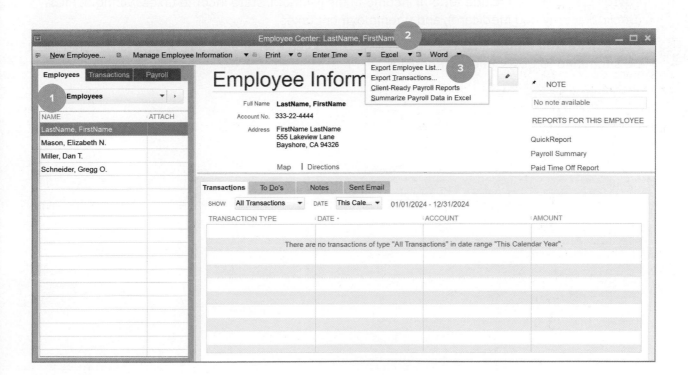

Section 8.6
Employee Navigation and Payroll Processing

If necessary, click the **Home** icon to view the Employees section of the Home Page.

To track time and process payroll in QuickBooks, we will use the Employees section of the Home Page. The Employees section of the Home Page is a flowchart of payroll transactions. As the flowchart indicates, there are four main steps to processing payroll using QuickBooks:

1. **Enter Time.** QuickBooks permits you to track employee time worked to use in processing payroll and billing customers. Simply enter time worked by employees. If the time-tracking feature is turned off, this icon will not appear.

2. **Pay Employees.** Select employees to pay and create their paychecks.

3. **Pay Payroll Liabilities.** Pay payroll tax liabilities due governmental agencies such as the IRS. Payroll tax liabilities include federal income taxes withheld, state income taxes withheld, FICA (Social Security and Medicare), and unemployment taxes.

4. **Process Payroll Forms.** Process payroll forms including Forms 940, 941, W-2, and W-3 that must be submitted to governmental agencies.

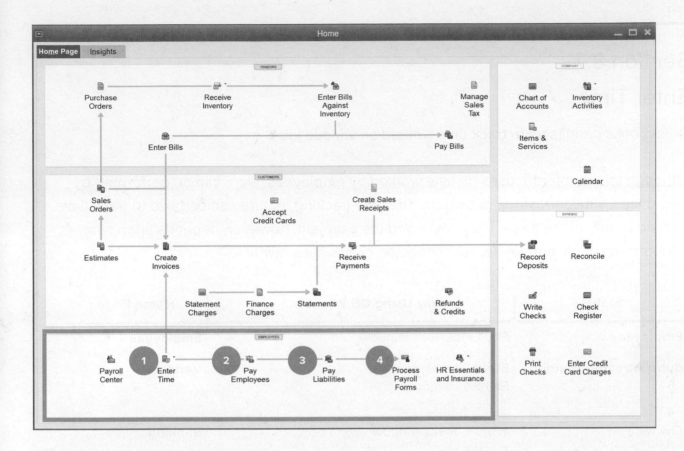

QuickBooks also has an Employee Center and a Payroll Center to help us manage employee and payroll information.

- **Employee Center.** The Employee Center can be accessed from the Navigation Bar and, as shown in the prior section of this chapter, contains the Employee List with employee information, such as address and Social Security number.

- **Payroll Center.** The Payroll Center is part of the Employee Center and is used to manage payroll and tax information, including information about wages, benefits, and withholding. The Payroll Center can be accessed by clicking the Payroll Center icon in the Employees section of the Home Page or by selecting the Payroll tab from the Employee Center.

Section 8.7
Enter Time

QuickBooks permits us to track time worked on various jobs.

Although this chapter focuses on time worked by employees, work can be performed by employees, subcontractors, or owners. The time-tracking feature can be used to track time worked by any of the three. How we record the payment, however, depends upon who performs the work: employee, subcontractor, or business owner.

Status	Pay Using QB Window...	Home Page
Employee	Pay Employees window	**Employees**
Subcontractor (Vendor)	Enter Bills window Pay Bills window	**Vendors**
Owner	Write Checks window	**Banking**

It is important that we determine the status of the individual performing the work. The status determines whether we record payments to the individual as an employee paycheck, vendor payment, or owner withdrawal.

> **Employees. Employees complete Form W-4 when hired. Form W-2 summarizes annual wages and tax withholdings.**

> **Independent Contractors. No tax withholdings are necessary for independent contractors. Tax Form 1099-MISC summarizes payments.**

> **Owner. If a stockholder is also an employee, wages are recorded as payroll. If not wages, then payment to the stockholder is a dividend.**

When employees use time tracking, the employee records the time worked on each job. The time data is then used to:

1. Prepare paychecks
2. Bill customers for time worked on specific jobs

QuickBooks Pro and QuickBooks Premier provide three different ways to track time.

1. **Time Single Activity.** Use the Stopwatch to time an activity and enter the time data. QuickBooks automatically records the time on the employee's weekly timesheet.
2. **Weekly Timesheet.** Use the weekly timesheet to enter time worked by each employee on various jobs during the week.
3. **Online Timesheets.** Enter billable hours from any Internet-connected computer. Download the timesheets into QuickBooks to process paychecks.

TIME SINGLE ACTIVITY

You will use the QuickBooks Stopwatch feature to time how long it takes you to complete payroll activities in this chapter.

To start the Stopwatch:

1   From the Employees section of the Home Page, select the **Enter Time** icon

2   Select **Time/Enter Single Activity**

3   When the Time/Enter Single Activity window appears, select Date: **12/15/2024**. You can use the Stopwatch to time activities for today's date only. However, for this activity, use the programmed date for the sample company: 12/15/2024.

4   From the Name drop-down list, select your **LastName, FirstName**

5   If the work was for a particular job or customer, we would enter the job or customer name and the service item, then click Billable. In this case, your time is not billable to a particular customer's job, so **uncheck Billable**.

6   Select Payroll Item: **Regular Pay**

7   Enter Notes: **Process payroll**

8 Click the **Start** button to start the stopwatch

9 Leave the window open while you complete the following payroll activities

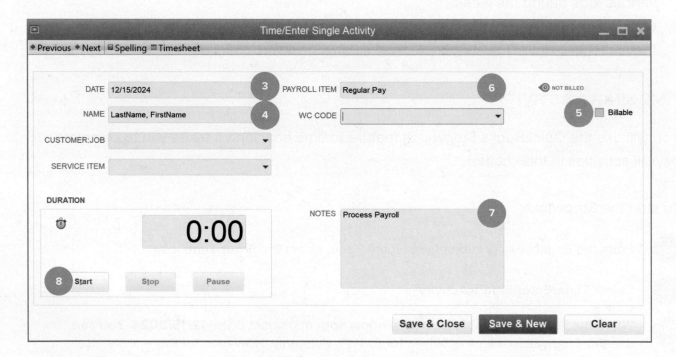

TIMESHEET

Rock Castle Construction pays employees biweekly. The last payday was December 15, 2024. The current pay period is December 16 through December 29, 2024 with paychecks due to be issued on on December 29, 2024.

Use the timesheet to enter the hours you worked for Rock Castle Construction during the last pay period. To use QuickBooks timesheet feature:

1   In the Employees section of the Home Page, select **Enter Time**

2   Select **Use Weekly Timesheet**

3   Select Week Of: **Dec 16 to Dec 22, 2024**

4   From the Name drop-down list, select your **LastName, FirstName**

5   From the Payroll Item drop-down list, select **Regular Pay**

6   Because your time is not billable to a specific customer or job, **uncheck** the **Billable?** field in the last column to indicate these charges will not be transferred to an invoice.

7   Enter **7** hours for each of the following dates for a total of 35 hours for the week:
- **Monday, December 16**
- **Tuesday, December 17**
- **Wednesday, December 18**
- **Thursday, December 19**
- **Friday, December 20**

8   Click the **Next** button in the upper left corner of the Weekly Timesheet window to advance to the timesheet for the week of **Dec 23 to Dec 29, 2024**

9   Select **Copy Last Sheet**.

10 Verify Payroll Item is **Regular Pay** and **Billable?** Is unchecked to mark your hours as nonbillable.

11 Enter **6** hours for each of the following dates for a total of 30 hours for the week:
- **Monday, December 23**
- **Tuesday, December 24**
- **Thursday, December 26**
- **Friday, December 27**
- **Saturday, December 28**

12 Click **Save & New** to record your hours and display a new timesheet

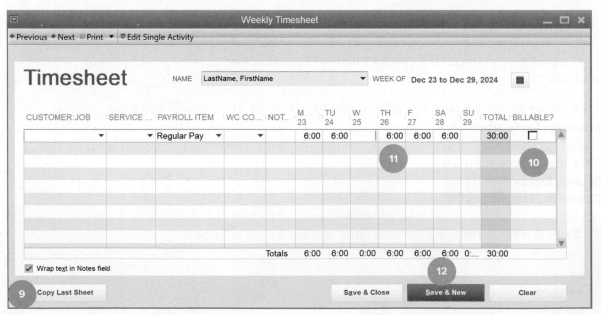

> Use Copy Last Sheet if the timesheet does not change much from week to week.

> If your time was billable to a specific customer or job, then select Customer: Job name and the Service Item.

C8.7.1 Time by Name Report. To view the time that you worked, create a Time by Name report as follows.

1 From the Navigation Bar, select **Reports** > **Jobs, Time & Mileage** > **Time by Name**

2 Select Dates: **12/16/2024 To 12/29/2024**

3 Select **Run**

4 Export the report to **Excel** or **print** the Time by Name report

If time is billable to a specific customer or job, this is indicated on the weekly timesheet. For example, Elizabeth Mason, a Rock Castle Construction employee, worked on the Teschner sun room; therefore, her hours are billable to the Teschner sun room job.

To enter billable hours on Elizabeth Mason's weekly timesheet:

1 On the new timesheet, select Employee Name: **Elizabeth N. Mason**. (Elizabeth Mason's name appears twice in the list, once as a vendor, and again as an employee. For the timesheet, be certain to select the employee, Elizabeth N. Mason.)

2 Click the **Previous** button in the upper left corner of the Weekly Timesheet window to change the timesheet dates to **Dec 16 to Dec 22, 2024**

3 To record time billable to a specific customer:
- Select Customer: Job: **Teschner, Anton: Sun Room**
- Select Service Item: **Framing**

4 Complete Elizabeth's weekly timesheet for framing the sunroom as follows. Notice that if the Customer: Job or Service Item changes, the time is entered on a new line in the timesheet. On the next blank line in the timesheet enter the following hours:

- **Monday, December 16**   8 hours

5 Check: **Billable?**

6 In the timesheet enter the following installation work that Elizabeth performed on the Teschner sun room. Notice that if the Customer: Job or Service Item changes, the time is entered on a new line in the timesheet.
- Select Customer: Job: **Teschner, Anton: Sun Room**
- Select Service Item: **Framing**
- Enter hours worked: **2 hours Tuesday, December 17**
- Check **Billable?**

7
- Select Customer: Job: **Teschner, Anton: Sun Room**
- Select Service Item: **Installation**
- Enter hours worked: **6 hours Tuesday, December 17**
- Check **Billable?**

8 Record **8** hours for each of the following dates that Elizabeth worked billable hours on **installing** the Teschner sun room:
- **Wednesday, December 18**
- **Thursday, December 19**
- **Friday, December 20**

9 Click the **Next** button to record Elizabeth N. Mason's hours and advance to the timesheet for the week of **Dec 23 to Dec 29, 2024**

10 Complete Elizabeth's weekly timesheet for **framing** the sun room as follows.

• **Monday, December 23**	**8 hours**
• **Tuesday, December 24**	**8 hours**
• **Thursday, December 26**	**8 hours**
• **Friday, December 27**	**6 hours**

11 Click **Save & Close** to record the time sheet and close the Weekly Timesheet window

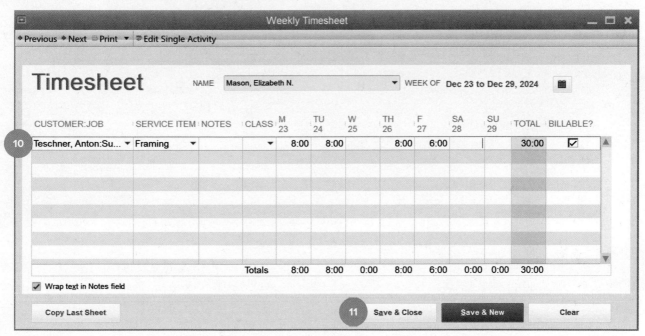

C8.7.2 Time by Name Report. To view the time that you and Elizabeth Mason worked, create a Time by Name report as follows.

1   From the Navigation Bar, select **Reports** > **Jobs, Time & Mileage** > **Time by Name**

2   Select Dates: **12/16/2024 To 12/29/2024**

3   Select **Run**

4   Export the report to **Excel** or **print** the Time by Name report

Later in the chapter, we will cover how to transfer billable tracked time to a customer's sales invoice.

Section 8.8

Pay Employees

After entering time worked, the next step is to create employee paychecks. QuickBooks offers the following QuickBooks payroll services to streamline payroll calculations and processing:

- Basic Payroll
- Enhanced Payroll
- Assisted Payroll

QUICKBOOKS PAYROLL SERVICES

QuickBooks offers three levels of payroll services for the entrepreneur to use with QuickBooks software: QuickBooks Basic, Enhanced, or Assisted Payroll. When we subscribe to a payroll service, QuickBooks requires that we have an Internet connection. Then QuickBooks automatically calculates payroll tax deductions.

If using a QuickBooks payroll service for a business, turn on the payroll auto update feature of QuickBooks to ensure you have the latest tax tables. If you update payroll when using this text, your answers may not be the same as the check figures so ask your instructor if you should update payroll.

Features of the three levels of payroll services for entrepreneurs are summarized as follows.

QuickBooks Payroll Plan	Features
Basic Payroll	• Create paychecks using automatic calculation of payroll tax deductions • Tax forms are not automatically prepared or filed • Entrepreneur must complete the tax forms or work with an accountant on payroll tax filings • Entrepreneur must pay payroll taxes
Enhanced Payroll	• Create paychecks using automatic calculation of payroll tax deductions • Federal and state payroll taxes are calculated in Quickbooks • Generates payroll tax forms for filings automatically • e-File and e-Pay taxes • e-File W-2's at year end
Assisted Payroll	• Payroll specialist assists in payroll setup • Company enters hours employees worked and runs payroll • Intuit files payroll tax forms and payments • Intuit pays any penalties

CREATE PAYCHECKS

The QuickBooks payroll service is active for the sample company file, Rock Castle Construction.

To create paychecks for Rock Castle Construction using the QuickBooks payroll service:

1 From the Employees section of the Home Page, click the **Pay Employees** icon to display the Employee Center: Payroll Center window

2 Notice that the following three tabs on the right side of the Payroll Center correspond to icons in the Employee section of the Home Page:
- Pay Employees
- Pay Liabilities
- File Forms

3 In the Pay Employees section, select: **Start Unscheduled Payroll**. We can schedule payroll to run at regular times, such as every week. In that case, we would select Start Scheduled Payroll.

4 When the Enter Payroll Information window appears, notice there are three steps listed at the top of the window: **Enter Payroll Information -> Review & Create Paychecks -> Print & Distribute Paychecks**

5 Select Pay Period Ends: **12/29/2024**. This is the last day of this pay period. If the Pay Period Change window appears, click **No** to change the date without updating the hours worked.

6 Select Check Date: **12/29/2024**

7 Select Bank Account: **10100 Checking**

8 Select Employee: **Elizabeth N. Mason**

9 Click **Continue**

10 When the Review and Create Paychecks window appears, notice that the tax withholding amounts appear automatically because Rock Castle uses a payroll service. If we were calculating payroll taxes manually, we must enter the withholding amounts manually.

11 Select **Open Paycheck Detail**

12 Notice in the Preview Paycheck window that the QuickBooks payroll service automatically calculates payroll amounts

13 If direct deposit was used for employee paychecks, we would select Use Direct Deposit

14 Select **Save & Close** to close the Preview Paycheck window

15 If we wanted to create the paycheck, we would select Create Paychecks. In this case, select **Finish Later**.

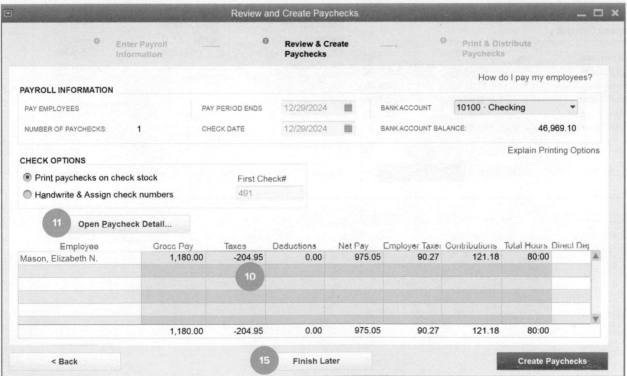

> If a message appears about updating QuickBooks before using payroll, update QuickBooks and then proceed. If you are not able to use QuickBooks payroll tax tables, then manually enter amounts shown in the Create Paychecks window.

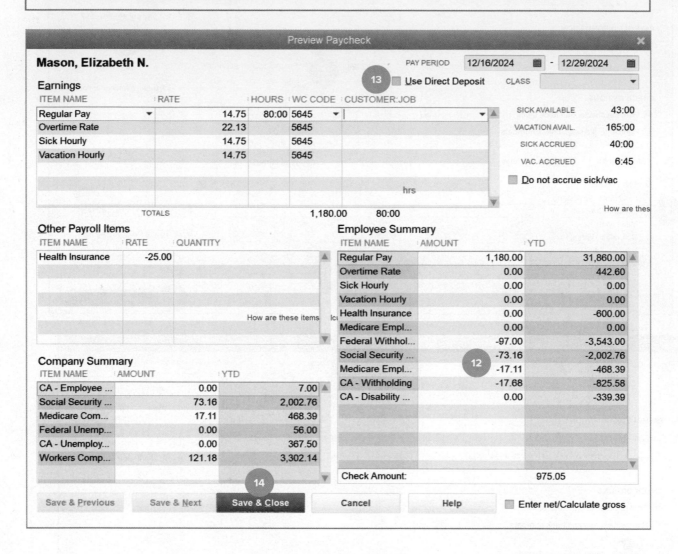

Section 8.9

Pay Payroll Liabilities

Payroll liabilities include amounts for:

- Federal income taxes withheld from employee paychecks
- State income taxes withheld from employee paychecks
- FICA (Social Security and Medicare, including both the employee and the employer portions)
- Unemployment taxes

Federal income taxes, state income taxes, and the employee portion of FICA are withheld from the employee, and the company has an obligation (liability) to remit these amounts to the appropriate tax agency. The employer share of FICA and unemployment taxes are payroll taxes the employer owes.

To pay the payroll tax liability:

1 If the Employee Center: Payroll Center window is already displayed, select the **Pay Liabilities** tab. (If the Employee Center: Payroll Center window is not already displayed, select the **Pay Liabilities** icon in the Employees section of the Home Page.)

2 In the Pay Taxes & Other Liabilities section of the Employee Center: Payroll Center window, you can view the upcoming scheduled payments for payroll liabilities. If any payments were due, you would select the payroll liabilities to pay, then click View/Pay. In the Due Date column, you can see that no payments are currently due for Rock Castle Construction.

3 Leave open the Employee Center: Payroll Center window

We will process payroll liability payments in the chapter exercises.

Section 8.10

File Payroll Tax Forms

Notice that the third section of the Payroll Center is File Forms. Basically, payroll forms summarize the amount of payroll withholdings that have been collected and remitted.

Payroll tax forms include:

- **Federal Form 940: Employer's Annual Federal Unemployment (FUTA) Tax Return.** This form summarizes the amount of unemployment tax paid and due by the employer.

- **Federal Form 941: Employer's Quarterly Federal Tax Return.** Filed with the IRS, this form summarizes the amount of federal income tax, Social Security, and Medicare withheld from employee paychecks for the quarter.

- **Federal Form 944: Employer's Annual Federal Tax Return.** Filed with the IRS, this form summarizes the amount of federal income tax, Social Security, and Medicare withheld from employee paychecks for the year. Form 944 is used by very small employers instead of filing Form 941 each quarter.

- **Form W-2: Wage and Tax Statement.** Before the end of January, an employer must provide W-2s to employees that summarize amounts paid for salaries, wages, and withholdings for the year.

- **Form W-3: Transmittal of Wage and Tax Statements.** Filed with the Social Security Administration, this form is a summary of all an employer's W-2 forms.

Close the Employee Center: Payroll Center window.

We will process payroll tax forms in the chapter exercises.

Section 8.11

Transfer Time to Sales Invoices

Billable time can be transferred to a specific customer's invoice, as shown in the Home Page by an arrow going from the Enter Time icon to the Create Invoices icon.

If we are using tracked time to bill customers, then the tasks are performed in the following order:

1   **Enter Time.** Time that is tracked by QuickBooks can be used to process payroll and bill customers. Enter time worked by employees, designating billable time to the specific customer and job.

2   **Transfer Time to Sales Invoices.** Record tracked time on an invoice for the appropriate customer and job.

3   **Pay Employees.** Select employees to pay and create their paychecks.

4   **Pay Payroll Liabilities.** Pay payroll tax liabilities due governmental agencies.

5   **Process Payroll Forms.** Process payroll forms that must be submitted to governmental agencies.

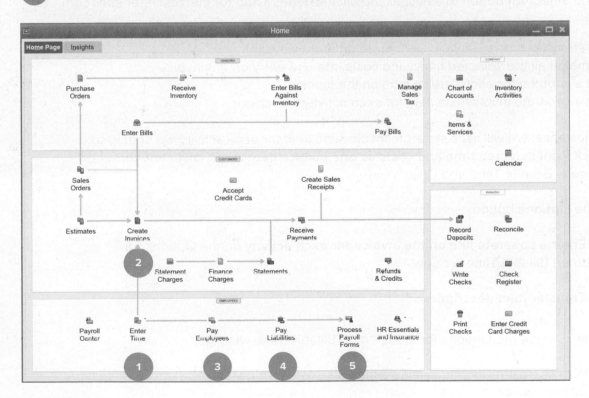

First, we must enter time worked, then open the Create Invoices window for the customer, and select the time billable to that customer. For the Teschner sun room job, we have already entered Elizabeth Mason's time.

To transfer billable time to the Teschner invoice:

1. Open the Create Invoices window by clicking the **Create Invoices** icon in the Customers section of the Home Page

2. From the Create Invoices window, select the customer job to be billed. In this instance, select Customer: Job: **Teschner, Anton: Sun Room**

3. If the following Billable Time/Costs window appears, select: **Select the outstanding billable time and costs to add to this invoice?**

4. Click **OK**

5. When the Choose Billable Time and Costs window appears, click the **Time** tab. Notice that items, expenses, and mileage can also be tracked and billed to specific customer jobs.

6. Click the **Select All** button to select all the billable times listed for the Teschner sun room job

7. We can transfer time to an invoice in three different ways:
   1. Combine all the selected times and costs into one entry on the invoice
   2. List a subtotal for each service item on the invoice
   3. List a separate invoice line item for each activity you check

   In this instance, we will list a separate invoice line item for each activity we check, so **uncheck Print selected time and costs as one invoice item** in the lower left corner of the Choose Billable Time and Costs window.

8. Click the **Options** button

9. Select **Enter a separate line on the invoice for each activity** on the Options for Transferring Billable Time window

10. Select **Transfer item descriptions**

11. Click **OK** to close the Options for Transferring Billable Time window

12. Click **OK** to close the Choose Billable Time and Costs window and add the labor cost to the Teschner invoice

13   Select Template: **Rock Castle Invoice**

14   Select Invoice Date: **12/27/2024**

15   Uncheck **Email Later**. Check **Print Later**.

16   Select **Save** and leave the Create Invoices window open

If you had not entered the billable time when you opened the invoice, **you can click the Add Time/Costs button to add billable time later.**

Notice that items, expenses, and mileage can also be tracked and billed to specific customer jobs.

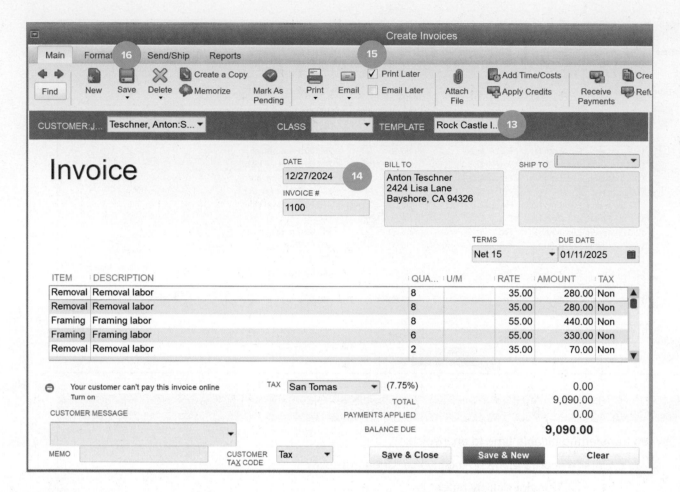

C8.11.1 Invoice Journal Entry. To view the journal entry that QuickBooks created behind the screen for the invoice entered and saved using the Create Invoices onscreen form, complete the following steps.

1 From the Create Invoices onscreen form, select the **Reports** tab

2 Select the **Transaction Journal** icon

3 Export the Transaction Journal report to **Excel** or **print** the report

4 **Close** the Transaction Journal window

> ⏱ **Stop the Stopwatch now by clicking the Stop button and then clicking Clear. Close the Stopwatch window.**

Section 8.12
Payroll Reports

In addition to providing assistance with filing payroll tax forms with federal, state, and local governmental agencies, QuickBooks also provides payroll reports for owners and managers to use to answer the following questions:

- How much did we pay our employees and pay in payroll taxes? (Payroll reports)
- How much time did we spend classified by employee and job? (Project reports)

Payroll reports can be accessed in the following ways:

1. **Employee Center.** (Select Employees (Navigation Bar) > Reports for this Employee.)

2. **Report Center.** (Select Reports (Navigation Bar) > Employees & Payroll.)

3. **Reports Menu.** (Select Reports Menu > Employees & Payroll.)

PAYROLL REPORTS: HOW MUCH DID WE PAY FOR PAYROLL?

The payroll reports list the amounts paid to employees and the amounts paid in payroll taxes.

C8.12.1 Payroll Summary Report. To print the Payroll Summary report:

1. Select **Reports** in the Navigation Bar

2. In Grid view, select **Employees & Payroll**

3. Select **Payroll Summary**

4. Select Dates: **This Month** From: **12/01/2024** To: **12/31/2024**

5. Select **Run**

6 Export to **Excel** or **print** the report

7 **Close** the Payroll Summary Report window

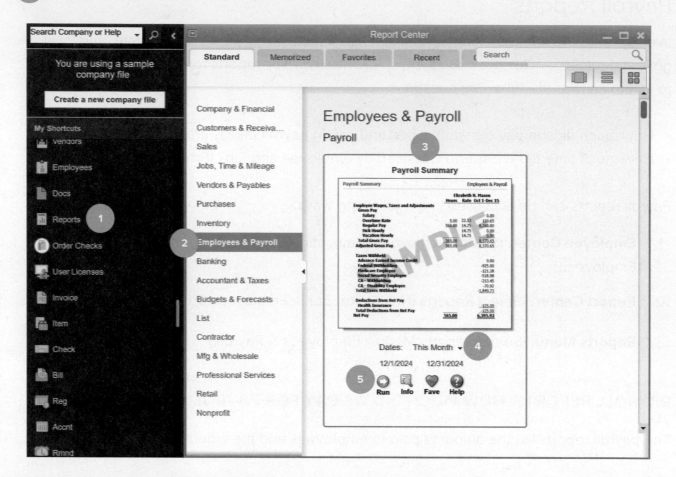

C8.12.2 Payroll Transaction Detail Report. The Payroll Transaction Detail report lists details about payroll transactions for the period and provides summary payroll totals. This report can be used if preparing payroll liability forms manually. To print the Payroll Transaction Detail report that provides detail about withholdings and deductions from employee paychecks:

1 Select **Reports** in the Navigation Bar

2 In Grid view, select **Employees & Payroll**

3 Select **Payroll Transaction Detail**

4   Select Dates: **This Month** From: **12/01/2024** To: **12/31/2024**

5   Select **Run**

6   Export to **Excel** or **print** the report

7   **Close** the Payroll Transaction Detail Report window

PROJECT REPORTS: HOW MUCH TIME DID WE USE?

Four different project reports are available in QuickBooks:

1. **Time by Job Summary Report.** Lists time spent on each job.
2. **Time by Job Detail Report.** Lists time by category spent on each job.
3. **Time by Name Report.** Lists amount of time worked by each employee.
4. **Time by Item Report.** Lists time worked on a particular job by service category.

C8.12.3 Time By Job Summary Report. To print the Time by Job Summary report:

1   From the Report Center, select: **Jobs, Time & Mileage > Time by Job Summary**

2   Export to **Excel** or **print** the Time by Job Summary report for **This Month** From: **12/01/2024** To: **12/31/2024**

3   **Highlight** the job requiring the most time for December 2024

> **To create a report detailing time spent on a specific job: 1. Report Center 2. Jobs, Time & Mileage 3. Time by Job Detail 4. Filter for Customer & Job**

Section 8.13
Back Up QuickBooks Files

BACK UP QBB

Save a backup of your Chapter 8 file [using the file name: **YourName Chapter 8 Backup.QBB**.

QBW WORKFLOW

If you are using the QBW approach, leave your QBW file open and proceed directly to Exercise 8.1.

QBB RESTORE

If you are using the QBB approach and ending your computer session now, close your QBW file and exit QuickBooks. When you restart, you will restore your backup file to complete Exercise 8.1.

Section 8.14

Accounting Essentials: Payroll Liabilities and Payroll Taxes

Accounting Essentials summarize important foundational accounting knowledge that may be useful when using QuickBooks

What are payroll liabilities?

- Payroll liabilities include two types of amounts:
    1. Amounts withheld from employee paychecks that must be paid to third parties
    2. Payroll tax expenses owed by the business

- Payroll liabilities include:
    - Federal income taxes withheld from employee paychecks
    - State income taxes withheld from employee paychecks
    - FICA (Social Security and Medicare, including both the employee and the employer portions)
    - Unemployment taxes

- Federal income taxes, state income taxes, and the employee portion of FICA are withheld from the employee, and the company has an obligation (liability) to remit these amounts to the appropriate tax agency. The employer share of FICA and unemployment taxes are payroll taxes the employer owes.

Payroll Liabilities (Federal)	Withheld from Employee Pay	Payroll Tax Expense Owed by Business	Reported on Tax Form
Federal Income Taxes	X X		941 Quarterly 944 Annual
FICA (SS + MEDICARE)	X X	X X	941 Quarterly 944 Annually
Federal Unemployment Tax		X	940 Annual

What are payroll tax forms?

- Basically, payroll forms summarize the amount of payroll withholdings that have been collected and remitted.
- Payroll tax forms include:
    - Federal Form 940: Employer's Annual Federal Unemployment (FUTA) Tax Return. This form summarizes the amount of unemployment tax paid and due by the employer.
    - Federal Form 941: Employer's Quarterly Federal Tax Return. Filed with the IRS, this form summarizes the amount of federal income tax, Social Security, and Medicare withheld from employee paychecks for the quarter.
    - Federal Form 944: Employer's Annual Federal Tax Return. Filed with the IRS, this form summarizes the amount of federal income tax, Social Security, and Medicare withheld from employee paychecks for the year. Form 944 is used by very small employers instead of filing Form 941 each quarter.
    - Form W-2: Wage and Tax Statement. Before the end of January, an employer must provide W-2s to employees that summarize amounts paid for salaries, wages, and withholdings for the year.
    - Form W-3: Transmittal of Wage and Tax Statements. Filed with the Social Security Administration, this form is a summary of all an employer's W-2 forms.

Exercise 8.1 Track time

 Rock Castle Construction

BACKSTORY

When sorting through the payroll documents that Mr. Castle gave you, you find the following unentered time for Dan Miller and Gregg Schneider.

Timesheet

Dan Miller	Salary	M Dec 16	TU Dec 17	W Dec 18	TH Dec 19	F Dec 20
Pretell: 75 Sunset	Framing	8	8	7	4	
Cook: 2nd Story	Installation				4	8

Dan Miller	Salary	M Dec 23	TU Dec 24	W Dec 25	TH Dec 26	F Dec 27
Pretell: 75 Sunset	Framing	8	8	8	8	3
Pretell: 75 Sunset	Installation					5

Timesheet

Gregg Schneider	Salary	M Dec 16	TU Dec 17	W Dec 18	TH Dec 19	F Dec 20
Cook: 2nd Story	Installation	6	6		2	
Pretell: 75 Sunset	Framing		2	8	6	8

Gregg Schneider	Salary	M Dec 23	TU Dec 24	W Dec 25	TH Dec 26	F Dec 27
Pretell: 75 Sunset	Framing	8	8	8	8	
Pretell: 75 Sunset	Installation					8

E8.1.1 QuickBooks File

If you will be using the same computer and the same Chapter 8.QBW file:

1. If your Chapter 8.QBW file is not already open, open it by selecting **File** > **Open Previous Company**. Select your **Chapter 8.QBW file**. If a QuickBooks Information window appears with a message about the sample company file, click **OK**.

2. Update the company name to **YourName Exercise 8.1 Rock Castle Construction** by selecting **Company Menu** > **My Company**.

> If you are not using the same computer that you used for Chapter 8, you will need to restore your Chapter 8 Backup.QBB file using the instructions in Appendix B: Back Up and Restore QuickBooks Files. After restoring, update the company name to YourName Exercise 8.1 Rock Castle Construction.

E8.1.2 Enter Time

1. Enter the hours employee **Dan T. Miller** worked using QuickBooks weekly timesheet

2. Enter the hours employee **Gregg O. Schneider** worked using QuickBooks weekly timesheet

E8.1.3 Time by Name Report

1. From the Navigation Bar, select **Reports** > **Jobs, Time & Mileage** > **Time by Name**

2. Select Dates: **12/16/2024 To 12/29/2024**

3. Select **Run**

4. Export the report to **Excel** or **print** the Time by Name report

E8.1.4 Back Up Exercise 8.1

Save a backup of your Exercise file using the file name: **YourName Exercise 8.1 Backup.QBB**. See Appendix B: Back Up and Restore QuickBooks Files for instructions.

Exercise 8.2 Payroll Liabilities and Forms

 Rock Castle Construction

BACKSTORY

"Payroll tax forms always give me a headache," Mr. Castle rubs his temples, muttering as he rushes past your cubicle. *"You can take care of those this year, can't you?"* he shouts over your cubicle wall.

You nod and reply confidently, *"Consider it done, Mr. Castle,"* to the back of his head as he rushes to his next appointment.

E8.2.1 QuickBooks File

If you will be using the same computer and the same QBW file:

1. Select your **QBW file**.

2. Update the company name to **YourName Exercise 8.2 Rock Castle Construction** by selecting **Company Menu > My Company**.

> If you are not using the same computer that you used for Chapter 8 and Exercise 8.1, you will need to restore your latest prior Backup.QBB file using the instructions in Appendix B: Back Up and Restore QuickBooks files. After restoring, update the company name to YourName Exercise 8.2 Rock Castle Construction.

E8.2.2 Pay Payroll Liabilities

To pay the payroll tax liability related to federal Forms 941/944:

1. Select the **Pay Liabilities** icon in the Employees section of the Home Page

2. In the Employee Center: Payroll Center window, select **Pay Liabilities** tab

3. In the Other Activities section, select **Create Custom Payments**

4. Select Dates: **12/01/2024 Through: 12/31/2024**

5. Select **OK**

6. In the Pay Liabilities window, select **To be printed**

7. Select Bank Account: **Checking**

8. Select Check Date: **12/15/2024**

9. Select: **Review liability check to enter expenses/penalties**

10.   Select: **All Payroll Items except Health Insurance**. Scroll down if necessary to view and select Payroll Items.

11.   Select **Payroll Liabilities Report.** Export the report to **Excel**. Close the Payroll Liabilities Balances report window.

12.   Normally, we could select Create on the Pay Liabilities window to create the checks to pay the payroll liabilities. In this case, select **Cancel** on the Pay Liabilities window.

13.   **Close** the Employee Center: Payroll Center window

E8.2.3 Payroll Transactions by Payee Report

1.   From the Report Center, export to **Excel** or **print** the Payroll Transactions by Payee report for This Calendar Year **From: 01/01/2024 To: 12/31/2024**

E8.2.4 Back Up Exercise 8.2

Save a backup of your Exercise file using the file name: **YourName Exercise 8.2 Backup.QBB**. See Appendix B: Back Up and Restore QuickBooks Files for instructions.

Exercise 8.3 Transfer Time to Sales Invoices

 Rock Castle Construction

BACKSTORY

" By the way, did I mention that I need a current sales invoice for the Jacobsen Kitchen job? Make sure all labor charges have been posted to the invoice," Mr. Castle shouts over the top of your cubicle as he rushes past.

E8.3.1 QuickBooks File

If you will be using the same computer and the same QBW file:

1.   Select your **QBW file**.

2.   Update the company name to **YourName Exercise 8.3 Rock Castle Construction** by selecting **Company Menu > My Company**.

> If you are not using the same computer that you used for Chapter 8, Exercise 8.1 and Exercise 8.2, you will need to restore your latest prior Backup.QBB file using the instructions in Appendix B: Back Up and Restore QuickBooks files. After restoring, update the company name to YourName Exercise 8.3 Rock Castle Construction.

E8.3.2 Transfer Time to Sales Invoice

Transfer time worked to the related Jacobsen Kitchen sales invoice as follows.

1. From the Customers section of the Home Page, click the **Create Invoices** icon

2. Transfer billable time and items to a sales invoice dated **12/22/2024** for the **Jacobsen Kitchen** job

3. From the Choose Billable Time and Costs window, click the **Time** tab, then click the **Select All** button to transfer employee time worked to the invoice. Select **Options button > Combine activities with the same service item and rate**.

4. On the Invoice, deselect **Email later**. Select **Print Later**.

4. **Save** the invoice

5. From the Create Invoices onscreen form, select the **Reports** tab

6. Select the **Transaction Journal** icon

7. Export the Transaction Journal report to **Excel** or **print** the report

8. **Close** the Transaction Journal window

E8.3.3 Time by Job Detail Report

The Time by Job Detail report provides information about time worked on each job. This report is useful for tracking that the time worked on a job is going as planned.

1. Export to **Excel** or **print** the Time by Job Detail report for 2024

2. **Highlight** any items on the report that are billable to specific jobs, yet still unbilled

E8.3.4 Back Up Exercise 8.3

Save a backup of your Exercise file using the file name: **YourName Exercise 8.3 Backup.QBB**. See Appendix B: Back Up and Restore QuickBooks Files for instructions.

PROJECT 8.1

Larry's Landscaping 🌴

As an accounting consultant for Larry's Landscaping complete the following to enter employees and payroll transactions for the company.

🌐 QuickBooks SatNav

The objective of Project 8.1 is to facilitate your mastery of QuickBooks Desktop. As shown in the following QuickBooks SatNav, Project 8.1 focuses on QuickBooks transactions related to employees and payroll.

QuickBooks SatNav

QuickBooks Settings

Company Settings
Chart of Accounts

QuickBooks Transactions

Banking
Customers & Sales
Vendors & Expenses
Employees & Payroll

QuickBooks Reports

Reports

P8.1.1 QuickBooks File

1. Use either your QuickBooks Company file (QBW) or restore the backup file (QBB) that you completed for Project 7.1. (If you have issues with your QuickBooks file, contact your instructor.)

2. Update the Company Name to: **YourName Project 8.1 Larry's Landscaping**

P8.1.2 Prepare Paychecks

1. Prepare and create (but do not print) the following paychecks for Larry's Landscaping. (Select the Pay Employees icon > Start Unscheduled Payroll.)

Pay Period Ends	**12/29/2024**
Check Date	**12/29/2024**
Employee	**Duncan Fisher**
Paycheck Amount	**$1,179.83**
Pay Period Ends	**12/29/2024**
Check Date	**12/29/2024**
Employee	**Jenny Miller**
Paycheck Amount	**$1,327.16**
Pay Period Ends	**12/29/2024**
Check Date	**12/29/2024**
Employee	**Shane Hamby**
Paycheck Amount	**$1,723.84**

(Note that paycheck amounts may vary slightly from amounts shown here due to QuickBooks Payroll Service updates for withholdings.)

P8.1.3 Reports

1. Export to **Excel** the Journal report for December 29, 2024
2. Export to **Excel** the Payroll Summary report for Larry's Landscaping for December 16 - 29, 2024
3. Export to **Excel** the Payroll Transaction Detail report for December 16 - 29, 2024
4. Export to **Excel** the Payroll Transactions by Payee report for December 16 - 29, 2024

P8.1.4 Back Up Project 8.1

Save a backup of your Project file using the file name: **YourName Project 8.1 Backup.QBB**. See Appendix B: Back Up and Restore QuickBooks Files for instructions.

Design elements: Dog icon: ©josep perianes jorba/Shutterstock; paint roller icon: ©Netti Buletti/Shutterstock; other icons/symbols: ©Carboxylase/Shutterstock

Chapter 9

QuickBooks Adjustments

 Rock Castle Construction

BACKSTORY

"Looks like we are going to need to bring our records up to date before preparing reports. So you are going to need to get up to speed on making adjusting entries, since no one else in the company knows how to make adjustments." Mr. Castle informs you early one morning.

"Ok, Mr. Castle, I'll take care of it," you reply with a smile. You had anticipated this was coming so you had started working on learning adjusting entries even before Mr. Castle mentioned it.

Chapter 9

Learning Objectives

Chapter 9 covers QuickBooks adjustments, adjusting entries to bring accounts up to date before preparing financial statements. In this chapter, you will learn about the following topics:

- Accounting Cycle
- Trial Balance
- Adjusting Entries
  - Why Do We Make Adjusting Entries?
  - How Do We Make Adjusting Entries?
  - When Do We Make Adjusting Entries?
- Using QuickBooks to Make Adjusting Entries
  - Using the Journal to Record Adjusting Entries
  - View Adjusting Journal Entries
  - Memorize Adjusting Entries
- Types of Adjusting Entries
- Prepaid Items: Related Expense and Asset Accounts
- Unearned Items: Related Revenue and Liability Accounts
- Accrued Expenses: Related Expense and Liability Accounts
- Accrued Revenues: Related Revenue and Asset Accounts
- Accounting Essentials: Accounting Adjustments and Corrections

Section 9.1

 QuickBooks SatNav

QuickBooks SatNav is your satellite navigation for QuickBooks, assisting you in navigating QuickBooks

QuickBooks SatNav divides QuickBooks into three processes:

1. **QuickBooks Settings.** This includes Company Settings when setting up a new QuickBooks company and the Company Chart of Accounts.

2. **QuickBooks Transactions.** This includes recording transactions in QuickBooks. Transaction types can be categorized as Banking, Customers and Sales, Vendors and Expenses, and Employees and Payroll. In basic terms, recording transactions involves recording money in and money out.

3. **QuickBooks Reports.** QuickBooks reports are the output of the system, such as commonly used financial statements of Balance Sheet, Income Statement, and Statement of Cash Flows.

Chapter 9 focuses on make adjustments necessary before preparing reports as shown in the following QuickBooks SatNav.

QuickBooks SatNav

 QuickBooks Settings

Company Settings
Chart of Accounts

QuickBooks Transactions

Banking
Customers & Sales
Vendors & Expenses
Employees & Payroll

 QuickBooks Reports

Reports

Section 9.2

Start QuickBooks and Open QuickBooks Company

START QUICKBOOKS

To start QuickBooks software, click the **QuickBooks** icon on your desktop. If a QuickBooks icon does not appear on your desktop, from Microsoft® Windows® click **Start** button > **QuickBooks** > **QuickBooks Premier Accountant Edition**.

> **QuickBooks Accountant** includes all the features of QuickBooks Pro plus features for client services. If you use QuickBooks Pro, your screens may appear slightly different than those appearing in this text.

RESTORE QBB STARTER FILE

Restore the QBB Starter file for this chapter as follows.

1. Select **File** > **Restore**

2. Using the directions in Appendix B: Back Up and Restore QuickBooks Files, restore **CHAPTER 9 STARTER.QBB**

3. After restoring, update the company name to **YourName Chapter 9 Rock Castle Construction** by selecting **Company Menu** > **My Company**

Section 9.3

Accounting Cycle

The accounting cycle is a series of accounting activities that a business performs each accounting period.

> **An accounting period** can be one month, one quarter, or one year.

The accounting cycle usually consists of the following steps.

- **Chart of Accounts.** The Chart of Accounts is a list of all accounts used to accumulate information about assets, liabilities, owners' equity revenues, and expenses. Create a Chart of Accounts when the business is established and modify the Chart of Accounts as needed over time.
- **Transactions.** During the accounting period, record transactions with customers, vendors, employees, and owners.
- **Trial Balance.** A Trial Balance lists each account and the account balance at the end of the accounting period. Prepare a Trial Balance to verify that the accounting system is in balance—total debits should equal total credits. An unadjusted Trial Balance is a Trial Balance prepared before adjustments.
- **Adjustments.** At the end of the accounting period before preparing financial statements, make any adjustments necessary to bring the accounts up to date. Adjustments are entered in the Journal using debits and credits.
- **Adjusted Trial Balance.** Prepare an Adjusted Trial Balance (a Trial Balance after adjustments) to verify that the accounting system still balances. If additional account detail is required, print the general ledger (the collection of all the accounts listing the transactions that affected the accounts).
- **Financial Statements.** Prepare financial statements for external users (Profit & Loss, Balance Sheet, and Statement of Cash Flows). Prepare income tax summary reports and management reports.

Section 9.4

Trial Balance

The Trial Balance is a listing of all of a company's accounts and the ending account balances. The purpose of the Trial Balance is to verify account balances and that the accounting system balances. On a Trial Balance, all debit ending account balances are listed in the debit column and credit ending balances are listed in the credit column. If the accounting system balances, total debits equal total credits.

A Trial Balance is often prepared both before adjustments (Trial Balance) and after adjustments (Adjusted Trial Balance).

C9.4.1 Trial Balance. To view and print the Trial Balance for Rock Castle Construction:

1. Select **Reports** in the Navigation Bar

2. Select **Accountant & Taxes**

3. Select **Trial Balance**

4. Select Date Range: **This Fiscal Quarter** From: **10/01/2024** To: **12/31/2024**

5. Select **Run**

6. Export to **Excel** or **print** the report

7. **Close** the Trial Balance

Section 9.5
Adjusting Entries

WHY DO WE MAKE ADJUSTING ENTRIES?

Adjusting entries record adjustments necessary to bring the accounts up to date at the end of an accounting period. We want to make adjusting entries before preparing financial reports so the accounts reflected on the reports are up to date.

HOW DO WE MAKE ADJUSTING ENTRIES?

Adjustments are also called Adjusting Entries because the way we enter adjustments is by making entries in the Journal. Adjusting entries are entered in the onscreen QuickBooks Journal using debits and credits.

Some companies use QuickBooks to maintain their financial system throughout the year and then have an accountant prepare the adjusting entries at year end to enter into QuickBooks.

WHEN DO WE MAKE ADJUSTING ENTRIES?

Adjusting entries are dated the last day of the accounting period. Typically, we prepare adjusting entries after we prepare a Trial Balance to verify that our accounts are in balance. The Trial Balance lists all accounts with their debit and credit balances. This permits us to see that our total debits equal our total credits before making adjusting entries.

Section 9.6

Using QuickBooks To Make Adjusting Entries

USING THE JOURNAL TO RECORD ADJUSTING ENTRIES

We can use the QuickBooks onscreen Journal to enter adjusting entries.

To make adjusting entries:

1 Select the **Accountant Menu**

2 Select **Make General Journal Entries**

3 When the Make General Journal Entries window appears, select Date: **12/31/2024**

4 Enter **Entry No**: **ADJ2024.1**

5 **Check** the **Adjusting Entry** box

6 On Line 1 select Account to Debit: **60900 Depreciation Expense**

7 Enter the Debit Amount: **50,000.00**

8 On Line 2 select Account to Credit: **17000 Accumulated Depreciation**

9 Enter the Credit Amount if the amount does not appear automatically: **50,000.00**

10 Select the **Save** icon and leave the Make General Journal Entries window open

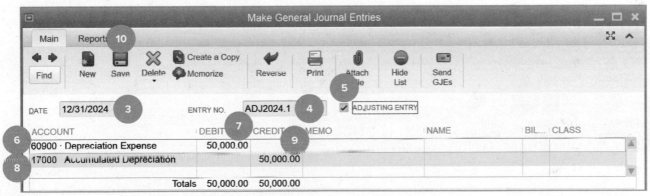

When making journal entries, including adjusting entries, accountants generally list Debits before Credits. Note that QuickBooks may not always list Debits before Credits in journal entries.

VIEW ADJUSTING JOURNAL ENTRIES

To view journal entries we recorded, display the Journal report. The Journal report also contains journal entries for all transactions recorded using onscreen forms, such as sales invoices. QuickBooks automatically converts transactions recorded in onscreen forms into journal entries with debits and credits.

If we are using QuickBooks Accountant Edition, we can view only the adjusting entries as follows by selecting the Adjusting Journal Entries report from the Report Center.

Another way to view the adjusting journal entries is from the Make General Journal Entries window as follows.

C9.6.1 Adjusting Journal Entries. To view the Adjusting Journal Entries report for the adjusting entry for depreciation that we just entered:

1 From the open Make General Journal Entries window, select the **Reports** tab

2 Select **Transaction Journal**

3 Export to **Excel** or print the **Journal**

4 **Close** the Journal window

MEMORIZE ADJUSTING ENTRIES

We can save our adjusting entries as memorized transactions. This saves us time. We will still need to update the amount of the adjustment, if needed.

To save an adjusting entry as a memorized transaction from the journal screen:

① From the open Make General Journal Entries window, select **Main > Memorize** to save the adjusting entry as a memorized transaction that can be reused

② Enter Template Name: **Adjusting Entry Depreciation**. (Since the Memorized Transactions are listed alphabetically, we want to name the Template so it automatically sorts in a way that is easy for us to find it.)

③ Select: **Add to my Reminders List** so we will be reminded to use the Memorized Transaction Template to make the adjusting entry.

④ Select How Often: **Annually**

⑤ Enter Next Date: **12/31/2025**

⑥ Select **OK**

To use the memorized transaction, select **Lists Menu > Memorized Transaction List**.

Section 9.7
Types of Adjusting Entries

If we use the accrual basis of accounting to calculate profits, the following four types of adjusting entries may be necessary.

1. **Prepaid items.** Items that are prepaid, such as prepaid insurance or prepaid rent.

2. **Unearned items.** Items that a customer has paid us for, but we have not provided the product or service.

3. **Accrued expenses.** Expenses that are incurred but not yet paid or recorded.

4. **Accrued revenues.** Revenues that have been earned but not yet collected or recorded.

The accrual basis of accounting attempts to match expenses with the revenue (income) they generate. The cash basis records revenues (income) when cash is received and records expenses when cash is paid. The accrual basis attempts to record revenue (income) in the accounting period when it is earned (the product or service is provided) regardless of when the cash is received. The accrual basis attempts to record expenses in the accounting period it is incurred regardless of when the cash is paid.

Depreciation is a special type of prepaid item involving fixed assets, such as equipment. Depreciation is the allocation of an asset's cost over its useful life. Depreciation can be calculated in a number of different ways. For more information about calculating depreciation for tax purposes, go to www.irs.gov.

Section 9.8

Prepaid Items: Related Expense and Asset Accounts

Prepaid items are items that are paid in advance, such as prepaid insurance or prepaid rent. An adjustment may be needed to record the amount of the prepaid item that has not expired at the end of the accounting period. For example, an adjustment may be needed to record the amount of insurance that has not expired as Prepaid Insurance (an asset with future benefit) and the amount of insurance that has expired as Insurance Expense.

Adjusting entries for prepaid items typically affect an Expense account and an Asset account. Examples of related Expense and Asset accounts used for prepaid item adjusting entries are as follows.

Prepaid Items	Expense Account	Asset Account
Prepaid Insurance	Insurance Expense	Prepaid Insurance
Prepaid Rent	Rent Expense	Prepaid Rent
Office Supplies	Office Supplies Expense	Office Supplies

Basically we want to make certain that the amounts in the related Expense account (such as Insurance Expense) and Asset account (Prepaid Insurance) are appropriate.

The adjusting entry is a Journal entry recording the amount that needs to be transferred between the two accounts, an Expense account and an Asset account, to show the appropriate balance in each account.

Whether a debit or credit increases or decreases an account depends upon the type of account.

Account Type	Debit	Credit
Asset	Increase	Decrease
Liabilities	Decrease	Increase
Equity	Decrease	Increase
Revenues (Income)	Decrease	Increase
Expenses	Increase	Decrease

For example, if we need to make an adjusting entry to increase Insurance Expense and decrease Prepaid Insurance for $1,000, we would determine whether to debit or credit the accounts as follows:

Account	Account Type	Increase or Decrease?	Debit or Credit?	Amount
Insurance Expense	Expense	Increase	Debit	$1,000
Prepaid Insurance	Asset	Decrease	Credit	$1,000

An example of an adjusting entry for a prepaid item using the QuickBooks Journal follows.

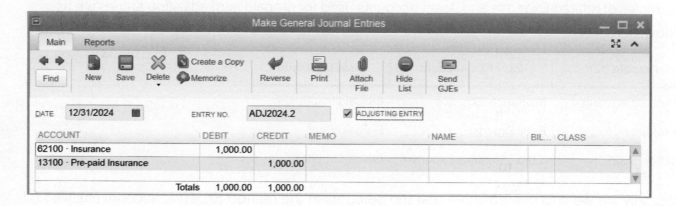

Section 9.9
Unearned Items: Related Revenue and Liability Accounts

Unearned items consist of revenue that we have not earned. If a customer pays in advance of receiving a service, such as when a customer makes a deposit, our business has an obligation (liability) to either provide the service in the future or return the customer's money. An adjustment may be necessary to bring the revenue account and unearned revenue (liability) account up to date.

Unearned Items	Revenue Account	Liability Account
Unearned Rent Revenue	Rent Revenue	Unearned Revenue
App Subscription	App Subscription Revenue	Unearned App Subscription Revenue

The adjusting entry is a Journal entry recording the amount that needs to be transferred between the two accounts, a Revenue account and a Liability account, to show the appropriate balance in each account.

For example, if we need to make an adjusting entry to increase Rent Revenue and decrease Unearned Revenue for $2,000, we would determine whether to debit or credit the accounts as follows:

Account	Account Type	Increase or Decrease?	Debit or Credit?	Amount
Rent Revenue	Revenue	Increase	Credit	$2,000
Unearned Revenue	Liablity	Decrease	Debit	$2,000

An example of an adjusting entry for unearned revenue using the QuickBooks Journal follows.

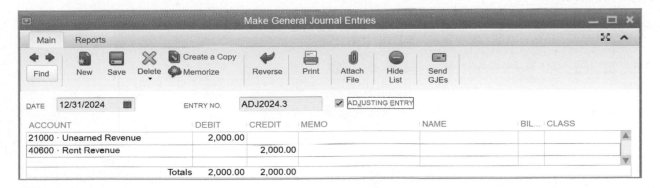

Section 9.10

Accrued Expenses: Related Expense and Liability Accounts

Accrued expenses are expenses that are incurred but not yet paid or recorded. Examples of accrued expenses include accrued interest expense (interest expense that has been incurred but not yet paid).

Accrued Expenses	Expense Account	Liability Account
Accrued Interest Incurred	Interest Expense	Interest Payable
Accrued Taxes Payable	Tax Expense	Taxes Payable

The adjusting entry is a Journal entry recording the amount that needs to be transferred between the two accounts, an Expense account and a Liability account, to show the appropriate balance in each account.

If we need to make an adjusting entry to increase Interest Expense and increase Interest Payable for $3,000, we would determine whether to debit or credit the accounts as follows:

Account	Account Type	Increase or Decrease?	Debit or Credit?	Amount
Interest Expense	Expense	Increase	Debit	$3,000
Interest Payable	Liablity	Increase	Credit	$3,000

An example of an adjusting entry for accrued interest expense using the QuickBooks Journal follows.

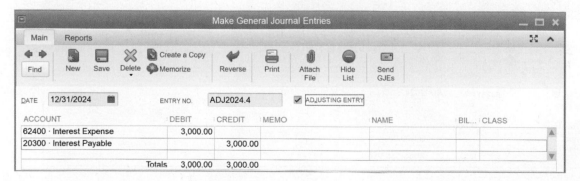

Section 9.11

Accrued Revenues: Related Revenue and Asset Accounts

Accrued revenues are revenues that have been earned but not yet collected or recorded. Examples of accrued revenues include interest revenue that has been earned but not yet collected or recorded.

Accrued Revenues	Revenue Account	Asset Account
Accrued Interest Earned	Interest Revenue	Interest Receivable
Accrued Rent Revenue	Rent Revenue	Rent Receivable

The adjusting entry is a Journal entry recording the amount that needs to be transferred between the two accounts, a Revenue account and an Asset account, to show the appropriate balance in each account.

If we need to make an adjusting entry to increase Interest Revenue and increase Interest Receivable for $4,000, we would determine whether to debit or credit the accounts as follows:

Account	Account Type	Increase or Decrease?	Debit or Credit?	Amount
Interest Revenue	Revenue	Increase	Credit	$4,000
Interest Receivable	Asset	Increase	Debit	$4,000

An example of an adjusting entry for accrued interest revenue using the QuickBooks Journal follows.

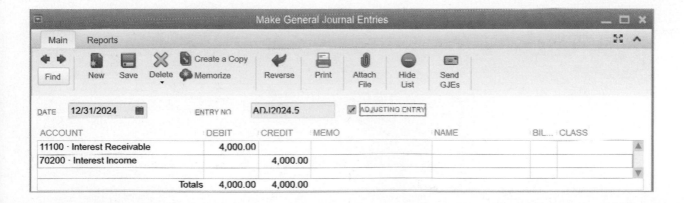

Section 9.12
Back Up QuickBooks Files

BACK UP QBB

Save a backup of your Chapter 9 file using the file name: **YourName Chapter 9 Backup.QBB**.

QBW WORKFLOW

If you will be using the same computer to complete Chapter 9 QuickBooks exercises, just as in a business workflow, you can continue to use the same QBW file.

If you are using the QBW approach, leave your QBW file open and proceed directly to Exercise 9.1.

QBB RESTORE

If you are using the QBB approach and ending your computer session now, close your QBW file and exit QuickBooks. When you restart, you will restore your backup file to complete Exercise 9.1.

Section 9.13

Accounting Essentials: Accounting Adjustments and Corrections

Accounting Essentials summarize important foundational accounting knowledge that may be useful when using QuickBooks

Why are adjusting entries necessary?

- When the accrual basis of accounting is used, adjusting entries are often necessary to bring the accounts up to date at the end of the accounting period. The accrual basis records revenue (income) when it is earned (when products and services are provided to customers) regardless of when the cash is received from customers. So at year-end there may be revenue that has not been recorded that has been earned, such as interest revenue. The accrual basis records expenses when they are incurred (the benefits have expired) regardless of when the cash is paid. So again, at year-end there may be expenses that have been incurred, but not recorded, such as interest expense.

- The accrual basis is often viewed as a better measure of profit than the cash basis. The cash basis records revenue (income) when the cash is received and records expenses when the cash is paid.

In double-entry accounting, how do we know whether to use a debit or credit for adjusting entries?

- Whether a debit or credit increases or decreases an account depends upon the type of account.

Account Type	Debit	Credit
Assets	Increase	Decrease
Liabilities	Decrease	Increase
Equity	Decrease	Increase
Revenues (Income)	Decrease	Increase
Expenses	Increase	Decrease

What are corrections?

- Corrections, or correcting entries, fix mistakes in the accounting system. Adjusting entries, on the other hand, are not mistakes, but updates that are required to bring accounts to their correct balance as of a certain date.

How do we make a correction using journal entries?

- For example, assume the Cash account should have been debited for $200.00 and the Professional Fees Revenue account credited for $200.00. However, the following incorrect entry was made for $2,000.00 instead of $200.00.

Incorrect Entry	Account	Amount
Debit	Cash	$2,000.00
Credit	Professional Fees Revenue	$2,000.00

- Often the easiest way for us to correct an error is to make two correcting entries in the Journal:

    1. **Eliminate the effect of the incorrect entry by making the opposite journal entry with Correcting Entry 1:**

Correcting Entry 1	Account	Amount
Debit	Professional Fees Revenue	$2,000.00
Credit	Cash	$2,000.00

    2. **After eliminating the effect of the incorrect entry, make the following Correcting Entry 2 that should have been made initially:**

Correcting Entry 2	Account	Amount
Debit	Cash	$200.00
Credit	Professional Fees Revenue	$200.00

How do we correct errors on saved documents, such as invoices or purchase orders?

- Once a document has been saved, we can use one of three approaches to correct the error:
    1. **Display** the document, correct the error, then save the document again.
    2. **Void** the erroneous document, then create a new document. Voiding keeps a record of the document, but changes the amounts to zero.
    3. **Delete** the erroneous document, then create a new document. Deleting the document erases the document from our system.
- Typically, options 1 or 2 are preferable because we have a better audit trail showing changes.

Exercise 9.1 Adjusting Entry Prepaid Insurance

 Rock Castle Construction

BACKSTORY

At December 31 Rock Castle Construction needs to make an adjusting journal entry to record $148.83 of Liability Insurance that has expired during the month of December. Use Entry No. ADJ2024.2. Use the following accounts to make the adjusting entry.

13100   Prepaid Insurance

62120   Liability Insurance Expense

E9.1.1 QuickBooks File

If you will be using the same computer and the same Chapter 9.QBW file:

1. If your Chapter 9.QBW file is not already open, open it by selecting **File > Open Previous Company**. Select your **Chapter 9.QBW file**. If a QuickBooks Information window appears with a message about the sample company file, click **OK**.

2. Update the company name to **YourName Exercise 9.1 Rock Castle Construction** by selecting **Company Menu > My Company**.

> If you are not using the same computer that you used for Chapter 9, you will need to restore your Chapter 9 Backup.QBB file using the instructions in Appendix B: Back Up and Restore QuickBooks Files. After restoring, update the company name to YourName Exercise 9.1 Rock Castle Construction.

E9.1.2 Prepaid Insurance Adjustment

Complete the following table.

Account	Account Type	Increase or Decrease?	Debit or Credit?	Amount
Insurance Expense	Expense	1. _____	2. _____	3. $_____
Prepaid Insurance	Asset	4. _____	5. _____	6. $_____

E9.1.3 Plan Adjusting Journal Entry

Complete the following.

1. _____

2. _____

3. _____

4. _____

E9.1.4 Enter Adjusting Journal Entry

Next, enter the adjusting journal entry into the QuickBooks Journal.

1. Select **Accountant Menu > Make General Journal Entries**

2. Enter the adjusting journal entry using the information you prepared in the prior activity

3. From the open Make General Journal Entries window, select the **Reports tab > Transaction Journal**

4. Export to **Excel** or print the **Journal**

E9.1.5 Back Up Exercise 9.1

Save a backup of your Exercise file using the file name: **YourName Exercise 9.1 Backup.QBB**. See Appendix B: Back Up and Restore QuickBooks Files for instructions.

Exercise 9.2 Adjusting Entry Unearned Revenue

 Rock Castle Construction

BACKSTORY

On December 1, 2024 Rock Castle Construction received $3,000 cash for unused storage space it leased to a subcontractor. Mr. Castle locked the cash in the office safe, and it was not recorded in QuickBooks. So the $3,000 amount needs to be recorded as petty cash and recorded as unearned rental revenue.

The $3,000 payment was for three months of rent, beginning December 1, 2024. An adjusting entry is needed to bring accounts up to date at December 31 and record the amount of rent revenue that has been earned as of December 31.

Use Entry No. ADJ2024.3. Use the following accounts to make the adjusting entry. Add new accounts as needed.

21000   Unearned Revenue

40600   Rent Revenue

E9.2.1 QuickBooks File and Journal Entry

If you will be using the same computer and the same QBW file:

1. Select your **QBW file**.

2. Update the company name to **YourName Exercise 9.2 Rock Castle Construction** by selecting **Company Menu > My Company**.

3. Using the Journal (select **Accountant Menu > Make General Journal Entries**), make a journal entry to record the **$3,000** as an increase in Account: **10400 Petty Cash** and an increase in Account: **21000 Unearned Revenue**.
   - Select Date: **12/01/2025**
   - Enter Entry No. **1123**
   - **Uncheck Adjusting Entry**

5. From the open Make General Journal Entries window, select the **Reports tab > Transaction Journal**

6. Export to **Excel** or print the **Journal**

E9.2.2 Unearned Revenue Adjustment

For the adjusting entry to record unearned rent revenue at December 31, 2025, complete the following table.

Account	Account Type	Increase or Decrease?	Debit or Credit?	Amount
Rent Revenue	Income	1. _____	2. _____	3. $_____
Unearned Revenue	Liability	4. _____	5. _____	6. $_____

E9.2.3 Plan Adjusting Journal Entry

Complete the following.

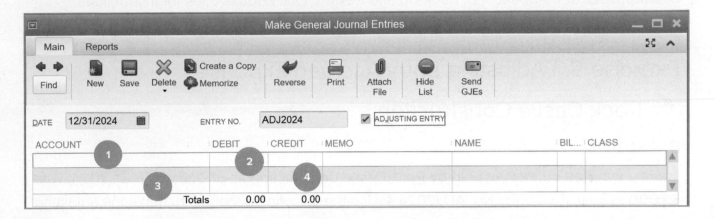

1. _____

2. _____

3. _____

4. _____

E9.2.4 Enter Adjusting Journal Entry

Next, enter the adjusting journal entry into the QuickBooks Journal.

1. Select **Accountant Menu > Make General Journal Entries**

2. Enter the adjusting journal entry using the information you prepared in the prior activity

3. From the open Make General Journal Entries window, select the **Reports tab > Transaction Journal**

4. Export to **Excel** or print the **Journal**

E9.2.5 Back Up Exercise 9.2

Save a backup of your Exercise file using the file name: **YourName Exercise 9.2 Backup.QBB**. See Appendix B: Back Up and Restore QuickBooks Files for instructions.

Exercise 9.3 Adjusting Entry Accrued Expenses

 Rock Castle Construction

BACKSTORY

Interest incurred but not yet paid by Rock Castle Construction as of December 31, 2024, was $3,000 in total. Use Entry No. ADJ2024.4. Use the following accounts to make the adjusting entry. Add new accounts as needed.

20300   Interest Payable

62420   Loan Interest (Expense)

E9.3.1 QuickBooks File

If you will be using the same computer and the same QBW file:

1.   Select your **QBW file**.

2.   Update the company name to **YourName Exercise 9.3 Rock Castle Construction** by selecting **Company Menu > My Company**.

If you are not using the same computer that you used for Chapter 9 and Exercises 9.1 - 9.2, you will need to restore your latest prior Backup.QBB file using the instructions in Appendix B: Back Up and Restore QuickBooks files. After restoring, update the company name to YourName Exercise 9.3 Rock Castle Construction.

E9.3.2 Accrued Expense Adjustment

Complete the following table.

Account	Account Type	Increase or Decrease?	Debit or Credit?	Amount
Interest Expense	Expense	1. _____	2. _____	3. $_____
Interest Payable	Liability	4. _____	5. _____	6. $_____

E9.3.3 Plan Adjusting Journal Entry

Complete the following.

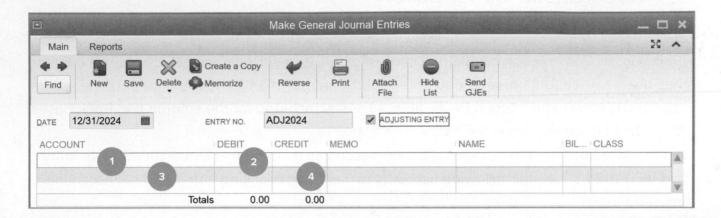

1. _____

2. _____

3. _____

4. _____

E9.3.4 Enter Adjusting Journal Entry

Next, enter the adjusting journal entry into the QuickBooks Journal.

1.   Select **Accountant Menu > Make General Journal Entries**

2.   Enter the adjusting journal entry using the information you prepared in the prior activity

3.   From the open Make General Journal Entries window, select the **Reports tab > Transaction Journal**

4.   Export to **Excel** or print the **Journal**

E9.3.5 Back Up Exercise 9.3

Save a backup of your Exercise file using the file name: **YourName Exercise 9.3 Backup.QBB**. See Appendix B: Back Up and Restore QuickBooks Files for instructions.

Exercise 9.4 Adjusting Entry Accrued Revenue

 Rock Castle Construction

BACKSTORY

Rock Castle Construction has earned interest of $400 as of December 31, 2024. This interest has been earned, but not recorded or received. Interest of $400 needs to be recorded as an accrued revenue and Interest Receivable, an asset, recorded for the amount that Rock Castle Construction will receive in the future.

An adjusting entry is needed to bring accounts up to date at December 31. Use Entry No. ADJ2024.5. Use the following accounts to make the adjusting entry. Add new accounts as needed.

11100   Interest Receivable

70200   Interest Income

E9.4.1 QuickBooks File

If you will be using the same computer and the same QBW file:

1. Select your **QBW file**.

2. Update the company name to **YourName Exercise 9.4 Rock Castle Construction** by selecting **Company Menu > My Company**.

> If you are not using the same computer that you used for Chapter 9 and Exercises 9.1 - 9.3, you will need to restore your latest prior Backup.QBB file using the instructions in Appendix B: Back Up and Restore QuickBooks files. After restoring, update the company name to YourName Exercise 9.4 Rock Castle Construction.

E9.4.2 Accrued Revenue Adjustment

Complete the following table.

Account	Account Type	Increase or Decrease?	Debit or Credit?	Amount
Interest Revenue	Income	1. _____	2. _____	3. $_____
Interest Receivable	Asset	4. _____	5. _____	6. $_____

E9.4.3 Plan Adjusting Journal Entry

Complete the following.

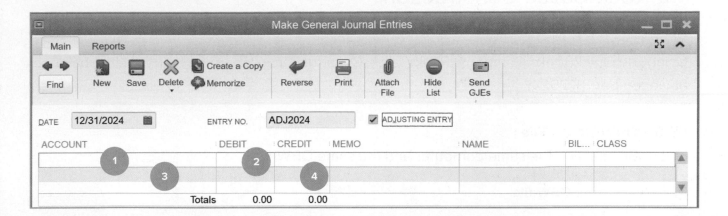

1. _____

2. _____

3. _____

4. _____

E9.4.4 Enter Adjusting Journal Entry

Next, enter the adjusting journal entry into the QuickBooks Journal.

1.   Select **Accountant Menu > Make General Journal Entries**

2.   Enter the adjusting journal entry using the information you prepared in the prior activity

3.   From the open Make General Journal Entries window, select the **Reports tab > Transaction Journal**

4.   Export to **Excel** or print the **Journal**

E9.4.5 Back Up Exercise 9.4

Save a backup of your Exercise file using the file name: **YourName Exercise 9.4 Backup.QBB**. See Appendix B: Back Up and Restore QuickBooks Files for instructions.

Exercise 9.5 Adjusted Trial Balance

 Rock Castle Construction

BACKSTORY

Using the QuickBooks Company, Rock Castle Construction, prepare an adjusted trial balance at December 31, 2024.

E9.5.1 QuickBooks File

If you will be using the same computer and the same QBW file:

1.   Select your **QBW file**.

2.   Update the company name to **YourName Exercise 9.5 Rock Castle Construction** by selecting **Company Menu > My Company**.

> **If you are not using the same computer that you used for Chapter 9 and Exercises 9.1 - 9.4, you will need to restore your latest prior Backup.QBB file using the instructions in Appendix B: Back Up and Restore QuickBooks files. After restoring, update the company name to YourName Exercise 9.5 Rock Castle Construction.**

E9.5.2 Adjusted Trial Balance

1.   From the Report Center, select **Accountant & Taxes > Adjusted Trial Balance**

2.   Select Date: **This Month 12/01/2024 To 12/31/2024**. Select **Run**.

3.   Export to **Excel** or **print** the Adjusted Trial Balance

4.   **Highlight** the adjustments and any adjusted trial balance account balances that changed as a result of adjustments

E9.5.3 Back Up Exercise 9.5

Save a backup of your Exercise file using the file name: **YourName Exercise 9.5 Backup.QBB**. See Appendix B: Back Up and Restore QuickBooks Files for instructions.

Exercise 9.6 Debits and Credits

Enter either Increase or Decrease in the following table to complete it.

- **Increase**
- **Decrease**

Account Type	Debit	Credit
Assets	_____	_____
Liabilities	_____	_____
Equity	_____	_____
Revenues (Income)	_____	_____
Expenses	_____	_____

PROJECT 9.1

Larry's Landscaping

As an accounting consultant for Larry's Landscaping complete the following to record adjustments to bring accounts up to date for the company.

💡 **Troubleshooting QuickBooks and Correcting Errors are crucial QuickBooks skill to acquire. Troubleshooting resources include:**
- **www.My-QuickBooks.com > QuickBooks Troubleshooting (QT) Tips**
- **Chapter 17, Quick Review Guide, contains tips on Correcting Errors**
- **Appendix D, QuickBooks Troubleshooting (QT), provides you with an effective troubleshooting process**

🌐 QuickBooks SatNav

The objective of Project 9.1 is to facilitate your mastery of QuickBooks Desktop. Project 9.1 focuses on adjustments that is required as part of the report preparation process.

QuickBooks SatNav

⚙ QuickBooks Settings

⚙ Company Settings
⚙ Chart of Accounts

QuickBooks Transactions

💰 Banking
💰 Customers & Sales
💰 Vendors & Expenses
💰 Employees & Payroll

📊 QuickBooks Reports

📊 Reports

P9.1.1 QuickBooks File

1. Use either your QuickBooks Company file (QBW) or retore the backup file (QBB) that you completed for Project 8.1. (If you have issues with your QuickBooks file, contact your instructor.)

2. Update the Company Name to: **YourName Project 9.1 Larry's Landscaping**

P9.1.2 Trial Balance

1. Export to **Excel** the Trial Balance report for Larry's Landscaping for This Fiscal Quarter, October 1 to December 31, 2024

P9.1.3 Adjusting Entries

1. Enter the following adjusting entries for Larry's Landscaping.

Date	**12/31/2024**
Entry Number	**A108**
Account to Debit	**6700 Depreciation (Expense)**
Account to Credit	**1520 Accumulated Depreciation – Truck**
Amount	**$600.00**

Date	**12/31/2024**
Entry Number	**A109**
Account to Debit	**6900 Insurance (Expense)**
Account to Credit	**Prepaid Insurance**
Amount	**$180**

2. Export to **Excel** the Adjusting Journal Entries report for December 31, 2024. (Select: Report Center > Accountant & Taxes > Adjusting Journal Entries.)

P9.1.4 Reports

1. Export to **Excel** the Adjusted Trial Balance for Larry's Landscaping at December 31, 2024

2. **Highlight** the adjustments and any adjusted trial balance account balances that changed as a result of adjustments

P9.1.5 Back Up Project 9.1

Save a backup of your Project file using the file name: **YourName Project 9.1 Backup.QBB**. See Appendix B: Back Up and Restore QuickBooks Files for instructions.

Design elements: Dog icon: ©josep perianes jorba/Shutterstock; paint roller icon: ©Netti Buletti/Shutterstock; other icons/symbols: ©Carboxylase/Shutterstock

Chapter 10

QuickBooks Reports

🔨 Rock Castle Construction

BACKSTORY

" *I need an income tax summary report ASAP—*" Mr. Castle barks as he races past your cubicle. In a few seconds he charges past your cubicle again. " *Don't forget to adjust the accounts first. You'll need to use those confounded debits and credits!*

"*Also, I need a P&L, balance sheet, and cash flow statement for my meeting with the bankers this afternoon. Throw in a graph or two if it'll make us look good.*"

Smiling, you push the Send button on your smartphone to send Mr. Castle the links to the financials. Then you send him a text message.

Chapter 10

Learning Objectives

Chapter 10 explores QuickBooks reports. In this chapter, you will learn about the following topics:

- Financial Reports: Results of the Accounting Cycle
- Trial Balance
- Adjusting Entries
- Adjusted Trial Balance
- Memorized Reports
- Financial Statements
    - Profit and Loss
    - Balance Sheet
    - Statement of Cash Flows
- Tax Reports
    - Income Tax Preparation Report
    - Income Tax Summary Report
    - Income Tax Detail Report
- Management Reports
    - Cash Flow Forecast
- Financial Insights
- Accounting Essentials: Financial Reports

Section 10.1

 QuickBooks SatNav

QuickBooks SatNav is your satellite navigation for QuickBooks, assisting you in navigating QuickBooks

QuickBooks SatNav divides QuickBooks into three processes:

1. **QuickBooks Settings.** This includes Company Settings when setting up a new QuickBooks company and the Company Chart of Accounts.

2. **QuickBooks Transactions.** This includes recording transactions in QuickBooks. Transaction types can be categorized as Banking, Customers and Sales, Vendors and Expenses, and Employees and Payroll. In basic terms, recording transactions involves recording money in and money out.

3. **QuickBooks Reports.** QuickBooks reports are the output of the system, such as commonly used financial statements of Balance Sheet, Income Statement, and Statement of Cash Flows.

Chapter 10 focuses on preparing reports as shown in the following QuickBooks SatNav.

QuickBooks SatNav

⚙ QuickBooks Settings

⚙ Company Settings
⚙ Chart of Accounts

QuickBooks Transactions

Banking
Customers & Sales
Vendors & Expenses
Employees & Payroll

📊 QuickBooks Reports

📊 Reports

💡 **Accounting Essentials appear at the end of the chapter. Tip: Preview Accounting Essentials <u>before</u> completing the chapter and then review Accounting Essentials <u>after</u> completing the chapter.**

Section 10.2

Start QuickBooks and Open QuickBooks Company

START QUICKBOOKS

To start QuickBooks software, click the **QuickBooks** icon on your desktop. If a QuickBooks icon does not appear on your desktop, from Microsoft® Windows® click **Start** button > **QuickBooks** > **QuickBooks Premier Accountant Edition**.

> **QuickBooks Accountant** includes all the features of QuickBooks Pro plus features for client services. If you use QuickBooks Pro, your screens may appear slightly different than those appearing in this text.

RESTORE QBB STARTER FILE

Restore the QBB Starter file for this chapter as follows.

1 Select **File > Restore**

2 Using the directions in Appendix B: Back Up and Restore QuickBooks Files, restore **CHAPTER 10 STARTER.QBB**

3 After restoring, update the company name to **YourName Chapter 10 Rock Castle Construction** by selecting **Company Menu > My Company**

Section 10.3

Financial Reports: Results of the Accounting Cycle

As mentioned in the prior chapter, the accounting cycle is a series of accounting activities that a business performs each accounting period.

> **An accounting period** can be one month, one quarter, or one year.

The accounting cycle usually consists of the following steps.

- **Chart of Accounts.** The Chart of Accounts is a list of all accounts used to accumulate information about assets, liabilities, owners' equity, revenues, and expenses. Create a Chart of Accounts when the business is established and modify the Chart of Accounts as needed over time. (The Chart of Accounts was discussed in Chapters 1 and 2 of this text.)
- **Transactions.** During the accounting period, record transactions with customers, vendors, employees, and owners. (Transactions were explored in Chapters 3, 4, 5, 6, 7, and 8 of this text.)
- **Trial Balance.** A Trial Balance lists each account and the account balance at the end of the accounting period. Prepare a Trial Balance to verify that the accounting system is in balance—total debits should equal total credits. An unadjusted Trial Balance is a Trial Balance prepared before adjustments.
- **Adjustments.** At the end of the accounting period before preparing financial statements, make any adjustments necessary to bring the accounts up to date. Adjustments are entered in the Journal using debits and credits. (Adjustments were covered in Chapter 9 of this text.)
- **Adjusted Trial Balance.** Prepare an Adjusted Trial Balance (a Trial Balance after adjustments) to verify that the accounting system still balances. If additional account detail is required, print the general ledger (the collection of all the accounts listing the transactions that affected the accounts).
- **Financial Statements.** Prepare financial statements for external users (Profit & Loss, Balance Sheet, and Statement of Cash Flows). Prepare income tax summary reports and management reports.

Section 10.4
Trial Balance

The Trial Balance is a listing of all of a company's accounts and the ending account balances. A Trial Balance is often prepared before making adjustments to verify account balances and that the accounting system balances. Preparing a Trial Balance was covered in Chapter 9.

Section 10.5

Adjusting Entries

The QuickBooks Journal is used to record adjustments. Adjustments are often necessary to bring the accounts up to date at the end of the accounting period. If we use the accrual basis of accounting to calculate profits, the following four types of adjusting entries may be necessary.

1. **Prepaid items.** Items that are prepaid, such as prepaid insurance or prepaid rent.
2. **Unearned items.** Items that a customer has paid us for, but we have not provided the product or service.
3. **Accrued expenses.** Expenses that are incurred but not yet paid or recorded.
4. **Accrued revenues.** Revenues that have been earned but not yet collected or recorded.

To make an adjusting entry using the Journal to record depreciation expense for 2024 on Rock Castle Construction Furniture and Equipment:

1. Select the **Accountant Menu**

2. Select **Make General Journal Entries**

3. From the Make General Journal Entries window, select Date: **12/31/2024**

4. Enter Entry No: **ADJ2024.6**

5. **Check** the **Adjusting Entry** box

6. Select Account to Debit: **60900 Depreciation Expense**

7. Enter Debit amount: **10,000.00**

8. Select Account to Credit: **17000 Accumulated Depreciation**

9. If it does not appear automatically, enter Credit amount: **10,000.00**.

10. **Save** the adjusting journal entry

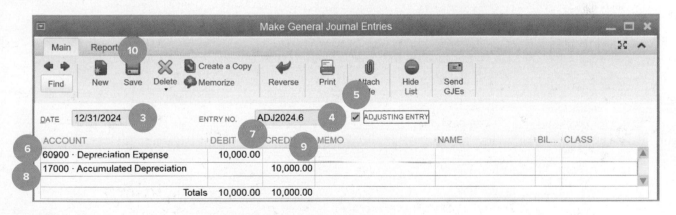

C10.5.1 Adjusting Journal Entries. To view the Adjusting Journal Entries report for the adjusting entry for depreciation that we just entered:

1   From the open Make General Journal Entries window, select the **Reports** tab

2   Select **Transaction Journal**

3   Export to **Excel** or print the **Journal**

4   **Close** the Journal window

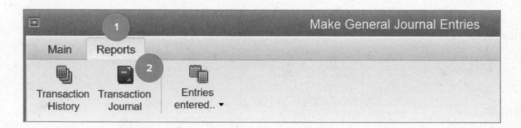

For more detailed information about adjusting entries, see Chapter 9.

Section 10.6

Adjusted Trial Balance

The Adjusted Trial Balance is prepared to verify that the accounting system still balances after adjusting entries are made, and that the adjustments have been made appropriately.

C10.6.1 Adjusted Trial Balance. Additional required adjusting entries were already entered in Chapter 9 to bring Rock Castle Construction's accounts up to date. To verify the adjustments, print an Adjusted Trial Balance as follows:

1. From the Navigation Bar, select **Reports**

2. Select **Accountant & Taxes**

3. Select **Adjusted Trial Balance**

4. Select Date: **12/31/2024**

5. Select **Run**

6. Notice the Unadjusted (Trial) Balance columns contain account balances *before* adjusting entries

7. Notice the Adjustments columns contain the amounts for adjusting entries at December 31, 2024

8. Notice the Adjusted (Trial) Balance columns contain account balances *after* adjusting entries

9. Export to **Excel** or **print** the Adjusted Trial Balance

Leave the Adjusted Trial Balance report open on your screen.

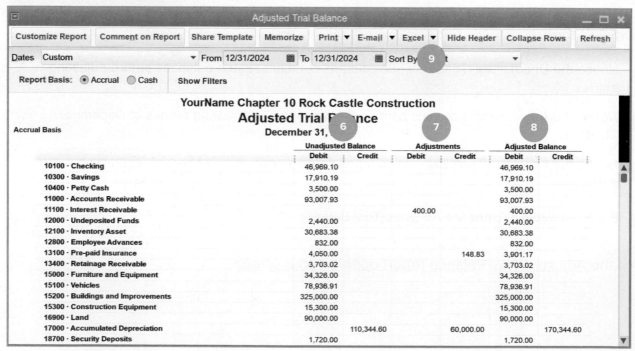

Section 10.7

Memorized Reports

When we prepare reports, we can create memorized reports for future use. To memorize a report, first create the report and then use the memorize feature of QuickBooks.

For example, Rock Castle Construction could save time in the future by memorizing reports, such as the Adjusted Trial Balance.

CREATE A MEMORIZED REPORT

To create a memorized Adjusted Trial Balance report for Rock Castle Construction:

1 To memorize the Adjusted Trial Balance open on your screen from the prior activity, select the **Memorize** button

2 In the Name Field enter **Rock Castle Construction Adjusted Trial Balance**

3 Select Save in Memorized Report Group: **Accountant**

4 Click **OK**

5 **Close** the Adjusted Trial Balance window

USE A MEMORIZED REPORT

To use a memorized report:

1 Select the **Memorized** tab at the top of the Report Center window

2 Select **Accountant** on the left of the Report Center window

3 When the Memorized List window appears, double-click on **Rock Castle Construction Adjusted Trial Balance** to display the Adjusted Trial Balance

4 At this point, we would make any changes as needed, such as the date. In this case, select **Cancel** since we have already exported the Adjusted Trial Balance.

Section 10.8
Financial Statements

Financial statements are standardized financial reports given to bankers and investors. The three main financial statements are the Profit & Loss, Balance Sheet, and Statement of Cash Flows.

PROFIT AND LOSS

The Profit and Loss Statement lists sales (sometimes called revenues) and expenses for a specified accounting period. Profit, or net income, can be measured two different ways:

1. **Cash basis.** A sale is recorded when cash is collected from the customer. Expenses are recorded when cash is paid.
2. **Accrual basis.** Sales are recorded when the good or service is provided regardless of when the cash is collected from the customer. Expenses are recorded when the cost is incurred or expires, even if the expense has not been paid.

QuickBooks permits you to prepare the Profit and Loss Statement using either the accrual or the cash basis. QuickBooks also permits you to prepare Profit and Loss Statements monthly, quarterly, or annually.

C10.8.1 Profit and Loss Statement. To prepare a Profit and Loss Statement for Rock Castle Construction using the accrual basis:

1. From the Report Center, select **Company & Financial** > **Profit & Loss Standard**

2. Select Date: **This Fiscal Year**. Select **Run**.

3. Click the **Customize Report** button. Click the **Display** tab, and then select Report Basis: **Accrual**. Click **OK**.

4. Export to **Excel** or **print** the Profit and Loss Statement

5. **Close** the Profit & Loss window

BALANCE SHEET

The Balance Sheet presents a company's financial position on a particular date. The Balance Sheet can be prepared at the end of a month, quarter, or year. The Balance Sheet lists:

1. **Assets.** What a company owns. On the Balance Sheet, assets are recorded at their historical cost, the amount you paid for the asset when you purchased it. Note that historical cost can be different from the market value of the asset, which is the amount the asset is worth now.

2. **Liabilities.** What a company owes. Liabilities are obligations that include amounts owed vendors (accounts payable) and bank loans (notes payable).

3. **Owners' equity.** The residual that is left after liabilities are satisfied. Also called net worth, owners' equity is increased by owners' contributions and net income. Owners' equity is decreased by owners' withdrawals (or dividends) and net losses.

C10.8.2 Balance Sheet. To prepare a Balance Sheet for Rock Castle Construction at 12/31/2024:

① From the Report Center, select **Company & Financial > Balance Sheet Standard**

② Select Date: **This Fiscal Year**. Select **Run**.

③ Export to **Excel** or **print** the Balance Sheet

④ **Close** the Balance Sheet window

⑤ **Highlight** the second single largest asset listed on the Balance Sheet

STATEMENT OF CASH FLOWS

The Statement of Cash Flows summarizes cash inflows and cash outflows for a business over a period of time. Cash flows are grouped into three categories:

1. **Cash flows from operating activities.** Cash inflows and outflows related to the company's primary business, such as cash flows from sales and operating expenses.
2. **Cash flows from investing activities.** Cash inflows and outflows related to acquisition and disposal of long-term assets.
3. **Cash flows from financing activities.** Cash inflows and outflows to and from investors and creditors (except for interest payments). Examples include: loan principal repayments and investments by owners.

C10.8.3 Statement of Cash Flows. To print the Statement of Cash Flows for Rock Castle Construction:

1. From the Report Center, select **Company & Financial > Statement of Cash Flows**

2. Select Date: **This Fiscal Year**. Select **Run**.

3. Export to **Excel** or **print** the Statement of Cash Flows

4. **Close** the Statement of Cash Flows window

5. **Highlight** the following items on the Statement of Cash Flows:
   - Net cash provided by Operating Activities
   - Net cash provided by Investing Activities
   - Net cash provided by Financing Activities

Section 10.9
Tax Reports

QuickBooks provides two different approaches that you can use when preparing your tax return.

1. Create your QuickBooks income tax reports and then enter the tax information on your income tax return or into your tax software.
2. Export your QuickBooks accounting data to tax software, such as TurboTax software, and then use TurboTax to complete your income tax return.

Three different income tax reports are provided by QuickBooks:

1. **Income Tax Preparation report.** Lists the assigned tax line for each account.
2. **Income Tax Summary report.** Summarizes income and expenses that should be listed on a business income tax return.
3. **Income Tax Detail report.** Provides more detailed information about the income or expense amount appearing on each tax line of the Income Tax Summary report.

INCOME TAX PREPARATION REPORT

Before printing the Income Tax Summary report, check your QuickBooks accounts to see that the correct Tax Line is selected for each account.

C10.9.1 Income Tax Preparation Report. An easy way to check the Tax Line specified for each account is to print the Income Tax Preparation report as follows.

1. From the Report Center, select **Accountant & Taxes** > **Income Tax Preparation**

2. Select Date: **This Tax Year**. Select **Run**.

3. Export to **Excel** or **print** the income Tax Preparation report

4. **Close** the Income Tax Preparation window

To determine if the correct tax line has been entered for each account, compare the tax lines listed on the Income Tax Preparation report with the business income tax return.

For example, if we wanted to change the Tax Line for the Postage account from Unassigned to the appropriate Tax Line:

1. From the Home Page, select **Chart of Accounts**

2. From the Chart of Accounts window, right-click on the account: **63100 Postage**

3. Select **Edit Account**

4. When the Edit Account window appears, change the Tax-Line Mapping from Unassigned to: **Other Deductions: Postage & delivery**

5. To save the changes, click **Save and Close**

6. **Close** the Chart of Accounts window

INCOME TAX SUMMARY REPORT

After we confirm that the Tax Line for each account is correct, we are ready to print an Income Tax Summary report. The Income Tax Summary report lists sales and expenses that should appear on the business federal tax return filed with the IRS.

A business can use the information on the Income Tax Summary report to manually complete its income tax return. A sole proprietorship files Schedule C (attached to the owner's personal 1040 tax return). A corporation files Form 1120. A subchapter S corporation files Form 1120S.

INCOME TAX DETAIL REPORT

If you want to view detail for the line items shown on the Income Tax Summary report, we could display the Income Tax Detail report.

Section 10.10

Management Reports

Reports used by management do not have to follow a specified set of rules such as the Internal Revenue Code. Instead, management reports are prepared as needed to provide management with information for making operating and business decisions.

Management reports include:

- Cash flow forecast
- Accounts receivable aging (See Chapter 5)
- Accounts payable aging (See Chapter 6)
- Inventory reports (See Chapter 7)
- Budgets (See Chapter 15)

CASH FLOW FORECAST

QuickBooks permits you to forecast cash flows. This enables you to project whether you will have enough cash to pay bills when they are due. If it appears that you will need additional cash, then you can arrange for a loan or line of credit to pay your bills. The Cash Flow Forecast report lists projected cash inflows and cash outflows.

C10.10.1 Cash Flow Forecast. To prepare a Cash Flow Forecast report for Rock Castle Construction:

1. From the Report Center, select: **Company & Financial > Cash Flow Forecast**

2. Select Date: **Next 4 Weeks**. Click **Run**.

3. Export to **Excel** or **print** the Cash Flow Forecast report

4. **Close** the Cash Flow Forecast window

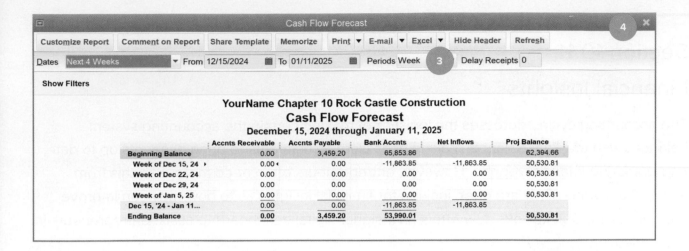

We can also email reports. For example, a client might email QuickBooks reports to the accountant for review. To email a QuickBooks report, select the Email button at the top of the Reports window.

Section 10.11

Financial Insights

The accounting cycle addresses the logistics of making certain the accounting system balances with the Trial Balance, making necessary adjustments to bring accounts up to date, and preparing financial reports. However, entrepreneurs often need more than this from financial software. They are often looking for financial insights as to how they can improve their business. QuickBooks now offers an Insights digital dashboard to assist entrepreneurs in this endeavor.

To use QuickBooks Insights:

1 From the Home Page, select: **Insights**

2 Select the **arrow** to the right of the screen to advance to the next insight

3 Notice in the yearly comparison how Rock Castle's income has increased in 2024

4 Select the **right** arrow again to advance to the next insight

5 This insight shows the top customers by sales, listing Brian Cook as the top customer. Although sales by customers are important, profitability by customer might be even more important for business success.

6 Notice the graph showing the breakdown for Expenses. Select **This Fiscal Year** to see the proportion of expenses for Job Expenses, Payroll Expenses, Depreciation Expense and Other Accounts.

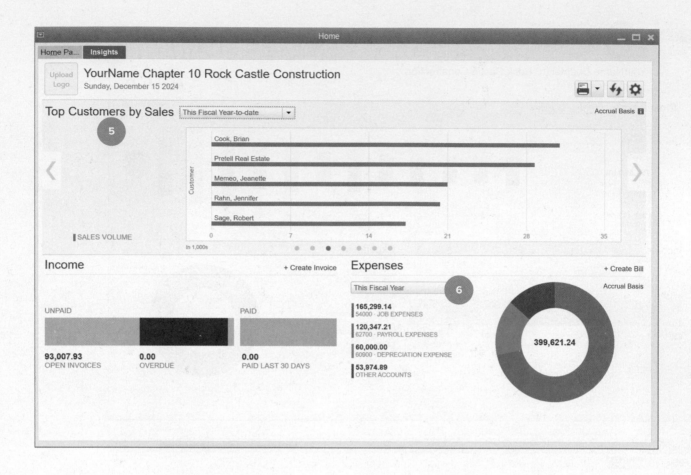

Section 10.12

Back Up QuickBooks Files

BACK UP QBB

Save a backup of your Chapter 10 file using the file name: **YourName Chapter 10 Backup.QBB**.

QBW WORKFLOW

If you will be using the same computer to complete Chapter 10 QuickBooks exercises, just as in a business workflow, you can continue to use the same QBW file.

If you are using the QBW approach, leave your QBW file open and proceed directly to Exercise 10.1.

QBB RESTORE

If you are using the QBB approach and ending your computer session now, close your QBW file and exit QuickBooks. When you restart, you will restore your backup file to complete Exercise 10.1.

Section 10.13

Accounting Essentials: Financial Reports

Accounting Essentials summarize important foundational accounting knowledge that may be useful when using QuickBooks

What is the objective of financial reporting?

The objective of financial reporting is to provide information to external users for decision making.

What are three types of financial reports a business prepares?

1. **Financial statements.** Financial statements are reports used by investors, owners, and creditors to make decisions. A banker might use the financial statements to decide whether to make a loan to a company. A prospective investor might use the financial statements to decide whether to invest in a company.

   The three financial statements most frequently used by external users are:

   - **Profit and Loss** (also referred to as the P & L or Income Statement) lists income and expenses, summarizing the income a company has earned and the expenses incurred to earn the income.
   - **Balance Sheet** lists assets, liabilities, and owners' equity, summarizing what a company *owns* and *owes* on a particular date.
   - **Statement of Cash Flows** lists cash flows from operating, investing, and financing activities of a business.

2. **Tax forms.** The objective of the tax form is to provide information to federal and state tax authorities. When preparing tax returns, a company uses different rules from those used to prepare financial statements. When preparing a federal tax return, use the Internal Revenue Code.

   Tax forms include the following:

   - Federal income tax return
   - State tax return

- Federal Payroll Forms 940, 941/944, W-2, W-3
- Federal Form 1099

3. **Management reports.** Management reports are used by internal users (managers) to make decisions regarding company operations. These reports are created to satisfy a manager's information needs.

Examples of reports that managers use include:
- Cash budget that projects amounts of cash that will be collected and spent in the future. (Note a Statement of Cash Flows focuses on cash inflows and outflows in the *past*. A Cash Budget focuses on expected cash flows in the *future*.)
- Accounts receivable aging report that lists the age and balance of customer accounts receivable so accounts are collected in a timely manner.

Exercise 10.1 Profit and Loss, Vertical Analysis

 Rock Castle Construction

BACKSTORY

You vaguely recall from your college accounting course that performing financial statement analysis can reveal additional useful information. Since Mr. Castle asked for whatever additional information he might need, you decide to print a vertical analysis of the Profit and Loss Statement using QuickBooks.

E10.1.1 QuickBooks File

If you will be using the same computer and the same Chapter 10.QBW file:

1. If your Chapter 10.QBW file is not already open, open it by selecting **File > Open Previous Company**. Select your **Chapter 10.QBW file**. If a QuickBooks Information window appears with a message about the sample company file, click **OK**.

2. Update the company name to **YourName Exercise 10.1 Rock Castle Construction** by selecting **Company Menu > My Company**.

> If you are not using the same computer that you used for Chapter 10, you will need to restore your Chapter 10 Backup.QBB file using the instructions in Appendix B: Back Up and Restore QuickBooks Files. After restoring, update the company name to YourName Exercise 10.1 Rock Castle Construction.

E10.1.2 Profit and Loss, Vertical Analysis

Prepare a customized Profit and Loss Statement that shows each item on the statement as a percentage of sales (income):

1. From the Report Center, select **Company & Financial > Profit & Loss Standard**

2. Select Dates: **This Fiscal Year**. Click **Run**.

3. To customize the report, click the **Customize Report** button

4. When the Modify Report window appears, select **Display** tab

5. Select: **% of Income**

6. Click **OK**

7. Export to **Excel** or **print** the report

8. **Highlight** the single largest income (revenue) item as a percentage of income

9. **Highlight** the profit margin (net income as a percentage of sales)

10. Memorize the Profit & Loss Vertical Analysis report. Save in the Memorized Report Group: **Accountant**.

E10.1.3 Income and Expense Graph

QuickBooks provides you with the ability to easily graph profit and loss information. A graph is simply another means to communicate financial information in a visual form.

To create an Income and Expense Graph for Rock Castle Construction:

1. From the Report Center, select **Company & Financial > Income & Expense Graph**

2. Select Dates: **This Fiscal Year**. Click **Run** to display the QuickInsight: Income and Expense Graph window.

3. Select the **By Account** button.

4. The upper section of the QuickInsight: Income and Expense Graph window displays a bar chart of income and expense by month for the fiscal year. Answer the following question about the bar chart: In which month of the year did Expenses exceed Income?

5. The lower section of the QuickInsight: Income and Expense Graph window displays a pie chart showing the relative proportion of each expense as a percentage of total expenses. Answer the following question about the pie chart: Job Expenses are what percentage of Total Expenses?

6. The lower section of the QuickInsight: Income and Expense Graph window displays a pie chart showing the relative proportion of each expense as a percentage of total expenses. Answer the following question about the pie chart: What percentage do Payroll Expenses represent as a percentage of Total Expenses?

7. **Close** the QuickInsight: Income and Expense Graph window

E10.1.4 Back Up Exercise 10.1

Save a backup of your Exercise file using the file name: **YourName Exercise 10.1 Backup.QBB**. See Appendix B: Back Up and Restore QuickBooks Files for instructions.

Exercise 10.2 Balance Sheet, Vertical Analysis

 Rock Castle Construction

BACKSTORY

Also, you decide to prepare a customized Balance Sheet that displays each account on the Balance Sheet as a percentage of total assets. This vertical analysis indicates the proportion of total assets that each asset represents. For example, inventory might be 30 percent of total assets. Vertical analysis also helps to assess the percentage of assets financed by debt versus owners' equity.

E10.2.1 QuickBooks File

If you will be using the same computer and the same QBW file:

1. Select your **QBW file**.

2. Update the company name to **YourName Exercise 10.2 Rock Castle Construction** by selecting **Company Menu > My Company**.

> If you are not using the same computer that you used for Chapter 10 and Exercise 10.1, you will need to restore your latest prior Backup.QBB file using the instructions in Appendix B: Back Up and Restore QuickBooks files. After restoring, update the company name to YourName Exercise 10.2 Rock Castle Construction.

E10.2.2 Balance Sheet, Vertical Analysis

Prepare a customized Balance Sheet that shows each account as a percentage of total assets.

1. From the Report Center, select: **Company & Financial** > **Balance Sheet Standard**

2. Select Dates: **This Fiscal Year.** Click **Run.**

3. Select the **Customize Report button** > **Display tab** > **% of Column**

4. Export to **Excel** or **print** the customized Balance Sheet

5. **Highlight** the asset that represents the second largest percentage of total assets

6. **Highlight** the percentage of assets financed with debt. (Hint: What is the percentage of total liabilities?)

E10.2.3 Back Up Exercise 10.2

Save a backup of your Exercise file using the file name: **YourName Exercise 10.2 Backup.QBB**. See Appendix B: Back Up and Restore QuickBooks Files for instructions.

Exercise 10.3 Financial Analysis

 Rock Castle Construction

BACKSTORY

" Last year, the bank told us we had money in the bank, but QuickBooks told us we were broke and had no money in our Checking account to pay bills." Mr. Castle casts you a look as he rushes past your cubicle—a look that warns you to be ready to answer a QuickBooks question.

"We had to hire an accountant last year to find the missing cash in QuickBooks." Rock Castle now pauses as you anticipated the upcoming question.*" Will we need to hire an accountant this year to find the missing cash or can you show me the money?"*

Rapidly, you reply, *"Mr. Castle, this year we know where all our cash is."* When you look up to show him some QuickBooks reports, Mr. Castle is already back in his office on the phone.

E10.3.1 QuickBooks File

If you will be using the same computer and the same QBW file:

1. Select your **QBW file**.

2. Update the company name to **YourName Exercise 10.3 Rock Castle Construction** by selecting **Company Menu** > **My Company**.

If you are not using the same computer that you used for Chapter 10, Exercise 10.1 and Exercise 10.2, you will need to restore your latest prior Backup.QBB file using the instructions in Appendix B: Back Up and Restore QuickBooks files. After restoring, update the company name to YourName Exercise 10.3 Rock Castle Construction.

E10.3.2 General Ledger: Show Me the Money

To show Mr. Castle the money, complete the following steps.

1. Display a General Ledger report (**Report Center > Accountant & Taxes > General Ledger**) for Rock Castle Construction for December 15 to December 31, 2024

2. To display all accounts in use with a balance, select **Customize Report button > Display tab > Advanced > In Use > Report Date > OK**

3. To filter for all asset accounts, select **Customize Report button > Filters tab> Account > All assets > Include split detail? No > OK**

4. Export to **Excel** or **print** the General Ledger report using the filter

5. **Highlight** the account on your General Ledger report where you think the accountant found the missing cash last year

E10.3.3 Ratios

In addition to the QuickBooks reports you will be providing Mr. Castle, you decide that preparing ratio analysis for him will provide additional insight into Rock Castle Construction operations.

Using your QuickBooks reports from this chapter and exercises, calculate the following ratios.

1. The Current Ratio is used as a measure of how well current assets cover the current liabilities that will be due within the next year. If an enterprise has $2 in current assets for each $1 in current liabilities, the current ratio is stated as 2:1.

    Calculate the Current Ratio (Current Assets/Current Liabilities) for Rock Castle Construction. Round to 1 decimal place. _____:_____

2. The debt ratio focuses on the percentage of company assets financed with debt as opposed to equity. For example, a debt ratio of 40% indicates that 40 percent of the enterprise's assets are financed with debt. Too high a debt ratio can indicate increased risk of default on the debt.

    Calculate the Debt Ratio (Total Liabilities/Total Assets) for Rock Castle Construction. _____%

3. The profit margin shows the percentage of each sales dollar that is left in profit. For example, a profit margin of 10% indicates that on average, 10 cents of each dollar of sales is profit. Profit margin varies greatly by industry with some industries, such as discount stores, having low profit margins.

    Calculate the Profit Margin (Net Income or Net Profit/Total Sales) for Rock Castle Construction for this fiscal year. _____%

4. Prepare a brief email to Rock Castle summarizing the results of your ratio analysis and outlining your conclusions, comments, or recommendations based on your analysis.

E10.3.4 Back Up Exercise 10.3

Save a backup of your Exercise file using the file name: **YourName Exercise 10.3 Backup.QBB**. See Appendix B: Back Up and Restore QuickBooks Files for instructions.

Exercise 10.4 Income Tax Preparation Report

 Rock Castle Construction

BACKSTORY

In order to cross check the change to the Tax Line for 63100 Postage account that you completed in this chapter, you decide to run another Income Tax Preparation report.

E10.4.1 QuickBooks File

If you will be using the same computer and the same QBW file:

1. Select your **QBW file**.

2. Update the company name to **YourName Exercise 10.4 Rock Castle Construction** by selecting **Company Menu > My Company**.

> If you are not using the same computer that you used for Chapter 10 and Exercise 10.1 - 10.3 you will need to restore your latest prior Backup.QBB file using the instructions in Appendix B: Back Up and Restore QuickBooks files. After restoring, update the company name to YourName Exercise 10.4 Rock Castle Construction.

E10.4.2 Income Tax Preparation Report

Prepare an Income Tax Preparation report for Rock Castle Construction at December 31, 2024.

1. From the Report Center, select: **Accountant & Taxes > Income Tax Preparation**

2. Select Dates: **This Tax Year.** Click **Run**.

3. Export to **Excel** or **print** the report

4. Verify and **highlight** the changed tax line item for account: **63100 Postage**

5. **Close** the Income Tax Preparation report

E10.4.3 Back Up Exercise 10.4

Save a backup of your Exercise file using the file name: **YourName Exercise 10.4 Backup.QBB**. See Appendix B: Back Up and Restore QuickBooks Files for instructions.

PROJECT 10.1

Larry's Landscaping

As an accounting consultant for Larry's Landscaping complete the following to create QuickBooks reports.

💡 **Troubleshooting QuickBooks and Correcting Errors** are crucial **QuickBooks** skill to acquire. **Troubleshooting resources include:**
- **www.My-QuickBooks.com > QuickBooks Troubleshooting (QT) Tips**
- **Chapter 17, Quick Review Guide, contains tips on Correcting Errors**
- **Appendix D, QuickBooks Troubleshooting (QT), provides you with an effective troubleshooting process**

🌐 QuickBooks SatNav

The objective of Project 10.1 is to facilitate your mastery of QuickBooks Desktop. Project 10.1 focuses on QuickBooks Reports.

QuickBooks SatNav

 QuickBooks Settings

Company Settings
Chart of Accounts

QuickBooks Transactions

Banking
Customers & Sales
Vendors & Expenses
Employees & Payroll

QuickBooks Reports

Reports

P10.1.1 QuickBooks File

1. Use either your QuickBooks Company file (QBW) or restore the backup file (QBB) that you completed for Project 9.1. (If you have issues with your QuickBooks file, contact your instructor.)

2. Update the Company Name to: **YourName Project 10.1 Larry's Landscaping**

P10.1.2 Profit and Loss

1. Export to **Excel** the Profit and Loss Standard report for January 1 to December 31, 2024

2. On the Profit and Loss report, **highlight** the item that generates the most income (revenue) for Larry's Landscaping

3. Export to **Excel** the Profit and Loss Standard report for January 1 to December 31, 2024 with a vertical analysis showing each item as a percentage of income

4. **Highlight** the item that generates the second largest amount of income (revenue) as a percentage of income for Larry's Landscaping

5. **Highlight** the profit margin (net income as a percentage of sales)

P10.1.3 Balance Sheet

1. Export to **Excel** the Balance Sheet Standard report as of December 31, 2024

2. Export to **Excel** the Balance Sheet Standard report with a vertical analysis showing each account as a percentage of total assets as of December 31, 2024

3. On the vertical analysis Balance Sheet, **highlight** the asset that represents the largest percentage of total assets

4. On the vertical analysis Balance Sheet, **highlight** the asset that represents the second largest percentage of total assets

5. **Highlight** the percentage of assets financed with debt. (Hint: What is the percentage of total liabilities?)

P10.1.4 Statement of Cash Flows

1. Export to **Excel** the Statement of Cash Flows report for January 1 to December 31, 2024

2. On the Statement of Cash Flows, **highlight** Net cash provided by Operating Activities

3. On the Statement of Cash Flows, **highlight** Net cash provided by Financing Activities

4. On the Statement of Cash Flows, **highlight** Net change in cash for the period

P10.1.5 Accounts Receivable Aging

1. Export to **Excel** the Accounts Receivable (A/R) Aging Summary at December 31, 2024

2. **Highlight** any accounts receivable owed to Larry's Landscaping by customers that are 1 - 30 days past due

P10.1.6 Accounts Payable Aging

1. Export to **Excel** the Accounts Payable (A/P) Aging Summary at December 31, 2024

2. **Highlight** any accounts payable owed by Larry's Landscaping to vendors that are 1 - 30 days past due

P10.1.7 Back Up Project 10.1

Save a backup of your Project file using the file name: **YourName Project 10.1 Backup.QBB**. See Appendix B: Back Up and Restore QuickBooks Files for instructions.

Chapter 11

QuickBooks Service Company

 Paint Palette

BACKSTORY

Lately, you've considered starting your own business and becoming an entrepreneur. You have been looking for a business opportunity that would use your talents to make money.

While working at Rock Castle Construction, you've overheard conversations that some of the customers are dissatisfied with the quality of the paint jobs. In addition, you believe there is a demand for custom painting. You know that Rock Castle Construction lost more than one job because it could not find a subcontractor to do custom painting.

One morning when you arrive at work, you hear Mr. Castle's voice booming throughout the office. "That's the second time this month!" he roars into the telephone. *"How are we supposed to finish our jobs on time when the painting subcontractor doesn't show up?!"* Mr. Castle slams down the phone.

That morning you begin to seriously consider the advantages and disadvantages of starting your own painting service business. Perhaps you could pick up some work from Rock Castle Construction. You could do interior and exterior painting for homes and businesses including custom-painted murals while continuing to work part-time for Rock Castle Construction maintaining its accounting records. Now that you have learned QuickBooks, you can quickly enter transactions and create the reports Mr. Castle needs, leaving you time to operate your own painting service business.

When you return from lunch, you notice Angel Merriman in Mr. Castle's office. Then you overhear Mr. Castle telling her, *"We would like to help you, Ms. Merriman, but we don't have anyone who can do a custom-painted seascape on your office wall. If I hear of anyone who does that type of work, I'll call you."*

You watch as the two of them shake hands and Ms. Merriman walks out the front door. Sensing a window of opportunity, you turn to Mr. Castle and ask, *"Would you mind if I help out Ms. Merriman with the mural?"*

Mr. Castle nods his approval. *"If it keeps one of our customers happy, then I'm happy. Plus she has a very successful cybersecurity business—Angel Merriman Associates."*

You swiftly pursue Ms. Merriman into the parking lot.

"Ms. Merriman—"

She stops and turns to look at you. *"Ms. Merriman—I understand that you are looking for someone to paint a seacape mural for your office."*

"Yes, as a matter of fact, I am." Angel pauses, then continues, *"Look, I spend much of my time working in my office in highly challenging cybersecurity situations, so I need some stress relief in my surrounding environment. I decided on a seascape mural for my office."*

"Sounds reasonable. I'd like to bid on the job."

With a sparkle in her eye, Ms. Merriman asks, *"How soon can you start?"*

"As soon as I get off work this afternoon!" you reply. *"Would you like a bid on the job?"*

Without hesitation, Ms. Merriman replies, *"I trust you will be fair to your first customer."*

When you reenter the office building, Mr. Castle is waiting for you. *"Congratulations,"* he says. Handing you a note, he adds, *"By the way, here is a customer you should call — Tracey Kari's black Labrador, Odin, somehow managed to squeeze through a cat door to get inside and redecorate the laundry and workroom with dirty paws. Kari would like the walls repainted with some type of marbled faux painting to conceal the damage."*

"Thanks, Mr. Castle. I'll do that right away," you reply as you head toward your cubicle.

Walking back to your cubicle, you quickly make start-up decisions:

1. To use the sole proprietorship form of business.
2. To name your business Paint Palette.
3. To use environmentally friendly paints and European painting techniques (faux and murals) for competitive advantage.
4. To invest in a computer so that you can use QuickBooks to maintain the accounting records for your business.

Now you will have two sources of income:

- Wages from Rock Castle Construction reported on your W-2 and attached to your 1040 tax return.
- Income from your painting business reported on a Schedule C attached to your 1040 tax return.

So you decide to treat yourself to a reward—a new smartphone—and use social media marketing to reach new customers for your new business endeavor.

Preferring to use your savings rather than take out a bank loan, you invest $10,000 of your savings to launch Paint Palette. Then you prepare the following list of items your business will need.

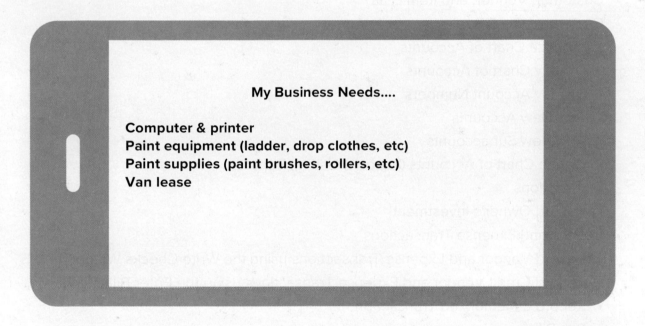

My Business Needs....

Computer & printer
Paint equipment (ladder, drop clothes, etc)
Paint supplies (paint brushes, rollers, etc)
Van lease

Chapter 11

Learning Objectives

Chapter 11 covers the following QuickBooks topics:

- Create New Company
- QuickBooks Company Setup
- Add the People You Do Business With
- Add the Products and Services You Sell
- Add Your Bank Accounts
- Customer, Vendor, and Item Lists
- Customize QuickBooks
- Customize Chart of Accounts
  - Display Chart of Accounts
  - Display Account Numbers
  - Add New Accounts
  - Add New Subaccounts
  - Create Chart of Accounts (Account Listing) Report
- Transactions
  - Record Owner's Investment
- Vendor and Expense Transactions
  - Record Vendor and Expense Transactions using the Write Checks Window
  - Record Credit Vendor and Expense Transactions using the Enter Bills Window
  - Record a Memorized Transaction
  - Pay Bills
- Customer and Sales Transactions
  - Customize Invoice
  - Create Invoice
  - Receive Payment
  - Make Deposit
  - Invoice History Tracker
- Adjusting Entries
- Reports
- Close the Accounting Period

Section 11.1

 QuickBooks SatNav

The objective of this chapter is to facilitate your mastery of QuickBooks Desktop. We will cover setting up a new QuickBooks service company, customize the QuickBooks Chart of Accounts, enter QuickBooks transactions, and create reports. This chapter provides the opportunity to integrate knowledge of QuickBooks Desktop through all three phases of the QuickBooks SatNav.

As shown in the following QuickBooks SatNav, Chapter 11 QuickBooks Service Company covers all three processes: QuickBooks Settings, QuickBooks Transactions, and QuickBooks Reports.

QuickBooks SatNav

⚙ QuickBooks Settings

> ⚙ Company Settings

> ⚙ Chart of Accounts

QuickBooks Transactions

> Banking

> Customers & Sales

> Vendors & Expenses

> Employees & Payroll

📊 QuickBooks Reports

> 📊 Reports

Section 11.2

New QuickBooks Service Company

In this chapter, you will set up a new service company in QuickBooks by completing the following steps:

- **EasyStep Interview.** Use the EasyStep Interview to enter information and preferences for the new company. Based on the information entered, QuickBooks automatically creates a Chart of Accounts.

- **Create Lists.**

  - **Customer List.** In the Customer List, enter information about customers to whom you sell products and services.

  - **Vendor List.** In the Vendor List, enter information about vendors from whom you buy products, supplies, and services.

  - **Item List.** In the Item List, enter information about (1) products and services you sell to customers and (2) products and services you buy from vendors.

- **Customize the Chart of Accounts.** Modify the Chart of Accounts to customize it for your business.

- **Record Transactions.** Enter business transactions in QuickBooks using onscreen forms and the onscreen Journal.

- **Reports.** After preparing adjusting entries, print financial reports.

If you hired employees, you would also enter information into the Employee List. In this case, Paint Palette has no employees.

> **Download the Excel Report Template for Chapter 11 at www.My-QuickBooks.com, QB2021 link, at the Online Learning Center www.mhhe.com/kay2021, or if you are using Connect, see your Connect assignments for the Excel Report Template.**

Section 11.3

Create New Company

START QUICKBOOKS

To start QuickBooks software, click the **QuickBooks** icon on your desktop. If a QuickBooks icon does not appear on your desktop, from Microsoft® Windows® click **Start** button > **QuickBooks** > **QuickBooks Premier Accountant Edition**.

EASYSTEP INTERVIEW

To create a new company data file in QuickBooks, use the EasyStep Interview. The EasyStep Interview asks you a series of questions about your business. Then QuickBooks uses the information to customize QuickBooks to fit your business needs.

Four options for how to set up a new company are:

- Express Start: Recommended for new QuickBooks users, this option will ask you a few basic questions and do the rest for you.
- Detailed Start: This option lets you control the setup and fine-tune the company file to meet your specific needs.
- Create: This choice permits you to create quickly a new company file by copying the preferences and key lists from an existing company.
- Other Options: This option lets you convert data from Quicken or other accounting software to create a new QuickBooks company file.

Create a new QuickBooks company using the EasyStep Interview as follows:

1   Select **Create a new company**

2   When the QuickBooks Setup window appears, select **Detailed Start**

3   When the EasyStep Interview Enter Your Company Information window appears, enter Company Name: **YourName Paint Palette**. Press the **Tab** key, and QuickBooks will automatically enter the company name in the Legal name field. Since the company will do business under its legal name, the Company name and Legal name fields are the same.

4 Enter the company information.

Tax ID	**333-22-4444**
Address	**333 Universe Boulevard**
City	**Bayshore**
State	**CA**
Zip	**94326**
Phone	**800-555-1358**
Email	**<Enter your email address>**

5 Select **Next**

6 In the Select Your Industry window, select **General Service-based Business**

7 Select **Next**

8 When the How Is Your Company Organized? window appears, select **Sole Proprietorship.**

How your business entity is organized (Sole Proprietorship, Partnership, Limited Liability Partnership (LLP), Limited Liability Company (LLC), C Corporation, S Corporation, or Non-Profit) determines which tax form and tax lines you use.

9 Select **Next**

10 Select the first month of your fiscal year: **January**

11 Select **Next**

12 In the Set Up Your Administrator Password window:
- Enter your administrator **password**
- Retype the **password**

13 Select **Next**. When the Create Your Company File window appears, click **Next** to choose a file name and location to save your company file.

14 When the Filename for New Company window appears, select Save in: **Desktop**

15 Enter File name: **YourName Chapter 11**

16 Click **Save**

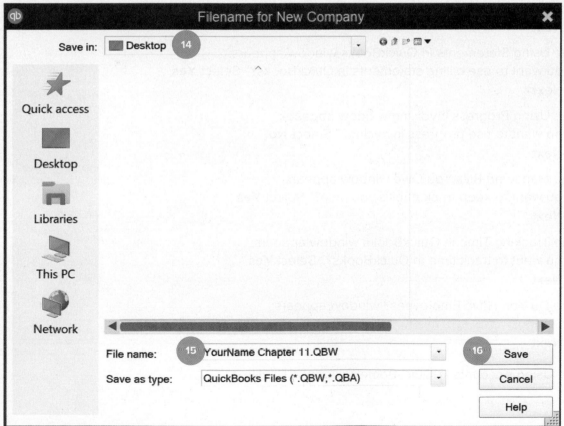

> **New Company from Existing Company. On the File Menu, notice the New Company from Existing Company File option. This choice permits you to create quickly a new company file by copying the preferences and key lists from an existing company.**

The My Shortcuts window should appear on the left side of your QuickBooks company screen. The next section of the EasyStep Interview is to customize QuickBooks by turning on features to fit your business needs.

1   When the Customizing QuickBooks For Your Business window appears, click **Next**

2   When the What Do You Sell? window appears:
- Select **Services only**
- Click **Next**

3   When asked "Do you charge sales tax?"
- Select **No**
- Click **Next**

4   When asked "Do you want to create estimates in QuickBooks?"
- Select **Yes**
- Click **Next**

5   When the Using Statements in QuickBooks window appears:
- "Do you want to use billing statements in QuickBooks?" Select **Yes**
- Click **Next**

6   When the Using Progress Invoicing window appears:
- "Do you want to use progress invoicing?" Select **No**
- Click **Next**

7   When the Managing Bills You Owe window appears:
- "Do you want to keep track of bills you owe?" Select **Yes**
- Click **Next**

8   When the Tracking Time in QuickBooks window appears:
- "Do you want to track time in QuickBooks?" Select **Yes**
- Click **Next**

9   When the Do You Have Employees? window appears:
- Select **No**
- Click **Next**

10   Read the Using Accounts in QuickBooks window. Click **Next**.

11 When the Select a Date to Start Tracking Your Finances window appears:
- Select **Use today's date or the first day of the quarter or month**
- Enter Date **01/01/2025**
- Click **Next**

12 When the Review Income and Expense Accounts window appears, scroll down to review the accounts, then click **Next**

13 When the Congratulations! window appears, click **Go to Setup**

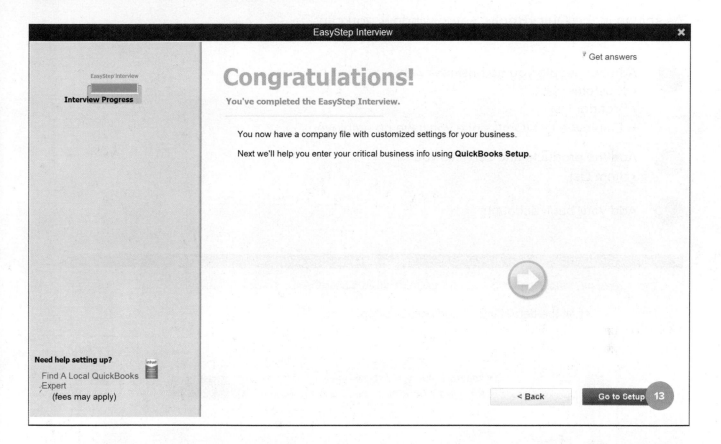

Section 11.4

QuickBooks Company Setup

After the EasyStep Interview is finished, you can start using the QuickBooks company file or you can finish the company setup using the following QuickBooks Setup window.

As shown in the QuickBooks Setup window, you can:

1 Add the people you do business with:
- Customer List
- Vendor List
- Employee List (Omit since you have no employees.)

2 Add the products and services you sell
- Item List

3 Add your bank accounts

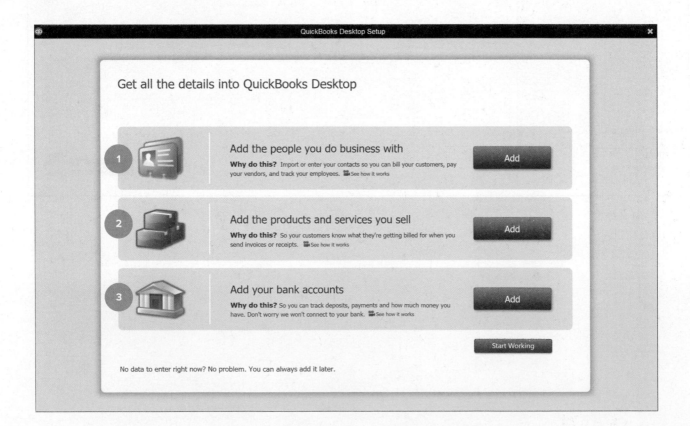

After completing these steps, you can customize your QuickBooks company file by completing the following:

1. Complete the company information
2. Customize preferences
3. Customize your Chart of Accounts

Section 11.5

Add The People You Do Business With

As you know from Chapter 5, the Customers List contains information about the customers to whom you sell services. In addition, the Customers List also contains information about jobs or projects for each customer. Currently, Paint Palette has two customers:

1. Angel Merriman Associates, who needs a custom seascape mural for her office
2. Tracey Kari, who needs faux painting in a laundry and workroom

As you know from Chapter 6, the Vendor List contains information about vendors from whom you buy products and services. Paint Palette needs to add Evan Paint Supplies as a vendor.

To add customers, vendors, and employees to your QuickBooks company file:

1. In the Add the People You Do Business With section of the QuickBooks Setup window, click the **Add** button
2. You have several options for how to add information about people you do business with as shown in the following Add the People You Do Business With window. Select **Paste from Excel or enter manually**.
3. Select **Continue**
4. When the Select Who to Add window appears, enter the following information about your first customer, Angel Merriman Associates.

Name	**Angel Merriman Associates**
Company Name	**Angel Merriman Associates**
First Name	**Angel**
Last Name	**Merriman**
Email	**angelmerrimanassociates@www.com**
Phone	**415-555-7579**
Address	**623 Thorsmork Road**
City, State, Zip	**Bayshore, CA 94326**
Contact Name	**Angel Merriman**

5. Select **Customer** radio button for Angel Merriman Associates

6 Move to the next line and enter the following information about Evan Paint Supplies

Name	**Evan Paint Supplies**
Company Name	**Evan Paint Supplies**
Email	**evanpaint@www.com**
Phone	**415-555-0301**
Address	**565 Steve Street**
City, State, Zip	**Bayshore, CA 94326**
Contact Name	**Evan Henry**

7 Select **Vendor** radio button for Evan Paint Supplies

8 Click **Continue**

9 If you had opening balances, you could enter those now. Instead, click **Continue**

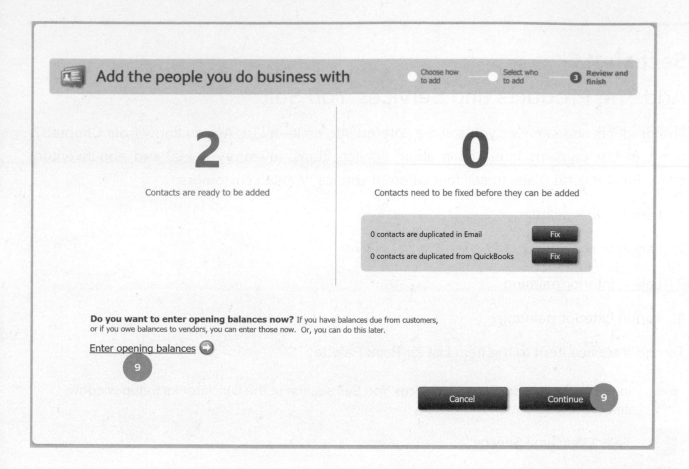

Section 11.6

Add The Products and Services You Sell

The products and services you sell are entered into an Item List. As you know from Chapter 7, the Item List contains information about service items, inventory items, and non-inventory items. Paint Palette plans to sell four different service items to customers:

1.   Labor: mural painting

2.   Labor: faux painting

3.   Labor: interior painting

4.   Labor: exterior painting

To add a service item to the Item List for Paint Palette:

1   In the Add the Products and Services You Sell section of the QuickBooks Setup window, select the **Add** button

2   Select Item type **Service**

3   Select **Continue**

4   Enter the following information about the new service item:

Name	**Labor**
Description	**Painting Labor**
Price	**0.00**

5   Click **Continue**

6   Click **Continue** again to return to the QuickBooks Setup window

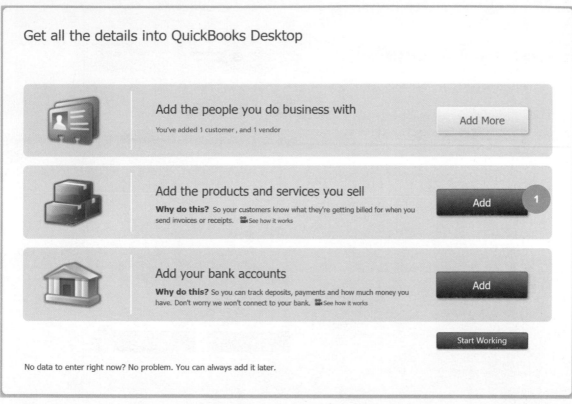

Get all the details into QuickBooks Desktop

Add the people you do business with
You've added 1 customer , and 1 vendor

[Add More]

Add the products and services you sell
Why do this? So your customers know what they're getting billed for when you send invoices or receipts. 📹 See how it works

[Add] ①

Add your bank accounts
Why do this? So you can track deposits, payments and how much money you have. Don't worry we won't connect to your bank. 📹 See how it works

[Add]

[Start Working]

No data to enter right now? No problem. You can always add it later.

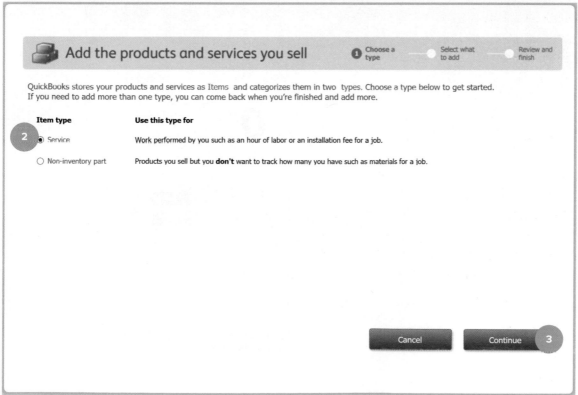

Add the products and services you sell

❶ Choose a type   Select what to add   Review and finish

QuickBooks stores your products and services as Items and categorizes them in two types. Choose a type below to get started. If you need to add more than one type, you can come back when you're finished and add more.

Item type	Use this type for
② ⦿ Service	Work performed by you such as an hour of labor or an installation fee for a job.
◯ Non-inventory part	Products you sell but you **don't** want to track how many you have such as materials for a job.

[Cancel]   [Continue] ③

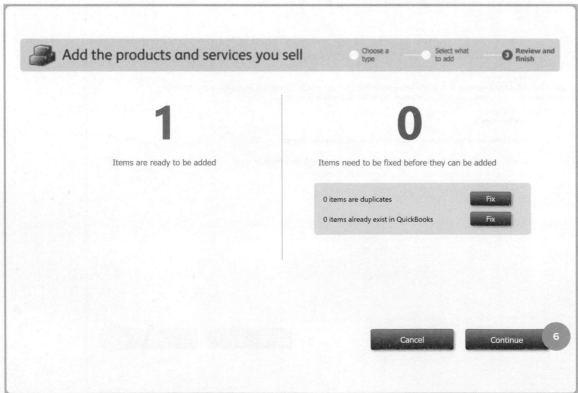

Section 11.7

Add Your Bank Accounts

Bank accounts in QuickBooks are used to track your company's deposits, payments, and current bank balances. A QuickBooks company file can have more than one bank account. For example, some companies use one bank account for payroll and another bank account for all other banking items.

To add a bank account for Paint Palette:

1 In the Add Your Bank Accounts section of the QuickBooks Setup window, click the **Add** button

2 Enter the following information about Paint Palette's bank account

Account Name	**Checking**
Account Number	**123456789**
Opening Balance	**0.00**
Opening Balance Date	**01/01/2025**

3 Select **Continue**

4 When asked if you want to order checks designed for QuickBooks, select **No Thanks**

5 Click **Continue** to return to the QuickBooks Setup window

6 Select **Start Working** at the bottom of the QuickBooks Setup window

7 When the New Feature Tour window appears, select **Vendor** to explore the new **Receipt Management** feature.

8 From the New Feature Tour window, select **Banking** to explore the **Advanced Bank Feeds** feature.

9 **Close** the New Feature Tour window

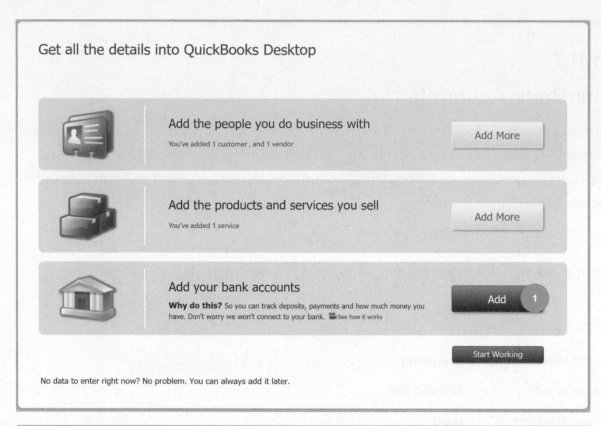

Get all the details into QuickBooks Desktop

Add the people you do business with
You've added 1 customer , and 1 vendor

[Add More]

Add the products and services you sell
You've added 1 service

[Add More]

Add your bank accounts
Why do this? So you can track deposits, payments and how much money you have. Don't worry we won't connect to your bank. ▣ See how it works

[Add] ①

[Start Working]

No data to enter right now? No problem. You can always add it later.

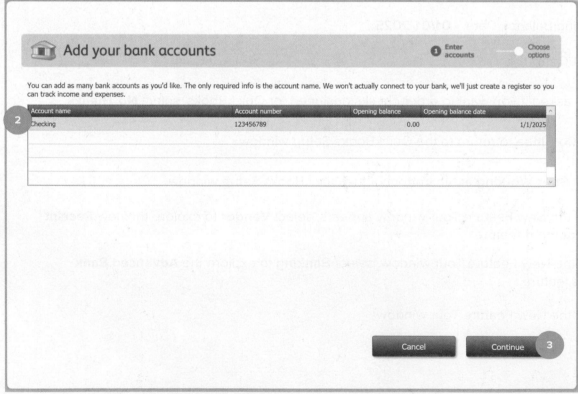

🏛 Add your bank accounts

❶ Enter accounts — Choose options

You can add as many bank accounts as you'd like. The only required info is the account name. We won't actually connect to your bank, we'll just create a register so you can track income and expenses.

Account name	Account number	Opening balance	Opening balance date
Checking	123456789	0.00	1/1/2025

[Cancel] [Continue] ③

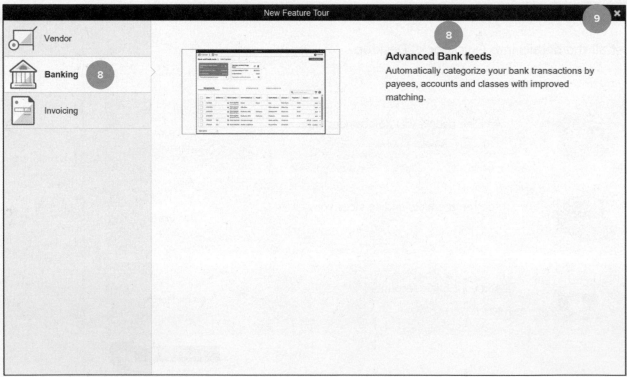

Section 11.8

Customer, Vendor, and Item Lists

CUSTOMER LIST

C11.8.1 Customer List. Before exporting the Customer List, let's add a new job for Angel Merriman Associates.

1 To add a new job, first display the Customer Center by selecting **Customers** on the Navigation Bar

2 Select Angel Merriman Associates in the Customers & Jobs List, then **right-click** to display the pop-up menu. Select **Add Job**.

3 Enter the following information into the New Job window:

Job Name	**Office**
Opening Balance	**0.00**
As of	**01/01/2025**
Job Description	**Office Seascape Mural**
Job Type <Add New>	**Mural**
Job Status	**Awarded**
Start Date	**01/03/2025**

4 Click **OK** to save

5 To export to Excel or print the Customer List, click the **Excel** button at the top of the Customer Center

6 Click **Export Customer List**

7 Select **Replace an existing worksheet**

8 **Browse** for **YourName CH11 REPORTS** Excel file

9 Select worksheet: **C11.8.1 CUS**

10 Select **Advanced**

11 Uncheck **Space between columns**

12 Check **Row height**

13 Uncheck **Include QuickBooks Export Guide worksheet with helpful advice**

14 Select **On printed report and screen**

15 Click **OK**

16 Select **Export**

17 If an Export Report Alert window appears asking if you want to continue, select **Do not display this message in the future > Yes**

18 **Close** the Customer Center

VENDOR LIST

C11.8.2 Vendor List. To export the Vendor List for Paint Palette:

1 Display the Vendor Center by selecting **Vendors** on the Navigation Bar

2 Select the **Excel** button at the top of the Vendor Center

3 Select **Export Vendor List**

4 Export to **Excel** the Vendor List

5 **Close** the Vendor Center

Item List

C11.8.3 Item List. To export the Item List for Paint Palette:

1 Display the Report Center by selecting **Reports** on the Navigation Bar

2 Select **List**

3 Select **Item Listing**

4 Select Date **01/01/2025**

5   Select **Run**

6   With the Item Listing report displayed on your screen, export to **Excel**.

⚠ When exporting to Excel, remember to select Advanced Excel Options:
- Uncheck **Space between columns**
- Uncheck **Include QuickBooks Export Guide worksheet with helpful advice**
- Select **On printed report and screen**

7   **Close** the Item Listing window and the Report Center window

Section 11.9
Customize QuickBooks

Notice that the Home Page for Paint Palette differs from the Home Page for Rock Castle Construction in the following ways:

1 The Vendors section of the Home Page for Paint Palette does not include Purchase Orders, Receive Inventory, and Enter Bills Against Inventory icons. During the company setup, you indicated that Paint Palette was a service company. Since you will not be selling a product, you will not be tracking inventory for resale.

2 Also notice that the Employees section does not include the Pay Employees, Pay Liabilities, and Process Payroll Forms icons. During the company setup, you indicated that there were no employees so these icons are not needed for Paint Palette.

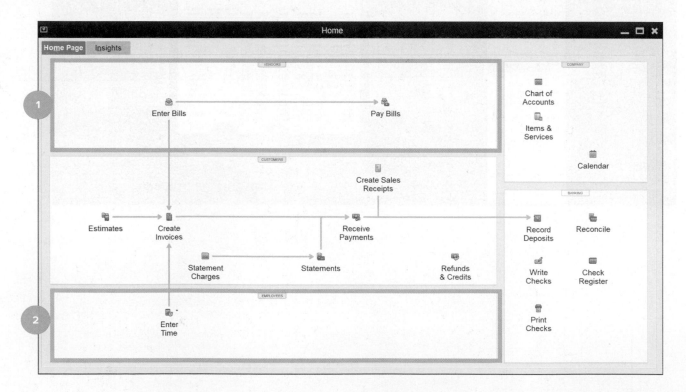

Next, we will customize QuickBooks for Paint Palette by entering company information and customizing preferences.

ENTER COMPANY INFORMATION

To enter additional company information:

1   Select **My Company** on the Navigation Bar

2   Select **Edit**

3   Update the Company Name: **YourName Chapter 11 Paint Palette**

4   Click **OK**

5   Verify Income Tax Form: **Form 1040 (Sole Proprietor)**

6   **Close** the My Company window

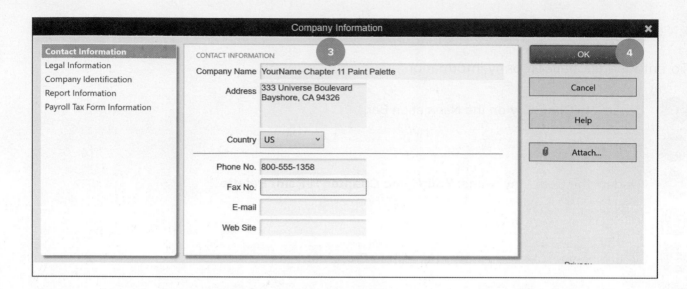

CUSTOMIZE QUICKBOOKS PREFERENCES

To customize your QuickBooks preferences:

1 Select **Edit Menu** > **Preferences** > **General** > **My Preferences**

2 Select Default Date to Use for New Transactions: **Use the last entered date as default**

3 Select **Desktop View** > **My Preferences** > **Show Home Page when opening a company file**

4 To customize the appearance of your QuickBooks, select **Company File Color Scheme**

5 Click **OK** to close the Preferences window

Section 11.10

Customize Chart of Accounts

The Chart of Accounts is a list of all the accounts Paint Palette will use when maintaining its accounting records. The Chart of Accounts is like a table of contents for accounting records.

In the EasyStep Interview, when you selected General Service-based Business as the type of industry, QuickBooks automatically created a Chart of Accounts for Paint Palette. Then QuickBooks permits you to customize the Chart of Accounts to fit your accounting needs.

Display Chart of Accounts

To display the following Chart of Accounts window:

1 Click **Chart of Accounts** icon in the Company section of the Home Page

2 Notice that the Chart of Accounts does not list the account numbers

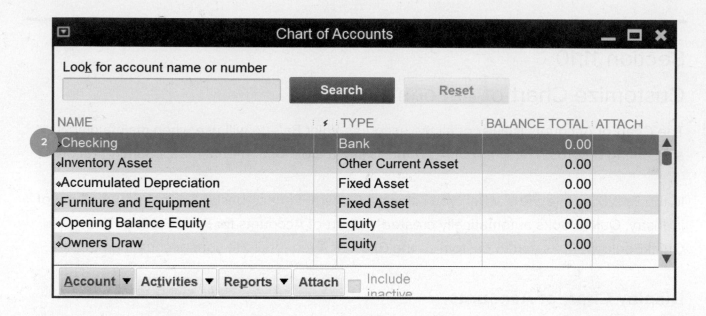

DISPLAY ACCOUNT NUMBERS

Display account numbers in the Chart of Accounts by completing the following steps:

1. Select **Edit Menu**

2. Select **Preferences**

3. When the Preferences window appears, select the **Accounting** icon on the left scrollbar

4. Select the **Company Preferences** tab

5. Select **Use account numbers**

6. Uncheck **Warn if transactions are 30 day(s) in the future**

7. Click **OK** to close the Preferences window

8. Your Chart of Accounts should now display account numbers preceding the account titles

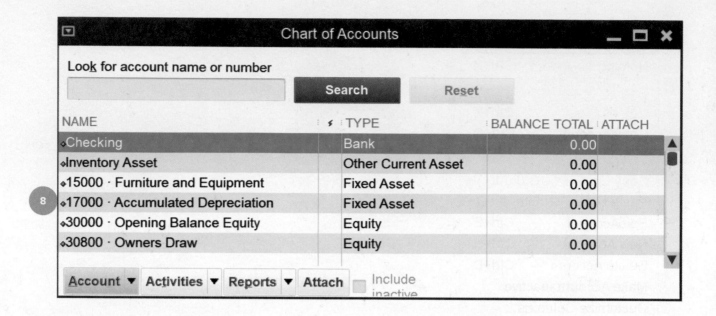

ADD NEW ACCOUNTS

Paint Palette will be purchasing a new computer. To account for the computer, you will need to add the following three accounts to the Chart of Accounts:

Account	**Computer**
Subaccount	**Computer Cost**
Subaccount	**Accumulated Depreciation Computer**

The Computer Cost subaccount contains the original cost of the computer. The Accumulated Depreciation subaccount for the computer accumulates all depreciation recorded for the computer over its useful life. The parent account, Computer, will show the net book value of the computer (cost minus accumulated depreciation).

> **Fixed Asset Item List.** If your business has a large number of fixed asset accounts, you can use the Fixed Asset Item List to track fixed asset information.

To add new accounts to the Chart of Accounts for Paint Palette:

1 From the Chart of Accounts window, **right-click** to display the pop-up menu. Then select **New**.

2 From the Add New Account: Choose Account Type window, select **Fixed Asset (major purchases)**

3 Click **Continue**

4 When the Add New Account window appears, select Account Type: **Fixed Asset**

5 Enter Account Number: **14100**

6 Enter Account Name: **Computer**

7 Enter Description: **Computer**

8 Select Tax Line: **<Unassigned>**

9 Click **Save & New** to enter another account

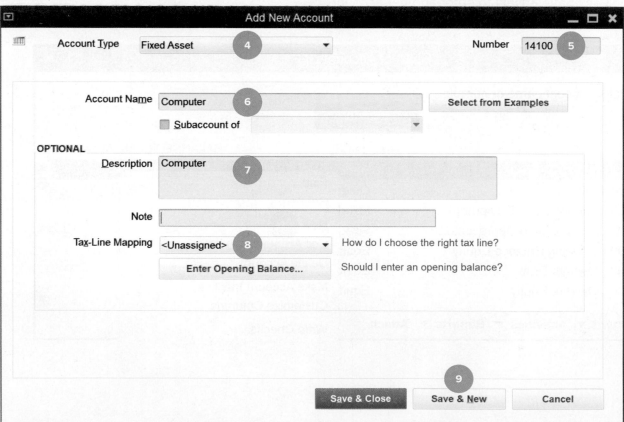

ADD NEW SUBACCOUNTS

When a blank Add New Account window appears, add a Computer Cost subaccount as follows:

1 Select Account Type: **Fixed Asset**

2 Enter Account Number: **14200**

3 Enter Account Name: **Computer Cost**

4 Check Subaccount of: **14100 – Computer**

5 Enter Description: **Computer Cost**

6 Select Tax Line: **<Unassigned>**

7 Click **Save & New** to add another subaccount

8 Add the Accumulated Depreciation Computer subaccount by entering the following information in the Add New Account window:

Account No.	**14300**
Account Type	**Fixed Asset**
Account Name	**Accumulated Depr Computer**
Subaccount of	**14100 Computer**
Account Description	**Accumulated Depreciation Computer**
Tax Line	**Unassigned**

9 Click **Save & Close** to close the Add New Account window

CREATE CHART OF ACCOUNTS (ACCOUNT LISTING) REPORT

C11.10.1 Chart of Accounts. To create the Chart of Accounts (Account Listing) report, complete the following steps:

1 From the Report Center select **List (or Accountant & Taxes) > Account Listing**

2 Select Date: **01/01/2025**. Select **Run**.

3 Export to **Excel** or **print** the Chart of Accounts

4 **Close** the Account Listing and Report Center windows

5 **Close** the Chart of Accounts window

Section 11.11

Transactions

Next we will enter business transactions for Paint Palette's first year of operations. These include transactions with the owner, customers, and vendors.

RECORD OWNER'S INVESTMENT

To launch your new business, you invest $10,000 in Paint Palette. In order to keep business records and your personal records separate, you open a business Checking account at the local bank for Paint Palette. You then deposit your personal check for $10,000 in the business Checking account.

In Chapters 3 and 4 you recorded deposits using the Record Deposits icon in the Banking section of the Home Page. You can also record deposits directly in the Check Register. QuickBooks then transfers the information to the Make Deposits window.

C11.11.1 Deposit Journal Entry. To record the deposit to Paint Palette's Checking account using the Make Deposits window, complete the following steps:

1. Click the **Record Deposits** icon in the Banking section of the Home Page

2. In the Make Deposits window, select Deposit To: **Checking**

3. Select Date: **01/01/2025**

4. On the Received From drop-down list, select **<Add New>**. Select **Other**, then click **OK**. Enter Name: **YourName**. Click **OK**.

5. Account: **30000: Opening Balance Equity**. Press the **Tab** key.

6. Memo: **Invested $10,000 in business**

7. Check No.: **1001**

8. Payment Method: **Check**

9   Amount: **10,000.00**

10   Select the **Save** icon at the top of the Make Deposits window

11   Select the **Journal** icon at the top of the Make Deposits window

12   Export the Transaction Journal to **Excel** or **print** the report

13   **Close** the Transaction Journal window and the Make Deposits window

Section 11.12

Vendor and Expense Transactions

Vendor and expense transactions can be either purchases made with a check or credit card or credit purchases on account that will be paid later.

RECORD VENDOR AND EXPENSE TRANSACTIONS USING THE WRITE CHECKS WINDOW

Paint Palette purchased a computer for $2,000. Because Paint Palette paid by check at the purchase, you can use the Write Checks window to record the purchase.

C11.12.1 Check Journal Entry. To record the computer purchase using the Write Checks window:

1. Click the **Write Checks** icon in the Banking section of the Home Page

2. In the following Write Checks window, select Bank Account: **Checking**

3. Select Date: **01/01/2025**

4. Pay to the Order of <Add New Vendor>: **Cornell Technologies**

5. Amount: **2000.00**

6. Account: **14200 Computer Cost**

7. Check: **Print Later**

8. Select the **Save** icon at the top of the Write Checks window

9. Select the **Reports tab > Transaction Journal**

10. Export the Transaction Journal report to **Excel** or **print** the report

11. **Close** the Transaction Journal and Write Checks windows

RECORD CREDIT VENDOR AND EXPENSE TRANSACTIONS USING THE ENTER BILLS WINDOW

When items are purchased on credit, a two-step process is used to record the purchase in QuickBooks.

	Action	Record Using...	Result
1	**Enter bill when received**	Enter Bills window	QuickBooks records an expense (or asset) and records an obligation to pay the bill later (accounts payable).
2	**Pay bill when due**	Pay Bills window	QuickBooks reduces accounts payable when the bill is paid. Bills can be paid using a check, credit card, or debit card.

C11.12.2 Bill Journal Entry. Next, we will enter bills for items Paint Palette purchased on credit. The first bill is for paint and supplies that Paint Palette purchased for the Merriman job.

1. Click the **Enter Bills** icon in the Vendors section of the Home Page

2. Select Date: **01/03/2025**

3. Select Vendor: **Evan Paint Supplies**

4. Enter Amount Due: **540.00**

5. Select Terms: **Net 30**

6. Click the **Expenses** tab

7. Select Account <Add New>: **64800 Paint Supplies Expense**

8. Select Customer & Job: **Angel Merriman Associates: Office**

9. Verify that **Billable** is checked

10 Select the **Save** icon at the top of the Enter Bills window. If asked if you want to make the change in payment terms permanent, select **Yes**.

11 Select the **Reports tab > Transaction Journal**

12 Export the Transaction Journal report to **Excel** or **print** the report

13 From the Enter Bills window, select **Save & New**

Notice that QuickBooks records the bill as accounts payable, indicating that Paint Palette has an obligation to pay these amounts to vendors. QuickBooks increases liabilities (accounts payable) on the company's Balance Sheet.

RECORD A MEMORIZED TRANSACTION

Often a transaction is recurring, such as monthly rent or utility payments. QuickBooks' memorized transaction feature permits you to memorize or save recurring transactions.

Paint Palette leases a van for a monthly lease payment of $336. You will use a memorized transaction to reuse each month to record the lease payment.

C11.12.3 Bill Journal Entry. To create a memorized transaction, first, enter the transaction in QuickBooks. To enter the bill for the van lease payment for Paint Palette:

1 From the open Enter Bills window on your screen, enter the following information about the van lease bill.

Date	**01/05/2025**
Vendor <Add New>	**Joseph Leasing**
Amount Due	**$336.00**
Terms	**Net 30**
Account	**67100 Rent Expense**
Memo	**Van lease**

2 Select **Memorize** icon at the top of the Enter Bills window

3 When the Memorize Transaction window appears, select **Add to my Reminders List**

4 Select How Often: **Monthly**

5 Enter Next Date: **02/01/2025**

6 Click **OK** to record the memorized transaction

7 Select the **Save** icon at the top of the Enter Bills window. If asked if you want to make the change in payment terms permanent, select **Yes**.

8 Select the **Reports tab** > **Transaction Journal**

9 Export the Transaction Journal report to **Excel** or **print** the report

10 Click **Save & Close** to close the Enter Bills window and record the van lease

To use a memorized transaction:

1 Select **Lists Menu** > **Memorized Transaction List**

2 When the Memorized Transaction List window appears, **double-click** the memorized transaction you want to use

3 QuickBooks displays the Enter Bills window with the memorized transaction data already entered. You can make any necessary changes on the form, such as changing the date. To record the bill in QuickBooks, you would click Save & Close.

At this time, **close the Enter Bills window without saving.** Then **close** the Memorized Transaction List window. Later, you will use the memorized transaction in **Exercise 11.5** at the end of the chapter.

PAY BILLS

To pay bills already entered:

1 Click the **Pay Bills** icon in the Vendors section of the Home Page

2 When the Pay Bills window appears, select Show Bills: **Due on or before 02/04/2025**, then press the **Tab** key. (If a Warning window appears, click OK, and then select All Vendors from the Filter By drop-down list.)

3   Select to pay the **Evan Paint Supplies bill for $540.00** and the **Joseph Leasing Bill for $336.00**

4   Select Payment Method: **Check**

5   Select **To be printed**

6   Select Payment Account: **Checking**

7   Enter Payment Date: **01/05/2025**

8   Click **Pay Selected Bills** to record the bills selected for payment

9   Select **Done** to close the Payment Summary window

C11.12.4 Pay Bills Journal Entries. To view the journal entries that QuickBooks created behind the screen when bills were entered and selected for payment, complete the following steps.

1   From the Navigation Bar, select **Reports > Accountant & Taxes > Journal**

2   Select Dates: **01/03/2025 to 01/05/2025**

3   Select **Run**

4   Export the Journal report to **Excel** or **print** the report

5   **Close** the Journal window

ADDITIONAL VENDOR AND EXPENSE TRANSACTIONS

See **Exercise 11.5** for additional vendor and expense transactions for Paint Palette.

Section 11.13

Customer and Sales Transactions

When using QuickBooks, sales transactions are recorded using three steps.

	Action	Record Using...	Result
1	Prepare invoice to record charges for services provided customer	Create Invoices window	The invoice is used to bill the customer for services. QuickBooks records the services provided on credit as an account receivable (an amount to be received in the future).
2	Receive customer payment	Receive Payments window	QuickBooks reduces accounts receivable and increases undeposited funds.
3	Record bank deposit	Make Deposits window	QuickBooks transfers the amount from undeposited funds to the bank account.

CUSTOMIZE INVOICE

Create a Custom Invoice Template with a Service Date column. This permits Paint Palette to bill customers once a month for all services provided during the month, listing each service date separately on the invoice.

To create a Custom Invoice Template, complete the following steps:

1. Click the **Create Invoices** icon in the Customers section of the Home Page

2. Click the **Formatting** tab in the upper portion of the Create Invoices window

3. Select **Manage Templates**

4. In the Manage Templates window, select **Intuit Service Invoice**

5. Then click **Copy**

6. To change the invoice template name, select **Copy of: Intuit Service Invoice**

7. In the Template Name field, change the template name to: **Service Date Invoice**

8. Click **OK** to close the Manage Templates window

9   Verify the Selected Template is: **Service Date Invoice**

10   Click the **Additional Customization** button

11   To add a Service Date column to the custom template, when the Additional Customization window appears, click the **Columns** tab

12   For Service Date, check **Screen** and **Print**. If a Layout Designer message about overlapping fields appears, select OK. If an Overlapping Fields message appears, select Continue.

13   Enter Title for Service Date: **Date**

14   Renumber the Order so they appear as shown

15   Click the **Layout Designer** button, adjust the field sizes as needed, then select **OK** to close the Layout Designer window.

16   Click **OK** to close the Customization windows

17   To view the custom invoice, if necessary from the Create Invoices window, select Template: **Service Date Invoice**

18   Notice that the first column of the invoice is now the **Date** column

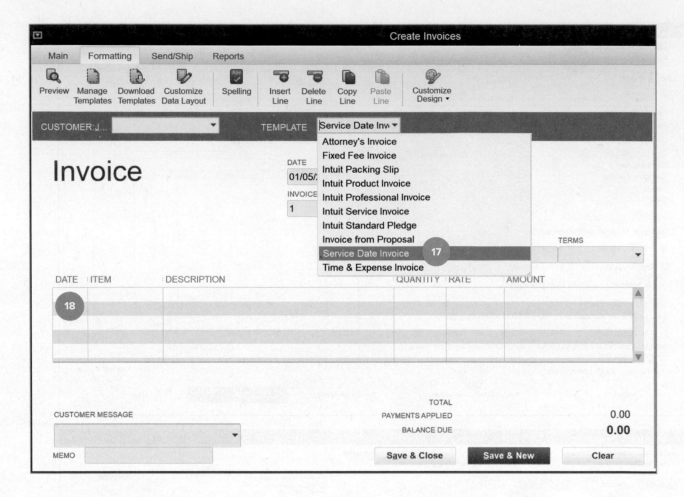

CREATE INVOICE

C11.13.1 Invoice Journal Entry. To create an invoice to record painting services provided by Paint Palette to Angel Merriman Associates during January:

1. If the Create Invoices window is not already open on your screen, select the **Create Invoices** icon in the Customers section of the Home Page

2. Select Customer & Job: **Angel Merriman Associates: Office**

3. When the Billable Time/Costs window appears to remind you the job has outstanding billable time, click **Select the outstanding billable time and costs to add to this invoice?**

4. Click **OK**

5. To select billable costs to apply to the Angel Merriman Associates invoice, from the Choose Billable Time and Costs window select the **Expenses** tab

6.   Enter Markup Amount or %: **40.0%**. (Be sure to enter %, otherwise $40 will be the markup.)

7.   Select Markup Account: **47900 – Sales**

8.   Check to select: **Evan Paint Supplies**

9.   Click **OK** to bill the Paint Supplies cost

10.   Select Template: **Service Date Invoice**

11.   Enter Invoice Date: **01/10/2025**

12.   The Angel Merriman Associates invoice will list Total Reimbursable Expenses of $756.00

13.   Next, enter the Service Date in the Create Invoices window: **01/05/2025**

14.   Select Item <Add New>: Type: **Service**. Item Name: **Labor Mural**. Subitem of: **Labor**. Description: **Labor Mural**. Rate: **50.00**. Account: **47900 Sales**.

15.   Quantity: **8** (hours)

16.   Enter Date (column): **01/07/2025**

17.   Select Item: **Labor Mural**

18.   Quantity: **8** (hours)

19.   Select **Print Later**

20.   Select the **Save** icon

21.   Select the **Reports tab**

22.   Select **Transaction Journal**

23.   Export to **Excel** or **print** the Transaction Journal

24.   **Close** the Transaction Journal and Create Invoices windows

RECEIVE PAYMENT

C11.13.2 Receive Payment Journal Entry. To record the Angel Merriman Associates payment for the invoice:

1 From the Customers section of the Home Page, click the **Receive Payments** icon

2 Select Received From: **Angel Merriman Associates: Office**

3 Enter Amount: **1556.00**. Verify that QuickBooks has selected the outstanding invoice.

4 Select Date: **01/13/2025**

5 Select Payment Method: **Check**

6 Enter Check No. **555**

7 Select **Save & New**

8 Select the **Find back arrow** to display the customer payment just recorded

9 Select **Reports tab > Transaction Journal**

10 Export the Transaction Journal report to **Excel** or **print** the report

11 **Close** the Transaction Journal and the Receive Payments windows

> **If a message appears regarding payment methods, select No.**

When a customer makes a payment, the customer's account receivable is reduced by the amount of the payment. In this case, the Angel Merriman Associates account receivable balance is reduced by $1,556.00.

MAKE DEPOSIT

C11.13.3 Deposit Journal Entry. To record the deposit of the customer's payment in the bank:

1 From the Banking section of the Home Page, click the **Record Deposits** icon

2 When the Payments to Deposit window appears, select the **payment from Angel Merriman Associates** for deposit

3 Click **OK** and the Make Deposits window appears

4 Select Deposit To: **Checking**

5 Select Date: **01/13/2025**

6 Verify the Amount is **$1556.00**

7   Select the **Save** icon at the top of the Make Deposits window

8   Select the **Journal** icon

9   Export the Transaction Journal report to **Excel** or **print** the report

10   **Close** the Transaction Journal and the Make Deposits windows

INVOICE HISTORY TRACKER

To view the Invoice History Tracker:

1   From the Customer section of the Home Page, click the **Create Invoices** icon

2   When the Create Invoices window appears, select the **Main tab > back arrow** to display the Merriman Associates: Office invoice

3   Select the **See History** link to display the Invoice History Tracker

4   The Invoice History Tracker displays the date the invoice was created

5   The Invoice History Tracker also lists the date and amount payment was received

6   The date and amount deposited is also listed on the Invoice History Tracker

7   If the invoice had been emailed, the Invoice History tracker would also display when the invoice was sent and viewed by the customer

8   Close the Invoice History Tracker window

9   Select **Save & Close** to close the Create Invoices window

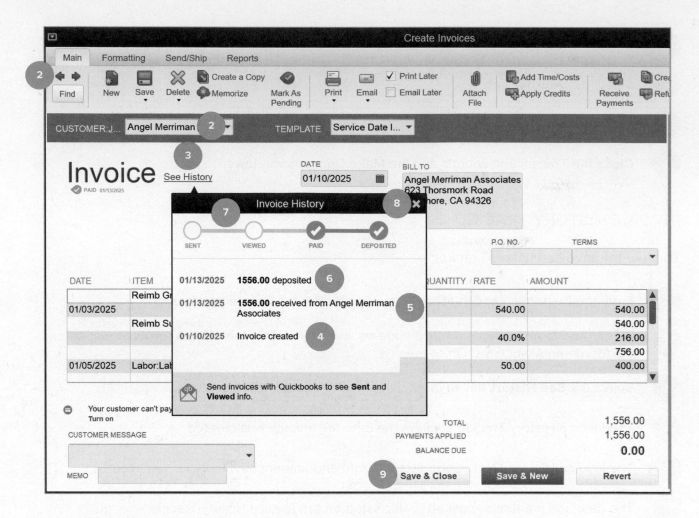

ADDITIONAL CUSTOMER AND SALES TRANSACTIONS

See **Exercise 11.6** for additional sales transactions for Paint Palette.

Section 11.14

Adjusting Entries

At the end of Paint Palette's accounting period, December 31, 2025, it is necessary to record adjustments to bring the company's accounts up to date as of year-end.

As discussed in Chapters 9 and 10, the process of making adjustments typically includes the following.

- **Trial Balance.** A Trial Balance lists each account and the account balance at the end of the accounting period. Prepare a Trial Balance to verify that the accounting system is in balance—total debits should equal total credits. An unadjusted Trial Balance is a Trial Balance prepared before adjustments.

- **Adjustments.** At the end of the accounting period before preparing financial statements, make any adjustments necessary to bring the accounts up to date. Adjustments are entered in the Journal using debits and credits. (Adjustments were covered in Chapter 9 of this text.)

- **Adjusted Trial Balance.** Prepare an Adjusted Trial Balance (a Trial Balance after adjustments) to verify that the accounting system still balances. If additional account detail is required, print the general ledger (the collection of all the accounts listing the transactions that affected the accounts).

The following adjustments are necessary for Paint Palette at December 31, 2025:
1. Depreciation expense for the computer for the year.
2. Depreciation expense for the painting equipment for the year.
3. The amount of paint supplies that are still on hand at year-end. Unused paint supplies should be recorded as assets because they have future benefit.

See **Exercise 11.7** for additional information about making adjusting entries for Paint Palette.

Section 11.15

Reports

The next step in the accounting cycle is to print financial reports. Usually, a company prints the following financial reports for the year:

- Profit & Loss (also known as the P & L or Income Statement)
- Balance Sheet
- Statement of Cash Flows

The Profit & Loss, the Balance Sheet, and the Statement of Cash Flows are financial statements typically given to external users, such as bankers and investors.

> **To print the financial statements, from the Report Center, select: Company & Financial.**

We will print financial statements for Paint Palette for the year 2025 in **Exercise 11.8**.

Section 11.16

Close the Accounting Period

When using a manual accounting system, closing entries are made in the General Journal to close the temporary accounts (revenues, expenses, and withdrawals or dividends). Closing entries are used in order to start the new year with a zero balance in the temporary accounts.

QuickBooks automatically closes temporary accounts to start each new year with $-0- balances in all temporary accounts (revenues, expenses, and dividends).

To prevent changes to prior periods, QuickBooks permits you to restrict access to the accounting records for past periods that have been closed. See **Exercise 11.9** for instructions on closing the accounting period in QuickBooks.

Section 11.17
Backup QuickBooks Files

BACK UP QBB

Save a backup of your Chapter 11 file using the file name: **YourName Chapter 11 Backup.QBB**. For further instructions on how to back up your file, *see* Appendix B: Back Up and Restore QuickBooks Files.

QBW WORKFLOW

If you will be using the same computer to complete Chapter 11 QuickBooks exercises, just as in a business workflow, you can continue to use the same QBW file.

If you are using the QBW approach, leave your QBW file open and proceed directly to Exercise 11.1.

QBB RESTORE

If you are using the QBB approach and ending your computer session now, close your QBW file and exit QuickBooks. When you restart, you will restore your backup file to complete Exercise 11.1.

Exercise 11.1 Chart of Accounts

 Paint Palette

BACKSTORY

In this exercise, you will add new accounts and subaccounts to Paint Palette's Chart of Accounts.

E11.1.1 QuickBooks File

If you will be using the same computer and the same Chapter 11.QBW file:

1. If your Chapter 11.QBW file is not already open, open it by selecting **File > Open Previous Company**. Select your **Chapter 11.QBW file**. If a QuickBooks Information window appears with a message about the sample company file, click **OK**.

2. Update the company name to **YourName Exercise 11.1 Paint Palette** by selecting **Company Menu > My Company**.

> **If you are not using the same computer that you used for Chapter 11, you will need to restore your Chapter 11 Backup.QBB file using the instructions in Appendix B: Back Up and Restore QuickBooks Files. After restoring, update the company name to YourName Exercise 11.1 Paint Palette.**

E11.1.2 Add Accounts

1. Add the following new accounts and subaccounts to the Chart of Accounts for Paint Palette. Click **Save & New** after entering each account.

Account Name	**Paint Supplies**
Account No.	**13000**
Account Type	**Other Current Asset**
Account Description	**Paint Supplies on Hand**
Tax Line	**Unassigned**
Account Name	**Equipment**
Account No.	**14400**
Account Type	**Fixed Asset**
Account Description	**Equipment**
Tax Line	**Unassigned**

Account Name	**Equipment Cost**
Account No.	**14500**
Account Type	**Fixed Asset**
Subaccount of:	**14400 Equipment**
Account Description	**Equipment Cost**
Tax Line	**Unassigned**

Account Name	**Accumulated Depr Equipment**
Account No.	**14600**
Account Type	**Fixed Asset**
Subaccount of:	**14400 Equipment**
Account Description	**Accumulated Depreciation Equipment**
Tax Line	**Unassigned**

2. Edit the following accounts to appear as follows for Paint Palette Chart of Accounts.

Account Name	**Depreciation Expense**
Account No.	**62400**
Account Type	**Expense**
Account Description	**Depreciation of equipment, buildings, and improvements**
Tax Line	**Schedule C: Other business expenses**

Account Name	**Paint Supplies Expense**
Account No.	**64800**
Account Type	**Expense**
Account Description	**Paint Supplies Expense**
Tax Line	**Schedule C: Supplies (not from COGS)**

3. Export to **Excel** or **print** the Chart of Accounts. (Select Report Center > List > Account Listing > January 13, 2025.)

E11.1.3 Back Up Exercise 11.1

Save a backup of your Exercise file using the file name: **YourName Exercise 11.1 Backup.QBB**. See Appendix B: Back Up and Restore QuickBooks Files for instructions.

Exercise 11.2 Customer List

 Paint Palette

In this exercise, you will add to Paint Palette's Customers List.

E11.2.1 QuickBooks File

If you will be using the same computer and the same QBW file:

1. Select your **QBW file**.

2. Update the company name to **YourName Exercise 11.2 Paint Palette** by selecting **Company Menu > My Company**.

> If you are not using the same computer that you used for Chapter 11 and Exercise 11.1, you will need to restore your latest prior Backup.QBB file using the instructions in Appendix B: Back Up and Restore QuickBooks files. After restoring, update the company name to YourName Exercise 11.2 Paint Palette.

E11.2.2 Add Customers

1. Add Tracey Kari to Paint Palette's Customer List.

Customer	**Kari, Tracey**
Opening Balance	**0.00**
As of	**01/01/2025**
Address Info:	
First Name	**Tracey**
Last Name	**Kari**
Main Phone	**415-555-1234**
Mobile	**415-555-9999**
Address	**99 Reyka Drive** **Bayshore, CA 94326**

Payment Settings:

Account No.	**1002**
Payment Terms	**Net 30**
Preferred Delivery Method	**E-mail**
Preferred Payment Method	**Check**

Additional Info:

Customer Type	**Referral**

2. Click **OK** to close the New Customer window

E11.2.3 Add Job

1. To add a new job, select: **Kari, Tracey**

2. **Right-click** to display pop-up menu. Select **Add Job**.

3. After entering the following job information, **close** the New Job window.

Job Info:

Job Name	**Laundry Workroom**
Opening Balance	**0.00**
As of	**01/01/2025**
Job Description	**Laundry Workroom Faux Painting**
Job Type \<Add New\>	**Faux Painting**
Job Status	**Pending**

4. From the Customer Center, export the Customer List to **Excel**.

5. **Close** the Customer Center

E11.2.4 Back Up Exercise 11.2

Save a backup of your Exercise file using the file name: **YourName Exercise 11.2 Backup.QBB**. See Appendix B: Back Up and Restore QuickBooks Files for instructions.

Exercise 11.3 Vendor List

🎨 Paint Palette

In this exercise, you will add to Paint Palette's Vendors List.

E11.3.1 QuickBooks File

If you will be using the same computer and the same QBW file:

1. Select your **QBW file**.

2. Update the company name to **YourName Exercise 11.3 Paint Palette** by selecting **Company Menu > My Company**.

> If you are not using the same computer that you used for Chapter 11, Exercise 11.1, and Exercise 11.2, you will need to restore your latest prior Backup.QBB file using the instructions in Appendix B: Back Up and Restore QuickBooks files. After restoring, update the company name to YourName Exercise 11.3 Paint Palette.

E11.3.2 Add Vendors

1. Edit the following vendor for the Paint Palette Vendor List.

Vendor	**Cornell Technologies**
Address Info:	
Company Name	**Cornell Technologies**
First Name	**Dan**
Last Name	**Cornell**
Main Phone	**415-555-8181**
Address	**108 Austin Avenue** **Bayshore, CA 94326**
Payment Settings:	
Account No.	**2002**
Payment Terms	**Net 30**
Credit Limit	**18000.00**

Tax Settings:

Vendor Tax ID	**37-4356781**

Additional Info:

Vendor Type	**Supplies**

2. Edit the following vendor for the Paint Palette Vendor List.

Vendor	**Joseph Leasing**

Address Info:

Company Name	**Joseph Leasing**
First Name	**Joseph**
Last Name	**Asher**
Main Phone	**415-555-0412**
Address	**13 Appleton Drive** **Bayshore, CA 94326**

Payment Settings:

Account No.	**2003**
Payment Terms	**Net 30**

Tax Settings:

Vendor Tax ID	**37-1726354**

Additional Info:

Vendor Type <Add New>	**Leasing**

3. From the Vendor Center, export the Vendor List to **Excel**

4. **Close** the Vendor Center

E11.3.3 Back Up Exercise 11.3

Save a backup of your Exercise file using the file name: **YourName Exercise 11.3 Backup.QBB**. See Appendix B: Back Up and Restore QuickBooks Files for instructions.

Exercise 11.4 Item List

🎨 Paint Palette

In this exercise, you will add to Paint Palette's Item List.

E11.4.1 QuickBooks File

If you will be using the same computer and the same QBW file:

1. Select your **QBW file**.

2. Update the company name to **YourName Exercise 11.4 Paint Palette** by selecting **Company Menu > My Company**.

> If you are not using the same computer that you used for Chapter 11, and Exercises 11.1 - 11.3, you will need to restore your latest prior Backup.QBB file using the instructions in Appendix B: Back Up and Restore QuickBooks files. After restoring, update the company name to YourName Exercise 11.4 Paint Palette.

E11.4.2 Add Items

1. Add the following items to Paint Palette's Item List. Click **Next** after entering each item.

Item Type	**Service**
Item Name	**Labor Faux**
Subitem of	**Labor**
Description	**Labor Faux Painting**
Rate	**42.00**
Account	**47900 – Sales**

Item Type	**Service**
Item Name	**Labor Interior**
Subitem of	**Labor**
Description	**Labor Interior Painting**
Rate	**30.00**
Account	**47900 – Sales**

Item Type	**Service**
Item Name	**Labor Exterior**
Subitem of	**Labor**
Description	**Labor Exterior Painting**
Rate	**33.00**
Account	**47900 – Sales**

2.   Export the Item List to **Excel**. (From the Item List window, select Reports button > Item Listing.)

E11.4.3 Back Up Exercise 11.4

Save a backup of your Exercise file using the file name: **YourName Exercise 11.4 Backup.QBB**. See Appendix B: Back Up and Restore QuickBooks Files for instructions.

Exercise 11.5 Vendors and Expense Transactions

 Paint Palette

In this exercise, you will enter vendor and expense transactions for Paint Palette.

E11.5.1 QuickBooks File

If you will be using the same computer and the same QBW file:

1.   Select your **QBW file**.

2.   Update the company name to **YourName Exercise 11.5 Paint Palette** by selecting **Company Menu > My Company**.

> **If you are not using the same computer that you used for Chapter 11 and Exercises 11.1 - 11.4, you will need to restore your latest prior Backup.QBB file using the instructions in Appendix B: Back Up and Restore QuickBooks files. After restoring, update the company name to YourName Exercise 11.5 Paint Palette.**

E11.5.2 Record Vendor and Expense Transactions

Paint Palette entered into the following vendor and expense transactions during 2025.

1. Record the vendor and expense transactions for Paint Palette. (Select View > Open Window List to streamline transaction entry.)

Date	Transaction
01/06/2025	Paint Palette made a credit purchase of $1,100 from Evan Paint Supplies of painting equipment including ladders and drop cloths. The painting equipment is recorded as an asset because it will benefit more than one accounting period and will be depreciated over the useful life of the equipment. Use Account 14500 Equipment Cost to record the $1,100 purchase of painting equipment.
02/01/2025	Use the memorized transaction to record the bill for the February van lease to be paid later
02/28/2025	Paid following bills: • $1,100 Evan Paint Supplies bill • Van lease bill for February
03/01/2025	Received bill for van lease for March
03/30/2025	Paid van lease for March (Due: 03/31/2025)
04/01/2025	Received bill for van lease for April
04/04/2025	Purchased $150 of paint supplies on account from Evan Paint Supplies. Record as Paint Supplies Expense.
04/30/2025	• Paid van lease for April (Due: 05/01/2025) • Paid for paint supplies purchased on April 4
05/01/2025	Received bill for van lease for May
05/30/2025	Paid van lease for May (Due: 05/31/2025)
06/01/2025	Received bill for van lease for June
06/30/2025	Paid van lease for June (Due: 07/01/2025)
07/01/2025	Purchased $100 of paint supplies on account from Evan Paint Supplies. Record as Paint Supplies Expense.
07/01/2025	Received bill for van lease for July
07/30/2025	• Paid van lease for July (Due: 07/31/2025) • Paid for paint supplies purchased on July 1
08/01/2025	Received bill for van lease for August
08/31/2025	Paid van lease for August (Due: 08/31/2025)
09/01/2025	Received bill for van lease for September

09/02/2025	Purchased $86 of paint supplies on account from Evan Paint Supplies. Record as Paint Supplies Expense.
09/30/2025	• Paid September van lease (Due: 10/01/2025) • Paid for paint supplies purchased on 09/02/2025
10/01/2025	Received bill for van lease for October
10/30/2025	Paid van lease for October (Due: 10/31/2025)
11/01/2025	Received bill for van lease for November
11/30/2025	Paid van lease for November (Due: 12/01/2025)
12/01/2025	Received bill for van lease for December
12/19/2025	Purchased $180 of paint supplies on account from Evan Paint Supplies. Record as Paint Supplies Expense.
12/30/2025	Paid van lease for December (Due: 12/31/2025)

2. Export to **Excel** or **print** the Expenses by Vendor Detail report for 2025. (Report Center > Company & Financial > Expenses by Vendor Detail.)

3. Export to **Excel** or **print** the Check Detail report for 2025. (Report Center > Banking > Check Detail.)

E11.5.3 Back Up Exercise 11.5

Save a backup of your Exercise file using the file name: **YourName Exercise 11.5 Backup.QBB**. See Appendix B: Back Up and Restore QuickBooks Files for instructions.

Exercise 11.6 Customers and Sales Transactions

 Paint Palette

Paint Palette worked on four jobs:

- Angel Merriman Associates offices, Seascape Mural
- Angel Merriman Associates offices, Dome Ceiling with Sky and Clouds Mural
- Tracey Kari Laundry and Workroom, Marbled Faux Painting to cover wall damage
- Tracey Kari Sun Room, Countryside Mural

In this exercise, you will enter the customers and sales transactions for Paint Palette.

E11.6.1 QuickBooks File

If you will be using the same computer and the same QBW file:

1. Select your **QBW file**.

2. Update the company name to **YourName Exercise 11.6 Paint Palette** by selecting **Company Menu > My Company**.

> If you are not using the same computer that you used for Chapter 11 and Exercises 11.1 - 11.5, you will need to restore your latest prior Backup.QBB file using the instructions in Appendix B: Back Up and Restore QuickBooks files. After restoring, update the company name to YourName Exercise 11.6 Paint Palette.

E11.6.2 Sales Transactions and Deposit Summaries

1. Using the Service Date Invoice Template, record the customer and sales transactions for Paint Palette during the year 2025. (Select View > Open Window List to streamline transaction entry.)

Invoice Date	**02/28/2025**
Customer	**Angel Merriman Associates**
Job	**Office**
Service Date	**02/10/2025**
Item	**Labor: Mural**
Hours	**10**
Service Date	**02/11/2025**
Item	**Labor: Mural**
Hours	**9**
Service Date	**02/15/2025**
Item	**Labor: Mural**
Hours	**10**
Service Date	**02/18/2025**
Item	**Labor: Mural**
Hours	**11**

Service Date	**02/20/2025**
Item	**Labor: Mural**
Hours	**12**
Service Date	**02/22/2025**
Item	**Labor: Mural**
Hours	**10**

Payment Received & Deposited	**03/14/2025**
Check No.	**675**

Invoice Date	**03/31/2025**
Customer	**Angel Merriman Associates**
Job	**Office**
Service Date	**03/05/2025**
Item	**Labor: Mural**
Hours	**9**
Service Date	**03/09/2025**
Item	**Labor: Mural**
Hours	**10**
Service Date	**03/13/2025**
Item	**Labor: Mural**
Hours	**11**
Service Date	**03/20/2025**
Item	**Labor: Mural**
Hours	**10**
Service Date	**03/29/2025**
Item	**Labor: Mural**
Hours	**10**

Payment Received & Deposited	**04/15/2025**
Check No.	**690**
Invoice Date	**04/30/2025**
Customer	**Tracey Kari**
Job	**Laundry Workroom**
Service Date	**04/10/2025**
Item	**Labor: Faux**
Hours	**9**
Service Date	**04/15/2025**
Item	**Labor: Faux**
Hours	**9**
Service Date	**04/25/2025**
Item	**Labor: Faux**
Hours	**8**
Service Date	**04/29/2025**
Item	**Labor: Faux**
Hours	**8**
Payment Received & Deposited	**05/15/2025**
Check No.	**432**
Invoice Date	**05/30/2025**
Customer	**Tracey Kari**
Job	**Laundry Workroom**
Service Date	**05/11/2025**
Item	**Labor: Faux**
Hours	**8**
Service Date	**05/18/2025**

Item	**Labor: Faux**
Hours	**9**
Service Date	**05/25/2025**
Item	**Labor: Faux**
Hours	**8**
Payment Received & Deposited	**06/15/2025**
Check No.	**455**
Invoice Date	**06/30/2025**
Customer	**Angel Merriman Associates**
Job <Add New Job>	**Office Dome Ceiling**
Service Date	**06/10/2025**
Item	**Labor: Mural**
Hours	**10**
Service Date	**06/18/2025**
Item	**Labor: Mural**
Hours	**8**
Service Date	**06/27/2025**
Item	**Labor: Mural**
Hours	**10**
Payment Received & Deposited	**07/15/2025**
Check No.	**733**
Invoice Date	**07/31/2025**
Customer	**Angel Merriman Associates**
Job	**Office Dome Ceiling**
Service Date	**07/09/2025**

Item	**Labor: Mural**
Hours	**9**
Service Date	**07/18/2025**
Item	**Labor: Mural**
Hours	**8**
Service Date	**07/27/2025**
Item	**Labor: Mural**
Hours	**8**
Payment Received & Deposited	**08/15/2025**
Check No.	**750**
Invoice Date	**08/31/2025**
Customer	**Angel Merriman Associates**
Job	**Office Dome Ceiling**
Service Date	**08/08/2025**
Item	**Labor: Mural**
Hours	**8**
Service Date	**08/18/2025**
Item	**Labor: Mural**
Hours	**9**
Service Date	**08/22/2025**
Item	**Labor: Mural**
Hours	**10**
Payment Received & Deposited	**09/15/2025**
Check No.	**782**

Invoice Date	**10/31/2025**
Customer	**Tracey Kari**
Job <Add New Job>	**Sun Room**
Service Date	**10/10/2025**
Item	**Labor: Mural**
Hours	**8**
Service Date	**10/20/2025**
Item	**Labor: Mural**
Hours	**5**
Service Date	**10/22/2025**
Item	**Labor: Mural**
Hours	**6**
Payment Received & Deposited	**11/16/2025**
Check No.	**685**
Invoice Date	**11/30/2025**
Customer	**Tracey Kari**
Job	**Sun Room**
Service Date	**11/11/2025**
Item	**Labor: Mural**
Hours	**11**
Service Date	**11/18/2025**
Item	**Labor: Mural**
Hours	**6**
Service Date	**11/27/2025**
Item	**Labor: Mural**
Hours	**9**

Payment Received & Deposited	**12/15/2025**
Check No.	**725**

2. Export to **Excel** or **print** the Income by Customer Detail report for 2025. (Report Center > Company & Financial > Income by Customer Detail.)

3. Export to **Excel** or **print** the Deposit Detail report for 2025. (Report Center > Banking > Deposit Detail.)

E11.6.3 Back Up Exercise 11.6

Save a backup of your Exercise file using the file name: **YourName Exercise 11.6 Backup.QBB**. See Appendix B: Back Up and Restore QuickBooks Files for instructions.

Exercise 11.7 Adjustments

 Paint Palette

In this exercise, you will first print a Trial Balance and then record adjusting entries for Paint Palette.

E11.7.1 QuickBooks File

If you will be using the same computer and the same QBW file:

1. Select your **QBW file**.

2. Update the company name to **YourName Exercise 11.7 Paint Palette** by selecting **Company Menu > My Company**.

> If you are not using the same computer that you used for Chapter 11 and Exercises 11.1 - 11.6, you will need to restore your latest prior Backup.QBB file using the instructions in Appendix B: Back Up and Restore QuickBooks files. After restoring, update the company name to YourName Exercise 11.7 Paint Palette.

E11.7.2 Trial Balance

The purpose of the Trial Balance is to determine whether the accounting system is in balance (debits equal credits).

Create a Trial Balance for Paint Palette at December 31, 2025.

1. From the Report Center select **Accountant & Taxes > Trial Balance**

2. Select Dates **From: 12/31/2025 To: 12/31/2025**

3. Export to **Excel** or **print** the Trial Balance for Paint Palette

4. **Close** the Trial Balance window

E11.7.3 Adjusting Entries

At the end of the accounting period, it is necessary to make adjusting entries to bring a company's accounts up to date as of year-end. Three adjusting entries are needed for Paint Palette as of December 31, 2025.

1. To enter adjusting entries, select **Accountant Menu > Make General Journal Entries**

2. Next, use the Make General Journal Entries window to record the adjusting entry (A1) for depreciation expense on the computer for Paint Palette at December 31, 2025. The $2,000 computer cost will be depreciated over a useful life of five years. (Depreciation expense is calculated as $2,000/5 years = $400 per year.) Use Account 62400 and 14300 to record the adjusting entry.

3. Record an adjusting entry (A2) to record depreciation expense for the painting equipment for the year. The $1,100 painting equipment cost is depreciated using straight-line depreciation over four years with no salvage value. Use Account No. 62400 and 14600 to record the adjusting entry.

4. On December 31, 2025, you take an inventory of unused paint supplies on hand to learn that $100 of paint supplies are still on hand as of that date. Since the supplies were recorded as supplies expense when originally purchased, an adjusting entry is needed (A3). Use Account 13000 to record the $100 of unused paint supplies as an asset with future benefit.

5. Click **Save & Close** to save the adjusting journal entries

6. To create an Adjusting Journal Entries report on December 31, 2025, for Paint Palette, from the Report Center, select **Accountant & Taxes > Adjusting Journal Entries**

7. Select Dates: **12/31/2025 To 12/31/2025**

8. Export to **Excel** or **print** the Adjusting Journal Entries report

9. **Close** the Adjusting Journal Entries report

E11.7.4 Adjusted Trial Balance

An Adjusted Trial Balance is simply a Trial Balance printed after adjusting entries are recorded.

Create an Adjusted Trial Balance for Paint Palette at December 31, 2025 after adjusting entires are entered.

1. Export to **Excel** or **print** an Adjusted Trial Balance at December 31, 2025. (Report Center > Accountant & Taxes > Adjusted Trial Balance.)

2. On the Adjusted Trial Balance, **highlight** amounts affected by the adjusting entries

E11.7.5 Back Up Exercise 11.7

Save a backup of your Exercise file using the file name: **YourName Exercise 11.7 Backup.QBB**. See Appendix B: Back Up and Restore QuickBooks Files for instructions.

Exercise 11.8 Reports

 Paint Palette

In this exercise, you will print out financial statements for Paint Palette for the year 2025.

E11.8.1 QuickBooks File

If you will be using the same computer and the same QBW file:

1. Select your **QBW file**.

2. Update the company name to **YourName Exercise 11.8 Paint Palette** by selecting **Company Menu > My Company**.

> If you are not using the same computer that you used for Chapter 11 and Exercises 11.1 - 11.7, you will need to restore your latest prior Backup.QBB file using the instructions in Appendix B: Back Up and Restore QuickBooks files. After restoring, update the company name to YourName Exercise 11.8 Paint Palette.

E11.8.2 Journal

The Journal lists all the transactions entered, whether using an onscreen form or the Journal, in a debit and credit format. The Journal is often a useful tool when tracking errors or discrepancies in the accounting system.

Create a Journal for Paint Palette for 2025.

1. From the Report Center select **Accountant & Taxes** > **Journal**

2. Select Dates **From: 01/01/2025 To: 12/31/2025**

3. Export to **Excel** or **print** the Journal for Paint Palette

4. **Close** the Journal window

E11.8.3 Financial Statements

Create the following financial statements for Paint Palette for the year 2025.

1. Export to **Excel** or **print** the Profit & Loss, Standard

2. Export to **Excel** or **print** the Balance Sheet, Standard

3. Export to **Excel** or **print** the Statement of Cash Flows

E11.8.4 Back Up Exercise 11.8

Save a backup of your Exercise file using the file name: **YourName Exercise 11.8 Backup.QBB**. See Appendix B: Back Up and Restore QuickBooks Files for instructions.

Exercise 11.9 Close the Accounting Period

 Paint Palette

> **Complete Exercise 11.9 only after you have completed Exercise 11.8.**

To prevent changes to prior periods, QuickBooks permits you to restrict access to the accounting records for past periods that have been closed.

The QuickBooks Administrator can restrict user access to closed periods either at the time a new user is set up or later.

E11.9.1 QuickBooks File

If you will be using the same computer and the same QBW file:

1. Select your **QBW file**.

2. Update the company name to **YourName Exercise 11.9 Paint Palette** by selecting **Company Menu** > **My Company**.

> If you are not using the same computer that you used for Chapter 11 and Exercises 11.1 - 11.8, you will need to restore your latest prior Backup.QBB file using the instructions in Appendix B: Back Up and Restore QuickBooks files. After restoring, update the company name to YourName Exercise 11.9 Paint Palette.

E11.9.2 Close the Accounting Period

To enter the closing date in QuickBooks:

1. Select **Company Menu > Set Up Users and Passwords > Set Up Users**

2. If necessary, enter information for the QuickBooks Administrator, then click **OK**

3. When the following User List window appears, click the **Closing Date** button

4. Enter the closing date: **12/31/2025**

5. Notice that QuickBooks strongly recommends setting a password to protect transactions date on or before the closing date to prevent others from making changes in prior periods. Enter a password and make note of the password.

6. Click **OK** to close the Set Closing Date and Password window

7. Select **Close** to close the User List window

E11.9.3 Back Up Exercise 11.9

Save a backup of your Exercise file using the file name: **YourName Exercise 11.9 Backup.QBB**. See Appendix B: Back Up and Restore QuickBooks Files for instructions.

PROJECT 11.1

 Martin Consulting

BACKSTORY

Martin launched Martin Consulting to offer consulting and design services for social media marketing. The firm advises organizations regarding how to use internet marketing and social media tools, such as Facebook® and Instagram®, to market and promote their companies, products, and brands. Social media tools are revolutionizing marketing to promote dating services, spas, grocery stores, and even emergency rooms. Martin Consulting is poised to provide the expertise to assist organizations in capitalizing upon social media to gain a competitive advantage.

Martin has asked you to maintain the accounting records for Martin Consulting using QuickBooks Desktop software.

🌐 QuickBooks SatNav

The objective of Project 11.1 is to facilitate your mastery of QuickBooks Desktop. As shown in the following QuickBooks SatNav, Project 11.1 covers all three processes: QuickBooks Settings, QuickBooks Transactions, and QuickBooks Reports. This project provides you with the opportunity to integrate your knowledge of QuickBooks Desktop through all three phases of QuickBooks SatNav for a service company.

QuickBooks SatNav

 QuickBooks Settings

Company Settings
Chart of Accounts

QuickBooks Transactions

Banking
Customers & Sales
Vendors & Expenses
Employees & Payroll

QuickBooks Reports

Reports

P11.1.1 New Company Setup

Create a new company in QuickBooks for Martin Consulting using the following information.

1. Use the EasyStep Interview to set up a new QuickBooks company.

Company name	**YourName Project 11.1 Martin Consulting**
Federal tax ID	**123-45-6789**
Address	**333 Blue Avenue**
City	**Bayshore**
State	**CA**
Zip	**94326**
Phone	**415-555-2022**
Email	**<Enter your email address>**
Industry	**General Service-based Business**
Type of organization	**Sole Proprietorship**
First month of fiscal year	**January**
File name	**YourName Project 11.1**
What do you sell?	**Services only**
Sales tax	**No**
Estimates	**Yes**
Billing statements	**No**
Progress invoicing	**No**
Track bills you owe	**Yes**
Track time	**Yes**
Employees	**No**
Start date	**01/01/2025**
Use recommended accounts	**Yes**
Bank account name	**Checking**
Bank account number	**2345678901**
Bank account balance	**0.00 as of 01/01/2025**

2. Click **Start Working** to exit QuickBooks Setup

P11.1.2 Add Customers

1. Add the following customers to the Customers List.

Customer	**Petit, Mimi**
Address Info:	
First Name	**Mimi**
Last Name	**Petit**
Main Phone	**415-555-2160**
Address	**220 Alsace Avenue** **Bayshore, CA 94326**
Payment Settings:	
Account No.	**12700**
Payment Terms	**Net 15**
Preferred Delivery Method	**E-mail**
Preferred Payment Method	**Check**
Additional Info:	
Customer Type	**From advertisement**
Customer	**Luminesse Link**
Company Name	**Luminesse Link**
Address Info:	
First Name	**Luminesse**
Main Phone	**415-555-2222**
Address	**22 Beach Street** **Bayshore, CA 94326**
Payment Settings:	
Account No.	**13330**
Payment Terms	**Net 15**
Preferred Delivery Method	**E-mail**
Preferred Payment Method	**Check**

Additional Info:

Customer Type	**Referral**

Customer	**Bichotte Supplies**
Company Name	**Bichotte Supplies**

Address Info:

First Name	**Bichotte**
Main Phone	**415-555-4567**
Address	**810 Francais Drive**
	Bayshore, CA 94326

Payment Settings:

Account No.	**19900**
Payment Terms	**Net 15**
Preferred Delivery Method	**E-mail**
Preferred Payment Method	**Check**

Additional Info:

Customer Type	**Referral**

2. From the Customer Center, export to **Excel** the Customers List.

   ⚠ When exporting to Excel, remember to select Advanced Excel Options:
   - Uncheck **Space between columns**
   - Check **Row height**
   - Uncheck **Include QuickBooks Export Guide worksheet with helpful advice**
   - Select **On printed report and screen**

P11.1.3 Add Vendors

1. Add the following vendors to the Vendors List.

Vendor	**Joseph Leasing**
Opening Balance	**$0.00 as of 01/01/2025**
Address Info:	
Company Name	**Joseph Leasing**

Full Name	**Joseph Asher**
Main Phone	**415-555-0412**
Address	**13 Appleton Drive** **Bayshore, CA 94326**
Payment Settings:	
Account No.	**2700**
Payment Terms	**Net 30**
Tax Settings:	
Vendor Tax ID	**37-1726354**
Additional Info:	
Vendor Type	**Service Providers**

Vendor	**Angel Merriman Associates**
Opening Balance	**$0.00 as of 01/01/2025**
Address Info:	
Company Name	**Angel Merriman Associates**
Full Name	**Angel Merriman**
Main Phone	**415-555-7579**
Address	**623 Thorsmork Road** **Bayshore, CA 94326**
Payment Settings:	
Account No.	**4500**
Payment Terms	**Net 30**
Tax Settings:	
Vendor Tax ID	**37-3571656**
Additional Info:	
Vendor Type	**Suppliers**

2.   From the Vendor Center, export to **Excel** the Vendor List

P11.1.4 Add Items

1.   Add the following items to the Items List.

Item Type	**Service**
Item Name	**Internet Marketing**
Description	**Internet Marketing Consulting**
Rate	**90.00**
Income Account	**Sales**

Item Type	**Service**
Item Name	**Social Media Marketing**
Description	**Social Media Marketing Consulting**
Rate	**110.00**
Income Account	**Sales**

2.   Export to **Excel** or **print** the Item List. (Use Report Center > List > Item Listing.)

   ⚠ When exporting to Excel, remember to select Advanced Excel Options:
   * Uncheck **Space between columns**
   * Check **Row height**
   * Uncheck **Include QuickBooks Export Guide worksheet with helpful advice**
   * Select **On printed report and screen**

P11.1.5 Chart of Accounts

Complete the following for the Chart of Account.

1.   Set Accounting preferences to display account numbers in the Chart of Accounts

2.   Edit the Checking account in the Chart of Accounts to add the Account Number: **10100**

3.   From the Report Center, export to **Excel** the Chart of Accounts (Account Listing)

P11.1.6 Enter Transactions

Martin Consulting entered into the following transactions during January 2025.

1. Record the transactions for Martin Consulting. (Click View > Open Window List to streamline transaction entry.)

Date	Transaction
01/01/2025	Martin invested $36,000 in the business (Check No. 432)
01/01/2025	Paid $1,000 for rent expense to Joseph Leasing. (Record with the two-step method using the Enter Bills and Pay Bills windows.)
01/02/2025	Purchased computer equipment for $2,400 on account from Angel Merriman Associates (Account: Furniture & Equipment).
01/03/2025	Purchased copier/printer/fax machine for $720 on account from Angel Merriman Associates (Account: Furniture & Equipment).
01/06/2025	Using the Intuit Service Invoice template, recorded and emailed invoice to Luminesse Link for: • 20 hours of Internet marketing consulting • 15 hours of social media marketing consulting
01/08/2025	Emailed invoice to Bichotte Supplies for: • 18 hours of Internet marketing consulting • 18 hours of social media marketing consulting
01/10/2025	Emailed invoice to Mimi Petit for: • 6 hours of Internet marketing consulting
01/15/2025	Emailed invoice to Bichotte Supplies for: • 24 hours of social media marketing consulting
01/20/2025	Purchased and paid by check $400 for office technology supplies from Angel Merriman Associates. (Record as Office Supplies (Expense) using the Enter Bills and Pay Bills windows.)
01/20/2025	Received payment from Luminesse Link (Check No. 589) and recorded deposit
01/22/2025	Emailed invoice to Luminesse Link for: • 30 hours of Internet marketing consulting
01/22/2025	Received payment from Bichotte Supplies for Invoice No. 2 (Check No. 935) and recorded deposit
01/23/2025	Received payment from Mimi Petit (Check No. 1245) and recorded deposit
01/24/2025	Purchased and paid by check $133 for office technology supplies from Angel Merriman Associates. (Record as Office Supplies (Expense) using the Enter Bills and Pay Bills windows.)

01/27/2025	Emailed invoice to Mimi Petit for: • 10 hours of Internet marketing consulting • 10 hours of social media marketing consulting
01/28/2025	Received payment from Bichotte Supplies (Check No. 876) and recorded deposit
01/31/2025	Paid Angel Merriman Associates bill for $2,400 computer

2. Export to **Excel** or **print** the Deposit Detail report for January 2025

3. Export to **Excel** or **print** the Check Detail report for January 2025

4. Export to **Excel** or **print** the Income by Customer Detail report for January 2025. (Report Center > Company & Financial > Income by Customer Detail.)

5. Export to **Excel** or **print** the Expenses by Vendor Detail report for January 2025. (Report Center > Company & Financial > Expenses by Vendor Detail.)

P11.1.7 Adjusting Entries

1. Export to **Excel** or **print** the Trial Balance report at January 31, 2025

2. Enter adjusting entries at January 31, 2025, using the following information.

   ADJ1: The $2,400 computer is depreciated over 24 months using straight-line depreciation and no salvage value. Use Account No. 62400 Depreciation Expense and Account No. 17000 Accumulated Depreciation.

   ADJ2: The $720 copier/printer/fax is depreciated over 36 months using straight-line depreciation and no salvage value. Use Account No. 62400 Depreciation Expense and Account No. 17000 Accumulated Depreciation.

   ADJ3: Office technology supplies on hand at January 31, 2025, totaled $90. Add a new account, No. 13000 Office Supplies on Hand (Other Current Asset), to transfer $90 from the Office Supplies (Expense) account to Office Supplies on Hand (Other Current Asset) account.

3. From the Report Center, export to **Excel** or **print** the Adjusting Journal Entries for January 31, 2025

4. Export to **Excel** or print the Adjusted Trial Balance report at January 31, 2025

5. On the Adjusted Trial Balance report, **highlight** the amounts affected by the adjusting entries

P11.1.8 Financial Reports

Create the following reports for Martin Consulting.

1. Export to **Excel** or **print** the Journal for the month of January 2025

2. Export to **Excel** or **print** the Profit & Loss, Standard for the month of January 2025

3. Export to **Excel** or **print** the Balance Sheet, Standard at January 31, 2025

4. Export to **Excel** or **print** the Statement of Cash Flows for the month of January 2025

5. Export to **Excel** or **print** the Cash Flow Forecast for the next month, 02/01/2025 to 02/28/2025

P11.1.9 Back Up Project 11.1

Save a backup of your Project file using the file name: **YourName Project 11.1 Backup.QBB**. See Appendix B: Back Up and Restore QuickBooks Files for instructions.

PROJECT 11.2

✳Hermann LLC

BACKSTORY

Hermann LLC, a start-up business, provides carpet, rugs and tile cleaning using the latest hi-tech cleaning equipment guaranteed to leave floors sparkling clean and safely disinfected.

First, set up a new QuickBooks company file for Hermann LLC using the EasyStep Interview. Create the Customers List, Vendors List, and Items List for the new company. Then enter transactions for the company and create reports.

🌐 QuickBooks SatNav

The objective of Project 11.2 is to facilitate your mastery of QuickBooks Desktop. As shown in the following QuickBooks SatNav, Project 11.2 covers all three processes: QuickBooks Settings, QuickBooks Transactions, and QuickBooks Reports. This project provides you with the opportunity to integrate your knowledge of QuickBooks Desktop through all three phases of QuickBooks SatNav for a service company.

QuickBooks SatNav

QuickBooks Settings

- Company Settings
- Chart of Accounts

QuickBooks Transactions

- Banking
- Customers & Sales
- Vendors & Expenses
- Employees & Payroll

QuickBooks Reports

- Reports

P11.2.1 New Company Setup

Create a new company in QuickBooks for Hermann LLC using the following information.

1. Use the EasyStep Interview to set up a new QuickBooks company.

Company name	**YourName Project 11.2 Hermann LLC**
Federal tax ID	**130-13-3636**
Address	**99 Droit Street**
City	**Bayshore**
State	**CA**
Zip	**94326**
Main Phone	**415-555-1313**
Email	**<Enter your email address>**
Industry	**General Service-based Business**
Type of organization	**LLC Single-member LLC (Form 1040)**
First month of fiscal year	**January**
File name	**YourName Project 11.2**
What do you sell?	**Services only**
Sales tax	**No**
Estimates	**No**
Billing statements	**No**
Invoices	**Yes**
Progress invoicing	**No**
Track bills you owe	**Yes**
Track time	**Yes**
Employees	**No**
Start date	**01/01/2025**
Use recommended accounts	**Yes**
Bank account name	**Checking**
Bank account number	**1234567890**
Bank account balance	**0.00 as of 01/01/2025**

2.   Click **Start Working** to exit QuickBooks Setup

3.   Set preferences as follows:

   a.   Accounting preferences to **display account numbers** in the Chart of Accounts

   b.   Accounting preferences to **uncheck Warn if transactions are 30 day(s) in the future**

   c.   Checking preferences to Open the Make Deposits form with **Checking** account

   d.   Check preferences to Open the Pay Bills form with **Checking** account

P11.2.2 Add Customer and Job

1.   Add the following customer to the Customers List. (Use the Customer Center to add new customers.)

Customer	**Johann Enterprises**
Address Info:	
First Name	**Johann**
Last Name	**Westman**
Main Phone	**415-555-3334**
Address	**63 Westman Blvd** **Bayshore, CA 94326**
Payment Settings:	
Account No.	**1005**
Payment Terms	**Net 15**
Preferred Delivery Method	**E-mail**
Preferred Payment Method	**Check**
Additional Info:	
Customer Type	**From advertisement**

2.   Click **OK** to close the New Customer window

3.   To add a new job, select Johann Enterprises in the Customers List, then **right-click** to display the pop-up menu. Select **Add Job**.

4.   Enter the following job information.

Job Info:	
Job Name	**Rug cleaning**

Job Description	**Rug cleaning**
Job Type	**Commercial**
Job Status	**Awarded**

5. From the Customer Center, export to **Excel** or **print** the Customers List.

⚠ When exporting to Excel, remember to select Advanced Excel Options:
- Uncheck **Space between columns**
- Check **Row height**
- Uncheck **Include QuickBooks Export Guide worksheet with helpful advice**
- Select **On printed report and screen**

6. **Close** the Customer Center

P11.2.3 Add Vendors

1. Add the following vendors to the Vendor List.

Vendor	**Northern Lights Cleaning Supplies**
Opening Balance	**$0.00 as of 01/01/2025**
Address Info:	
Company Name	**Northern Lights Cleaning Supplies**
Full Name	
Main Phone	**415-555-7272**
Address	**360 Northern Lights Way** **Bayshore, CA 94326**
Payment Settings:	
Account No.	**2004**
Payment Terms	**Net 30**
Tax Settings:	
Vendor Tax ID	**37-6543219**
Additional Info:	
Vendor Type	**Supplies**

2. From the Vendor Center, export to **Excel** the Vendor List

P11.2.4 Add Items

1. Add the following items. Click **Next** after entering each item.

Item Type	**Service**
Item Name	**Rug Cleaning**
Description	**Rug Cleaning**
Account	**47900 – Sales**

Item Type	**Service**
Item Name	**3x5 Rug Cleaning**
Subitem of	**Rug Cleaning**
Description	**3x5 Rug Cleaning**
Rate	**63.00**
Account	**47900 – Sales**

Item Type	**Service**
Item Name	**5x7 Rug Cleaning**
Subitem of	**Rug Cleaning**
Description	**5x7 Rug Cleaning**
Rate	**81.00**
Account	**47900 – Sales**

Item Type	**Service**
Item Name	**8x10 Rug Cleaning**
Subitem of	**Rug Cleaning**
Description	**8x10 Rug Cleaning**
Rate	**154.00**
Account	**47900 – Sales**

2. Export to **Excel** or **print** the Item List as of January 1, 2025. (Use Report Center > List > Item Listing.)

    ⚠ When exporting to Excel, remember to select Advanced Excel Options:
    - Uncheck **Space between columns**
    - Check **Row height**
    - Uncheck **Include QuickBooks Export Guide worksheet with helpful advice**
    - Select **On printed report and screen**

P11.2.5 Customize Chart of Accounts

Edit the Chart of Accounts and enter opening balances as follows.

1. Add the following information to the Chart of Accounts.

Account	**Checking**
Account No.	**10100**

Account	**Cleaning Supplies**
Account No.	**13000**
Account Type	**Other Current Asset**
Account Description	**Cleaning Supplies**
Tax Line	**Unassigned**

Account	**Cleaning Equipment**
Account No.	**14400**
Account Type	**Fixed Asset**
Account Description	**Cleaning Equipment**
Tax Line	**Unassigned**

Account	**Cleaning Equipment Cost**
Account No.	**14500**
Account Type	**Fixed Asset**

Account Description	Cleaning Equipment Cost
Subaccount of	14400 Cleaning Equipment
Tax Line	Unassigned

Account	Cleaning Equipment Acc Depr
Account No.	14600
Account Type	Fixed Asset
Account Description	Cleaning Equipment Accumulated Depreciation
Subaccount of	14400 Cleaning Equipment
Tax Line	Unassigned

Account	Accounts Payable
Account No.	21000
Account Type	Accounts Payable
Account Description	Accounts Payable
Tax Line	Unassigned

Account	Supplies Expense
Account No.	64800
Account Type	Expense
Account Description	Supplies Expense
Tax Line	Schedule C: Supplies (not from COGS)

2. Export to **Excel** the Chart of Accounts (Account Listing) as of January 1, 2025. (Report Center > List > Account Listing.)

⚠ When exporting to Excel, remember to select Advanced Excel Options:
- Uncheck **Space between columns**
- Check **Row height**
- Uncheck **Include QuickBooks Export Guide worksheet with helpful advice**
- Select **On printed report and screen**

P11.2.6 Enter Transactions

During January, Hermann LLC entered into the transactions listed below.

1. Record the following transactions. (To streamline transaction entry, select: View > Open Window List.)

Date	Transaction
Date	**Transaction**
01/01/2025	Hermann invested $13,000 cash in the business. (Use the Make Deposits window with Account No 30000 and Check No 501.)
01/02/2025	Purchased and paid by check for $1,200 of cleaning equipment from Northern Lights Cleaning Supplies. (Use the Enter Bills and Pay Bills windows.)
01/05/2025	Purchased $200 of cleaning supplies on account from Northern Lights Cleaning Supplies. (Use Enter Bills window to record in Account No 64800 Supplies Expense.)
01/10/2025	Using the Intuit Service Invoice Template, record cleaning rugs for Johann Enterprises on account: • (5) 3 x 5 • (10) 5 x 7 • (8) 8 x 10
01/29/2025	Collected payment from Johann Enterprises for cleaning services (Check No. 580) and deposited customer payment

2. Export to **Excel** the Deposit Detail report for January 2025

3. Export to **Excel** the Check Detail report for January 2025

4. Export to **Excel** or **print** the Income by Customer Detail report for January 2025. (Report Center > Company & Financial > Income by Customer Detail.)

5. Export to **Excel** or **print** the Expenses by Vendor Detail report for January 2025. (Report Center > Company & Financial > Expenses by Vendor Detail.)

P11.2.7 Adjusting Entries

1. Export to **Excel** the Trial Balance report at January 31, 2025

2. Make adjusting entries at January 31, 2025.

    ADJ1: Make an adjusting entry at January 31, 2025, to record one month of depreciation for the cleaning equipment. The cleaning equipment cost $1,200 and has a five-year (60-month) life and no salvage value resulting in depreciation expense of $20 per month.

    ADJ2: Make an adjusting entry to record cleaning supplies of $40 on hand at January 31, 2025.

3. From the Report Center, export to **Excel** the Adjusting Journal Entries for January 31, 2025

4. Export to **Excel** the Adjusted Trial Balance report at January 31, 2025

5. On the Adjusted Trial Balance report, **highlight** the amounts affected by the adjusting entries

P11.2.8 Financial Reports

Export to **Excel** or **print** the following reports for Hermann LLC for January 2025.

1. Export to **Excel** the Journal for the month of January 2025

2. Export to **Excel** the Profit & Loss, Standard for the month of January 2025

3. Export to **Excel** the Balance Sheet, Standard at January 31, 2025

4. Export to **Excel** the Statement of Cash Flows for the month of January 2025

P11.2.9 Back Up Project 11.2

Save a backup of your Project file using the file name: **YourName Project 11.2 Backup.QBB**. See Appendix B: Back Up and Restore QuickBooks Files for instructions.

Design elements: Dog icon: ©josep perianes jorba/Shutterstock; paint roller icon: ©Netti Buletti/Shutterstock; other icons/symbols: ©Carboxylase/Shutterstock

Chapter 12

QuickBooks Service Company Case

Mookie The Beagle Spa™

BACKSTORY

Your friend and entrepreneur, Cy Walker, previously founded a business, Mookie The Beagle™ Concierge, that provides pet care and pet healthcare services. With an accompanying app that streamlined and simplified pet care, Mookie The Beagle™ Concierge became a financial success.

One of Cy's satisfied clients, Tracey Kari, encouraged Cy to start a pet grooming business. Tracey's black Labrador, Odin, performs at agility dog shows, and Tracey would like Cy to do doggie massages and pet grooming for Odin before and after shows.

After researching this business opportunity thoroughly, Cy is now ready to add a related business endeavor, Mookie The Beagle Spa™. Cy envisions the new business would provide mobile pet spa and grooming services. Cy developed a Mookie The Beagle Spa smartphone app to schedule spa appointments, coach pet parents about grooming maintenance between appointments, and more.

As Cy works on his business plan for the pet spa business, he realizes that a key to its financial success will be to have standing customer appointments on a regular basis to provide an ongoing revenue base. Cy receives a commitment from Tracey Kari for a standing appointment every month for his Labrador, Odin. Cy asks Kari to spread the word about the new pet spa with other pet owners. Soon, Cy has the following clients scheduled for standing appointments.

- Odin, Kari's black Labrador with his easy going temperament, has standing weekly appointments for grooming and massage with the understanding that Odin's appointments could vary with his agility dog show schedule.

- Maggie, a playful, smart, and affectionate cream Havanese, whose pet parent, Sherry Byran, plans to schedule monthly appointments, including a puppy cut trim.

- Angel Merriman, owner of Angel Merriman Associates a firm providing technology and cybersecurity services for Mookie The Beagle Spa, will commit to scheduling a minimum of a monthly shampoo and blow dry for her protective black and tan German Shepherd, Kuno. Angel informs Cy that additional grooming appointments are likely since Kuno's favorite pastime is rolling in muddy puddles.

- Mimi Petit will schedule a standing quarterly grooming appointment for her sweet-tempered, chocolate French Bulldog puppy, Bebe.

- Remy the Rescue Dog, recently adopted by Sandy Copper, is tentatively scheduled for quarterly grooming appointments for her coppery short hair plus relaxing massages for anxiety reduction. If the massages prove effective, Sandy is open to scheduling Remy for more frequent appointments.

To maintain the financial records for Mookie The Beagle Concierge, Cy Walker selected QuickBooks Online. For the new business venture, Cy would like to try QuickBooks Desktop. Since he knew you were using QBDT at your Rock Castle Construction position, he approached you to inquire if you were willing to set up his new company in QuickBooks Desktop. Cy could then compare and contrast QuickBooks Desktop and QuickBooks Online to see which he thinks is a better fit for his businesses going forward.

After goodnatured but heated negotiations, you and Cy reach an agreement: you will assist Cy with his QuickBooks Desktop needs, and he will assist you with marketing and promoting your painting business.

Download the Excel Report Template for Chapter 12 at www.My-QuickBooks.com, **QB2021** link, at the OLC www.mhhe.com/kay2021, or if you are using Connect, from Connect.

Chapter 12
Learning Objectives

Chapter 12 covers the following QuickBooks topics:

- Set Up New QuickBooks Company and Customize Chart of Accounts
- Customer List
- Vendor List
- Item List
- Customize Invoice Template
- Record Transactions
- Adjusting Entries
- Financial Reports
- Back Up QuickBooks Files

Section 12.1

 QuickBooks SatNav

The objective of this chapter is to facilitate mastery of QuickBooks Desktop for a QuickBooks service company. We will cover setting up a new QuickBooks service company, customize the QuickBooks Chart of Accounts, enter QuickBooks transactions, and create reports. This chapter provides the opportunity to integrate knowledge of QuickBooks Desktop through all three phases of the QuickBooks SatNav.

As shown in the following QuickBooks SatNav, Chapter 12 QuickBooks Service Company Case covers all three processes: QuickBooks Settings, QuickBooks Transactions, and QuickBooks Reports.

QuickBooks SatNav

⚙ QuickBooks Settings

⚙ Company Settings

⚙ Chart of Accounts

QuickBooks Transactions

Banking

Customers & Sales

Vendors & Expenses

Employees & Payroll

📊 QuickBooks Reports

Reports

Section 12.2

Set Up New QuickBooks Company and Customize Chart of Accounts

C12.2.1 Create New QuickBooks Company

Create a new company in QuickBooks for Mookie The Beagle™ Spa using the following information and the EasyStep Interview.

Company Name	**YourName Chapter 12 Mookie The Beagle Spa**
Tax ID	**123-45-6789**
Address	**432 Phoenician Way**
City	**Mountain View**
State	**CA**
ZIP	**94043**
Phone	**415-555-1111**
Email	**<Enter your email address>**
Industry	**General Service-based Business**
Type of organization	**Sole Proprietorship**
First month of fiscal year	**January**
File name	**YourName Chapter 12**
What do you sell?	**Services only**
Sales tax	**No**
Estimates	**No**
Billing statements	**No**
Invoices	**Yes**
Progress invoicing	**No**
Track bills you owe	**Yes**
Track time	**Yes**
Employees	**No**

Start date	**01/01/2025**
Use recommended accounts?	**Yes**
Bank account name	**Checking**
Bank account number	**9876543210**
Bank account balance	**0.00 as of 01/01/2025**

Verify the tax form, Form 1040 (Sole Proprietorship), for Mookie The Beagle™ Spa.

1 Select **Company Menu**

2 Select **My Company**

3 Select Income Tax Form: **Form 1040 (Sole Proprietor)**

C12.2.2 Display Account Numbers

Display Account Numbers in the Chart of Accounts for Mookie The Beagle Spa.

1 Select **Edit Menu**

2 Select **Preferences**

3 Select **Accounting**

4 Select **Company Preferences**

5 Select **Use Account Numbers**

C12.2.3 Update Chart of Accounts

1. Add the following accounts to the Chart of Accounts for Mookie The Beagle Spa.

Account No.	**14000**
Account Type	**Fixed Asset**
Account Name	**Pet Spa Equipment**
Account Description	**Pet Spa Equipment**
Tax Line	**Unassigned**

Account No.	**14100**
Account Type	**Fixed Asset**
Account Name	**Pet Spa Equipment Cost**
Subaccount of	**Pet Spa Equipment**
Account Description	**Pet Spa Equipment Cost**
Tax Line	**Unassigned**

Account No.	**14200**
Account Type	**Fixed Asset**
Account Name	**Pet Spa Equipment Acc Depr**
Subaccount of	**Pet Spa Equipment**
Account Description	**Pet Spa Equipment Accumulated Depreciation**
Tax Line	**Unassigned**

Account No.	**21000**
Account Type	**Credit Card**
Account Name	**VISA Credit Card**
Account Description	**VISA Credit Card**
Tax Line	**Unassigned**

Account No.	**64800**
Account Type	**Expense**
Account Name	**Supplies Expense**
Account Description	**Supplies Expense**
Tax Line	**Schedule C: Supplies (not from COGS)**

Account No.	**64810**
Account Type	**Expense**
Account Name	**Pet Spa Supplies Expense**
Subaccount of	**Supplies Expense**
Account Description	**Pet Spa Supplies Expense**
Tax Line	**Schedule C: Supplies (not from COGS)**

Account No.	**64820**
Account Type	**Expense**
Account Name	**Technology Supplies Expense**
Subaccount of	**Supplies Expense**
Account Description	**Technology Supplies Expense**
Tax Line	**Schedule C: Supplies (not from COGS)**

Account No.	**67000**
Account Type	**Expense**
Account Name	**Lease Expense**
Account Description	**Lease Expense for Vehicles and Equipment**
Tax Line	**Schedule C: Rent/lease vehicles, equip.**

2. Edit the following accounts in the Chart of Accounts for Mookie The Beagle Spa to appear as follows.

Account Name	**Checking**
Account No.	**10100**

Account No.	**62400**
Account Type	**Expense**
Account Name	**Depreciation Expense**
Account Description	**Depreciation on equipment, buildings, and improvements**
Tax Line <Change from Unassigned>	**Schedule C: Other business expenses**

Account No.	**67100**
Account Type	**Expense**
Account Name	**Rent Expense**
Account Description	**Rent paid for company offices or other structures used in the business**
Tax Line <Change from Schedule C: Rent/lease vehicles, equip.>	**Schedule C: Rent/lease other bus. prop.**

Account No.	**64900**
Account Type	**Expense**
Account Name	**Office Supplies**
Account Description	**Office supplies expense**
Tax Line <Verify>	**Schedule C: Office expenses**

Note that Account No 64900 Office Supplies (Expense) is mapped to the Tax Line Schedule C: Office Expenses. The accounts added previously, Account No 64810 Pet Supplies Expense and Account No 64820 Technology Supplies Expense, were mapped to a different tax line, Schedule C: Supplies (not from COGS). The separate accounts provide better tracking of expenses for future decision making.

C12.2.4 Create Chart of Accounts Report

Generate a Chart of Accounts report for Mookie The Beagle Spa.

1 From the Report Center, select **List > Account Listing** or select **Accountant & Taxes > Account Listing**

2 Export to **Excel** or **print** the Chart of Accounts (Account Listing) report for Mookie The Beagle Spa at 01/01/2025.

⚠ When exporting to Excel, remember to select Advanced Excel Options:
- Uncheck **Space between columns**
- Check **Row height**
- Uncheck **Include QuickBooks Export Guide worksheet with helpful advice**
- Select **On printed report and screen**

Section 12.3

Customer List

C12.3.1 Create Customer List

Using the following information, create a Customer List for Mookie The Beagle Spa. Note that Customer Type refers to how the customer learned about Mookie The Beagle Spa.

1. Using the following information, add a customer to Mookie The Beagle Spa Customer List.

Customer	**Merriman, Angel**
Opening Balance	**0.00 as of 01/01/2025**
Address Info:	
First Name	**Angel**
Last Name	**Merriman**
Mobile	**415-555-7579**
Address	**623 Thorsmork Road** **Bayshore, CA 94326**
Payment Settings:	
Account No.	**3001**
Payment Terms	**Net 30**
Preferred Delivery Method	**E-mail**
Preferred Payment Method	**Visa**
Additional Info:	
Customer Type <Add New>	**Direct Contact**

2. Add the following job for Angel Merriman. (Add jobs by selecting the customer in the Customer List, right- click > Add Job.)

Job Info:	
Job Name	**Kuno**
Job Description	**Kuno German Shepherd**
Job Type <Add New>	**Extra Large Pet**
Job Status	**Awarded**

3. Add another customer.

Customer	Kari, Tracey
Opening Balance	0.00 as of 01/01/2025

Address Info:

First Name	Tracey
Last Name	Kari
Mobile	415-555-9999
Address	99 Reyka Drive Bayshore, CA 94326

Payment Settings:

Account No.	3002
Payment Terms	Net 30
Preferred Delivery Method	E-mail
Preferred Payment Method	Check

Additional Info:

Customer Type	Referral

4. Add the following job for Tracey Kari.

Job Info:

Job Name	Odin
Job Description	Odin Black Labrador
Job Type <Add New>	Large Pet
Job Status	Awarded

5. Add a new customer.

Customer	Petit, Mimi
Opening Balance	0.00 as of 01/01/2025

Address Info:

First Name	Mimi
Last Name	Petit
Mobile	415-555-2160
Address	220 Alsace Avenue Bayshore, CA 94326

Payment Settings:

Account No.	**3003**
Payment Terms	**Net 30**
Preferred Delivery Method	**E-mail**
Preferred Payment Method	**Check**

Additional Info:

Customer Type <Add New>	**Internet**

6. Add the following job for Mimi Petit.

Job Info:

Job Name	**Bebe**
Job Description	**Bebe French Bulldog**
Job Type <Add New>	**Medium Pet**
Job Status	**Awarded**

7. Add a new customer.

Customer	**Copper, Sandy**
Opening Balance	**0.00 as of 01/01/2025**

Address Info:

First Name	**Sandy**
Last Name	**Copper**
Mobile	**415-555-4320**
Address	**720 Cuivre Drive** **Bayshore, CA 94326**

Payment Settings:

Account No.	**3004**
Payment Terms	**Net 30**
Preferred Delivery Method	**E-mail**
Preferred Payment Method	**Check**

Additional Info:

Customer Type <Add New>	**Social Media**

8. Add the following job for Sandy Copper.
    Job Info:

Job Name	**Remy**
Job Description	**Remy Rescue Dog**
Job Type	**Medium Pet**
Job Status	**Awarded**

9. Add a new customer.

Customer	**Byran, Sherry**
Opening Balance	**0.00 as of 01/01/2025**
Address Info:	
First Name	**Sherry**
Last Name	**Byran**
Mobile	**415-555-2222**
Address	**222 Mure Drive** **Bayshore, CA 94326**
Payment Settings:	
Account No.	**3005**
Payment Terms	**Net 30**
Preferred Delivery Method	**E-mail**
Preferred Payment Method	**Check**
Additional Info:	
Customer Type <Add New>	**Social Media**
Custom Field <Select Define Fields > Enter Label: Preferences > Check Customer > OK>	**Maggie Puppy Cut**

10. Add the following job for Sherry Byran.
    Job Info:

Job Name	**Maggie**
Job Description	**Maggie Cream Havanese**
Job Type <Add New>	**Small Pet**
Job Status	**Awarded**

C12.3.2 Export Customer List

From the Customer Center, export the Customer List to **Excel** or **print**.

Section 12.4
Vendor List

C12.4.1 Create Vendor List

Using the following information, create a Vendor List for Mookie The Beagle Spa.

1. Add a new vendor.

Vendor	**Angel Merriman Associates**
Opening Balance	**$0.00 as of 01/01/2025**
Address Info:	
Company Name	**Angel Merriman Associates**
First Name	**Angel**
Main Phone	**415-555-7579**
Address	**623 Thorsmork Road** **Bayshore, CA 94326**
Payment Settings:	
Account No.	**4001**
Payment Terms	**Net 30**
Print on Check as	**Angel Merriman Associates**
Tax Settings:	
Vendor Tax ID	**37-3571656**
Additional Info:	
Vendor Type	**Supplies**

2. Add new vendor.

Vendor	**Joseph Leasing**
Opening Balance	**$0.00 as of 01/01/2025**
Address Info:	
Company Name	**Joseph Leasing**
First Name	**Joseph**

Main Phone	**415-555-0412**
Address	**13 Appleton Drive** **Bayshore, CA 94326**
Payment Settings:	
Account No.	**4002**
Payment Terms	**Due on receipt**
Print on Check as	**Joseph Leasing**
Additional Info:	
Vendor Type <Add New>	**Leasing**

3. Add new vendor.

Vendor	**Bichotte Supplies**
Opening Balance	**$0.00 as of 01/01/2025**
Address Info:	
Company Name	**Bichotte Supplies**
First Name	**Bichotte**
Main Phone	**415-555-4567**
Address	**810 Francais Drive** **Bayshore, CA 94326**
Payment Settings:	
Account No.	**4003**
Payment Terms	**Net 30**
Print on Check as	**Bichotte Supplies**
Additional Info:	
Vendor Type	**Supplies**

4. Add new vendor.

Vendor	**Meta PetCare Supplies**
Opening Balance	**$0.00 as of 01/01/2025**
Address Info:	

Company Name	**Meta PetCare Supplies**
First Name	**Meta**
Main Phone	**415-555-1010**
Address	**10 Chassure Street** **Bayshore, CA 94326**
Payment Settings:	
Account No.	**4004**
Payment Terms	**Net 30**
Print on Check as	**Meta PetCare Supplies**
Additional Info:	
Vendor Type	**Suppliers**

C12.4.2 Export Vendor List

From the Vendor Center, export the Vendor List to **Excel** or **print**.

Section 12.5

Item List

C12.5.1 Add Items

Enter the following items in the Item List for Mookie The Beagle Spa. Use the Income account: **47900 Sales**.

SUBITEM OF	NAME	TYPE	SALES DESCRIPTION	SALES PRICE
Shampoo	Shampoo Small	Service	Shampoo small dog	$ 36
Shampoo	Shampoo Medium	Service	Shampoo medium dog	$ 45
Shampoo	Shampoo Large	Service	Shampoo large dog	$ 54
Shampoo	Shampoo Extra Large	Service	Shampoo extra large dog	$ 63
Conditioner	Conditioner Small	Service	Conditioner small dog	$ 10
Conditioner	Conditioner Medium	Service	Conditioner medium dog	$ 12
Conditioner	Conditioner Large	Service	Conditioner large dog	$ 18
Conditioner	Conditioner Extra Large	Service	Conditioner extra large dog	$ 22
Blow Dry	Blow Dry Small	Service	Blow dry small dog	$ 20
Blow Dry	Blow Dry Medium	Service	Blow dry medium dog	$ 27
Blow Dry	Blow Dry Large	Service	Blow dry large dog	$ 33
Blow Dry	Blow Dry Extra Large	Service	Blow dry extra large dog	$ 36
Doggie Massage	Short Massage	Service	Massage 15 minutes	$ 30
Doggie Massage	Medium Massage	Service	Massage 30 minutes	$ 55
Doggie Massage	Extended Massage	Service	Massage 60 minutes	$ 100
Grooming	Trim Coat	Service	Trim coat	$ 66
Grooming	Trim Nails	Service	Trim nails and file	$ 18

C12.5.2 Export Item List

From the Report Center, export the Item List to **Excel** or **print**.

Section 12.6

Customize Invoice Template

Create a Custom Invoice Template with a Service Date column for Mookie The Beagle Spa. (See Chapter 11, Section 11.13, for step-by-step instructions on how to create a custom invoice with a Service Date column.) The Service Date column permits the company to bill clients once a month for all services provided during the month, listing each service date separately on the invoice.

Section 12.7

Record Transactions

Mookie The Beagle Spa entered into the following transactions during the year.

C12.7.1 Enter Transactions

Record the following transactions for Mookie The Beagle Spa. Customers are billed monthly. To streamline transaction entry, use memorized transactions for recurring transactions as appropriate.

Date	Transaction
01/01/2025	Cy Walker invested $7,200 in the business. (Use the Make Deposits window and Check No 5555.)
01/01/2025	Paid $360 for van lease expense to Joseph Leasing for use as Mookie's new mobile Pet Spa. (Record with the two-step method using the Enter Bills and Pay Bills windows. Use the Lease Expense account.)
01/02/2025	Purchased pet spa equipment for $1,500 on account from Meta PetCare Supplies
01/03/2025	Purchased technology supplies for $210 on account from Angel Merriman Associates. (Use the Technology Supplies Expense account.)
01/06/2025	Purchased office supplies for $90 with a VISA credit card from Bichotte Supplies. (Use the Enter Credit Card Charges window and Office Supplies (Expense) account.)
01/08/2025	Purchased $135 of pet spa supplies on account from Meta PetCare to stock Mookie's new mobile Pet Spa. (Use the Pet Spa Supplies Expense account.)
01/10/2025	Purchased $80 of gasoline from FastFuel using VISA credit card. (Use the Enter Credit Card Charges window and the Automobile Expense account.)
01/20/2025	Paid by check Meta PetCare Supplies bills of $1,635 for January purchases
01/30/2025	Emailed invoice to customer for the following work performed in January. **Use the Service Date Invoice Template to record all work performed for the same customer during the month on a single invoice, indicating the date of service in the Date column.**

01/13/2025   Angel Merriman Job: Kuno
Services:
- Shampoo Extra Large
- Conditioner Extra Large
- Blow Dry Extra Large
- Trim Nails

01/20/2025   Angel Merriman Job: Kuno
Services:
- Extended Massage

01/21/2025   Sherry Byran Job: Maggie
Services:
- Trim Coat
- Shampoo Small
- Conditioner Small
- Blow Dry Small
- Medium Massage

01/27/2025   Tracey Kari Job: Odin
Services:
- Extended Massage
- Shampoo Large
- Conditioner Large
- Blow Dry Large
- Trim Nails

02/01/2025   Paid $360 for van lease expense to Joseph Leasing

02/09/2025   Received payment from Sherry Byran: Maggie (VISA 5555 5555 3333 5555 Exp 11/2027) for January invoice. Recorded deposit.

02/10/2025   Received payment from Angel Merriman: Kuno (VISA 5555 5555 5555 5555 Exp 01/2027) for January invoice. Recorded deposit.

02/11/2025   Received payment from Tracey Kari: Odin (Check 1200) for January invoice. Recorded deposit.

02/20/2025   Purchased $45 of pet spa supplies from Meta PetCare Supplies on account

02/23/2025   Paid VISA credit card bill for $170 (January purchases). (Use the Enter Bills window. Add VISA as a new vendor. Select Expense: Account 21000 Visa Credit Card. Then use Pay Bills window to pay the bill from the Checking account.)

02/28/2025   Emailed invoices to customers for the following work performed in February. **Use the Service Date Invoice Template to record all work performed for the same customer during the month on a single invoice, indicating the date of service in the Date column.**

02/02/2025   Tracey Kari Job: Odin
Services:
- Extended Massage
- Shampoo Large
- Conditioner Large
- Blow Dry Large
- Trim Nails

02/10/2025   Tracey Kari Job: Odin
Services:
- Extended Massage
- Shampoo Large
- Conditioner Large
- Blow Dry Large

02/13/2025   Sherry Byran Job: Maggie
Services:
- Trim Coat
- Shampoo Small
- Conditioner Small
- Blow Dry Small
- Trim Nails
- Medium Massage

02/16/2025   Mimi Petit Job: Bebe
Services:
- Shampoo Medium
- Conditioner Medium
- Blow Dry Medium
- Trim Nails
- Extended Massage

02/20/2025   Tracey Kari Job: Odin
Services:
- Extended Massage
- Shampoo Large
- Conditioner Large
- Blow Dry Large

02/27/2025   Tracey Kari Job: Odin
Services:
- Extended Massage
- Shampoo Large
- Conditioner Large
- Blow Dry Large

02/27/2025 Angel Merriman Job: Kuno
Services:
- Shampoo Extra Large
- Conditioner Extra Large
- Blow Dry Extra Large
- Extended Massage

03/02/2025 Paid Angel Merriman Associates for $210 of technology supplies purchased on account

03/02/2025 Paid $360 for van lease expense to Joseph Leasing

03/10/2025 Received the following payments for prior month invoices.
- Received payment from Angel Merriman: Kuno (VISA)
- Received payment from Tracey Kari: Odin (Check No. 1234)
- Received payment from Mimi Petit: Bebe (Check No. 178)
- Received payment from Sherry Byran: Maggie (VISA)
- Recorded deposits

03/14/2025 Paid Meta PetCare Supplies bill for $45

03/30/2025 Emailed invoices to customers for the following work performed in March. **Use the Service Date Invoice Template to record all work performed for the same customer during the month on a single invoice, indicating the date of service in the Date column.**

03/01/2025 Tracey Kari Job: Odin
Services:
- Extended Massage
- Shampoo Large
- Conditioner Large
- Blow Dry Large
- Trim Nails

03/08/2025 Tracey Kari Job: Odin
Services:
- Extended Massage
- Shampoo Large
- Conditioner Large
- Blow Dry Large

03/15/2025 Sherry Byran Job: Maggie
Services:
- Trim Coat
- Shampoo Small
- Conditioner Small
- Blow Dry Small
- Trim Nails
- Medium Massage

03/15/2025   Tracey Kari Job: Odin
              Services:
              • Extended Massage
              • Shampoo Large
              • Conditioner Large
              • Blow Dry Large

03/16/2025   Sandy Copper Job: Remy
              Services:
              • Shampoo Medium
              • Conditioner Medium
              • Blow Dry Medium
              • Trim Nails
              • Extended Massage

03/22/2025   Tracey Kari Job: Odin
              Services:
              • Extended Massage
              • Shampoo Large
              • Conditioner Large
              • Blow Dry Large

03/27/2025   Angel Merriman Job: Kuno
              Services:
              • Shampoo Extra Large
              • Conditioner Extra Large
              • Blow Dry Extra Large
              • Extended Massage

03/29/2025   Tracey Kari Job: Odin
              Services:
              • Extended Massage
              • Shampoo Large
              • Conditioner Large
              • Blow Dry Large

04/01/2025   Paid $360 for van lease expense to Joseph Leasing

04/10/2025   Received the following payments for prior month invoices.
              • Received payment from Angel Merriman: Kuno (VISA)
              • Received payment from Tracey Kari: Odin (Check No. 1342)
              • Received payment from Sandy Copper: Remy (Check No. 572)
              • Received payment from Sherry Byran: Maggie (VISA)
              • Recorded deposits

04/20/2025   Purchased $54 of gasoline from FastFuel using VISA credit card

04/30/2025   Emailed invoices to customers for the following work performed in April. **Use the Service Date Invoice Template to record all work performed for the same customer during the month on a single invoice, indicating the date of service in the Date column.**

        04/01/2025   Tracey Kari Job: Odin
                          Services:
- Extended Massage
- Shampoo Large
- Conditioner Large
- Blow Dry Large
- Trim Nails

        04/08/2025   Tracey Kari Job: Odin
                          Services:
- Extended Massage
- Shampoo Large
- Conditioner Large
- Blow Dry Large

        04/15/2025   Angel Merriman Job: Kuno
                          Services:
- Shampoo Extra Large
- Conditioner Extra Large
- Blow Dry Extra Large
- Trim Nails
- Medium Massage

        04/15/2025   Tracey Kari Job: Odin
                          Services:
- Extended Massage
- Shampoo Large
- Conditioner Large
- Blow Dry Large

        04/16/2025   Sherry Byran Job: Maggie
                          Services:
- Trim Coat
- Shampoo Small
- Conditioner Small
- Blow Dry Small
- Trim Nails
- Medium Massage

04/22/2025   Tracey Kari Job: Odin
Services:
- Extended Massage
- Shampoo Large
- Conditioner Large
- Blow Dry Large

04/27/2025   Angel Merriman Job: Kuno
Services:
- Shampoo Extra Large
- Conditioner Extra Large
- Blow Dry Extra Large
- Extended Massage

04/29/2025   Tracey Kari Job: Odin
Services:
- Extended Massage
- Shampoo Large
- Conditioner Large
- Blow Dry Large

04/30/2025   Sandy Copper Job: Remy
Services:
- Shampoo Medium
- Conditioner Medium
- Blow Dry Medium
- Extended Massage
- Trim Nails

05/01/2025   Paid $360 for van lease expense to Joseph Leasing

05/11/2025   Received the following payments for prior month invoices.
- Received payment from Angel Merriman: Kuno (VISA)
- Received payment from Tracey Kari: Odin (Check No. 1363)
- Received payment from Sherry Byran: Maggie (VISA)
- Received payment from Sandy Copper: Remy (Check No. 577)
- Recorded deposits

05/22/2025   Paid VISA credit card bill for $54

05/30/2025   Emailed invoices to customers for the following work performed in May.

05/01/2025   Tracey Kari Job: Odin
Services:
- Extended Massage
- Shampoo Large
- Conditioner Large
- Blow Dry Large
- Trim Nails

05/08/2025   Tracey Kari Job: Odin
Services:
- Extended Massage
- Shampoo Large
- Conditioner Large
- Blow Dry Large

05/15/2025   Angel Merriman Job: Kuno
Services:
- Shampoo Extra Large
- Conditioner Extra Large
- Blow Dry Extra Large
- Trim Nails
- Medium Massage

05/15/2025   Tracey Kari Job: Odin
Services:
- Extended Massage
- Shampoo Large
- Conditioner Large
- Blow Dry Large

05/16/2025   Mimi Petit Job: Bebe
Services:
- Shampoo Medium
- Conditioner Medium
- Blow Dry Medium
- Trim Nails
- Extended Massage

05/16/2025   Sherry Byran Job: Maggie
Services:
- Trim Coat
- Shampoo Small
- Conditioner Small
- Blow Dry Small
- Trim Nails
- Medium Massage

05/22/2025   Tracey Kari Job: Odin
Services:
- Extended Massage
- Shampoo Large
- Conditioner Large
- Blow Dry Large

05/27/2025   Angel Merriman Job: Kuno
Services:
- Shampoo Extra Large
- Conditioner Extra Large
- Blow Dry Extra Large
- Extended Massage

05/29/2025   Tracey Kari Job: Odin
Services:
- Extended Massage
- Shampoo Large
- Conditioner Large
- Blow Dry Large

06/01/2025   Paid $360 for van lease expense to Joseph Leasing

06/10/2025   Received the following payments for prior month invoices.
- Received payment from Angel Merriman: Kuno (VISA)
- Received payment from Tracey Kari: Odin (Check No. 1372)
- Received payment from Mimi Petit: Bebe (Check No. 210)
- Received payment from Sherry Byran: Maggie (VISA)
- Recorded deposits

06/30/2025   Emailed invoices to customers for the following work performed in June.

06/01/2025   Tracey Kari Job: Odin
Services:
- Extended Massage
- Shampoo Large
- Conditioner Large
- Blow Dry Large
- Trim Nails

06/15/2025   Angel Merriman Job: Kuno
Services:
- Shampoo Extra Large
- Conditioner Extra Large
- Blow Dry Extra Large
- Trim Nails
- Medium Massage

06/16/2025   Sherry Byran Job: Maggie
Services:
- Trim Coat
- Shampoo Small
- Conditioner Small
- Blow Dry Small
- Trim Nails
- Medium Massage

06/16/2025   Tracey Kari Job: Odin
Services:
- Extended Massage
- Shampoo Large
- Conditioner Large
- Blow Dry Large

06/27/2025   Angel Merriman Job: Kuno
Services:
- Shampoo Extra Large
- Conditioner Extra Large
- Blow Dry Extra Large
- Medium Massage

06/30/2025   Sandy Copper Job: Remy
Services:
- Shampoo Medium
- Conditioner Medium
- Blow Dry Medium
- Extended Massage
- Trim Nails

07/01/2025   Paid $360 for van lease expense to Joseph Leasing

07/10/2025   Received the following payments for prior month invoices.
- Received payment from Angel Merriman: Kuno (VISA)
- Received payment from Tracey Kari: Odin (Check No. 1381)
- Received payment from Sherry Byran: Maggie (VISA)
- Received payment from Sandy Copper: Remy (Check No. 589)
- Recorded deposits

07/20/2025   Purchased $63 of gasoline from FastFuel using VISA credit card

07/30/2025   Emailed invoices to customers for the following work performed in July.

        07/01/2025   Tracey Kari Job: Odin
        Services:
- Extended Massage
- Shampoo Large
- Conditioner Large
- Blow Dry Large
- Trim Nails

07/08/2025   Tracey Kari Job: Odin
              Services:
              • Extended Massage
              • Shampoo Large
              • Conditioner Large
              • Blow Dry Large
07/15/2025   Angel Merriman Job: Kuno
              Services:
              • Shampoo Extra Large
              • Conditioner Extra Large
              • Blow Dry Extra Large
              • Trim Nails
              • Medium Massage
07/16/2025   Sherry Byran Job: Maggie
              Services:
              • Trim Coat
              • Shampoo Small
              • Conditioner Small
              • Blow Dry Small
              • Trim Nails
              • Medium Massage
07/16/2025   Tracey Kari Job: Odin
              Services:
              • Extended Massage
              • Shampoo Large
              • Conditioner Large
              • Blow Dry Large
07/22/2025   Tracey Kari Job: Odin
              Services:
              • Extended Massage
              • Shampoo Large
              • Conditioner Large
              • Blow Dry Large
07/27/2025   Angel Merriman Job: Kuno
              Services:
              • Shampoo Extra Large
              • Conditioner Extra Large
              • Blow Dry Extra Large
              • Extended Massage
07/29/2025   Tracey Kari Job: Odin
              Services:
              • Extended Massage
              • Shampoo Large
              • Conditioner Large
              • Blow Dry Large

07/30/2025   Sandy Copper Job: Remy
Services:
- Shampoo Medium
- Conditioner Medium
- Blow Dry Medium
- Extended Massage
- Trim Nails

08/01/2025   Paid $360 for van lease expense to Joseph Leasing

08/10/2025   Received the following payments for prior month invoices.
- Received payment from Angel Merriman: Kuno (VISA)
- Received payment from Tracey Kari: Odin (Check No. 1390)
- Received payment from Sherry Byran: Maggie (VISA)
- Received payment from Sandy Copper: Remy (Check No. 595)
- Recorded deposits

08/22/2025   Paid VISA credit card bill for $63

08/31/2025   Emailed invoices to customers for the following work performed in August.

        08/01/2025   Tracey Kari Job: Odin
        Services:
- Extended Massage
- Shampoo Large
- Conditioner Large
- Blow Dry Large
- Trim Nails

        08/08/2025   Tracey Kari Job: Odin
        Services:
- Extended Massage
- Shampoo Large
- Conditioner Large
- Blow Dry Large

        08/15/2025   Angel Merriman Job: Kuno
        Services:
- Shampoo Extra Large
- Conditioner Extra Large
- Blow Dry Extra Large
- Trim Nails
- Extended Massage

08/16/2025   Mimi Petit Job: Bebe
Services:
- Shampoo Medium
- Conditioner Medium
- Blow Dry Medium
- Trim Nails
- Extended Massage

08/16/2025   Sherry Byran Job: Maggie
Services:
- Trim Coat
- Shampoo Small
- Conditioner Small
- Blow Dry Small
- Trim Nails
- Medium Massage

08/16/2025   Tracey Kari Job: Odin
Services:
- Extended Massage
- Shampoo Large
- Conditioner Large
- Blow Dry Large

08/22/2025   Tracey Kari Job: Odin
Services:
- Extended Massage
- Shampoo Large
- Conditioner Large
- Blow Dry Large

08/27/2025   Angel Merriman Job: Kuno
Services:
- Shampoo Extra Large
- Conditioner Extra Large
- Blow Dry Extra Large
- Extended Massage

08/29/2025   Tracey Kari Job: Odin
Services:
- Extended Massage
- Shampoo Large
- Conditioner Large
- Blow Dry Large

09/01/2025   Paid $360 for van lease expense to Joseph Leasing

09/10/2025 Received the following payments for prior month invoices.
- Received payment from Angel Merriman: Kuno (VISA)
- Received payment from Tracey Kari: Odin (Check No. 1350)
- Received payment from Mimi Petit: Bebe (Check No. 234)
- Received payment from Sherry Byran: Maggie (VISA)
- Recorded deposits

09/21/2025 Purchased $72 of pet spa supplies from Meta PetCare Supplies on account

09/30/2025 Emailed invoices to customers for the following work performed in September.

    09/01/2025 Tracey Kari Job: Odin
    Services:
- Extended Massage
- Shampoo Large
- Conditioner Large
- Blow Dry Large
- Trim Nails

    09/08/2025 Tracey Kari Job: Odin
    Services:
- Extended Massage
- Shampoo Large
- Conditioner Large
- Blow Dry Large

    09/15/2025 Angel Merriman Job: Kuno
    Services:
- Shampoo Extra Large
- Conditioner Extra Large
- Blow Dry Extra Large
- Trim Nails
- Medium Massage

    09/15/2025 Tracey Kari Job: Odin
    Services:
- Extended Massage
- Shampoo Large
- Conditioner Large
- Blow Dry Large

    09/16/2025 Sherry Byran Job: Maggie
    Services:
- Trim Coat
- Shampoo Small
- Conditioner Small
- Blow Dry Small
- Trim Nails
- Medium Massage

09/22/2025 Tracey Kari Job: Odin
Services:
- Extended Massage
- Shampoo Large
- Conditioner Large
- Blow Dry Large

09/27/2025 Angel Merriman Job: Kuno
Services:
- Shampoo Extra Large
- Conditioner Extra Large
- Blow Dry Extra Large
- Extended Massage

09/29/2025 Tracey Kari Job: Odin
Services:
- Extended Massage
- Shampoo Large
- Conditioner Large
- Blow Dry Large

09/30/2025 Sandy Copper Job: Remy
Services:
- Shampoo Medium
- Conditioner Medium
- Blow Dry Medium
- Extended Massage
- Trim Nails

10/01/2025 Paid $360 for van lease expense to Joseph Leasing

10/10/2025 Received the following payments for prior month invoices.
- Received payment from Angel Merriman: Kuno (VISA)
- Received payment from Tracey Kari: Odin (Check No. 1359)
- Received payment from Sherry Byran: Maggie (VISA)
- Received payment from Sandy Copper: Remy (Check No. 612)
- Recorded deposits

10/15/2025 Paid Meta PetCare Supplies bill for $72

10/30/2025   Emailed invoices to customers for the following work performed in October.

10/01/2025   Tracey Kari Job: Odin
Services:
- Extended Massage
- Shampoo Large
- Conditioner Large
- Blow Dry Large
- Trim Nails

10/15/2025   Angel Merriman Job: Kuno
Services:
- Shampoo Extra Large
- Conditioner Extra Large
- Blow Dry Extra Large
- Trim Nails
- Medium Massage

10/16/2025   Sherry Byran Job: Maggie
Services:
- Trim Coat
- Shampoo Small
- Conditioner Small
- Blow Dry Small
- Trim Nails
- Medium Massage

10/22/2025   Tracey Kari Job: Odin
Services:
- Extended Massage
- Shampoo Large
- Conditioner Large
- Blow Dry Large

10/27/2025   Angel Merriman Job: Kuno
Services:
- Shampoo Extra Large
- Conditioner Extra Large
- Blow Dry Extra Large
- Extended Massage

10/30/2025   Sandy Copper Job: Remy
Services:
- Shampoo Medium
- Conditioner Medium
- Blow Dry Medium
- Extended Massage
- Trim Nails

11/01/2025   Paid $360 for van lease expense to Joseph Leasing

11/10/2025   Received the following payments for prior month invoices.
- Received payment from Angel Merriman: Kuno (VISA)
- Received payment from Tracey Kari: Odin (Check No. 1368)
- Received payment from Sherry Byran: Maggie (VISA)
- Received payment from Sandy Copper: Remy (Check No. 621)
- Recorded deposits

11/30/2025   Emailed invoices to customers for the following work performed in November.

         11/01/2025   Tracey Kari Job: Odin
                        Services:
- Extended Massage
- Shampoo Large
- Conditioner Large
- Blow Dry Large
- Trim Nails

         11/08/2025   Tracey Kari Job: Odin
                        Services:
- Extended Massage
- Shampoo Large
- Conditioner Large
- Blow Dry Large

         11/15/2025   Angel Merriman Job: Kuno
                        Services:
- Shampoo Extra Large
- Conditioner Extra Large
- Blow Dry Extra Large
- Trim Nails
- Medium Massage

         11/15/2025   Tracey Kari Job: Odin
                        Services:
- Extended Massage
- Shampoo Large
- Conditioner Large
- Blow Dry Large

         11/16/2025   Sherry Byran Job: Maggie
                        Services:
- Trim Coat
- Shampoo Small
- Conditioner Small
- Blow Dry Small
- Trim Nails
- Medium Massage

11/18/2025   Mimi Petit Job: Bebe
Services:
- Shampoo Medium
- Conditioner Medium
- Blow Dry Medium
- Trim Nails
- Extended Massage

11/22/2025   Tracey Kari Job: Odin
Services:
- Extended Massage
- Shampoo Large
- Conditioner Large
- Blow Dry Large

11/27/2025   Angel Merriman Job: Kuno
Services:
- Shampoo Extra Large
- Conditioner Extra Large
- Blow Dry Extra Large
- Extended Massage

11/29/2025   Tracey Kari Job: Odin
Services:
- Extended Massage
- Shampoo Large
- Conditioner Large
- Blow Dry Large

12/01/2025   Paid $360 for van lease expense to Joseph Leasing

12/10/2025   Received the following payments for prior month invoices.
- Received payment from Angel Merriman: Kuno (VISA)
- Received payment from Tracey Kari: Odin (Check No. 1377)
- Received payment from Mimi Petit: Bebe (Check No. 261)
- Received payment from Sherry Byran: Maggie (Check No. 630)
- Recorded deposits

12/21/2025   Purchased $54 of gasoline from FastFuel using VISA credit card

12/30/2025   Emailed invoices to customers for the following work performed in December.

12/01/2025   Tracey Kari Job: Odin
                Services:
                - Extended Massage
                - Shampoo Large
                - Conditioner Large
                - Blow Dry Large
                - Trim Nails

12/15/2025   Angel Merriman Job: Kuno
                Services:
                - Shampoo Extra Large
                - Conditioner Extra Large
                - Blow Dry Extra Large
                - Trim Nails
                - Extended Massage

12/15/2025   Sherry Byran Job: Maggie
                Services:
                - Trim Coat
                - Shampoo Small
                - Conditioner Small
                - Blow Dry Small
                - Trim Nails
                - Medium Massage

12/20/2025   Tracey Kari Job: Odin
                Services:
                - Extended Massage
                - Shampoo Large
                - Conditioner Large
                - Blow Dry Large

12/20/2025   Sandy Copper Job: Remy
                Services:
                - Shampoo Medium
                - Conditioner Medium
                - Blow Dry Medium
                - Extended Massage
                - Trim Nails

C12.7.2 Export Deposit Detail Report

Export to **Excel** or **print** the Deposit Detail report for 2025.

C12.7.3 Export Check Detail Report

Export to **Excel** or **print** the Check Detail report for 2025.

C12.7.4 Export Customer Detail Report

Export to **Excel** or **print** the Income by Customer Detail report for 2025.

C12.7.5 Export Expenses by Vendor Detail Report

Export to **Excel** or **print** the Expenses by Vendor Detail report for 2025.

Section 12.8
Adjusting Entries

Make adjusting entries for Mookie The Beagle Spa.

C12.8.1 Export Trial Balance

1. Export to **Excel** or **print** the Trial Balance report for Mookie The Beagle Spa at December 31, 2025.

2. Verify that Account 12000 Undeposited Funds has a $0.00 balance. **Highlight** the $0.00 balance in the Undeposited Funds account. (Note that if there is a balance in the Undeposited Funds account, this indicates that a customer payment has been recorded as received, but has not been recorded as a bank deposit.)

C12.8.2 Adjusting Entries

Make adjusting entries for Mookie The Beagle Spa at December 31, 2025, using the following information.

1. **ADJ1:** A count of office supplies revealed $50 supplies on hand at December 31, 2025. (Add new account: 13100 Office Supplies on Hand, Other Current Asset.)

2. **ADJ2:** A count of pet spa supplies revealed $100 of supplies on hand at December 31, 2025 (Add new account: 13200 Pet Spa Supplies on Hand, Other Current Asset.)

3. **ADJ3:** The pet spa equipment cost $1,500 and has a five-year life and no salvage value. (Use account: 14200 Pet Spa Equipment Acc Depr.)

C12.8.3 Export Adjusting Journal Entries Report

Export to **Excel** or **print** the Adjusting Journal Entries report on December 31, 2025.

C12.8.4 Export Adjusted Trial Balance

Export to **Excel** or **print** the Adjusted Trial Balance report for Mookie The Beagle Spa at December 31, 2025.

C12.8.5 Adjusted Trial Balance

On the Adjusted Trial Balance report, **highlight** the amounts affected by the adjusting entries.

Section 12.9

Financial Reports

Prepare financial reports for Mookie The Beagle Spa.

C12.9.1 Export Profit and Loss by Job Report

Export to **Excel** or **print** the Profit and Loss by Job for the year 2025.

C12.9.2 Export Profit and Loss, Standard

Export to **Excel** or **print** the Profit and Loss, Standard for the year 2025.

C12.9.3 Export Balance Sheet, Standard

Export to **Excel** or **print** the Balance Sheet, Standard at December 31, 2025.

C12.9.4 Export Statement of Cash Flows

Export to **Excel** or **print** the Statement of Cash Flows for the year of 2025.

C12.9.5 Export Cash Flow Forecast

Export to **Excel** or **print** the Cash Flow Forecast for January 1, 2026 to January 31, 2026.

Section 12.10

Back up QuickBooks Files

Save a backup of your Chapter 12 file using the file name: **YourName Chapter 12 Backup.QBB**. For further instructions on how to back up your file, *see* Appendix B: Back Up and Restore QuickBooks Files.

Design elements: Dog icon: ©josep perianes jorba/Shutterstock; paint roller icon: ©Netti Buletti/Shutterstock; other icons/symbols: ©Carboxylase/Shutterstock

Chapter 13

QuickBooks Merchandise Company

 Paint Palette Store

BACKSTORY

After one year of operation, your painting service, Paint Palette, is receiving stellar reviews from satisfied customers. Your clients take photos of whatever they want for their wall murals (sunsets, waterfalls, beaches, and so on) and then text the photos to your smart phone. Then with your smart phone, you display the photo onto the wall to paint the mural. It saves you time, you no longer have to guess what the customer wants, and customer satisfaction couldn't be better. As a promotion, you created a digital gallery of your completed murals for your website and held a contest for your fans' favorite mural.

Your paint supplier is a small boutique paint shop, owned and operated by Sam Montroyal. He provides excellent customer service, delivers paint to a job when you run short, and custom mixes paint tints you use for your murals. To your dismay, you discover that Sam is planning to close the store and retire, taking his first vacation since he opened the store 20 years ago. After your initial disappointment, however, you see a business opportunity.

If you owned the paint store, you could make a profit on the markup from paint sales made to your Paint Palette clients. In addition, you are certain you could land some large commercial customers for whom you have worked, such as Rock Castle Construction. With your connections, you could sell paint to other customers, including paint contractors and homeowners.

Convinced there is a profitable market for custom-mixed paint, you approach Sam about purchasing his store. Sam agrees to sell the business to you for $20,000 cash. In addition, you agree to assume a $3,000 bank loan as part of the purchase agreement. You have some extra cash you can invest, and you decide to seek other investors to finance the remainder.

Joseph Asher of Joseph Leasing is a long-time customer of the paint store and owner of the store building. When he learns of your plans to buy the paint store business, he eagerly offers to invest.

Joseph suggests that you investigate incorporating the new business to provide limited liability to the owners. You vaguely recall discussion of limited liability in your college accounting class and decide to email your college accounting professor, Pat Vollenger, for more information.

Professor Vollenger's email reply:

Subject: Limited Liability

Corporations provide investors with limited liability. The most the investor can lose is the amount invested in the corporation's stock. If you invest in a corporation, your personal assets are protected from claims against the paint store.

For tax purposes, there are two different types of corporations:
S Corporation
C Corporation

A C Corporation's earnings are subject to double taxation. The profits of the corporation are taxed (Form 1120) and then the dividends received by investors are taxed on their 1040s.

If you meet the requirements to use an S Corporation, you can avoid this double taxation. An S Corporation files a Form 1020S and its earnings appear on your personal 1040 tax return, taxes at your personal income tax rate.

Best wishes on your new business venture!

Joseph and you form an S Corporation. Joseph buys $10,000 of stock, and you buy $10,000 of stock. The stock proceeds are used to purchase the business from Sam Montroyal. Until you can hire a store manager, you will manage the store. Paint Palette Store opens for business on January 1, 2026.

Chapter 13

Learning Objectives

Chapter 13 covers using QuickBooks for a merchandising company that sells products. In this chapter, you will learn about the following topics:

- Create New Company
  - EasyStep Interview
  - Complete Company Setup
- Add Bank Account
- Customize QuickBooks Preferences
- Customer, Vendor and Item Lists
  - Customer List
  - Vendor List
  - Item List: Inventory
  - Item List: Sales Tax Item
- Customize Chart of Accounts
- QuickBooks Opening Adjustments
- Vendors and Expenses Transactions
  - Equipment Purchases
  - Purchasing Cycle
  - Create a Purchase Order
  - Receive Inventory Items
  - Enter Bills
  - Pay Bills
  - Print Checks
- Customers and Sales Transactions
  - Sales Cycle
  - Create Invoices
  - Receive Payments
  - Make Deposits
- Adjusting Entries
- Financial Reports
- Back Up QuickBooks Files

Section 13.1
 QuickBooks SatNav

The objective of this chapter is to facilitate your mastery of QuickBooks Desktop. We will cover setting up a new QuickBooks merchandising company, customize the QuickBooks Chart of Accounts, enter QuickBooks transactions, and create reports. This chapter provides you with the opportunity to integrate your knowledge of QuickBooks Desktop through all three phases of the QuickBooks SatNav.

As shown in the following QuickBooks SatNav, Chapter 13 QuickBooks Merchandise Company covers all three processes: QuickBooks Settings, QuickBooks Transactions, and QuickBooks Reports.

QuickBooks SatNav

QuickBooks Settings

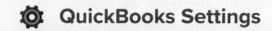

Company Settings

Chart of Accounts

QuickBooks Transactions

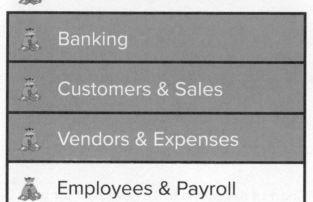

Banking

Customers & Sales

Vendors & Expenses

Employees & Payroll

QuickBooks Reports

Reports

Section 13.2

New QuickBooks Merchandising Company

A company can sell customers (1) a product or (2) a service. In Chapter 11, we maintained accounting records for a company that sells a service to customers. In this chapter, we will maintain an accounting system for a company that sells a product.

In Chapter 13, we will complete the following:

- **EasyStep Interview.** Use the EasyStep Interview to enter information and preferences for the new company. Based on the information entered, QuickBooks automatically creates a Chart of Accounts.
- **Create Lists.**
  - **Customer List.** In the Customer List, enter information about customers to whom you sell products and services.
  - **Vendor List.** In the Vendor List, enter information about vendors from whom you buy products, supplies, and services.
  - **Item List.** In the Item List, enter information about (1) products and services you sell to customers and (2) products and services you buy from vendors. Also we will create a sales tax item in the Item List.
- **Customize the Chart of Accounts.** Modify the Chart of Accounts to customize it for your business.
- **Record Transactions.** Enter business transactions in QuickBooks using onscreen forms and the onscreen Journal.
- **Create Reports.** After preparing adjusting entries, print financial reports.

If you hired employees, you would also enter information into the Employee List. In this case, there are no employees.

> **Download the Excel Report Template for Chapter 13 at www.My-QuickBooks.com, QB2021 link, at the OLC www.mhhe.com/kay2021, or if you are using Connect, from Connect.**

Section 13.3
Create New Company

START QUICKBOOKS

To start QuickBooks software, click the **QuickBooks** icon on your desktop. If a QuickBooks icon does not appear on your desktop, from Microsoft® Windows® click **Start** button > **QuickBooks** > **QuickBooks Premier Accountant Edition**.

EASYSTEP INTERVIEW

To create a new company data file in QuickBooks, use the EasyStep Interview. The EasyStep Interview asks you a series of questions about your business. Then QuickBooks uses the information to customize QuickBooks to fit your business needs.

Create a new QuickBooks company using the EasyStep Interview as follows:

1 Select **Create a new company**

2 When the QuickBooks Setup window appears, select **Detailed Start**

3 When the EasyStep Interview Enter Your Company Information window appears, enter Company Name: **YourName Chapter 13 Paint Palette Store**. Press the **Tab** key, and QuickBooks will automatically enter the company name in the Legal name field. Since the company will do business under its legal name, the Company name and Legal name fields are the same.

4 Enter the company information.

Tax ID	**37-9875602**
Address	**864 Venus Boulevard**
City	**Bayshore**
State	**CA**
Zip	**94326**
Email	**<Enter your email address>**

5   Select **Next**

6   In the Select Your Industry window, select **Retail Shop or Online Commerce**

7   Select **Next**

8   When the How Is Your Company Organized? window appears, select **S Corporation**

9   Select **Next**

10   Select the first month of your fiscal year: **January**

11   Select **Next**

12   In the Set Up Your Administrator Password window:
- Enter your administrator **password**
- Retype the **password**
- **Click Next**

13   When the Create Your Company File window appears, click **Next** to choose a file name and location to save your company file

14   When the Filename for New Company window appears, select Save in: **Desktop**

15   Enter File name: **YourName Chapter 13**

16   Click **Save**

The Navigation Bar and My Shortcuts window should appear on the left side of your QuickBooks company screen. The next section of the EasyStep Interview is to customize QuickBooks by turning on features to fit your business needs.

1   When the Customizing QuickBooks For Your Business window appears, click **Next**

2   What Do You Sell?
- Select **Products only**
- Click **Next**

3   How will you enter your sales in QuickBooks
- Select **Record each sale individually**
- Click **Next**

4   Do you charge sales tax?
- Select **Yes**
- Click **Next**

5   Do you want to create estimates in QuickBooks?
- Select **No**
- Click **Next**

6   Do you want to track sales orders before you invoice your customers?
- Select **No**
- Click **Next**

7   Do you want to use billing statements in QuickBooks?
- Select **No**
- Click **Next**

8   Do you want to use Invoices?
- Select **Yes**
- Click **Next**

9   Do you want to use progress invoicing?
- Select **No**
- Click **Next**

10   Do you want to keep track of bills you owe?
- Select **Yes**
- Click **Next**

11   Do you want to track inventory in QuickBooks?
- Select **Yes**
- Click **Next**

12   Do you want to track time in QuickBooks?
- Select **Yes**
- Click **Next**

13   Do You Have Employees?
- Select **No**
- Click **Next**

14   Read the Using Accounts in QuickBooks window. Click **Next**.

15 When the Select a Date to Start Tracking Your Finances window appears:
- Select **Use today's date or the first day of the quarter or month**
- Enter Date **01/01/2026**
- Click **Next**

16 When the Review Income and Expense Accounts window appears, click **Next**

17 When the Congratulations! window appears, click **Go to Setup**

COMPLETE THE COMPANY SETUP

Use the following checklist to complete the company setup:

- Add bank account
- Customize QuickBooks preferences
- Add customers
- Add vendors
- Add products and services as items
- Customize Chart of Accounts
- Enter opening adjustments

Section 13.4

Add Bank Account

Bank accounts in QuickBooks are used to track your company's deposits, payments, and current bank balances. A QuickBooks company file can have more than one bank account. For example, some companies use one bank account for payroll and another bank account for all other banking items.

To add a bank account for Paint Palette Store:

1 In the Add Your Bank Accounts section of the QuickBooks Setup window, click the **Add** button

2 Enter the following information about Paint Palette's bank account

Account Name	**Checking**
Account Number	**4567891230**
Opening Balance	**0.00**
Opening Balance Date	**01/01/2026**

3 Select **Continue**

4 When asked if you want to order checks designed for QuickBooks, select **No Thanks**

5 Click **Continue** to return to the QuickBooks Setup window

6 Select **Start Working** at the bottom of the QuickBooks Setup window

7 If the New Feature Tour window appears, **close** the New Feature Tour window

In setting up QuickBooks for Paint Palette Store, the next step is to customize QuickBooks preferences.

Section 13.5

Customize QuickBooks Preferences

You will customize QuickBooks for Paint Palette Store by customizing QuickBooks preferences. To customize preferences:

1 Select **Edit Menu > Preferences > General > My Preferences**

2 Select Default Date to Use for New Transactions: **Use the last entered date as default**

3 Select **Accounting > Company Preferences**. Select the following Accounting preferences.
- Select **Use account numbers**
- Uncheck **Use class tracking for transactions**
- Uncheck **Warn if transactions are 30 day(s) in the future**

4 Select **Checking > My Preferences**. Select default accounts to use.
- Open the Write Checks form with **Checking** account
- Open the Pay Bills form with **Checking** account
- Open the Pay Sales Tax form with **Checking** account
- Open the Make Deposits form with **Checking** account

5 Select **Desktop View > Company Preferences**. Verify the following preference settings. To change the settings for these preferences in the future, you would return to this screen.
- Estimates (off)
- Sales Tax (on)
- Sales Orders (off)
- Inventory (on)
- Payroll (off)
- Time Tracking (on)

6 Select **Sales Tax > Company Preferences**. Select Your Most Common Sales Tax Item: **State Tax**.

7 Click **OK** to save your customized preference settings

In setting up QuickBooks for Paint Palette Store, the next step is to enter information into lists for customers, vendors, and items.

Section 13.6

Customer, Vendor, and Item Lists

CUSTOMER LIST

When using QuickBooks to account for a merchandising company that sells a product to customers, you must indicate whether the specific customer is charged sales tax.

Paint Palette Store will sell to:

1. Retail customers, such as homeowners, who must pay sales tax

2. Wholesale customers, such as Tracey Kari Interiors, who resell the product and do not pay sales tax

Enter customer information in the Customer List.

 Create a Customer List for Paint Palette Store using the following information.

Customer	**Merriman, Angel**
Opening Balance	**0.00 as of 01/01/2026**
Address Info:	
First Name	**Angel**
Last Name	**Merriman**
Mobile	**415-555-7579**
Address	**623 Thorsmork Road** **Bayshore, CA 94326**
Payment Settings:	
Account No.	**3001**
Payment Terms	**Net 30**
Preferred Delivery Method	**E-mail**

Sales Tax Settings:

Tax Code	**Tax**
Tax Item	**State Tax**

Additional Info:

Customer Type	**Retail**

Special Interest

- In the Custom Fields section, select **Define Fields** > enter Label: **Special Interest** > select **Use for: Cust**
- In the Special Interest field you just created, enter **Seascapes**

<Add Job>

Job Name	**Custom Paint**
Job Description	**Custom Paint**
Job Type <Add New>	**Custom Paint**
Job Status	**Awarded**

2 **C13.6.1 Customer List.** From the Customer Center, export to **Excel** or **print** Paint Palette Store Customer List.

⚠ When exporting to Excel, remember to select Advanced Excel Options:
- Uncheck **Space between columns**
- Check **Row height**
- Uncheck **Include QuickBooks Export Guide worksheet with helpful advice**
- Select **On printed report and screen**

VENDOR LIST

Next, enter vendor information in the Vendor List.

1 Create a Vendor List for Paint Palette Store using the following information.

Vendor	**Evan Paint Supplies**
Opening Balance	**0.00 as of 01/01/2026**
Address Info:	
Company Name	**Evan Paint Supplies**

Full Name	**Evan Henry**
Main Phone	**415-555-0301**
Address	**565 Steve Street**
	Bayshore, CA 94326

Payment Settings:	
Account No.	**4001**
Payment Terms	**Net 30**
Print on Check as	**Evan Paint Supplies**
Credit Limit	**15,000.00**
Tax Settings:	
Vendor Tax ID	**37-7832541**
Additional Info:	
Vendor Type	**Suppliers**

C13.6.2 Vendor List. From the Vendor Center, export to **Excel** or **print** Paint Palette Store Vendor List

ITEM LIST: INVENTORY

Each of the inventory items that Paint Palette Store sells is entered in the QuickBooks Item List. Paint Palette Store will stock and sell paint inventory to both retail and wholesale customers. The store will charge retail customers the full price and charge wholesale customers a discounted price. Because the sales price varies depending upon the type of customer, instead of entering the sales price in the Item List, you will enter the sales price on the invoice at the time of sale.

Create an Item List for Paint Palette Store inventory using the following information.

Item Type	**Inventory Part**
Item Name	**Paint Base**
Description	**Paint Base**

COGS Account	**50000 – Cost of Goods Sold**
Income Account	**46000 – Merchandise Sales**
Asset Account	**12100 – Inventory Asset**
Qty on Hand	**0.00 as of 01/01/2026**
Item Type	**Inventory Part**
Item Name	**IntBase 1 gal**
Subitem of	**Paint Base**
Description	**Interior Paint Base (1 gallon)**
Cost	**10.00**
COGS Account	**50000 – Cost of Goods Sold**
Tax Code	**Tax**
Income Account	**46000 – Merchandise Sales**
Asset Account	**12100 – Inventory Asset**
Qty on Hand	**0.00 as of 01/01/2026**
Item Type	**Inventory Part**
Item Name	**ExtBase 1 gal**
Subitem of	**Paint Base**
Description	**Exterior Paint Base (1 gallon)**
Cost	**11.00**
COGS Account	**50000 – Cost of Goods Sold**
Tax Code	**Tax**
Income Account	**46000 – Merchandise Sales**
Asset Account	**12100 – Inventory Asset**
Qty on Hand	**0.00 as of 01/01/2026**
Item Type	**Inventory Part**
Item Name	**Paint Tint**
Description	**Paint Tint**
COGS Account	**50000 – Cost of Goods Sold**
Income Account	**46000 – Merchandise Sales**

Asset Account	**12100 – Inventory Asset**
Qty on Hand	**0.00 as of 01/01/2026**

Item Type	**Inventory Part**
Item Name	**Stock Tint**
Subitem of	**Paint Tint**
Description	**Stock Paint Tint**
Cost	**3.00**
COGS Account	**50000 – Cost of Goods Sold**
Tax Code	**Tax**
Income Account	**46000 – Merchandise Sales**
Asset Account	**12100 – Inventory Asset**
Qty on Hand	**0.00 as of 01/01/2026**

Item Type	**Inventory Part**
Item Name	**Custom Tint**
Subitem of	**Paint Tint**
Description	**Custom Paint Tint**
Cost	**5.00**
COGS Account	**50000 – Cost of Goods Sold**
Tax Code	**Tax**
Income Account	**46000 – Merchandise Sales**
Asset Account	**12100 – Inventory Asset**
Qty on Hand	**0.00 as of 01/01/2026**

C13.6.3 Item List. Export to **Excel** or **print** the Item List as of January 1, 2026. (Use Report Center > List > Item Listing.)

⚠ When exporting to Excel, remember to select Advanced Excel Options:
- Uncheck **Space between columns**
- Check **Row height**
- Uncheck **Include QuickBooks Export Guide worksheet with helpful advice**
- Select **On printed report and screen**

ITEM LIST: SALES TAX ITEM

A merchandiser selling products to consumers must charge sales tax. A sales tax item is created in the Item List with the rate and tax agency information.

To enter a sales tax item:

1. In the Item List window, **double-click** on **State Sales Tax**

2. When the Edit Item window appears, enter Tax Rate: **9.0%**

3. Enter Tax Agency: **California State Board of Equalization**

4. Click **OK**

5. If a Vendor Not Found window appears, select: **Quick Add**. If necessary, click **OK** again to close the Edit Item window.

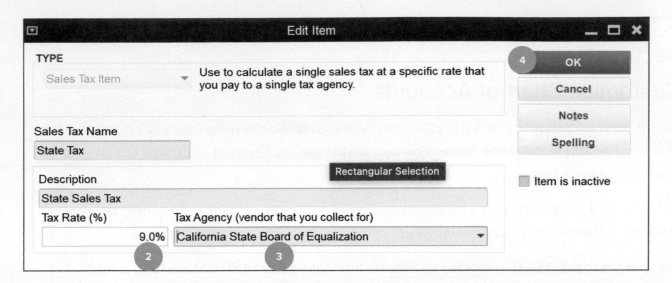

In setting up QuickBooks for Paint Palette Store, the next step is to customize the Chart of Accounts.

Section 13.7

Customize Chart of Accounts

Based on your answers in the EasyStep Interview, QuickBooks automatically creates a Chart of Accounts for Paint Palette Store. You can customize the Chart of Accounts to suit your specific business needs.

Because you are purchasing an existing business, some accounts have opening balances. Opening balances for Paint Palette Store at January 1, 2026, appear as follows.

You purchased $10,000 in stock and Joseph purchased $10,000 in stock for a total of $20,000.

PAINT PALETTE STORE
Balance Sheet

Assets:		
Checking	$	4,200
Supplies on Hand		2,600
Store fixtures		9,000
Paint mixing equipment		7,200
Total Assets	$	23,000
Liabilities & Equity:		
Notes payable	$	3,000
Capital stock (opening balance equity)		20,000
Total Liabilities & Equity	$	23,000

Customize the Chart of Accounts and enter opening balances as follows:

1 If needed, display account numbers in the Chart of Accounts. Select **Edit Menu > Preferences > Accounting > Company Preferences > Use account numbers**.

2 Enter the opening balance for the company Checking account:

- To open the Chart of Accounts, click the **Chart of Accounts** icon in the Company section of the Home Page
- Select **Checking** account
- **Right-click** to display the pop-up menu
- Select **Edit Account**
- When the Edit Account window for the Checking account appears, enter Account No.: **10100**
- Select **Enter Opening Balance**
- Enter Statement Ending Balance: **$4,200**
- Statement Ending Date: **01/01/2026**
- Click **OK**
- Click **Save & Close** to close the Edit Account window

3 Add the following accounts and opening balances to the Chart of Accounts. Abbreviate account titles as shown.

Account No.	**26000**
Account Type	**Other Current Liability**
Account Name	**Notes Payable**
Account Description	**Notes Payable**
Tax Line	**B/S-Liabs/Eq.: Other current liabilities**
Opening Balance	**$3,000 as of 01/01/2026**

Account No.	**12500**
Account Type	**Other Current Asset**
Account Name	**Supplies on Hand**
Account Description	**Supplies on Hand**
Tax Line	**B/S-Assets: Other current assets**
Opening Balance	**$2,600 as of 01/01/2026**

Account No.	**14000**
Account Type	**Fixed Asset**
Account Name	**Store Fixtures**
Account Description	**Store Fixtures**

Tax Line	**B/S-Assets: Buildings/oth. depr. assets**
Opening Balance	**$0 as of 01/01/2026**

Account No.	**14100**
Account Type	**Fixed Asset**
Account Name	**Store Fixtures Cost**
Subaccount of	**Store Fixtures**
Account Description	**Store Fixtures Cost**
Tax Line	**B/S-Assets: Buildings/oth. depr. assets**
Opening Balance	**$9,000 as of 01/01/2026**

Account No.	**14200**
Account Type	**Fixed Asset**
Account Name	**Store Fixtures Accumulated Depr**
Subaccount of	**Store Fixtures**
Account Description	**Store Fixtures Accumulated Depreciation**
Tax Line	**B/S-Assets: Buildings/oth. depr. assets**
Opening Balance	**$0 as of 01/01/2026**

Account No.	**14300**
Account Type	**Fixed Asset**
Account Name	**Paint Mixing Equipment**
Account Description	**Paint Mixing Equipment**
Tax Line	**B/S-Assets: Buildings/oth. depr. assets**
Opening Balance	**$0 as of 01/01/2026**

Account No.	**14400**
Account Type	**Fixed Asset**
Account Name	**Paint Mixing Equipment Cost**
Subaccount of	**Paint Mixing Equipment**
Account Description	**Paint Mixing Equipment Cost**

Tax Line	**B/S-Assets: Buildings/oth. depr. assets**
Opening Balance	**$7,200 as of 01/01/2026**

Account No.	**14500**
Account Type	**Fixed Asset**
Account Name	**Paint Mixing Equipment Acc Depr**
Subaccount of	**Paint Mixing Equipment**
Account Description	**Paint Mixing Equipment Accumulated Depreciation**
Tax Line	**B/S-Assets: Buildings/oth. depr. assets**
Opening Balance	**$0 as of 01/01/2026**

Account No.	**14600**
Account Type	**Fixed Asset**
Account Name	**Paint Tint Equipment**
Account Description	**Paint Tint Equipment**
Tax Line	**B/S-Assets: Buildings/oth. depr. assets**
Opening Balance	**$0 as of 01/01/2026**

Account No.	**14700**
Account Type	**Fixed Asset**
Account Name	**Paint Tint Equipment Cost**
Subaccount of	**Paint Tint Equipment**
Account Description	**Paint Tint Equipment Cost**
Tax Line	**B/S-Assets: Buildings/oth. depr. assets**
Opening Balance	**$0 as of 01/01/2026**

Account No.	**14800**
Account Type	**Fixed Asset**
Account Name	**Paint Tint Equipment Acc Depr**
Subaccount of	**Paint Tint Equipment**
Account Description	**Paint Tint Equipment Accumulated Depreciation**

Tax Line   **B/S-Assets: Buildings/oth. depr. assets**

Opening Balance   **$0 as of 01/01/2026**

(4) From the Chart of Accounts window, edit the following accounts to update the tax lines:
- 10100 Checking: **B/S-Assets: Cash**
- 60200 Automobile Expense: **Other Deductions: Auto and truck**
- 60400 Bank Service Charges: **Other Deductions: Bank charges**
- 62400 Depreciation Expense: **Other Deductions: Other deductions**
- 63300 Insurance Expense: **Other Deductions: Insurance**
- 63500 Janitorial Expense: **Other Deductions: Janitorial & cleaning**
- 64900 Office Supplies: **Other Deductions: Office expenses**
- 66700 Professional Fees: **Other Deductions: Legal & professional fees**
- 68100 Telephone Expense: **Other Deductions: Telephone**
- 68600 Utilities: **Other Deductions: Utilities**

(5) **Re-sort** the chart of accounts. (Select Account button > Re-sort List.)

(6) **C13.7.1 Chart of Accounts.** From the Report Center, export to **Excel** or **print** the Chart of Accounts (Account Listing) report for Paint Palette Store.

Section 13.8

QuickBooks Opening Adjustments

As discussed in Chapter 1, accounting systems use double-entry accounting where each entry must balance. In general, when an existing company with opening balances is set up in QuickBooks accounting software, as accounts receivable, accounts payable, and item balances are entered, QuickBooks offsets these entries with a balancing effect to other accounts.

For example, as customer accounts receivable opening balances are entered, QuickBooks offsets these to an Uncategorized Income account. As vendor accounts payable opening balances are entered, QuickBooks offsets these to an Uncategorized Expense account. As item opening balances are entered, QuickBooks offsets these to an Opening Balance Equity account. When opening balances are entered for all other accounts in the Chart of Accounts, QuickBooks offsets these to the Opening Balance Equity account.

For new start-up companies, the opening balances are zero. For existing companies that have opening balances, QuickBooks offsets these opening balances. Thus, when setting up existing companies in QuickBooks, the following opening adjustments must be recorded using journal entries.

1. When accounts receivable opening balances create Uncategorized Income, use an opening adjustment to transfer the Uncategorized Income to the Opening Balance Equity account.

2. When accounts payable opening balances create Uncategorized Expenses, use an opening adjustment to transfer the Uncategorized Expenses to the Opening Balance Equity account.

3. Opening balances for inventory items and all other accounts are offset by QuickBooks in the Opening Balance Equity account. At this point the balance in the Opening Balance Equity account consists of the transfers from Uncategorized Income and Uncategorized Expenses plus offsets from Inventory items and all other accounts. Use an opening adjustment to transfer the balance in the Opening Balance Equity account to the Capital Stock account.

> **Notice** the description for the Opening Balance Equity account (No. 30000): Opening balances during setup post to this account. The balance of this account should be zero after completing your setup.

The following diagram summarizes the transfer of offsets used for opening balances in QuickBooks.

A/R Balances	→	Uncategorized Income	→			
A/P Balances	→	Uncategorized Expenses	→	Opening Balance Equity	→	Capital Stock
Item Balances	→					
Other Balances	→					

Next, prepare the opening adjustments for Paint Palette Store.

① **C13.8.1 Trial Balance.** Export to **Excel** or **print** a Trial Balance report for Paint Palette Store dated 01/01/2026.
- Compare your Trial Balance report to the check figures to verify your account balances are correct.
- Note that QuickBooks records the offsetting amount to the opening account balances in an Opening Balance Equity account.
- Since Paint Palette Store did not have any opening balances for customers or vendors, there is no Uncategorized Income or Uncategorized Expense accounts shown on the Trial Balance report.
- Supplies on Hand have future benefit and are recorded in an asset account, No. 12500. Later, Supplies that have been used and the benefits expired will be recorded in a Supplies Expense account.

② Transfer the Opening Balance Equity account balance to the Capital Stock account using a journal entry debiting the Opening Balance Equity account and crediting the Capital Stock account

③ Select **Save & Close** to close the Make General Journal Entries window

④ **C13.8.2 Adjusted Trial Balance.** Export to **Excel** or **print** the Adjusted Trial Balance (after the opening adjustment) on 01/01/2026. Verify that the Opening Balance Equity account balance was transferred to the Capital Stock account.

⑤ **C13.8.3 Balance Sheet Standard.** Export to **Excel** or **print** a Balance Sheet, Standard for Paint Palette Store dated 01/01/2026.

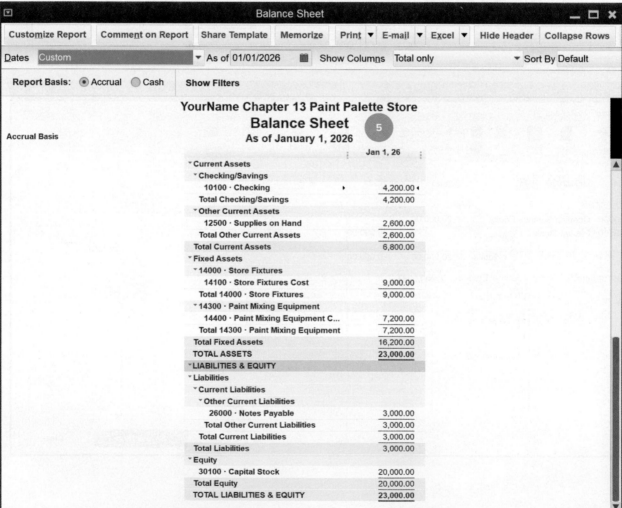

Section 13.9
Vendors and Expenses Transactions

EQUIPMENT PURCHASES

On January 1, 2026, Paint Palette Store purchased computerized paint tint matching equipment from Evan Paint Supplies with a $2,400 check.

C13.9.1 Check Journal Entry. To record the paint tint matching equipment purchase:

1. Use the Write checks window to record the purchase of the paint tint equipment in Account No. 14700

2. Select the **Save** icon at the top of the Write Checks window

3. Select the **Reports tab** > **Transaction Journal**

4. Export the Transaction Journal report to **Excel** or **print** the report

PURCHASING CYCLE

The purchasing cycle for a merchandising company consists of the following transactions:

1. Create a purchase order to order inventory.

2. Receive the inventory items ordered and update inventory.

3. Enter the bill in QuickBooks when the bill is received.

4. Pay the bill.

Next, you will record each of the above transactions in the purchasing cycle for Paint Palette Store.

CREATE A PURCHASE ORDER

The first step in the purchasing cycle is to create a purchase order which is sent to the vendor to order inventory. The purchase order provides a record of the type and quantity of item ordered.

Paint Palette Store needs to order 50 gallons of Interior Base Paint. To order the paint, Paint Palette Store must create a purchase order indicating the item and quantity desired.

C13.9.2 Purchase Order Journal Entry. To create a purchase order in QuickBooks:

1. Click the **Purchase Orders** icon in the Vendors section of the Home Page

2. Select Vendor: **Evan Paint Supplies**

3. Select Template: **Custom Purchase Order**

4. Enter Date: **01/02/2026**

5. Enter the item ordered, by selecting Item: **Interior Paint Base (1 gallon)**

6. Enter Quantity: **50**. Automatically, $10.00 should appear in the Rate column and $500.00 appear in the Amount column.

7. Select: **Print Later**

8. Select the **Save** icon at the top of the Create Purchase Orders window

9. Select the **Reports tab > Transaction Journal**

10. Export the Transaction Journal report to **Excel** or **print** the report

RECEIVE INVENTORY ITEMS

When the inventory items that have been ordered are received, record their receipt in QuickBooks. QuickBooks will then add the items received to the Inventory account.

On January 05, 2026, Paint Palette Store received 45 gallons of interior paint base from Evan Paint Supplies.

C13.9.3 Receive Inventory Journal Entry. To record the inventory items received from Evan Paint Supplies:

1 Click the **Receive Inventory** icon in the Vendors section of the Home Page. Select **Receive Inventory without Bill**.

2 When the Create Item Receipts window appears, select Vendor: **Evan Paint Supplies**

3 If a purchase order for the vendor exists, QuickBooks displays the following Open POs Exist window. Click **Yes** to receive against an open purchase order for Evan Paint Supplies.

4 When the Open Purchase Orders window appears, select **Purchase Order No. 1** dated **01/02/2026**

5 Click **OK**

6 The Create Item Receipts window will appear. Enter Date: **01/05/2026**

7 The quantity received (45 gallons) differs from the quantity ordered (50 gallons). Enter Quantity: **45**.

8 Click the **Save** icon and leave the Create Item Receipts window open

9 Select the **Reports tab > Transaction Journal**

10 Export the Transaction Journal report to **Excel** or **print** the report

ENTER BILLS

Bills can be entered in QuickBooks when the bill is received or when the bill is paid. (For more information, see Chapters 6 and 7.)

Paint Palette Store will enter bills in QuickBooks when bills are received. At that time, QuickBooks records an obligation to pay the bill later (account payable). QuickBooks tracks bills due. If you use the reminder feature, QuickBooks will even remind you when it is time to pay bills.

C13.9.4 Enter Bill Journal Entry. Paint Palette Store previously received 45 1-gallon cans of interior paint base. To record the associated bill when it is received:

1. Click the **Enter Bills Against Inventory** icon in the Vendors section of the Home Page

2. When the following Select Item Receipt window appears, select Vendor: **Evan Paint Supplies**

3. Select Item Receipt corresponding to the bill (**Date: 01/05/2026**)

4. Click **OK**

5. When the following Enter Bills window appears, make any necessary changes. In this case, change the date to **01/09/2026** (the date the bill was received).

6. The Amount Due of **$450.00** should agree with the amount shown on the vendor's bill received. (The Items tab should also display $450.00. Select the Expenses tab and verify there is no Account selected.)

7. Click the **Save** icon. If asked if you want to record your changes, select **Yes**. Leave the Enter Bills window open.

8. From the Enter Bills form, select the **Reports tab > Transaction Journal**

9. Export the Transaction Journal report to **Excel** or **print** the report

When you enter bills, QuickBooks automatically adds the amount of the bill to Accounts Payable, reflecting your obligation to pay the bills later.

> If the items and the bill were received at the same time, use the Receive Item with Bill window.

PAY BILLS

After receiving an inventory item and entering the bill in QuickBooks, the next step is to pay the bill when due. Paint Palette Store will pay the bills for paint and paint tint that have been received and recorded.

C13.9.5 Pay Bills Journal Entries. To pay bills in QuickBooks:

1 Click the **Pay Bills** icon in the Vendors section of the Home Page

2 When the Pay Bills window appears:
- Select: **Show All Bills**
- Select bill from **Evan Paint Supplies**
- Select **Checking** account
- Select Payment Method: **To be Printed**
- Select Payment Date: **01/09/2026**

3 Click **Pay Selected Bills** to close the Pay Bills window

4 When the Payment Summary window displays, if we wanted to print the checks, we would select Print Checks. In this case, select **Done**.

5 From the Navigation Bar, select **Reports** > **Accountant & Taxes** > **Journal**

6 Select Date: **01/09/2026**

7 Export the Journal report to **Excel** or **print** the report

PRINT CHECKS

After selecting bills to pay, if checks are required, you can prepare checks in two different ways:

1. Write the checks manually, or

2. Print the checks using QuickBooks. If you use QuickBooks to print checks, preprinted check forms are inserted in the printer before printing.

Section 13.10

Customers and Sales Transactions

SALES CYCLE

The sales cycle for a merchandising company consists of the following transactions:

1. Create an invoice to record the sale and bill the customer.

2. Receive the customer payments.

3. Deposit the customer payments in the bank.

Next, you will record each of these transactions in QuickBooks for Paint Palette Store.

CREATE INVOICES

When inventory is sold to a customer, the sale is recorded on an invoice in QuickBooks. The invoice lists the items sold, the quantity, and the price. In addition, if the product is sold to a retail customer, sales tax is automatically added to the invoice.

C13.10.1 Invoice Journal Entry. To create an invoice:

① Click the **Create Invoices** icon in the Customers section of the Home Page

② Using the Intuit Product Invoice Template, create an invoice for the following sales made by Paint Palette Store.

Sale of 40 gallons of interior paint to Angel Merriman

Date	**01/11/2026**
Customer: Job	**Angel Merriman: Custom Paint**
Terms	**Net 30**
Quantity	**40 gallons**
Item Code	**Interior Paint Base (1 gallon)**
Price Each	**60.00**
Tax	**State Tax**

3   Select **Print Later**

4   Select the **Save** icon

5   Select the **Reports tab** > **Transaction Journal**

6   Export to **Excel** or **print** the Transaction Journal

RECEIVE PAYMENTS

When a credit sale is recorded, QuickBooks records an account receivable at the time the invoice is created. The account receivable is the amount that Paint Palette Store expects to receive from the customer later.

C13.10.2 Receive Payment Journal Entry. To record a payment received from a customer:

1   Click the **Receive Payments** icon in the Customers section of the Home Page

2   Record the following payments received by Paint Palette Store from a customer.

Date Received	**01/11/2026**
Customer: Job	**Angel Merriman: Custom Paint**
Amount Received	**2616.00**
Payment Method	**Check**
Check No.	**1001**

3   Select **Save & New**

4   Select the **Find back arrow** to display the customer payment just recorded

5   Select **Reports tab** > **Transaction Journal**

6   Export the Transaction Journal report to **Excel** or **print** the report

---

If a customer pays cash at the time of sale, it can be recorded using the Sales Receipts window.

MAKE DEPOSITS

When the customer's payment is deposited in Paint Palette Store's Checking account, record the bank deposit in QuickBooks.

C13.10.3 Deposit Journal Entry. To record a bank deposit:

1. Click the **Record Deposits** icon in the Banking section of the Home Page

2. On January 12, 2026, record the deposit of customer payments received from **Angel Merriman**. Select Deposit To: **Checking**.

3. Select the **Save** icon at the top of the Make Deposits window

4. Select the **Journal** icon

5. Export the Transaction Journal report to **Excel** or **print** the report

Section 13.11
Adjusting Entries

Before preparing financial statements for Paint Palette Store for January, it is necessary to record adjustments to bring the company's accounts up to date.

> **Before making adjusting entries, prepare a Trial Balance to see if the accounting system is in balance (debits equal credits).**

The following adjustments are necessary for Paint Palette Store at January 31, 2026:

1. **ADJ1:** The store fixtures cost of $9,000 will be depreciated over a 10-year useful life with no salvage value. Depreciation expense is $75 per month. (See Exercise 13.6.)

2. **ADJ2:** The paint mixing equipment cost of $7,200 will be depreciated over a 5-year useful life with no salvage value. Depreciation expense is $120 per month. (See Exercise 13.6.)

3. **ADJ3:** The computer paint tint equipment cost of $2,400 will be depreciated over a 5-year useful life with no salvage value. Depreciation expense is $40 per month. (See Exercise 13.6.)

4. **ADJ4:** A count of supplies on hand at the end of January totaled $500. The Supplies on Hand account balance before adjustment is $2,600, so Supplies on Hand (Account 12500) should be decreased by $2,100. An adjusting entry is required to transfer $2,100 from the Supplies on Hand account to a Supplies Expense account. So the adjusting entry will increase (debit) Supplies Expense (Account 64800) by $2,100, and decrease (credit) Supplies on Hand (Account 12500) by $2,100. (See Exercise 13.6.)

5. **ADJ5:** The adjusting entry to record interest expense for January 2026 and the liability for interest payable is $10. To record this adjustment, add Other Current Liability account: Account No. 21000 Interest Payable. (See Exercise 13.6.)

Next, use the Make General Journal Entries window to practice recording the adjusting entry for depreciation expense for Paint Palette Store at January 31, 2026. Depreciation expense for the Store Fixtures is $75 per month.

① Select **Accountant Menu > Make General Journal Entries**. If a message about numbering journal entries appears, click **OK**.

② To record the entry for depreciation in the General Journal, select Date: **01/31/2026**

③ Entry No.: **ADJ1**

④ Select **Adjusting Entry**

⑤ Enter Account: **62400**. Press the **Tab** key to advance the cursor to the Debit column.

⑥ Enter **75.00**

⑦ Enter Account: **14200**

⑧ Enter Credit: **75.00**

⑨ Normally, we would select Save & Close, but in this case select **Clear**. Then **close** the Make General Journal Entries window. We will enter and save the adjusting entry in the exercises.

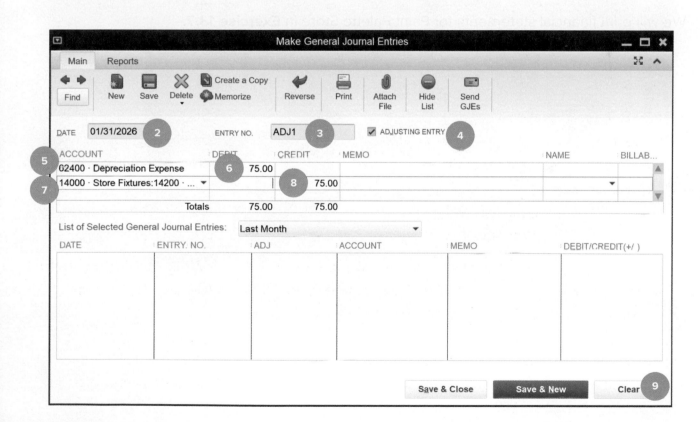

Section 13.12

Financial Reports

The next step in the accounting cycle is to print financial reports. Usually, a company prints the following financial reports for the year:

- Profit & Loss (also known as the P & L or Income Statement)
- Balance Sheet
- Statement of Cash Flows

The Profit & Loss, the Balance Sheet, and the Statement of Cash Flows are financial statements typically given to external users, such as bankers and investors.

To print the financial statements, from the Report Center, select: Company & Financial

We will print financial statements for Paint Palette Store in **Exercise 13.7**.

Section 13.13
Back Up QuickBooks Files

BACK UP QBB

Save a backup of your Chapter 13 file using the file name: **YourName Chapter 13 Backup.QBB**. For further instructions on how to back up your file, *see* Appendix B: Back Up and Restore QuickBooks Files.

QBW WORKFLOW

If you will be using the same computer to complete Chapter 13 QuickBooks exercises, just as in a business workflow, you can continue to use the same QBW file.

If you are using the QBW approach, leave your QBW file open and proceed directly to Exercise 13.1.

QBB RESTORE

If you are using the QBB approach and ending your computer session now, close your QBW file and exit QuickBooks. When you restart, you will restore your backup file to complete Exercise 13.1.

Exercise 13.1 Chart of Accounts

 Paint Palette Store

BACKSTORY

In this exercise, you will add a new account to Paint Palette Store's Chart of Accounts.

E13.1.1 QuickBooks File

If you will be using the same computer and the same Chapter 13.QBW file:

1.   If your Chapter 13.QBW file is not already open, open it by selecting **File > Open Previous Company**. Select your **Chapter 13.QBW file**. If a QuickBooks Information window appears with a message about the sample company file, click **OK**.

2.   Update the company name to include **YourName Exercise 13.1** by selecting **Company Menu > My Company**.

> **If you are not using the same computer that you used for Chapter 13,** you will need to restore your **Chapter 13 Backup.QBB file using the instructions in Appendix B: Back Up and Restore QuickBooks Files. After restoring, update the company name to include YourName Exercise 13.1.**

E13.1.2 Add Account

1.   Add the following new account to the Chart of Accounts for Paint Palette Store.

Account Name	**Supplies Expense**
Account No.	**64800**
Account Type	**Expense**
Account Description	**Supplies Expense**
Tax Line	**Other Deductions: Supplies**

2.   **Re-sort** the Chart of Accounts. (Select Account button > Re-sort List.)

3.   Export to **Excel** or **print** the Chart of Accounts. (Select Report Center > List > Account Listing. Use Date: 01/01/2026.)

E13.1.3 Back Up Exercise 13.1

Save a backup of your Exercise file using the file name: **YourName Exercise 13.1 Backup.QBB**. See Appendix B: Back Up and Restore QuickBooks Files for instructions.

Exercise 13.2 Customer List

 Paint Palette Store

In this exercise, you will add to Paint Palette Store's Customer List.

E13.2.1 QuickBooks File

If you will be using the same computer and the same QBW file:

1. Select your **QBW file**.

2. Update the company name to include **YourName Exercise 13.2** by selecting **Company Menu > My Company**.

> If you are not using the same computer that you used for Chapter 13 and Exercise 13.1, you will need to restore your latest prior Backup.QBB file using the instructions in Appendix B: Back Up and Restore QuickBooks files. After restoring, update the company name to include YourName Exercise 13.2.

E13.2.2 Add Customers

1. Add the following customers to Paint Palette Store's Customer List.

Customer	**Tracey Kari Interiors**
Address Info:	
Company Name	**Tracey Kari Interiors**
First Name	**Tracey**
Main Phone	**415-555-9999**
Address	**99 Reyka Drive** **Bayshore, CA 94326**
Payment Settings:	
Account No.	**3005**
Payment Terms	**Net 30**
Preferred Delivery Method	**E-mail**

Sales Tax Settings:

Tax Code	**Non**
Tax Item	**State Tax**

Additional Info:

Customer Type	**Wholesale**
Special Interest	**Scandinavian Design**

<Add Job>

Job Name	**Custom & Stock Paint**
Job Description	**Custom & Stock Paint**
Job Type	**Commercial**
Job Status	**Awarded**

Customer	**Rock Castle Construction**

Address Info:

Company Name	**Rock Castle Construction**
Mr./Ms./...	**Mr**
First Name	**Rock**
Last Name	**Castle**
Main Phone	**415-555-7272**
Mobile	**415-555-5679**
Address	**1735 County Road** **Bayshore, CA 94326**

Payment Settings:

Account No.	**3003**
Payment Terms	**Net 30**
Preferred Delivery Method	**E-mail**

Sales Tax Settings:

Tax Code	**Non**
Tax Item	**State Tax**

Additional Info:

Customer Type	**Wholesale**
Special Interest	**Various**

<Add Job>

Job Name	**Custom Paint**
Job Description	**Custom Paint**
Job Type	**Commercial**
Job Status	**Awarded**
Customer	**Sandy Copper Textiles**
Address Info:	
Company Name	**Sandy Copper Textiles**
First Name	**Sandy**
Main Phone	**415-555-4320**
Address	**720 Cuivre Drive**
	Bayshore, CA 94326
Payment Settings:	
Account No.	**3004**
Payment Terms	**Net 30**
Preferred Delivery Method	**E-mail**
Sales Tax Settings:	
Tax Code	**Tax**
Tax Item	**State Tax**
Additional Info:	
Customer Type	**Retail**
Special Interest	**Industrial**
<Add Job>	
Job Name	**Custom Paint**
Job Description	**Custom Paint**
Job Type	**Commercial**
Job Status	**Awarded**

2. From the Customer Center, export to **Excel** or **print** Paint Palette Store Customer List

E13.2.3 Back Up Exercise 13.2

Save a backup of your Exercise file using the file name: **YourName Exercise 13.2 Backup.QBB**. See Appendix B: Back Up and Restore QuickBooks Files for instructions.

Exercise 13.3 Vendor List

🎨 Paint Palette Store

In this exercise, you will add to Paint Palette Store's Vendors List.

E13.3.1 QuickBooks File

If you will be using the same computer and the same QBW file:

1. Select your **QBW file**.

2. Update the company name to include **YourName Exercise 13.3** by selecting **Company Menu > My Company**.

> **If you are not using the same computer that you used for Chapter 13, Exercise 13.1, and Exercise 13.2, you will need to restore your latest prior Backup.QBB file using the instructions in Appendix B: Back Up and Restore QuickBooks files. After restoring, update the company name to include YourName Exercise 13.3.**

E13.3.2 Add Vendors

1. Add the following vendors to the Vendor List for Paint Palette Store.

Vendor	**Joseph Leasing**
Opening Balance	**0.00 as of 01/01/2026**
Address Info:	
Company Name	**Joseph Leasing**
First Name	**Joseph**
Main Phone	**415-555-0412**
Address	**13 Appleton Street** **Bayshore, CA 94326**
Payment Settings:	
Account No.	**4002**
Payment Terms	**Net 30**
Tax Settings:	
Vendor Tax ID	**37-1726354**

Additional Info:

Vendor Type <Add New>	**Leasing**

Vendor	**Crystalline Paints**
Opening Balance	**0.00 as of 01/01/2026**

Address Info:

Company Name	**Crystalline Paints**
First Name	**Crystal**
Main Phone	**415-555-9988**
Address	**99 Beryl Avenue**
	Bayshore, CA 94326

Payment Settings:

Account No.	**4003**
Payment Terms	**Net 30**

Tax Settings:

Vendor Tax ID	**37-1726355**

Additional Info:

Vendor Type	**Suppliers**

2. From the Vendor Center, export the Vendor List to **Excel**

E13.3.3 Back Up Exercise 13.3
Save a backup of your Exercise file using the file name: **YourName Exercise 13.3 Backup.QBB**. See Appendix B: Back Up and Restore QuickBooks Files for instructions.

Exercise 13.4 Vendors and Expenses Transactions

 Paint Palette Store

In this exercise, you will enter vendors and expenses transactions for Paint Palette Store.

E13.4.1 QuickBooks File

If you will be using the same computer and the same QBW file:

1. Select your **QBW file**.

2. Update the company name to include **YourName Exercise 13.4** by selecting **Company Menu > My Company**.

> If you are not using the same computer that you used for Chapter 13, and Exercises 13.1 - 13.3, you will need to restore your latest prior Backup.QBB file using the instructions in Appendix B: Back Up and Restore QuickBooks files. After restoring, update the company name to include YourName Exercise 13.4.

E13.4.2 Purchase Orders

Paint Palette Store entered into the following purchase orders for Paint Palette Store during January 2026.

1. Using the Purchase Order icon, enter the following purchase orders.

Vendor	**Evan Paint Supplies**
Date	**01/15/2026**
Item	**Exterior Paint Base (1 gallon)**
Quantity	**100**

Vendor	**Crystalline Paints**
Date	**01/18/2026**
Item	**Custom Tint**
Quantity	**70 (cartons)**
Item	**Stock Tint**
Quantity	**70 (cartons)**

Vendor	**Evan Paint Supplies**
Date	**01/19/2026**
Item	**Interior Paint Base (1 gallon)**
Quantity	**100**

2. **Close** the Create Purchase Orders window

3. Export to **Excel** or **print** the Open Purchase Orders Detail report from January 1 to January 20, 2026

E13.4.3 Receive Inventory Items

Paint Palette Store entered into the following vendor and expense transactions during January 2026.

1. Record the following inventory items received.

Vendor	**Evan Paint Supplies**
Date Items Received	**01/16/2026**
PO No.	**1**
Item	**Interior Paint Base (1 gallon)**
Quantity	**5**

Vendor	**Evan Paint Supplies**
Date Items Received	**01/21/2026**
PO No.	**4**
Item	**Interior Paint Base (1 gallon)**
Quantity	**100**

Vendor	**Crystalline Paints**
Date Items Received	**01/21/2026**
PO No.	**3**
Item	**Custom Tint**
Quantity	**70 (cartons)**
Item	**Stock Tint**
Quantity	**70 (cartons)**

2. **Close** the Create Item Receipts window

3. Export to **Excel** or **print** the Item Listing from the Report Center as of January 21, 2026, showing the quantity on hand for each item in inventory. (Select Reports > List > Item Listing.)

E13.4.4 Enter Bills Against Inventory

Record the following bills received against inventory items for Paint Palette Store.

1. Using the Enter Bills Against Inventory icon, enter the following bill.

Vendor	**Evan Paint Supplies**
Date Bill Received	**01/22/2026**
Terms	**Net 30**
PO No.	**1**
Item	**Interior Paint Base (1 gallon)**
Quantity	**5**

2. Export to **Excel** the Transaction Journal for the above bill entered against inventory

3. Enter the following bill.

Vendor	**Evan Paint Supplies**
Date Bill Received	**01/22/2026**
Terms	**Net 30**
PO No.	**4**
Item	**Interior Paint Base (1 gallon)**
Quantity	**100**

4. Export to **Excel** the Transaction Journal for the above bill entered against inventory

5. Enter the following bill.

Vendor	**Crystalline Paints**
Date Bill Received	**01/22/2026**
Terms	**Net 30**
PO No.	**3**
Item	**Custom Tint**
Quantity	**70 (cartons)**
Item	**Stock Tint**
Quantity	**70 (cartons)**

6. Export to **Excel** the Transaction Journal for the above bill entered against inventory

E13.4.5 Enter Bill

Paint Palette Store received the following bill from Joseph Leasing for January rent.

1. Use the Enter Bills icon to enter the Joseph Leasing bill for January rent.

Vendor	**Joseph Leasing**
Date Bill Received	**01/12/2026**
Terms	**Net 30**
Amount Due	**$1,000.00**
Account	**67100 Rent Expense**

2. Record the bill for rent as a memorized transaction. With the Enter Bills window still open, click the **Memorize** icon. Select How Often: **Monthly**. Next Date: **02/12/2026**.

3. Select the **Save** icon

4. From the Enter Bills form, select the **Reports tab > Transaction Journal**

5. Export the Transaction Journal report to **Excel** or **print** the report

E13.4.6 Pay Bills

After entering the purchase order, receiving the inventory item, and recording the bill, the next step is to pay the bill.

To pay bills for Paint Palette Store at January 30, 2026, complete the following.

1. Select the **Pay Bills** icon in the Vendors section of the Home Page

2. When the Pay Bills window appears:

    - Select: **Show All Bills**
    - Select bills from **Evan Paint Supplies** and **Crystalline Paints**
    - Select **Checking** account
    - Select Payment Method: **To be Printed**
    - Select Payment Date: **01/30/2026**

3. Click **Pay Selected Bills** to close the Pay Bills window

4. Export to **Excel** or **print** the Check Detail Report for January 2026

E13.4.7 Back Up Exercise 13.4

Save a backup of your Exercise file using the file name: **YourName Exercise 13.4 Backup.QBB**. See Appendix B: Back Up and Restore QuickBooks Files for instructions.

Exercise 13.5 Customers and Sales Transactions

 Paint Palette Store

In this exercise, you will enter customer and sales transactions for Paint Palette Store.

E13.5.1 QuickBooks File

If you will be using the same computer and the same QBW file:

1. Select your **QBW file**.

2. Update the company name to include **YourName Exercise 13.5** by selecting **Company Menu > My Company**.

> If you are not using the same computer that you used for Chapter 13 and Exercises 13.1 - 13.4, you will need to restore your latest prior Backup.QBB file using the instructions in Appendix B: Back Up and Restore QuickBooks files. After restoring, update the company name to include YourName Exercise 13.5.

E13.5.2 Create Invoices

In order to attract new commercial customers and build your new business, you offer introductory promotions to commercial customers. Create the following invoices for January for Paint Palette Store.

1. Sale of paint to Tracey Kari Interiors, a commercial customer.

Date	**01/22/2026**
Customer: Job	**Tracey Kari Interiors: Custom & Stock Paint**
Terms	**Net 30**
Quantity	**70 gallons**
Item Code	**Interior Paint Base (1 gallon)**
Price Each	**50.00**

Quantity	**35**
Item Code	**Custom Tint**
Price Each	**20.00**

Quantity	**35**
Item Code	**Stock Tint**
Price Each	**12.00**

Print Later	**Yes**
Tax	**Non**

2.   Export to **Excel** the Transaction Journal for the above invoice

3.   Sale of paint to Sandy Copper Textiles.

Date	**01/23/2026**
Customer: Job	**Sandy Copper Textiles: Custom Paint**
Terms	**Net 30**

Quantity	**30 gallons**
Item Code	**Interior Paint Base (1 gallon)**
Price Each	**60.00**

Quantity	**30**
Item Code	**Custom Tint**
Price Each	**25.00**

Print Later	**Yes**
Tax	**State Tax**

4.   Export to **Excel** the Transaction Journal for the above invoice

E13.5.3 Receive Payments

When Paint Palette Store receives a customer payment, QuickBooks reduces the customer's account receivable by the amount of the payment.

1. Record the following customer payment received by Paint Palette Store.

Date Received	**01/30/2026**
Customer: Job	**Tracey Kari Interiors: Custom & Stock Paint**
Amount Received	**4620.00**
Payment Method	**Check**
Check No.	**4567**

2. Select **Save & New**

3. Select the **Find back arrow** to display the customer payment just recorded

4. Select **Reports tab** > **Transaction Journal**

5. Export the Transaction Journal report to **Excel** or **print** the report

E13.5.4 Make Deposits

When a customer's payment is received, QuickBooks records it in the Undeposited Funds account. Next, make the deposit to transfer the funds from the Undeposited Funds account to the Checking account.

To make the deposit:

1. Click the **Record Deposits** icon in the Banking section of the Home Page

2. On January 30, 2026, record the deposit of the customer payment received from Tracey Kari Interiors. Select Deposit To: **Checking**.

3. Export to **Excel** or **print** the Transaction Journal report for this deposit

4. Export to **Excel** or **print** the Deposit Detail report for January 2026

E13.5.5 Back Up Exercise 13.5

Save a backup of your Exercise file using the file name: **YourName Exercise 13.5 Backup.QBB**. See Appendix B: Back Up and Restore QuickBooks Files for instructions.

Exercise 13.6 Adjustments

🎨 Paint Palette Store

In this exercise, you will first print a Trial Balance and then record adjusting entries for Paint Palette Store.

E13.6.1 QuickBooks File

If you will be using the same computer and the same QBW file:

1. Select your **QBW file**.

2. Update the company name to include **YourName Exercise 13.6** by selecting **Company Menu > My Company**.

> If you are not using the same computer that you used for Chapter 13 and Exercises 13.1 - 13.5, you will need to restore your latest prior Backup.QBB file using the instructions in Appendix B: Back Up and Restore QuickBooks files. After restoring, update the company name to include YourName Exercise 13.6.

E13.6.2 Trial Balance

The purpose of the Trial Balance is to determine whether the accounting system is in balance (debits equal credits).

Create a Trial Balance for Paint Palette Store at January 31, 2026.

1. From the Report Center select **Accountant & Taxes > Trial Balance**

2. Select Dates **From: 01/31/2026 To: 01/31/2026**

3. Export to **Excel** or **print** the Trial Balance for Paint Palette Store

4. **Close** the Trial Balance window

E13.6.3 Adjusting Entries

At the end of the accounting period, it is necessary to make adjusting entries to bring a company's accounts up to date as of year-end. The following adjusting entries are needed for Paint Palette Store at January 31, 2026.

1. To enter the following adjusting entries, select **Accountant Menu** > **Make General Journal Entries**

2. **ADJ1:** The store fixtures cost of $9,000 will be depreciated over a 10-year useful life with no salvage value. Depreciation expense is $75 per month.

3. **ADJ2:** The paint mixing equipment cost of $7,200 will be depreciated over a 5-year useful life with no salvage value. Depreciation expense is $120 per month.

4. **ADJ3:** The computer paint tint equipment cost of $2,400 will be depreciated over a 5-year useful life with no salvage value. Depreciation expense is $40 per month.

5. **ADJ4:** A count of supplies on hand at the end of January totaled $500. The Supplies on Hand account balance before adjustment is $2,600, so Supplies on Hand (Account 12500) should be decreased by $2,100. An adjusting entry is required to transfer $2,100 from the Supplies on Hand account to the Supplies Expense account. So the adjusting entry will increase (debit) Supplies Expense (Account 64800) by $2,100, and decrease (credit) Supplies on Hand (Account 12500) by $2,100.

6. **ADJ5:** The adjusting entry to record interest expense for January 2026 and the liability for interest payable is $10. To record this adjustment, add Other Current Liability account: Account No. 21000 Interest Payable.

7. From the Report Center, export to **Excel** or **print** the adjusting journal entries for Paint Palette Store for January 31, 2026

E13.6.4 Adjusted Trial Balance

An Adjusted Trial Balance is simply a Trial Balance printed after adjusting entries are recorded.

Create an Adjusted Trial Balance for Paint Palette Store at January 31, 2026 after adjusting entries are entered.

1. Export to **Excel** or **print** an Adjusted Trial Balance at January 31, 2026 (Report Center > Accountant & Taxes > Adjusted Trial Balance)

2. On the Adjusted Trial Balance, **highlight** amounts affected by the adjusting entries

E13.6.5 Back Up Exercise 13.6

Save a backup of your Exercise file using the file name: **YourName Exercise 13.6 Backup.QBB**. See Appendix B: Back Up and Restore QuickBooks Files for instructions.

Exercise 13.7 Reports

🎨 Paint Palette Store

In this exercise, you will prepare financial reports for Paint Palette Store for the January 2026.

E13.7.1 QuickBooks File

If you will be using the same computer and the same QBW file:

1. Select your **QBW file**.

2. Update the company name to include **YourName Exercise 13.7** by selecting **Company Menu > My Company**.

> If you are not using the same computer that you used for Chapter 13 and Exercises 13.1 - 13.6, you will need to restore your latest prior Backup.QBB file using the instructions in Appendix B: Back Up and Restore QuickBooks files. After restoring, update the company name to include YourName Exercise 13.7.

E13.7.2 Journal

The Journal lists all the transactions entered, whether using an onscreen form or the Journal, in a debit and credit format. The Journal is often a useful tool when tracking errors or discrepancies in the accounting system.

Create a Journal report for Paint Palette Store for January 2026.

1. From the Report Center select **Accountant & Taxes > Journal**
2. Select Dates **From: 01/01/2026 To: 01/31/2026**
3. Export to **Excel** or **print** the Journal for Paint Palette Store
4. **Close** the Journal window

E13.7.3 Financial Statements

Create the following financial statements for Paint Palette Store for the January 2026.

1. Export to **Excel** or **print** the Profit & Loss, Standard
2. Export to **Excel** or **print** the Balance Sheet, Standard
3. Export to **Excel** or **print** the Statement of Cash Flows

E13.7.4 Back Up Exercise 13.7

Save a backup of your Exercise file using the file name: **YourName Exercise 13.7 Backup.QBB**. See Appendix B: Back Up and Restore QuickBooks Files for instructions.

PROJECT 13.1

 Ella's Knittery

BACKSTORY

Ella Brewer, founder of Ella's Knittery, has asked if you would be interested in maintaining the accounting records for her knitting and yarn boutique. Ella, a business major at the local college, was encouraged by her grandmother to knit for stress relief. To her surprise, Ella discovered that her grandmother was right and knitting was more calming than yoga when she was stressed with her classes. Hoping to assist in funding her college education and put her business studies into practice, Ella decided to become an entrepreneur and open a knitting boutique with a small storefront near her college campus. To drive up her sales volume and profitability, she also plans to market and sell products online.

To distinguish her business from the competition, Ella offers unique, value priced yarns. For example, Ella stocks allergy friendly yarns made from linen and cotton, instead of wool yarns from sheep or alpaca. To streamline purchasing, Ella decided to buy inventory from two main vendors: Sandy Copper Textiles and Bella Italia Design. Sandy Copper provides Ella with trendy copper infused cotton yarns that are becoming increasingly popular because of the potential health benefits of copper infused textiles. Bella Italia Design offers fine Italian linen yarns in fashionable shades that Ella thinks will sell well. In addition, Ella researched knitting needles and decided to stock Bella Italia Design's interchangeable circular knitting needles that can be adjusted to different sizes. This keeps Ella's inventory costs low by eliminating the need to stock numerous knitting needles in various sizes that might never sell. The interchangeable needles Ella plans to stock are made of the highest quality materials of carbon fiber and olivewood for a smoother, better knitting experience.

To become an online influencer, Ella hired Martin Consulting to launch social media marketing for Ella's Knittery. Ella's marketing plan includes creating and offering online videos on meditative knitting.

In order to ensure proper security for her customers' financial data, Ella also hired Angel Merriman Associates to set up her network, provide technology services, and advise regarding cybersecurity measures to protect Ella's Knittery.

Ella would like to use QuickBooks Desktop software for her accounting records, converting from her current manual accounting system. After reaching agreement on your fee, Ella gives you the following information to enter into QuickBooks.

🌐 QuickBooks SatNav

The objective of Project 13.1 is to facilitate your mastery of QuickBooks Desktop. As shown in the following QuickBooks SatNav, Project 13.1 covers all three processes: QuickBooks Settings, QuickBooks Transactions, and QuickBooks Reports. This project provides you with the opportunity to integrate your knowledge of QuickBooks Desktop through all three phases of the QuickBooks SatNav.

🌐 **QuickBooks SatNav**

⚙ **QuickBooks Settings**

⚙ Company Settings
⚙ Chart of Accounts

💰 **QuickBooks Transactions**

💰 Banking
💰 Customers & Sales
💰 Vendors & Expenses
💰 Employees & Payroll

📊 **QuickBooks Reports**

📊 Reports

P13.1.1 New Company Setup

Create a new company in QuickBooks for Ella's Knittery using the following information.

1. Use the EasyStep Interview to set up a new QuickBooks company.

Company name	**YourName Project 13.1 Ella's Knittery**
Federal tax ID	**37-1872613**
Address	**36 Spring Street**
City	**Bayshore**
State	**CA**
Zip	**94326**
Main Phone	**415-555-3636**
Email	**<Enter your email address>**
Industry	**Retail Shop or Online Commerce**
Type of organization	**S Corporation**
First month of fiscal year	**January**
File name	**YourName Project 13.1**
What do you sell?	**Products only**
Enter sales	**Record each sale individually**
Sales tax	**Yes**
Estimates	**No**
Sales orders	**Yes**
Billing statements	**No**
Progress invoicing	**No**
Track bills you owe	**Yes**
Track inventory in QuickBooks	**Yes**
Track time	**Yes**
Employees	**No**
Start date	**01/01/2026**
Use recommended income and expense accounts	**Yes**
Bank account name	**Checking**
Bank account number	**3216549870**
Bank account balance	**0.00 as of 01/01/2026**

2. Click **Start Working** to exit QuickBooks Setup

3. **Display** account numbers in the Chart of Accounts

P13.1.2 Add Customers

1. Add Brigette Tricot to Ella's Knittery Customer List.

Customer	**Tricot, Brigette**
Address Info:	
First Name	**Brigette**
Last Name	**Tricot**
Main Phone	**415-555-9900**
Address	**99 College Avenue** **Bayshore, CA 94326**
Payment Settings:	
Account No.	**13000**
Payment Terms	**Net 15**
Preferred Delivery Method	**E-mail**
Preferred Payment Method	**Check**
Sales Tax Settings:	
Tax Code	**Tax**
Tax Item	**State Tax**

2. Next add Mimi Petit to Ella's Knittery Customer List.

Customer	**Petit, Mimi**
Address Info:	
First Name	**Mimi**
Last Name	**Petit**
Main Phone	**415-555-2160**
Address	**220 Alsace Avenue** **Bayshore, CA 94326**

Payment Settings:

Account No.	**15000**
Payment Terms	**Net 15**
Preferred Delivery Method	**E-mail**
Preferred Payment Method	**Check**

Sales Tax Settings:

Tax Code	**Tax**
Tax Item	**State Tax**

3. Click **OK**

4. From the Customer Center, export to **Excel** or **print** the Customer List.

⚠ When exporting to Excel, remember to select Advanced Excel Options:
- Uncheck **Space between columns**
- Check **Row height**
- Uncheck **Include QuickBooks Export Guide worksheet with helpful advice**
- Select **On printed report and screen**

5. **Close** the Customer Center

P13.1.3 Add Vendors

1. Add the following vendors to the Vendor List for Ella's Knittery.

Vendor	**Joseph Leasing**
Opening Balance	**$0.00 as of 01/01/2026**
Address Info:	
Company Name	**Joseph Leasing**
Full Name	**Joseph Asher**
Main Phone	**415-555-0412**
Address	**13 Appleton Drive** **Bayshore, CA 94326**
Payment Settings:	
Account No.	**2700**
Payment Terms	**Net 30**

Tax Settings:

Vendor Tax ID	**37-1726354**
Additional Info:	
Vendor Type <Add New>	**Leasing**

Vendor	**Bella Italia Design**
Opening Balance	**$0.00 as of 01/01/2026**
Address Info:	
Company Name	**Bella Italia Design**
Full Name	**Bella Italia**
Main Phone	**415-555-1270**
Address	**13 Marco Drive** **Bayshore, CA 94326**

Payment Settings:

Account No.	**5400**
Payment Terms	**Net 30**

Tax Settings:

Vendor Tax ID	**37-3571595**
Additional Info:	
Vendor Type	**Suppliers**

Vendor	**Sandy Copper Textiles**
Opening Balance	**$0.00 as of 01/01/2026**
Address Info:	
Company Name	**Sandy Copper Textiles**
Full Name	**Sandy Copper**
Main Phone	**415-555-4320**
Address	**720 Cuivre Drive** **Bayshore, CA 94326**

Payment Settings:

Account No.	**6300**
Payment Terms	**Net 30**

Tax Settings:

Vendor Tax ID	**37-1599515**

Additional Info:

Vendor Type	**Suppliers**

Vendor	**Bichotte Supplies**
Opening Balance	**$0.00 as of 01/01/2026**

Address Info:

Company Name	**Bichotte Supplies**
First Name	**Bichotte**
Main Phone	**415-555-4567**
Address	**810 Francais Drive**
	Bayshore, CA 94326

Payment Settings:

Account No.	**8100**
Payment Terms	**Net 30**

Tax Settings:

Vendor Tax ID	**37-1599517**

Additional Info:

Vendor Type	**Supplies**

Vendor	**Martin Consulting**
Opening Balance	**$0.00 as of 01/01/2026**

Address Info:

Company Name	**Martin Consulting**
First Name	**Martin**
Main Phone	**415-555-2022**

| Address | 333 Blue Avenue |
| | Bayshore, CA 94326 |

Payment Settings:

| Account No. | 7200 |
| Payment Terms | Net 30 |

Tax Settings:

| Vendor Tax ID | 123-45-6789 |

Additional Info:

| Vendor Type | Consultant |

| Vendor | Angel Merriman Associates |
| Opening Balance | $0.00 as of 01/01/2026 |

Address Info:

Company Name	Angel Merriman Associates
First Name	Angel
Main Phone	415-555-7579
Address	623 Thorsmork Road
	Bayshore, CA 94326

Payment Settings:

| Account No. | 9000 |
| Payment Terms | Net 30 |

Tax Settings:

| Vendor Tax ID | 37-3571656 |

Additional Info:

| Vendor Type | Consultant |

2.   From the Vendor Center, export to **Excel** or **print** the Vendor List

P13.1.4 Add Items

1. Add the following items for Ella's Knittery.

Item Type	**Inventory Part**
Item Name	**Italian Linen Yarn**
Description	**Italian Linen Yarn**
Income Account	**46000 – Merchandise Sales**

Item Type	**Inventory Part**
Item Name	**Italian Linen Yarn Orchid**
Subitem of	**Italian Linen Yarn**
Description	**Italian Linen Yarn Orchid**
Sales Price	**36.00 (per skein)**
Income Account	**46000 – Merchandise Sales**
Preferred Vendor	**Bella Italia Design**

Item Type	**Inventory Part**
Item Name	**Italian Linen Yarn Azure**
Subitem of	**Italian Linen Yarn**
Description	**Italian Linen Yarn Azure**
Sales Price	**33.00 (per skein)**
Income Account	**46000 – Merchandise Sales**
Preferred Vendor	**Bella Italia Design**

Item Type	**Inventory Part**
Item Name	**Italian Linen Yarn Snow**
Subitem of	**Italian Linen Yarn**
Description	**Italian Linen Yarn Snow**
Sales Price	**30.00 (per skein)**
Income Account	**46000 – Merchandise Sales**
Preferred Vendor	**Bella Italia Design**

Item Type	**Inventory Part**
Item Name	**Cotton Copper Yarn 2 ply**

| Description | Copper Infused Cotton Yarn 2 ply |
| Income Account | 46000 – Merchandise Sales |

Item Type	Inventory Part
Item Name	Cotton Copper Sunshine 2 ply
Subitem of	Cotton Copper Yarn 2 ply
Description	Copper Infused Cotton Yarn Sunshine 2 ply
Sales Price	19.00 (per skein)
Income Account	46000 – Merchandise Sales
Preferred Vendor	Sandy Copper Textiles

Item Type	Inventory Part
Item Name	Cotton Copper Yarn Sage 2 ply
Subitem of	Cotton Copper Yarn 2 ply
Description	Copper Infused Cotton Yarn Sage 2 ply
Sales Price	18.00 (per skein)
Income Account	46000 – Merchandise Sales
Preferred Vendor	Sandy Copper Textiles

Item Type	Inventory Part
Item Name	Cotton Copper Yarn 4 ply
Description	Copper Infused Cotton Yarn 4 ply
Income Account	46000 – Merchandise Sales

Item Type	Inventory Part
Item Name	Cotton Copper Yarn Pearl 4 ply
Subitem of	Cotton Copper Yarn 4 ply
Description	Copper Infused Cotton Yarn Pearl 4 ply
Sales Price	26.00 (per skein)
Income Account	46000 – Merchandise Sales
Preferred Vendor	Sandy Copper Textiles

Item Type	**Inventory Part**
Item Name	**Cotton Copper Yarn Silver 4 ply**
Subitem of	**Cotton Copper Yarn 4 ply**
Description	**Copper Infused Cotton Yarn Silver 4 ply**
Sales Price	**26.00 (per skein)**
Income Account	**46000 – Merchandise Sales**
Preferred Vendor	**Sandy Copper Textiles**

Item Type	**Inventory Part**
Item Name	**Knitting Needles**
Description	**Knitting Needles**
Income Account	**46000 – Merchandise Sales**

Item Type	**Inventory Part**
Item Name	**Knitting Needles IntCirc CF**
Subitem of	**Knitting Needles**
Description	**Interchangeable Circular Knitting Needles with Carbon Fiber Tips**
Sales Price	**27.00 (per set)**
Income Account	**46000 – Merchandise Sales**
Preferred Vendor	**Bella Italia Design**

Item Type	**Inventory Part**
Item Name	**Knitting Needles IntCirc OW**
Subitem of	**Knitting Needles**
Description	**Interchangeable Circular Knitting Needles with Olivewood Tips**
Sales Price	**36.00 (per set)**
Income Account	**46000 – Merchandise Sales**
Preferred Vendor	**Bella Italia Design**

2. From the Item List, enter the 9.0% sales tax rate as follows:
    *   **Double-click** on **State Tax** in the Item List
    *   Enter Tax Rate: **9.0%**
    *   Enter Tax Agency: **California State Board of Equalization**
    *   Click **OK**

3. Export to **Excel** or **print** the Item List as of January 1, 2026. (Use Report Center > List > Item Listing.)

    ⚠ When exporting to Excel, remember to select Advanced Excel Options:
    *   Uncheck **Space between columns**
    *   Check **Row height**
    *   Uncheck **Include QuickBooks Export Guide worksheet with helpful advice**
    *   Select **On printed report and screen**

P13.1.5 Customize Chart of Accounts

Edit the Chart of Accounts and enter opening balances as follows:

1. Enter the opening balance for the company Checking account:
    *   To open the Chart of Accounts, click the **Chart of Accounts** icon in the Company section of the Home Page
    *   Select **Checking** account. **Right-click** to display the pop-up menu.
    *   Select **Edit Account**
    *   When the Edit Account window for the Checking account appears, enter Account No.: **10100**
    *   Enter Opening Balance: **$6,000** as of **01/01/2026**
    *   Click **OK**

2. Add the following Notes Payable account and opening balance to the Chart of Accounts.

Account No.	**26000**
Account Type	**Other Current Liability**
Account Name	**Notes Payable**
Account Description	**Notes Payable**
Tax Line	**B/S-Liabs/Eq.: Other current liabilities**
Opening Balance	**$1,000 as of 01/01/2026**

3. From the Report Center, export to **Excel** or **print** the Chart of Accounts (Account Listing) report as of January 1, 2026, with opening balances for Ella's Knittery

4. Export to **Excel** or **print** a Trial Balance report for Ella's Knittery dated 01/01/2026. Verify your Trial Balance account balances are correct.

5. Transfer the Opening Balance Equity account balance to the Capital Stock account using a journal entry. Use Date: **01/01/2026** and Entry No.: **Open ADJ1**. Select **Save**. Export the opening balance adjusting entry to **Excel** by selecting the **Reports tab** > **Transaction Journal**.

6. Export to **Excel** or **print** the Adjusted Trial Balance (after opening adjustments) on 01/01/2026 to verify that the Opening Balance Equity account balance was transferred to the Capital Stock account

P13.1.6 Enter Transactions

Ella's Knittery entered into the following transactions during January 2026.

1. Record the transactions for Ella's Knittery.
   - Record all deposits to: **Checking**.
   - If necessary, change the Make Deposits default to **Checking**. (Select Edit Menu > Preferences > Checking > My Preferences > Open the Make Deposits form with 10100 Checking account.)

Date	Transaction
01/01/2026	Ella's Knittery paid $500 store rent to Joseph Leasing. Use Write Checks window.
01/01/2026	Purchased $180 of office supplies on account from Bichotte Supplies. Use Enter Bills window to record Office Supplies (Expense).
01/12/2026	Placed the following order with Sandy Copper Textiles. • 20 skeins Cotton Copper Infused Yarn Sunshine 2 ply at a cost of $5 each • 30 skeins Cotton Copper Infused Yarn Sage 2 ply at a cost of $5 each • 10 skeins Cotton Copper Infused Yarn Pearl 4 ply at a cost of $6 each • 10 skeins Cotton Copper Infused Yarn Silver 4 ply at a cost of $6 each (Click Yes if asked to update cost because costs were not entered when the items was entered in QuickBooks Inventory.)
01/15/2026	Received Copper Infused Cotton yarn ordered on 01/12/2026
01/16/2026	Ordered the following yarn from Bella Italia Design on account. • 50 skeins Italian Linen Yarn Orchid @ $13 each • 45 skeins Italian Linen Yarn Azure @ $11 each • 20 skeins Italian Linen Yarn Snow @ $10 each • 3 sets interchangeable circular knitting needles, carbon fiber @ $9 each • 2 sets interchangeable circular knitting needles, olivewood @ $8 each
01/18/2026	Received the Bella Italian items ordered on 01/16/2026

01/19/2026   Sold to Brigette Tricot on account:
- 10 skeins Cotton Copper Yarn Sunshine 2 ply
- 22 skeins Cotton Copper Yarn Sage 2 ply
- 2 skeins Cotton Copper Yarn Pearl 4 ply
- 2 skeins Cotton Copper Yarn Silver 4 ply
- 1 set interchangeable circular knitting needles, olivewood

Record the sale using the Create Invoices window.

01/19/2026   Received bill from Sandy Copper Textiles for Cotton Copper yarn received on 01/15/2026

01/20/2026   Angel Merriman finished providing technology and cybersecurity consulting services for Ella's Knittery and presented Ella with a bill for $300 due within 30 days. Use Enter Bills window to record in Account No 66700 Professional Fees (Expense).

1/20/2026   When discussing cybersecurity procedures for Ella's Knittery, Ella gave Angel Merriman a quick knitting lesson and then sold Angel the following items:
- 8 skeins of Cotton Copper yarn Silver 4 ply
- 1 set of interchangeable circular knitting needles, carbon fiber

Enter Angel Merriman as a new customer in the Customer List using the contact information for Angel Merriman Associates. (Note that Angel Merriman Associates will be a vendor in the Vendors List and Angel Merriman will be a customer in the Customers List.)

Record the sale using the Create Invoices window.

01/23/2026   When Sandy Copper reached out to Ella to see if she was pleased with the new copper infused yarn order, Ella learned that Sandy wanted to learn more about meditative knitting. Ella directed Sandy to her online videos and sold Sandy the following items:
- 1 set of interchangeable circular knitting needles, carbon fiber tips
- 1 set of interchangeable circular knitting needles, olivewood tips
- 20 skeins of Italian Linen Yarn Azure

Enter Sandy Copper as a new customer in the Customers List using the contact information for Sandy Copper Textiles. (Note that Sandy Copper Textiles will be a vendor in the Vendors List and Sandy Copper will be a customer in the Customers List.)

Record the sale using the Create Invoices window.

01/25/2026   Sold to Mimi Petit on account:
- 30 skeins of Italian Linen Yarn Orchid
- 22 skeins of Italian Linen Yarn Azure
- 9 skeins of Italian Linen Yarn Snow

Record the sale using the Create Invoices window.

01/25/2026	Paid Sandy Copper Textiles bill for Copper Infused Cotton yarn by check
01/25/2026	Received and deposited to the Checking account the customer payment from Brigette Tricot for sale of Copper Infused Cotton yarn on 01/19/2026 (Check No. 1200)
01/26/2026	Paid Bichotte Supplies bill by check
01/27/2026	Received and deposited to the Checking account the customer payment from Angel Merriman for sale on 01/20/2026 (Check No. 970)
01/30/2026	Received bill for $360 from Martin Consulting for social media marketing services provided for the month of January for promotion of Ella's Knittery on Facebook and Instagram. Use Enter Bills window to record in Account No 66700 Professional Fees (Expense).
01/30/2026	Received Bella Italia Design bill

2. Export to **Excel** or **print** the Deposit Detail report for January 2026

3. Export to **Excel** or **print** the Check Detail report for January 2026

4. Export to **Excel** or **print** the Transaction Detail by Account report for January 2026. (From the Report Center, select Accountant & Taxes > Transaction Detail by Account.)

P13.1.7 Adjusting Entries

1. Export to **Excel** or **print** the Trial Balance report for Ella's Knittery at January 31, 2026

2. Make adjusting entries for Ella's Knittery at January 31, 2026, using the following information.

   ADJ1: A count of supplies revealed $80 of supplies on hand. Since $180 of supplies were recorded as Office Supplies (Expense) when purchased and $80 still remain on hand unused, it is necessary to transfer $80 into an asset account, Office Supplies on Hand. Add a new account: 12500 Office Supplies on Hand as Account Type: Other Current Asset. Make the adjusting entry to transfer $80 from the Office Supplies (Expense) account to the Office Supplies on Hand account, an asset.

   ADJ2: Make an adjusting entry to record Interest Expense and Interest Payable for $12.00. Add a new account: 21000 Interest Payable as Account Type: Other Current Liability.

3. From the Report Center, export to **Excel** or **print** the Adjusting Journal Entries for January 31, 2026

4. Export to **Excel** or print the Adjusted Trial Balance report for Ella's Knittery at January 31, 2026. **Highlight** the amounts affected by the adjusting entries.

P13.1.8 Financial Reports

Create the following reports for Ella's Knittery.

1. Export to **Excel** or **print** the Journal for the month of January 2026

2. Export to **Excel** or **print** the Profit & Loss, Standard for the month of January 2026

3. Export to **Excel** or **print** the Balance Sheet, Standard at January 31, 2026

4. Export to **Excel** or **print** the Statement of Cash Flows for the month of January 2026

P13.1.9 Back Up Project 13.1

Save a backup of your Project file using the file name: **YourName Project 13.1 Backup.QBB**.
See Appendix B: Back Up and Restore QuickBooks Files for instructions.

PROJECT 13.2

 Johann Enterprises

BACKSTORY

Johann Enterprises sells trendy smartphone and tablet accessories including earbuds, bluetooth earpieces, portable speakers, and cases. The company is converting from a manual accounting system to QuickBooks Desktop beginning January 2026.

⊕ QuickBooks SatNav

The objective of Project 13.2 is to facilitate your mastery of QuickBooks Desktop. As shown in the following QuickBooks SatNav, Project 13.2 covers all three processes: QuickBooks Settings, QuickBooks Transactions, and QuickBooks Reports. This project provides you with the opportunity to integrate your knowledge of QuickBooks Desktop through all three phases of the QuickBooks SatNav.

🌐 **QuickBooks SatNav**

⚙️ **QuickBooks Settings**

| ⚙️ Company Settings |
| ⚙️ Chart of Accounts |

💰 **QuickBooks Transactions**

| 💰 Banking |
| 💰 Customers & Sales |
| 💰 Vendors & Expenses |
| 💰 Employees & Payroll |

📊 **QuickBooks Reports**

| 📊 Reports |

P13.2.1 New Company Setup

Create a new company in QuickBooks for Johann Enterprises using the following information.

1.   Use the EasyStep Interview to set up a new QuickBooks company.

Company name	**YourName Project 13.2 Johann Enterprises**
Federal tax ID	**30-1957546**
Address	**63 Westman Blvd**
City	**Bayshore**
State	**CA**
Zip	**94326**
Main Phone	**415-555-3334**
Email	**<Enter your email address>**
Industry	**Retail Shop or Online Commerce**
Type of organization	**S Corporation**
First month of fiscal year	**January**
File name	**YourName Project 13.2**
What do you sell?	**Products only**
Enter sales	**Record each sale individually**
Sales tax	**Yes**
Estimates	**No**
Sales orders	**Yes**
Billing statements	**No**
Invoices	**Yes**
Progress invoicing	**No**
Track bills you owe	**Yes**
Track inventory in QuickBooks	**Yes**
Track time	**Yes**
Employees	**No**
Start date	**01/01/2026**
Use recommended accounts	**Yes**

Bank account name	**Checking**
Bank account number	**7894561230**
Bank account balance	**0.00 as of 01/01/2026**

2. Click **Start Working** to exit QuickBooks Setup

3. Set preferences as follows:

- Accounting preferences to **Use account numbers** in the Chart of Accounts
- Accounting preferences to **uncheck Warn if transactions are 30 day(s) in the future**
- Checking preferences to Open the Make Deposits form with **Checking** account

P13.2.2 Add Customers

1. Add the following customers to the Customer List for Johann Enterprises.

Customer	**Petit, Mimi**
Address Info:	
First Name	**Mimi**
Last Name	**Petit**
Main Phone	**415-555-2160**
Address	**220 Alsace Avenue** **Bayshore, CA 94326**
Payment Settings:	
Account No.	**12700**
Payment Terms	**Net 15**
Preferred Delivery Method	**E-mail**
Preferred Payment Method	**Check**
Sales Tax Settings:	
Tax Code	**Tax**
Tax Item	**State Tax**
Additional Info:	
Customer Type	**Retail**

Customer	**Luminesse Link**
Company Name	**Luminesse Link**
Address Info:	
First Name	**Luminesse**
Main Phone	**415-555-2222**
Address	**22 Beach Street** **Bayshore, CA 94326**
Payment Settings:	
Account No.	**13330**
Payment Terms	**Net 15**
Preferred Delivery Method	**E-mail**
Preferred Payment Method	**Check**
Sales Tax Settings:	
Tax Code	**Non**
Tax Item	**State Tax**
Additional Info:	
Customer Type	**Wholesale**

Customer	**Bichotte Supplies**
Company Name	**Bichotte Supplies**
Address Info:	
First Name	**Bichotte**
Main Phone	**415-555-4567**
Address	**810 Francais Drive** **Bayshore, CA 94326**
Payment Settings:	
Account No.	**19900**
Payment Terms	**Net 15**
Preferred Delivery Method	**E-mail**
Preferred Payment Method	**Check**

Sales Tax Settings:

Tax Code   **Non**

Tax Item   **State Tax**

Additional Info:

Customer Type   **Wholesale**

2.   From the Customer Center, export to **Excel** the Customer List.

⚠ When exporting to Excel, remember to select Advanced Excel Options:
- Uncheck **Space between columns**
- Check **Row height**
- Uncheck **Include QuickBooks Export Guide worksheet with helpful advice**
- Select **On printed report and screen**

P13.2.3 Add Vendors

1.   Add the following vendors to the Vendor List.

Vendor   **Joseph Leasing**

Opening Balance   **$0.00 as of 01/01/2026**

Address Info:

Company Name   **Joseph Leasing**

Full Name   **Joseph Asher**

Main Phone   **415-555-0412**

Address   **13 Appleton Drive**
                                               Bayshore, CA 94326

Payment Settings:

Account No.   **2700**

Payment Terms   **Due on receipt**

Tax Settings:

Vendor Tax ID   **37-1726354**

Additional Info:

Vendor Type <Add New>   **Leasing**

Vendor	**Angel Merriman Associates**
Opening Balance	**$0.00 as of 01/01/2026**
Address Info:	
Company Name	**Angel Merriman Associates**
Full Name	**Angel Merriman**
Main Phone	**415-555-7579**
Address	**623 Thorsmork Road** **Bayshore, CA 94326**
Payment Settings:	
Account No.	**4500**
Payment Terms	**Net 30**
Tax Settings:	
Vendor Tax ID	**37-3571656**
Additional Info:	
Vendor Type	**Suppliers**

2.   From the Vendor Center, export to **Excel** the Vendor List

P13.2.4 Add Items

1.   Add the following items.

Item Type	**Inventory Part**
Item Name	**Bluetooth Earpiece**
Description	**Bluetooth Earpiece**
Cost	**6.00**
COGS Account	**50000 – Cost of Goods Sold**
Preferred Vendor	**Angel Merriman Associates**
Sales Price	**29.00**
Tax	**Tax**
Income Account	**46000 – Merchandise Sales**
Asset Account	**12100 – Inventory Asset**
Qty on Hand	**0 as of 01/01/2026**

Item Type	**Inventory Part**
Item Name	**Smartphone Case**
Description	**Smartphone Case**
Cost	**8.00**
COGS Account	**50000 – Cost of Goods Sold**
Preferred Vendor	**Angel Merriman Associates**
Sales Price	**42.00**
Tax	**Tax**
Income Account	**46000 – Merchandise Sales**
Asset Account	**12100 – Inventory Asset**
Qty on Hand	**0 as of 01/01/2026**

Item Type	**Inventory Part**
Item Name	**Portable Speaker**
Description	**Portable Speaker**
Cost	**30.00**
COGS Account	**50000 – Cost of Goods Sold**
Preferred Vendor	**Angel Merriman Associates**
Sales Price	**120.00**
Tax	**Tax**
Income Account	**46000 – Merchandise Sales**
Asset Account	**12100 – Inventory Asset**
Qty on Hand	**0 as of 01/01/2026**

2. From the Item List, enter the 9.0% sales tax rate as follows:
    - **Double-click** on **State Tax** in the Item List
    - Enter Tax Rate: **9.0%**
    - Enter Tax Agency: **California State Board of Equalization**
    - Click **OK**

3. Export to **Excel** or **print** the Item List as of January 1, 2026. (Use Report Center > List > Item Listing.)

    ⚠ When exporting to Excel, remember to select Advanced Excel Options:
    - Uncheck **Space between columns**
    - Check **Row height**
    - Uncheck **Include QuickBooks Export Guide worksheet with helpful advice**
    - Select **On printed report and screen**

P13.2.5 Customize Chart of Accounts

Edit the Chart of Accounts and enter opening balances as follows.

1. Add the following information to the Chart of Accounts with the opening balances as of 01/01/2026.

Account	**Checking**
Account No.	**10100**
Opening Balance	**$10,000**

Account	**Notes Payable**
Account No.	**26000**
Opening Balance	**$5000**
Account Type	**Other Current Liability**
Account Description	**Notes Payable**
Tax Line	**B/S-Liabs/Eq: Other current liabilities**

Account	**Office Supplies on Hand**
Account No.	**12500**
Opening Balance	**$450**
Account Type	**Other Current Asset**
Account Description	**Office Supplies on Hand**
Tax Line	**B/S-Assets: Other current assets**

Account	**Store Fixtures**
Account No.	**14000**
Opening Balance	**$0**
Account Type	**Fixed Asset**
Account Description	**Store Fixtures**
Tax Line	**B/S-Assets: Buildings/oth depr assets**

Account	**Store Fixtures Cost**
Account No.	**14100**
Opening Balance	**$5,500**
Account Type	**Fixed Asset**
Subaccount of	**Store Fixtures**
Account Description	**Store Fixtures Cost**
Tax Line	**B/S-Assets: Buildings/oth depr assets**

Account	**Store Fixtures Acc Depr**
Account No.	**14200**
Opening Balance	**$0**
Account Type	**Fixed Asset**
Subaccount of	**Store Fixtures**
Account Description	**Store Fixtures Accumulated Depreciation**
Tax Line	**B/S-Assets: Buildings/oth depr assets**

2. Edit the following account to update it as follows.

Account	**Office Supplies Expense**
Account No.	**64900**
Account Type	**Expense**
Account Description	**Office Supplies Expense**
Tax Line	**Other Deductions: Office Expenses**

3. From the Report Center, export to **Excel** or **print** the Chart of Accounts (Account Listing) report as of January 1, 2026.

4. Export to **Excel** or **print** a Trial Balance report dated 01/01/2026. Verify your Trial Balance account balances are correct.

5. Transfer the Opening Balance Equity account balance to the Capital Stock account using a journal entry. Use Entry No.: **Open ADJ1**. Select **Save**. Export the opening balance adjusting entry to **Excel** by selecting the **Reports tab > Transaction Journal**.

6. Export to **Excel** or **print** the Adjusted Trial Balance (after opening adjustments) to verify that the Opening Balance Equity account balance was transferred to the Capital Stock account.

P13.2.6 Enter Transactions

Johann Enterprises entered into the following transactions during January 2026.

1.   Record the following transactions.
      • Record all deposits to: **Checking**.
      • If necessary, change the Make Deposits default to **Checking**. (Select Edit Menu >
        Preferences > Checking > My Preferences > Open the Make Deposits form with 10100
        Checking account.)

Date	Transaction
01/01/2026	Paid $350 for store rent to Joseph Leasing. Use Write Checks window.
01/02/2026	Ordered the following from Angel Merriman Associates. • 900 Bluetooth earpieces • 360 smartphone cases • 100 portable speakers
01/04/2026	Received items ordered from Angel Merriman Associates on 01/02/2026
01/05/2026	Sold the following to Luminesse Link on account. • 600 Bluetooth earpieces • 180 smartphone cases
01/07/2026	Received bill from Angel Merriman Associates
01/08/2026	Sold the following to Bichotte Supplies on account. • 200 Bluetooth earpieces • 170 smartphone cases
01/11/2026	Sold the following to Mimi Petit on account. • 70 portable speakers • 50 Bluetooth earpieces
01/15/2026	Paid at time of purchase for $20 of office supplies from Carole Design Media. (Record using the Enter Bills and Pay Bills windows. Add new vendor: Carole Design Media. Use the Office Supplies on Hand account.)
01/22/2026	Received and deposited payment from Luminesse Link (Check No. 906)
01/23/2026	Received and deposited payment from Bichotte Supplies (Check No. 787)
01/25/2026	Sold the following to Luminesse Link on account. • 50 Bluetooth earpieces • 25 portable speakers
01/25/2026	Ordered 200 Bluetooth earpieces from Angel Merriman Associates
01/26/2026	Received and deposited payment from Mimi Petit (Check No. 321)
01/28/2026	Received items ordered from Angel Merriman Associates on 01/25/2026

01/28/2026	Received bill from Angel Merriman Associates
01/29/2026	Sold the following to Bichotte Supplies on account.
	• 150 Bluetooth earpieces
	• 3 portable speakers
01/30/2026	Paid Angel Merriman Associates bill due on 02/06/2026

2. Export to **Excel** the Deposit Detail report for January 2026

3. Export to **Excel** the Check Detail report for January 2026

P13.2.7 Adjusting Entries

1. Export to **Excel** the Trial Balance report at January 31, 2026

2. Make adjusting entries at January 31, 2026, using the following information.

    ADJ1: A count of office supplies revealed $270 on hand.

    ADJ2: January depreciation expense for store fixtures was $90.

    ADJ3: Interest expense and interest payable on the Notes Payable equaled $42.00. Add Account No. 21000 Interest Payable (Other Current Liability).

3. From the Report Center, export to **Excel** the Adjusting Journal Entries for January 31, 2026

4. Export to **Excel** the Adjusted Trial Balance report at January 31, 2026. **Highlight** the amounts affected by the adjusting entries.

P13.2.8 Financial Reports

Create the following reports.

1. Export to **Excel** the Accounts Receivable Aging Detail report at January 31, 2026

2. Export to **Excel** the Profit & Loss, Standard for the month of January 2026

3. Export to **Excel** the Balance Sheet, Standard at January 31, 2026

4. Export to **Excel** the Statement of Cash Flows for the month of January 2026

5. Export to **Excel** the Customer Balance Detail report for January 1 - 31, 2026

6. Export to **Excel** the Vendor Balance Detail report for January 1 - 31, 2026

P13.2.9 Back Up Project 13.2

Save a backup of your Project file using the file name: **YourName Project 13.2 Backup.QBB**.
See Appendix B: Back Up and Restore QuickBooks Files for instructions.

Design elements: Dog icon: ©josep perianes jorba/Shutterstock; paint roller icon: ©Netti Buletti/Shutterstock; other icons/symbols: ©Carboxylase/Shutterstock

Chapter 14

QuickBooks Merchandise Company Case

Mookie The Beagle Spa™ Supplies

BACKSTORY

Your friend and entrepreneur, Cy Walker, approaches you about a business opportunity. Cy would like to buy an existing pet supply business and relaunch as Mookie The Beagle Spa™ Supplies. The company would offer Mookie The Beagle branded merchandise for pet grooming, and eventually pet apparel. To further differentiate product offerings, the MTB spa products would be formulated to omit toxic ingredients often found in pet supplies.

Cy plans to keep operations lean by leasing storage space to stock merchandise for shipment to large retail customers and online consumers. This eliminates the need for an expensive brick and mortar storefront.

After negotiations, Cy and you agree to invest $11,000 each in stock of the company. You also enter into an arrangement with Cy to assist with QuickBooks Desktop for his newest business in exchange for spa services for Ozzie, your new curly apricot Goldendoodle.

> **Download the Excel Report Template for Chapter 14 at www.My-QuickBooks.com, QB2021 link.**

Chapter 14

Learning Objectives

Chapter 14 covers the following QuickBooks topics:

- Set Up New QuickBooks Company
- Customer List
- Vendor List
- Item List
- Customize the Chart of Accounts
- Record Opening Adjustments
- Record Transactions
- Adjusting Entries
- Financial Reports
- Back Up QuickBooks Files

Section 14.1
 QuickBooks SatNav

The objective of this chapter is to facilitate mastery of QuickBooks Desktop for a merchandising company. We will cover setting up a new QuickBooks merchandise company, customizing the QuickBooks Chart of Accounts, entering QuickBooks transactions, and creating reports. This chapter provides you with the opportunity to integrate your knowledge of QuickBooks Desktop through all three phases of QuickBooks SatNav for a merchandising company.

As shown in the following QuickBooks SatNav, Chapter 14 QuickBooks Service Company Case covers all three processes: QuickBooks Settings, QuickBooks Transactions, and QuickBooks Reports.

QuickBooks SatNav

QuickBooks Settings

Company Settings
Chart of Accounts

QuickBooks Transactions

Banking
Customers & Sales
Vendors & Expenses
Employees & Payroll

QuickBooks Reports

Reports

Section 14.2
Set Up New QuickBooks Company

C14.2.1 Create New QuickBooks Company

Create a new company in QuickBooks for Mookie The Beagle™ Spa Supplies using the following information and the EasyStep Interview.

Company Name	**YourName Chapter 14 Mookie The Beagle Spa Supplies**
Federal Tax ID	**37-7879146**
Address	**432 Phoenician Way**
City	**Mountain View**
State	**CA**
ZIP	**94043**
Email	**<Enter your own email address>**
Industry	**Retail Shop or Online Commerce**
Type of organization	**S Corporation**
First month of fiscal year	**January**
File name	**YourName Chapter 14**
What do you sell?	**Products only**
Enter sales	**Record each sale individually**
Sales tax	**Yes**
Estimates	**No**
Sales orders	**No**
Billing statements	**No**
Invoices	**Yes**
Progress invoicing	**No**
Track bills	**Yes**
Track inventory	**Yes**
Track time	**Yes**

Employees	**No**
Start date	**01/01/2026**
Use recommended accounts?	**Yes**
Bank account name	**Checking**
Bank account number	**4564564561**
Bank account balance	**0.00 as of 01/01/2026**

C14.2.2 Select Tax Return

Verify the tax form, 1120S (S Corporation), for Mookie The Beagle Spa™ Supplies.

1 Select **Company Menu**

2 Select **My Company**

3 Select Income Tax Form: **Form 1120S (S Corporation)**

C14.2.3 Display Account Numbers

Display Account Numbers in the Chart of Accounts for Mookie The Beagle Spa Supplies.

1 Select **Edit Menu**

2 Select **Preferences**

3 Select **Accounting**

4 Select **Company Preferences**

5 Select **Use Account Numbers**

6 Deselect **Warn if transactions are 30 day(s) in the future**

C14.2.4 Set Preferences

Set preferences for Mookie The Beagle Spa Supplies.

1 Select **Edit Menu**

2 Select **Preferences**

3 Select **Checking**

4 Select **My Preferences**

5 Select **Open Make Deposits form with Checking account**

Section 14.3

Customer List

C14.3.1 Create Customer List

Using the following information, create a Customer List for Mookie The Beagle Spa Supplies.

Customer	**Maddy's Marvels**
Opening Balance	**$0.00 as of 01/01/2026**
Address Info:	
Company Name	**Maddy's Marvels**
First Name	**Maddy**
Mobile	**415-555-2727**
Address	**27 Aquarian Rue** **Bayshore, CA 94326**
Payment Settings:	
Account No.	**30001**
Payment Terms	**Net 30**
Sales Tax Settings:	
Tax Code	**Non**
Additional Info:	
Customer Type	**Wholesale**
Customer	**Meta PetCare Supplies**
Opening Balance	**$0.00 as of 01/01/2026**
Address Info:	
Company Name	**Meta PetCare Supplies**
First Name	**Meta**
Main Phone	**415-555-1010**

| Address | **10 Chassure Street** |
| | **Bayshore, CA 94326** |

Payment Settings:

| Account No. | **30002** |
| Payment Terms | **Net 30** |

Sales Tax Settings:

| Tax Code | **Non** |

Additional Info:

| Customer Type | **Wholesale** |

| Customer | **Kari, Tracey** |
| Opening Balance | **$0.00 as of 01/01/2026** |

Address Info:

First Name	**Tracey**
Last Name	**Kari**
Mobile	**415-555-9999**
Address	**99 Reyka Drive**
	Bayshore, CA 94326

Payment Settings:

| Account No. | **30003** |
| Payment Terms | **Net 30** |

Sales Tax Settings:

| Tax Code | **Tax** |
| Tax Item | **State Tax** |

Additional Info:

| Customer Type <Add New> | **Online** |

Custom Field <Select Define Field > Enter
Label: Pet Name > Select Cust > Enter Label:
Pet Description > Select Cust > Select OK>

Pet Name	**Odin**
Pet Description	**Black Labrador**
Customer	**Byran, Sherry**
Opening Balance	**$0.00 as of 01/01/2026**
Address Info:	
First Name	**Sherry**
Last Name	**Byran**
Main Phone	**415-555-2222**
Address	**222 Mure Drive**
	Bayshore, CA 94326
Payment Settings:	
Account No.	**30004**
Payment Terms	**Net 30**
Sales Tax Settings:	
Tax Code	**Tax**
Tax Item	**State Tax**
Additional Info:	
Customer Type	**Online**
Pet Name	**Maggie**
Pet Description	**Cream Havanese**
Customer	**Copper, Sandy**
Opening Balance	**$0.00 as of 01/01/2026**
Address Info:	
First Name	**Sandy**
Last Name	**Copper**
Main Phone	**415-555-4320**

Address	**720 Cuivre Drive**
	Bayshore, CA 94326
Payment Settings:	
Account No.	**30005**
Payment Terms	**Net 30**
Sales Tax Settings:	
Tax Code	**Tax**
Tax Item	**State Tax**
Additional Info:	
Customer Type	**Online**
Pet Name	**Remy**
Pet Description	**Coppery Short Hair Rescue Dog**

Customer	**Merriman, Angel**
Opening Balance	**$0.00 as of 01/01/2026**
Address Info:	
First Name	**Angel**
Last Name	**Merriman**
Main Phone	**415-555-7579**
Address	**623 Thorsmork Road**
	Bayshore, CA 94326
Payment Settings:	
Account No.	**30006**
Payment Terms	**Net 30**
Sales Tax Settings:	
Tax Code	**Tax**
Tax Item	**State Tax**

Additional Info:

Customer Type	**Online**
Pet Name	**Kuno**
Pet Description	**Black and Tan German Shepherd**

C14.3.2 Export Customer List

Export the Customer List to **Excel** or **print**.

⚠ When exporting to Excel, remember to select Advanced Excel Options:

- Uncheck **Space between columns**
- Check **Row height**
- Uncheck **Include QuickBooks Export Guide worksheet with helpful advice**
- Select **On printed report and screen**

Section 14.4
Vendor List

C14.4.1 Create Vendor List
Using the following information, create a Vendor List for Mookie The Beagle Spa Supplies.

1. Add a new vendor.

Vendor	**Angel Merriman Associates**
Opening Balance	**$0.00 as of 01/01/2026**
Address Info:	
Company Name	**Angel Merriman Associates**
First Name	**Angel**
Last Name	**Merriman**
Main Phone	**415-555-7579**
Address	**623 Thorsmork Road** **Bayshore, CA 94326**
Payment Settings:	
Account No.	**4001**
Payment Terms	**Net 30**
Print on Check as	**Angel Merriman Associates**
Vendor Tax ID	**37-3571656**
Additional Info:	
Vendor Type	**Consultant**

2. Add new vendor.

Vendor	**Joseph Leasing**
Opening Balance	**$0.00 as of 01/01/2026**
Address Info:	
Company Name	**Joseph Leasing**
First Name	**Joseph**

Last Name	**Asher**
Main Phone	**415-555-0412**
Address	**13 Appleton Drive** **Bayshore, CA 94326**
Payment Settings:	
Account No.	**4002**
Payment Terms	**Net 30**
Print on Check as	**Joseph Leasing**
Vendor Tax ID	**37-1726354**
Additional Info:	
Vendor Type <Add New>	**Leasing**

3.   Add new vendor.

Vendor	**Toronto LLC**
Opening Balance	**$0.00 as of 01/01/2026**
Address Info:	
Company Name	**Toronto LLC**
First Name	**Tor**
Main Phone	**415-555-5377**
Address	**416 Wellington Drive** **Bayshore, CA 94326**
Payment Settings:	
Account No.	**4003**
Payment Terms	**Net 30**
Print on Check as	**Toronto LLC**
Additional Info:	
Vendor Type	**Suppliers**

C14.4.2 Export Vendor List
Export the Vendor List to **Excel** or **print**.

Section 14.5

Item List

C14.5.1 Enter Item List

Enter the following items in the Item List for Mookie The Beagle Spa Supplies.

Use the following information when entering inventory items:

- COGS Expense account: **50000 Cost of Goods Sold**

- Income account: **46000 Merchandise Sales**

- Tax Code: **Tax**

- Inventory asset account: **12100 Inventory Asset**

- Initial quantity on hand: **0.00 As of 01/01/2026**

SUBITEM OF	ITEM NAME	TYPE	DESCRIPTION	COST	SALES PRICE
Pet Spa Product	MTB Organic Oatmeal Shampoo	Inventory	Mookie The Beagle Organic Oatmeal Shampoo	$5	$21
Pet Spa Product	MTB Organic Coconut Conditioner	Inventory	Mookie The Beagle Organic Coconut Oil Conditioner	$6	$22
Pet Spa Product	MTB Leave-in Detangler	Inventory	Mookie The Beagle Leave-in Detangler Spray	$8	$20
Pet Spa Product	MTB Cologne	Inventory	Mookie The Beagle Cologne Deodorizer	$6	$15
Pet Spa Tool	MTB Hair Dryer	Inventory	Mookie The Beagle Grooming Hair Dryer	$10	$30
Pet Spa Tool	MTB Grooming Brush	Inventory	Mookie The Beagle Grooming Bristle Brush	$4	$12
Pet Spa Tool	MTB Grooming Comb	Inventory	Mookie The Beagle Grooming Steel Comb	$3	$16
Pet Spa Tool	MTB Grooming Scissors	Inventory	Mookie The Beagle Grooming Scissors	$6	$18
Pet Spa Tool	MTB Doggie Toothbrush Set	Inventory	Mookie The Beagle Doggie Toothpaste and Toothbrush Set	$2	$13
Pet Spa Tool	MTB Massage Brush	Inventory	Mookie The Beagle Massage Brush	$8	$54
Pet Spa Wipe	MTB Doggie Paw Wipes	Inventory	Mookie The Beagle Doggie Paw Wipes	$3	$9
Pet Spa Wipe	MTB Doggie Ear and Eye Wipes	Inventory	Mookie The Beagle Doggie Ear and Eye Wipes	$3	$9
Pet Spa Wipe	MTB Grooming Wipes	Inventory	Mookie The Beagle Grooming Wipes Multipurpose	$3	$9

C14.5.2 Enter Sales Tax Rate

From the Item List, enter the sales tax rate.

1. From the Item List, **double-click State Tax**

2. Enter Tax Rate: **9.0%**

3. Enter Tax Agency: **California State Board of Equalization**

4. Click **OK**

C14.5.3 Export Item List

1. Re-sort the Item List

2. From the Report Center, export the Item List to **Excel** or **print**.

⚠ When exporting to Excel, remember to select Advanced Excel Options:
- Uncheck **Space between columns**
- Check **Row height**
- Uncheck **Include QuickBooks Export Guide worksheet with helpful advice**
- Select **On printed report and screen**

Section 14.6

Customize the Chart of Accounts

Customize the Chart of Accounts for Mookie The Beagle Spa Supplies.

C14.6.1 Enter Checking Account Opening Balance

Enter the opening balance for the company Checking account in the Chart of Accounts for Mookie The Beagle Spa Supplies.

1. To open the Chart of Accounts, select the **Chart of Accounts** icon in the Company section of the Home Page

2. Select **Checking** account. **Right-click** to display the pop-up menu.

3. Select **Edit Account**

4. When the Edit Account window for the Checking account appears, enter Account No.: **10100**

5. Enter Opening Balance: **$2,500 as of 01/01/2026**

C14.6.2 Enter Accounts and Opening Balances

Add the following accounts and opening balances to the Chart of Accounts for Mookie The Beagle Spa Supplies.

Account No.	**26000**
Account Type	**Long Term Liability**
Account Name	**Notes Payable**
Account Description	**Notes Payable**
Tax Line	**B/S-Liabs/Eq.:L-T Mortgage/note/bonds pay**
Opening Balance	**$1,000 as of 01/01/2026**

Account No.	**12500**
Account Type	**Other Current Asset**
Account Name	**Office Supplies on Hand**
Account Description	**Office Supplies on Hand**
Tax Line	**B/S-Assets:Other current assets**
Opening Balance	**$900 as of 01/01/2026**

C14.6.3 Export Chart of Accounts

Using the Reports Center, export to **Excel** or **print** a Chart of Accounts (Account Listing) report for Mookie The Beagle Spa Supplies.

Section 14.7

Record Opening Adjustments

C14.7.1 Export Trial Balance

Export to **Excel** or **print** a Trial Balance report for Mookie The Beagle Spa Supplies dated 01/01/2026.

C14.7.2 Enter Opening Adjusting Journal Entry

Prepare the following opening adjustment entry using the Journal.

1 Transfer the Opening Balance Equity account balance to the Capital Stock account. Use Entry No. **Open ADJ1**. Use Date: **01/01/2026**.

2 Select **Save**

3 Select the **Reports tab > Transaction Journal**

4 Export the opening balance adjusting entry to **Excel**

C14.7.3 Export Adjusted Trial Balance

Export to **Excel** or **print** an Adjusted Trial Balance report after opening adjustments for Mookie The Beagle Spa Supplies dated 01/01/2026. Verify that the Opening Balance Equity account balance was transferred to the Capital Stock account.

Section 14.8
Record Transactions

Mookie The Beagle Spa Supplies entered into the following transactions during January 2026.

C14.8.1 Enter Transactions

Record the following transactions for Mookie The Beagle Spa. Use memorized transactions for recurring transactions.

Date	Transaction
01/01/2026	Cy invested $11,000 by e-check in stock of Mookie The Beagle Spa Supplies. You invested $11,000 by e-check in the stock of the business. Deposit the funds into the company Checking account. (Use Make Deposits window.)
01/01/2026	Paid $500 rent to Joseph Leasing for storage space lease. (Use the Write Checks window, then create a memorized transaction.)
01/02/2026	Purchased technology and cybersecurity services for $300 on account from Angel Merriman Associates. (Use Enter Bills window to record Professional Fees Expense.)
01/05/2026	Ordered following inventory from Toronto LLC: • 500 Mookie The Beagle Organic Oatmeal Shampoo • 200 Mookie The Beagle Organic Coconut Oil Conditioner • 80 Mookie The Beagle Leave-in Detangler • 50 Mookie The Beagle Hair Dryer • 50 Mookie The Beagle Grooming Brush • 90 Mookie The Beagle Massage Brush
01/07/2026	Received items ordered from Toronto LLC
01/08/2026	Sold the following to Maddy's Marvels on account: • 400 Mookie The Beagle Organic Oatmeal Shampoo • 120 Mookie The Beagle Organic Coconut Oil Conditioner • 50 Mookie The Beagle Leave-in Detangler • 30 Mookie The Beagle Hair Dryer • 27 Mookie The Beagle Grooming Brush • 60 Mookie The Beagle Massage Brush

01/09/2026   Sold the following to Meta PetCare Supplies on account:
- 90 Mookie The Beagle Organic Oatmeal Shampoo
- 65 Mookie The Beagle Organic Coconut Oil Conditioner
- 30 Mookie The Beagle Leave-in Detangler
- 12 Mookie The Beagle Hair Dryer
- 8 Mookie The Beagle Grooming Brush
- 20 Mookie The Beagle Massage Brush

01/12/2026   Received bill from Toronto LLC for inventory received on 1/07/2026

01/16/2026   Paid Toronto LLC bill for inventory purchased

01/18/2026   Sold the following online to Tracey Kari and received credit card payment at time of sale. (VISA 5555 5555 5555 5555 Exp: 05/2027) Include sales tax on this sale. (Use Create Invoices, Receive Payments and Make Deposits windows.)
- 3 Mookie The Beagle Organic Oatmeal Shampoo
- 3 Mookie The Beagle Organic Coconut Oil Conditioner
- 2 Mookie The Beagle Grooming Brush
- 2 Mookie The Beagle Hair Dryer
- 2 Mookie The Beagle Massage Brush

01/21/2026   Ordered following inventory from Toronto LLC:
- 30 Mookie The Beagle Doggie Toothpaste and Toothbrush Set
- 300 Mookie The Beagle Doggie Paw Wipes
- 300 Mookie The Beagle Doggie Ear and Eye Wipes
- 300 Mookie The Beagle Grooming Wipes

01/22/2026   Received items ordered from Toronto LLC on 01/21/2026

01/23/2026   Sold the following online to Sherry Byran and received credit card payment at time of sale. (VISA 7777 7777 7777 7777 Exp: 07/2027) Include sales tax on this sale. (Use Create Invoices, Receive Payments and Make Deposits windows.)
- 3 Mookie The Beagle Grooming Wipes
- 5 Mookie The Beagle Doggie Paw Wipes
- 2 Mookie The Beagle Massage Brush
- 1 Mookie The Beagle Doggie Toothpaste and Toothbrush Set

01/23/2026   Sold the following online to Sandy Copper and received credit card payment at time of sale. (VISA 6666 6666 6666 6666 Exp: 06/2026) Include sales tax on this sale. (Use Create Invoices, Receive Payments and Make Deposits windows.)
- 10 Mookie The Beagle Grooming Wipes
- 10 Mookie The Beagle Doggie Paw Wipes
- 1 Mookie The Beagle Grooming Brush
- 1 Mookie The Beagle Massage Brush
- 1 Mookie The Beagle Doggie Toothpaste and Toothbrush Set

| 01/23/2026 | Sold the following online to Angel Merriman and received credit card payment at time of sale. (MasterCard 2222 2222 2222 2222 Exp: 02/2027) Include sales tax on this sale. (Use Create Invoices, Receive Payments and Make Deposits windows.) |

- 20 Mookie The Beagle Grooming Wipes
- 20 Mookie The Beagle Doggie Paw Wipes
- 1 Mookie The Beagle Grooming Brush
- 1 Mookie The Beagle Massage Brush
- 1 Mookie The Beagle Doggie Toothpaste and Toothbrush Set

01/26/2026 Received and deposited payment from Meta PetCare Supplies (Check No. 1313)

01/28/2026 Received and deposited payment from Maddy's Marvels (Check No. 2700)

01/28/2026 Sold the following to Maddy's Marvels on account:
- 25 Mookie The Beagle Doggie Toothpaste and Toothbrush Set
- 250 Mookie The Beagle Doggie Paw Wipes
- 200 Mookie The Beagle Doggie Ear and Eye Wipes
- 250 Mookie The Beagle Grooming Wipes

01/30/2026 Received bill from Toronto LLC for inventory received on 1/22/2026

01/30/2026 Paid $500 to Joseph Leasing for storage space lease for February rental

C14.8.2 Export Deposit Detail Report

Export to **Excel** or **print** the Deposit Detail report for January 2026.

C14.8.3 Export Check Detail Report

Export to **Excel** or **print** the Check Detail report for January 2026.

C14.8.4 Export Transaction Detail by Account Report

Export to **Excel** or **print** the Transaction Detail by Account report for January 2026.

Section 14.9

Adjusting Entries

Make adjustments at January 31, 2026 to bring accounts up to date before preparing financial reports for Mookie The Beagle Spa Supplies.

C14.9.1 Export Trial Balance

Export to **Excel** or **print** the Trial Balance report for Mookie The Beagle Spa Supplies at January 31, 2026.

C14.9.2 Enter Adjusting Journal Entries

Make adjusting entries for Mookie The Beagle Spa Supplies at January 31, 2026, using the following information.

1. **ADJ1:** Record as a prepaid asset the February 2026 rent paid that was expensed in January 2026. Add Account 13000 Prepaid Rent, Other Current Asset.

2. **ADJ2:** A count of office supplies on hand reveals that $700 of supplies are still on hand at January 31, 2026.

3. **ADJ3:** Interest expense and interest payable at January 31, 2026, on Notes Payable was $29. Add Account No. 21000, Interest Payable.

C14.9.3 Export Adjusting Journal Entries Report

Export to **Excel** or **print** the Adjusting Journal Entries report at January 31, 2026.

C14.9.4 Export Adjusted Trial Balance

Export to **Excel** or **print** the Adjusted Trial Balance report for Mookie The Beagle Spa Supplies at January 31, 2026. **Highlight** amounts affected by the adjusting entries.

Section 14.10

Financial Reports

Prepare financial reports for Mookie The Beagle Spa Supplies for January 2026.

C14.10.1 Export Journal

Export to **Excel** or **print** the Journal for the month of January 2026.

C14.10.2 Export Profit and Loss, Standard

Export to **Excel** or **print** the Profit and Loss, Standard for the month of January 2026.

C14.10.3 Export Balance Sheet, Standard

Export to **Excel** or **print** the Balance Sheet, Standard at January 31, 2026.

C14.10.4 Export Statement of Cash Flows

Export to **Excel** or **print** the Statement of Cash Flows for the month of January 2026. Highlight the following on the Statement of Cash Flows report:

- Net cash provided by Operating Activities
- Net cash provided by Financing Activities
- Net cash increase for the period

C14.10.5 Export Accounts Receivable Aging Summary

Export to **Excel** or **print** the Accounts Receivable Aging Summary at January 31, 2026.

C14.10.6 Export Accounts Payable Aging Summary

Export to **Excel** or **print** the Accounts Payable Aging Summary at January 31, 2026.

Section 14.11

Back Up QuickBooks Files

Save a backup of your Chapter 14 file using the file name: **YourName Chapter 14 Backup.QBB**. For further instructions on how to back up your file, *see* Appendix B: Back Up and Restore QuickBooks Files.

Design elements: Dog icon: ©josep perianes jorba/Shutterstock; paint roller icon: ©Netti Buletti/Shutterstock; other icons/symbols: ©Carboxylase/Shutterstock

Chapter 15

Advanced QuickBooks Features for Accountants

 Paint Palette

BACKSTORY

During the month of January 2026 you continue to operate your painting service, Paint Palette, while still managing the Paint Palette Store. In order to plan better, you would like to create a budget for Paint Palette for the coming year and want to learn more about using the QuickBooks budget feature.

In the new year, several commercial customers have approached you about custom painting for their offices and businesses. Moreover, you continue to get referrals from satisfied customers. However, the new customers want bids and estimates before they award contracts, so you would like to start using the QuickBooks estimates feature. Also, since some of these new jobs will require months to complete, you want to use the QuickBooks progress billing feature to bill customers as the job progresses in order to bring in a steady cash flow for your business.

Furthermore, you continue to provide QuickBooks consulting services for a variety of accounting clients. Therefore, to improve customer service for your QuickBooks clients, you continue to expand your knowledge and learn more about other advanced features of QuickBooks designed for the accounting professional.

Chapter 15
Learning Objectives

Chapter 15 explores advanced QuickBooks features used by accountants. In this chapter, you will learn about the following topics:

- Budgets
- Estimates
- Progress Billing
- Credit Card Sales
- Bad Debts
- Audit Trail
- Accountant's Copy
- Ask My Accountant
- Accounting Essentials: Bad Debts

Section 15.1

Introduction

This chapter covers some of the more advanced features of QuickBooks that are of interest to the accounting professional. These features include setting up budgets, progress billing, and the audit trail.

Section 15.2
Start QuickBooks and Open QuickBooks Company

START QUICKBOOKS

To start QuickBooks software, click the **QuickBooks** icon on your desktop. If a QuickBooks icon does not appear on your desktop, from Microsoft® Windows® click **Start** button > **QuickBooks** > **QuickBooks Premier Accountant Edition**.

RESTORE QBB

Restore the backup (QBB) file for this chapter as follows.

1 Select **File** > **Restore**

2 Using the directions in Appendix B: Back Up and Restore QuickBooks Files, restore the **CHAPTER 15 STARTER.QBB** file. (If a password is requested, use KayQB2021.)

3 After restoring, update the company name tp **YourName Chapter 15 Paint Palette** by selecting **Company Menu** > **My Company**

Section 15.3

Budgets

As Paint Palette enters its second year of operation, planning for future expansion is important to its continued success. You develop the following budget for 2026.

- January sales are expected to be $6,500. Sales are expected to increase by 5% each month thereafter.
- Paint supplies expense is budgeted at $45 per month.
- The van lease will be $350 per month. (Use Account No. 67100.)

To prepare budgets for Paint Palette using QuickBooks:

1 Select **Company Menu**

2 Select **Planning & Budgeting**

3 Select **Set Up Budgets**

4 In the Create New Budget window, select the year: **2026**

5 Select budget type: **Profit and Loss**

6 Select **Next**

7 Select **No additional criteria**

8 Select **Next**

9 Select **Create budget from scratch**

10 Click **Finish**

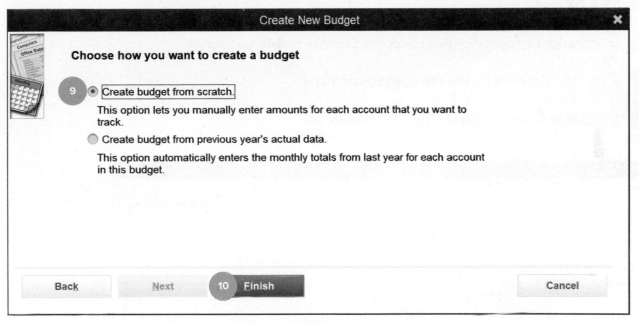

When the Set Up Budgets window appears:

1. Enter **6500.00** for 47900 Sales account in the Jan26 column

2. Click the **Copy Across** button

3. Click the **Adjust Row Amounts** button

4. When the Adjust Row Amounts window appears, select Start at: **Currently selected month**

5. Select: **Increase each remaining monthly amount in this row by this dollar amount or percentage**

6. Enter **5.0%**

7. Check: **Enable compounding**

8. Click **OK**

9. Enter budget amounts for Paint Supplies Expense of **$45** per month

10. Enter Rent Expense for the van of **$350** per month

11. Click **OK** to close the Set Up Budgets window

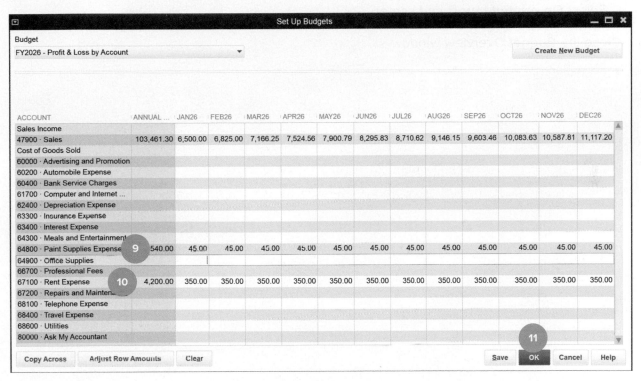

C15.3.1 Budget. Export to **Excel** or **print** the budget you created for Paint Palette:

1 From the Report Center select **Budgets & Forecasts** > **Budget Overview**

2 Select Dates: **01/01/2026 To: 12/31/2026**. Click **Run**.

3 Select: **FY2026 – Profit and Loss by Account** > **Next**

4 Select Report Layout: **Account by Month** > **Next** > **Finish**

5 Export to **Excel** or **print** the Budget Overview report.

⚠ When exporting to Excel, remember to select Advanced Excel Options:
- Uncheck **Space between columns**
- Check **Row height**
- Uncheck **Include QuickBooks Export Guide worksheet with helpful advice**
- Select **On printed report and screen**

6 **Close** the Budget Overview window

Section 15.4
Estimates

Often customers ask for a bid or estimate of job cost before awarding a contract. Paint Palette needs to estimate job costs that are accurate in order not to overbid and lose the job or underbid and lose money on the job.

To prepare a job cost estimate for Paint Palette:

1   Click the **Estimates** icon in the Customers section of the Home Page

2   In the Create Estimates window that appears, from the drop-down Customer List, select **<Add New>**

3   Enter Customer Name: **Snaps Café**

4   Enter Company Name: **Snaps Café**

5   Enter First Name: **Skal**

6   Enter Address:
1111 Skylar Blvd
Bayshore, CA 94326

7   Click the Job Info tab, then enter Job Status: **Pending**

8   Click **OK** to close the New Customer window

9   To enter estimate information in the Create Estimates window, select Template: **Custom Estimate**

10   Select Date: **01/05/2026**

11   Enter Item: **Labor: Exterior Painting**

12   Enter Quantity **60**

13   Enter a second Item: **Labor: Interior Painting**

14   Enter Quantity: **86**

15   Click **Save & Close** to close the Create Estimates window

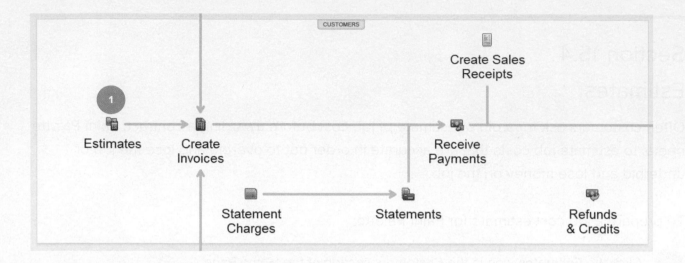

Section 15.5

Progress Billing

When undertaking a job that lasts a long period of time, a business often does not want to wait until the job is completed to receive payment for its work. The business often incurs expenses in performing the job that must be paid before the business receives payment from customers. This can create a cash flow problem. One solution to this problem is progress billing.

Progress billing permits a business to bill customers as the job progresses. Thus, the business receives partial payments from the customer before the project is completed.

After you give Snaps Café your estimate of the paint job cost, Snaps awards you the contract. The job will last about three weeks. However, instead of waiting three weeks to bill Snaps, you bill Snaps every week so that you will have cash to pay your bills.

To use progress billing in QuickBooks, first you must turn on the preference for progress invoicing.

To select the preference for progress invoicing:

1. Select **Edit Menu**

2. Select **Preferences**

3. Select **Jobs & Estimates**

4. Select **Company Preferences**

5. Select **Yes** to indicate you want to use Progress Invoicing

6. Check **Don't print items that have zero amount**

7. Click **OK** to save the Progress Invoicing preference and close the Preferences window. Click **OK** if a warning window appears.

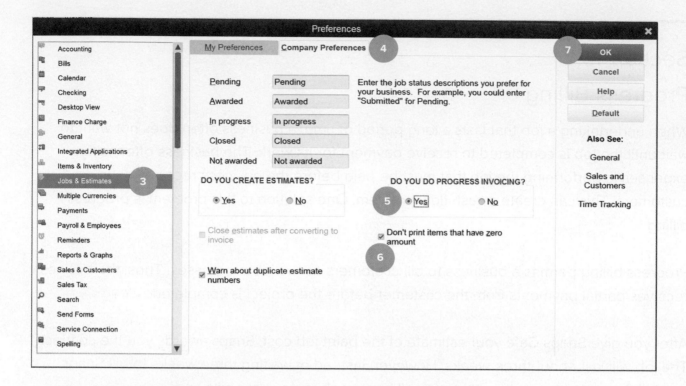

After selecting the Progress Invoicing preference, the Progress Invoice template is now available in the Create Invoices window.

C15.5.1 Progress Invoice. To create a progress invoice:

1 Click the **Create Invoices** icon in the Customers section of the Home Page

2 When the Create Invoices window appears, select Customer: **Snaps Café**

3 Select the **Snaps Café** estimate to invoice

4 Click **OK**

5 When the Create Progress Invoice Based On Estimate window appears, select: **Create invoice for the entire estimate (100%)**

6 Click **OK**

7 When the following Create Invoices window appears, the template should now be: **Progress Invoice**

8 Enter the number of hours actually worked on the Snaps Café job
- Enter Exterior Painting Labor Quantity: **20**
- Enter Interior Painting Labor Quantity: **0**

9 Select the **Save** icon

10 Select the **Reports tab** at the top of the Create Invoices window

11 Select **Transaction Journal**

12 Export to **Excel** or **print** the Transaction Journal report

13 Click **Save & Close** to close the Create Invoices window. If a message appears, click **Yes** to record changes to the invoice.

C15.5.2 Progress Invoice. The following week you complete the exterior painting for Snaps Café and work 17 hours on interior painting. Create another progress invoice for Snaps Café by completing the following steps.

1. Display the Create Invoices window and select Customer: **Snaps Café**

2. Select the **Snaps Café** estimate to invoice, then click **OK**

3. When the Create Progress Invoice Based On Estimate window appears, select **Create invoice for selected items or for different percentages of each item**

4. Click **OK**

5. When the Specify Invoice Amounts for Items on Estimate window appears, Check: **Show Quantity and Rate**

6. Check: **Show Percentage**

7. Enter Exterior Painting Quantity: **40**

8. Enter Interior Painting Quantity: **18**

9. Click **OK** to record these amounts on the progress invoice

10. When the Create Invoices window appears, change the date of the progress invoice to: **01/12/2026**

11. Select the **Save** icon

12. Select the **Reports tab > Transaction Journal**

13. Export to **Excel** or **print** the Transaction Journal

14. Click **Save & Close** to close the Create Invoices window

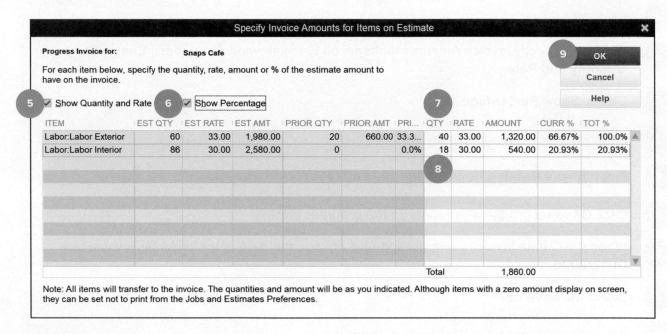

Customer payments received on progress invoices are recorded in the same manner as customer payments for standard invoices (see Chapter 5).

Section 15.6
Credit Card Sales

As a convenience to your customers, you agree to accept credit cards as payment for services you provide. Snaps Café would like to make its first payment using a VISA credit card.

In QuickBooks, you record credit card payments in the same manner that you record a payment by check; however, instead of selecting Check as the payment method, you select the type of credit card used.

C15.6.1 Deposit Journal Entry. To record a credit card sale using QuickBooks:

1. Click the **Receive Payments** icon in the Customers section of the Home Page

2. When the Receive Payments window appears, select Received From: **Snaps Café**. QuickBooks will automatically display any unpaid invoices for Snaps Café.

3. Select Invoice **11** for **660.00**

4. Enter Date: **01/30/2026**

5. Select Payment Method: **CREDIT DEBIT**

6. When the Enter Card Information window appears, select Payment: **Visa**

7. Enter Card Number: **19991999191999**

8. Enter Exp Date: **12/2026**

9. Select **Done**

10. To record the customer payment and close the Receive Payments window, click **Save & Close**

11. Since you are not using the Merchant Account Services, when the credit card payment is deposited at the bank on 01/30/2026, record the deposit just as you would a check or cash deposit. Click the **Record Deposits** icon in the Banking section of the Home Page > From the Payments to Deposit window, select **Snaps Café payment** for deposit > click **OK**.

12 From the Make Deposits window, select the **Save** icon

13 Select the **Journal** icon

14 Export to **Excel** or **print** the Deposit Journal report

15 **Close** the Journal report and the Make Deposits windows

If the specific credit card is not listed on the Payment Method List, **select Add New, then enter the name of the credit card.**

Banks will accept bank credit card payments, such as Visa or Mastercard, the same as a cash or check deposit. **You can record the credit card payment as a deposit to your checking account.**

Section 15.7
Bad Debts

When Skal paid the bill for $660 for Snaps Café, he tells you that his business has plummeted. To your dismay, he informs you his café is closing and he will not be able to pay you the remainder that he owes. You decide to write off the Snaps Café remaining account balance as uncollectible.

Paint Palette uses the direct write-off method and records the uncollectible accounts expense when an account actually becomes uncollectible. To accomplish this, first we will create an account for tracking uncollectible accounts expense and then write off the customer's uncollectible account receivable.

To add a Bad Debt Expense account to the Chart of Accounts for Paint Palette, complete the following steps:

1. Click the **Chart of Accounts** icon in the Company section of the Home Page

2. Add the following account to the Chart of Accounts:

Account Type	**Expense**
Account No.	**67000**
Account Name	**Bad Debt Expense**
Tax Line	**Schedule C: Bad debts from sales/services**

Next, record the write-off of the uncollectible account receivable. There are three different methods to record a bad debt using QuickBooks:

1. Make a journal entry to remove the customer's account receivable (credit Accounts Receivable) and debit either Bad Debt Expense (direct write-off method) or the Allowance for Uncollectible Accounts (allowance method).
2. Use the Credit Memo window to record uncollectible accounts.
3. Use the Receive Payments window (Discounts And Credits icon) to record the write-off of the customer's uncollectible account. Use this method if you charged sales tax on the transaction written off.

To record the write-off of an uncollectible account receivable using the Receive Payments window (method 3 above), first change the preference for automatically calculating payments as follows:

1 Select **Edit Menu**

2 Select **Preferences**

3 Select **Payments**

4 Select **Company Preferences**

5 Uncheck **Automatically calculate payments**

6 Select **OK** to close the Preferences window

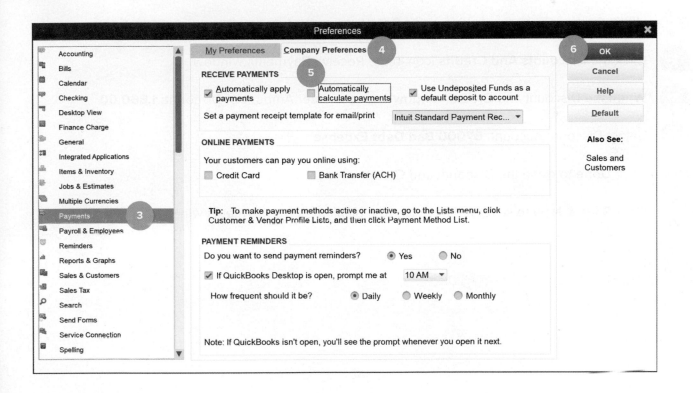

To record the write-off of an uncollectible account receivable using the Receive Payments window, complete the following steps:

1. Click the **Receive Payments** icon in the Customers section of the Home Page

2. When the Receive Payments window appears, select Received From: **Snaps Café**

3. Leave the Payment Amount as **$0.00**

4. Enter Date: **01/30/2026**

5. Enter Memo: **Write off Uncollectible Account**

6. Select the outstanding invoice dated: **01/12/2026**

7. Because the Amount field is $0.00, a warning may appear. Click **OK**.

8. Highlight the invoice by clicking on its **Date** field

9. Click the **Discounts And Credits** icon in the Receive Payments window

10. When the Discount and Credits window appears, enter Amount of Discount: **1,860.00**

11. Select Discount Account: **67000 Bad Debt Expense**

12. Click **Done** to close the Discount and Credits window

13. Click **Save & New** to save and advance to a blank Receive Payments window

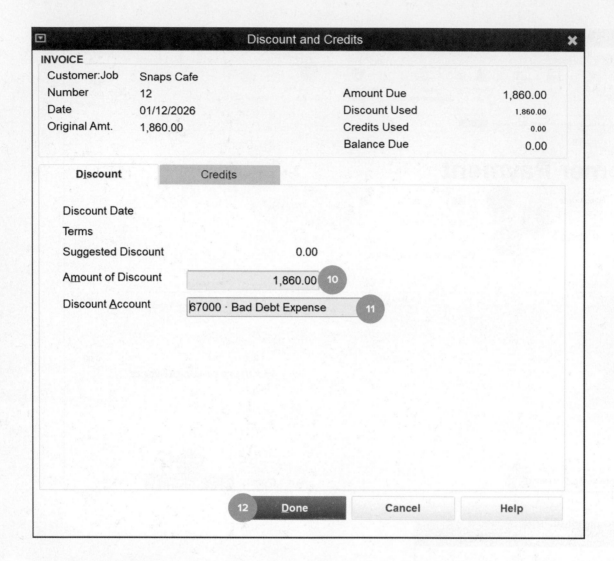

C15.7.1 Bad Debt Expense Journal Entry. To view the Journal entry that QuickBooks makes behind the screen when bad debt expense is recorded in this manner:

1. Select the **back Find arrow** until the Snaps Cafe Receive Payment of $0.00 appears on the screen

2. Select the **Reports** tab

3. Select **Transaction Journal**

4. Export to **Excel** or **print** the Transaction Journal report

5. **Close** the Transaction Journal report and the Receive Payments windows

The Accounts Receivable Aging Summary report (discussed in Chapter 5) provides information about the age of customers' accounts receivable which can be useful for tracking and managing collections.

To reduce uncollectible customer accounts, some companies adopt a policy that requires customers to make a deposit or advance payment before beginning work on a project. In addition, companies often evaluate the creditworthiness of customers before extending credit.

Section 15.8

Audit Trail

The Audit Trail feature of QuickBooks permits you to track all changes (additions, modifications, and deletions) made to your QuickBooks records. When used appropriately, the Audit Trail feature improves internal control by tracking any unauthorized changes to accounting records. The owner (or manager) should periodically review the Audit Trail for discrepancies or unauthorized changes. The Audit Trail report is especially useful if you have more than one user for QuickBooks. This report permits you to determine which user made which changes.

Access to the Audit Trail should be restricted to only the QuickBooks Administrator.

When you export the Audit Trail report to Excel, you can perform further analysis with the Auto Filter feature shown in the following example.

To illustrate how an accounting clerk, Ima M. Bezler, might attempt to embezzle funds, assume Ima pockets a customer's cash payment. If Ima just keeps the cash payment, the customer would receive another bill and possibly contact the company to complain, triggering an investigation into the customer's account activity. So Ima deletes any record of the customer's bill from QuickBooks.

Instead of deleting the bill, Ima might try to write off the customer's account as uncollectible in order to ensure the customer does not receive another bill.

To test the Audit Trail feature, first record a customer invoice to Angel Merriman Associates.

1 Select the **Create Invoices** icon

2 Select Template: **Service Date Invoice**

3 Select Invoice Date: **02/01/2026**

4   Select Customer Job: **Angel Merriman Associates Office Dome Ceiling**

5   Select Service Date: **02/01/2026**

6   Select Item: **Labor: Mural**

7   Select Quantity: **3 hours**

8   Select **Save & Close** to close invoice

On 02/02/2026, Angel Merriman Associates pay the bill in cash. If Ima decides to keep the cash and delete the invoice (so that Angel Merriman Associates would not receive another bill), the Audit Trail maintains a record of the deleted invoice.

To delete the invoice:

1   Display the Angel Merriman Associates invoice that you just created

2   Select **Edit Menu**

3   Select **Delete Invoice**

4   When asked if you are sure, select **OK**

The Audit Trail report will list the original transaction to record the invoice and the change to delete the customer's invoice.

To prepare the Audit Trail report:

1   From the Report Center, select **Accountant & Taxes**

2   Select **Audit Trail**

3   Select Dates: **All**

4   Select: **Run**

To create a filter to display **2026** transactions:

1 Select **Customize Report > Filters**

2 Remove Selected Filter: **Entered/Modified Today**

3 Choose Filter: **Date**

4 Select Date From: **01/01/2026 To: 12/31/2026**

5 Click **OK** to close the Modify Report window

C15.8.1. Audit Log. To export the Audit Trail to Excel with autofiltering:

1 Click the **Excel** button at the top of the Audit Trail window

2 Select: **Create New Worksheet**

3 Select **Replace an existing worksheet**

4 Select workbook: **YourLastName FirstName CH15 REPORTS.xls**

5 Select sheet: **C15.8.1 AUDIT**

6 Select the **Advanced** tab on the Send Report to Excel window

7 Uncheck: **Space between columns**

8 Check: **Auto Outline (allows collapsing/expanding)**

9 Check: **Auto Filtering (allows custom data filtering)**

10 Uncheck: **Include QuickBooks Export Guide worksheet with helpful advice**

11 Select Show report header: **On printed report and screen**

12 Select **OK** to close the Advanced Excel Options window

13 Select **Export**

14 **Highlight** the record of the deleted invoice dated 02/01/2026

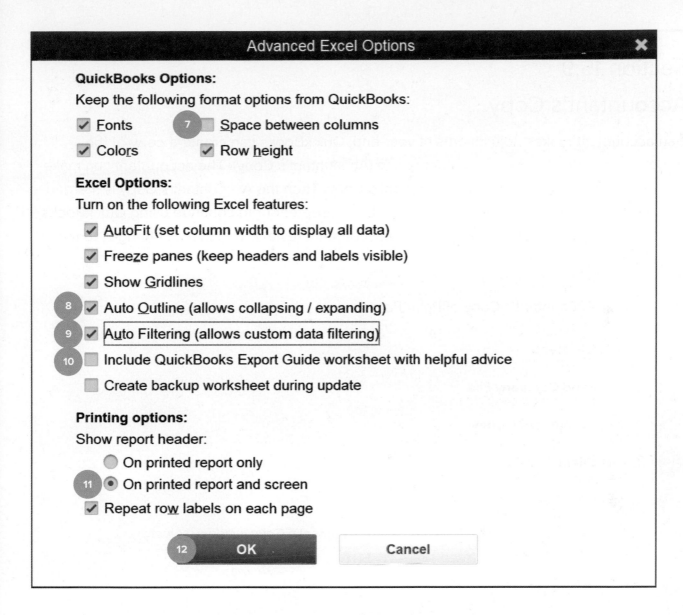

Notice in the Audit Trail report exported to Excel including the Auto Filter feature, each column heading becomes a drop-down list. This permits you to sort or select a filter of your choice from the drop-down lists. For example, you could use the Auto Filter to track all items recorded by a specific user (Last Modified by field).

To track deleted or changed items in the Audit Trail report, you can filter on the status of transactions to display Latest, Prior, or Deleted transactions (State field).

Note that the Audit Trail feature requires more storage for larger files because both original transactions and changed transactions are saved. So the Audit Trail feature may slow processing time.

Section 15.9

Accountant's Copy

If an accountant makes adjustments at year-end, QuickBooks can create a copy of the company data files for the accountant to use (Accountant's Copy). The accountant can make adjustments and changes to the Accountant's Copy. Then the Accountant's Copy is merged with the original company data. This permits the entrepreneur to continue using QuickBooks to record transactions at the same time the accountant reviews and makes changes to the records.

To create an Accountant's Copy of Paint Palette:

1. Select **File Menu**

2. Select **Send Company File**

3. Select **Accountant's Copy**

4. Select **Client Activities**

5. Select **Save File**

6. After reading the information on the Save Accountant's Copy window, select **Accountant's Copy**

7. Select **Next**

8. Select Dividing Date: **Custom 12/31/2026**

9. Normally you would select Next. In this case, select **Cancel**.

QuickBooks creates a copy of the QuickBooks company file for the accountant's temporary use. After the accountant has made necessary adjustments to the Accountant's Copy, the Accountant's Copy is then merged with the QuickBooks company data file, incorporating the accountant's changes into the company's records.

Section 15.10

Ask My Accountant

In the Chart of Accounts is an account entitled Ask My Accountant. Entrepreneurs using QuickBooks can use this account to record items when they are uncertain how to record specific items properly. The items can be recorded in this account and the accountant can review these items and record them properly before financial statements are prepared.

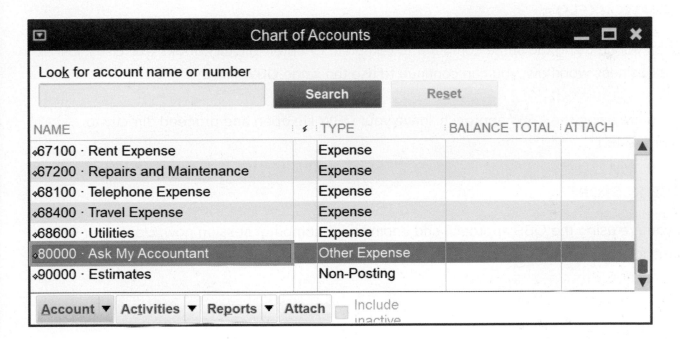

Section 15.11
Back Up QuickBooks Files

BACK UP QBB

Save a backup of your Chapter 15 file using the file name: **YourName Chapter 15 Backup.QBB**.

QBW WORKFLOW

If you will be using the same computer to complete Chapter 15 QuickBooks exercises, just as in a business workflow, you can continue to use the same QBW file.

If you are using the QBW approach, leave your QBW file open and proceed directly to Exercise 15.1.

QBB RESTORE

If you are using the QBB approach and ending your computer session now, close your QBW file and exit QuickBooks. When you restart, you will restore your backup file to complete Exercise 15.1.

Section 15.12

Accounting Essentials: Bad Debts

Accounting Essentials summarize important foundational accounting knowledge that may be useful when using QuickBooks

What happens if a customer does not pay an accounts receivable balance?

- When a customer does not pay the accounts receivable balance, then it is called a bad debt or uncollectible account.
- At the time a credit sale occurs, it is recorded as an increase to sales and an increase to accounts receivable.
- Occasionally a company is unable to collect a customer payment and must write off the customer's account as a bad debt or uncollectible account. When an account is uncollectible, the account receivable is written off or removed from the accounting records.

What are two methods used to account for bad debts?

- There are two different methods that can be used to account for bad debts:
    1. **Direct write-off method.** This method records bad debt expense when it becomes apparent that the customer is not going to pay the amount due. If the direct write-off method is used, the customer's uncollectible account receivable is removed and bad debt expense is recorded at the time a specific customer's account becomes uncollectible. The direct write-off method is used for tax purposes.
    2. **Allowance method.** The allowance method estimates bad debt expense and establishes an allowance or reserve for uncollectible accounts. When using the allowance method, uncollectible accounts expense is estimated in advance of the write-off. The estimate can be calculated as a percentage of sales or as a percentage of accounts receivable. (For example, 2% of credit sales might be estimated to be uncollectible.) This method should be used if uncollectible accounts have a material effect on the company's financial statements used by investors and creditors.

Exercise 15.1 QuickBooks Apps

The Intuit App Center features apps that work with QuickBooks, including apps that permit you to access your QuickBooks company data on your mobile phone.

1.   From the Help Menu, select **App Center: Find More Business Solutions**

2.   From the Apps for QuickBooks Desktop Marketplace window, select your favorite app.

3.   Summarize for your accounting clients why you consider your choice a worthwhile app for QuickBooks.

Exercise 15.2 Accountant Center

A QuickBooks feature designed for accounting professionals is the Accountant Center. To learn more about this feature:

1.   To open the Accountant Center, from Accountant Menu, select **Accountant Center**.

2.   From the Tools section of the Accountant Center window, select two Accountant tools and write a short email to send to your accounting firm staff summarizing information about how these tools can be used.

PROJECT 15.1

 Martin Consulting

Project 15.1 is a continuation of Project 11.1.

BACKSTORY

Martin Consulting provides consulting and design services to companies using social media marketing. The firm advises companies regarding how to use internet marketing and social media tools, such as Facebook® and Instagram®, to market and promote their companies, products, and brands.

 QuickBooks SatNav

The focus of Project 15.1 is mastery of QuickBooks Desktop budgets, a type of report.

🌐 QBO SatNav

⚙️ QBO Settings

⚙️ Company Settings
⚙️ Chart of Accounts

💰 QBO Transactions

💰 Banking
💰 Customers & Sales
💰 Vendors & Expenses
💰 Employees & Payroll

📊 QBO Reports

📊 Reports

P15.1.1 Open Company and Update Company Name

1. To start Project 15.1, either:
    * Open your Project 11.1 QuickBooks Company file (YourName Project 11.1.QBW) or
    * Restore your Project 11.1 Backup file (YourName Project 11.1 Backup.QBB)
    If you have issues with your QuickBooks file, contact your instructor for assistance.

2. Update the QuickBooks Company name to **YourName Project 15.1 Martin Consulting**.

P15.1.2 Create a Profit and Loss Budget

Create a Profit and Loss Budget for Martin Consulting for the year 2026.

1. Enter the following budget items and amounts for 2026.

Account No.	**47900**
Account	**Sales**
January 2026 Budget Amount	**$15,000**

Account No.	**64900**
Account	**Office Supplies (Expense)**
Monthly 2026 Budget Amount	**$200**

Account No.	**67100**
Account	**Rent Expense**
Monthly 2026 Budget Amount	**$1000**

2. With Account No 47900 Sales row selected, click **Adjust Row Amounts** > select **Currently selected month** > **2%** monthly increase > **Enable compounding**.

3. Export to **Excel** the Profit and Loss Budget Overview report for 2026

P15.1.3 Back Up Project 15.1

Save a backup of your Project file using the file name: **YourName Project 15.1 Backup.QBB**.

See Appendix B: Back Up and Restore QuickBooks Files for instructions.

PROJECT 15.2

 ## YourName Botanicals

BACKSTORY

Botanicals is your retail and online store specializing in unique orchid designs for special occasions. Your botanical designs, in addition to orchids, use a variety of relatively low cost supplies. So it's not practical to track inventory of the numerous small supply items on an individual basis. However, to ensure you have an adequate markup, you plan to track inventory of the higher cost orchids. Then you plan to charge a design service fee that covers your time and the cost of supplies used. You will record supplies purchased and then count supplies on hand at the end of the accounting period to determine the amount of supplies used for the month. This approach offers design flexibility and also permits tracking of the orchid inventory.

You offer the following orchid design services:
- Wedding
- Anniversary
- Birthday
- Special Event
- Commercial Design

Angel Merriman Associates, a cybersecurity firm, has agreed to use the Commercial Orchid Design for their offices. Tracey Kari Interiors is planning to use your orchid designs, not only in his offices, but also as gifts for his clients to celebrate completion of their interior design projects. Ella Brewer, owner of Ella's Knittery, is planning to use your orchid designs to decorate her knitting boutique.

Instead of purchasing a brick and mortar store, you are leasing a small studio from Joseph Asher where you can create and display your orchid designs and meet with customers as needed. Martin Consulting is providing social media marketing services to launch and promote your business. You are using QuickBooks Desktop for your financial system.

🌐 QuickBooks SatNav

Project 15.2 is a comprehensive project that facilitates your mastery of QuickBooks Desktop. As shown in the following QuickBooks SatNav, Project 15.2 covers all three processes: QuickBooks Settings, QuickBooks Transactions, and QuickBooks Reports. This project provides you with the opportunity to integrate your knowledge of QuickBooks Desktop through all three phases of QuickBooks SatNav.

 QuickBooks SatNav

QuickBooks Settings

Company Settings

Chart of Accounts

 QuickBooks Transactions

Banking

Customers & Sales

Vendors & Expenses

Employees & Payroll

QuickBooks Reports

Reports

P15.2.1 New Company Setup

Create a new company in QuickBooks using the following information.

1. Use the EasyStep Interview to set up a new QuickBooks company.

Company name	**YourName Project 15.2 Botanicals**
Federal tax ID	**12-1234567**
Address	**222 Market Street**
City	**Bayshore**
State	**CA**
Zip	**94326**
Main Phone	**415-258-1356**
Email	**<Enter your email address>**
Industry	**Retail Shop or Online Commerce**
Type of organization	**S Corporation**
First month of fiscal year	**January**
File name	**YourName Project 15.2**
What do you sell?	**Both products and services**
How will you enter sales?	**Record each sale individually**
Sales tax	**Yes**
Estimates	**Yes**
Sales orders	**No**
Billing statements	**No**
Progress invoicing	**Yes**
Track bills you owe	**Yes**
Track inventory in QuickBooks	**Yes**
Track time	**Yes**
Employees	**No**
Start date	**01/01/2026**

Use recommended accounts	**Yes**
Bank account name	**Checking**
Bank account number	**8945612307**
Bank account balance	**0.00 as of 01/01/2026**

2. Click **Start Working** to exit QuickBooks Setup

3. Set preferences as follows:

   - Accounting preferences to **Use account numbers** in the Chart of Accounts

   - Accounting preferences to **uncheck Warn if transactions are 30 day(s) in the future**

   - Checking preferences to Open the Make Deposits form with **Checking** account

P15.2.2 Add Customer & Job

1. Add the following customers to the Customer List.

Customer	**Angel Merriman Associates**
Address Info:	
Company Name	**Angel Merriman Associates**
First Name	**Angel**
Last Name	**Merriman**
Main Phone	**415-555-7579**
Address	**623 Thorsmork Road** **Bayshore, CA 94326**
Payment Settings:	
Account No	**10001**
Payment Terms	**Net 30**
Sales Tax Settings:	
Tax Code	**Tax**
Tax Item	**State Tax**

Customer	**Tracey Kari Interiors**
Address Info:	
Company Name	**Tracey Kari Interiors**
First Name	**Tracey**
Last Name	**Kari**
Main Phone	**415-555-9999**
Address	**99 Reyka Drive** **Bayshore, CA 94326**
Payment Settings:	
Account No	**10002**
Payment Terms	**Net 30**
Sales Tax Settings:	
Tax Code	**Tax**
Tax Item	**State Tax**

Customer	**Ella's Knittery**
Address Info:	
Company Name	**Ella's Knittery**
First Name	**Ella**
Last Name	**Brewer**
Main Phone	**415-555-3636**
Address	**36 Spring Street** **Bayshore, CA 94326**
Payment Settings:	
Account No	**10003**
Payment Terms	**Net 30**
Sales Tax Settings:	
Tax Code	**Tax**
Tax Item	**State Tax**

2. From the Customer Center, export to **Excel** the Customer List.

    ⚠ When exporting to Excel, remember to select Advanced Excel Options:
    - Uncheck **Space between columns**
    - Check **Row height**
    - Uncheck **Include QuickBooks Export Guide worksheet with helpful advice**
    - Select **On printed report and screen**

P15.2.3 Add Vendors

1. Add the following vendors to the Vendor List.

Vendor	**Joseph Leasing**
Opening Balance	**$0.00 as of 01/01/2026**
Address Info:	
Company Name	**Joseph Leasing**
Full Name	**Joseph Asher**
Main Phone	**415-555-0412**
Address	**13 Appleton Drive** **Bayshore, CA 94326**
Payment Settings:	
Account No.	**2700**
Payment Terms	**Net 30**
Tax Settings:	
Vendor Tax ID	**37-1726354**
Additional Info:	
Vendor Type <Add New>	**Leasing**
Vendor	**Martin Consulting**
Opening Balance	**$0.00 as of 01/01/2026**
Address Info:	
Company Name	**Martin Consulting**
First Name	**Martin**
Main Phone	**415-555-2022**

Address	**333 Blue Avenue**
	Bayshore, CA 94326
Payment Settings:	
Account No.	**3300**
Payment Terms	**Net 30**
Tax Settings:	
Vendor Tax ID	**123-45-6789**
Additional Info:	
Vendor Type <Add New>	**Consultant**
Vendor	**Orchid Express**
Opening Balance	**$0.00 as of 01/01/2026**
Address Info:	
Company Name	**Orchid Express**
First Name	**Kai**
Main Phone	**415-555-4567**
Address	**63 Jardin Lane**
	Bayshore, CA 94326
Payment Settings:	
Account No.	**6300**
Payment Terms	**Net 30**
Tax Settings:	
Vendor Tax ID	**37-3571667**
Additional Info:	
Vendor Type	**Suppliers**
Vendor	**Blooming Design**
Opening Balance	**$0.00 as of 01/01/2026**
Address Info:	
Company Name	**Blooming Design**

Contact	**Bloom**
Main Phone	**415-555-8900**
Address	**678 Summers Avenue** **Bayshore, CA 94326**
Payment Settings:	
Account No.	**8100**
Payment Terms	**Net 30**
Tax Settings:	
Vendor Tax ID	**37-3527667**
Additional Info:	
Vendor Type	**Suppliers**

2. From the Vendor Center, export to **Excel** the Vendor List

P15.2.4 Add Items

1. Add the following items.

Item Type	**Inventory Part**
Item Name	**Orchid Small**
Description	**Orchid Small**
Income Account	**46000 – Merchandise Sales**
Item Type	**Inventory Part**
Item Name	**Orchid Small Yellow**
Description	**Orchid Small Yellow**
Cost	**10.00**
COGS Account	**50000 – Cost of Goods Sold**
Preferred Vendor	**Orchid Express**
Sales Price	**60.00**
Tax	**Tax**

Income Account	46000 – Merchandise Sales
Asset Account	12100 – Inventory Asset
Qty on Hand	0 as of 01/01/2026

Item Type	Inventory Part
Item Name	Orchid Small Purple
Description	Orchid Small Purple
Cost	10.00
COGS Account	50000 – Cost of Goods Sold
Preferred Vendor	Orchid Express
Sales Price	75.00
Tax	Tax
Income Account	46000 – Merchandise Sales
Asset Account	12100 – Inventory Asset
Qty on Hand	0 as of 01/01/2026

Item Type	Inventory Part
Item Name	Orchid Large
Description	Orchid Large
Income Account	46000 – Merchandise Sales

Item Type	Inventory Part
Item Name	Orchid Large Yellow
Description	Orchid Large Yellow
Cost	20.00
COGS Account	50000 – Cost of Goods Sold
Preferred Vendor	Orchid Express
Sales Price	100.00
Tax	Tax

Income Account	**46000 – Merchandise Sales**
Asset Account	**12100 – Inventory Asset**
Qty on Hand	**0 as of 01/01/2026**

Item Type	**Inventory Part**
Item Name	**Orchid Large Purple**
Description	**Orchid Large Purple**
Cost	**20.00**
COGS Account	**50000 – Cost of Goods Sold**
Preferred Vendor	**Orchid Express**
Sales Price	**110.00**
Tax	**Tax**
Income Account	**46000 – Merchandise Sales**
Asset Account	**12100 – Inventory Asset**
Qty on Hand	**0 as of 01/01/2026**

Item Type	**Service**
Item Name	**Wedding Orchid Design**
Description	**Wedding Orchid Design**
Rate	**200.00**
Tax Code	**Tax**
Income Account <Add new>	**48000 – Service Sales**

Item Type	**Service**
Item Name	**Anniversary Orchid Design**
Description	**Anniversary Orchid Design**
Rate	**100.00**
Income Account	**48000 – Service Sales**

Item Type	**Service**
Item Name	**Birthday Orchid Design**
Description	**Birthday Orchid Design**
Rate	**90.00**
Income Account	**48000 – Service Sales**

Item Type	**Service**
Item Name	**Special Event Orchid Design**
Description	**Special Event Orchid Design**
Rate	**100.00**
Income Account	**48000 – Service Sales**

Item Type	**Service**
Item Name	**Commercial Orchid Design**
Description	**Commercial Orchid Design**
Rate	**150.00**
Income Account	**48000 – Service Sales**

2. From the Item List, enter the 9.0% sales tax rate as follows:
   - **Double-click** on **State Tax** in the Item List
   - Enter Tax Rate: **9.0%**
   - Enter Tax Agency: **California State Board of Equalization**
   - Click **OK**

3. Export to **Excel** or **print** the Item List as of January 1, 2026. (Use Report Center > List > Item Listing.)

   ⚠ When exporting to Excel, remember to select Advanced Excel Options:
   - Uncheck **Space between columns**
   - Check **Row height**
   - Uncheck **Include QuickBooks Export Guide worksheet with helpful advice**
   - Select **On printed report and screen**

P15.2.5 Customize Chart of Accounts

Edit the Chart of Accounts and enter opening balances as follows.

1. Add the following information to the Chart of Accounts with the opening balances as of 01/01/2026.

Account	**Checking**
Account No.	**10100**
Opening Balance	**$0.00**

Account	**Design Supplies on Hand**
Account No.	**11100**
Opening Balance	**$0.00**
Account Type	**Other Current Asset**
Account Description	**Design Supplies on Hand**
Tax Line	**B/S-Assets: Other current assets**

Account	**Design Supplies Expense**
Account No.	**61300**
Opening Balance	**$0.00**
Account Type	**Expense**
Account Description	**Design Supplies Expense**
Tax Line	**Other Deductions: Supplies**

Account	**Studio Furniture & Equipment**
Account No.	**14400**
Opening Balance	**$0.00**
Account Type	**Fixed Asset**
Account Description	**Studio Furniture & Equipment**
Tax Line	**B/S-Assets: Buildings/oth. depr. Assets**

Account	**Studio Furniture & Equipment Cost**
Account No.	**14500**
Opening Balance	**$6,000**
Account Type	**Fixed Asset**
Subaccount of	**Studio Furniture & Equipment**

Account Description	**Studio Furniture & Equipment Cost**
Tax Line	**B/S-Assets: Buildings/oth. depr. Assets**
Account	**Studio Furniture&Equip Acc Depr**
Account No.	**14600**
Opening Balance	**$0.00**
Account Type	**Fixed Asset**
Subaccount of	**Studio Furniture & Equipment**
Account Description	**Studio Furniture & Equipment Accumulated Depreciation**
Tax Line	**B/S-Assets: Buildings/oth. depr Assets**

2. From the Report Center, export to **Excel** the Chart of Accounts (Account Listing) report as of January 1, 2026

3. **Export** to Excel or **print** a Trial Balance report dated 01/01/2026. Verify your Trial Balance account balances are correct.

4. Transfer the Opening Balance Equity account balance to the Capital Stock account using a journal entry. Use Entry No.: **Open ADJ1**. Select **Save**. Export the opening balance adjusting entry to **Excel** by selecting the **Reports tab > Transaction Journal**.

5. Export to **Excel** or **print** the Adjusted Trial Balance (after opening adjustments) to verify that the Opening Balance Equity account balance was transferred to the Capital Stock account.

P15.2.6 Enter Transactions

YourName Botanicals entered into the following transactions during January 2026.

1. Record the following transactions.
    - Record all deposits to: **10100 Checking**.
    - If necessary, change the Make Deposits default to **10100 Checking**. (Select Edit Menu > Preferences > Checking > My Preferences > Open the Make Deposits form with 10100 Checking account).
    - For invoiced items, including Orchids and Design Fees, use **Taxable > State Tax**. (Note that some states tax only products, while other states may tax products and services. In this specific case, the Design Fees are simply part of the price of the arrangement sold and considered taxable.)

Date	Transaction
01/01/2026	You invest $8,000 (Check No. 101) in Capital Stock of the business

01/01/2026	Botanicals takes out a bank loan from City Bank for $10,000, to be repaid within 1 year. (Use Make Deposits window. Add new Account No. 26100 Note Payable.)
01/01/2026	Received the bill and paid one month's studio rental ($400) to Joseph Leasing. (Use Enter Bills and Pay Bills windows.)
01/01/2026	Purchased $500 of design supplies from Blooming Design on account. (Since you are not tracking inventory of design supplies, record Design Supplies Expense using the Enter Bills window instead of the Purchase Order and Receive Inventory windows.)
01/02/2026	Ordered 24 large orchids from Orchid Express in the following shades: • 12 purple small orchids • 12 yellow small orchids
01/04/2026	Received order in full from Orchid Express for small orchids
01/05/2026	Sold Ella's Knittery 3 Commercial Orchid Design arrangements on account. Prepare an invoice with the following items: • 3 Commercial Orchid Design Fee • 6 Orchids Small Yellow • 6 Orchids Small Purple
01/06/2026	Received payment by e-check from Ella's Knittery for 01/05/2026 invoice and deposited the funds
01/07/2026	Ordered 12 dozen (144) large orchids from Orchid Express in the following shades: • 72 purple large orchids • 72 yellow large orchids
01/07/2026	Provided an estimate of 20 Wedding Orchid Design arrangements for Ella Brewer with the following items. Add New Customer: Ella Brewer. Add New Job: Wedding. Job Status: Pending. Tax: State Tax. Terms: 50% due at time of awarding job and 50% due upon completion. • 20 Wedding Orchid Design Fee • 30 Orchids Large Yellow • 30 Orchids Large Purple
01/07/2026	Paid Blooming Design for design supplies
01/08/2026	Received order in full from Orchid Express for large orchids
01/09/2026	Received bill from Orchid Express for small orchids
01/11/2026	Sold 6 Commercial Orchid Design arrangements to Tracey Kari Interiors on account. Prepare an invoice with the following items: • 6 Commercial Orchid Design Fee • 6 Orchids Large Yellow
01/11/2026	Awarded wedding job from Ella Brewer. Update Job Status to: Awarded.

01/11/2026	Sold 22 Commercial Orchid Designs to Angel Merriman Associates on account. Prepare an invoice with the following items: • 22 Commercial Orchid Design Fee • 66 Orchids Large Yellow • 66 Orchids Large Purple
01/12/2026	Received bill from Orchid Express for large orchids
01/12/2026	Sent Ella Brewer progress invoice for 50% of the Wedding job. Select OK if warnings appear regarding Orchid Inventory.
01/12/2026	Set a reminder to order orchids for Ella Brewer wedding. Select Company menu > To Do List > To Do arrow > New To Do > select Type: Task > Priority: high > With Vendor: Orchid Express > Due 01/13/2026 > Time: 8:00 AM > Details: Order Orchids for Ella Brewer Wedding > Status: Active > OK.
01/12/2026	Paid the following bills: • Paid Orchid Express for orchids ordered on 01/03/2026 • Paid Orchid Express for orchids ordered on 01/07/2026
01/13/2026	Ordered large orchids for Ella Brewer Wedding job from Orchid Express in the following shades: • 30 purple large orchids • 30 yellow large orchids
01/14/2026	Received e-check payment from Ella Brewer and deposited funds
01/15/2026	Sold 3 Special Event Orchid Design arrangements to Tracey Kari Interiors on account. Prepare an invoice with the following items: • 3 Special Event Orchid Design Fee • 3 Orchids Small Purple • 3 Orchids Small Yellow
01/15/2026	Received e-check payment from Tracey Kari Interiors for full amount of Commercial Orchid Designs and deposited the funds
01/16/2026	Received order in full from Orchid Express for large orchids
01/19/2026	Received bill from Orchid Express for large orchids
01/22/2026	Sent Ella Brewer invoice for completing the Wedding job
01/22/2026	Received e-check payment from Ella Brewer for completing Wedding job and deposited funds
01/30/2026	Sold 2 Special Event Orchid Design arrangements to Tracey Kari Interiors on account. Prepare an invoice with the following items: • 2 Special Event Orchid Design Fee • 2 Orchids Small Purple • 2 Orchids Small Yellow

01/30/2026	Received bill for $330 from Martin Consulting for social media marketing services provided for the month of January for promotion of Botanicals on Facebook and Instagram. Use Enter Bills window to record in Account No 66700 Professional Fees (Expense).
01/30/2026	When Martin of Martin Consulting dropped off his bill for the month, you sold him 1 Birthday Orchid Design arrangement, and he personally selected the orchids he would like in the arrangement. Add new customer: Martin. Tax: State Sales Tax. Prepare an invoice with the following items: • 1 Birthday Orchid Design Fee • 2 Orchids Large Purple
01/30/2026	Received payment by e-check from Tracey Kari Interiors for 01/15/2026 invoice and deposited the funds
01/31/2026	Record Martin's e-check payment for Birthday Orchid Design and deposited funds

2. Export to **Excel** the Deposit Detail report for January 2026

3. Export to **Excel** the Check Detail report for January 2026

4. Export to **Excel** the Transaction Detail by Account report for January 2026. (From the Report Center, select Accountant & Taxes > Transaction Detail by Account.)

P15.2.7 Adjusting Entries

1. Export to **Excel** the Trial Balance report at January 31, 2026

2. Make adjusting entries at January 31, 2026, using the following Information.

   ADJ1: Studio Furniture & Equipment depreciation expense is $100 per month ($6,000 cost / 60 months = $100 per month). Use Account No 62400 Depreciation Expense and Account No 14600 Studio Furniture & Equipment Accumulated Depreciation.

   ADJ2: Design Supplies on hand at the end of January 2026 totaled $150

3. From the Report Center, export to **Excel** the Adjusting Journal Entries for January 31, 2026

4. Export to **Excel** the Adjusted Trial Balance report at January 31, 2026. **Highlight** the amounts affected by the January 31, 2026 adjusting entries.

P15.2.8 Financial Reports

Create the following reports.

1. Export to **Excel** the Journal for the month of January 2026

2. Export to **Excel** the Profit & Loss, Standard for the month of January 2026

3. Export to **Excel** the Balance Sheet, Standard at January 31, 2026

4. Export to **Excel** the Statement of Cash Flows for the month of January 2026. Highlight the following amounts on the Statement of Cash Flows:
   - Net cash provided by Operating Activities
   - Net cash provided by Investing Activities
   - Net cash provided by Financing Activities
   - Net cash increase for period

5. Export to **Excel** the Customer Balance Detail report for January 1 - 31, 2026

6. Export to **Excel** the Vendor Balance Detail report for January 1 - 31, 2026

7. Create and export to **Excel** a Profit and Loss Budget (Budget Overview report) for 2026 based on the following information.
   - January projected Merchandise Sales: $22,000. Monthly expected increase: 5% (compounding).
   - January projected Service Sales: $9,200. Monthly expected increase 5% (compounding).
   - Monthly Design Supplies Expense for 2026: $350
   - Monthly Rent Expense for 2026: $400

P15.2.9 Back Up Project 15.2

Save a backup of your Project file using the file name: **YourName Project 15.2 Backup.QBB**.

See Appendix B: Back Up and Restore QuickBooks Files for instructions.

Design elements: Dog icon: ©josep perianes jorba/Shutterstock; paint roller icon: ©Netti Buletti/Shutterstock; other icons/symbols: ©Carboxylase/Shutterstock

Chapter 16

QuickBooks Desktop Versus QuickBooks Online

Your QuickBooks consulting business continues to grow as satisfied clients refer new clients. While most of your clients need the added functionality and features of QuickBooks Desktop software, a few clients have asked you about anytime, anywhere QuickBooks Online. Your challenge is to find the best fit to meet your clients' needs while at the same time keeping your consulting service operations streamlined and efficient. To make informed recommendations to your clients, you realize you need to learn more about the various QuickBooks options offered by Intuit.

Chapter 16

Learning Objectives

Chapter 16 compares and contrasts QuickBooks Desktop with QuickBooks Online. In this chapter, you will learn about the following topics:

- Ask My Accountant: Which QuickBooks Should I Use?
- How Can Our Accounting Firm Streamline Our QuickBooks Consulting?
- What Are My QuickBooks User Options?
  - QuickBooks Desktop: Pro, Premier, or Enterprise
  - QuickBooks Online
- What Are My QuickBooks Accountant Options?
  - QuickBooks Desktop Accountant
  - QuickBooks Online Accountant

Section 16.1

Ask My Accountant: Which QuickBooks Should I Use?

To meet different QuickBooks users' needs, Intuit offers several different versions of QuickBooks. If you are an accountant advising different clients on the best fit between their needs and QuickBooks version, then a general knowledge of the different types of QuickBooks available becomes vital to provide sound client advice.

In general, QuickBooks versions can be divided into two broad categories:

- **QuickBooks User.** Businesses and organizations that use QuickBooks to maintain their accounting and financial records.

- **QuickBooks Accountant.** Accountants who provide accounting and financial services to multiple clients who use QuickBooks.

Since QuickBooks offers several different options (summarized in the following table), QuickBooks users often turn to their accountants for recommendations about which QuickBooks to use. The QuickBooks version that the client uses dictates which QuickBooks version the client's accountant must use. As the accountant making recommendations, you will need to consider not only how the recommendation affects your client, but also how the recommendation will impact your client services operations.

QuickBooks Versions	QuickBooks Desktop (QBDT)	QuickBooks Online (QBO)
Client/User	QuickBooks Pro QuickBooks Premier QuickBooks Enterprise	QuickBooks Online
Accounting Firm	QuickBooks Desktop Accountant	QuickBooks Online Accountant

When making client recommendations, keep in mind the difference between client needs and wants. Needs are critical; wants are wishes. Stay focused on needs first, so you do not become distracted and sidetracked with client wants, which can keep you from meeting client needs. An easy way to do this is to make two lists with needs on one list and wants on another list. After needs are addressed, then wants can be considered. Prepare your client to face tradeoffs, such as tighter control over data security versus anytime, anywhere access. Your role is to summarize the features and tradeoffs, assisting clients with finding a good fit, even if they do not attain 100% of what they thought they wanted.

Section 16.2

How Can Our Accounting Firm Streamline Our QuickBooks Consulting?

Which QuickBooks version your clients use affects your consulting services operations. Some accounting firms relate war stories about clients using an array of QuickBooks Desktop software of various editions of QuickBooks. This approach to QuickBooks consulting requires the accounting firm to maintain all the various versions of the client software and track which clients use which versions. This can become a logistical nightmare for an accounting firm since it must have not only all the QuickBooks editions operational but also staff trained on the multiple versions.

Other accounting firms take a more streamlined, proactive approach when working with multiple clients that use QuickBooks. These firms recommend to clients which QuickBooks edition to use based on the best fit for the client while still keeping it manageable for the firm. Some accountants move all their clients to the next edition of QuickBooks at the same time. For example, after the 2021 QuickBooks edition is released in fall of 2020 and the accounting firm has thoroughly tested the new edition, the firm moves all clients to QuickBooks 2021 on January 1, 2021. This approach permits the accounting firm to test the new software for possible issues, install updates, and create workarounds before moving clients to the new edition. Since many clients are on a calendar year starting January 1, this timeline permits a nice cutoff. Also, this approach streamlines firm operations since now all clients and the firm are in sync, using the same version of QuickBooks.

This proactive approach requires the accounting firm to communicate clearly with clients, working as a team with clients to prepare and transition them to the new version. Firms that use this proactive approach often state that it requires time and effort to do so, but much less time than trying to maintain multiple versions of QuickBooks for multiple clients. If clients start moving to the new edition as soon as it is released, clients may encounter unexpected issues that the accounting firm has not had time to thoroughly investigate and resolve. Some firms even provide training for clients as they transition them to the new version, summarizing differences and new features to proactively prepare clients for what to expect. This can minimize client errors in working with the new version and save the firm from unexpected disruptions and surprises.

Although features and functionality of QuickBooks options can be expected to change over time, the following sections summarize information about some of the QuickBooks options for clients and accountants. For additional updates about each of these options, see www.Intuit.com.

Section 16.3

What Are My QuickBooks User Options?

A QuickBooks user is a business, entrepreneur, or not-for-profit organization that uses QuickBooks to maintain accounting and financial records for that entity. A QuickBooks user has two basic options:

- QuickBooks Desktop

- QuickBooks Online

QuickBooks is designed for business use, not personal finance. For personal financial records of the business owners, personal financial apps should be used, such as Quicken (Intuit's predecessor to QuickBooks) or Mint (now owned by Intuit).

If the QuickBooks user selects the QuickBooks Desktop option, then there are several additional choices to consider that are summarized next.

QUICKBOOKS DESKTOP: PRO, PREMIER, OR ENTERPRISE

QuickBooks Desktop software can be installed on the hard drive of desktop computers, laptops, or servers controlled by the user (client). If QuickBooks is installed on a network, it can be accessed by multiple QuickBooks users. QuickBooks Desktop software can be purchased using different approaches:

1. **Software download.** Since new desktop computers and laptops increasingly do not have CD drives, users can purchase a QuickBooks software key code and download the QuickBooks software using an Internet browser.

2. **Subscription.** Instead of purchasing QuickBooks software, the user can choose to pay a monthly subscription fee to use the software. The QuickBooks software is still downloaded to the desktop computer or laptop, but when the user decides to stop paying the monthly fee, the user's access to the QuickBooks software is blocked.

In general, QuickBooks Desktop offers several advantages over QuickBooks Online including:

- Additional features and functionality not offered by QuickBooks Online

- User control over desktop computer access and security

- User control over backups and access to backup data files

- Portability of backup and portable QuickBooks files

- Remote access to QuickBooks Desktop

- Navigation features to streamline use, such as the My Shortcuts Icon Bar and the Home Page with flowcharts

- Intuit offers the following different editions of the QuickBooks Desktop software to meet specific user needs, including:

  - QuickBooks Pro
  - QuickBooks Premier
  - QuickBooks Enterprise

QuickBooks Pro is a good option for small businesses that do not require industry-specific features because it is less expensive.

QuickBooks Premier offers more advanced features than QuickBooks Pro and permits you to customize QuickBooks by selecting a version with industry-specific features. QuickBooks Premier has different industry versions from which you can choose including the following.

- Contractor
- Manufacturing and Wholesale
- Nonprofit
- Professional Services
- Retailers
- General Business

QuickBooks Enterprise Solutions is designed for mid-size companies that have outgrown QuickBooks Premier. QuickBooks Enterprise can be used to track inventory at multiple locations and consolidate reports from multiple companies.

QUICKBOOKS ONLINE

Accessed using a browser and the Internet, QuickBooks Online typically has fewer features and functionality than the QuickBooks Desktop version. With QuickBooks Online, there is no software to install on your computer hard drive or local server. The main advantage to QuickBooks Online is its anytime, anywhere use, so long as Internet access is available. Factors to consider when using QuickBooks Online include:

- Internet connection needs to be a secure connection with data in transit encrypted. Using an open WiFi at a café or a hotel when traveling to access QuickBooks Online, while convenient, places data in transit at risk. Your login, password, and confidential financial data could be viewed by others.

- Fewer features and functionality than QuickBooks Desktop with features that will continue to change as QuickBooks Online is dynamically updated.

- The convenience of dynamic updates that occur automatically without needing to download and install.

- Loss of control over when updates occur, which may result in the need to learn new updates at unplanned times.

- Convenience of not needing to remember to make backup files.

- Loss of control over backup files.

QuickBooks Online Mobile App permits you to access your QuickBooks Online financial records from your iPad®, iPhone® or Android™ device.

Section 16.4

What Are My QuickBooks Accountant Options?

Designed for accountants serving multiple clients, Intuit offers two QuickBooks Accountant options:

- QuickBooks Desktop Accountant

- QuickBooks Online Accountant

Which option the accountant chooses is typically dictated by client use because QuickBooks Desktop files are not compatible with QuickBooks Online. For example, if all the accounting firm's clients use QuickBooks Desktop software, then the accounting firm would use QuickBooks Accountant Desktop version. If the clients use QuickBooks Online, then the accountant would need to use QuickBooks Online Accountant. Some accounting firms have clients using QuickBooks Desktop versions and other clients using QuickBooks Online, so those accounting firms must use both QuickBooks Accountant Desktop and QuickBooks Online Accountant to be able to work with both types of clients.

QUICKBOOKS DESKTOP ACCOUNTANT

QuickBooks Desktop Accountant is the software provided free with this text if purchased new. Like QuickBooks Desktop software, QuickBooks Accountant in the Desktop edition is installed on the hard drive of desktop computers, laptops, or network servers. The QuickBooks Accountant edition permits the accountant to toggle between different Desktop user editions of QuickBooks. This permits the accountant to view whatever edition of QuickBooks (QuickBooks Pro, QuickBooks Premier, and so on) that a particular client uses. For additional features of QuickBooks Accountant in the Desktop edition, see Chapter 15.

QUICKBOOKS ONLINE ACCOUNTANT

QuickBooks Online Accountant is designed for accounting firms that provide services to multiple clients who use QuickBooks Online. QuickBooks Online Accountant is accessed using the Internet and a browser and permits the accountant to collaborate with several different clients, viewing their QuickBooks Online companies. QuickBooks Online Accountant, at this time, does not use the Home Page navigational feature. In addition, there are fewer features and functionality with the QuickBooks Online Accountant version than the QuickBooks Accountant Desktop version. The main advantage to QuickBooks Online Accountant is the anytime, anywhere access when an Internet connection is available. Of course, since the accountant is responsible for maintaining the confidentiality of client financial data, the Internet connection needs to be a secure connection with data in transit encrypted. Using an open WiFi connection risks data in transit (such as your login, password, and confidential client financial data) being viewed by others. Since accounting firms have a responsibility to maintain client data confidentiality and security, this is a serious concern.

For more information about QuickBooks Online, visit www.My-QuickBooks.com, select My QBO Link.

Exercise 16.1 QuickBooks Online Versus QuickBooks Desktop

Compare and contrast QuickBooks Online and QuickBooks Desktop.

1. What are the advantages of QuickBooks Online versus QuickBooks Desktop for the user?

2. What are the disadvantages of QuickBooks Online versus QuickBooks Desktop?

Exercise 16.2 QuickBooks Online Accountant Versus QuickBooks Desktop Accountant

Compare and contrast QuickBooks Online Accountant and QuickBooks Desktop Accountant.

1. What are the advantages of QuickBooks Online Accountant versus QuickBooks Desktop Accountant?

2. What are the disadvantages of QuickBooks Online Accountant versus QuickBooks Desktop?

Exercise 16.3 QuickBooks Client

If a client is using QuickBooks Online, what are the corresponding QuickBooks options for the accountant to use?

Design elements: Dog icon: ©josep perianes jorba/Shutterstock; paint roller icon: ©Netti Buletti/Shutterstock; other icons/symbols: ©Carboxylase/Shutterstock

Chapter 17

Quick Review Guide

For your convenience, this Quick Review Guide is designed for you as:

- A user friendly review guide for frequently used QuickBooks tasks
- A review guide to enhance your prep for the QuickBooks User Certification examination

This Quick Review Guide contains step-by-step instructions for frequently used QuickBooks tasks, providing you with a convenient, easy-to-use resource that summarizes essential tasks. The chapters in *Computer Accounting with QuickBooks* are designed as tutorials for you to initially learn the accounting software, providing numerous screen captures and detailed instructions. To improve long-term retention of your software skills, exercises and projects are designed with fewer instructions to test your understanding and, when needed, to develop your skill at quickly locating additional information to complete the task. The ability to seek out information as needed is an increasingly important skill in the rapidly changing business environment, and the design of *Computer Accounting with QuickBooks* seamlessly facilitates your development of this crucial skill.

In addition, the Quick Review Guide is designed to enhance your preparation for the QuickBooks User Certification exam. Organized around the 10 domains covered on the QuickBooks User Certification exam, this Quick Review Guide is designed to guide you in quickly reviewing key material efficiently.

Chapter 17

Learning Objectives

Chapter 17 is a QuickBooks Review Guide that covers the following topics:

- QuickBooks User Certification Exam Review Guide
- QuickBooks Setup
  - Install QuickBooks Software
  - Register QuickBooks Software
  - Start QuickBooks Software
  - Set Up New Company
  - Set Up New Company from Existing Company
  - Customize Home Page
  - Set Up Lists
- QuickBooks Utilities and General Product Knowledge
  - How to Navigate QuickBooks
  - Back Up Company File (QBB)
  - Restore Company File (QBB0
  - Save Portable Company File (QBM)
  - Open Portable Company File (QBM)
  - Change Company Name
  - View Version and Release Number
  - Update QuickBooks Software
  - Update QuickBooks Company File
  - Use Single-User and Multi-User Modes
  - Open Company File (QBW)
  - Close QuickBooks Company File (QBW)
  - Exit QuickBooks Software
  - Password Protect QuickBooks
  - Customize QuickBooks with Preferences
- List Management
  - Manage QuickBooks Lists
  - Add New Entries
  - Delete Entries

- Edit Entries
- Merge Entries
- Import Lists from Excel
- Export Lists to Excel
- Items
  - How to Use QuickBooks Items
  - Use Different Types of Items
  - Add Items
  - Edit Items
  - Enter an Item Selling for a Specified Price
  - Enter an Item Selling for Different Prices
- Sales (Customer Transactions)
  - Use the Customer Center
  - Enter Customer Information
  - Add New Job
  - Invoice Customers
  - Receive Customer Payments
  - Deposit Customer Payments
  - Create Sales Receipts
  - Create Statements
  - Create Progress Invoice
  - Record a Customer Credit
  - Account for Bounced NSF Check
- Purchases (Vendor Transactions)
  - Use the Vendor Center
  - Enter Vendor Information
  - Enter Items
  - Create Purchase Orders
  - Receive Items
  - Enter Bills Against Inventory
  - Enter Bills
  - Pay Bills by Check
  - Print Checks
  - Write Checks

- Pay with Credit Card
- Pay with Debit Card
- Pay with Online Bank Payment
- Record Vendor Credit
- How to Set Up, Collect, and Pay Sales Tax
- Reconcile Bank Statement
- Payroll (Employee Transactions)
  - Ways to Process Payroll with QuickBooks
  - How to Set Up Payroll
  - Add Payroll Item
  - Edit Payroll Item
  - Enter Employee Information
  - Track Time for Payroll
  - Track Time for Invoicing Customers
  - Track Sick and Vacation Time
  - Set Up Payroll Schedules
  - Pay Employees
  - Pay Payroll Liabilities
  - Prepare Payroll Forms
- Reports
  - Use the Report Center
  - Customize Reports
  - Export Reports to Excel
  - Memorize Reports
  - Print Trial Balance
  - Print General Journal
  - Print General Ledger
  - Print Income Statement
  - Print Balance Sheet
  - Print Statement of Cash Flows
- Basic Accounting
  - Basic Financial Statements
  - Difference Between Cash and Accrual
  - Enter New Accounts

- Enter Beginning Account Balances
- Print Chart of Accounts
- Journal Entries
- Adjusting Entries
- Correcting Entries
- Closing
- Customization/Saving Time and Shortcuts
  - Memorize Transactions
  - Set Up Multiple Users with Access
  - Create Custom Fields
  - Customize an Invoice

QuickBooks User Certification Exam Review Guide

After you have completed prior chapters of *Computer Accounting with QuickBooks*, use this Quick Review Guide to review for the QuickBooks User Certification examination.

WHAT IS THE QUICKBOOKS CERTIFICATION USER EXAMINATION?

The QuickBooks User Certification exam is an online exam that is proctored at authorized testing centers. The exam consists of multiple choice questions or simulations. The QuickBooks User Certification examination is a certification focused on QuickBooks users. The QuickBooks ProAdvisor certification is a different certification that is focused more on accountants who provide advisory services to QuickBooks clients.

> To learn more about the QuickBooks Certification exam, go to Certiport.com and search for QuickBooks Certified User. This text covers QuickBooks Desktop certification.

WHAT IS ON THE QUICKBOOKS USER CERTIFICATION EXAMINATION?

The QuickBooks User Certification exam covers 10 domains. The following table provides you with information about coverage of the QuickBooks User Certification exam domains, content and approximate coverage.

QuickBooks User Certification Domain
1 QuickBooks Setup
2 QuickBooks Utilities and General Product Knowledge
3 List Management
4 Items
5 Sales
6 Purchases
7 Payroll
8 Reports
9 Basic Accounting
10 Customization and Saving Time

WHY CONSIDER TAKING THE QUICKBOOKS USER CERTIFICATION EXAMINATION?

Passing the QuickBooks User Certification examination can add another credential to your resume. Employers often look for credentials that indicate skill and knowledge level as a baseline for employment.

HOW CAN THE QUICK GUIDE HELP ME REVIEW FOR THE QUICKBOOKS USER CERTIFICATION EXAMINATION?

This Quick Review Guide is mapped to the 10 domains of the QuickBooks User Certification exam to streamline your review for the exam.

The Quick Review Guide domain mapping to the QuickBooks User Certification follows.

Quick Review Guide Section	QuickBooks User Certification Domain	% of Exam
17.1	QuickBooks Setup	6%
17.2	QuickBooks Utilities and General Product Knowledge	10%
17.3	List Management	6%
17.4	Items	8%
17.5	Sales	10%
17.6	Purchases	10%
17.7	Payroll	12%
17.8	Reports	16%
17.9	Basic Accounting	10%
17.10	Customization and Saving Time	12%

WHAT IS AN EFFECTIVE REVIEW ACTION PLAN?

Consider the following action plan to increase the effectiveness of your review. Note that simply reading the instructions assists your review but deeper learning occurs when you actually complete the steps using the QuickBooks software.

1. Complete prior chapters of *Computer Accounting with QuickBooks*.

2. Download the file: **CHAPTER 17 STARTER.QBB** from www.mhhe.com/kay2021.

3. Restore the **CHAPTER 17 STARTER.QBB** file following the instructions in Appendix B for restoring a file. When restoring, use the filename **YourName Chapter 17.QBW**.

   ⚠ *Important Note:*
   - *When restoring a QBB file if QuickBooks requires you to create a password in order to continue, create your own password and record the password in a secure location, such as the inside cover of your textbook*

- *When restoring QuickBooks QBB files, if a password is requested:*
  - *Try using User ID: Admin and leave the Password field blank*
  - *If you are using the QBB Starter files and QuickBooks requires a password and QuickBooks will not accept the password field blank, try User ID: Admin and Password: KayQB2021*
  - *If none of the above approaches permit you to restore the QBB file, see your instructor*

4. Read and then complete the steps contained in this Quick Review Guide using the **YourName Chapter 17.QBW** file. To practice some of the tasks, simply insert realistic data to complete the forms.

   - Consider reviewing the Quick Review Guide a minimum of three times to improve your retention of the material.

   - Mark any tasks that you found challenging for later practice.

5. Try a practice exam.

   - Ask your instructor to provide you with a Chapter 17 Exam as an opportunity to practice multiple choice questions.

   - If you register to take the QuickBooks User Certification exam at www.Certiport.com, you will be provided with a code that permits you to take practice exams before you take the certification examination. Take a practice exam and see how well you do.

HOW DO I OBTAIN MORE INFORMATION ABOUT THE QUICKBOOKS USER CERTIFICATION EXAMINATION?

For more information, see www.Certiport.com or go to www.My-QuickBooks.com and click on QB Certified User.

Section 17.1
QuickBooks Setup

INSTALL QUICKBOOKS SOFTWARE

To install QuickBooks software, follow the step-by-step directions provided at www.My-QuickBooks.com or Appendix A: Install and Activate QuickBooks Software.

ACTIVATE QUICKBOOKS SOFTWARE

Activate QuickBooks software at the time you install the software, following the directions provided at www.My-QuickBooks.com or Appendix A: Install and Activate QuickBooks Software.

Failure to activate QuickBooks software within the first 30 days may result in the software no longer functioning. To avoid this, activate the software at the time you install it. If you fail to activate QuickBooks software within 30 days and you are locked out from using the software, select **Help Menu > Activate QuickBooks**.

START QUICKBOOKS SOFTWARE

1. Click the QuickBooks desktop icon or click **Start > QuickBooks > QuickBooks Premier Accountant Edition** (or **QuickBooks Pro**).

2. If necessary, close the QuickBooks Learning Center window to begin using QuickBooks.

SET UP NEW COMPANY

1. Select **File Menu > New Company**.

2. Select **Detailed Start**. Follow the onscreen instructions to complete the EasyStep Interview to set up a new company. Also see Chapters 11 and 13.

3. Complete the QuickBooks Setup to add bank accounts, vendors, customers, employees, and items. Also see Chapters 11 and 13.

SET UP NEW COMPANY FROM EXISTING COMPANY

1. Select **File Menu** > **New Company from Existing Company File**.

2. Select **Browse**.

3. Select **a company to copy from**.

4. Enter **a name for the new company**.

5. Select **Create Company**.

6. Select **Save**.

CUSTOMIZE HOME PAGE

1. Select **Edit Menu** > **Preferences** > **Desktop View** > **Company Preferences**.

2. Select feature icons to appear on the Home Page.

SET UP LISTS

1. Select **Lists Menu** > **Add/Edit Multiple List Entries**.

2. Select **List** (Customers, Vendors, Service Items, Inventory Parts, Non-Inventory Parts, or Inventory Assemblies).

3. **Customize columns** to display.

4. Paste from Excel or type to add or edit the list.

5. Select **Save Changes**.

Section 17.2

QuickBooks Utilities and General Product Knowledge

HOW TO NAVIGATE QUICKBOOKS

There are three basic ways to navigate QuickBooks:

1. Home Page

2. Menus

3. Navigation or Icon Bar with My Shortcuts.

See Chapter 1 for information about the three ways to navigate QuickBooks.

BACK UP COMPANY FILE (QBB)

Backup company files (QBB) are compressed company files. Typically, you will want to back up your company at regular intervals. To save a QuickBooks backup company file:

1. Select **File Menu > Back Up Company > Create Local Backup**.

2. Select **Local backup > Next**.

3. If requested, select location of backup file. Click **OK**.

4. Select **Use this Location**.

5. Select **Save it now > Next**.

6. Select location and backup filename (QBB). Click **Save**.

Also see Appendix B: Back Up and Restore QuickBooks Files and Chapter 1.

RESTORE COMPANY FILE (QBB)

Typically you restore a backup company file when the QuickBooks QBW file fails. For purposes of this text, you will restore a backup file when you use the QBB Restore approach. For more information, see Appendix B: Back Up and Restore QuickBooks Files and Chapter 1.

To restore a QuickBooks backup company file:

1. Select **File Menu > Open or Restore Company**.

2. Select **Restore a backup copy > Next**.

3. Select **Local backup > Next**.

4. Select location of backup file and backup file name. Select **Open > Next**.

5. Select location and name of restored file. If saving to the hard drive, try saving to your desktop to make it easier to find the QBW file later. If QuickBooks will not recognize your desktop, then save to the location that QuickBooks defaults to automatically for restoring the file. Make a note of the path and directory.

6. Click **Save**.

7. Click **OK**.

SAVE PORTABLE COMPANY FILE (QBM)

Portable company files (QBM) permit you to move your QuickBooks company file from one computer to another. To save a portable QuickBooks company file:

1. Select **File Menu > Create Copy**.

2. Select **Portable company file > Next**.

3. Enter the location and filename, then click **Save**.

4. Select **OK** to close and reopen your QuickBooks company file.

OPEN PORTABLE COMPANY FILE (QBM)

To open a QuickBooks portable company file:

1. Select **File Menu > Open or Restore Company**.

2. Select **Restore a portable file > Next**.

3. Select the location and portable company file name (QBM) to open. Select **Open > Next**.

4. Enter the QuickBooks working filename (QBW) and location.

5. Click **Save**.

CHANGE COMPANY NAME

1. Select **Company Menu** > **My Company**. Or select **My Company** from My Shortcuts Navigation (Icon) Bar.

2. Select **Edit** icon.

3. Update Company Name.

4. Click **OK**.

VIEW VERSION AND RELEASE NUMBER

1. With QuickBooks software running, press the **CTRL** and **1** keys at the same time (**CRTL+1**).

2. In the Product field of the Product Information window, find the version and release. (Example: QuickBooks Accountant R3P indicates the version is QuickBooks Accountant. R3P indicates it is release 3.)

3. The Product Information window also displays the License number and Product number. If your QuickBooks Desktop has been activated, the word, ACTIVATED, will appear after your License number.

UPDATE QUICKBOOKS SOFTWARE

To update QuickBooks software, first download the updates and then install the updates. To download the updates:

1. Verify that you have an Internet connection.

2. Select **Help Menu** > **Update QuickBooks Desktop**.

3. Click the **Options** tab.

4. If you would like QuickBooks to automatically update each time you connect to the Internet, select **Yes** for Automatic Update.

5. In the Updates section of the Options screen, select Updates: **Maintenance Releases, Help, Accountant, Data Protect**. Ask your instructor if you should select Payroll updates to download. If you download payroll updates, your answers may not match the text answers for payroll assignments.

6. To download an update, select **Update Now** tab > **Get Updates**. If asked if you want to update QuickBooks, click **Yes**.

To install the QuickBooks update:

1. **Exit** QuickBooks software, then **reopen** QuickBooks software.

2. At the prompt to install the update, select **Yes**.

3. After the update completes, **restart** your computer.

UPDATE QUICKBOOKS COMPANY FILE

To update your company file created using a previous version of QuickBooks (for example, to update a QuickBooks company file created in QuickBooks 2019 to QuickBooks 2021):

1. **Back up** your company file.

2. Using the newer version of QuickBooks, such as QuickBooks 2021 software, select **File Menu > Open or Restore Company**.

3. Select **Restore a backup copy > Next**.

4. Select **Local backup > Next**.

5. Select location of backup file for prior version of QuickBooks and backup file name. Select **Open > Next**.

6. When asked if you want to update the file, enter **YES** and click **OK**.

USE SINGLE-USER AND MULTI-USER MODES

1. If you are in multi-user mode, to switch to single-user mode select **File Menu > Switch to Single-user Mode > Yes**.

2. If you are in single-user mode, to switch to multi-user mode select **File Menu > Switch to Multi-user Mode > Yes**.

OPEN COMPANY FILE (QBW)

To open a QuickBooks company file (QBW) that is on the hard drive (C:) or that has been restored to the C: drive:

1. After QuickBooks software is open, select **File Menu > Open or Restore Company**.

2. Select **Open a company file (QBW) > Next**.

3. Select the company file and location. Click **Open**.

CLOSE QUICKBOOKS COMPANY FILE (QBW)

1. Select **File Menu**.

2. Click **Close Company**.

EXIT QUICKBOOKS SOFTWARE

1. Select **File Menu**.

2. Click **Exit**.

PASSWORD PROTECT QUICKBOOKS

1. Select **Company Menu** > **Set Up Users and Passwords** > **Set Up Users**.

2. Select **Add User** (or Edit User).

3. Enter **User Name**.

4. Enter **Password**.

5. Confirm **Password**.

6. Select **Next**. Select the appropriate QuickBooks user access settings.

7. Click **Finish**.

CUSTOMIZE QUICKBOOKS WITH PREFERENCES

To customize QuickBooks to fit your accounting software needs, you can select preferences as follows:

1. Select **Edit Menu** > **Preferences**.

2. From the left scroll bar Preferences window, select the category:

    *   Accounting
    *   Bills
    *   Calendar
    *   Checking

- Desktop View
- Finance Charge
- General
- Integrated Applications
- Items & Inventory
- Jobs & Estimates
- Multiple Currencies
- Payments
- Payroll & Employees
- Reminders
- Reports & Graphs
- Sales & Customers
- Sales Tax
- Search
- Send Forms
- Service Connection
- Spelling
- Tax: 1099
- Time & Expenses

3. Select the **My Preferences** tab or the **Company Preferences** tab.

4. Enter the preference settings you desire to customize QuickBooks.

5. When finished selecting preferences, click **OK**.

Section 17.3

List Management

MANAGE QUICKBOOKS LISTS

QuickBooks uses lists to record and organize information about:

- Customers
- Vendors
- Items (such as services, inventory, and non-inventory)
- Employees
- Other

There are several different ways to manage lists in QuickBooks. For example, the Customer List can be accessed from the Customer Center and the Vendor List accessed from the Vendor Center. Another option is to manage lists using the Add/Edit Multiple List Entries window as follows.

ADD NEW ENTRIES

To add new entries using the Add/Edit Multiple List Entries window:

1. Select **Lists Menu > Add/Edit Multiple List Entries**.

2. Select a type of list (such as Vendor) from the **List** drop-down menu.

3. **Customize Columns** to display in the list.

4. Enter or paste from Excel to add to the list.

5. Click **Save Changes**.

DELETE ENTRIES

To delete entries from a list using the Add/Edit Multiple List Entries window:

1. Select **Lists Menu > Add/Edit Multiple List Entries**.

2. Select a type of list (such as Customer) from the **List** drop-down menu.

3. Select the entry to delete.

4. **Right-click > Delete Line**.

5. Click **Save Changes**.

Note that typically entries related to transactions, such as customer entries related to invoices, cannot be deleted.

EDIT ENTRIES

To edit entries in a list using the Add/Edit Multiple List Entries window:

1. Select **Lists Menu > Add/Edit Multiple List Entries**.

2. Select a type of list (Customer, Vendor, and so on) from the **List** drop-down menu.

3. **Customize Columns** to display in the list.

4. Enter changes to the list entries.

5. Click **Save Changes**.

MERGE ENTRIES

To merge or combine entries on a list:

1. Select type of list (Customer, Vendor, Employee, or Item) from the **List** drop-down menu.

2. If your list has two names for the same vendor, for example, but one is misspelled, select the misspelled vendor name on the list, **right-click** then select **Edit**.

3. Type the correct name.

4. Click **OK**.

5. Click **Yes** when asked if you would like to merge this entry with the other entry with the same name.

After merging, only the correct name will appear on the list. QuickBooks will also merge the transactions for the two entries. Note that when merging accounts for the Chart of Accounts, only accounts with the same type (Income, Expense, and so on) can be merged.

IMPORT LISTS FROM EXCEL

To import lists of customers, vendors, accounts, or items from Microsoft Excel into QuickBooks:

1. Back up the QuickBooks company file.

2. Select **File Menu > Utilities > Import > Excel Files**.

3. When the Add/Edit Multiple List Entries window appears if you select **Yes**, QuickBooks will take you to the **Lists Menu > Add/Edit Multiple List Entries** to add/edit multiple lists. Further instructions follow in the next section.

4. If you select **No**, the Add Your Excel Data to QuickBooks window will appear.

5. From the Add Your Excel Data to QuickBooks window, click **Advanced Import** button.

6. Select the **Set up Import tab > Select A File > Mappings**.

7. Click the **Preference** tab. Select how to handle duplicates and errors.

8. Click **Preview**. Make appropriate corrections.

9. Click **Import**.

Another way to import data into Excel is using the Add/Edit Multiple List feature:

1. Select **Lists > Add/Edit Multiple List Entries**.

2. Select List (Customers, Vendors, Service, Inventory or Non-Inventory).

3. **Customize Columns** to display.

4. Paste from Excel or type to add or edit the list.

5. Select **Save Changes**.

You can also import data from Excel from the specific center. For example, to import the Customer List from Excel:

1. From the **Customer Center**, click the **Excel** button.

2. Select **Import from Excel**.

3. When the Add/Edit Multiple List Entries window appears, if you select **Yes**, QuickBooks will take you to the **Lists Menu > Add/Edit Multiple List Entries** to add/edit multiple lists.

4. If you select **No**, the Add Your Excel Data to QuickBooks window will appear. From this window, select the appropriate **type of data you want to add to QuickBooks** button.

5. Follow the onscreen instructions to copy your data into a spreadsheet formatted to work with QuickBooks.

6. **Save** the Excel file.

EXPORT LISTS TO EXCEL

You can export data to Microsoft Excel for customers, vendors, inventory items, transactions, payroll summary, and reports. For example, to export customer data to a new Excel workbook:

1. Click **Customers** on the Icon Bar.

2. Display the **Customer List**.

3. Click the **Excel** button. Select **Export Customer List**.

4. Select **Create new worksheet > in new workbook > Export**.

5. When the Excel file opens, save the Excel file.

Section 17.4

Items

HOW TO USE QUICKBOOKS ITEMS

The QuickBooks Item List is used to track items purchased and sold. Types of items include:
- Service
- Inventory Part
- Inventory Assembly
- Non-inventory Part
- Group
- Discount
- Sales Tax Item

USE DIFFERENT TYPES OF ITEMS

When adding items to the Item List, the appropriate type of item is selected. This cannot be changed later. The three main types of items frequently used are service, non-inventory part, and inventory part.

- **Service item:** Use this item type for services you purchase or sell, such as labor, consulting hours, or professional fees.
- **Non-inventory part item:** Use this item type for goods you buy but don't need to track the quantity, such as office supplies or materials for a specific customer job that you will charge back to the customer.
- **Inventory part item:** Use this item type for goods you purchase, track as inventory, and resell to customers.

ADD ITEMS

1. From the **Company** section of the Home Page, click the **Items & Services** icon.

2. **Right-click** to display the pop-up menu. Select **New**.

3. Enter item information.

4. To enter another item, click **Next**.

5. When finished, click **OK**.

EDIT ITEMS

1. From the **Company** section of the Home Page, click the **Items & Services** icon.

2. After selecting the item you would like to edit, **right-click** to display the pop-up menu. Select **Edit** Item.

3. Edit item information.

4. When finished, click **OK**.

ENTER AN ITEM SELLING FOR A SPECIFIED PRICE

When a specific item is typically sold at the same specified price, that price can be entered in the Item List. This specified sales price will automatically appear on invoices when this item is selected.

To enter an item that sells at a specified price:

1. From the **Company** section of the Home Page, click the **Items & Services** icon.

2. **Right-click** to display the pop-up menu. Select **New**.

3. Select **Item Type**.

4. Enter item information.

5. Enter **Sales Price**. When the Sales Price is entered in the Item List, then this sales price will automatically appear on invoices when this item is selected. Note that this automatic price can be changed on the invoice when needed for a specific sale.

6. To enter another item, click **Next**.

7. When finished, click **OK**.

ENTER AN ITEM SELLING FOR DIFFERENT PRICES

When a specific item is typically sold at different prices, the price for that item can be left blank in the Item List. When the item is selected for sale on an invoice, the sales price will automatically appear as $0.00. Then you enter the price required for the specific sale on the invoice.

To enter an item that sells for different prices:

1. From the **Company** section of the Home Page, click the **Items & Services** icon.

2. **Right-click** to display the pop-up menu. Select **New**.

3. Select **Item Type**.

4. Enter item information.

5. Enter **Sales Price: 0.00**. When a Sales Price of $0.00 is entered for an item in the Item List, then $0.00 will automatically appear as the sales price on invoices when this item is selected. You can enter whatever price is required for the specific sale on the invoice.

6. To enter another item, click **Next**.

7. When finished, click **OK**.

Section 17.5

Sales (Customer Transactions)

USE THE CUSTOMER CENTER

1. Click **Customers** on the Navigation (Icon) Bar or click Customers in the Customers section of the Home Page.

2. From the Customer Center, you can view your Customer: Job List, enter new customers, edit current customers listed, enter new transactions, print or export to Excel, view transactions and contacts.

ENTER CUSTOMER INFORMATION

1. Click **Customers** on the Navigation (Icon) Bar or click Customers in the Customers section of the Home Page.

2. Select **New Customer & Job > New Customer**.

3. Enter customer information.

4. Click **OK** to save and close the window.

ADD NEW JOB

1. Select the specific customer from the Customer List in the Customer Center.

2. With the customer selected, **right-click** to display the pop-up menu. Select **Add Job**.

3. Enter the Job Name and other job information.

4. Click **OK** to save and close the window.

INVOICE CUSTOMERS

1. From the **Customers** section of the Home Page, click the **Create Invoices** icon.

2. Enter invoice information.

3. Click the **Print** icon to print the invoice or the **Email** icon to email the invoice.

4. Click **Save & New** to enter another invoice or **Save & Close** to close the window.

RECEIVE CUSTOMER PAYMENTS

1. From the **Customers** section of the Home Page, click the **Receive Payments** icon.

2. Enter receipt information.

3. Click **Save & New** to enter another receipt or **Save & Close** to close the window.

DEPOSIT CUSTOMER PAYMENTS

1. From the **Banking** section of the Home Page, click **Record Deposits**.

2. Select **Payments to Deposit**, then click **OK**.

3. Select **Bank Account**. Enter **Date** and deposit information.

4. Click **Print** to print the deposit summary.

5. Click **Save & Close**.

CREATE SALES RECEIPTS

1. From the **Customers** section of the Home Page, click the **Create Sales Receipts** icon.

2. Enter receipt information.

3. Click **Save & New** to enter another receipt or **Save & Close** to close the window.

CREATE STATEMENTS

1. From the **Customers** section of the Home Page, click the **Statements** icon.

2. Select Statement Date, Statement Period, and Customer.

3. If requested, in the Select Additional Options section you can choose to show invoice item detail on the statement.

4. Click **Print** to print the invoice or **Email** to email the invoice.

5. Click **Close** to close the window.

CREATE PROGRESS INVOICE

1. Select **Edit > Preferences > Jobs & Estimates > Company Preferences**. Select Do you create estimates? **Yes**. Select Do you do progress invoicing? **Yes**.

2. From the **Customers** section of the Home Page, click the **Create Invoices** icon.

3. Select Template: **Progress Invoice**.

4. Select appropriate Customer and Job.

5. When asked, select appropriate estimate.

6. Enter the quantity or percentage of work completed to be billed.

7. Click **Save & New** to enter another receipt or **Save & Close** to close the window.

RECORD A CUSTOMER CREDIT

1. From the **Customers** section of the Home Page, click the **Refunds & Credits** icon.

2. Select the appropriate Customer and Job.

3. Enter credit information.

4. Click **Save & New** to enter another refund/credit or **Save & Close** to close the window.

ACCOUNT FOR BOUNCED NSF CHECK

When a customer check is returned by the bank because the customer has insufficient funds to cover the check, you must account for:

- The returned check
- Any bank fees you are charged by the bank
- Any fees you charge the customer for the NSF check

How you account for an NSF check depends upon which QuickBooks version you use. If you are using a QuickBooks version that has a bounced check feature, complete the following steps to account for the NSF check.

1. From the **Customers** section of the Home Page, select the **Receive Payments** icon.

2. From the Receive Payments window, select the customer payment associated with the bounced check. For example, find the customer payment for **Abercrombie, Kristy: Remodel Bathroom** on **12/15/2024** for **$7633.28**.

3. The Pmt. Method must have **Check** selected for the **Record Bounced Check** icon to be active in the Receive Payments window.

4. With the customer transaction for the bounced check appearing in the Receive Payments window, select the **Record Bounced Check** icon. (Note: if your Receive Payments window does not display a Bounced Check button: (1) the Pmt. Method was not Check, or (2) your QuickBooks version may not offer this feature.)

5. In the What did the bank charge you for this bounced check? section of the Manage Bounced Check window, enter amount for **Bank Fee**.

6. Enter **Date**.

7. Enter Expense Account: **60600 – Bank Service Charges**.

8. In the How much do you want to charge your customer? section of the Manage Bounced Check window, enter amount for **Customer Fee**.

9. Select **Next**.

10. A Bounced Check Summary window should appear summarizing what will happen in QuickBooks when you record the bounced check. QuickBooks will perform a series of steps to account for the bounced check:

    - The original customer invoice is marked unpaid.

    - The customer payment is stamped: Bounced Check.

    - The customer's bounced check that was deposited in your account will be deducted from your bank account. (A journal entry is made to increase accounts receivable and decrease your Checking account.)

    - The fee the bank charges you for bounced checks will be deducted from your bank account. (A journal entry is made to increase the Bank Service Charge Expense account and reduce your Checking account by the amount you are charged for the bank's NSF fee.)

    - A new invoice is created to charge the customer for the bounced check fee.

11.   Select **Finish**.

12.   Select **Save & Close** to close the Receive Payments window.

To create a collection letter to send the customer regarding a bounced check:

1.   From the Customer List in the **Customer Center**, select the customer to receive the bounced check collection letter.

2.   At the top of the Customer Center, click the **Word drop-down arrow > Prepare Letter to [Customer Name]**.

3.   In the Choose a Letter Template window, select **Bounced Check**.

4.   Follow the onscreen instructions in the Letter and Envelopes wizard to create the customer's bounced check letter.

If your version of QuickBooks does not have the bounced check feature, approaches to account for the NSF check include the following:

- Create a credit memo for the NSF check and offset it against the corresponding customer invoice
- Create a new invoice for the NSF check including the bounced check fee charged the customer

The following instructions are an example of how to use a new invoice to account for an NSF check if your QuickBooks version does not have the bounced check feature.

First, create an item for tracking bounced (NSF) checks:

1.   From the **Company** section of the Home Page, select **Items & Services**.

2.   Select **Item** button > **New**.

3.   Select Type: **Other Charge**.

4.   Enter Item Name/Number: **Bounced Check**.

5.   In the Amount or % field, leave: **0.00**.

6.   In the Account field, select: **Checking**.

7.   Click **Next** to enter another item. Leave the New Item window open.

Next create an item to track bad check charges that you charge customers for bounced checks.

1. With the New Item window still open, select Type: **Other Charge**.

2. Enter Item Name/Number: **Bad Check Charge**.

3. In the Amount or % field, leave: **0.00**.

4. In the Account field, select: **<Add New>**.

5. Select Account Type: **Income**.

6. Enter Account Name: **Returned Check Charges**.

7. Select **Save & Close** to close the Add New Account window. The Account field should now display Returned Check Charges.

8. Click **OK** to close the New Item window.

The next task is to re-invoice the customer for the bounced check plus any returned check charges.

1. From the **Customers** section of the Home Page, select **Create Invoices**.

2. From the customer drop-down list, select the customer and job related to the bounced check.

3. Select Item: **Bounced Check**.

4. In the Amount field, enter the amount of the bounced check. Note that this will reduce your bank account by the amount of the bad check.

5. Move to the second line item. Select Item: **Bad Check Charge**.

6. In the Amount field, enter the amount of returned check charges you want to recover from the customer.

7. The rest of the invoice can be completed as you normally would.

8. Select **Save & Close**.

Another related task is to see that any NSF fees the bank charges your company are recorded when you reconcile your company bank statement.

Section 17.6
Purchases (Vendor Transactions)

USE THE VENDOR CENTER

1. Select **Vendors** on the Navigation (Icon) Bar or select Vendors in the Vendors section of the Home Page.

2. From the Vendor Center, you can view your Vendor List, enter new vendors, edit current vendors listed, enter new transactions, print or export to Excel, view transactions and contacts.

ENTER VENDOR INFORMATION

1. Select **Vendors** on the Navigation (Icon) Bar or select Vendors in the Vendors section of the Home Page.

2. From the **Vendor Center**, click the **New Vendor** button > **New Vendor**.

3. Enter vendor information.

4. Click **OK** to save and close the window.

ENTER ITEMS

1. From the **Company** section of the Home Page, click the **Items & Services** icon.

2. **Right-click** to display the pop-up menu. Select **New**.

3. Select type of item.

4. Enter item information.

5. To enter another item, click **Next**.

6. When finished, click **OK**.

CREATE PURCHASE ORDERS

1. After entering items into the Item List, to record the purchase of inventory, from the **Vendors** section of the Home Page, click **Purchase Orders**.

2. Enter purchase information.

3. To enter another purchase order, click **Save & New**.

4. When finished, click **Save & Close**.

RECEIVE ITEMS

1. From the **Vendors** section of the Home Page, click **Receive Inventory**.

2. Select **Receive Inventory with Bill** or **Receive Inventory without Bill**.

3. Select the vendor. If asked if you want to match against outstanding purchase orders, click **Yes**.

4. Enter the remaining information.

5. To enter another item received, click **Save & New**.

6. When finished, click **Save & Close**.

ENTER BILLS AGAINST INVENTORY

1. From the **Vendors** section of the Home Page, click **Enter Bills Against Inventory**.

2. Select the vendor and choose the Item Receipt that corresponds to the bill.

3. Enter the remaining information.

4. To enter another bill, click **Save & New**.

5. When finished, click **Save & Close**.

Enter Bills

1. From the **Vendors** section of the Home Page, click **Enter Bills**.

2. Select the vendor.

3. Enter bill information.

4. Select Expenses or Items tab and select the appropriate account.

5. To enter another bill, click **Save & New**.

6. When finished, click **Save & Close**.

THE PAY BILLS BY CHECK

1. From the **Vendors** section of the Home Page, click **Pay Bills**.

2. Select **Show all bills**.

3. Select bills to pay.

4. Enter **Payment Date**.

5. Select Method: **Check**. Select appropriate Checking account.

6. Click **Pay Selected Bills**.

PRINT CHECKS

1. Select **File Menu** > **Print Forms** > **Checks** (or click the **Print Checks** icon in the **Banking** section of the Home Page).

2. Select **Bank Account**.

3. Enter **First Check Number**.

4. Select checks to print.

5. Click **OK**.

6. Select **Check Style**.

7. Click **Print**.

WRITE CHECKS

1. From the **Banking** section of the Home Page, click **Write Checks**.

2. Select **Bank Account**.

3. Enter **Check Date** and remaining check information.

4. Enter **Account** and **Amount**.

5. Select **Print Later**.

6. Click **Print** to print the checks.

PAY WITH CREDIT CARD

1. From the **Vendors** section of the Home Page, click **Pay Bills**.

2. Select **Show all bills**.

3. Select bills to pay.

4. Enter **Payment Date**.

5. Select Method: **Credit Card**. Select appropriate account.

6. Click **Pay Selected Bills**.

PAY WITH DEBIT CARD

1. From the **Vendors** section of the Home Page, click **Pay Bills**.

2. Select **Show all bills**.

3. Select bills to pay.

4. Enter **Payment Date**.

5. Select Method: **Check**.

6. Select **Assign check number**.

7. Select appropriate Checking account.

8. Click **Pay Selected Bills**.

9. Assign check number **DC** for Debit Card. Click **OK**.

PAY WITH ONLINE BANK PAYMENT

1. From the **Vendors** section of the Home Page, click **Pay Bills**.

2. Select **Show all bills**.

3. Select bills to pay.

4. Enter **Payment Date**.

5. Select Method: **Online Bank Pmt**. Select appropriate account.

6. If appropriate, select **Include reference number**.

7. Click **Pay Selected Bills**.

RECORD VENDOR CREDIT

To record a vendor credit:

1. From the **Vendors** section of the Home Page, click **Enter Bills**.

2. Select **Credit** (instead of Bill) near the top of the Enter Bills window.

3. From the drop-down list, select the appropriate **vendor**.

4. Enter the **credit amount**.

5. Select the **account** used to record the initial expense or item.

6. To enter another vendor credit, click **Save & New**.

7. When finished, click **Save & Close** to save the credit memo.

To apply the credit memo against a specific bill:

1. From the **Vendors** section of the Home Page, click **Pay Bills**.

2. Select the bill that you would like to apply the credit to.

3. If the amount of the credit needs to be adjusted, select **Set Credits**.

4. Enter amount of credit in the **Amount To Use** column for the bill(s).

5. Click **Done** to close the Discount and Credits window.

6. Select any other bills to pay.

7. Click **Pay Selected Bills**.

8. Select **Done** or **Print Checks** to close the Payment Summary window.

HOW TO SET UP, COLLECT, AND PAY SALES TAX

To set up sales tax:

1. Select **Edit Menu** > **Preferences** > **Sales Tax** > **Company Preferences** (or from the **Vendors** section of the Home Page, select **Manage Sales Tax** > **Sales Tax Preferences**).

2. Select Do you charge sales tax? **Yes**.

3. Select **Add sales tax item**. Enter and save sales tax item information for each county or sales tax district where you collect sales tax.

4. Select your most common **sales tax item** from the drop-down list.

5. Select **Accrual** or **Cash Basis** as appropriate for When Do You Owe Sales Tax?

6. Select appropriate answer for When Do You Pay Sales Tax?

7. Click **OK** to close the Preferences window.

8. When entering customer information into the Customer List, select the appropriate sales tax settings for the specific customer from the New/Edit Customer window by selecting **Sales Tax Settings** tab > **Tax Code** > **Tax Item**.

To collect sales tax:

1. When using the Create Invoices or Create Sales Receipts windows, enter the customer information and items sold. The Tax column should automatically reflect the sales tax settings entered in the Customer List for the specific customer.

2. If necessary, select the appropriate sales tax item from the Tax drop-down list on the Create Invoices or Create Sales Receipts windows.

To pay sales tax:

1. From the **Vendors** section of the Home Page select **Manage Sales Tax** > **Pay Sales Tax**.

2. From the Pay Sales Tax window, enter the **Pay From Account**.

3. Select **Check Date**.

4. Select **Show sales tax due through** date.

5. Check the sales taxes to pay.

6. Click **OK**, then print checks to pay sales taxes.

Reconcile Bank Statement

1. From the **Banking** section of the Home Page, click **Reconcile**.

2. Select **Bank Account**.

3. Enter **Statement Date** and **Ending Balance**.

4. Enter **Service Charges** and **Interest Earned**.

5. Click **Continue**.

6. Check deposits and checks that appear on the bank statement.

7. Click **Reconcile Now**.

Section 17.7
Payroll (Employee Transactions)

WAYS TO PROCESS PAYROLL WITH QUICKBOOKS

There are two general ways that a company can process payroll using QuickBooks:

- Manually calculate payroll taxes.

- Use a QuickBooks payroll service.

QuickBooks offers three different levels of payroll services:

1. **Basic Payroll.** Basic payroll service creates paychecks using automatic calculation of payroll tax deductions. Tax forms for filings are not automatically prepared so the entrepreneur must complete the tax forms or work with an accountant on payroll tax filings.

2. **Enhanced Payroll.** Enhanced payroll service creates paychecks using automatic calculation of payroll tax deductions and generates payroll tax forms for filings automatically.

3. **Assisted Payroll.** Assisted payroll service automatically calculates payroll tax deductions and processes and files payroll tax forms and payments for the entrepreneur.

HOW TO SET UP PAYROLL

1. Select **Edit Menu > Preferences > Payroll & Employees > Company Preferences > Full Payroll**.

2. Enter **Employee Defaults**.

3. Click **OK** to close the Preferences window.

4. Select **Employees Menu > Payroll Setup**.

5. Complete the QuickBooks Payroll Setup.

See Chapters 8 for more information about payroll setup.

ADD PAYROLL ITEM

1. Select **Employees Menu** > **Manage Payroll Items** > **New Payroll Item**.

2. Select **EZ Setup** > **Next**.

3. Select type of payroll item, such as Insurance Benefits. Click **Next**.

4. After the Payroll Setup Interview loads, select the appropriate payroll items, such as Health Insurance. Click **Next**.

5. Answer any remaining questions about the payroll item(s).

6. Select **payees**, appropriate **accounts**, and **payment frequency**.

7. Click **Finish**.

EDIT PAYROLL ITEM

To edit a payroll item:

1. Select **Employees Menu** > **Manage Payroll Items** > **View/Edit Payroll Item List** to open the Payroll Item List.

2. Select the specific payroll item you would like to edit. **Right-click** and select **Edit**.

3. If necessary, edit the name of the payroll item. Click **Next**.

4. Answer the questions regarding the payroll item, then click **Next**.

5. Click **Finish**.

Next, enter employee information as needed for payroll item deductions.

ENTER EMPLOYEE INFORMATION

1. Select **Employees** on the Icon Bar.

2. From the **Employee Center**, click the **New Employee** button.

3. Enter employee information.

4. Click **Next** to enter another employee or click **OK** to save and close the window.

TRACK TIME FOR PAYROLL

1. From the **Employees** section of the Home Page, select **Enter Time** icon > **Use Weekly Timesheet**.

2. Select **Employee Name**.

3. Select **Week**.

4. Enter time worked (if needed, select customer and service item).

5. To enter another timesheet, click **Save & New**.

6. Click **Print** to print the timesheets.

7. When finished, click **Save & Close**.

TRACK TIME FOR INVOICING CUSTOMERS

See the preceding Track Time for Payroll for instructions on entering time using the weekly timesheet.

To transfer time worked to customer invoices:

1. From the **Customers** section of the Home Page, select **Create Invoices**.

2. Select the customer and job from the Customer: Job drop-down list.

3. If necessary, select **Add Time/Costs**.

4. When the Billable Time/Costs window appears, click: **Select the outstanding billable time and costs to add to this invoice?** Click **OK**.

5. Select **Time** tab. Select time to transfer to the invoice and appropriate options. Click **OK**.

6. Complete the rest of the invoice.

7. When finished, click **Save & Close**.

TRACK SICK AND VACATION TIME

To track sick and vacation time for employees, when setting up payroll, select the appropriate options for sick and vacation time. To adjust sick or vacation time for a specific employee:

1. Select **Employees** on the (Navigation) Icon Bar or select Employees in the Employees section of the Home Page.

2. From the Employee List, double-click on the employee's name to open the Edit Employee window.

3. Select **Payroll Info** tab.

4. Select Sick Hourly, Sick Salary, Vacation Hourly or Vacation Salary from the Item Name drop-down list.

5. Select sick and vacation options as needed.

6. When finished, click **OK** to close the Sick and Vacation window.

7. Click **OK** to close the Edit Employee window.

SET UP PAYROLL SCHEDULES

1. From the **Employees** section of the Home Page, select **Payroll Center**.

2. If this is the first scheduled payroll, from the **Pay Employees** section, select **Start Scheduled Payroll > Set up Now**.

3. If a payroll schedule already exists and you are adding another payroll schedule, from the **Pay Employees** section, select **New** from the Payroll Schedules drop-down.

4. In the New Payroll Schedule window, enter the name for the payroll schedule.

5. Enter how often you will pay employees on this schedule.

6. Select what date should appear on paychecks for this pay period.

7. Click **OK**.

PAY EMPLOYEES

1. From the **Employees** section of the Home Page, click **Pay Employees**.

2. In the **Pay Employees** section of the Employee Center: Payroll Center window, select **Start Scheduled Payroll** or **Start Unscheduled Payroll**.

3. In the Enter Payroll Information window, enter **Pay Period Ends** and **Check Date**.

4. Select **Employee name**. Select **Open Paycheck Detail**.

5. Enter withholding and deduction amounts. Select **Save & Close**.

6. Continue until all employee paychecks are completed. Then click **Continue**.

7. Click **Create Paychecks**.

8. Click **Print Paychecks** to print the paychecks.

PAY PAYROLL LIABILITIES

1. From the **Employees** section of the Home Page, select **Pay Liabilities**.

2. In the **Pay Liabilities** section, select payroll liabilities you would like to pay.

3. Select **View/Pay**.

4. Select **E-payment** or **Check**.

5. When finished, click **Save & Close**.

PREPARE PAYROLL FORMS

1. From the **Employees** section of the Home Page, select **Process Payroll Forms**.

2. Select **Federal form** or **State form**. Click **OK**. (Forms available to select depends upon the payroll service.)

3. Choose the form you want to use.

4. Click **OK**.

Section 17.8
Reports

USE THE REPORT CENTER

You can access the Report Center in the following ways:

1. Select **Reports** from the Navigation (Icon) Bar > My Shortcuts.

2. Select **Reports Menu** > **Report Center**.

After opening the Report Center to display a report:

1. Select the report type.

2. Select the report.

3. Select **Date**.

4. Click **Run**.

CUSTOMIZE REPORTS

1. From the **Report Center**, display the desired report.

2. Select **Customize Report** near the top of the report window.

3. Select from **Display**, **Filters**, **Header/Footer**, and **Fonts & Numbers** tabs to customize your report.

4. Select **OK**.

EXPORT REPORTS TO EXCEL

To export reports to Microsoft Excel:

1. Using the **Report Center**, display the desired report.

2. Click the **Excel** button at the top of the report window.

3. Select **Create New Worksheet** or **Update Existing Worksheet** as appropriate.

4. If you are replacing a worksheet in an existing worksheet, select **Replace Existing Worksheet.** Select the appropriate workbook and sheet.

5. If you would like to add Auto Outline or Auto Filtering to your Excel worksheet, select **Advanced**. Select **Auto Outline** and/or **Auto Filtering**. Select **OK**.

6. Click **Export**.

7. When the Excel file opens, save the Excel file.

MEMORIZE REPORTS

1. From the **Report Center**, display the report that you wish to memorize.

2. Select **Memorize** at the top of the report window.

3. In the Memorize Report window, enter the **Name** you wish to use for the report.

4. Select **Save in Memorized Report Group** and specify the group.

5. Click **OK**.

6. Close the report window.

PRINT TRIAL BALANCE

1. From the **Report Center**, select **Accountant & Taxes > Trial Balance**.

2. Select **Dates**.

3. Click **Run** icon.

4. Click **Excel** or **Print**.

PRINT GENERAL JOURNAL

1. From the **Report Center**, select **Accountant & Taxes > Journal**.

2. Select **Dates**.

3. Click **Run** icon.

4. Click **Excel** or **Print**.

PRINT GENERAL LEDGER

1. From the **Report Center**, select **Accountant & Taxes > General Ledger**.

2. Select **Dates**.

3. Click **Run** icon.

4. Select **Customize Report > Advanced**. Select to show only accounts **In Use**.

5. Click **Excel** or **Print**.

PRINT INCOME STATEMENT

1. From the **Report Center**, select **Company & Financial**.

2. Under the **Profit & Loss (Income Statement)** section, select **Profit & Loss Standard**.

3. Select **Dates**.

4. Click **Run** icon.

5. Select **Customize Report > Display** tab. Select the type of Report Basis needed for your income statement: **Accrual** or **Cash**. Click **OK**.

6. Click **Excel** or **Print**.

PRINT BALANCE SHEET

1. From the **Report Center**, select **Company & Financial**.

2. Under the **Balance Sheet & Net Worth** section, select **Balance Sheet Standard**.

3. Select **Dates**.

4. Click **Run** icon.

5. Click **Excel** or **Print**.

PRINT STATEMENT OF CASH FLOWS

1. From the **Report Center**, select **Company & Financial**.

2. Under the **Cash Flow** section, select **Statement of Cash Flows**.

3. Select **Dates**.

4. Click **Run** icon.

5. Click **Excel** or **Print**.

Section 17.9
Basic Accounting

BASIC FINANCIAL STATEMENTS

Three basic financial statements often used when evaluating an organization's performance are:

1. Income statement (also called Profit and Loss or P & L). The income statement measures revenues and expenses over a period of time, such as one year.

2. Balance sheet (also called a statement of financial position). The balance sheet measures assets (items with future benefit), liabilities (obligations), and owner's equity (the residual left when liabilities are subtracted from assets).

3. Statement of cash flows. The statement of cash flows has three main sections: cash flows from operations, cash flows from financing activities, and cash flows from investing activities.

To create these three main financial statements, see preceding Section 17.8 Reports.

DIFFERENCE BETWEEN CASH AND ACCRUAL

The cash basis and accrual basis are two different ways of measuring revenues and expenses. The cash basis uses cash inflows and cash outflows. For example, an income statement on the cash basis measures cash inflows received for revenues and cash outflows paid for expenses.

The accrual basis uses the matching principle to measure revenues and expenses. In general when the accrual basis is used, revenues are recorded when the goods or services are provided to the customer (earned). Expenses are matched against revenues earned.

To select Accrual basis for a report:

1. From the **Report Center**, open the desired report, such as the income statement.

2. Select **Customize Report > Display** tab.

3. Select Report Basis: **Accrual**.

4. Select **OK**.

5. **Print** or **export** the report to Excel.

To select Cash basis for a report:

1. From the **Report Center**, open the desired report, such as the income statement.

2. Select **Customize Report > Display** tab.

3. Select Report Basis: **Cash**.

4. Select **OK**.

5. **Print** or **export** the report to Excel.

ENTER NEW ACCOUNTS

1. From the **Company** section of the Home Page, click the **Chart of Accounts** icon.

2. **Right-click** to display the pop-up menu. Select **New**.

3. Enter **Type of Account**, **Account Number**, **Name**, **Description**, and **Tax Line**.

4. Click **Save & New** to enter another account.

5. Click **Save & Close** to close the Add New Account window.

ENTER BEGINNING ACCOUNT BALANCES

1. If the account has a beginning balance, when entering the new account, from the Add New Account (or Edit Account) window, select the **Enter Opening Balance** button.

2. Enter the **Opening Balance** and the **As of Date** for the beginning balance.

3. Click **OK**.

PRINT CHART OF ACCOUNTS

1. From the **Report Center**, select **Accountant & Taxes > Account Listing**.

2. Enter **Date**, select **Run**, then **Excel** or **Print**.

JOURNAL ENTRIES

1. Select **Accountant Menu > Make General Journal Entries**. (For QuickBooks Pro, select **Company Menu > Make General Journal Entries**.)

2. Enter **Date**, **Entry Number**, **Accounts**, and **Debit** and **Credit** amounts.

3. Click **Save & New** to enter another journal entry.

4. Click **Save & Close** to close the Make General Journal Entries window.

ADJUSTING ENTRIES

1. Select **Accountant Menu > Make General Journal Entries**. (For QuickBooks Pro, select **Company Menu > Make General Journal Entries**.)

2. Enter **Date**, **Entry Number (ADJ#)**, **Accounts**, and **Debit** and **Credit** amounts.

3. **Check** the **Adjusting Entry checkbox**.

4. Click **Save & New** to enter another journal entry.

5. Click **Save & Close** to close the Make General Journal Entries window.

CORRECTING ENTRIES

To correct an error, make two correcting entries in the Journal:

1. Eliminate the effect of the incorrect entry by making the opposite journal entry.

   For example, assume the Cash account should have been debited for $200.00 and the Professional Fees Revenue account credited for $200.00. However, the following incorrect entry was made for $2,000.00 instead of $200.00.

Debit	Cash	2,000.00
Credit	Professional Fees Revenue	2,000.00

   To eliminate the effect of the incorrect entry, make the following entry:

Debit	Professional Fees Revenue	2,000.00
Credit	Cash	2,000.00

2. After eliminating the effect of the incorrect entry, make the following correct entry that should have been made initially:

Debit	Cash	200.00
Credit	Professional Fees Revenue	200.00

In addition to correcting entries, QuickBooks provides a number of additional ways to correct errors. For more information about correcting errors in QuickBooks, see <u>My-Quickbooks.com</u>, QB Issue Resolution.

CLOSING

Before closing a fiscal period, prepare adjusting entries and print all reports needed. To close the fiscal period:

1. Select **Edit Menu** > **Preferences** > **Accounting** > **Company Preferences**.

2. In the Closing Date section, select **Set Date/Password**.

3. Enter the **Closing Date**. If desired, enter and confirm the **Closing Date Password**.

4. Click **OK**.

Section 17.10
Customization/Saving Time and Shortcuts

MEMORIZE TRANSACTIONS

1. Enter the transaction into the appropriate form (Enter Bill, Create Invoice, and so on).

2. Select the **Memorize** icon.

3. Enter **Name** for the memorized transaction.

4. Select **How Often**.

5. Select **Next Date**.

6. Click **OK**.

SET UP MULTIPLE USERS WITH ACCESS

1. Select **Company Menu > Set Up Users and Passwords > Set Up Users**.

2. Select **Add User** (or **Edit User**).

3. Enter **User Name**.

4. Enter **Password**.

5. Confirm **Password**.

6. Select **Next**. Then complete the following QuickBooks user access settings.

7. Click **Finish**.

CREATE CUSTOM FIELDS

1. Open the appropriate list, such as customer, vendor, or employee list.

2. With your cursor over the list, **right-click** and select **New** or **Edit**.

3. Select the **Additional Info** tab > **Define Fields**.

4. In the Label column of the Setup Custom Fields for Names window, enter the name you wish to use for the custom field.

5. Select Use for: **Customer**, **Vendor** and/or **Employee**.

6. Click **OK** to close the Set up Custom Fields for Names window.

7. Click **OK** to close the customer, vendor, or employee window.

CUSTOMIZE AN INVOICE

First, create a copy of an existing invoice template:

1. From the **Customers** section of the Home Page, select **Create Invoices**.

2. Select the **Create a Copy** icon near the top of the Create Invoices window.

3. If a QuickBooks Information window appears informing you that a duplicate invoice has been created, click **OK** to close it.

Next, customize the layout of the duplicate invoice template:

1. Select the **Template** that you wish to customize.

2. Select the **Formatting** tab near the top of the Create Invoices window.

3. Select the **Customize Data Layout** icon.

4. Select Basic Customization, Layout Designer, or appropriate tabs (Header, Columns, Prog Cols (Progress Invoice Columns), Footer, or Print) to customize your invoice.

5. When finished, click **OK**.

Chapter 18

QuickBooks Consulting Project

Chapter 18 provides an opportunity to apply the knowledge and skills you have acquired thus far to an authentic QuickBooks project. You will assume the role of a consultant providing QuickBooks consulting services to a client. This project provides an opportunity for realistic, valuable practical experience to better prepare you for professional employment as well as enhance your resume.

The chapter contains a project management framework to guide you through the development of an accounting system for entrepreneurs or not-for-profits using QuickBooks Desktop accounting software. The system development approach provided in this chapter can be used with various types of organizations, allowing for flexibility to customize the system to meet the specific needs of the entrepreneur or not-for-profit.

Consistent with a sound project management approach, the consulting project is divided into seven milestones. Each milestone should be reviewed by your instructor before you proceed to the next milestone. In addition, the QuickBooks Consulting Project Approval form should be signed by the client as each step is completed and approved.

Chapter 18
Learning Objectives

Chapter 18 introduces a QuickBooks Consulting Project, including the following seven milestones used for project development:

- Milestone 1 Proposal
- Milestone 2 Company Setup
- Milestone 3 Customer, Vendor, Employee, and Item Lists
- Milestone 4 Memorized Transactions
- Milestone 5 Memorized Reports
- Milestone 6 Documentation and Client Instructions
- Milestone 7 Presentation

The project management framework for developing a real QuickBooks accounting system consists of the following seven milestones.

Milestone 1. Develop a proposal. In this milestone, you will identify a real-world client (either a small business or a not-for-profit organization) that needs assistance in establishing an accounting system using QuickBooks. After identifying the client, gather information from the client and develop a plan for a QuickBooks accounting system that will meet the client's needs.

Milestone 2. Develop a prototype or sample QuickBooks accounting system for the client. Set up a company in QuickBooks with a sample Chart of Accounts for the client to review. After obtaining approval of the Chart of Accounts from the client and your instructor, enter beginning balances for the accounts.

Milestone 3. Develop sample QuickBooks lists for customers, vendors, items, and employees. Obtain client and instructor approval for the lists and enter the list information.

Milestone 4. Enter sample transactions to test the prototype and then memorize the transactions in QuickBooks to save them for future use.

Milestone 5. Identify the reports that the client needs and then create memorized reports using QuickBooks.

Milestone 6. Develop documentation for the project including instructions for client use.

Milestone 7. Present the final project first to your class and then to the client.

This project can be completed individually or in teams. Ask your instructor which approach you will be using.

Section 18.1

Milestone 1 Proposal

For Milestone 1, you will create a project proposal. The purpose of the proposal is twofold. First, it forces you, the consultant, to plan the project from start to finish. Second, the proposal serves to improve communication between you and your client. When the client reads your proposal, there is an opportunity for the client to further clarify any misunderstandings. Furthermore, the client may think of additional information or user requirements that were not mentioned earlier.

Complete the following steps to create a project proposal:

1. Identify a real QuickBooks project.

2. Gather project information and user requirements.

3. Write the project proposal.

IDENTIFY QUICKBOOKS PROJECT

The first step is to identify an actual client who needs a QuickBooks accounting system. The client can be an entrepreneur, small business, or not-for-profit organization. For example, the client can be a friend or relative who operates a small business and needs an updated accounting system. Some colleges have Service Learning Coordinators who assist in matching student volunteers with charitable organizations needing assistance.

> ⚠ **Note: It is important to inform the client that this is a class project and all work should be reviewed by his or her own accountant to verify appropriateness. Check with your instructor to see if your instructor or college requires a client waiver, indicating that the client will have all work reviewed and approved by an appropriate professional.**

GATHER QUICKBOOKS PROJECT INFORMATION AND USER REQUIREMENTS

After identifying the client, the next step is to interview the client to determine specific accounting needs and user requirements. Communication is extremely important to the process of designing and developing a successful accounting system. Listening to the client's needs and then communicating to the client the possible solutions are part of the ongoing development process. If clients are not familiar with accounting or QuickBooks, they may not be able to communicate all of their needs. This requires you to gather enough information from the client to identify both the need and the solution.

To make the most effective use of your client's time during the interview, prepare in advance. Before the interview, review all seven milestones of the project to identify the types of information you need to collect. For example, when gathering information for the Customer List, what customer fields does the client need? Also review the QuickBooks New Company Setup (see Chapters 11 and 13) to make certain you ask your client the questions you will need to answer when setting up the new company QuickBooks file for your client.

When collecting information about the Chart of Accounts, first identify the tax return filed by the enterprise. This will help you determine the accounts that are needed for tax purposes. Then, collect information about the assets, liabilities, equity, revenue and expense accounts that the company currently uses. Also, collect information about the beginning balances for accounts with opening balances.

> ⚠ **Note: All information the client shares with you is confidential and should not be shared with anyone else. If you need to share information of a confidential nature with your instructor, first ask the client's permission.**

Prior to your interview, create your own User Requirements Checklist for gathering information from the client. A sample checklist follows.

Milestone 1 User Requirements Checklist

- Organization name
- Type of business (industry)
- Chart of Accounts information
- Type of Tax Return Filed: Schedule C, Form 1120 or Form 1120S
- Beginning account balances
- Customer List information
- Vendor List information
- Employee List information
- Item List information
- Types of transactions to be recorded
- Types of reports needed
- Users of the QuickBooks system and security access

PREPARE QUICKBOOKS CONSULTING PROJECT PROPOSAL

After gathering information from the client, write a proposal that describes your plan for designing and developing your project. The proposal is a plan of what you intend to accomplish and how you will accomplish it.

Your proposal should have a professional appearance and tone that communicates to your client your competency and your enthusiasm for his or her project. Components of the proposal include:

1. **Cover Letter.** In the cover letter, you can thank the client for the opportunity to work together on this QuickBooks project, provide a brief introduction about yourself, summarize the main points in your proposal, and provide your contact information if the client has questions.

2. **Executive Summary.** The Executive Summary should include the following.

   - The project name, your name, client name, and the date.

   - Project objectives and initial feasibility assessment.

   - Possible solutions that would meet project objectives.

   - Your recommendation for the project and supporting rationale.

   See the following Executive Summary Template for more information.

Executive Summary Template

Company Name	[Your consulting name and logo]
Contact Name	[Your name]
Date	[Date of proposal]
Client	[Client name]
Project Name	[QuickBooks project name]
Objectives	[Paragraph 1 contains a concise summary of the project objectives and the initial feasibility assessment.]
Possible Solutions	[Paragraph 2 briefly summarizes possible solutions that satisfy the project objectives.]
Recommendation	[Paragraph 3 contains your recommendation and supporting rationale.]

3. **Proposal Report.** Include the following headings and sections.

    *   **Overview and Objectives.** Briefly describe the client organization and operations. Identify the client's user requirements for an accounting system. For example, the client needs accounting records for tax purposes. Evaluate the feasibility of meeting the organization's needs with QuickBooks and the objectives of this project.

    *   **Scope of Services.** Outline the services that you will provide for the client. What accounting features of QuickBooks will be implemented? Accounts receivable? Accounts payable? Specify the services you will provide the client. Will you provide implementation and setup? Conversion assistance?

    *   **Client Responsibilities.** Clearly specify any responsibilities or information that the client will need to provide.

    *   **Cost/Benefit Analysis.** Provide a summary of the costs associated with the project that the client might expect to occur. Provide information about the benefits that might be expected, including financial and nonfinancial benefits. For example, estimated time that the client might save in maintaining accounting records might be considered both a financial and nonfinancial benefit.

    *   **Timeline.** Identify and list the major tasks involved in completing the project. Include a timeline with completion dates for each task. See the sample format below.

Task	Projected Completion Date
1.	
2.	
3.	
4.	
5.	
6.	
7.	

- **Recommendation.** State your recommendation and provide a short summary including any disclaimers or remaining challenges. End the proposal on a positive, upbeat note.

Submit the proposal to both the client and your instructor. Obtain approval from both the client and your instructor. Ask the client to sign off on the proposal using the approval form that appears at the end of Chapter 18.

Section 18.2

Milestone 2 Company Setup

In this milestone, you will set up a prototype or sample company for the client to review and revise.

1. Based on the information collected from the client, set up a new company and customize the Chart of Accounts for the company.

2. Submit the Chart of Accounts to your instructor for review and recommendations.

3. Have the client review the Chart of Accounts and make recommendations. Ask the client to sign off on the Chart of Accounts using the approval form.

4. After obtaining approval from both the client and instructor, enter beginning balances for the accounts.

Note: Nonprofits use fund accounting. Use subaccounts or the class tracking preference for fund accounting. In addition, Intuit offers a fund accounting version of QuickBooks.

Section 18.3

Milestone 3 Customer, Vendor, Employee and Item Lists

After the Chart of Accounts has been approved, develop lists (customer, vendor, employee, and item) for the client.

1. After consulting with the client, list the customer information (fields) needed for each customer. If necessary, create user-defined fields in QuickBooks to accommodate the client's needs.

2. List the information needed by the organization for each vendor. Create any user-defined fields that are needed for vendors.

3. List the employee information needed by the organization for each employee. Determine any payroll items needed to accurately record payroll. If applicable, collect payroll year-to-date information.

4. Determine the items (inventory, non-inventory, and service items) required to meet the organization's needs. List the information needed for each item.

5. After obtaining approval for the lists from the client and your instructor, enter information for the following:

   - Customer List
   - Vendor List
   - Employee List
   - Item List
   - Payroll year-to-date information

Section 18.4

Milestone 4 Memorized Transactions

Complete the following steps for Milestone 4.

1. Determine the types of transactions the client will enter in QuickBooks (for example: cash sales, credit card sales, purchase orders).

2. Enter test or sample transactions in QuickBooks. Obtain client and instructor approval of the results.

3. Modify forms as needed to meet the client's needs. For example, if the client needs a Date column on the invoice, customize the invoice by following the instructions in Chapter 11.

4. After obtaining the client's approval for transactions, create memorized transactions for the transactions that will be repeated periodically.

> **Customizing the Chart of Accounts. As you develop the accounting system, you may find that further customization of the Chart of Accounts is needed to meet specific business needs. In your final project, highlight any new accounts added.**

It is important that you and the client reach an agreement regarding what you will complete before you turn the project over to the client. Discuss with the client whether you will be entering only a few sample transactions or entering all transactions for the year to date. For example, if entering all transactions is too time consuming, you may agree that you will enter only sample transactions and the client will enter the real transactions after you submit the final project.

Section 18.5

Milestone 5 Memorized Reports

Complete the following steps for Milestone 5.

1. Determine which reports the client needs. Review Chapters 5 through 10 to obtain information about the different reports that QuickBooks can generate. You may need to make the client aware of the reports that are available in QuickBooks and then let the client select the reports that would be useful.

2. Obtain client and instructor approval for the reports.

3. After obtaining approval concerning the reports, create and memorize the reports using QuickBooks.

Section 18.6

Milestone 6 Documentation and Client Instructions

Create documentation for the client. Include a history of the project development as well as instructions that the client will need. For example, instructions regarding how and when to back up and restore company files are essential. Providing instructions on how to use memorized transactions and memorized reports is also advisable.

An easy way to provide the client with adequate instructions is to recommend existing training materials to the client and then simply reference pages in the training materials. For example, if the client obtains a copy of this book, you may wish to reference pages of the text for each task the client will be performing.

Other documentation that the client might find useful is the QuickBooks Year-End Guide. To view the Year-End Guide, select **Help** menu > **Year-End Guide**.

QuickBooks Help. Provide the client with instructions for using QuickBooks Help feature.

Be prepared for clients to ask if they may call if they need your assistance in the future. Adequate user instructions (Milestone 6) are essential in reducing the client's future dependence on you.

Section 18.7
Milestone 7 Presentation

There are three parts to this milestone:

1. Make any final changes to your project.

2. Make the project presentation to your class.

3. Make a project presentation to the client.

The presentation to your instructor and classmates is practice for the final presentation to the client. You may want to ask your classmates for suggestions you can incorporate into your final presentation for the client.

A suggested outline for the project presentation follows:

1. **History and Overview.** Provide background about the client and the client's needs as an introduction for your presentation.

2. **Demonstration.** If the room has projection equipment, demonstrate your QuickBooks project. Display memorized transactions, memorized reports, and lists for the class and/or client to view. Remember to use test/sample data for the class presentation instead of actual client data that is confidential.

3. **Examples.** Present examples of the documentation and client instructions you are providing the client (see Milestone 6).

4. **Cost/Benefit and Advantages/Disadvantages.** Briefly present advantages and disadvantages of using QuickBooks for this particular project as well as associated costs and benefits.

5. **Summary.** Present concluding remarks to summarize the major points of your presentation.

6. **Questions and Answers.** Provide classmates or the client an opportunity to ask questions about the project. In preparing for your presentation, you will want to anticipate possible questions and prepare appropriate answers.

QuickBooks Consulting Project Approval

Milestone	Approved	Date
1. Proposal		
2. Company Setup and Chart of Accounts		
3. Lists: Customers, Vendors, Employees and Items		
4. Memorized Transactions		
5. Memorized Reports		
6. Documentation		
7. Final Presentation		

Notes:

Appendix A

Install and Activate QuickBooks Software

Install QuickBooks Software

To obtain QuickBooks Desktop 2021 software for students to accompany your *Computer Accounting with QuickBooks 2021* text:

1 Go to **https://intuit.me/mh-desktop**. Note: if you have any issue with this url, go to www.mhhe.com/kay2021 for additional information and updates.

2 Follow the onscreen instructions to complete the Intuit request form for your QuickBooks Desktop 2021 student software. Be sure to select the version for this text: **QuickBooks Desktop 2021**.

3 After you receive email confirmation from Intuit, follow the instructions provided to download your QuickBooks software installer to your computer desktop. If you don't receive the confirmation email, check your Spam folder.

⚠ **Before installing QuickBooks Desktop software** verify that your Windows operating system is compatible with the QuickBooks Desktop software. Note that QuickBooks Desktop 2021 is not compatible with Windows 7 or earlier.

After downloading your QuickBooks Desktop 2021 software installer and verifying that your Windows operating system is compatible with QBDT 2021, install the QBDT 2021 software as follows:

1 If the installer does not open automatically, double-click on the QuickBooks Desktop 2021 installer to start installation. Follow the onscreen instructions. After the installer is loaded, to accept the license agreement and proceed with installation, select **Accept & Continue**.

2 When prompted to **enter your License Number and Product Number,** copy and paste the license and product numbers from the Intuit email. Then select **Next**.

3 When the Choose your installation type window appears, select **Express > Next**.

4 Follow the onscreen instructions and select **Install** to install the QuickBooks software.

5 Various screens will appear while the QuickBooks software is installing. When the Installation Complete window appears, select **Open QuickBooks**.

6 After QuickBooks starts, if the Activate Quickbooks Desktop Now window appears, select **Begin Activation**. Follow the onscreen instructions to activate QuickBooks.

Intuit QuickBooks Desktop Installer

Welcome to QuickBooks

Complete your QuickBooks installation with just a few steps. For smooth installation, it is a good idea to close any open programs, especially virus protection programs.

Once the installer is loaded, accept the license agreement to continue.
View License Agreement

Accept & Continue   Cancel

Sample download notification email

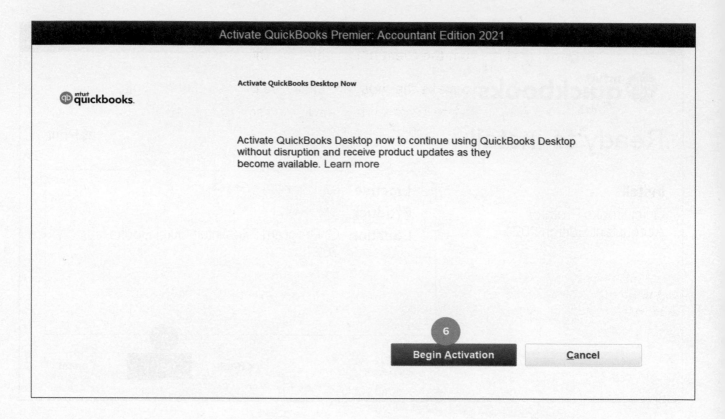

Occasionally the information for obtaining the software from Intuit changes. If you experience issues downloading and installing your QuickBooks Desktop 2021 software, Another site to check for possible updates to download the QuickBooks software is www.mhhe.com/kay2021, select QuickBooks Software Download, and then follow instructions provided.

Another option to obtain information about possible additional updates:

1. Go to **www.My-QuickBooks.com**

2. Select **QB2021** link

3. Scroll down to **Download and Install QuickBooks Software**

4. Follow the instructions to download and install the QuickBooks software

5. **Activate the QuickBooks software following the instructions provided**

> QuickBooks Support. QuickBooks Desktop Installation Support: 888-222-7276. QuickBooks Desktop Registration Support 800-316-1068.

> ⚠ **Activate QuickBooks software** with Intuit after installing or you will be locked out of the software. If activated, you will be able to use the QuickBooks software for up to 1 year. If you fail to activate the software, you will be locked out of the software and unable to use it.

> **QuickBooks Accountant** software that comes with your text is Windows-based software. If you have a Mac, see your instructor. Also, go to www.My-QuickBooks.com. Select QB & My Mac for options.

> If you already have another version of QuickBooks software installed on your computer, you can select to replace it with the newer version or to install both versions. If your QuickBooks software fails to install, try uninstalling any prior versions of QuickBooks and then reinstalling QuickBooks 2021 software.

> QuickBooks Support. QuickBooks Desktop Installation Support: 888-222-7276. QuickBooks Desktop Registration Support 800-316-1068.

Activate QuickBooks Software

Three ways to activate your QuickBooks software are:

1. Activate the software when you install it
2. Select **Help menu** > **About QuickBooks** > **CTRL + R + P**
3. Activate your QuickBooks software by phone at 800-316-1068 and select the appropriate menu option

If you are locked out from using the software, try selecting **Help menu** > **About QuickBooks** > **CTRL + R + P**. If that is unsuccessful, try uninstalling and reinstalling the QuickBooks software.

> ⚠ **Activate your QuickBooks software!** Failure to activate your QuickBooks trial version software will result in the software no longer functioning.

Appendix B

Back Up and Restore QuickBooks Files

QuickBooks File Versions

QuickBooks software uses a company file to store information about a specific enterprise. Thus, you can use the QuickBooks software installed on your computer with many different company files. This is similar to using Microsoft Excel software, for example, with many different Excel data files.

The different versions of QuickBooks company files are summarized in the following table.

Extension	QuickBooks File
QBW	**QuickBooks for Windows.** You can think of this file as a QuickBooks working file. This is the file version that you use to enter transactions and data. It is usually saved to the hard drive of your computer.
QBB	**QuickBooks Backup.** A QuickBooks Backup file should be created at regular intervals in case your QBW file fails or is destroyed. The QBB file version is a compressed file and cannot be opened directly. Furthermore, you cannot enter transactions directly into a QBB file. Instead, you must unzip the file first by restoring the file into a QBW file version.
.QBM	**QuickBooks Mobile.** A QuickBooks Mobile file, also called a QuickBooks Portable file, is used to move a QuickBooks file to another computer. Like the QBB backup file version, the .QBM file version is compressed and must be unzipped and restored into a QBW file version before it can be used to enter data.
QBX	**QuickBooks Accountant.** A QuickBooks Accountant Copy is identified with a QBX extension. This version of the company file is given to the accountant. The accountant can make changes, such as adjusting entries, to the QBX version of the company file while the QBW company file is used to continue entering transactions.

QuickBooks File Management

QuickBooks file management involves managing your QuickBooks company files to ensure the security and integrity of your QuickBooks accounting system.

In a typical business workflow, you use the same QBW computer file on the same computer. Sound file management includes making backups as part of a disaster recovery plan. A good backup system is to have a different backup for each business day: Monday backup, Tuesday backup, Wednesday backup, and so on. Then if it is necessary to use the backup file and the Wednesday backup, for example, fails, the company has a Tuesday backup to use. Furthermore, it is recommended that a business store at least one backup at a remote location.

If a company's QBW file fails, then you must restart by restoring your most recent QBB file version. The backup file (QBB) is compressed and must be converted to a working file (QBW) before you can use it to enter data or transactions.

The following diagrams illustrate when you will back up and restore for purposes of this text. Note that we will be using a new QBB Starter file provided with the text for each chapter (except Chapters 11, 12, 13, 14, 16, and 18). For the projects, instead of restarting each project by restoring a Starter file, we will continue to use our QBW file.

QUICKBOOKS CHAPTER & EXERCISES		
QBW	**QBB STARTER FILES**	**QBB BACKUP FILES**
Start		
↓		
Restore QBB STARTER FILE	← CHAPTER 1 QBB STARTER FILE	
↓		
Complete Chapter 1		
↓		
Back Up		→ QBB BACKUP FILE
↓		
Complete Exercise 1.1		
↓		
Back Up		→ QBB BACKUP FILE
↓		
Repeat		
↓		
Restore QBB STARTER FILE	← CHAPTER 2 QBB STARTER FILE	
↓		
Complete Chapter 2		
↓		
Back Up		→ QBB BACKUP FILE
↓		
Repeat		
↓		
End		

QUICKBOOKS PROJECTS		
QBW	**QBB STARTER FILE**	**QBB BACKUP FILES**
Start		
↓		
Restore PROJECT 1.1 QBB STARTER FILE	← PROJECT 1.1 QBB STARTER FILE	
↓		
Open QBW File		
↓		
Complete Project 1.1		
↓		
Back Up		→ QBB BACKUP FILE
↓		
Complete Project 2.1 Using Same QBW File		
↓		
Back Up		→ QBB BACKUP FILE
↓		
Repeat		
↓		
End		

Back Up QuickBooks Files

Throughout the text you will be instructed when to back up your QuickBooks file.

To save a backup (QBB) file:

1 With your QuickBooks file (*.QBW) open, click **File**

2 Select **Back Up Company**

3 Select **Create Local Backup**

4 When the Create Backup window appears, select **Local backup**

5 Select **Options** to specify your backup settings

6 If asked where to save your files, to make it easier to find your backup files, click the **Browse** button

7 Select **Desktop**. Click **OK** to close the Browse for Folder window.

8 Select **Add the date and time of the backup to the file name (recommended)**

9 Select **Complete verification (recommended)**

10 Click **OK** again to close the Backup Options window. Select **Use this Location** if a QuickBooks warning window appears.

11 Select **Next**

12 Select **Save it now**

13 Select **Next**

14 When the Save Backup Copy window appears, the Save in field should automatically show: **Desktop**

15 Update the File name field as shown to: **YourName Chapter 1 (Backup)**. Depending on your operating system settings, the file extension .QBB may appear automatically. If the .QBB extension does not appear, *do not type it*.

16 The Save as type field should automatically appear as **QBW Backup (*.QBB)**

17 Select **Save**

18 If a QuickBooks Desktop Information message appears, click **OK**

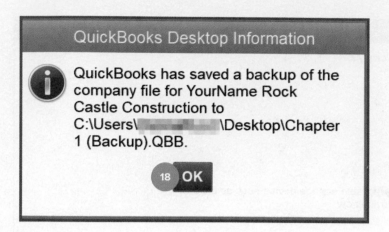

You can schedule a backup every time you close a QuickBooks company file or at regular intervals.

Restore QuickBooks Files

At the beginning of chapters 1 through 10 and 15 and 17, you will be asked to restore a Starter file provided for you with the text. Ask your instructor for the location of the Starter files to download.

Another time you might need to restore a QuickBooks file is if you need to switch computers. Then you will back up your QBW file and then restore the QBB backup file you created to another computer.

A third reason you might need to restore a QuickBooks file is if you realize you have an error that you are unable to track and fix. In this case if you have a QBB file, you would roll back to the most recent QBB file and restore it.

For your convenience, QuickBooks (QBB) Starter files accompany *Computer Accounting with QuickBooks 2021.*

Go to www.mhhe.com/kay2021 to download the Starter files from the Online Learning Center.

To stay organized, consider adding a folder to your Desktop: QBB STARTER FILES. Then copy the QBB STARTER files to that folder.

For Connect users, the Starter Files are accessible through your Connect Chapter Assignments.

⚠ **Desktop (QBDT) QBB Files are compressed backup files that can be restored and used. To use QBB Starter files, the compressed file must be restored following the instructions here. Since it is a compressed file, you cannot open and use the QuickBooks Starter files by simply clicking on the file. Instead you must follow the instructions here to unzip and restore the data file before using it.**

⚠ *Important Note regarding passwords:*

- *When restoring a QBB file if QuickBooks requires you to <u>create</u> a password in order to continue, create your own password and record the password in a secure location, such as the inside cover of your textbook*

- *When restoring QuickBooks QBB files, if a password is requested:*
    1. *Try using User ID: Admin and leave the Password field blank*
    2. *If you are using the QBB Starter files and QuickBooks requires a password and QuickBooks will not accept the password field blank, try User ID: Admin and Password: KayQB2021*
    3. *If none of the above approaches permit you to restore the QBB file, see your instructor*

To restore a backup QBB file to a QBW file:

1   From the No Company Open window, select **Open or restore an existing company**. (If the Let's get your business set up quickly! window appears first, select **Other Options > Open Existing File**.)

2   Select **Restore a backup copy**

3   Click **Next**

4   When the Open or Restore Company window appears, select **Local backup**

5   Click **Next**

6   Identify the location of the **CHAPTER 1 STARTER.QBB** file. If you copied the CHAPTER 1 STARTER file to your desktop, select the **Look in** field to find the location of the .QBB file on your desktop.

7   Select the file: **CHAPTER 1 STARTER.QBB**

8   The Files of type field should automatically display: **QBW Backup (*.QBB)**

9   Click **Open**

10   When the Open or Restore window appears, click **Next**

11   Identify the file name and location of the QBW company file. To save the QBW (working file) on your desktop, select the location to save in: **Desktop**. (Another option is to save your QBW files to Users > Public > Public Documents > Intuit > QuickBooks > Company Files. Be sure you have permissions to save to a folder.)

12   Enter QBW File name: **YourName Chapter 1**. (Insert your name in the QBW file name so you can identify your files.)

13   The Save as type field should automatically appear as **QuickBooks Files (*.QBW)**

14   Click **Save**

15   Click **OK** when the QuickBooks Desktop Information window appears notifying you that **You're opening a QuickBooks sample file**

Change Company Name

So that your name automatically appears on reports and checks, update the Company Name setting to add your name to the company name.

To change a company name in QuickBooks, complete the following:

1. From My Shortcuts on the Navigation Bar, select **My Company**

2. When the My Company window appears, select **Edit**

3. When the Company Information window appears, update the Company Name field to: **YourName Chapter 1 Rock Castle Construction**

4. Select **OK** to close the Company Information window

5. **Close** the My Company window

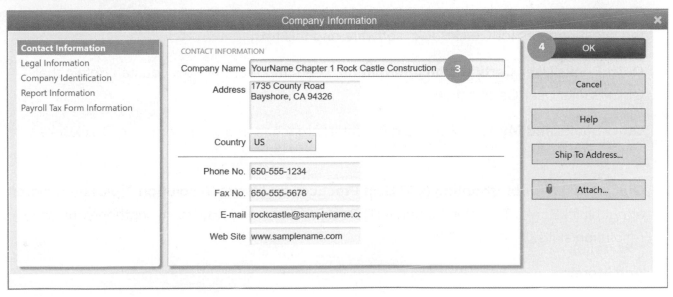

Appendix C

www.My-QuickBooks.com

Go to www.My-QuickBooks.com to view the QuickBooks website to accompany *Computer Accounting with QuickBooks*.

www.My-QuickBooks.com includes:

- **Excel Report Templates.** Use the Excel report templates to create digital QuickBooks reports instead of paper printouts for your assignments.

- **QuickBooks Videos.** View videos on QuickBooks topics such as back up, restore, and much more.

- **Computer Accounting with QuickBooks Updates.** Check out Updates to stay current with the latest updates for QuickBooks software and this text.

- **QuickBooks User Certification Information.** Learn more about how you can obtain the QuickBooks User Certification.

- **QuickBooks and My Mac.** Explore different approaches and ideas for using QuickBooks with your Mac.

- **QuickBooks Troubleshooting (QT) Best Practices and Issue Resolution Tips.** Learn more about QuickBooks Troubleshooting (QT) Best Practices and how to strengthen your issue resolution skills.

- **And More....**

Appendix D

QuickBooks Troubleshooting

This appendix summarizes resources to assist you with QuickBooks Troubleshooting (QT) including:

- QuickBooks Help
- QuickBooks Tool Hub
- QuickBooks Troubleshooting (QT) Best Practices

QuickBooks Help

To use the Quickbooks Help Menu:

1 Select **Help** on the Menu Bar to display the drop-down menu of Help features

2 Select **QuickBooks Desktop Help** from the Help Menu, and the Have a Question? window will appear

3 At the top of the Have a Question? window, you can type in your question and then view the results

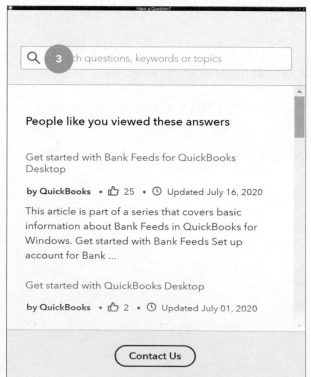

QuickBooks Tool Hub

QuickBooks Tool Hub is a new feature that is a launchpad for QuickBooks Desktop troubleshooting tools. The QuickBooks Tool Hub is where you can find tools for fixing QuickBooks Desktop issues.

To download and install the QuickBooks Tool Hub:

1. Select **Help** on the Menu Bar to display the drop-down Help menu

2. From the Help menu select **QuickBooks Tool Hub: Fix Setup and File Issues**. If you receive an error message, select **Retry**.

3. Follow the onscreen instructions to **download** the QuickBooks Tool Hub, saving it to your Downloads folder or to your Desktop where you can find it easily

4. **Open** the downloaded file named **QuickBooksToolHub.exe**

5. Follow the instructions on your screen to **install** the QuickBooks Tool Hub

6. After installed, to open the QuickBooks Tool Hub, **double-click on the QuickBooks Tool Hub icon** that appears on your desktop. If the icon does not automatically appear on your desktop, use your Windows search feature to search for the QuickBooks Tool Hub app.

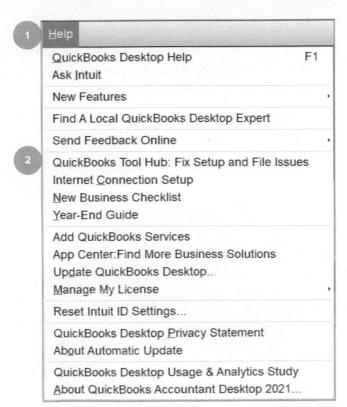

> **Note: Intuit recommends using QuickBooks Tool Hub on Windows 10, 64-bit for the best experience.**

The QuickBooks Tool Hub organizes the tools into categories for different types of problems. To view the tools for the various categories select the tabs on the left hand side of the Tool Hub.

To use the QuickBooks Tool Hub:

1. Select **Home** tab to view a summary of the tool categories

2. Select the **Company Files Issues** tab. These tools include the QuickBooks File Doctor to repair common company data file issues.

3. Select the **Network Issues** tab. Under this tab you will find QuickBooks tools to address issues with your network or computers on your network.

4. Select the **Program Problems** tab. These QuickBooks tools resolve performance issues, such as the program crashing, or printing and PDF issues.

5. Select the **Installation Issues** tab. Click this tab to resolve issues with installing and uninstalling QuickBooks Desktop software.

6. Select the **Password Reset** tab. Use this tab if you need to use the password reset tool to reset your QuickBooks Desktop password.

7. Select the **Help & Support** tab. Click this tab to contact QuickBooks support if you have not resolved your issue with the Tool Hub. Also, manage your Intuit QuickBooks account.

8. Select the **Advanced Tools** tab. This tab contains Windows shortcuts for common tasks in troubleshooting QuickBooks errors.

9. Select **Installed Version - Check for Updates** to find the latest updates to the QuickBooks Tool Hub

10. **Close** the QuickBooks Tool Hub by selecting the **X** in the upper right corner of the Tool Hub

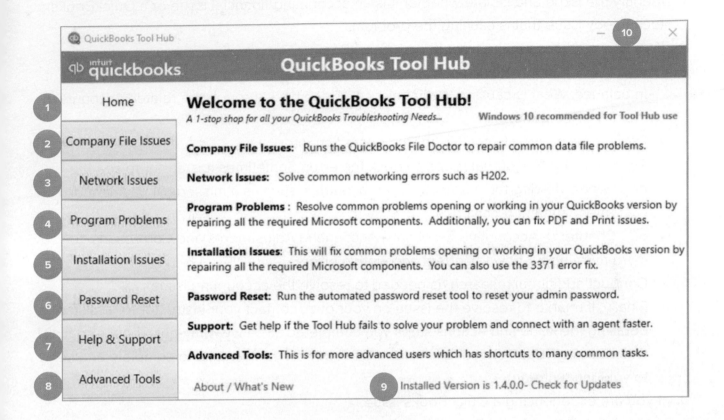

QuickBooks Troubleshooting (QT) Best Practices

QuickBooks Troubleshooting (QT) Best Practices can increase your chances of success at troubleshooting QuickBooks. One QT Best Practice is to use a structured, process approach to QuickBooks Troubleshooting to streamline the troubleshooting process and increase effectiveness in resolving issues.

QuickBooks Troubleshooting (QT) Process

QuickBooks Troubleshooting (QT) Process, like any business process, can be thought of as a blueprint that depicts pathways of related activities to reach a goal as efficiently as possible. In the case of QuickBooks Troubleshooting, your goal is to resolve the QB issue as efficiently as possible by using a QT Process blueprint of defined activities.

Consider the following example of a QT Process that you can customize to create your own QT process.

1. Identify the issue and isolate whether it is an accounting/financial issue or a QuickBooks technology issue that is causing the problem.

2. If you have an accounting error in your QuickBooks company file:
   - Isolate and identify the specific accounting issue. For example, is your trial balance not in balance. What is causing the imbalance? Trace back through the related accounts to identify discrepancies.
   - Review Accounting Essentials for the related chapter.
   - Try displaying the journal report to track the error. Sometimes it is easier to see the error when viewing the associated journal entries, such as a missed bill payment or customer payment received.
   - See Chapter 9, Accounting Essentials, Accounting Adjustments and Corrections, to learn more about how to correct accounting errors.
   - Conduct additional research as needed to resolve the accounting issue.
   - Finally, if unable to resolve the issue on your own, contact your instructor for assistance, detailing the issue and actions steps you completed. (See www.my-quickbooks.com, QT QuickBooks Troubleshooting link, for a QT form that you can use to complete and send to your instructor.)

3. If you are experiencing a QuickBooks issue:
   - Isolate and identify the QuickBooks issue.
   - Review related QuickBooks Chapter and Section.
   - Verify QuickBooks tasks were completed correctly.
   - Check out Updates for your Computer Accounting with QuickBooks edition at www.My-QuickBooks.com > select QB2021 link > scroll down to Updates section. Or go to the OLC at www.mhhe.com/kay2021. See if an update resolves the issue.
   - Resolve QuickBooks issue by researching the issue using QuickBooks Help, QuickBooks Tool Hub, and QuickBooks Community. If you received a specific error code, such as H202, search for that code in QuickBooks Community.
   - Finally, if unable to resolve the issue on your own, contact your instructor for assistance, detailing the issue and actions steps you completed. (See www.my-quickbooks.com, QT QuickBooks Troubleshooting link, for a QT form that you can use to complete and send to your instructor.)

For more QuickBooks Troubleshooting Best Practices, go to www.my-quickbooks.com, QT QuickBooks Troubleshooting link.

QUICKBOOKS TROUBLESHOOTING PROCESS MAP

	1	
	Identify Issue and Isolate whether an Accounting Issue or a QuickBooks Issue	
2		**3**
Accounting Issue?		**QuickBooks Issue?**
↓		↓
Isolate and Identify Specific Accounting Issue		**Isolate and Identify QuickBooks Issue**
↓		↓
Review Accounting Essentials		**Review Relevant QuickBooks Chapter and Section**
↓		↓
Create Journal Report to Track Error		**Verify QuickBooks Tasks Were Completed Correctly**
↓		↓
See Chapter 9, Accounting Essentials, to Learn How to Correct Accounting Errors		**Check out Updates for Your Text Online**
↓		↓
If Not Resolved, Conduct Additional Research		**If Not Resolved, Conduct Additional Research Using:** • **QuickBooks Help** • **QuickBooks Tool Hub** • **QuickBooks Community**
↓		↓
Finally, Contact Your Instructor using QT Form Online		**Finally, Contact Your Instructor Using QT Form Online**

Index